ADVANCE PRAISE FOR
Communicology for the Human Sciences

"We are in a world where scholars increasingly define themselves away from all other realms of thought except some cramped field of expertise whose walls relentlessly move in like some torture-room dreamt by Edgar Alan Poe. In the face of this, Richard L. Lanigan's commitment is to think phenomenologically to give us the open-air insight that communication is by human consciousnesses, to others, about matters whose truth is in our mutual world. In this book we have so much evidence of the wide, breathing fruitfulness of this effort of communicology."
—*Peter Ashworth, Emeritus Professor Department of Psychology Sociology and Politics, Sheffield Hallam University, Sheffield, England*

"A wonderful commemorative volume to honor Richard L. Lanigan, one of the most important American semiotic phenomenologists. This superb volume demonstrates the range of Lanigan's influence, from communicology to ethics, through phenomenology and semiotics. A must-read for whoever is interested in philosophy of communication at its best."
—*François Cooren, Professor, Université de Montréal, Canada, Past ICA President (2010-2011), ICA Fellow*

"For 50 years, Richard L. Lanigan has been developing a communicology for the human sciences, an approach to communication studies grounded in phenomenology. This Festschrift adds an amazing collection of original articles to his approach, written by his mentors, students, and friends. It leads the reader through a surprising diversity of topics that communicology invites, discussing its philosophical roots and relating it to semiotics, linguistics, ethics, mental health, the future of communicability, and more, all the way to the coding of qualitative data."
—*Klaus Krippendorff, Gregory Bateson Professor Emeritus for Cybernetics, Language and Culture, The Annenberg School for Communication, University of Pennsylvania*

"Voices across three generations celebrate the work of Richard L. Lanigan, a giant in scholarship, service and humanity. In dialogue with American pragmatism and continental philosophy, Lanigan the philosopher and communicologist investigates the phenomenological foundations of communication inspiring new pathways in research as represented by the authors in this volume. An extraordinary enterprise marking the overwhelming importance of communication today with its singular responsibilities for theorists and practitioners alike, in the face of its pervasiveness and consequence not only for humankind but for life overall."
—*Susan Petrilli, Professor of Philosophy and Theory of Languages, University of Bari Aldo Moro, Italy, Visiting Research Fellow at the University of Adelaide, Australia*

"Inspired by Richard L. Lanigan—a philosopher, scholar, teacher, mentor, and friend to many—the contributors of this volume take us in diverse and thought-provoking directions: from epistemological foundations to formative logics, from embodied practice to ethical comportment. As a result, communicology emerges as a coherent and innovative discipline vital for the human sciences. In today's fragmented and fractured world, reading this book is a heuristic and healing experience."
—*Galina Sinekopova, Professor and Director of Graduate Studies, Department of Communication, Eastern Washington University*

"This Festschrift in honor of Richard L. Lanigan's 50-year legacy offers contributions by his colleagues and students to disciplines he has advanced, being a perpetual beginner himself, who merges communicology as a science of human discourse with semiotic phenomenology. It is a journey to the (inter)subjectivity of the intentional self which paves the way to a helical model of man's reasoning and becoming. Every researcher in anthropological philosophy, cognitive sciences, and linguistics should read this volume."
—*Zdzisław Wąsik, Professor in Linguistic Semiotics and Communicology, Adam Mickiewicz University in Poznań, Poland*

Communicology for the Human Sciences

This book is part of the Peter Lang Media and Communication list.
Every volume is peer reviewed and meets
the highest quality standards for content and production.

PETER LANG
New York • Bern • Frankfurt • Berlin
Brussels • Vienna • Oxford • Warsaw

Communicology for the Human Sciences

Lanigan and the Philosophy
of Communication

Andrew R. Smith, Isaac E. Catt & Igor E. Klyukanov,
Editors

PETER LANG
New York • Bern • Frankfurt • Berlin
Brussels • Vienna • Oxford • Warsaw

Library of Congress Cataloging-in-Publication Data

Names: Smith, Andrew R., editor. | Catt, Isaac E., editor. |
Klyukanov, Igor E., editor. | Lanigan, Richard L., honouree.
Title: Communicology for the human sciences: Lanigan and the
philosophy of communication / edited by
Andrew R. Smith, Isaac E. Catt & Igor E. Kluykanov.
Description: New York: Peter Lang, 2018.
Includes bibliographical references and index.
Identifiers: LCCN 2017013150 | ISBN 978-1-4331-4115-7 (pbk.: alk. paper)
ISBN 978-1-4331-4374-8 (hardback: alk. paper) |
ISBN 978-1-4331-4114-0 (ebook pdf)
ISBN 978-1-4331-4372-4 (epub) | ISBN 978-1-4331-4373-1 (mobi)
Subjects: LCSH: Communication—Philosophy. | Phenomenology. |
Semantics (Philosophy).
Classification: LCC P91.25.P48 | DDC 302.2/01—dc23
LC record available at https://lccn.loc.gov/2017013150
DOI 10.3726/b10835

Bibliographic information published by **Die Deutsche Nationalbibliothek**.
Die Deutsche Nationalbibliothek lists this publication in the "Deutsche
Nationalbibliografie"; detailed bibliographic data are available
on the Internet at http://dnb.d-nb.de/.

The paper in this book meets the guidelines for permanence and durability
of the Committee on Production Guidelines for Book Longevity
of the Council of Library Resources.

∞

© 2018 Peter Lang Publishing, Inc., New York
29 Broadway, 18th floor, New York, NY 10006
www.peterlang.com

All rights reserved.
Reprint or reproduction, even partially, in all forms such as microfilm,
xerography, microfiche, microcard, and offset strictly prohibited.

Printed in the United States of America

A Festschrift
for
Richard L. Lanigan
Professor, Colleague, Mentor, Friend

The philosopher is a perpetual beginner. This means that [s]he accepts nothing as established from what men [*sic*] or scientists think they know. This also means that philosophy itself must not take itself as established in the truths it has managed to utter, that philosophy is an ever-renewed experiment of its own beginning, that it consists entirely in describing this beginning, and finally, that radical reflection is conscious of its own dependence on an unreflected life that is its initial, constant, and final situation.

—Maurice Merleau-Ponty. *Phenomenology of Perception*, trans. Donald A. Landes (New York: Routledge, 2012), xxviii.

This book is dedicated to perpetual beginners.
ARS, IEC and IEK

Table of Contents

List of Tables and Figures xv
Foreword: Speaking and Semiotics xvii
    Calvin O. Schrag
Acknowledgements xxi
Introduction: Communicology: What's in a Name? 1
    Isaac E. Catt, Igor E. Klyukanov, and Andrew R. Smith

Section One: Founding(s)

Chapter One: Decolonizing Research Praxis: Embodiment, Border Thinking
    and Theory Construction in the Human Sciences 23
    Andrew R. Smith

Chapter Two: Lanigan's "Encyclopedic Dictionary": Key Concepts, Insights,
    and Advances 49
    Corey Anton

Chapter Three: Communicability as Ground of Communicology: Impulses
    and Impediments 71
    Horst Ruthrof

Chapter Four: The Human, the Family, and the *Vécu* of Semiotic
    Phenomenology: Lanigan's Communicology in the Context of Life Itself ... 93
    Frank Macke

Section Two: Tropologic(s)

Chapter Five: Communicational Aspects in Experimental Phenomenological
    Studies on Cognition: Theory and Methodology 111
    William B. Gomes

Chapter Six: The Monstrosity of Adduction 133
    Igor E. Klyukanov

Chapter Seven: Is Martin Heidegger's Fourfold a Semiotic Square? 147
    Alexander Kozin
Chapter Eight: Communicology and the Practice of Coding in Qualitative
    Communication Research 159
    Eric E. Peterson and Kristin M. Langellier

Section Three: Trans/formations

Chapter Nine: Emmanuel Levinas: The Turning of Semioethics 179
    Ronald C. Arnett, Susan Mancino, and Hannah Karolak
Chapter Ten: Mental Health in the Communication Matrix: A Semiotic
    Phenomenology of Depression Medicine 201
    Isaac E. Catt
Chapter Eleven: Decolonial Phenomenological Practice: Communicology
    Across the Cultural and Political Borders of the North-South and West-
    East Divides 221
    Jacqueline M. Martinez
Chapter Twelve: In the Context of Communicology: Issues of Technical Risk
    Communication About Sustainability 243
    Hong Wang

Section Four: Voicing Bodies/Embodying Voices

Chapter Thirteen: Authoring Life Writing as a Technology of the Self:
    A Communicological Perspective on the Concept of Voice 267
    Deborah Eicher-Catt
Chapter Fourteen: Communicative Possibilities in/of a Glance................. 283
    Pat Arneson
Chapter Fifteen: Laban and Lanigan: Shall We Dance? 299
    Maureen Connolly and Tom D. Craig
Chapter Sixteen: Lexis Agonistic and Lexis Graphike: Translation from Library
    Document to Museum Monument 313
    Thaddeus Martin

Section Five: Horizons of Communicability

Chapter Seventeen: The Subject at Hand 327
    Vincent Colapietro

Chapter Eighteen: Being in Speech: Inferentialism, Historicism, and
    Metaphysics of Intentionality 351
    Jason Hannan
Chapter Nineteen: The Theory of Perfective Drift 369
    Johan Siebers
Afterword: Richard L. Lanigan: A Fifty Year Legacy 391
    Thomas J. Pace, Jr.

Appendix A: Richard L. Lanigan's Biography and Curriculum Vitae 397
Appendix B: Richard L. Lanigan's Publications, Presentations, Thesis and
    Dissertation Direction 427
Index 493

Tables and Figures

Table 5.1:	Classificatory Criteria of Statements for the Seven Cases Selected from the Study	121
Table 13.1:	Foucault's Semiotic and Phenomenological Oppositions/Appositions of Language and Discourse	269
Figure 5.1:	Verbalizations of the Participants with High Scores on Raven Test	122
Figure 5.2:	Verbalizations of the Participants with Low Scores on the Raven Test	123
Figure 6.1:	Four Kinds of Reasoning	139
Figure 6.2:	Four Forms of Judgment	139
Figure 7.1:	The Semiotic Square	149
Figure 12.1:	Technical Risk Communication Model as Semiosis of a Peircean Sign	248
Figure 12.2:	Assumed Link Between "Inform" and "Change"	250
Figure 19.1	A Helical Model of Communication [Based on Dance (1967)]	380
Figure 19.2	The Play of Perception	381
Figure 19.3	Yin and Yang	383
Figure 19.4	Model of Perfective Drift	385
Figure 19.5	Star of David with the Event Cone	386

Tables and figures

Foreword

Speaking and Semiotics

CALVIN O. SCHRAG

Richard Lanigan's long career in the philosophy of communication has covered a quite extensive terrain. One of the prominent features of this career has been his achievement of the convergence of a phenomenology of speech with a science of semiotics without incorporating the one into the other and thus curtailing the contributions of each. This has proceeded in such a way as to avoid the linguistic empiricism of speech act theory on the one hand and semiotic reductionism on the other hand. The background of the story concerns the tension between a phenomenology of language and a science of linguistics, which, as is well known, has its origins in the thought of Ferdinand de Saussure and his distinctions between individual speech utterances *(la parole)*, the spoken language *(la langue)*, and the history of language as a semiotic structural system *(le langage)*. In advancing his project of providing a model for modern linguistics it was necessary for Saussure to sort out *la langue* and *le langage* as the proper objects of investigation so as to lay the foundations for a structuralist theory of linguistic science.

What catches the eye of the reader of Lanigan's consummate literary production is that both the issue of a phenomenology of the event of speaking and ruminations on semiotic structures are addressed, as becomes evident when we compare side by side his two works *Speech Act Phenomenology* and *Speaking and Semiology: Approaches to Semiotics*. His phenomenological roots are deep and consequential, primarily as the result of his early interests and careful studies in the existential phenomenology of Maurice Merleau-Ponty. It was Merleau-Ponty who gave voice to the embodied *parole*, the concrete existential event with its primacy of what he called "the lived body as expression and speech." Lanigan came to defend this Pontyian position on speech as an embodied event against the linguistic empiricism of speech act theory, in which the diversified holism of the embodied event of speaking suffers a pulverization into discrete elemental representations of locutions, illocutions, and perlocutions. These atomistic representations offer little toward a comprehension of the embodied praxis of communication. To achieve an understanding of the dynamics of communication one needs to work one's way around the constraints of linguistics modeled after an empirically grounded representational elementarism.

Lanigan's interrogations of the contributions of semiotics follows the lines of an analysis similar to that of his uses of phenomenology for approaching the communicative function of the event of speaking. In the case of semiotics we are apprized of the dangers of developing a theory of the sign that might gravitate us into a semiotic reductionism, which like a linguistic empirical elementarism would occlude the positive resources of communication. A semiotics that congeals into a theory of signs founded on a grammatological function within a signifier/signified infrastructure loses the event of speaking and the embodied speaker as readily as does an empirically based linguistic elementarism. Plainly enough, the science of linguistics has its own positive story to tell. The semiotic forms and rules within phonemics, morphemics, syntactics, and lexicography provide legitimate data for scientific investigations. An objectification of semiotic structures and relations is indeed required for a constitution of linguistics as a science. And such a constitution can happily proceed without reference to a speaking subject and the concrete event of speaking. It is thus appropriate to speak of *le langage* as comprising a synchronic structural system. But this should not be done at the expense of losing the diachronic dimension within the procession of speech events, occluding the upsurge of meaning in the word as being spoken (*la parole*).

Much has to do here with the need to remain attuned to a phenomenology of speaking, which alone can deliver the dynamics of semantics as the augmentation of meaning. Syntactics requires the accompaniment of semantics with its sentential and narratival expression by a *speaking subject*, saying *to* someone, something *about* something. Only in such a moment can we unify meaning and reference within the dialectics of a genuine communicative event. It is this unity of meaning and reference voiced by a speaking subject that is torn asunder when structural semiotics is extended into a philosophical program of *structuralism*, auguring toward a unity of the human sciences encompassing anthropology, sociology, psychology. psychiatry, and literary theory—with sundry proclamations of the death of man, the elimination of authorial meaning, the dissolution of the speaking subject, etc. All this is brought to the fore in Claude Levi-Strauss's reductionist claim that the ultimate goal of the human sciences "is not to constitute, but to dissolve man." In semiotic reductionism the abstracted forms and laws of syntax replace the intentionality of speaking by a phenomenological subject. Such a destiny ill serves the functioning of an intentionality-laden speaking in the communicative venture, and in the end sacrifices both any robust phenomenology of the speech event and the proper role of a system-oriented science of semiotics. Richard Lanigan has shown us how to avoid this double edged danger by keeping the phenomenological speech event and the system of semiotics within their proper perspectives.

Acknowledgements

This Festshrift for Richard L. Lanigan was conceived as a result of the colloquium *The Cultural Matrix of Communicology* sponsored by the Department of Communication at Eastern Washington University in May 2014. Thanks to Gary Krug, department chair, Vickie Shields, Dean of the College of Social Sciences, co-editor Igor Klyukanov, Galina Sinekopova, and the university staff who organized that meeting, which included a number of the contributors to this volume. We wish to thank all the contributors, who enthusiastically produced original and compelling essays in honor of Richard in a relatively short period of time. Many of these scholars earned their doctorates under Richard's tutelage, and that of Thomas J. Pace in the philosophy of communication program at Southern Illinois University, Carbondale, between the years of 1976 and 1998. The initial work on the volume was made possible by a sabbatical leave for Andrew R. Smith at Edinboro University in the Fall of 2014. The editing and production of the manuscript would have taken much longer without the persistent, high-quality work of Raffaele Fusulan and Dorothy Noel, graduate assistants in the Department of Communication Studies at Edinboro University. The editors' appreciation for their dedicated efforts is immeasurable.

EDITORS

Isaac E. Catt (PhD, Philosophy of Communication, Southern Illinois University, Carbondale, 1982) is Visiting Scholar, Simon E. Silverman Phenomenology Center and Department of Communication & Rhetorical Studies, Duquesne University,

Pittsburgh, PA, USA. His research awards include the Donald H. Ecroyd Award for Research and Scholarship from the Pennsylvania Communication Association. Awards from the National Communication Association include Top Journal Article, Top Book Chapter, and Top Conference Paper in Philosophy of Communication and Top Conference Paper in the Semiotics Division. His many publications include guest editorship of several journals and *Communicology: The New Science of Embodied Discourse* with Deborah Eicher-Catt. He is author of *Embodiment in the Semiotic Matrix: Communicology in Peirce, Dewey, Bateson, and Bourdieu* (Fairleigh Dickinson University Press, 2017). Professor Catt is a member of the interdisciplinary European network of scholars on Social Uncertainty, Precarity and Insecurity (SUPI). He is Past President of the Semiotic Society of America, Fellow and Founding Member of the International Communicology Institute, member of numerous editorial boards and reviewer for several publishers. icatt309@comcast.net

Igor E. Klyukanov (PhD, Saratov State University [Russia], 1999) is Professor of Communication in the Department of Communication Studies at Eastern Washington University. He served as an Associate Editor of *The American Journal of Semiotics* and is the Founding Editor of *Russian Journal of Communication* (Taylor & Francis). He is interested in communication theory, philosophy of communication, semiotics, general linguistics, and translation studies. His works have been published in U.S., Russia, England, Spain, Costa Rica, Serbia, Bulgaria, India, and Morocco. His textbook *Principles of Intercultural Communication* (Boston, Pearson Education, 2005) has been adopted by over 30 Colleges and Universities in the United States. His monograph *A Communication Universe: Manifestations of Meaning, Stagings of Significance* (Lexington Books, 2010) won the 2012 NCA Philosophy of Communication Division 2012 Best Book Award. He is also the Translator and Editor of Mikhail Epstein's book *The Transformative Humanities: A Manifesto* (Bloomsbury, 2012). iklyukanov@ewu.edu

Andrew R. Smith (PhD, Philosophy of Communication, Southern Illinois University, 1990) is Professor and Graduate Program Head in the Department of Communication, Journalism and Media at Edinboro University where he also coordinates the Graduate Certificate in Conflict Management. He served as Senior Fulbright Fellow (1998–1999) and Fulbright Specialist (2011) at the Faculty of Letters, Mohammed V University, Rabat, Morocco, and is a member of the Research Group on Language, Culture and Development through the Centre for Doctoral Studies in Rabat. He is a Fellow in the International Communicology Institute and received the Donald H. Ecroyd Award for Research and Scholarship from the Pennsylvania Communication Association in 2016. He was recognized as advisor of the year at Edinboro in 2009. He is editor of *Radical Conflict: Essays in Violence, Intractability and Communication* (Lexington Books), coeditor of *Recovering Pragmatism's Voice: The Classical Tradition, Rorty and the Philosophy of Communication*

(SUNY), and author of numerous essays with focus on human rights, freedom of speech, intercultural learning, and the philosophy of communication, many of which can be found at https://edinborouniversity.academia.edu/AndrewRSmith. arsmith@edinboro.edu

CONTRIBUTORS

Corey Anton (PhD, Purdue University, 1998) is Professor of Communication Studies at Grand Valley State University and a Fellow of the International Communicology Institute. He is author of *Selfhood and Authenticity* (2001, SUNY Press), *Sources of Significance: Worldly Rejuvenation and Neo-Stoic Heroism* (2010, Purdue University Press), *Communication Uncovered: General Semantics and Media Ecology* (2011, IGS Press) and is the editor of *Valuation and Media Ecology: Ethics, Morals, and Laws* (2010, Hampton Press), co-editor (along with Lance Strate) of *Korzybski and...* (2012, IGS press), and co-editor (along with Robert K. Logan & Lance Strate) of *Taking Up McLuhan's Cause: Perspectives on Media and Formal Causality* (2017, Intellect Publishing). He is also past Editor of the journal *Explorations in Media Ecology*. antonc@gvsu.edu

Pat Arneson (PhD, Ohio University, 1987) is a Professor in the Department of Communication & Rhetorical Studies at Duquesne University in Pittsburgh, PA. Arneson is author of *Communicative Engagement and Social Liberation: Justice Will Be Made* (2014). She is co-editor with Ronald C. Arnett of *Philosophy of Communication Ethics: Alterity and the Other* (2014), editor of *Perspectives on Philosophy of Communication* (2007) and *Exploring Communication Ethics: Interviews with Influential Scholars in the Field* (2007), and co-author with Ronald C. Arnett of *Dialogic Civility in a Cynical Age: Community, Hope, and Interpersonal Relationships* (1999). She has published over 50 book chapters, journal articles, encyclopedia entries, or research reports and serves on editorial boards for several professional journals. arneson@duq.edu

Ronald C. Arnett (PhD, Ohio University, 1978) is Chair and Professor of the Department of Communication & Rhetorical Studies, The Patricia Doherty Yoder and Ronald Wolfe Endowed Chair in Communication Ethics, and Henry Koren, C.S.Sp., Endowed Chair for Scholarly Excellence (2010–2015) at Duquesne University. He is the author/coauthor/coeditor of fourteen books, including his most recent work, *Levinas's Rhetorical Demand: The Unending Obligation of Communication Ethics* (2017, Southern Illinois University Press). He is the recipient of six book awards, including the 2013 Top Book Award for *Communication Ethics in Dark Times: Hannah Arendt's Rhetoric of Warning and Hope* from the Communication Ethics Division of the National Communication Association. arnett@duq.edu

Vincent Colapietro (PhD, Philosophy, Marquette University, 1983) is Liberal Arts Research Professor at the Pennsylvania State University (University Park). One of his main areas of research is pragmatism, with emphasis on Peirce. Though devoted to developing a semiotic perspective rooted in Peirce's seminal work, Colapietro draws upon a number of other authors and perspectives (including Bakhtin, Jakobson, and Bourdieu as well as such movements as phenomenology, hermeneutics, and deconstruction). He is the author of *Peirce's Approach to the Self* (1989), *A Glossary of Semiotics* (1993), and *Fateful Shapes of Human Freedom* (2003) as well as numerous essays. He has served as President of the Charles S. Peirce Society, the Metaphysical Society of America, and the Semiotic Society of America. (vxc5@psu.edu)

Maureen Connolly (PhD University of Alberta, 1990) is a Professor of Physical Education and Kinesiology, in the Faculty of Applied Health Sciences at Brock University. Her ongoing interests include narrative and Arts based inquiry, poetic and bodily expressive modalities and how these function across scholarly, pedagogic and other creative outlets. A university and national teaching award winner and a 2009 Erasmus Mundus scholar, Maureen's teaching and research include curriculum, stressed embodiment, dance & movement education, and Freirian approaches to teaching and learning. Her theoretical dispositions are semiotic, phenomenological, post/anti-colonial, irreverent and quixotic. Maureen enjoys training, reading, writing, laughing, and authentic interpersonal engagement. mconnolly@brocku.ca

Thomas D. Craig (PhD, Religion, Vanderbilt University, 1991; PhD, Philosophy of Communication, Southern Illinois University, Carbondale, 1997) is a Communication scholar and photographer specializing in the role of the moving body through the activities of daily life. Research areas include Communicology and Culture, Phenomenologies of the Body, Critical Disability Theory, Deaf Sociality, Fundamentalisms. He is adjunct Professor in the Centre for Applied Disability Studies at Brock University, he also is a Founding Member, Fellow, and Director of Integrated Media for the International Communicology Institute. tcraig@start.ca

Deborah Eicher-Catt (PhD, Philosophy of Communication, Southern Illinois University, Carbondale, 1996) is Professor and Program Coordinator, Department of Communication Arts & Sciences and the Women's and Gender Studies minor, Pennsylvania State University, York. Her research explores the intersections of Communicology, narrative, and feminism. She is Fellow and founding member of the International Communicology Institute, past chair of the Philosophy of Communication Division for the National Communication Association, and co-editor (with Isaac E. Catt) of *Communicology: The New Science of Embodied Discourse.* She is an award-winning author and teacher receiving in 2012 the Donald Ecroyd Research and Scholarship Award and in 2016 the Teaching Fellow Award from

Pennsylvania State University. She is currently Vice-President of the Semiotic Society of America. dle4@psu.edu

William Barbosa Gomes (PhD, Southern Illinois University, Carbondale, 1983) is Professor of epistemology and history of psychology at the Universidade Federal do Rio Grande do Sul, Porto Alegre—Brazil. He is a licensed psychologist by the Universidade Católica de Pernambuco, Recife, Brazil (1971). At SIU, he studied with Dr. Richard Lanigan (semiotic phenomenology) and with Dr. Emil Spees (higher education). His publications include studies on semiotic phenomenology, experimental phenomenology and cognition, psychotherapeutic effectiveness, history of psychology, and curriculum development. He served as consultant to the National Coordination for Improvement of Higher Education, founder and first editor of *Psychology: Research and Review* (SpringOpen), and president of the Brazilian National Association for Research and Postgraduate Studies in Psychology (2012–2014). gomesw@ufrgs.br

Jason Hannan (PhD, Carleton University, 2010) is Associate Professor in the Department of Rhetoric and Communications at the University of Winnipeg. He is the editor of *Philosophical Profiles in the Theory of Communication* (Peter Lang, 2012) and *Truth in the Public Sphere* (Lexington, 2016). His research interests include bioethics and medical humanities, posthumanism and critical animal studies, and the intersection of rhetoric and political theory. j.hannan@uwinnipeg.ca

Hannah Karolak (ABD, Duquesne University) studies communication ethics and philosophy of communication. She is the author or co-author of two articles (one in press), four book chapters (two in press) and one book review. She has research interests in communication ethics and philosophy of communication. She is the recipient of the 2016 Donald Clark Edwards Award for Service from Duquesne University and the co-recipient (with Susan Mancino) of the 2015 Applied Urban Communication Research Grant for a project entitled "Memorials and Ironic Sites: Urban Communication Ethics in Local, National, and International Communities." Her current research explores communication ethics and counterterrorism in organizational contexts. cherico865@duq.edu

Alexander Kozin (PhD, Philosophy of Communication, Southern Illinois University, Carbondale, 2002) is Research Fellow and Manager, Centre for Literature and Philosophy, University of Sussex, UK. From 2003 to 2009 he was Research Fellow at the Freie Universität Berlin, Germany. His current interests reside at the juncture of phenomenology, semiotics, literature, and visual arts. He has published in *Janus Head, Text and Talk, Law and Critique, National Identity, Russian Journal of Communication, Journal of East European Philosophy, Law and Social Inquiry, Semiotica, International Journal for the Semiotics of Law* and other academic journals. Currently he is working on two book projects: *Alien Modalities in the Philosophy of Edmund Husserl* and *The Sense of Translation*. alex.kozin@gmx.net

Kristin M. Langellier (PhD, Southern Illinois University, 1980) is Emerita Professor in the Department of Communication and Journalism at the University of Maine. She studied with Richard Lanigan and completed a dissertation on *The Audience of Literature: A Phenomenological Poetic and Rhetoric*. Her research interests are narrative performance, family storytelling, and cultural identity. She has numerous article-length publications and two co-authored books: *Storytelling in Daily Life: Performing Narrative* (Temple UP, 2004); and *Somalis in Maine: Crossing Cultural Currents*. She is former Editor of *Text and Performance Quarterly* and former Mark and Marcia Bailey Professor at the University of Maine. kristin_langellier@maine.edu

Frank Macke (PhD, Philosophy of Communication, Southern Illinois University, Carbondale, 1993) is Professor of Semiotics, Rhetoric, and Communication Theory at Mercer University. He is Fellow and Founding Member of the International Communicology Institute. His essays have appeared in *Philosophy Today*, *The Journal of Phenomenological Psychology*, *Communication Education*, and *The American Journal of Semiotics*, and is the author of *The Experience of Human Communication: Body, Flesh, and Relationship*. He completed a degree (M. F. T.) in psychotherapy and psychoanalysis, human development, and family systems in 2006 from the School of Medicine at Mercer University, and served as Chair of the Commission on Semiotics and Communication of the National Communication Association, and Chair of the Philosophy of Communication Division of the NCA in 2016. fmacke@bellsouth.net

Susan Mancino (ABD, Duquesne University) is studying rhetoric, communication ethics, and philosophy of communication. Susan is the co-editor on an upcoming encyclopaedia on communication ethics with Ronald C. Arnett and Annette Holba (forthcoming with Peter Lang) and author or co-author of five articles (one of which is in press) and four book chapters (one of which is in press). Her work appears in national and international journals including *Review of Communication*, *Empedocles: The European Journal for the Philosophy of Communication*, and *Listening: Journal of Communication, Religion, and Ethics*. She is the recipient of the 2016 Wilhelm S. Wurzer Scholarship Award and co-recipient of the 2015 Applied Urban Communication Research Grant with Hannah Karolak. mancinos@duq.com

Thaddeus Martin (PhD, Philosophy of Communication, Southern Illinois University, Carbondale, 1992) is an Instructional Designer for Ellie Mae and an adjunct faculty at Modesto Junior College in Modesto, California. He received his B.A. in Philosophy at California State University, Chico. He took a course in Philosophy of Communication with Dr. Isaac Catt, and as a result continued studying at CSU, Chico to receive his M.A. in Interpersonal and Organizational Communication. He then studied with Dr. Tom Pace and with Dr. Richard Lanigan at Southern Illinois University, Carbondale, and received his PhD in Philosophy of Speech Communication from SIU Carbondale in 1992. Although he now works primarily in the private sector, he continues to read and write from a communicological perspective. thad.martin@dh.com

Jacqueline M. Martinez (PhD, Philosophy of Communication, Southern Illinois University, Carbondale, 1992) is currently Associate Professor of Communicology at Arizona State University. She has been a Fellow of the International Communicology Institute since 2000, and is a past president of the Interdisciplinary Coalition of North American Phenomenologists. She is the author of Phenomenology of Chicana Experience and Identity: Communication and Transformation in Praxis (2000, Rowman and Littlefield), and Communicative Sexualities: A Communicology of Sexual Experience. Some of her articles appear in Hypatia, Semiotica, and The American Journal of Semiotics. jmartinez@asu.edu

Thomas J. Pace (PhD, University of Denver, 1957) is Professor Emeritus from Southern Illinois University, Carbondale, where he served as Director of Graduate Studies for twenty years, retiring in 1994. From 1963 to 1965 he was a visiting postdoctoral scholar in philosophy and communication at Northwestern University. At SIU-C he directed fifty dissertations in Philosophy of Communication, Communication Theory, Rhetoric and Public Address, Discussion, General Semantics, Interpersonal Communication and Political Communication. He was one of the first to receive the Amoco Great Teaching Award at SIU-C, and upon retirement the NCA Wallace Bacon Lifetime Teaching Excellence Award. Central States Communication Association selected him to the Hall of Fame for Emeritus Professors, and the Illinois Communication and Theater Association awarded him the Edith Harrod Award and the W.P. Sanford Award for distinguished service and outstanding achievement to the profession. tjpacejr@frontier.com

Eric E. Peterson (PhD, Southern Illinois University, 1980) is Professor Emeritus in the Department of Communication and Journalism at the University of Maine. He studied with Richard Lanigan and completed his dissertation, *A Semiotic Phenomenology of Performing*. His published research draws upon traditions in the human sciences to examine communication phenomena that range from media consumption and identity politics to pedagogy and classroom communication. He has co-authored work with Kristin M. Langellier on storytelling and narrative performance, including their book, *Storytelling in Daily Life: Performing Narrative* (Temple UP, 2004) and a series of journal essays and book chapters on family storytelling. eric.peterson@maine.edu

Horst Ruthrof (PhD, Rhodes, 1969) is Professor Emeritus at Murdoch University, a Fellow of the Australian Academy of the Humanities and a Fellow of the Communicology Institute in Washington, D.C. With over 100 papers in philosophical, literary, linguistic, and semiotic journals, he is also the author of *The Reader's Construction of Narrative* (1981; 2016); *Pandora and Occam: On the Limits of Language and Literature* (1991; 2017); *Semantics and the Body: Meaning from Frege to the Postmodern* (1997; 1998); *The Body in Language* (2000; 2015); and *Language and Imaginability* (2014). His current project is *Language as Social Process: A Phenomenological Account*. H.Ruthrof@murdoch.edu.au

Calvin Schrag (PhD, Philosophy, Harvard University, 1957). Calvin O. Schrag is the George Ade Distinguished Professor of Philosophy Emeritus of Purdue University. He is a graduate of Yale and Harvard, a Fulbright Scholar at Heidelberg and Oxford Universities, a Guggenheim Fellow at the University of Freiburg, and a co-founder of the international philosophical quarterly Continental Philosophy Review. His published works have been translated into eleven foreign languages, of which the most recently published are *The Self After Postmodernity* (1999), *God as Otherwise Than Being: Toward a Semantics of the Gift* (2002), *Convergence Amidst Difference: Philosophical Conversations Across National Boundaries* (2004), *Doing Philosophy with Others: Conversations, Reminiscences, and Reflections* (2010), and *Reflections on the Religious, the Ethical, and the Political* (edited by Michael Paradiso-Michau with Interview, 2011). cschrag@purdue.edu

Johan Siebers (PhD, Philosophy, Leiden University, 1998) is Associate Professor of Philosophy and Religion at Middlesex University London and Associate Fellow and Director of the Ernst Bloch Center for German Thought at the School of Advanced Study, University of London. He has been a fellow of the International Communicology Institute since 2008. Johan founded *Empedocles: European Journal for the Philosophy of Communication*, as well as the Philosophy of Communication Section of the European Communication Research and Education Association (ECREA). He is Vice-President of the Ernst Bloch Gesellschaft (Ludwigshafen). His main research and publication interests are in philosophy of communication, history of German philosophy, metaphysics and critical theory. Johan.Siebers@sas.ac.uk

Hong Wang (PhD, Philosophy of Communicaiton, Southern Illinois University, Carbondale, 2002) is Associate Professor in the Department of Human Communication Studies at Shippensburg University, USA. She has been a Fellow of the International Communicology Institute since 2007. She serves on InSITE Conference International Board of Reviewers and a reviewer for Pennsylvania Communication Annual. Her major research interests include self-translating mechanism in intercultural communication, functionalities of cultural codes in computer-mediated communication, and the effects of embodiment in environmental communication that are reflected in her publications in American Journal of Semiotics, Journal of International Informing Science, and China Media Research, among others. howang@ship.edu. HoWang@ship.edu

COMMUNICOLOGY FOR THE HUMAN SCIENCES: LANIGAN AND THE PHILOSOPHY OF COMMUNICATION

Chapter Abstracts and Key Words

Part I. Founding(s)

Chapter 1. Andrew R. Smith, "Decolonizing Research Praxis: Embodiment, Border Thinking and Theory Construction in the Human Sciences." The essay configures both a philosophical introduction and a methodological orientation to human science research that can serve those who are doing empirical and/or eidetic work. Richard Lanigan's development of semiotic phenomenology has paved the way for a broadening of both phenomenology and semiotics, expanding in complementary fashion the epistemological horizons of each. The author argues that abductive and adductive logics are tropic in nature and function, and fundamental to critically reflecting on and de-positioniong prejudices, ascertaining working hypotheses, developing experimental work, imaginatively varying findings, and establishing reality-posits both abstract and concrete. The essay links eidetic science with theory construction in communicology, and shows how research can be grounded empirically and philosophically through methodological principles associated with both semiotics and phenomenology that advances a decolonizing research praxis.

Key Words: eidetic and empirical research, abduction, adduction, phenomenological epoché, epistemology, human science, communicability, Maurice Merleau-Ponty, Edmund Husserl, Hans Georg Gadamer.

Chapter 2. Corey Anton, "Lanigan's 'Encyclopedic Dictionary': Key Concepts, Insights, and Advances". Few works are more stimulating and more indispensable for any communicologist than Richard L. Lanigan's classic, "Communicology: An Encyclopedic Dictionary of the Human Sciences." In this heady text, Lanigan brings together and synthesizes important ideas from a wide swath of traditions and thinkers. He has accomplished what many scholars would have thought too bold of a project: a synergistic integration of semiotics and phenomenology. The present chapter draws heavily upon the Encyclopedic Dictionary to clarify how information theory is a subset of communication theory, one that has grown into human communication processes. My review shows how longitudinal intentionalities operate within Gestalten and phenomenological appresentation to vitally contribute to both perceptual processes and human communication. It also reveals how the evolutionary development of denotative utterances releases information from communicative contexts and bears upon the reversibility between perception and expression. Finally, it outlines the crucial role played by alphabetic literacy and literate-based technologies in increasingly transforming communication into an informational system, one where the "poetic function," the "metalinguistic function," and the "referential function," gain increasing relevance and come to rival the other discourse functions (i.e., emotive, conative, phatic).

Key Words: alphabetic literacy, analogic, appresentation, context, denotation, digital, eidetic, gestalt, iconic signs, indexical signs, invariance, marked vs. unmarked terms, paradigmatic axis, syntagmatic axis, play, writing

Chapter 3. Horst Ruthrof, "Communicability as Ground of Communicology: Impulses and Impediments." My contribution to this Festschrift for Richard Lanigan argues communicability as the necessary ground of communicology. The chapter opens with a minimal definition of communicability conditions requiring at least: social reciprocity; the ontic heteronomy of consciousness; intentionality; aboutness and voice; introjection and intention-reading; imaginability as projection of mental scenarios; and an intersubjective mentalism as methodological precondition. On this baseline of communicology, I address a series of impediments in the way of Lanigan's project. I identify such hurdles to human communicology as Frege's collapsing natural language meaning into formal sense; Saussure's radical arbitrariness; syntactocentrism of psycholinguistics; anonymized sentence meanings; the reduction of human communication to biology and other obstacles. Positive impulses in support of communicology are drawn from Dilthey's Geisteswissenschaften; Kant's schematism and his dialectic of reflective and teleological reasoning; Peirce's hypoiconicity; and Ingarden's ontic heteronomy of compound cultural phenomena.

Key Words: imaginability as variation of perception under social guidance; social reciprocity; aboutness; voice; implicit deixis; introjection; projection of mental scenarios; meanings as indirectly public; intersubjective intentionality; intersubjective mentalism

Chapter 4. Frank Macke, "The Human, the Family, and the Vécu of Semiotic Phenomenology: Lanigan's Communicology in the Context of Life Itself." One of the things that I take to be most powerful about Richard Lanigan's work is the manner in which it positions the messiness and mystification of human experience in the scheme of both semiotics and phenomenology. Reflecting on the concept of the "icon" as a general problematic of cultural semiotics, Lanigan (1993) writes: "within the context of communication and culture the most visible icon is the conscious experience we have of a child in the family. There is no better person upon whom we can focus our attention to investigate the problematic of how communication and culture come to thematize one another in daily life." Besides Lanigan, no one in the field that academia now recognizes as "communication studies" had ever considered the lived communicative experience (vécu is the preferred French term) of children and families (other than as behavioral abstractions) prior to the 1990s. The lingering aspects of infantile attachment and childhood/adolescent adjustment now preoccupy me as I think through the directions of communicology as an academic field and as a modality of addressing human science issues. For over three decades, the link between Merleau-Ponty and Foucault has been articulated in a depth by Lanigan that, in my judgment, finds no parallel in the human sciences. Lanigan's interpretation of Foucault's theory of discourse, particularly as it intertwines with his communicological interpretation of Margaret Mead's cultural theory of the family, enables thinking about the Self and Other—and what would appear, on the surface of things, to be relations of rational actors entailed in purposeful activity—to enter into new worlds of insight. It is this particular conceptual interconnection (with additional context from the recent work of Bernard Stiegler) that I will explore in this Festschrift contribution.

Key Words: family system, structure, icon, Murray Bowen, David Lynch, Charles Sanders Peirce, normality, Margaret Mead, prefigurative culture, intergenerational conflict

Part II. Tropologic(s)

Chapter 5. William Gomes, "Communicational Aspects in Experimental Phenomenological Studies on Cognition: Theory and Methodology." Neokantians of the late 19th century Baden school, resumed the theory that knowledge differed by conceptual characteristics of their objects. They emphasized the Kantian difference between phenomenon (capta) and noumenon (data). This theoretical understanding led to two methodological views, idiographic methods for the study of capta and nomological methods for study of data. A century later in his work on theory and methodology in the human sciences Richard Lanigan reaffirmed the difference, but resized the relationship between objects and their conceptual characteristics. According to Lanigan, theory implies the conjunction between an eidetic model (realization) and an empirical model (actualization). Thus, the eidetic model would be analytical (deduction, sufficiency) and critical (adduction, necessity); and the empirical model would be experimental (induction, actuality), and experiential (abduction, possibility). In turn, methodology would be the conjunction, yet contrast, between quantity (what is real) as the truth condition method, and quality (what appears) as a necessary and sufficient condition method. This chapter will describe and demonstrate how this epistemological primacy guided a fertile empirical research program, anticipating what is now recognized in cognitive science as the first person perspective (experiential) and third person perspective (experimental). In theoretical terms, the scope of what is named experimental phenomenology will be illustrated by empirical studies on the reversible relation between capta and data on psychotherapeutic effectiveness, and by cognitive studies of external manifestations of internal conversations. In methodological terms, these studies meet the logical requirements of abduction (why experiential?), induction (why experimental?), deduction (why analytical?), and adduction (why critical?).

Key Words: Gomes theory, methodology, experimental phenomenology, internal conversation, memory, human communication

Chapter 6. Igor E. Klyukanov, "The Monstrosity of Adduction." In this chapter I look at anomaly representing the limit of human experience, distinguishing it from both abnormal and paranormal. I argue that anomaly presents itself as monstrosity—something appearing before us yet prior to sense. The monster is a divine omen and foreboding known through its effect; anomaly thus can only be felt. I also investigate how the immediate presence of "monstrosity" challenges our traditional logic and calls for a special kind of reasoning. I claim that monstrosity can be best explained by adduction as "an extreme case" of our perceptual judgments. Although Ch. S. Peirce used the term "adduction", he never seemed to clearly differentiate between hypothesis (read as abduction) and abduction (read as adduction). I attempt to do this in my chapter by drawing on Richard Lanigan's writings (1992; 1995; 2005). I find his conceptualization of adduction extremely insightful and heuristic. Based on these ideas, I map out the four kinds of reasoning—induction, deduction, abduction, and adduction—onto the Semiotic Square and show where paradox and anomaly fit there. Finally, following Lanigan's treatment of "the Critical as the use of adductive logic", I show that monstrosity, too, "requires necessity": it is the ultimate external test that calls for synthetic reasoning which supplies new ideas.

Key Words: paradox, anomaly, monstrosity, phenomenology, adduction, abduction, semiosis, liminal, Immanuel Kant, Charles Sanders Peirce, Richard Lanigan

Chapter 7. Alexander Kozin, "Is Martin Heidegger's 'Fourfold' a Semiotic Square?" This chapter examines the possibility of a semiotic reading of Martin Heidegger's concept of the fourfold (das Geviert) which he discusses in several of his writings on language. An invitation to such an examination is called both by the phenomenologist's expressed interest in signification and the uncanny resemblance of his fourfold to Algirdas-Julien (A.-J.) Greimas' semiotic square. Yet, as I would like to argue, Greimas' objective and method, although related to Heidegger's approach to signification, are different enough as to suggest that Heidegger created a unique semiotic model. I elaborate this model focusing on its main components (e.g., "set terms"), relations (e.g., "unfolding"), and functions (e.g., "un-concealment"). I also provide an exemplar of fourfolding: Paul Bowles' novel The Sheltering Sky. The main purpose of this study is to bring attention to the semiotic strand in Heidegger's philosophy vis-à-vis literary aesthetics.

Key Words: fourfold, semiotic square, isotopy, actant, unfolding, unconcealment

Chapter 8. Eric E. Peterson and Kristin M. Langellier, "Communicology and the Practice of Coding in Qualitative Communication Research." Qualitative communication researchers take up the challenges of systematic analysis of interviews, documents, and participant observation. In analysis, the researcher identifies units of data that are meaningful or significant. With the advent of computer-assisted data analysis, emphasis has shifted to taking up this process as the practice of coding. Codes, from this perspective, are a shorthand way to distinguish, label, organize, and categorize qualitative data. This essay uses semiotic phenomenology to critique the practice of coding which emphasizes explicit content over lived meaning, common-sense knowledge over interpretive understanding, saying over doing, information over communication, and data over capta. In short, coding conflates the order of experience with the order of analysis that a communicology-based understanding of codes would address. We draw on examples of empirical research to illustrate the value of communicology in cultivating alternatives to coding for qualitative communication research.

Key Words: coding, qualitative inquiry, research methods, discourse analysis, storytelling

Part III. Trans/formations

Chapter 9. Ronald C. Arnett, Susan Mancino, and Hannah Karolak, "Emmanuel Levinas: The Turning of Semioethics." This essay explicates Emmanuel Levinas's "ethics as first philosophy" as a performative phenomenon that commences with the face of the Other as sign (an ethics of optics) that shifts one's attention to an ethical echo of "I am my brother's keeper" (an audio ethic). This encounter transforms an "originative I" into a "derivative I"* charged with unending responsibility and obligation to and for a particular Other. The performative phenomenon of Levinas's ethics project frames connections to: (1) communication and communicology, and (2) semioethics and rhetoric. We turn to a communicological understanding of communicative experience as we encounter the experience of Levinas's groundbreaking project on ethics. The experience of his work permits one to sense signification beyond the words. This essay explicates, via communicology, the signification of Levinas's undertaking. [*Ronald C. Arnett, Communication Ethics in Dark Times: Hannah Arendt's Rhetoric of Warning and Hope (Carbondale: Southern Illinois University Press, 2013)]

Key Words: communicology, semiotic phenomenology, Richard Lanigan, Emmanuel Levinas, semioethics, semiotics, human science, phenomenology

Chapter 10. Isaac E. Catt, "Mental Health in the Communication Matrix: A Semiotic Phenomenology of Depression Medicine." This chapter explores Richard L. Lanigan's claim that the reversibility and reflexivity of perception and expression provide the logic foundations for the human sciences. This profound idea is applied in the context of mental health. Ontological and epistemological presuppositions of depression medicine are exposed. Depression is the paradigm exemplar of modern psychiatry, and its treatment through antidepressant drugs is a prototype rationalizing the prevailing mechanistic culture. The purposes of the critique are to provide a clearing for informed decision-making and to restore a needed dialogue between psychiatry and communicology. A semiotic phenomenology of mental health is described focusing on depression, the medical disease model is interrogated by examining a particular narrative, and the conscious experience of being on the drugs is compared to experiencing depression. A sense of disconnection, of lost communication with the social world is found essential to both. Communication is positioned as a central concern of depression medicine and of mental health in general.

Key Words: Pierre Bourdieu, Bernard Stiegler, existence and experience, asynchronous expression and perception, ecology of communication, antidepressants, feelings of being, epistemic pathology

Chapter 11. Jacqueline M. Martinez, "Decolonial Phenomenological Practice: Communicology across the Cultural and Political Borders of the North-South and West-East Divides." My concern in the present work is to consider how communicology, as an interdisciplinary and decolonial phenomenology, constitutes a philosophical practice that has the capacity to adequately engage the cultural, historical and political borders that create tacit hierarchies of meaning and value across the north-south and east-west global divides. Taking up Enrique Dussel's Ethics of Liberation, this communicological approach features the problematic of embodiment as a condition of contingency in which the immediacy of lived-experience becomes actualized within historical and cultural contexts that always exceed the perceptive capacities carried within the immediacy of the communicative-experience of the person. Specifying the terms and conditions of this cultural (semiotic), historical (temporal), and axiological (political) situation is beyond consciousness as it emerges within the immediacy of communicative-experience. Efforts to specify these terms and conditions often lend themselves to critical practices that disregard their own terms of communicative engagement. My effort is to demonstrate how a communicological approach provides a more adequate way of intervening in the reproduction of cultural hierarchies of difference, and to show how a such an approach allow us sort through the problems of assessing our capacity to adequately interrogate the very terms and conditions through which our communication with others both enables and constrains our ability to cross the cultural and political borders that are at work in the immediacy of communicative-experience.

Key Words: cultural communicoloy, decolonial phenomenology, liberation ethics, scientific inquiry, capacity vs. actuality, Enrique Dussel, Charles Sanders Peirce

Chapter 12. Hong Wang, "In the Context of Communicology: Issues of Technical Risk Communication about Sustainability." The concept of intentional arc originates from Merleau-Ponty's concern for body-mind-world, whereby a well-trained body can take charge, and does what it needs to do outside the range of consciousness, or in other words, thoughts are generated without mental representation. By looking into the intentional arc of the general American public the author argues that environmental education needs to re-design its approach from information focus to communication focus. The first part of the paper describes the semiotic features of the EPA's website presentation pertaining to the "zero nature". The paper moves on to reduce the intentional arc or embodied conditions of the general public, who lives in this complex interplay of the different worlds where meanings have to be personally sought after. In the final section I discuss how the technical risk communication fails its purpose from the perspective of communicology. I conclude that embodied intentional arc presents a big challenge to performing environmental sustainability. Communication rather than information transmission will better prepare the public for living a sustainable life.

Key Words: information vs. communication, embodied experience, intentional arc, mediation, Peirce's model of sign, representation, semiotic plausibility, sustainability

Part IV. Voicing Bodies/Embodying Voices

Chapter 13. Deborah Eicher-Catt, "Authoring Life Writing as a Technology of the Self: A Communicological Perspective on the Concept of Voice." This paper problematizes a number of theoretical issues surrounding the popular performance of feminist life writing, in particular investigating how it relates to the feminist concept of "voice." To begin, I argue that current theorizing on life writing is too narrowly focused on its linguistic nature. Drawing from the works of Michel Foucault, I develop a more nuanced epistemology of life writing employing a Communicological lens, paying tribute to the insights of Richard L. Lanigan. I argue that such an epistemological stance expands our current understanding of life writing because it allows us to view it as a dialectical practice of discourse thereby fully appreciating it as a communication phenomenon (not merely a linguistic enactment). I describe how life writing is best understood as proceeding from a combinatory discursive logic, one that accentuates it as a semiotic process and phenomenological event, i.e., embodied communicative experience. Doing so begins to expose life writing's inherent dialectical movement in practice between life writing and what I call writing life. I use Foucault's dialectic of the "voiceless name" and the "nameless voice" (and Lanigan's interpretation of Foucault on this phenomenon), to provide a more insightful analysis of the life writing process as an issue of voice. We discover that when viewed as a discursive practice (and not merely a practice of discourse), voice enacts its true authorship. I argue that it is only through this new theoretical lens that we can understand life writing as a powerful technology of the self that feminists claim it to be.

Key Words: life writing, technology of the self, Michel Foucault, nameless voice, voiceless name, feminist theory, authorship, discursive logic.

Chapter 14. Pat Arneson, "Communicative Possibilities in/of a Glance." In this essay, I consider philosophical differences between gaze and glance. Particular attention is paid to gaze in the works of Jean-Paul Sartre, Michel Foucault, and Jacques Lacan. Edward S. Casey's work on glance opens possibilities for understanding the relationship between philosophy and human communication. I address the role of one's attentiveness in glancing with particular attention to visual and mental glancing in his work. A communicological perspective on glancing is offered, emphasizing the perceptual component of communicology. An embodied event of glancing is examined as it communicatively orients a person in her lived-world.

Key Words: gaze, glance, possibility, communicative event, Edward S. Casey, Richard L. Lanigan, Jean-Paul Sartre, Michel Foucault, Jacques Lacan, Maurice Merleau-Ponty

Chapter 15. Maureen Connolly and Tom D. Craig, "Laban and Lanigan: Shall We Dance?" The authors use examples of bodily expressive movement in everyday life as a site for a semiotic phenomenological elucidation blending Rudolf Laban's movement analysis with Richard Lanigan's embedded tripartite methodology of description, reduction, and interpretation. In so doing, we hope to disclose cultural norms and inscriptions, the body as socially volatile sign, and the sign system/s that hold these together.[i] In effect, we offer a semiotic choreological exploration of an embodied poetics of practice. We will be weaving a semiotic phenomenological description (using Lanigan's tripartite approach) with a Laban movement analysis while acknowledging the necessity of both being embedded within a cultural context that also informs the bodily-expressive examples that are the focus of the analysis. For this paper we explore the movement experience of "pressing", a basic effort action that combines time, weight, space and flow and that also carries and expresses cultural norms and inscriptions. We describe and examine pressing in basic and more elaborated forms, and hope to engage the reader in its embodied intricacies and complexities.

Key Words: recursive analysis, liminality, ambiguity, socially volatile body, embodied intersectionality, expressive bodies, Rudolf Laban

Chapter 16. Thaddeus Martin, "Lexis Agonistic and Lexis Graphike: Translation from Library Document to Museum Monument." In the context of Communicology, the Vietnam Memorial and Wyoming's Independence Rock are placed in semiotic phenomenological apposition as a discourse practice to illustrate the inscription contest of lexis agonistike, or "performative style," vs. lexis graphike, or "written style." Foucault's concepts of the Library or Document, or what Lanigan describes as the voiceless name (Asyndeton), and of the Museum or Monument, or what Lanigan describes as the nameless voice (Prosopopoeia) are used to explicate this contest. The contest reveals what Foucault would describe as the limits and forms of the "sayable," of conservation, of memory, of reactivation, and of appropriation. The Vietnam Memorial is meant by the State to be a Museum or Monument, but is really a Library or Document via the human touch of embodiment; Independence Rock is meant by the State to be a Library or Document, but is really a Museum or Monument as the rock itself, like our bodies, slowly fades/wares away.

Key Words: asyndeton, prosopopoeia, lexis agonistike, lexis graphike, library, museum, postmodern, Gemeinschaft and Gesellschaft, document, monument, Michel Foucault, Aristotle, semiotics, phenomenology

Part V. Horizons of Communicability

Chapter 17. Vincent Colapietro, "The Subject at Hand." Peirce's dialogical understanding of semiosis encompasses not only a semiotic understanding of dialogue but also a Platonic vision of Logos. In practical terms, this vision of Logos translates into an acknowledgment of the power of reality to elicit recognition, not merely to invite inquiry. Despite our finitude, fallibility, and indeed "depravity," we are, even at our worst, unwitting witnesses to an encompassing reality in whose depths the very roots of our being are to be found. Even our errors have their truth. In most processes of communication, the participants are guided by a sense of salience. At the very least, an implicit question ("How is this relevant to the subject at hand?") directs them. Even a communicative exchange given to free association is one in which the hope of discovering a more subtle network of ordinarily unnoticed saliences tends to be operative. Of course, exchanges not abandoning themselves to such association can also be often ones in which a kaleidoscopic series of cursory topics, momentarily touched upon, unfolds. In a variety of ways, a conception of reality as that which is at our beck and call takes hold. Granting reality itself a say in what we say about it smacks of a fantastic anthropomorphism. Or so our modernist sensibility immediately disposes us to think. But what if our sense of salience is, in effect, a witness to the presence of the subject(s) at hand, to their power to insinuate themselves in our discourses? This has little to do with the force of actuality, though what little it has to do with this is hardly negligible. It has most to do with the power of reality to win our recognition. If this is so, then the subject at hand, the topic about which we are communicating, is not amorphous, inert stuff waiting to be shaped in any form whatsoever by the adventitious will of capricious interpreters; rather it is a dynamic, form-giving or –generating power. The subject at hand is itself a participant in our discourses. What would it mean to accord it such a status in communication? Given my interests and expertise, I know of no better way of honoring Richard Lanigan's singular contribution to contemporary thought than by exploring this Peircean suggestion.

Key Words: Mikhail Bakhtin, communication, dialogism, experience, *logos*, *Natur- v. Geistwissenschaften*, Charles Sanders Peirce, phenomenology, pragmatism, realism (and anti-realism), reality, Richard Rorty, semiotics, signs, subjectivity

Chapter 18. Jason Hannan, "Being in Speech: Inferentialism, Historicism, and Metaphysics of Intentionality." This chapter explores the thought of Robert Brandom, one of the most important philosophers in the English-speaking world. Like Richard Lanigan, Brandom's thought is devoted to illuminating the nature of consciousness. But whereas Lanigan works through the tradition of phenomenology, Brandom works through the tradition of historicism. The first part of this chapter explores Brandom's answer to a deceptively simple question: what does it mean to be a creature of speech? The second part provides a more detailed account of Brandom's historicism. The third part reviews the political implications of Brandom's thought for democracy. In the final part, I argue that Brandom's model of historicism and Lanigan's model of a semiotically inflected phenomenology provide two paradigms for a posthumanist ethics and politics.

Key Words: historicism, pragmatism, intentionality, speech, reasoning, phenomenology, object-oriented ontology, posthumanism, animals

Chapter 19. Johan Siebers, "The Theory of Perfective Drift." In this paper I outline a philosophy of communication which seeks to articulate and connect (a) a processual view of communication and (b) a view of communication that emphasizes the various ways in which wholeness is an often problematic but never absent dimension of communicative acts. The paper builds on Lanigan's seminal work in drawing the implications of Merleau-Ponty's existentialist phenomenology for communication theory by arguing that there is a specifically philosophical dimension to understanding communication as both direct intuition and as a reflexive relation constitutive of subjectivity, which requires its own modes of expression, articulation and indeed conceptual analysis. Once the difference between philosophies of communication and other approaches to communication has been established, the outlines of the theory of perfective drift are sketched by reference to process philosophy and a re-interpretation of F. Dance's helical model of communication. The implications of the theory for a critical theory of communicative praxis are indicated in the conclusion.

Key Words: Maurice Merleau-Ponty, Ernst Bloch, process philosophy, phenomenology of communication, metaphysics of communication, subjectivity, helix model

Introduction

Communicology: What's in a Name?

ISAAC E. CATT, IGOR E. KLYUKANOV, AND ANDREW R. SMITH

The term *communicology* is now widely accepted internationally as the appropriate designation for the study of embodied human discourse, as elaborated in the work of Richard L. Lanigan, especially in *The Human Science of Communicology*.[1] The prefix is derived from the Latin *communis*, what is held in common and constructed in common, and of course the Greek suffix *ology* specifies the logic(s) of discourse in a field of study that engages objects (and subjects) of inquiry. Communicology is a human science discipline that is underwritten by a substantial intellectual tradition in the philosophy of communication. The authors of chapters in this book offer ample evidence for the claim that the range of communicology entails all of human lived experience, but with focus on interrelated domains of communication including the intrapersonal (corporeal-self domain), interpersonal (self-other domain), social (group-organizational domain), and cultural (traditional, mediated, artistic, national and political).[2]

While still drawing on and influencing diverse disciplines in the human sciences and testing disciplinary limits, the specific aim of this collection is not to establish a unified science through integration of theory, but to demonstrate a range of scholarship responding to and extending the seminal work of Richard L. Lanigan. Ultimately, research in different domains shows that humans can only be understood ontologically as communicative beings; put differently, the humanity of every person is inherently communicable. There are multifarious constraints on experience, but the drive to communicate is just as strong for the person with a severe neural disability, or one who by extreme circumstance is confined and prevented from interacting with anyone, as it is for an able-bodied person. We live to communicate with other persons but also with natural, mystical, and imaginary worlds. Unlike some psycholinguists and cognitive neuroscientists, however, who argue for a biological foundation for the acquisition of language, communicologists see language in an active sense and recognize languaging as one among several expressive semiotic capabilities that a person embodies.[3] Certainly, meaning in language is an abstraction, whereas the full sense of the word communication implies an eidetic linguistic habitus necessarily grounded in an empirical embodied habitus. As a symbolic representation of culture, language assumes meaning when in use.

Given these capabilities for creative languaging and other forms of semiosis for persons living in complex worlds with other human and non-human beings, what are the limits of this relative newcomer to the human sciences? By definition, a discipline must have recognized boundaries. It is obvious that communication inquiry has the potential to be connected to anything and everything, but the principal focus here is embodied meaning in human expression and perception in all domains specified above, whose manifestations in discourse seek to describe, analyze, interpret and improve human relations. Given its breadth of concerns and problematics, communicology shares boundaries with its disciplinary cousins including philosophy, psychology, psychiatry, sociology, linguistics and anthropology, which have influenced its development from the beginning. The study of persons in the communication matrix is sufficiently complex and broad as it incorporates knowledge from all these disciplines and more. An interest in experimentation with ideas and experiences is firmly grounded in the tradition of American pragmatism stemming from the works of Charles Sanders Peirce, John Dewey, William James, George Herbert Mead and others.

There is a difference between coherence and integration. Communicology offers coherent theory and does not attempt to connect communication to the entire universe. It appears that attempts to unify science and theory will always be with us, but communicology respects the limits of its disciplinary cousins, while seeking meaningful dialogue with them to advance knowledge of lived worlds and human relations. Communicologists resist the all too easy temptation to close off a universe of discourse by means of scholasticism, which employs the art of rendering certain subject matter off limits by means of elite and exclusionary naming. In other words, and as the authors in this book exemplify, disciplinary boundaries define communities of shared interest, while creating linkages for innovative research and shared knowledge.

At communicology.org, the website for the International Communicology Institute, there is a brief and useful chronology tracing significant publications relevant to the discipline. However, intellectual histories of this relatively new field are still in the making. They will no doubt specify converging interests from multiple disciplines, describe several paradigms of influence, and mention prominent thinkers some of whom do not take discourse as their initial focus of attention. There may be competing interpretations of where such histories should begin, arguments about whether a particular scholar is really a communicologist, and differences of opinion concerning the time and place where it can be said that communicology proper emerged. No single history will exhaust the discussion; more likely most will have something useful to offer. Our point here is that communicology has deeper roots than some might suppose, the most obvious of which are linked to the tradition of rhetoric. By way of introduction, then, we will draw attention to other traditions, while recognizing that the task will remain incomplete.

Communicologists strive to be open-minded by means of phenomenological methodology. This form of rigorous systematic reflection seeks to radically reflect on and set aside, or bracket, presuppositions for the purpose of grounding tentative claims, posing theories, and advancing working hypotheses. Then, too, we are self-conscious of our fallibility. The world perceived, after all, is a mediated reality filtered by signifying relations, the study of which is semiotics. Communicology employs combinatory logic of both phenomenology and semiotics.

We believe the word *communicology* is an improvement over other references to the field such as communication studies, which does not roll off the tongue with ease, or communications associated primarily with technology and media studies. Neither of these latter names arises from a specific and synthetic philosophical foundation, nor does the ambiguous term communication. Indeed, communicology is distinguished from mainstream theory and research in communication in numerous important ways, even while offering an inclusive umbrella name for the advancement of philosophically informed scientific inquiry. Undoubtedly, communication scholars in the United States are familiar with the social science of communication but less familiar with the human science of communication and may want to identify the latter as merely a subset within the myriad of qualitative approaches derived from the humanities. While the humanities generally influence communicology, the discipline is proposed not as another method but rather as living philosophy grounded in the rigorous, systematic application of semiotics and phenomenology. Mainstream scholars may conceive phenomenology as another word for introspection, and, if they recognize semiotics at all, might locate it as a narrow method for media analysis. We should not be surprised. It takes time to recognize a new paradigm and then to grasp what may be its radical implications for the standard ways of thinking and the routines of scholarly practices. This is true even if the accepted vocabulary is problematized; for example, the word *empirical* means something quite different in the USA version of social science than it means to William James who proposed a "radical empiricism" that we know today as phenomenology. Scholars of intercultural communication have long thematized and distinguished levels and degrees of resistance to new ideas, with acceptance of change being a primary exemplar of culture.[4] While the USA is said to be more receptive to change than many other countries (nations, of course, are not the boundaries of culture), this does not suggest that new ideas meet with no resistance or automatically become lasting features of US culture. For instance, some scholars in cultural studies drawing selectively on Pierre Bourdieu have recently suggested that phenomenology is dead. And, when the print media in the United States wrote their epitaphs for the last undergraduate program in semiotics at Brown University they said farewell to what they conceived as an obscure interest in linguistics with irrelevant origins in the Medieval Period. More recently, the obituary for Umberto Eco in the *New York Times* recognized his international status as a renowned scholar of the humanities and duly noted his many novels, but also referenced his strange fascination with the "arcane" subject "semiotics." By contrast, thinkers like Maurice Merleau-Ponty, Pierre Bourdieu, Michel Foucault and Richard Lanigan draw on several intellectual traditions and rely upon semiotics as a synthetic logic in addition to an analytic logic.[5] Disciplinary animosities among philosophy, anthropology, psychology, and sociology are thus transcended. Oppositions between philosophies of experience and philosophies of logic are reconsidered as *a*ppositions that inform and draw from one another with dynamic boundaries between and among them, rather than territorial oppositions. This critical turn has a history.

Here we will supplement and complement the intellectual history of communicology provided at communicology.org and elaborated in Lanigan's seminal essay on "The Yale School of Communicology" which constitutes the point of departure for the essays in this book.[6] We recognize that histories of the mainstream discipline of communication have been written and have legitimacy, certainly, but the history of communicology is distinct, largely invisible to the mainstream narrative of rhetoric and social science, taking shape in parallel fashion to them. The history of any discipline, communicology included, is a story of people and ideas that create an intellectual heritage. This heritage is perhaps unavoidably chronological as usually rendered, but reality is always a bit different. The strands of the narrative overlap, as American pragmatism meets continental philosophy and a synthesis commences that results ineluctably in today's communicology.

This history begins in altogether different times and places—the Metaphysical Club in Boston where Charles S. Peirce spoke and the Universities of Göttingen and Freiburg in Germany where Edmund Husserl worked; it incorporates unique threads of several disciplines, especially philosophy, linguistics, anthropology and psychiatry; it includes names unknown or unrecognized as "communication" scholars such as Peirce, Dewey, Husserl, Sapir, Merleau-Ponty, Foucault, Bourdieu; and it draws upon their work in ways that may be surprising to mainstream scholars. Above all, communicology is described as an organic outgrowth of philosophy of consciousness applied as a human science of experience and behavior. The intellectual history adumbrates the influence of early American pragmatism as it intersects with continental philosophy and psychiatry. This lineage takes us from Peirce to

John Dewey, Edward Sapir, Benjamin Lee Whorf, Harry Stack Sullivan, and to Jürgen Ruesch and Gregory Bateson in mid-20th century. Given the interconnection of these traditions, the central focus is on the meeting ground of semiotics and phenomenology in the communication matrix of person, society, and culture. In this brief history we foreground Ruesch and Bateson, because Lanigan designated their joint work in *Communication: The Social Matrix of Psychiatry* as the first coherent theoretical statement of communicology in the modern period. Many communicologists take this book as a starting point for their eidetic and empirical research in the late 20th and early 21st centuries, as this volume's essays, which encompass all of the disciplinary cousins mentioned above illustrate. Ruesch and Bateson are incorporated into the mainstream as pioneers in cybernetics-information theory, but they should also be seen as synthesizers of general semantics, pragmatism, phenomenology, semiotics, and culturology.[7]

Of course, all of the above moved concurrently if not in concert with the development of French and German philosophy involving Merleau-Ponty, Jürgen Habermas and the Frankfurt School, and others in contemporary continental philosophy. In fact, many of the ideas promulgated in American pragmatism may now be seen as highly compatible with continental thinking, such as Dewey's take on habits and conduct and Bourdieu's concept of habitus. The groundwork has been laid and the essays in the volume mark out the frontiers of the field.

We recognize that the word *communicology* itself is subject to interpretation. The Department of Communicology at University of Hawaii, Manoa, several universities granting degrees in communicology in Europe, professional and academic associations in Scandinavia, and budding journals lay their own claims to the name. Our claim is an alternative and readers will have to judge the history and intellectual basis provided for competing histories of this name. Just as (some of) the US scholars discuss the social scientific bias by addressing communication from more humanistic perspectives, in Russia and possibly elsewhere in the world, the study of communication today is being shaped within social science traditions. Clarification of terminology is important, given that the social science of communication is a broader concept in Europe than it is in the US, where it generally names the information science of message production, reception and exchange. A telling example is how "communicology" is conceptualized in Russia. The new Russian scientific journal *Communicology* positions itself as focusing "on the theory and practice of public relations, media and communications, the basic theory of communication, sociology of mass communications, image making skills, as well as problems of formation of non-material values (image, publicity, brand, reputation, etc.)."[8] As should be clear, the discipline of communicology we are advancing here does not cohere with a narrow focus on message processing exemplified by this "communications" paradigm.

To the contrary, communicology as a discipline in the human sciences incorporates information theory as a subset of communication theory. The intent is not to substitute human science for social science, but rather the inclusive goal of establishing a logical hierarchy in which the human science interest in meaning is embedded in and through expression, and perception takes precedence over the social science emphasis on information and message exchange. This shift in interest changes the focus of inquiry to the social and cultural conditions that give rise to what we conceive as messages. We must begin, therefore, with philosophy of communication. A philosopher's task is to ask fundamental questions and a communicologist consistently conducts inquiry with ontology, epistemology, axiology, and logic in mind. Whether synchronic or diachronic, a historicity or history, communicology's narrative is always sensitive to the operative intentionalities, institutional relations, and structural constraints associated with socio-cultural practices and individual agency. If that sounds like pragmatism, then it well should. If it seems a synthesis of the two great movements of continental philosophy, structuralism and phenomenology, then that is intended as well.

Given our own historical moment, we cannot know whether C. S. Peirce and fellows are the least cognizant of the enormity of their enterprise when they convene in Boston in the early 1870s to establish The Metaphysical Club.[9] The United States in the aftermath of the civil war is teeming with cultural conflicts in the process of fulfilling its supposed manifest destiny, which as we know includes the final conquering of the heretofore-indigenous populations all the way to the Pacific Ocean. Education is under development as a distinctive institution among others, and the first doctoral degrees in the newly unified nation are not yet awarded. Naturally, the nation looks to its ancestral background for models. In this context Peirce, his friend William James, Oliver Wendell Holmes, Chauncey Wright and others gather regularly to discuss European philosophy. It is relevant to mention that there are many exchanges during this time among German and American scholars particularly. Thousands of scholars travel across the ocean in both directions. Both Peirce and James spend significant time in Europe.

From these beginnings American pragmatism is born, a new contribution to philosophy. Yet, it must be understood that Kant, Hegel, Schiller and others would remain major influences in this new configuration of thought. Already, the study of language, then philology, is in their sight, as is hermeneutics. Signs were of importance in figuring issues of perception and expression. Phenomenology is a familiar term, which Peirce refers to as phaneroscopy, and Hegel's version is a tacit influence on pragmatism. Edmund Husserl is scarcely known in the USA during this time. Already, the subject of communication is a major issue in discussions of the new pragmatists, though the nexus of their conceit was just beginning to arrive. By 1898, James formalizes pragmatism as a movement in thought and credits the lesser-known Peirce as the originator of this philosophy, though Peirce rejects James' interpretation and renames his conception pragmaticism.[10]

Ferdinand de Saussure may be better known to scholars of communication whose interest is in cultural studies and who therefore frequently ground their work in structuralism and post-structuralism.[11] Despite his contributions to the life of signs in society, however, Saussure is not a communication scholar and is much less relevant to the discipline than is Peirce.[12] Saussure is a linguist who studies languages within a dualistic psychology; he is not a semiotician who studies theory of language in use. Saussure's version of cultural inquiry limits interest in *parole* and instead emphasizes *langue*, and at that, actually *langage* as idealization of signifying systems or what he called semiology. German and French scholars Karl Bühler and Emile Benveniste are prominent among speech theorists who unlike Saussure emphasize speech, but Roman Jakobson is perhaps better known to American communicologists.[13] Jakobson's model of communication based on Peirce's work translates the linguistic terminology of *langue* and *parole* to code and message. Jakobson understands Peirce's focus on semiotic phenomenology as the very essence of pragmatism. Semiotics, Peirce's word and the modern term for study of signs, employs phenomenology as methodology to describe verbal and nonverbal codes in use, and in speech.[14] This is to say, Peirce, like today's linguistic pragmatists, understands the importance of context as a dialectical construction of code and message in a matrix of sign embodiment, though we should note that semiotics is seldom mentioned in mainstream communication research.[15]

Peirce's contributions far exceed what we are able to say here, but it is worth noting that he emphasizes habit formation as a process of codification through signifying practices. The latter consists of irreducible triadic structures of sign-object-interpretant at their base such that a process of semiosis or sign action in discourse is always already underway in any form of communication. Rather than relying on positivist presuppositions that bifurcate person and world, subject and object, perception and expression in Cartesian fashion, and rather than presupposing the "social" that "constructs reality," the social itself is understood as an "interpretant" (Peirce's term for the effect of signifying relations). That is, society is a symbolic outcome of culture simultaneously affirmed and challenged in the predispositions of speakers who flexibly and creatively engage their worlds. As such, being human takes cultural precedence over any "natural" conception of human being in an ongoing process of persons interacting with each other's expressions. Each individual is taken as a "sign" of personhood to the other; their reciprocal comprehension of otherness as also "human" is entirely dependent on the taking of the other in the perception of expression as a sign. We are signs to one another and thus to ourselves.[16]

Dewey is a student of Peirce at Johns Hopkins and, though sometimes subtle, the influence of his teacher is generally palpable in Dewey's philosophy, psychology and educational experimentation. Dewey writes essays directly on semiotics, particularly notable being critical responses to his friend George H. Mead's student Charles Morris.[17] Under Mead's direction Morris begins his sojourn in semiotics, which he links with efforts seeking unified theory and behaviorism, both rejected by Dewey. Like his mentor, Dewey understands the necessity of the phenomenology of the sign in the study of communication. In this respect, his philosophy of consciousness is worldly and similar to that of existential phenomenologists such as Merleau-Ponty. Both learn from their respective predecessors Peirce and Husserl the fallibility of the search for absolute beginnings. In fact, a principal difference between Saussure and Peirce is precisely that the former's semiology is based on dualism, whereas Peirce's semiotics is grounded in "continuism," an ongoing communicative process.[18] This is to say that, with Dewey and later Merleau-Ponty, there is reversibility of person and world, experience is the reflexive condition of consciousness, and that body and sign are co-figured in the cultural-semiotic process and embodied-phenomenological event of communication. Particularly in his seminal essay on the reflex arc in psychology (which should be required reading for communication students) Dewey presages not only the critique of behaviorism but also a principal theme of Merleau-Ponty as described in Dreyfus's discussion of the same arc of communication decades later.[19] Dewey emphasizes habits as the predispositions of custom incorporated and altered in verbal and nonverbal discourse.[20] This same theme is continued and critically elaborated by Pierre Bourdieu in a number of works.[21]

Next comes Edward Sapir, another scholar whose significance to communication and to pragmatism is insufficiently recognized. Sapir studies with Franz Boas, our first culturologist, by which we mean a scholar whose focus is the logic of culture. Known as the first anthropologist in the USA, he already transcends the discipline with the prescient realization later formalized by Sapir, then Benjamin Lee Whorf, which consists in a distinct logic of experience and behavior, and, while each culture is capable of understanding every other culture, their semiotic systems *obligate* them to habitual patterns of social practices. Whorf's specific concern is that "natural logics" or habits of culture could act as blinders on embodied perceptions reified as semiotic expressions.[22] Contrary to popular but unexamined views in communication studies the two linguists never suggest that language inherently determines thought nor do they distinguish language separate from culture. Following their actual semiotics, it is more reasonable to conclude that they specifically oppose linguistic determinism or habitual logics that might prevent us from understanding the expressive systems of other cultures as equally legitimate. Incommensurability of thought can be overcome but it requires effort against the tendency to pre-consciously accept the taken-for-granted perceptions of culture that are reifications of language (and other semiotic systems as well).[23] Rather, language is considered a primary but nonexclusive symbolic semiotic system, a code of culture. Sapir and Whorf are in fact in clear allegiance with Hegel who posits language as "the actuality of culture"[24] and Alfred Korzybki's general semantics in the theoretical position that language is meaningless when it lacks reference to empirical grounds in nonverbal discourse.[25] The semiotic connection is scarcely noticed by many critics. However, Sapir's empirical studies of indigenous tribes in Canada, then his exposure to pragmatism at the University of Chicago assures us that Boasian teachings made lasting impressions on him. Following Boas, he does not divorce linguistics from culture and neither of them from communication. The combined influences lead him to two important realizations. First, all experience is semiotic, which he announces explicitly in his pivotal essay on symbolism.[26] Second, it is a fool's errand to speak of culture as an abstraction set aside from language in use, and likewise, any explanation of the individual person is false when disconnected from the culture in which every person's experience is embedded, a communicological conception.[27]

In Chicago Sapir comes under the considerable sway of pragmatism, and it now seems naturally so given the compatibility of Boas' thinking with Dewey's. Again, however, Sapir is not typically connected to pragmatism or semiotics. While in Illinois, Sapir learns that the already famous interpersonal psychiatrist Harry Stack Sullivan is to give a lecture. Sapir seeks to meet him, and they subsequently become fast friends and colleagues. Sullivan studies with Sapir, but it is a mutual arrangement, for Sapir uses Sullivan's work to discuss culture. Sullivan is phenomenologically informed and makes psychiatry focus on interpersonal communication by means of studying signs in clinical practice.[28] Though Sullivan receives mention in interpersonal communication studies, his phenomenology of signs in psychiatric practice remains to be appreciated in the discipline. Sapir and Sullivan advance the idea that society is an abstract concept, a context always to be determined by the interdependence of culture and person. The tension therein creates a matrix of the semiotic and phenomenological. Thus, they seek a "fusion" of the study of culture and psychiatry. It is not to be fulfilled because of several factors, ultimately Sapir's untimely death.[29]

We return, then, to Ruesch and Bateson whose collaboration produces the book *Communication* previously mentioned. This work provides the first comprehensive theory of human communication and is a fundamental text in communicology. We have already mentioned the levels of inquiry in communicology that derive from the networks of discourse described in this book. While the text is frequently cited by communicologists, we wish to draw attention to largely neglected but important aspects of their work. The collaboration of an anthropologist (Bateson) with a psychiatrist (Ruesch) is modeled on the Sapir and Sullivan relationship, which features the same combination and produces some reversal of roles in both cases. Sapir contributes to the first issue of Sullivan's new journal in psychiatry and finds himself writing significant essays on the fusion idea.[30] It is rightly said that he is an anthropologist who writes about psychiatry. Sullivan extrapolates the psychiatric dimension to speak broadly of social, national and international matters. In parallel fashion, it is rightly said that he is a psychiatrist who writes about culture.[31] The same may be said about the later scholars. Bateson, as is well recognized, works with Ruesch in psychiatry at the Langley Porter Institute. He is an anthropologist who practices psychotherapy. Ruesch writes extensively about culture, especially nonverbal codes of behavior.[32] The reversal of the authors in both instances mirrors what they have to say about the reversible and reflexive relationship of culture and communication. Both collaborations employ the insights of semiotics and phenomenology in pragmatism. The term "matrix" in the subtitle of the communication book is no accident, and neither is focus on the social or semantic level of discourse. Peirce, Dewey, Sapir, and Ruesch and Bateson all use the term "matrix" to name the intersection of body and sign in society.[33] A matrix in general is a nexus of interactions that are constraints, sign boundaries that are two-sided; the boundaries define, identify and distinguish interiority and exteriority, self and other. Peirce describes the matrix in discussions of the interpretant and symbol as "the womb of the future,"[34] an apt metaphor given that the homeworld of the person encounters the other of discourse in the matrix.

Peirce and Husserl have some limited familiarity with each other, but unfortunately they never meet and never have an opportunity to fully engage each other's work. Wilbur Marshall Urban is yet another professor at Yale University who not coincidentally uses Sapir's research in support of his work. Urban makes it his task to bring Husserl and Ernst Cassirer's thinking to the United States. Cassirer is among the greatest philosophers of culture whose work is scarcely referenced in communication studies. In fact, Cassirer makes the physical journey and joins the faculty at Yale. Urban's book, *Language and Reality*, interprets both Husserl and Cassirer and is another fundamental contribution to communicology. Central to his synthesis is that a person's perception and cultural expression are two interrelated levels of consciousness that occur in social context. Thus what we perceive is what we *mean*. This, of course, becomes a theme of Merleau-Ponty as well who posits that we are "condemned to *sense* [embodiment]," but he adds that "there is nothing that we can do or say that does not require a name [sign] in history."[35] Already in this statement the seeds are planted for his extensive theoretical work further employing the combinatory logic of semiotics and phenomenology.[36] Merleau-Ponty's student Bourdieu thematizes this Peircean compatible idea throughout his works in which he is concerned with the dialectics of embodiment and objectification. For Bourdieu, habitus is inescapably "a product of history"[37] as the "sensible," naturally, that is to say culturally, gravitates toward the "reasonable."[38] In Peirce this is the progressive but recursive movement of semiosis exemplified in the perception to expression semiotic phenomenological process of objects of thought from icon, to index, to symbol and normatively from aesthetics, to ethics, to logic.[39] Urban employs a quite similar phenomenological methodology to interpret the essential symbolism in Husserl as well as Cassirer. Cassirer, it must be remembered, describes a movement from myth (parole), to spirit (sign), to symbol (logos) and in this way stimulates a contemporary communicologist to associate his ideas with Peirce.[40] As Lanigan indicates, symbolism is Urban's term, common in the historic moment for semiotics. Lanigan argues that Ruesch and Bateson offer an application of this theory in their work together. That Ruesch is acquainted with Cassirer is evident in his avant-garde work in communication where he applies the idea of symbolic forms to understand communication.[41] Thus we may say with Lanigan that the levels of discourse we encounter in Ruesch and Bateson result from "the power of human speech to constitute conditions of subjective and intersubjective consciousness, principally the human ability to displace space and time referents by means of linguistic and semiotic symbols."[42]

This is to say also that Peircean ideas underwrite the mid-20th century work of Bateson and Ruesch. In fact, Bateson's work is suffused with language and ideas that appear to be drawn from Peirce, though this connection is instead probably inherited through his readings of Morris, Sapir, Whorf and Korzybski, as well as Ruesch's background studies of Dewey.[43] Specifically, at each level of discourse we have the encounter of existence with experience. Thus, the fundamental media of communication are: self as other, interpersonal other, social other and cultural other.[44] The word media is used here in its exact sense, referencing the levels of embodied existence encountering signs of the other in experience. Encounters of perception and expression in the social world are *mediations,* signs of the other in discourse.[45] We meet the other at the four levels mentioned. This does not imply that a completed consciousness sets off on a deliberate journey into the world of others; to the contrary, as Dewey and Bourdieu later describe, *hexis* and *habitus*, personal experience and cultural predispositions, are formed from the interpenetration of the encounters. While communicologists divide the territory for purposes of inquiry, the lived experience of communication is embodied and takes in the world and participates in its social practices in an all-at-once manner. No person is cultural, then social, then interpersonal, and so on. The world is always experientially taken in all at once. Lanigan's position on this is clear and profound in constancy with Husserl as he envisions phenomenology "the ground of both philosophy and science."[46]

Lanigan's history references Husserl's London lectures of 1922 as a starting point for communicology because it is here that the founder of phenomenology makes explicit the fact that the doublet "conscious experience," grounded as it is in the intentionality of a correlate phenomenal field, implies communication. Peirce's concept of semiosis may be read similarly, the action of signs in discourse being another way of discussing the sense and reason of intentionality. Recall that in Dewey and Dreyfus this is a reflex arc.

Among Urban's students at Yale is Lanigan's future teacher at the University of New Mexico, Hubert Griggs Alexander. Alexander's text, *The Language and Logic of Philosophy*, is another book that was required reading in doctoral classes taught by Lanigan in the philosophy of communication program at Southern Illinois University at Carbondale, Illinois in the USA.[47] Lanigan was and remains a mentor and friend to the editors of this volume. Along with the other authors in this book we are proud to offer this text as a humble memento to his profound and prolific contributions to philosophy of communication and communicology. We are very gratified professionally and personally to be a part of this intellectual heritage and philosophical movement.

OVERVIEW OF THE BOOK

Though inspired by Richard Lanigan, the essays here do not simply repeat his work or provide an exegesis of it; they are original to the volume and extend research in communicology in innovative and experimental ways. Calvin Schrag, whose own work has cut new paths in phenomenological research on communication, authors the Foreword and recognizes Lanigan's nuanced linkage of semiotics and the speaking subject. The Afterword is provided by Thomas J. Pace, Lanigan's mentor and colleague at Southern Illinois University for 30 years who, with Lanigan, established the first doctoral program in the philsophy of communication in the United States. The book is divided into five sections, based organically on the essays submitted. The editors did not solicit contributions based on the themes marked by the work's headings; the themes emerged from the essays submitted. The summary that follows is elaborated thematically by section heading with a brief explanation of how each chapter fits under that heading.

Founding(s)

Founding(s) and finding(s) rather than foundations, though certainly the latter term is pertinent, as we do seek to establish parameters for scholarship in communicology. That said, what has been found is not only what is given (*data*) in the sense of material data in the world or in human relations, but what the inquirer takes (*capta*) from his or her dynamic relations with others in the world, and what he or she does (*acta*) with it. Andrew R. Smith's essay "Decolonizing Research Praxis: Embodiment, Border Thinking and Theory Construction in the Human Sciences" provides an introduction to the epistemological basis for doing human science research on communication topics, and explains the relations between semiotics and phenomenology in doing this research with an interest in advancing theory construction that links eidetic and empirical dimensions of scholarship.

Corey Anton's essay, "Lanigan's Encyclopedic Dictionary" provides an overview of primary concepts associated with the work of both Lanigan and especially Roman Jakobson, arguing that critical features of Jakobson's model enables critical reflection on how technology increasingly structures human perception and expression. Horst Ruthrof's contribution, "Communication as Ground of Communicology" draws on a multitude of influences primarily from the German tradition of communicology to reveal the kinds of philosophical impediments that resist recognition of the primacy of communication, arguing that communicability is fundamental to all of the human sciences. And finally, Frank Macke's essay focuses on the contributions of French communicology, especially the work of Merleau-Ponty and Foucault, to address the fundamental problem of self-other relations stemming from the family, a focus that is foundational when we consider that all forms of communication develop primordially from this relation.

Tropologic(s)

Every field of study requires grounding in logic as well as a disciplinary language. The logics associated with communicology, however, go beyond the standard inductive and deductive approaches operative in the social sciences, and emphasize adductive and abductive logics as well. As William Gomes illustrates in his essay "Communicational Aspects in Experimental Studies on Cognition," those logics, poetic in nature and function, advance experimental work in the psychology of communication that is distinct from what researchers typically think of regarding experimentation. Igor E. Klyukanov takes the problem of logic into a new dimension by linking Peirce's and Lanigan's respective conceptions of adduction as a way to both clarify what that logic fully entails, and how its application addresses the distinctive problem of paradox and anomaly. Alexander Kozin, who, like Klyukanov draws on the semiotic square as a method for explication, applies it in complementary fashion to Heidegger's notion of the 'fourfold' and Paul Bowles's literary masterpiece *The Sheltering Sky*. The literary emphasis here focuses on lived meaning, and Eric Peterson and Kristin Langellier argue in "Communicology and the Practice of Coding in Qualitative Communication Research" that such meaning is integral to doing interpretive research. They offer alternatives to the notion of coding that do not conflate the order of experience with the order of analysis.

Trans/formations

The problem of change invokes the primary issues of self-other relations, and requires both transcendence of habituated practices and the emergence of new formations that advance an ethical life. Ronald Arnett, Susan Mancino and Hannah

Karolak in "Levinas and the Turning of Semioethics" take up this challenge of change as a performative phenomenon driven by the face of the other as sign. This problematic of the other and its trans/formative impact on self is exemplified, as Isaac E. Catt argues in his essay "Mental Health in the Communication Matrix," in the increasing dependency on anti-depressant medicine that wards off the effects of other persons in human relationship. Catt advances the idea that communication understood in terms of a matrix of human relations is central to sustaining mental health outside of the medical paradigm. Whereas Catt's emphasis is on interpersonal and familial relations, Jacqueline Martinez addresses the historical and political problematics of trans/formation through her critical analysis of the reproduction of cultural hierarchies based on identity and movement across borders and boundaries. She shows how a communicological approach aids in interventions against injustice associated with such hierarchies. Finally, Hong Wang in "At the Intersection of Intentional arcs—Issues of Technical Risk Communication about Climate Change" argues that environmental education must change radically from a purely information theoretic model about climate, to a communication theoretic model that enables a more decisive response to the planet's climate crises.

Voicing Bodies/Embodying Voices

The phenomenon of voice and embodiment permeates all essays in the volume, but those in this section make explicit claims concerning the reversible relation between voice and body in one dimension, and body and world in a more expansive dimension. Deborah Eicher-Catt in "Authoring Life Writing as a Technology of the Self" focuses on feminist life writing as a dialectical practice of discourse that involves embodied communicative experience in writing life through the voice(s) heard in that practice. Pat Arneson in her essay, "Communicative Possibilities in/of a Glance" addresses a voice that can be heard in a glance, with emphasis on the perceptual component of communication that creates of glancing an embodied event that orients a person in the life-world. Maureen Connolly and Tom D. Craig in "Laban and Lanigan: Shall we Dance?" work with movement analysis to disclose the body as a socially volatile sign with focus on the intricacies and complexities of pressing. To round out this section, Thaddeus Martin takes up the voices of monuments in "Lexis Agonistic and Lexis Graphike" with focus on the appositions between the Vietnam War Memorial and Independence Rock that mark the limits of the sayable.

Horizons of Communicability

As suggested earlier in this introduction, all disciplines have edges, boundary zones that touch upon other distinct fields of study that mark possibilities for recognizing new problematics and opportunities for inquiry. The volume ends with focus on horizons that push communicology into new territory that is not necessarily subsumed by the heritages it comes out of, but still illustrates the imaginative and experimental thinking that is so integral to verdant linkages between American pragmatism and continental philosophy. Vincent Colapietro, in "The Subject at Hand" seeks to uncover what is ordinarily unnoticed, unrecognized, in-communicable but still salient with a reality that is often sublime. How can we bear witness in discourse to that which resists discourse? He draws on Peirce especially to address this question of the subject-at-hand that is a dynamical, form-giving, object. Jason Hannan takes a similar tact in addressing some of the problematics associated with object-oriented ontology, albeit through the work primarily of Robert Brandom's historicism, which he contrasts with a semiotic approach to phenomenology in advancing a posthumanist ethics and politics. The final essay in the volume, Johan Siebers' "The Theory of Perfective Drift" draws upon Merleau-Ponty's existential philosophy and Lanigan's semiotic phenomenology to advance inquiry into the powers of direct intuition and the reflexive relations constitutive of subjectivity with an interest in advancing a critical theory of communicative praxis.

NOTES

1. Richard L. Lanigan, *The Human Science of Communicology: A Phenomenology of Discourse in Foucault and Merleau-Ponty* (Pittsburgh: Duquesne University Press, 1992).
2. This distinction between levels of communication and the specification of networks associated with them was first advanced by Jürgen Ruesch and Gregory Bateson; see their essay "Individual, Group, and Culture: A Review of the Theory of Communication," in *Communication: The Social Matrix of Psychiatry* (New York: Norton, 1951), 273–289. See also Deborah Eicher-Catt and Isaac E. Catt, eds., *Communicology: The New Science of Embodied Discourse* (Madison, NJ: Fairleigh Dickinson University Press, 2010). Andrew R. Smith argues that the national constitutes a separate, fifth, level of communication, and that the conflation of the national and the cultural is problematical politically; see "Discord in Intercultural Negotiation: Toward an Ethic of Communicability," in *Ferment in the Intercultural Field: Axiology/Value/Praxis. Intercultural and International Communication Annual*, vol. 26, ed. W. Starosta and G.-M. Chen (Thousand Oaks: Sage, 2003), 106.
3. Igor Klyukanov, *A Communication Universe: Manifestations of Meaning, Stagings of Significance* (New York: Lexington Press, 2010). See particularly chapter 5, 93–116.
4. See Smith, "Discord in Intercultural Negotiation," 91–130.
5. Michael Grenfell, *Pierre Bourdieu: Agent Provocateur* (New York: Continuum, 2004), 13.

6. Richard L. Lanigan, "Husserl's Phenomenology in America (USA): The Human Science Legacy of Wilbur Marshall Urban and the Yale School of Communicology," *Schutzian Research* 3 (2011): 203–217.
7. Ruesch and Bateson, "Individual, Group, and Culture".
8. V.F. Kuznetsov, "Communicology Journal. The Start-Up," *Politstudies*, http://www.politstudies.ru/en/article/4888 (accessed February 5, 2017).
9. Louis Menand, *The Metaphysical Club: A Story of Ideas in America* (New York: Farrar, Straus and Giroux, 2001).
10. Menand, *Metaphysical Club*, 354.
11. Ferdinand de Saussure, *Course in General Linguistics* (New York: McGraw-Hill, 1966).
12. Georges Deledalle, *Charles S. Peirce's Philosophy of Signs: Essays in Comparative Semiotics* (Bloomington: Indiana University Press, 2000), 100–113.
13. Roman Jakobson, "Langue and Parole: Code and Message," in *On Language: Roman Jakobson*, ed. Linda R. Waugh and Monique Monville-Burston (Cambridge, MA: Harvard University Press, 1990), 80–109.
14. Roman Jakobson, "The Speech Event and the Functions of Language," in *On Language: Roman Jakobson*, ed. Linda R. Waugh and Monique Monville-Burston (Cambridge, MA: Harvard University Press, 1990), 69–79.
15. Isaac E. Catt and Deborah Eicher-Catt, "Semiotics in Mainstream Communication Studies: A Review of Principal USA Journals in the Context of Communicology," *The Review of Communication* 12, no. 3 (2012): 176–200.
16. See Charles S. Peirce, "Pragmatism," in *The Essential Peirce: Selected Philosophical Writings*, ed. The Peirce Edition Project, vol. 2 (1893–1913) (Bloomington: Indiana University Press, 1998), 398–433.
17. John Dewey, "A Confused Semiotic," in *Knowing and the Known* (Boston: Beacon Press, 1949), 233–269. See also Dewey's "Peirce's Theory of Linguistic Signs, Thought and Meaning," *The Journal of Philosophy* 43, no. 4 (1946): 85–95.
18. Deledalle, *Charles S. Peirce's Philosophy*, 107.
19. John Dewey, "The Reflex Arc Concept in Psychology," *Psychological Review* 3 (1896): 357–370. Hubert Dreyfus, "Intelligence without Representation-Merleau-Ponty's Critique of Mental Representation: The Relevance of Phenomenology to Scientific Representation," *Phenomenology and the Cognitive Sciences* 1, no. 4 (2002): 367–383. These articles have the common theme of reflexivity in conscious experience as understood through phenomenology.
20. John Dewey, *Human Nature and Conduct* (New York: Henry Holt and Company, 1922).
21. Isaac E. Catt, *Embodiment in the Semiotic Matrix: Communicology in Peirce, Dewey, Bateson, and Bourdieu* (Madison, NJ: Fairleigh Dickinson University Press, 2017). Bourdieu did not read American pragmatism or Dewey specifically before developing his ideas concerning *habitus*. However, he read Dewey later and found his discussion of habits compatible.
22. Benjamin Lee Whorf, *Language, Thought and Reality* (Cambridge, MA: MIT Press, 1956). See particularly "Science and Linguistics," 207–219. For a historical review of these philosophical ideas see John Leavitt, *Linguistic Relativities: Language Diversity and Modern Thought* (London: Cambridge, 2011).
23. Catt, *Embodiment*.
24. Lanigan, "Husserl's Phenomenology," 207.
25. Alfred Korzybski, "The Role of Language in Perceptual Processes," in *Perception as an Approach to Personality*, ed. Robert R. Blake and Glenn V. Ramsey (New York: The Ronald Press Company,

1951), 170–205. This posthumously published article is important to understand General Semantics, because of the role of nonverbal discourse in Korzybski's thinking. See also Horst Ruthrof, *Semantics and the Body: Meaning from Frege to the Postmodern* (Toronto: University of Toronto Press, 1997) and Ruthrof's *The Body in Language* (London: Cassell, 2000) for a contemporary discussion of these ideas as they evolve in 20th century philosophy.
26. Edward Sapir, "Symbolism," in *The Psychology of Culture* (New York: Mouton de Gruyter, 2002), 219–238.
27. Edward Sapir, "Psychological Aspects of Culture," in *The Psychology of Culture* (New York: Mouton de Gruyter, 2002), 175–190.
28. Harry Stack Sullivan, *The Psychiatric Interview* (New York: Norton, 1970). See chapter VIII in which Sullivan describes how psychiatrists are to interpret the semiotics of patient behavior, 173–197.
29. Harry Stack Sullivan, *The Fusion of Psychiatry and Social Science* (New York: Norton, 1964).
30. Edward Sapir, "The Contribution of Psychiatry to an Understanding of Behavior in Society," *American Journal of Sociology* 42, no. 6 (1937): 862–870.
31. F. Barton Evans III, *Harry Stack Sullivan: Interpersonal Theory and Psychotherapy* (New York: Routledge, 1996).
32. Jürgen Ruesch and Weldon Kees, *Nonverbal Communication* (Berkeley: University of California Press, 1956).
33. Catt, *Embodiment*.
34. See Charles S. Peirce, "Sundry Logical Conceptions," in *The Essential Peirce: Selected Philosophical Writings*, ed. The Peirce Edition Project, vol. 2 (1893–1913) (Bloomington: Indiana University Press, 1998), 269.
35. Maurice Merleau-Ponty, "Preface," in *Phenomenology of Perception*, trans. Donald A. Landes (New York: Routledge, 2012), xxxiv.
36. Richard L. Lanigan, *Phenomenology of Communication: Merleau-Ponty's Thematics in Communicology and Semiology* (Pittsburgh: Duquesne University Press, 1988).
37. Pierre Bourdieu, *Outline of a Theory of Practice*, trans. Richard Nice (London: Cambridge, 1972), 82.
38. Bourdieu, *Outline of a Theory of Practice*, 78.
39. Edward S. Petry Jr., "The Origin and Development of Peirce's Concept of Self Control," *Transactions of the Charles S. Peirce Society* 28, no. 4 (1992): 667–690. That the movement of semiosis requires phenomenology is clarified in a number of places. See Gary Fuhrman, "Peirce's Retrospectives on his Phenomenological Quest," *Transactions of the Charles S. Peirce Society* 49, no. 4 (2013): 490–508; Vincent Colapietro, *Peirce's Approach to the Self: A Semiotic Perspective on Human Subjectivity* (Albany: SUNY, 1989), and Lenore Langsdorf and Andrew R. Smith, eds., *Recovering Pragmatism's Voice: The Classical Tradition, Rorty, and the Philosophy of Communication* (Albany: SUNY, 1995).
40. See for example Deborah Eicher-Catt and Isaac E. Catt, "Peirce and Cassirer 'Life' and 'Spirit': A Communicology of Religion," *The Journal of Communication and Religion* 36, no. 2 (2013): 77–106.
41. Jürgen Ruesch, *Semiotics and Human Relations* (The Hague: Mouton, 1972). See chapter 7, "The Social Control of Symbolic Systems," 277–300.
42. Lanigan, "Husserl's Phenomenology," 205.
43. Note the many references to Dewey in the index to Ruesch's *Semiotics and Human Relations*.

44. Isaac E. Catt, "Culture in the Conscious Experience of Communication," *Journal of Communication Ethics, Religion and Culture* 48, no. 2 (2013): 99–119.
45. Isaac E. Catt, "The Signifying World Between Ineffability and Intelligibility: Body as Sign in Communicology," *The Review of Communication* 11, no. 2 (2011): 122–144. Among the propositions concerning embodiment in communicology advanced here is the idea that the body is a channel and medium of discourse. See p. 135.
46. Lanigan, "Husserl's Phenomenology," 205.
47. Hubert G. Alexander, *The Language and Logic of Philosophy* (Albuquerque: University of New Mexico Press, 1967).

BIBLIOGRAPHY

Alexander, Hubert G. *The Language and Logic of Philosophy*. Albuquerque: University of New Mexico Press, 1967.

Bourdieu, Pierre. *Outline of a Theory of Practice*. Translated by Richard Nice. London: Cambridge, 1972.

Catt, Isaac E. "Culture in the Conscious Experience of Communication." *Journal of Communication Ethics, Religion and Culture* 48, no. 2 (2013): 99–119.

Catt, Isaac E. *Embodiment in the Semiotic Matrix: Communicology in Peirce, Dewey, Bateson, and Bourdieu*. Madison, NJ: Fairleigh Dickinson University Press, 2017.

Catt, Isaac E. "The Signifying World Between Ineffability and Intelligibility: Body as Sign in Communicology." *The Review of Communication* 11, no. 2 (2011): 122–144.

Catt, Isaac E., and Deborah Eicher-Catt. "Semiotics in Mainstream Communication Studies: A Review of Principal USA Journals in the Context of Communicology." *The Review of Communication* 12, no. 3 (2012): 176–200.

Colapietro, Vincent. *Peirce's Approach to the Self: A Semiotic Perspective on Human Subjectivity*. Albany: SUNY, 1989.

Deledalle, Georges. *Charles S. Peirce's Philosophy of Signs: Essays in Comparative Semiotics*. Bloomington: Indiana University Press, 2000.

De Saussure, Ferdinand. *Course in General Linguistics*. New York: McGraw-Hill, 1966.

Dewey, John. "A Confused Semiotic." In Dewey, John and Bentley, Arthur F. *Knowing and the Known*. Boston, MA: Beacon Press, 1949: 233–69.

Dewey, John. *Human Nature and Conduct*. New York: Henry Holt, 1922.

Dewey, John. "Peirce's Theory of Linguistic Signs, Thought and Meaning." *The Journal of Philosophy* 43, no. 4 (1946): 85–95.

Dewey, John. "The Reflex Arc Concept in Psychology." *Psychological Review* 3 (1896): 357–370.

Dreyfus, Hubert. "Intelligence without Representation—Merleau-Ponty's Critique of Mental Representation: The Relevance of Phenomenology to Scientific Representation." *Phenomenology and the Cognitive Sciences* 1, no. 4 (2002): 367–383.

Eicher-Catt, Deborah, and Isaac E. Catt. *Communicology: The New Science of Embodied Discourse*. Madison, NJ: Fairleigh Dickinson University Press, 2010.

Eicher-Catt, Deborah, and Isaac E. Catt. "Peirce and Cassirer 'Life' and 'Spirit': A Communicology of Religion." *The Journal of Communication and Religion* 36, no. 2 (2013): 77–106.

Evans III, F. Barton. *Harry Stack Sullivan: Interpersonal Theory and Psychotherapy*. New York: Routledge, 1996.

Fuhrman, Gary. "Peirce's Retrospectives on his Phenomenological Quest." *Transactions of the Charles S. Peirce Society* 49, no. 4 (2013): 490–508.

Grenfell, Michael. *Pierre Bourdieu: Agent Provocateur*. New York: Continuum, 2004.

Jakobson, Roman. "Langue and Parole: Code and Message." In *On Language: Roman Jakobson*, edited by Linda R. Waugh and Monique Monville-Burston, 80–109. Cambridge, MA: Harvard University Press, 1990.

Jakobson, Roman. "The Speech Event and the Functions of Language." In *On Language: Roman Jakobson*, edited by Linda R. Waugh and Monique Monville-Burston, 69–79. Cambridge, MA: Harvard University Press, 1990.

Klyukanov, Igor. *A Communication Universe: Manifestations of Meaning, Stagings of Significance*. New York: Lexington Press, 2010.

Korzybski, Alfred. "The Role of Language in Perceptual Processes." In *Perception as an Approach to Personality*, edited by Robert R. Blake and Glenn V. Ramsey, 170–205. New York: The Ronald Press Company, 1951.

Kuznetsov, V. F. "Communicology Journal. The Start-Up." *Politstudies*. Accessed February 5, 2017. http://www.politstudies.ru/en/article/4888

Langsdorf, Lenore, and Andrew R. Smith. *Recovering Pragmatism's Voice: The Classical Tradition, Rorty and the Philosophy of Communication*. Albany: SUNY, 1995.

Lanigan, Richard L. *The Human Science of Communicology: A Phenomenology of Discourse in Foucault and Merleau-Ponty*. Pittsburgh, PA: Duquesne University Press, 1992.

Lanigan, Richard L. "Husserl's Phenomenology in America (USA): The Human Science Legacy of Willbur Marshall Urban and the Yale School of Communicology." *Schutzian Research* 3 (2011): 203–217.

Lanigan, Richard L. *Phenomenology of Communication: Merleau-Ponty's Thematics in Communicology and Semiology*. Pittsburgh, PA: Duquesne University Press, 1988.

Leavitt, John. *Linguistic Relativities: Language Diversity and Modern Thought*. London: Cambridge, 2011.

Menand, Louis. *The Metaphysical Club: A Story of Ideas in America*. New York: Farrar, Straus and Giroux, 2001.

Merleau-Ponty, Maurice. "Preface." In *Phenomenology of Perception*. Translated by Donald A. Landes. New York: Routledge, 2012.

Peirce, Charles S. "Pragmatism." In *The Essential Peirce: Selected Philosophical Writings*, edited by The Peirce Edition Project. Bloomington: Indiana University Press, 1998.

Peirce, Charles S. "Sundry Logical Conceptions." In *The Essential Peirce: Selected Philosophical Writings*, edited by The Peirce Edition Project, 269. Bloomington: Indiana University Press, 1998.

Petry, Edward S., Jr. "The Origin and Development of Peirce's Concept of Self Control." *Transactions of the Charles S. Peirce Society* 28, no. 4 (1992): 667–690.

Ruesch, Jürgen. *Semiotics and Human Relations*. The Hague: Mouton, 1972.

Ruesch, Jürgen, and Gregory Bateson. "Individual, Group, and Culture: A Review of the Theory of Communication." In *Communication: The Social Matrix of Psychiatry*, edited by Jürgen Ruesch and Gregory Bateson. New York: Norton, 1951.

Ruesch, Jürgen, and Weldon Kees. *Nonverbal Communication*. Berkeley: University of California Press, 1956.

Ruthrof, Horst. *The Body in Language*. London: Cassell, 2000.

Ruthrof, Horst. *Semantics and the Body: Meaning from Frege to the Postmodern.* Toronto: University of Toronto Press, 1997.

Sapir, Edward. "The Contribution of Psychiatry to an Understanding of Behavior in Society." *American Journal of Sociology* 42, no. 6 (1937): 862–870.

Sapir, Edward. "Psychological Aspects of Culture." In *The Psychology of Culture*, edited by Judith T. Irvine. New York: Mouton de Gruyter, 2002: 175–190.

Sapir, Edward. "Symbolism." In *The Psychology of Culture*, edited by Judith T. Irvine. New York: Mouton de Gruyter, 2002: 219–38.

Smith, Andrew R. "Discord in Intercultural Negotiation: Toward an Ethic of Communicability." In *Ferment in the Intercultural Field: Axiology/Value/Praxis. Intercultural and International Communication Annual*, vol. 26, edited by W. Starosta and G.-M. Chen, 106. Thousand Oaks: Sage, 2003.

Sullivan, Harry Stack. *The Fusion of Psychiatry and Social Science.* New York: Norton, 1964.

Sullivan, Harry Stack. *The Psychiatric Interview.* New York: Norton, 1970.

Whorf, Benjamin Lee. *Language, Thought and Reality.* Cambridge, MA: MIT Press, 1956.

SECTION ONE

Founding(s)

CHAPTER ONE

Decolonizing Research Praxis

Embodiment, Border Thinking and Theory Construction in the Human Sciences

ANDREW R. SMITH

> It is a commonplace among human scientists that in many cultures the very concepts of 'culture' and 'communication' are embodied in the same word. Why this is so sets the boundary condition for examining the mutual influence of culture as a process of value transmission and communication as a process of value constitution.[1]
> —Richard L. Lanigan

> Epistemic disobedience and border thinking are the pillars of de-racializing and de-sexualizing (that is, decolonizing) knowledge, feelings and understanding.[2]
> —Walter Mignolo

Richard Lanigan's development of "semiotic phenomenology"[3] has paved the way for a broadening of both phenomenology and semiotics, expanding in complementary fashion the epistemological horizons of each, linking onto existential, hermeneutic, ethnographic, rhetorical, critical-cultural and postcolonial theories and methods. There are two branches of this approach. The *empirical* is concerned with the description and interpretation of lived experience (*Lebenswelt*) and social life (*Mitwelt*) as understood through the explication of contextualized meaning. The interest is in formulating propositions concerning the competing truths of everyday life, public contestations over public and private goods, rights claims and institutional duties, aesthetic and mediated realities, political discourses and actions, and also sublimities of injustices that lack recognized idioms for expression. From a decolonial view, it is this latter that requires the most urgent border thinking and epistemic disobedience on behalf of *the just*.

Complementarily, *eidetic* science involves the postulation of new conceptual frames, fresh ways of thinking, and innovative systems of thought that enable researchers to ground their empirical work philosophically. Eidetic and empirical are recursive forms of research, informing and mutually influencing one another. Empirical work without a philosophical framework is just as groundless as eidetic work that has no relevance to lived experience. My interest here is to show how research praxis in human science can be grounded empirically *and* eidetically through an orientation that entails decolonizing *and* systematically exposing the ever-increasing systemic occupation and exploitation of life worlds, including the non-human.

No research project is value-free, and those who make a claim otherwise are likely oblivious to the influence of prejudices and presuppositions on their postulations and conceptual schemes, an ignorance that is precarious at best and often dangerous in the field. The generation of new insights, understandings, knowhow, failures as well as achievements in the context of doing human science field research involves a consideration of what constitutes the good(s) of that work in private and public realms, an orientation that enjoins the pragmatistic sensibility that Charles Sanders Peirce insisted should inform one's ethical and critical bearings.[4] The ultimate interest in such research is to develop valid reflective judgments and propositions about private troubles and public struggles that emerge in everyday life, but only insofar as one has the capacity to *listen* over extended periods of time. The researcher, in the approach advanced here, is most primordially an addressee.

Grasping border thinking and epistemic disobedience requires new ways of seeing and speaking, listening and sensing, imagining and linking; it requires engaging abductive and adductive "tropologics" that enable insight and conceptualization of problems of those seeking venues to voice their struggles in the face of apparatuses of power. The field work for my own research has, over the last twenty years, focused on Morocco where I have lived, taught, and become actively engaged with human rights activists, journalists, scholars and others seeking peaceful constitutional reform and deliberative democracy. As such, my research and writing addresses authoritarian practices, national security regimens, border crossings, the suppression and expression of speech, cyber-activism and related rights claims that I continue to work at providing a credible and worthy account of, on their own terms culturally, politically and communicatively.

This emic approach is in keeping with a decolonial production of knowledge, though it may seem to exemplify an attempt to "speak for others" from significantly different cultural worlds, an approach to research roundly criticized by postcolonial and cultural critics. To work beyond the substance of participants' lived experiences, setting aside or even forgetting the way they have suffered history, using the material(s) they have generously provided as 'grist' to create a meta-theoretical architectonic, does disservice and even violence to the integrity of their narratives. I take up this problematic in the final section of the essay, arguing that meta-theory has a place in the decolonizing project addressing damages and wrongs on a broader spectrum, with regard especially to changing institutional norms, applying or altering international law, rethinking peace, equitability and reconciliation, and so on.

In sum, this chapter attempts to provide a philosophical and epistemological orientation that serves human science researchers in formulating and engaging empirical and eidetic projects that explicate truths and critically address injustices that have resulted from form(s) of colonization. We should keep in mind throughout that inquiry from the communicological perspective advanced by Lanigan can engage phenomena that are intimately familiar, perceived on the horizon, or anything discoverable. We begin, then, with an overview of the contentious but productive relationship between social/behavioral and human sciences, specifically with regard to how each defines and engages objects of, and subjects for, inquiry.

CONTRASTING LOGICS OF SOCIAL AND HUMAN SCIENCES

The Greek term *epistemé* refers to knowledge, and every claim to knowledge presupposes some form of *logos*. Of course *logos* in its original sense refers to discourse, not simply logic, as no knowledge is possible without meaningful communication through shared signs and common codes that make valid inference possible. In this section I elaborate on the complementary relationship between social and human sciences, then focus on their respective logics with emphasis on abduction and adduction.

Social and Human Sciences

Social science from its very inception contended with arrangements of centralized power that imposed ways of thinking on scholars and entire populations. In order to radically depart from classical metaphysics and the mystification of realities based on empirically untestable postulations and illegitimate claims, the modern social scientific enterprise developed an approach to establishing the truth of reality-posits that involved a form of invention. Here one begins with the concept of the thing itself that is hypostatized as real. Put another way, the thing itself becomes equivocated through the correspondence theory of truth with the symbolic universe that enables conceptualization of it. To hypostatize is to invent, but not to fabricate out of thin air. Based on observable phenomena, the social scientist tests probabilities through measurements of extent, magnitude, impact and other forces across sampling units. The interest is in establishing verisimilitude between an analytic construct and a reality-posit that has been hypostatized—e.g. polling numbers (analytic construct) point to relative favorability (reality-posit) of candidates. The goal, of course, is establishing facts, explaining a phenomenon and achieving verifiable knowledge. Resulting statements about tendencies and patterns recognized as fact are typically referred to as data speaking for themselves—QED (*quad erat demonstrandum*; which was to be demonstrated). The approach is generally referred to as "phenomenalism," which conforms to the Law of Identity and the Law of Contradiction, as Lanigan elaborates it.[5]

Social scientific procedures and practices have provided an important basis for challenging classical conceptions of society and elitist postulations of Right, Good, True and Great that ensure entitlements for the privileged while colonizing and disenfranchising millions globally. It also provides working theories for testing and experimentation to gain insight on singular instances, and can serve as the basis for countering exploitative tendencies of the most powerful. But its objectivist underpinnings have been challenged over the years as it has become widely acknowledged that human beings—their psychologies, relationships, societies, histories, practices, tendencies, cultures and forms of communication—cannot be justly *posited* in the same way as physical or natural phenomena, even when acknowledging margins of error. Societies' structural forces, arrangements of power, institutional sets of relations, rules for interaction, cultural patterns, normative practices, and systems of signs and meanings may be recognized and described impartially, but the objectification of persons, groups, and collectivities can also advance misguided policies and practices with attendant forms of institutionalized subjugation.

This deleterious situation is certainly not the fault of social scientific practices; any substantiated knowledge no matter how obtained can be used for wicked purposes. The difference here is that the phenomenological emphasis on lived experience eschews any objectivist trappings, favoring instead intersubjective knowledge in the investigation of the singularity of an event, experience and/or phenomenon. Likewise, semiotics is something much more than a taxonomic sorting out of signs, codes, meanings, and significances (*signifiance*); it is instead a way of *figuring the event* of lived experience through verbal, visual and other sensory and sensible means. It is not understood, at least in the tradition of American pragmatism or continental and Russian philosophy, as a two-world representationalism. In linking semiotics and phenomenology, Lanigan and contributors to this volume recognize the integrative whole of human being-in-the-world through analysis of concrete phenomena, eidetically and empirically, and critical reflection on attendant values, interests, needs, desires, and positions.

In short, the phenomenological contrast to objectivism is not subjectivism or relativism; it is intersubjectivism, as Richard Bernstein emphasizes in his seminal work,[6] grounded in a self that is configured by and through others. The interest is to understand meanings, make sense (*Sinn*) of that which persons (including the researcher) live through, in order to comport ourselves in relation to the phenomenon while imagining what the consequences of our conceptions might be. Rather than beginning with invention and hypostatization, the human science researcher generates questions, or working hypotheses, based on directly experienced, intersubjectively recognized, and textually available materialities. Such forms are not constructs, observed from a distance, but concretized through human interaction and embodied communication—so much so that the researcher may only realize after-the-fact that an event worthy of inquiry has happened or *is happening*. The working hypotheses are not generated in order to confirm how well one can predict, control, or categorize in a deductive sense, but to embark on an expedition of learning through a process of questioning persons, groups, texts, artifacts, rumblings, and historicities, seeking validation of *that which* the dynamic field for research is sensibly and significantly offering, has offered, or may offer.[7]

An experimental attitude is required, but not necessarily one that involves manipulation of subjects and determining variables.[8] Rather the researcher trusts that those persons with whom one engages in research are fully capable of openly reflecting upon, explicating and interpreting their own experiences, observations, and perspectives in relation to the phenomenon. They are also capable of providing perspectives on the researcher's perceptions and interpretations. The result is conceptualization of events, actions, practices, conditions, and situations that enable the researcher to come to a deeper understanding and *involvement with* a phenomenon that would not be available otherwise. Rather than elicit rules for conversation and interaction, or predictions based on a rhetorical situation, semiotic phenomenology invites participants to be fully engaged in a radical reflection on lived experience and social reality as manifest through expressive form of semiosis.

William James termed such an approach to research "radical empiricism" that goes beyond participant observation in the conventional sense, toward a deeper endowment by and through others and events, in a dynamic field that takes up and disposes the researcher in unforeseen ways, beyond intention, design or power to control. This radical empirical engagement, then, serves as the ground for "true" knowledge in the pragmatic sense, as Charlene Haddock Seigfried elaborates:

> The distinctiveness of James's view of knowledge is best expressed as arising from its attempt to describe knowing as it exists concretely in contrast to the popular or usual epistemological view, which only describes the results taken abstractly. Reflection on the storm of controversy raised over the pragmatic theory of truth led him to realize that "concreteness as radical as ours is not so obvious. The whole originality of pragmatism, the whole point in it, is its use of the concrete way of seeing." The concrete level of analysis is also called the "practical and psychological view."[9]

And so findings are not abstract disembodied statements removed from lived experience, but embodied propositions, thematic expressions of meaning fully fleshed out and understood as forms of action.

In the phenomenological construction of perceived reality, discourse and action are not *given* (like data sitting ready for plucking from the world), but *taken* and constructed, worked through and lived, presented situationally (*Darstellung*) and fallibly as *capta*. Instead of QED or that which was to have been demonstrated, a phenomenological approach ends with QEI (*quad erat inveniendum*; which was to be found out).[10] Such an end does not establish identity once and for all, or knowing *with certainty* via language (*Verstehen*), but remains subject to refinement and elaboration through the *Law of Participation*[11] that involves conversation, argumentation and dialogical engagement—reasoning, feeling, valuing, learning communicatively (*Verstand*), and remaining open to the unexpected no matter how much it may displace, throw one out of context, or disrupt an otherwise elegant design.

Abduction and Adduction

Semiotic phenomenological research participates reflexively in a decolonizing praxis to the extent that it engages in radical empiricism self-critically (fallibly and often precariously) through abductive and adductive logics *understood as discourses* of insight and discovery. Abduction and adduction are not linked to entirely separate kinds of inquiry than deduction and induction, but stages that orient inductive elaborations of theory and deductive testing of propositions and postulations.[12] Induction, central to scientific reasoning, moves from particulars of selected sample(s) [*case*] to common attributes [*result*] that establish probabilities of relation generalized to larger populations [*rule*]. Deduction, integral to normal science, works from the general [*rule*; first premise or proposition] to the particular [*case*; instance that comes under the rule] in order to demonstrate conclusively the reality of some referent [*result*; a necessary conclusion]. In contrast, abductive and adductive inferences, as Lanigan puts it, reflect more precisely the Aristotelian notion of the enthymeme whereby "the syllogism is formally deficient [rule] and materially uncertain [result] as a judgment [case]"; even though both abduction and adduction follow the same formula of rule + result = case, "abduction is a *particular* and *a posteriori* claim whereas adduction is a *universal* and *a priori* claim."[13] It is important here to elucidate these logics and their orientations to phenomena as perceived and judged by a researcher; along with Peirce, the philosophy of Maurice Merleau-Ponty is of particular import in this regard.

Merleau-Ponty's mention of abduction and adduction helps to situate the operational foci of these logics in terms of judgments that arise from sense experience in everyday life that serves as the ground of perception: "Now, on the whole, the significance of adduction is that the organism turns toward the stimulus and is attracted by the world—of abduction that it turns away from the stimulus and withdraws toward its centre."[14] He refers in this context to experimental evidence of persons who react differently to similar stimuli depending on the color of the background the stimulus is produced in, and argues that sensation is intentional and differential, rather than mechanical and similar as different persons put significances back into the world in relation to the color coding. Sensation is therefore intentional not passively received, Merleau-Ponty argues, "because I find that in the sensible a certain rhythm of existence is put forward—abduction or adduction— and, following up this hint, and stealing into the form of existence which is thus suggested to me, I am brought into relation with an external being, whether it be to open myself to it or to shut myself off from it."[15] The phenomenon manifests as a rhythm of existence, a tonality in the Peircian sense, and one abstracts *qualities* understood as signs that radiate a certain mode of existence separate from human perception. Nevertheless, the inquirer "does not posit them as objects, but enters into a sympathetic relation with them, makes them his [sic] own and finds in them his [sic] momentary law."[16] The abstractive and associative process of perception from the stimulus toward one's "centre" is abductive and *aesthetic*—an object, event or other is *grasped*; putting that experience back into the world conceptually is adductive and *intentional*—a significance is *performed*.

Given these grounds for understanding the aesthetic and intentional movements of abductive and adductive logics, how are they operative concretely in human science research? Klaus Krippendorf provides some good working examples, arguing specifically with regard to abduction that it will "proceed across logically distinct domains, from particulars of one kind to particulars of another kind."[17] Such a metonymic association or procession means that one must *imagine relations and linkages where previously there were none*. Abduction is *speculative*, involving poiesis and aesthesis, because it is an act that abstracts and imagines (perceives, associates, judges) relations and conditions of objects and beings, generating working hypotheses; while adduction is *rhetorical* because any abductive inference is inherently fallible, requiring the researcher to test out the significances posited as realities. Insights do not come from nowhere. The elements of any hypothesis, Peirce argues, are in our minds beforehand; it is putting together what has not been put together before that "flashes the insight before our contemplation."[18] The following are examples adapted from various sources that suggest the indexical nature of abductive inference.[19]

- One infers the ideologies and actual intentions of political leaders from the metaphors used in their speeches or tweets
- One infers whether someone is lying from his or her tones and gestures (an amalgamation of nonverbal cues).

- One infers another's degree of sobriety based on slurs of speech or the look in his or her eyes.
- One infers media bias based on a comparison of editorial sources or sites.
- One infers hierarchical relationship in a formal organizational setting based on where persons are sitting in relation to one another in a room.
- One infers the political affiliations of persons based on their social media posts.
- One infers a person's social status based on his or her form of address.

Some researchers argue that abduction begins with a body of data (facts, observations, stimuli, givens),[20] though as Merleau-Ponty makes clear, any body of sensible data cannot and should not be isolated, but instead interpreted in terms of a background or, in Husserlian terms, both a field and a horizon that condition its apprehension:

> An analysis which would try to isolate the perceived content would find nothing; for all consciousness of something, as soon as this thing ceases to be an indeterminate existence, as soon as it is identifiable and recognizable (...) presupposes the apprehension of a meaning through the lived impression which is not *contained* in the consciousness and is not a real part of it. The matter of knowledge becomes a *borderline-notion* posed by consciousness in its reflection upon itself, and not a component of the act of knowing. But from then on perception is a variety of intellection and, in all its positive aspects, a judgment.[21]

Pragmatically, to research kinship patterns for example, one must have a working hypothesis, passing theory or operative *meaning* [Rule] of kinship, which situates perception of and orientation toward [Result] instances [Case] that may challenge the presumptive meanings one arrives with. The singular instance changes the way we think—abductively—about the presumed meanings, and that thinking is fallible as Peirce emphasized, requiring further inquiry and validation. In this sense, the notion of "grounded theory," where one presumably enters the field as a blank slate and constructs theory through the accumulation of "data," is problematical as it presupposes that the researcher has no preconceptions, meanings, questions, passing theories or working hypotheses associated with the phenomenon. This is not to say that something surprising might not occur in the field as an event that does not fit into the passing theory—it will, or should, which is the point of doing research in the first place. Normal science seeks to confirm existing theory or innovate on that theory; radical empiricism seeks to challenge existing preconceptions and alter in a deeper, more incisive way how we think, feel, affect, value, and engage a phenomenon.

In phenomenology, then, research design develops from ideas and meanings about and experiences with the context one is working within. The context suggests the contours of the field in which one will conduct the research, and marks out the horizon of possible propositions concerning the phenomenon of interest. Knowledge of the context must also be embedded, of course, in the traditions of a discipline which determines or at least constrains the kinds of analytical constructs that can be legitimately produced. In posing research questions and/or working hypotheses, one seeks answers, and those answers come thematically through narrative accounts of lived experiences, reflections on interactions that the researcher engages in, observations and accounts of practices, serendipitous occurrences, unexpected events, textual materials such as pamphlets, instructions and media representations. The sets or samples selected, informed by conceptual frames that launch the inquiry, provide the actual ground for making inferences about practices, attitudes, beliefs, values, obligations, desires, feelings, relationships, worldviews, and so on—quasi-transcendental realities that are not empirically observable but are certainly operative in the social world. Such realities, as Richard Shweder puts it:

> (…) can be imagined, but never seen or deduced, for they are construction of our own making, which sometimes succeed in binding us to the underlying reality they imagine by giving us an intellectual tool—metaphor, a premise, an analogy, a category—with which to live, to arrange our experience, and to interpret our experiences so arranged. In other words, the abductive faculty is the faculty of imagination, which comes to the rescue of sensation and logic by providing them with the intellectual means to see through experience and leap beyond empty syllogisms and tautologies to some creative representation of an underlying reality that might be grasped and reacted to, even if that imagined reality cannot be found, proved, or disproved by inductive or deductive rule-following.[22]

In sum, speculative rhetoric (abductive + adductive inferential practices) as it functions at the heart of semiotic phenomenology requires that the researcher continually work through differentiations in combination [Law of Non-contradiction], and attempt to parse the meanings of terms, phrases, propositions, practices, arguments, contextual slippage, styles, processes and procedures with a driving interest in recognizing associations, variations and linkages that were previously invisible or incommunicable [Law of Participation]. In so doing, one engages the singular instance (the "case") and questions how it runs counter to what was previously thought to be the case, what might have been the case, and/or what could be the case. As such, semiotic phenomenological research encounters negativity in all instantiations—through the negative inherent in the grammaticality of language, the invariances of structural relations, and what might be termed "intentional negativity" or that which is "hidden in speech, the lack acknowledged by the logician and the analyst that runs through discourse and grants it its referential power."[23] Such negativity, in the qualified Hegelian sense elaborated by many post-structural thinkers, is immensely creative and productive.

THE PROBLEM OF RESEARCHING OTHERS

Over the last several decades philosophers, sociologists, anthropologists, historians, communicologists, critical theorists, feminist and literary critics and many others in the arts, letters, and human sciences—East and West, South and North—have discussed in painstaking detail the problems associated with researching others whose histories and practices are significantly different from one's own. The range of concerns can be condensed into three *topoi*: (1) the privileged and biased position from which the researcher works; (2) the accuracy or "truth" of descriptions and interpretations; and (3) the researcher's responsibility for immediate and long-term impacts of involvement, conceptions and findings in the field. Abdellah Hammoudi puts it succinctly with regard to ethnographic research in authoritarian contexts:

> An ethnography of forms of domination and submission that play themselves out in important social sectors required a parallel work of introspection. Power relations, tactics, and strategies could not be written about without reaching a threshold where they made themselves manifest to, and unsettled, the investigator's sense of self. (…) This personal introspection—one which recognizes the subject's ethical and political accountability even as it abdicates a transcendental subjectivity—becomes inseparable from the ethnographic inspection of human action and meaning.[24]

Personal introspection that recognizes and engages ethical and political accountability is a crucial part of doing semiotic phenomenological research, and points to the influence of a radical hermeneutic influence on any such inquiry, including the ethnographic.[25] Hammoudi's reference to transcendental subjectivity is an allusion to the phenomenology of Edmund Husserl, whose conception of eidetic science stands as a foundation upon which all phenomenological inquiry should, at some point, come to terms for understanding how phenomena are embedded empirically through primordial (temporal) experience.

The problems Husserl confronted in elucidating the operations of intentionality (consciousness of...) that constitute phenomena led to an account of meaning-constituting acts.[26] The experience of time is crucial for understanding Husserl's notion of meaning in an object. We are "capable of grasping intentionally, in continually new moments, what is no longer existing"[27] and through this grasping we are able to apprehend temporal existence as such: "The object is not a genuinely concrete part of the phenomenon; in its temporality it has something which cannot at all be found in the phenomenon or reduced to the phenomenon. And yet it is constituted within the phenomenon. It is presented therein and is evidently given as 'existing' there."[28] In short, the phenomenon of temporal existence, which grounds all perception and expression and through which "seeing extends" itself in order to constitute an object of inquiry and distinguish between the act of constituting and the constituted itself, is equiprimordial with *intentionality*. Although

Husserl's philosophy of transcendental subjectivity has been roundly criticized as idealism, he in fact had in mind a very realist interest in ensuring that philosophy takes its rightful place as a rigorous science.[29] As Hammoudi suggests, recognition of Husserl's notion of intentionality is crucial for the human science researcher engaged in making sense of meaning-constituting acts.

The legitimacy of subjectively bracketing one's prejudices, referred to in Husserl's work as the phenomenological epoché, is also problematical and has been sufficiently criticized in later continental philosophy to not deter us here.[30] The most prudent course of action with regard to addressing the issue of researcher prejudice or bias, while not falling prey to the objectivist illusion, is, in my view, to follow Gadamer's reformulations of the epoché. This approach, familiar to many in communicology but worthy of elaboration here, involves recognizing certain prejudices as useful for situating existing knowledge and informing questioning. The task is to radically reflect on one's "fore-meanings," making them problematical such that one does not blindly discover or simply justify what one preconsciously expects or unconsciously imposes.

Gadamer argues that "fore-meanings" and "prejudices" come into view not through intuitive means, but through engagement with alterity. Prejudices are neither to be "doubted" in the strict Cartesian sense nor "bracketed" in the Husserlian sense but made known and utilized reflexively for questioning and understanding. Gadamer states that:

> (...) this kind of sensitivity involves neither "neutrality" with respect to content nor the extinction of one's self, but the foregrounding and appropriation of one's own fore-meanings and prejudices. The important thing is to be aware of one's own bias, so that the text [object of inquiry] can present itself in all its otherness and thus assert its own truth against one's own fore-meanings.[31]

If one's unreflective bias dominates, in this line of thinking, then one merely projects the familiar onto the strangeness of the "text," event, or other(s) rather than allowing alterity to speak—an expression heard or configured against fore-meanings. *Learning something new* and interpreting it reflectively (not neutrally or objectively) becomes possible through dialogical engagement.

Gadamer develops his idea of fore-meanings out of Heidegger's notions of fore-having (*Vorhabe*), fore-conception (*Vorgriff*) and fore-sight (*Vorsicht*). The recognition of how fore-structures operate in the understanding is requisite for prudent interpretation (the "as-structure"). The interpretive struggle with meaning and the recognition of fallibility and mortality are, in turn, necessary to live an authentic existence as Heidegger conceives it.[32] For the research to be hermeneutical, the researcher should note how findings run counter to what was presupposed; for it to be critical, one should account for what Michel Foucault refers to as the complex heterogeneous workings of power that impinge upon perception, judgment, and discursive and non-discursive meanings— the *dispositif.*

> What I'm trying to pick out with this term is, firstly, a thoroughly heterogeneous ensemble consisting of discourse, institutions, architectural forms, regulatory decision, laws, administrative measures, scientific statements, philosophical, moral and philanthropic propositions—in short, the said as much as the unsaid. Such are the elements of the apparatus. The apparatus itself is the system of relations that can be established between these elements. Secondly, what I am trying to identify in this apparatus is precisely the nature of the connection that can exist between these heterogeneous elements. (…) Thirdly, I understand by the term "apparatus" as sort of—shall we say—formation which has as its major function at a given historical moment that of responding to an urgent need. The apparatus thus has a dominant strategic function.[33]

Fore-meanings emerge reflectively through the engagement with alterity; correlatively, knowing how the external heterogeneous forces and relations of the *dispositif* frame perception and judgment will not be realized until that engagement begins. This, of course begs the question of knowing what to research, and being capable of developing well-grounded working hypotheses.

Suffice to say that one does not embark on semiotic phenomenological research without first engaging alterity and the ensemble sufficiently to generate questions (working hypotheses, passing theories) that ignite further inquiry and commitment to a field that has its dynamic forces of meaning and significance, an agency of its own. What emerges for the researcher, how he or she perceives and is able to describe the "what is happening," is inevitably bound up not only with his or her own prejudices as Gadamer conceives them, but also the force of the *dispositif* manifest in a field of significations, relations and forces which impinge unremittingly on disposition, perception and understanding of the field and others (and ultimately on others' perceptions of, and cooperation with the researcher). That *dispositif* is put into relief through sustained engagement with alterity, whereby avenues for inquiry open up, relationships are built, connections established, understandings shared, know-how embodied, perceptions altered, and complexity of identity and interests enjoined.

It goes without saying that identity is multiple, and becomes more complex with each engagement of alterity. A person embodies and expresses voices and influences depending on salient addressees, contexts, demands at the moment, gender, ethnicity, sexuality, nationality, socio-economic capacity, age, religion or its lack, and other traditions and characteristics associated with primary and secondary socialization such as family upbringing, education, career path, political involvement, and so on.[34] Whereas Foucault takes these multiple forces and reveals how they express relations of power and knowledge, Pierre Bourdieu depicts how they help construct or otherwise feed into one's habitus, the "durable and transposable dispositions" through which one functions and masters the vicissitudes of everyday life, acquires modes of operation and improvisation, and effectively becomes a genius at social relations.[35] The postcolonial concern about imposition of hegemonic power structures and ethnocentric bias that presumes subjects engaged cannot speak for themselves, presupposes in turn that one cannot adapt to and become an integral part of a very different social or cultural world. In adapting to a distinctive cultural world, one takes on the flesh (bodily *hexis* in Bourdieu's nomenclature) of that habitus, recognizing and in fact *feeling* the forces and relations of heterogeneous ensembles. Such an immersion, which involves transgressing boundaries (*hrig* in Arabic),[36] learning actively and openly, recognizing fallibility, and living or working precariously, is a prerequisite for the kind of decolonizing research praxis advanced here.

The objectivist concern has traditionally emphasized the degree to which a researcher mitigates or even eliminates the influences of his or her own habitus (an impossible task) and disconnects self from the heterogeneous apparatus (equally impossible) in order to better report the *quiddity* of that which presents itself. Though certainly a noble effort, the phenomenological perspective maintains that how one enters the field *ipso facto* affects or influences that field, creates new ripples and wrinkles in relational systems and structures; just as important is the critical struggle of recognizing how the field itself takes one up and alters the research design or plan. The field, in the ethnographic sense, is a dynamic force that cannot be reduced formalistically. *How* one enters a field is contingent not only on how one has already been influenced by a habitus, but as suggested previously and worth repeating, *how the new field one enters orients or dis-poses the researcher in unanticipated ways.* This principle emphasizes the idea that a field, in and for itself, does indeed have an agency that supersedes the individual intent or agency of a researcher or artist. As Franz Fanon argued, one estranges oneself from that which is most familiar, the better to understand how it determines what one says and does, and the better to say and do something else, something more inventive and experimental, something perhaps unexpected that will make a difference for shaping public goods. A researcher should move, in Merleau-Ponty's terms, from unreflective embeddedness in the influences of "speech spoken" (*parole parlée*, the language of repetition essential to the operation of any apparatus) to the radical reflection associated with "speech speaking" (*parole parlante*, the speech of creative intelligence, an openness to learning, and new concept formation).[37]

Not being critically reflective of one's own prejudices and traditions on one hand, and not being attentive *in situ* to how a field takes one up, on the other, can result in serious distortions in how findings are formulated and communicated. Partiality, in both senses of the word, is an unavoidable problem. Grappling with it should be an ongoing reflective, creative, insightful endeavor; not recognizing or taking account of it constitutes an ethical lapse.[38] The stakes are high for any person interested in practicing a semiotic phenomenological approach to inquiry and analysis based on work in different or even familiar social, institutional, or cultural worlds or texts. Researchers who are not inhabitants (or residents) of a place, who are not "cut from the same cloth" as the people they are engaging, and who have little interest in adapting to the place and peoples, seeking quick results that can be reported or published, *inevitably* present a highly partial, distorted, and colonizing view, wittingly or unwittingly.[39]

The problem is actually much deeper and more elusive than this, however, especially for ethnographic and critical-cultural work in and through previously unfamiliar fields. The problem is not only a matter of a non-inhabitant of a place speaking credibly *for* the inhabitants, or that the researcher makes a claim to seeing things which inhabitants cannot.[40] Given the asymmetrical relationship, it also becomes a matter of how inhabitants perceive and intentionally engage with the researcher, who is able to enter, move, and exit in ways that natives of the place may not, cannot or will not. The researcher's very presence may be an index of wealth and privilege, linked reflexively to an imperialist attitude or agenda *whether part of the researcher's individual intentions or not*. His or her own motility and bodily bearing (*hexis*) among others in the social world reflects not only difference, but inequality, a symbolic violence in itself that supersedes any intention or motivation. Such unequal positionality and privilege, the perception of this by inhabitants and participants in research, obliges radical reflection not merely on self, but on all the ways in which relationships are established, observations made, events known and engaged, accounts logged, senses and judgments made. Given the fluctuating, unstable, uncertain, indeterminate realm of communicative contact, hypotheses and judgments are continually subject to revision by virtue of the contested and contesting field that dramatically impinges upon the human science project.

My purpose in addressing these issues is not to throw cold water on researchers' interests. It is rather to press the issue of positionality and privilege, the obligation[41] to take account of it, and to recognize that research must be first and foremost in the interests of others rather than self. The researcher, in this respect, should offer self *as a donation* in the Levinasian sense, with humility and long-term engagement and shared survival values in mind. Through such sacrifice, participants in research become partners, even co-researchers, with common interest in getting their views and voices right.[42] In response to the legitimate and constructive concerns of cultural and postcolonial theorists, I wish to emphasize that: a) truth is relative to each society's established procedures for verification, and these procedures should be recognized and respected as long as they do not violate persons' autonomy and dignity; b) it is impossible not to be prejudicial in the perception and description of events and texts, the actions and discourses of others, and this limitation should be understood as a problematic that, through radical reflection, is a source for learning, questioning, formulating new perspectives and practices, and contributing back to the field and others; and c) the best we can do in conducting human science research is to work on constructing a picture whose discursive claims can be linked consistently and coherently through dialogical engagement, and always with a critically reflexive sense of the just. That is to say, as Shweder emphasizes, after research and engagement over years or even decades, one should still feel obliged to take analysis and interpretation back to the participants and others of the place. Contention, argumentation, agreement, qualification ensue. All reporting or publishing of work, then, is never final for the dynamical interpretant of the singular case. But is there such a thing as *final* interpretant? Peirce, Merleau-Ponty, Lanigan and others argue that there is, and that research should push beyond the theory of the case to come to terms with it, a problematical move for decolonizing praxis.

THEORY CONSTRUCTION

In other work I have detailed the methods and procedures for collecting and analyzing materials, and several other essays in this volume detail the description, reduction and interpretation process associated with semiotic phenomenology. Rather than repeating the process or elaborating on the empirical procedure, I will discuss its utility for theory construction. Still, some background on doing empirical work is necessary to set up the approach to theoretical and meta-theoretical (eidetic) work.

All researchers seek or should seek to present issues and results in discourse that expresses an accurate sense of meanings associated with communicative actions, events, practices, relations and forces of an inquiry. The researcher engages from macroscopic (communal and collective) and microscopic (existential and interpersonal) loci, with a driving interest to describe and interpret aspects of the phenomenon narratively. One engages the dynamic object as Peirce put it, living realities manifest in and through signs perceived and expressed. Reality does not exist outside of the sign which functions in conjunction with operative personal, interpersonal, social, and cultural codes, and remains elusive if one is not initiated to a place, tradition, or set of texts. The researcher's purpose is to gain access, learn the semiotic systems (verbal and nonverbal signs, normative practices, social codes, genres of discourse), reveal their operations to self through and for others who validate or further question the analysis or interpretation. The researcher seeks broadly to disclose a vibrant constellation of meanings, practices, beliefs, regularities of practice, *ideologemes*—conceived as signs that are *integral to*, not separate from or isomorphic with the phenomenon. Following Merleau-Ponty and Peirce, the understanding of "signs" elaborated in this volume is that they do not stand *in place of* but are *part and parcel of* the emergence, constitution and understanding of any phenomenon.

Since human science research is concerned with engaging, describing, analyzing, synthesizing and interpreting narrative accounts of everyday life that have significance, the researcher seeks personal retrospective descriptions of what people know, what they have lived through, believe or practice in some respect or capacity. Retrospection requires, in Merleau-Ponty's sense of temporality, both "retention" of lived experience and "protention" through discourse and impending action; he interprets these notions from Husserl in a new light:

> Husserl uses the terms protention and retention for the intentionalities which anchor me to an environment. They do not run from a central *I*, but from my perceptual field itself, so to speak, which draws along in its wake its own horizon of retentions, and bites into the future with its protentions. I do not pass through a series of instances of now, the images of which I preserve and which, placed end to end, make a line. With the arrival of every moment, its predecessor undergoes a change: I still have it in hand and it is still there, but already it is sinking away below the level of presents; in order to retain it, I need to reach through a thin layer of time.[43]

As persons discuss their involvements, practices, know-how and mark out their experience of and perspective on a phenomenon (in interviews, conversations, stories on-the-cusp, focus group settings, tribal meetings, conferences or other venues) they reach through a "thin layer of time" and experience that world in terms of a perceptual field that is continually unfolding as they speak and listen. That world unfolds narratively, and may contest other narrative accounts. Retrospection develops threads of insight that can be stitched metonymically with other accounts to generate what Richard Shweder refers to as reality-posits. In this sense retrospection should not be thought of as a process of introspection where through contemplation one arrives at the essence of the thing (i.e. intuitionism), but as anamnesis, a form of action whereby a person comes to terms dialogically (*parole parlante*) with how he or she is constituting or suffering a phenomenon temporally, spatially, linguistically and bodily. To work in this way, in fields that one adapts to over many years, or in familiar ones now made strange, involves a nomadic approach to research in the Deleuzian sense, but that does *not* mean it does not contribute through its findings to knowledge grounded in scientific methods and procedures.

Agonistic involvement in research is fundamental to any decolonizing praxis, and requires affective, aesthetic, ethical, and political concern and commitment, especially when studying a divisive or polemical phenomenon in fields previously unfamiliar. Incessant questioning, listening, learning gestural meaning and tonalities of people, places, and spaces is also fundamental. Such a locus for inquiry continually elaborates new material, taking up the fortuitous again into a meaningful whole, as Merleau-Ponty emphasized. In individual retrospections, whether through everyday conversation on-the-cusp or in more formal interviews, focus should be not only on verbal content but also intonation, elision, hesitation, contradiction, punctuation as well as metaphor, metonymy, irony, analogy, synechdoche and other tropes.[44] To the extent that a person's perspective shifts or is self-contradictory, or capabilities for language and understanding are inhibited, or prejudices and consequences of utterances and actions are not fully recognized, then the "truth" of any instance of a phenomenon will also be distorted, slanted or confused. There *will* be contradictory accounts and interpretations. The accuracy of findings will not be given objectively, but remain to be interpreted by the researcher in dialogical engagement with others. Attentiveness and probing allows participants in the research to think imaginatively and critically, encourages them to understand their own thematizing acts, and fosters insight on operative intentionalities. Working tropologically is instrumental for qualitatively verifiable insight, understanding, analysis and theory construction; it requires working with the materiality or "flesh" of the inquiry.

Theory construction understood conventionally and inductively as a systematic process comes at the "end" of the work of analysis and interpretation of findings (of *capta*, what has been taken, lived through and engaged in doing research). It is incumbent upon the researcher to advance a theory of the singular case in order to address its specific problematics and thematics, and do justice to its singularity from a so-called "emic" point of view. From a decolonial perspective, extending this singularity to, or weaving it into a meta-theoretical or etic perspective may seem to do it an injustice, given meta-theories' reductionistic and selective tendencies and procedures. But to synthesize is not to destroy, it is to work at abstracting teeming essences, finding linkages, and creating idioms that may in fact do further justice to the phenomenon and others related to it. To make the meta-theoretical move, then, one proceeds according to a more inverted structure, recognizing the double role of Interpretation. In situating the singularity of the phenomenon in a body of history, one opens onto more general propositions, postulates, and rules in the Peircian sense. This is how eidetic work is launched.

Recall that in doing semiotic phenomenological analysis and interpretation of materials gathered *empirically*, one also begins with interpretation based on what one has perceived, engaged, lived through, and manifested through radical reflection. Here fore-meanings open onto the heterogeneous apparatuses or *dispositif(s)* that situate one as researcher and influence the kinds of questions one asks. Since the engagement of (or confrontation with) alterity is a necessary condition for such reflection, one gains insight to the extent that he or she is able to also begin to recognize and articulate those *dispositif(s)* that impinge upon the phenomenon engaged, for others as well as self, eliciting what is shared and what is differentiated. As a deeper understanding is gained through lived experiences and interactions with others, questioning of materials deepens and broader theoretical questions emerge.

One is working at a meta-level to the extent that one develops through critique a theory of the theory of the case, engaging in "etic" analysis across interpretations (theories of related cases), critically engaging interpretations, showing how they inform one's thinking, and finding a compelling narrative voice at the level of theory.[45] Such reflection begins by clarifying the conceptual framework driven by the ends of the empirical study or studies. One begins, then, with a Description of the empirically-based interpretation(s) (the theory of the case), that highlights new or *altered* problematics and questions based on comparative and critical work. One should always keep in mind that the interpretations so described have been developed through similar reductions (synthesis, thematization) of the empirical description(s) engaged, so a valid claim to doing "grounded meta-theory" can be made. As Lanigan puts it, this first phase of constructing meta-theory involves a Description that *thematizes* the results of research, which involves the interpretation of the reduction of descriptions of sign(s). In building meta-theory, *begin again* with a summary of where you ended up conceptually with the empirical work, then compare it to others imaginatively and critically to make a claim for doing human science that seeks the just as well as truth(s).

There is, indeed, an important imaginative and artistic part of doing human scientific work. Narratives, fragments of narratives, stories, and stories within stories are the heart of radical empirical analysis, all thematic development revolves around tropes. In meta-theory construction, one must abstract and re-conceptualize this thematic content in terms of the new theoretical problematics and questions posed. In semiotic terms, the thematic content at the empirical level constituted the signifieds imbued with meaning and significance. Now, in doing meta-theory construction, those *signifieds become signifiers* of broader, more general concerns. As Lanigan puts it, the Reduction *abstracts* the interpretation of the reduction of the description of signifier(s), which is to emphasize this moment of semiotic transformation through abstraction of that which has been found and interpreted. The goal, for Peirce, is to move from the interpretation of the dynamic interpretant (the "object" or singular case) to a final interpretant in meta-theory construction; elaborating such rules and laws in any field is what makes it a science.

It is important to never forget the singularity of the event, a remembering that marks the anamnesis associated with the object of inquiry that the researcher lives and works with. The phenomenon is not external, but lived bodily, in flesh and bones, with compelling and opposing historicities; one works for an interpretation of findings that places the phenomenon "back" into a body of history. The phenomenon, in all of its complexity, is grounded in operative and sometimes contradictory micro-histories, and reveals broader ethical, political, and philosophical questions and concerns. Instances of patronage, kinship, harassment, loyalty, friendship, corruption, confinement, discrimination, rights claims, border crossings, migration, security regimens, deliberative democracy, mental health, family dynamics, nonhuman relations, or any other phenomenon analyzed through radical empirical research should be an investiture, requiring sacrifice of self, and embodied research engagement over time that includes critical reflexivity. The final interpretant in the Peircian view, understood in this meta-theoretical way, resituates the theorist's *responsibility for the persons, places, texts and historicities associated with the phenomenon.* No critical meta-theory perspective should be offered without a deep sense of obligation to persons and places engaged.[46]

A critical perspective is situated immanently, based on the terms abstracted from the empirical explication of the phenomenon, terms that signify and are linked inextricably to that phenomenon's extension of attributes. In Lanigan's terms, this final step constitutes an Interpretation that *explicates* the interpretation of the reduction of the description of signified(s). Proposing some final interpretant requires we move from the dynamical interpretant (that developed at the end of empirical work) toward a meta-theory that a community of scholars can consider, contest or accede to. To be valid it should be grounded eidetically and empirically in meanings and experiences of those who/that which, has/have been vigorously engaged and researched diachronically, over and in time, not merely at one time.

CONCLUSION

In this attempt at a philosophical guide to doing semiotic phenomenology, I have drawn on the work of Richard Lanigan and other sources in the history of phenomenology and semiotics in order to provide a systematic and hopefully accessible approach to research and theory construction in communicology. To advance a decolonizing research praxis, we start from where we are, at this moment, toward a horizon of meaning that compels inquiry but also presents sometimes insuperable boundaries and borders. To be drawn to and taken by the field, one approaches and thinks through these boundaries, often sacrificing self in the process. To be a researcher in the tradition outlined here, one is *taken* in every sense of being human.

To conclude, I want to emphasize that the existential basis suggested for research in the continental and pragmatic traditions referenced in this chapter, is oriented and in fact founded on intersubjective relations, the swirl of multiple voices, and competing realities of everyday life. It also involves recognition of and accounting for heterogeneous influences and apparatuses of power that impinge upon the research. Radical empirical analysis associated with decolonial research praxis involves most primordially an immersion in the complexity of a world that encompasses rhetorical/textual, interpersonal/intercultural, social/political, artistic/performative and mass mediated genres and dimensions. One enters such a complex field only to be consumed by it, which means one must work to find pathways and lines of inquiry (and at times lines of flight) that may not be part of a preconceived research design.

The human science of communicology, drawing as it does on complementary cultural and intellectual traditions, and providing conceptual and methodological tools for making sense of the world, is broad enough to encompasses all such dimensions and directions, engaging the empirical and existential through immanent and defetishizing critique toward the eidetic and meta-theoretical.[47] The global context of semiotic phenomenology, as developed by Richard Lanigan and elaborated herein, encompasses these genres and interests.

NOTES

1. Richard L. Lanigan, "Communicology and Culturology: Roland Posner's Semiosphere," in *Sign Culture / Zeichen Kultur*, ed. Ernst W. B. Hess-Lüttich (Würzburg: Verlag Königshausen and Neuman GmbH, 2012), 266.
2. Walter Mignolo, "Time to Bleed," *Chronic*, June 30, 2016 in *Arts & Pedagogy*. http://chimurengachronic.co.za/time-to-bleed-an-extended-conversation-with-walter-mignolo/
3. Although Lanigan discusses epistemology in various sources, the definitive explanation of semiotic phenomenology can be found in Richard L. Lanigan, *Phenomenology of Communication: Merleau-Ponty's Thematics in Communicology and Semiology* (Pittsburgh, PA: Duquesne University Press, 1988); and *The Human Science of Communicology: A Phenomenology of Discourse in Foucault and Merleau-Ponty* (Pittsburgh, PA: Duquesne University Press, 1992); see also "Semiotic Phenomenology: A Theory of Human Communication Praxis," *Journal of Applied Communication Research* 10 (1982): 62–73.
4. See Vincent Colapietro's essay, "The Subject at Hand," in this volume.
5. Lanigan, *Human Science*, 85, 98, Appendix A. The Law of Identity postulates that "a thing is always itself in the same time/place;" the Law of Contradiction states that "one thing cannot be *another* thing in the same time/place;" Lanigan argues that the Law of Non-Contradiction ("a thing cannot both be and not be at the same time/place") subsumes the other two Laws and sets up "the analogue logic rule of *differentiation by combination* in contrast to the 'digital logic' of Contradiction" (emphases in original; 194–195) that leads to what Lévi-Bruhl refers to as the Law of Participation.
6. For a discussion on false dichotomy between objectivism and subjectivism (in the guise of relativism) see Richard Bernstein, *Beyond Objectivism and Relativism: Science, Hermeneutics, Practice* (Philadelphia: University of Pennsylvania Press, 1988); for a discussion of hermeneutics and social science in a cross-cultural context, see Richard Bernstein, "The Hermeneutics of Cross-Cultural understanding," in *Cross-Cultural Conversation*, ed. A. N. Balslev (Atlanta, GA: The Scholars Press, 1992), 29–42.
7. For an instance of such an approach while doing fieldwork in Morocco, see my essay "*Sedq* in Morocco: On Communcability, Patronage and Partial Truth," *Cultural Critique* 51 (2002): 101–142.
8. For an introduction to *experimental* phenomenology, see Donald Ihde, *Experimental Phenomenology* (New York: G. P. Putnam and Sons, 1977).
9. See Charlene Haddock Seigfried, "Devising Ends Worth Striving For: William James and the Reconstruction of Philosophy," in *Recovering Pragmatism's Voice: The Classical Tradition, Rorty and the Philosophy of Communication*, ed. Lenore Langsdorf and Andrew R. Smith (Albany: State University of New York, 1995), 117. References to James in this quotation are from: William James, "The Meaning of Truth," in *The Works of William James*, ed. Frederick H. Burkhardt,

F. Bowers, and I. K. Skrupskelis (Cambridge, MA: Harvard University Press, 1975), 79–86, 115–16, 23n6.
10. See Lanigan, *Phenomenology*, 5, 6, 16.
11. See the discussion of the Law of Participation in Richard L. Lanigan, "Appendix A: Lévi-Bruhl and the Human Science 'Law of Participation'," in *Human Science of Communicology*, 191–196.
12. Ahti-Veikko Pietarinen and Francesco Bellucci, "New Light on Peirce's Conceptions of Retroduction, Deduction, and Scientific Reasoning," *International Studies in the Philosophy of Science* 28, no. 4 (2014): 353–373.
13. Richard L. Lanigan, "From Enthymeme to Abduction: The Classical Law of Logic and the Postmodern Rule of Rhetoric," in *Recovering Pragmatism's Voice: The Classical Tradition, Rorty and the Philosophy of Communication*, ed. Lenore Langsdorf and Andrew R. Smith (Albany: State University of New York, 1995), 54.
14. Maurice Merleau-Ponty, *The Phenomenology of Perception*, trans. Colin Smith, trans revisions Forrest Williams and David Guerière (London: Routledge and Kegan Paul, 1986; original publication 1962), 213.
15. Merleau-Ponty, *Phenomenology*, 213–214.
16. Merleau-Ponty, *Phenomenology*, 214. He refers to his previous discussion in *The Structure of Behavior*, trans. Alden L. Fisher (Pittsburgh: Duquesne University Press, 1983; original publication 1942), 200; here he takes up issues related to the Kantian notion of the transcendental esthetic, and asks, in the end "How, as a matter of fact, are we to conceive the relations of the 'given' and 'thought,' the operation of consciousness on inert 'things' which pure sensations would be, the connection of 'affection' and knowledge and the connection of sensible and intellectual consciousness? In the final analysis, then, there will be no sensible consciousness, no hiatus between the esthetic and the analytic, and no naturized consciousness."
17. Klaus Krippendorf, *Content Analysis: An Introduction to its Methodology*, 3rd ed. (Los Angeles: Sage, 2012); 41–42.
18. Charles Sanders Peirce, *Collected Papers of Charles Sanders Peirce*, ed. C. Hartshorne, P. Weiss, and A. W. Burks (Cambridge, MA: Harvard University Press, 1966), vol. 5, 181.
19. This list is adapted and extended based on Krippendorf, *Content Analysis*.
20. Krippendorf, *Content Analysis*, 42.
21. Merleau-Ponty, *Structure of Behavior*, 200–201 (emphasis added).
22. Richard Shweder, *Thinking Through Cultures: Expeditions in Cultural Psychology* (Cambridge, MA: Harvard University Press, 1991), 360n.
23. Jean-François Lyotard, *Discourse, Figure*, trans. Antony Hudek and Mary Lydon. (St. Paul: University of Minnesota Press, 2010), 119.
24. Abdellah Hammoudi, *Master and Disciple: The Cultural Foundations of Moroccan Authoritarianism* (Chicago, IL: University of Chicago Press, 1997), vii.
25. See John Caputo, *Radical Hermeneutics* (Bloomington: Indiana University Press, 1986). For distinctions between conservative, liberal and radical hermeneutics, see Robert Young, *Intercultural Communication: Pragmatics, Geneology, Deconstruction* (Philadelphia, PA: Multilingual Matters, 1996).
26. For elaboration on the Husserlian notion of pure science of transcendental subjectivity, and its limitations as developed by Mohanty, for doing intercultural research, see my essay "Phenomenology of Intercultural Communication," in *Japanese and Western Phenomenology*, ed. P. Blosser, E. Shimonmisse, L. Embree, and H. Kojime (Boston, MA: Kluwer Academic Publishers, 1993), 235–248.

27. Edmund Husserl, *Ideas: A General Introduction to Pure Phenomenology*, trans. W. R. Boyce Gibson (New York: Humanities Press, 1967), 52.
28. Edmund Husserl. *The Idea of Phenomenology*, trans. William P. Alston and George Nakhnikian (The Hague: Martinus Nijhoff, 1964), 53.
29. Edmund Husserl. *Phenomenology and the Crisis of Philosophy* [*Philosophy as Rigorous Science* and *Philosophy and the Crisis of European Man*], trans. Quentin Lauer (New York: Harper, 1965).
30. See Merleau-Ponty, *Phenomenology*; Lanigan, *Phenomenology*; *Human Science*
31. Hans-Georg Gadamer, *Truth and Method*, Second Rev. ed., trans Joel Weinsheimer and Donald G. Marshall (New York: Crossroads, 1992), 269.
32. See Martin Heidegger, *Being and Time*, trans. John Macquarrie and Edward Robinson (San Francisco: Harper and Row, 1962), 188–195, 210–214.
33. Michel Foucault, "Confessions of the Flesh," in *Power/Knowledge: Selective Interviews and Other Writings 1972-1977*, ed. Colin Gordon, trans. Colin Gordon, Leo Marshall, John Mepham, Kate Soper (New York: Pantheon, 1977), 194–195.
34. See Fred Evans, *The Multivoiced Body: Society and Communication in an Age of Diversity* (New York: Columbia University Press, 2008).
35. Pierre Bourdieu, *Language and Symbolic Power*, ed. John Thompson, trans. Gino Raymon and Matthew Adamson (Cambridge, MA: Harvard University Press, 1990).
36. See Andrew R. Smith, "Transformational Pragmatics in the MENA Uprisings: Reterritorialization in Morocco," in *Communication and Conflict Transformation: Local to Global Engagements*, ed. Thomas Matyok and Petter Kellett (New York: Lexington Books, 2017), 291–322.
37. See Lanigan, *Phenomenology*, 62, 163.
38. See James Clifford, "On Ethnographic Allegory," in *Writing Culture: The Poetics and Politics of Ethnography*, ed. J. Clifford and E. Marcus (Berkeley: University of California Press, 1986), 98–121. James Clifford, "Introduction: Partial Truths," in *Writing Culture*, 1–26; Andrew R. Smith, "Discord in Intercultural Negotiation: Toward an Ethic of Communicability," in *Ferment in the Intercultural Field: Axiology/Value/Praxis. Intercultural and International Communication Annual*, vol. 26 (Los Angeles: Sage, 2003), 91–130; "Geertz's Characterizations of Moroccans: Some Critical Concerns," in *The Moroccan Character: Studies in Honor of Mohammed Abu-Talib*, ed. A. Youssi, M. Dahbi, and L. Haddad (Rabat, Morocco: AMAPATRIL), 86–97.
39. Edward Said, "Identity, Negation, Violence," *New Left Review* 171 (1989); *Orientalism* (New York: Vintage Books, 1978); "Representing the Colonized: Anthropology's Interlocutors," *Critical Inquiry* 15, no. 2 (1989): 205–125; Gayatri Spivak, *In Other Worlds: Essays in Cultural Politics* (New York: Methuen, 1987); Spivak, *The Post-colonial Critic: Interviews, Strategies, Dialogues*, ed. Sarah Harasym (New York: Routledge, 1990).
40. See Linda Alcoff, "The Problem of Speaking for Others," *Cultural Critique* 20 (1990): 5–32. Talal Asad, "Two European Images of Non-European Rule," in *Anthropology as Colonial Encounter*, ed. Talal Asad (Atlantic Highlands, NJ: Humanities Press, 2005), 103–118; with regard to critical research and analysis see Andrew R. Smith and Fadoua Loudiy, "Testing the Red Lines: On the Liberalization of Speech in Morocco," *Human Rights Quarterly* 27, no. 3 (2005): 1069–1119.
41. The quasi-Levinasian notion of obligation as John Caputo develops it in *Against Ethics: Contributions to a Poetics of Obligation with Constant Reference to Deconstruction* (Bloomington: Indiana University Press, 1992); see Emmanuel Levinas, *Otherwise than Being or Beyond Essence*, trans. Alphonso Lingis (The Hague: Kluwer Academic Publishers, 1990).
42. My research and writing in and about Morocco over the past twenty years has aspired to meet these standards. In addition to work already cited, see Andrew R. Smith, Fadoua Loudiy, and

Kristin Thomas, "Agonistic Discourse(s) in the Sahara Conflict: The Right to have Rights," in *Radical Conflict: Essays on Violence, Intractability and Communication*, ed. Andrew R. Smith (New York: Lexington Books, 2016), 201–230.
43. See Merleau-Ponty, *Phenomenology*, 416.
44. Richard L. Lanigan, "Verbal and Non-verbal Codes of Communicology: The Foundation of Interpersonal Agency and Efficacy," in *Communicology: The New Science of Embodied Discourse*, ed. Deborah Eicher-Catt and Isaac E. Catt (Madison: Fairleigh Dickinson University Press, 2010).
45. For an example of elaborating such a narrative voice around the concept of "radical conflict," see Andrew R. Smith, "On Radical Conflict," in *Radical Conflict: Essays on Violence, Intractability and Communication*, ed. Andrew R. Smith (New York: Lexington Books, 2016), xv–xxix.
46. See Andrew R. Smith, "Dialogue in Agony: The Problem of Communication in Authoritarian Regimes," *Communication Theory* 18, no. 1 (2008): 160–185.
47. See Andrew R. Smith, "Seyla Benhabib: Foundations of Critical Communication Theory and Praxis," in *Philosophical Profiles in the Theory of Communication*, ed. Jason Hannan (New York: Peter Lang, 2011), 35–63.

BIBLIOGRAPHY

Alcoff, Linda. "The Problem of Speaking for Others." *Cultural Critique* 20 (1991): 5–32.
Asad, Talal, ed. *Anthropology and the Colonial Encounter.* New York: Prometheus Books, 1995.
Bernstein, Richard. *Beyond Objectivism and Relativism: Science, Hermeneutics, and Praxis.* Philadelphia: University of Pennsylvania Press, 1988.
Bernstein, Richard. "The Hermeneutics of Cross-cultural Understanding." In *Cross-Cultural Conversation*, edited by A. N. Balslev, 29–42. Atlanta, GA: The Scholars Press, 1996.
Bourdieu, Pierre. *Language and Symbolic Power.* Edited by John Thompson and Translated by Gino Raymon and Matthew Adamson. Cambridge, MA: Harvard University Press, 1990.
Caputo, John. *Against Ethics. Contributions to a Poetics of Obligation with Constant Reference to Deconstruction.* Bloomington: Indiana University Press, 1993.
Caputo, John. *Radical Hermeneutics.* Bloomington: University of Indiana Press, 1987.
Clifford, James. "Introduction: Partial Truths." In *Writing Culture: The Poetics and Politics of Ethnography*, edited by James Clifford and E. Marcus, 1–26. Berkeley: University of California Press, 1986.
Clifford, James. "On Ethnographic Allegory." In *Writing Culture: The Poetics and Politics of Ethnography*, edited by J. Clifford and E. Marcus, 98–121. Berkeley: University of California Press, 1986.
Evans, Fred. *The Multivoiced Body: Society and Communication in an Age of Diversity.* New York: Columbia University Press, 2008.
Foucault, Michel. "The Confessions of the Flesh." In *Power/Knowledge: Selected Interviews & Other Writings.* Edited by Colin Gordon; translated by Colin Gordon, Leo Marshalll, John Mepham, Kate Soper. New York: Pantheon Books, 1980.
Foucault, Michel. "The Subject and Power." In *Michel Foucault: Beyond Structuralism and Hermeneutics*, edited by Hubert Dreyfus and Paul Rabinow, 208–226. Chicago, IL: University of Chicago Press, 1982.
Gadamer, Hans-Georg. *Truth and Method.* Translated by J. Weinsheimer and D. G. Marshall. New York: Crossroad, 1992.
Hammoudi, Abdellah. *Master and Disciple: The Cultural Foundations of Moroccan Authoritarianism.* Chicago, IL: University of Chicago Press, 1997.

Heidegger, Martin. *Being and Time.* Translated by John Macquarrie and Edward Robinson. San Francisco, CA: Harper and Row, 1962.
Husserl, Edmund. *The Idea of Phenomenology.* Translated by William P. Alston and George Nakhnikian. The Hague: Martinus Nijhoff, 1964.
Husserl, Edmund. *Ideas: A General Introduction to Pure Phenomenology.* Translated by W. R. Boyce Gibson. New York: Humanities Press, 1967.
Husserl, Edmund. *Phenomenology and the Crisis of Philosophy* [*Philosophy as Rigorous Science* and *Philosophy and the Crisis of European Man*]. Translated by Quentin Lauer. New York: Harper, 1965.
Ihde, Donald. *Experimental Phenomenology.* New York: G. P. Putnam's Sons, 1977.
James, William. "The Meaning of Truth." In *The Works of William James*, edited by Frederick H. Burkhardt, F. Bowers, and I. K. Skrupskelis, 79–86. Cambridge, MA: Harvard University Press, 1975.
Krippendorf, Klaus. *Content Analysis: An Introduction to Its Methodology.* 3rd ed. Los Angeles, CA: Sage, 2012.
Lanigan, Richard L. "Communicology and Culturology: Roland Posner's Semiosphere." In *Sign Culture / Zeichen Kultur*, edited by Ernst W. B. Hess-Lüttich, 265–282. Würzburg: Verlag Königshausen and Neuman GmbH, 2012.
Lanigan, Richard L. "From Enthymeme to Abduction: The Classical Law of Logic and the Postmodern Rule of Rhetoric." In *Recovering Pragmatism's Voice: The Classical Tradition, Rorty, and the Philosophy of Communication*, edited by Lenore Langsdorf, L. and Andrew R. Smith, 49–70. Albany: State University of New York Press, 1995.
Lanigan, Richard L. *The Human Science of Communicology: A Phenomenology of Discourse in Foucault and Merleau-Ponty.* Pittsburgh, PA: Duquesne University Press, 1992.
Lanigan, Richard L. *Phenomenology of Communication: Merleau-Ponty's Thematics in Communicology and Semiology.* Pittsburgh, PA: Dusquesne University Press, 1988.
Lanigan, Richard L. "Semiotic Phenomenology: A Theory of Human Communication Praxis." *Journal of Applied Communication Research* 10 (1982): 62–73.
Lanigan, Richard L. "Verbal and Non-verbal Codes of Communicology: The Foundation of Interpersonal Agency and Efficacy." In *Communicology: The New Science of Embodied Discourse*, edited by Deborah Eicher-Catt and Isaac E. Catt. Madison: Fairleigh Dickinson University Press, 2010.
Levinas, Emmanuel. *Otherwise Than Being or Beyond Essence.* Translated by Alphonso Lingis. Boston, MA: Kluwer Academic Publishers, 1991.
Lyotard, Jean-François. *Discourse, Figure*, 119. Translated by Antony Hudek and Mary Lydon. St. Paul: University of Minnesota Press, 2010.
Merleau-Ponty, Maurice. *The Phenomenology of Perception.* Translated by Colin Smith; translation revisions by Forrest Williams and David Guerrière. London: Routledge and Kegan Paul, 1986.
Merleau-Ponty, Maurice. *Signs.* Translated by R. C. McLeary. Evanston, IL: Northwestern University Press, 1964.
Merleau-Ponty, Maurice. *The Structure of Behavior.* Translated by Alden L. Fisher. Pittsburgh, PA: Duquesne University Press, 1983.
Peirce, Charles Sanders. *Collected Papers of Charles Sanders Peirce.* Edited by Charles Hartshorne, Paul Weiss, and A. W. Burks. Cambridge, MA: Harvard University Press, 1966.
Pietarinen, Ahti-Veikko, and Francesco Bellucci. "New Light on Peirce's Conceptions of Retroduction, Deduction, and Scientific Reasoning." *International Studies in the Philosophy of Science* 28, no. 4 (2014): 353–373.

Ricoeur, Paul. "Phenomenology and the Social Sciences." *The Annals of Phenomenological Sociology* 1 (1975): 145–159.
Said, Edward. "Identity, Negation, Violence." *New Left Review* I (September/October, 1988): 171.
Said, Edward. *Orientalism*. New York: Vintage Books, 1978.
Said, Edward. "Representing the Colonized: Anthropology's Interlocutors." *Critical Inquiry* 15, no. 2 (1989): 205–225.
Schrag, Calvin. *Radical Reflection and the Origin of the Human Sciences*. West Lafayette, IN: Purdue University Press, 1980.
Seigfried, Charlene Haddock. "Devising Ends Worth Striving For: William James and the Reconstruction of Philosophy." In *Recovering Pragmatism's Voice: The Classical Tradition, Rorty and the Philosophy of Communication*, edited by Lenore Langsdorf and Andrew R. Smith, 117. Albany: State University of New York, 1995.
Shweder, Richard A. *Thinking through Cultures: Expeditions in Cultural Psychology*. Cambridge, MA: Harvard University Press, 1991.
Smith, Andrew R. "Dialogue in Agony: The Problem of Communication in Authoritarian Regimes." *Communication Theory* 18, no. 1 (2008): 160–185.
Smith, Andrew R. "Discord in Intercultural Negotiation: Toward an Ethic of Communicability." In *Ferment in the Intercultural Field: Axiology/Value/Praxis. Intercultural and International Communication Annual*. Vol. 26, edited by William Starosta and Guo-Ming Chen, 91–130. Los Angeles, CA: Sage, 2003.
Smith, Andrew R. "Geertz's Characterizations of Moroccans: Some Critical Concerns." In *The Moroccan Character: Studies in Honor of Mohammed Abu-Talib*, edited by A. Youssi, M. Dahbi, and L. Haddad, 86–97. Rabat, Morocco: AMAPATRIL, 2003.
Smith, Andrew R. "The Limits of Communication: Lyotard and Levinas on Otherness." In *Transgressing Discourses: Communication and the Voice of Other*, edited by Michael Huspek and Gary Radford, 327–351. Albany: State University of New York Press, 1997.
Smith, Andrew R. "Phenomenology of Intercultural Communication." In *Japanese and Western Phenomenology*, edited by P. Blosser, E. Shimonmisse, L. Embree, and H. Kojime, 235–248. Boston, MA: Kluwer Academic Publishers, 1993.
Smith, Andrew R. "*Sedq* in Morocco: On Communicability, Patronage and Partial Truth." *Cultural Critique* 51 (2002): 101–142.
Smith, Andrew R. "Seyla Benhabib: Foundations of Critical Communication Theory and Praxis." In *Philosophical Profiles in the Theory of Communication*, edited by Jason Hannan, 35–63. New York: Peter Lang, 2011.
Smith, Andrew R. "Transformational Pragmatics in the MENA Uprisings: Reterritorialization in Morocco." In *Communication and Conflict Transformation: Local to Global Engagements*, edited by Thomas Matyok and Petter Kellett, 291–322. New York: Lexington Books, 2017. Smith, Andrew R. "On Radical Conflict." In *Radical Conflict: Essays on Violence, Intractability and Communication*, edited by Andrew R. Smith, xv–xxix. New York: Lexington Books, 2016.
Smith, Andrew R., and Fadoua Loudiy. Testing the Red Lines: On the Liberalization of Speech in Morocco. *Human Rights Quarterly* 27, no. 3 (2005): 1069–1119.
Smith, Andrew R., Fadoua Loudiy, and Kristen Thomas, "Agonistic Discourse(s) in the Sahara Conflict: The Right to have Rights." In *Radical Conflict: Essays on Violence, Intractability and Communication*, edited by Andrew R. Smith, 201–230. New York: Lexington Books, 2016.
Spivak, Gaytri. *In Other Worlds: Essays in Cultural Politics*. New York: Methuen, 1987.

Spivak, Gaytri. *The Post-colonial Critic: Interviews, Strategies, Dialogues.* Edited by Sarah Harasym. New York: Routledge, 1990.

Young, Robert. *Intercultural Communication: Pragmatics, Geneology, Deconstruction.* Philadelphia, PA: Multilingual Matters, 1996.

CHAPTER TWO

Lanigan's "Encyclopedic Dictionary"

Key Concepts, Insights, and Advances

COREY ANTON

> All consciousness is synergistic in this way: the moment that you move from step one to step two, you have simultaneously invented (experienced) step three —that is, the relationship between steps one and two.[1]
> —Richard Lanigan

> The vertical structure of consciousness combines with the horizontal essence of experience as an orthogonal nexus.[2]
> —Richard Lanigan

> Truth is not, therefore, merely eidetic or empirical, but both, and synergistically so.[3]
> —Richard Lanigan

It is a delight and an honor to be included in this Festschrift honoring Richard L. Lanigan. Although I was not one of his students, his writings have informed a good number of my publications and, I should add that I have benefitted personally from Richard generously sharing his time and insights with me on more than one occasion.[4] The work of his that I find myself returning to again and again, the one that offers the greatest challenges but also yields the greatest rewards, is his "Communicology: An Encyclopedic Dictionary of the Human Sciences".[5] Few works are as heuristically rich, as theoretically dense, and as widely applicable. An extraordinary resource for anyone seriously interested in communication theory, Lanigan's "Encyclopedic Dictionary" offers technical vocabulary for comprehending and comparatively assessing the practices, logics, and methodologies within the natural and social sciences. It overviews the common ground used (both qualitative and quantitative) when scholars advance claims regarding knowledge and/or understanding. Given space limitations, little justice can be given to its overall scope, range, and comprehensiveness; the whole is simply beyond address here. My more modest goal is to make evident the value of Lanigan's semiotic phenomenology, a qualitative methodology that attempts to understand sign-systems as they are lived and experienced in embodied consciousness within concrete contexts.

The present chapter pulls amply from the Encyclopedic Dictionary to clarify how information theory is a subset of communication theory, one that has grown into human communication processes. Part of the task here is to show how longitudinal intentionalities synergistically operate within Gestalten and phenomenological appresentation to vitally contribute to both perceptual processes and human communication. Another part is to show how the evolutionary development of denotative utterances worked to release information from communicative contexts and also bore upon the reversibility between perception and expression. Finally, I outline the crucial role played by alphabetic literacy and literate-based technologies (e.g., dictionaries and encyclopedias) in increasingly transforming communication into an informational system, one where the discourse functions aligned to the linguistic realm (i.e. the "poetic function," the "metalinguistic function," and the "referential function,") gain increasing relevance and come to rival the discourse functions aligning mainly to speech/communication (i.e., emotive, conative, phatic).[6]

Before advancing directly to Lanigan's "Encyclopedic Dictionary," I wish to contextualize his work amongst a few of what I take to be his many scholarly influences. I limit my review to four scholarly traditions (omitting the obvious connections to Merleau-Ponty and Foucault). The first comes from Jürgen Ruesch and Gregory Bateson, especially *The Social Matrix of Psychiatry*. Ruesch and Bateson successfully overcame the separation of psychology (i.e., the individual) and sociology (i.e., the collective) by turning attention to common ground: communication. Whereas earlier orientations largely had focused on either the individual or the collective, either psychological factors within persons or social forces and influences between persons, Ruesch and Bateson reveal how both of these phenomena (and more) can be grasped simultaneously by adequately understanding human communication.

Second, Edward Hall's work, especially his *Beyond Culture*, accounts for the vibrant relationships between and among information, context, and culture. Hall, too, eschews focus on either the individual or the collective, and he stresses that both the collective and the individual need to be approached through context. Hall provides a model and theory of the relationship between information and context (where context is both internal and external), which furthermore allows for integrative and comparative studies of culture. One can, for example, talk about differences between East and West within a common framework. Hall's work also incorporates a time element as well as addresses the mediating role of technologies. For all of these reasons, it effectively combats overly reductive and simplistic orientations to communication.

Third, Elmar Holenstein's book *Roman Jakobson's Approach to Language*, offers much useful technical background on Jakobson. Furthermore, whereas European lines of humanities scholarship traditionally divided into two groups, on the one hand, adherents to linguistics, structuralism, and semiotics (Saussure, Levi-Strauss, Hjelmslev) and, on the other, adherents to phenomenology (Husserl, Heidegger, Merleau-Ponty), Holenstein shows how Jakobson's work, as a whole, reconciles the division between transpersonal, socio-cultural structure and personal, lived-through conscious experience. No other single book has been as helpful to me in grasping Lanigan's semiotic phenomenology.

Finally, of nearly equal importance to Holenstein's summations of Jakobson is Anthony Wilden's work, especially *System and Structure*. Wilden reveals the relationship between analog and digital communication and thereby undercuts the rigid division between systems (e.g. process, change) and structures (e.g. pattern, stability). Also useful is his *The Rules Are No Game: The Strategy of Communication*, and its final chapter, on "Context Theory." Wilden, with solid command over the ideas of Bateson and Lacan, demonstrates how communication, with its "both/and" analog logic, incorporates and internally employs—but also can become tyrannized by—the "either/or" digital logic of information.

CONTEXTUAL BACKGROUNDS: GESTALT PROCESSES AND APPRESENTATION

Among the earliest and arguably most crucial entries in Lanigan's "Encyclopedic Dictionary" are the following two:

> COMMUNICATION THEORY = binary analogue logic that constitutes *possibility* differentiation (i.e., certainty) by combination; simply formulated as "a choice of context"; strictly formulated as "the choice of a context by relation which entails a choice by correlation"; formalized as: {Both [Both/And] And [Either/Or]}.[7]

And,

> INFORMATION THEORY = digital logic that constitutes *probability* differentiation (i.e., reduces uncertainty) by exclusion; simply formulated as "a context of choice"; strictly formulated as "the context of a choice by correlation which entails a context by relation"; formalized as: {Either [Either/Or] Or [Both/And]}.[8]

One way to take hold of the above distinctions is to recall that actual lived-through experience offers, as William James observed, "a much-at-onceness" from which perceptual and conceptual processes carve out the contexts within which more refined and precise deliberations and choices might be made. Only by first delimiting (i.e., choosing) *both* the system *and* its elements can we begin to structure those situated digital contexts in which we can choose *either* one item *or* another. As Lanigan elsewhere writes, "… (1) a Choice of Context as a *combinatory analog apposition* always precedes (2) a Context of Choice as a *disjunctive digital opposition* …"[9]

These distinctions can be grasped both more broadly and more directly by stepping back to reconsider some basics of Gestalt psychology as well as Husserl's work on appresentation and time-consciousness. By these orientations, the technical expression, "binary analogue logic that constitutes *possibility* differentiation by combination," suggests temporal processes (i.e., longitudinal intentionalities) that include many modes of Gestalt-like combinatory contrasts (appositions and oppositions, including perceptual, linguistic, and eidetic variations) whereby differentiation by combination constitutes an experienced sense of what is, as well as what is possible.[10] That also means that any figure stands in various relationships with its grounds such that the figure retains some degree of context-dependence, and context-dependence is an inclusive mode of "differentiation by combination." Additionally, any figure, as a kind of semiotic unit, stands in a paradigmatic relation to other similar yet absent items of its kind, meaning that the empirical presence of a figure stands in analog relation to its eidetic (i.e., perceptually absent) form. A perceived whole, a figure within a ground, stands both in a spatial and temporal relation to whatever is empirically contiguous (i.e., various syntagmatic connections), while also standing in paradigmatic relation (i.e., eidetic relation) to other similar yet absent elements. For example: I have a cube in my hand. No matter how I rotate it or change my perspective on it, I can see only three sides of it at one time. Nevertheless, I experience the whole cube. The sides seen and/or felt are variations presented perceptually but the unseen and unfelt sides are appresented eidetically. We thus can experience a sense of a "whole cube" despite empirically encountering only partial variants within a series of adumbrations. The perceptual world accordingly has intersubjective thickness, spatial depth, and temporal duration. Hence, we can move our eyes and/or our hands over an object, and therein the combinations across profiles, with their various conjunctions, increase certainty regarding various possibilities of the object.

Speech, too, is a movement, one with its own means of changing positions or shifting perception so that an object of concern can be more completely and articulately disclosed.[11] Just as a given patch of colored cloth bears slightly different hues when placed against different background textures, colors, or in different lighting, so, too, do phonemes, morphemes, words, and phrases (all enunciated with varying degrees of volume, of intensity and of tonality) gain their meaning by *combination*, both in combination with other phonemes, morphemes, words, and phrases as well as in combination with various non-verbal elements and contexts.

Time-consciousness and memory (as forms of longitudinal intentionality) seem to be the common condition for these synergistic relations between (a) "part" and "whole," (b) "empirical" and "eidetic," and (c) "variation" and "invariance."[12]

The reversibility of perception and expression seems, in many respects, to be an outgrowth of the fact that the body is a *network* of sensory capacities and one sense can reflect synesthetically upon another. Just as we can turn our heads to look in the direction of something heard, or we can rub our eyes when our vision is not clear, we can talk about any perceived Gestalten.[13] This not only leads to greater perceptual acuity; it also enables expressions regarding what remains empirically absent to be combined with immediately perceived situations.[14] We can combine elements (perceived and/or expressed, empirical and/or eidetic) and thereby talk and think about different kinds of parts and wholes. We can speak about what otherwise would remain remote in space and time, just as we can imaginatively rearrange empirically perceived situations without physically moving any objects. With simple assertions such as, "The ink is black," we can predicate substances, tearing asunder what remains empirically inseparable.

The term "analogic" underscores notions of continuous and contiguous positive values, gradations of emotion, energy level, and attention.[15] Analogic dimensions pervade the distinctive features within spoken communication, both inherent and prosodic: ("sonority," "protensity," and "tonality" as well as "force," "quantity," and "tone," respectively). Such elements always have a particular magnitude, and much of our relational communication is done analogically, with indexes and icons. Our communication also includes emotional states and expressed values that have an embodied style not reducible to "either/or" conditions except as those can be represented symbolically. But the term "analogic" also trades upon notions of analogy, metaphor, and/or structural similarity. Hence, the notion of "*binary* analogue" seems to mean that humans, in addition to dealing with analogue differences, can integrate digital distinctions into various kinds of analogical relations.

Clear examples of "digital logic" are best grasped by probability theory within mathematics or by information theory within computer science. In both these cases, the presence of one discrete element excludes other probable elements. Uncertainty can be reduced within such closed-systems by sequences of exclusionary questions (either "yes" or "no"). The information system is closed and its elements (the code) remain fixed according to pre-determined values; they are not subject to creative innovation or recontextualization. They are, on their own terms, meaningless.[16]

Other examples of information theory can be found in True/False and/or Multiple-Choice tests. Such exams make students face contexts of choice, where questions are worded so that information (i.e., data) is given depending upon the items selected. But communication, as choice of context, would need to include opportunities for responses that recontextualize or rephrase the question and/or the possible responses. A student might say, "Can't this question be *both* true *and* false?" or "Shouldn't there be another option listed in the possible responses?" or "What does word 'X' mean?" or perhaps, "There seems to be a typo in this question." This point is underscored in the subtitle to the opening chapter of Lanigan's *The Human Science of Communicology*, which reads: "Can an American Do Semiotic Phenomenology?"[17] If we accept the question at its face value, we find ourselves led into the logic of "either/or": an American either can (or cannot) do semiotic phenomenology. But, if, in grasping his point, we do not accept the wording of the question or want further clarification and/or wish to redefine any word by making substitutions along the paradigmatic axis, we must engage not only in the original context of choice but must invoke a choice of context.

Information theory deals with established values and boundaries whereas communication theory can take given values and boundaries (or not), and also introduce new values and boundaries themselves. Communication, then, is a form of both action and possible abstracting within the world of particulars and continuity. Hence, any information given by "a context of choice" is produced only by closed-system operations, whereas communication is fundamentally an open-system, one having not only "a choice of context," but also, according to temporal processes, the means by which the code itself and the overall system boundaries remain open and fruitfully ambiguous.

All of the above implies that the emergence of denotation makes a significant evolutionary revision—a radical acceleration of the possibility of experiencing, producing, and distributing information. The evolutionary development of denotative propositions signifies one of the unique qualities of human language, a vital component of "time-binding."[18] Humans, as sheer organisms, always find themselves installed within an immediately surrounding environment, one disclosed according to the abstracting capacities of the senses. In very concrete ways, each sensory modality carries a recontextualization with it, a new definition of the situation, a revised sense of the overall context. The perceptually disclosed immediate environment was, and perhaps remains, the original and perennial "context of choice," and some forms of nascent information are generated according to organismal goal-seeking (i.e., making selections and combinations) from within that largely analogical context. But, with the dawn of denotation (and predication too), the context itself, along with the meaning of information, was subject to radical expansion and ongoing revision.[19]

DENOTATION AND THE EVOLUTION OF INFORMATION WITHIN COMMUNICATION

Evolutionarily speaking, as communicative processes made more and more room for denotative elements, both signifier and signified were increasingly doubled over both eidetically and empirically. Denotation, that is, carries an "empirical/

eidetic doublet" both in language and in the realm of "objects" we can talk about.[20] Consider, for example, the denotative word, "apple." On the one hand, the word, the sound-complex "apple," is eidetically separated from all of the variations in pronunciation, volume, pitch, rate, intonation, accent, etc.; the word can be recognized as the word it is despite the fact that it always appears in varied guises. On the other hand, any actual particular apple that I am able to hold and recognize as an apple (no matter its size, thickness, color, or shape) is, to that effect, a member of a category, a token of a type. Although I can hold an apple in my hand, any particular one held does not liquidate the signified *apple*. Denotation, therefore, implies that both the word and the thing have become idealized into discrete informational units and yet both remain haunted by very real absences.

The evolutionary emergence of denotation (and predication)—including verbal Gestalten that now can transcend their local contexts of utterance as well as nonverbal Gestalten (either empirically perceivable, or available by inner recollection and/or imagination)—inaugurated "information" as distinct (or eidetically separable) from communication.[21] Moreover, the phenomena associated with denotative utterances and predication, on at least two different fronts, encompass a great deal more than individual words referring to objects or abstracted elements. Underscoring the gestalt nature of perception and communication, we first should stress that each and every object—whether referring to objects in the world or to linguistic objects or imaginary objects—has its context. This is why Jakobson uses the term "context" to designate the referential function of discourse. Second, with historical hindsight and the benefit of modern literacy studies, we today can appreciate how the poetic possibilities of syntactically combining abstracted (i.e., possible) denotative elements fundamentally opened up the human world. Said otherwise, without grammar and syntax—and without metalinguistic resources—denotation arguably would have remained a highly limited and insular affair, and predication could not have emerged.[22]

Among the most important breakthroughs in modern linguistics, already alluded to in Jakobson's and Holenstein's works respectively, was the discovery of the syntagmatic and paradigmatic axes.[23] Although the two axes are sometimes limited to linguistic analysis, they imply much more. As Lanigan makes evident throughout many of his writings, they refer, respectively, to the horizontal axis (present/empirical, speaker and listener, syntax and grammar, esctatical temporality, metonymy) and the vertical axis (absent/eidetic, code and context, semantics and reference, historicity, metaphor).[24] Lanigan also points out, in stressing the importance of Levi-Bruhl's work, that syntagmatic and paradigmatic operations constitute the basic structure of "pre-logical" thought; they resonate within and throughout countless cultural practices. As identified by Sir James George Frazer, forms of sympathetic magic (of "contagion" and of "similarity") comprise the ground of "reasoning" within many traditional rituals and sayings.

For Saussure, the paradigmatic axis (i.e., the synchronic) was not only set in a dichotomous relationship to the syntagmatic axis (i.e., the diachronic), but the former was privileged over the latter. One of Jakobson's significant contributions, his focus on the message and the poetic function in discourse, was to undercut this dichotomy and to reverse this privilege. He recognized that the code holds only the necessary conditions (the elements) but not yet the sufficient conditions (functions) for communication.[25] Hence, just as context-dependence fundamentally precedes any possible decontextualization, so too, the nonverbal syntagm, both temporally and logically, paves the way for the growth and development of the paradigmatic axis.

This claim can be clarified, in part, by recalling Bateson's account of mammalian play and metacommunicative framing. The critical transition came with the historical emergence of play frames (i.e., iconic coding systems) from the world of symptomatic mood-signs (i.e., indexicals). Bateson knew, when he went to the Fleishhacker Zoo, that he would not find denotative propositions. But he did not anticipate grasping what he later would call "the onion-skin," the beginning of logical types, categories, classifications, typologies, and codification schemas—what might be called "ideas *about* relation-states" rather than merely "managed relation-states."[26] The first kinds of signs, largely indexical, are symptomatic and context-bound, including forms of aggression found in pre-mammalian organisms. The "playful nip" emerges as a metonymic sign (a synecdoche), meaning that it is both an early moment of the syntagmatic axis within interaction and an iconic sign (paradigmatic) of a type of behavior.[27] The play frame, by engaging in metacommunicative iconic sign use, fortifies the paradigmatic axis with a growing repertoire of possible responses within concrete interaction.

We can appreciate the difference yet relationship between the face-to-face situation within which any communication occurs (i.e. a syntagmatic relation in its own right and something that well predates the emergence of denotative language properly speaking) and the syntagmatic axis of language, a relatively late evolutionary accomplishment. The initial basic unit then, the whole that operates in presentia, is the syntagm, and it includes "addresser" and "addressee" as well as their "contact" within any co-present nonverbal situation.[28] It incorporates all situational elements as they synergistically combine, here and now. Susanne K. Langer contributes significantly to this line of thought. Her account of the origin of language tracks the development from indexical signs to iconic signs to presentational symbolic forms to denotative utterances.[29] She also notes how iconic signs can become symbolic ones through "emendations" that rely upon countless indexicals. She writes:

> All discourse involves two elements, which may be called, respectively, the context (verbal or practical) and the novelty. The novelty is what the speaker is trying to point out or to express. For this purpose he will use any word that serves him. The word may be apt, or it may be

> ambiguous, or even new; the context, seen or stated, modifies it and determines just what it means. Where a precise word is lacking to designate the novelty which the speaker would point out, he resorts to the powers of logical analogy, and uses a word denoting something else that is a presentational symbol for the thing he means; the context makes it clear that he cannot mean the thing literally denoted, and must mean something else symbolically …. Whether it is to be taken in a literal or a metaphorical sense has to be determined by the context.[30]

Langer here roughly accounts for how "the stock" of any language must have grown evolutionarily and socio-historically. Many words have emerged through ostensible definition within locally perceived contexts and came to be weaned from those contexts of original utterance and used for novel employment in new situations. People thereby generate new meanings by invoking already known words in combination with novel situations (verbal or extra-verbal) and/or by expressing what a particular combination of novelty and context would allow.

It is from within this context that we can appreciate the robust value of the distinction between "marked" and "unmarked terms." In defining a "marked term," Lanigan states that it is a "statement of P (…) a position (opposition); a first term explains itself, hence marks itself in a position which simultaneously opposes it to other possible positions of similar terms … what a dictionary does for words/ideas."[31] On the other hand, in defining an "unmarked term" we must recognize both a general meaning and a specific meaning. The general meaning is a "non-statement of P," whereas the specific meaning is a "statement of non-P." Lanigan's "Encyclopedic Dictionary" further clarifies the meaning of an "unmarked term" as follows:

> an apposition; a second term explains a first term, hence the "unmarked" second term explains the now "marked" first term … in short, marked meaning and specific unmarked meaning stand in an apposition in which Communication Theory (choice of context) entails Information Theory (context of choice) (…) Apposition, for example, is what an encyclopedia does for words/ideas.[32]

As one moves from linguistics to semiotics, the theoretical potency of the marked/unmarked distinction becomes even more evident. Just as we must distinguish between the syntagm of a face-to-face interaction and any linguistic syntagm, so, too, we must grasp the utility of the marked/unmarked pair for semiotic study, not merely for linguistic analysis.

The value of the marked/unmarked distinction within linguistics comes from the fact that all languages have abundant nouns and verbs, but not all languages liberally employ adjectives and adverbs. Many languages have separate and distinct words for what in English would be a common noun modified by an adjective. For example, there might be separate words for raw meat (e.g., sashimi) as well as cured meat (e.g., jerky). This makes the marked/unmarked pair incredibly helpful for trying to grasp universals of comparative linguistics. This also implies that the marked/unmarked term pair designates a linguistic function largely aligned to both the empirical/eidetic pair and the variation/invariant pair.[33]

Any context (physical or verbal) seems to have much that is understood, implied, or simply taken-for-granted, which also means much that remains *unsaid* (by omission and/or by unstated opposition). Such is the range of the unmarked. As the eidetic and invariant, the unmarked refers to what is, *generally*, "non-statement of P" and more specifically, a "statement of non-P." This implies the marked is an empirical attempt to register variation, marking the otherwise ambiguous taken-for-granted meaning of the unmarked by making explicit the variation: "statement of P." Notice that as we move from the semiotic to the linguistic, we find various grammatical and syntactical hierarchies emerging atop the verbal/nonverbal hierarchy.[34] This further suggests that verbal communication occurs along a continuum of high context to low context, and whatever is unstated can be brought into discourse and marked, but, soon enough—of course depending upon context—what had been marked can assume the status of an unmarked term.

The evolutionary transitions just outlined, broadly reviewed, move from nondenotative communicative messages, to denotation, to denotative propositions, to an overgrowth and establishment of a set of relatively stable intersubjective sensibilities regarding possibilities of the code. Said simply: marked terms, become, in time, part of the background repertoire that amounts to the paradigmatic axis. That is, roughly, what Langer's account suggests: through various forms of metaphorical and metonymical extension, of "emendation," the overall stock of language grows. This fact is rather obvious if we keep in mind that most words, as discrete lexical units, can be found in the dictionary and are defined by other words.

This insight also helps to illustrate the existential primacy of "message" over "code" and thus to reveal the potency of the poetic function. Consider how William Gass uses words such as "paper" and "raisins," words normally employed as nouns, as verbs. He writes that "wet leaves paper a street" and that "the habit of anger raisins the heart." Here, "speech spoken" (the code) is drawn upon only to be transcended by "speech speaking" (the message) and is reincorporated into the code as a new possibility for expression.[35]

Any discussion of the poetic function of discourse faintly points to the tension between the transpersonal system and existing individuals, meaning that messages shared between addresser and addressee are, at least to some extent, interchangeable—both within public dialogue and consciousness—because both are mediated by the code. The unsaid words, the similar and substitutable elements of the system, the redundancy features of the code, all are the "in abstentia" elements of transformation that make translation possible. Moreover, when we speak with others in interaction (interpersonal communication), we give expressions; we produce messages that have been constituted out of empirical contexts of choice.

When listeners perceive messages and attempt to break them down to their constituent coded elements, they seek the invariant (eidetic) meaning—the meaning that is not reducible to any one empirically perceptible message. When others try to tell us what we have told them and they seek to do so by putting it into their own words, the redundancy features are what facilitate our mutual recognition of the coded invariance beyond and/or behind any empirically shared messages. The eidetic sphere—a historical coagulation, "the code"—invisibly haunts the empirically heard and seen messages of the human world.

When speaking with others—or even with ourselves in the mode of discourse known as thought—we change positions and slide back and forth between addresser and addressee. Most basically, the addresser, through selection and combination, constructs a context while the addressee takes that context and analyzes it to detect its constituents. For the addresser, the choice of context occurs within an ascending scale of freedom (or within a descending scale of code dependence) by combining the units of language along the paradigmatic axis (from the zero freedom of distinctive features to the very minimal freedom of phonemes to increased freedom with words to the rangy and nearly unlimited liberty that comes with utterances), whereas the addressee perceives the expressed message as coded along the syntagmatic axis—as a context of choice to be analyzed moving from the utterance to the words to the phonemes to distinctive features.[36] For the addressee, because of different pronunciations, mispronunciations, dialects and such, an initial hermeneutic layer demands the task of hearing any words as "the words they are" from the acoustical whole comprising the message. This already implies a digital logic of information theory. But within communication theory, because addressee and addresser are reversible, we must also take account of the redundancy features: the semantic meaning of each word, the syntactical meaning of the words taken together as well as the pragmatic meaning of the utterance in a real (or imagined) context that is more than verbal.[37] Intersemiotically speaking, the "in abstentia" code includes all of the perceptions and/or possible expressions that are similar and/or substitutable.[38] Some of the paradigmatic elements are defined by not being their opposite, whereas others appear along an axis of varied similarity; some parts of the "in abstentia" code haunting the paradigmatic axis are oppositional whereas other parts are analogous. Nevertheless, all elements are in apposition.

ALPHABETIC LITERACY AND AUTONOMOUS DISCOURSE

Communication theory and information theory can hardly be separated within the wholly oral world. Admittedly, however, we ought to recognize that the earliest "information revolutions" occurred with the dawn of denotation, predication, and denotative propositions. Denotative utterances, arguably a uniquely human achievement, generate the conditions for abstract information-sharing well beyond symptomatic displays and other forms of nonlinguistic communication. Note, here, that the word "denotation" is commonly set in opposition to the word "connotation," and refers primarily to the dictionary definition of a word rather than any subjective meaning that a word might have for a speaker or listener.

Of Jakobson's six functions of communication, the "referential" function (context) and "the metacommunication" function (code) are, arguably, the latest to develop to maturity and the most naturally allied to linguistics, literacy, and the concerns of "information." An overall implication is that literacy, especially modern alphabetic text, increasingly transformed human communication into an information system. The earlier dominant functions of communication (i.e., "emotive," "conative," and "phatic") slowly came to be rivaled first by the "poetic" and ultimately by the "metalinguistic" and the "referential" functions. These claims might be defended by appealing, first, to ontogeny and children's acquisition of language. One piece of evidence comes from noting that the vocative and the imperative are among the earlier acquisitions in childhood.[39] Another comes from recognizing that the emotive and conative functions occur on phonic as well as grammatical and lexical levels. A final piece of evidence comes from the fact that modern literate parents often try to hide information from young children by spelling out certain words. In such cases, the children have access to the emotive, conative and phatic functions, and even, perhaps, a bit of the poetic function. But what not-yet-literate children are lacking are the redundancy features aligned with the metalinguistic and referential functions of literate discourse. In this way, parents can use spelling as a furtive code, at least for a while, to prevent their children from knowing what they are talking about.

Consider some of differences between a phoneme and a letter of the alphabet. Phonemes are communicative elements which constitute meaning by combination, and yet, they are nothing in themselves; they are utterly context-bound, gain significance only through apposition or opposition, and do not retain any distinct meaning independent of their context of occurrence. Letters of the alphabet (and written words), on the other hand, turn the phonemic material of interaction into a digital information system. They retain their identity and basic minimal meaning regardless of their context. Perhaps it helps to consider Lanigan's research project, "Guess at the Words".[40] This chapter lucidly demonstrates the logic of both communication theory and information theory in concrete operation. The research protocol that Lanigan includes in his review of the "historical characteristics of hermeneutic experience," relies upon, but does not "spell out," a complex history of literacy: how phonemes differ from many kinds of visual signs, how phonetic text and/or alphabetic text differs from pictographic and ideographic writing, how modern literacy is a detribalizing and psychologically isolating (individuating) practice, how the standardization of spelling was made possible through wide distributions of dictionaries, etc.[41]

Literacy, alphabetic print in particular, revolutionized the world of information and communication. It seems to be the main culprit in fostering the illusion that "information transfer" amounts to communication. It grounds, stabilizes, ratifies, and gives institutional tenacity to the code. Denotation, without a doubt, revolutionized human possibilities for information production and sharing, but alphabetic literacy exponentially expanded those possibilities. Discourse thus seems to slide quite naturally toward information transfer insofar as people consciously operate by the belief that anything said can also be written down. But much caution needs to be exercised here: language cannot be reduced to a definite number of words a person possesses; it is, on the contrary, the capacity to make novel distinctions within open-ended situations.[42] So, too, alphabetic literacy is not merely recognizing or knowing a certain number of visual signs; it is grasping the reversible phonetic principle that whatever can be said can be written, and whatever is written can be uttered. Literate spoken utterances thereby always carry some mystique of quasi-autonomous, context independence. Whether any particular words are actually written down or not, modern literates sense that they could be written down and/or looked up in a dictionary. Literacy so pervade contemporary culture that some people claim that a word not appearing in "the dictionary" is no word at all. In these simple ways, literacy helps to generate the sense that communication boils down to "information sharing."

The story still to be written within communicology is how alphabetic translation, dictionaries, encyclopedias, and "the grapholect" have shaped not only the structure of language and communication but furnished the material symbols to remake the modern Western mind.[43] Speech and thought have been made over in the image of the alphabet, and one of the main ways that this has occurred is through a shrinking or narrowing of the horizontal axis. Analytical discernment and nuanced word-choice often dominates literate discourse. In stark contrast, early oral discourse had no notion of "verbatium," and ideas themselves remained the basic unit of commerce within spoken interaction. They were understood through shared spatial and temporal contexts and were generally conveyed by well-known expressions, clichés and/or oral formula.[44]

Lanigan often uses Merleau-Ponty's distinction between "speech spoken" and "speech speaking." Whereas the former refers to already sedimented language—thought crystallized within expressions already accomplished but now available for recirculation—the latter refers to the living moments of articulation and crystallization. This also implies that "speech speaking" aligns, at least somewhat, to Jakobson's privileging of the poetic function and to his stressing the malleability of the code. One of the more significant and important changes in the history of Western literacy—and one of great relevance within this context—is a reversal in the meaning of the word "poetry".[45] Plato expressed concerns regarding poetry in the ancient world, but his concerns were largely with the over-reliance upon oral formula, upon cliché (i.e., speech spoken). Hence, certain kinds of changes were occurring to the noetic economy of Western consciousness. Today, by the time of Jakobson, the poetic has become aligned with individual expression and with the capacity to innovate and creatively adapt to the situation, a kind of "speech speaking."

Summarizing all of the ways that modern eidetic and noetic economies have been shaped by alphabetic literacy surpasses the scope of the present chapter, but a few key changes and/or reorientations are listed here: reducing speech's reliance upon rhyme and rhythm, reducing fear of novelty and forgetfulness, introducing the distinction between paraphrase and verbatium, detribalizing individuals, increasing capacities of sustained introspection, accumulating skeptical knowledge, fostering the sensation of articulate private thought, increasing means for functional anonymity, providing systematic means for ordering and prioritizing information, funding possibilities of mass education, generating conditions for universal translation, narrowing of unit linguistic analysis from oral clichés and expressions to individual words down to individual letters (e.g., on the one hand, the advocacy for and development of universal spelling, and on the other hand, linguistic science and Derrida's *différance*), giving rise to silent reading, and finally, setting the conditions for the development of modern sciences including phenomenology, linguistics, semiotics, and communicology.

CLOSING REMARKS

If we take a big-history perspective and ask how people, in the modern Western world, got where they find themselves today, we should take note of a couple of items. First, hominid tool-use goes back around 2.5 million years, and controlled use of fire goes back around a million years. I do not know of a reputable scholar who will place human language back that far. Most scholars identify the origin of language with the possibilities that come through denotative propositions, and they place its beginnings, maybe, as far back as 100,000 years ago. A more conservative and popular estimate is that denotative language, as it is known today first emerged about 40,000 years ago. Writing, in various forms, is only about 10,000 years old, and alphabetic script is only about 3,000 years old. The *Oxford English Dictionary* (O.E.D.) did not appear until the middle of the 19th century. Hence, it was not until a few centuries after Gutenberg's printing press that we find the embodied possibilities of mass education, public schooling, and standardized testing. All of these evolutionary and historical milestones should be kept in mind as we try to understand how information theory evolved and developed within communication theory. For those of us who study, those who read and write, such transitions should be of great interest.[46]

Novice teachers sometimes try to get students to reflect upon communicative processes by proclaiming, "There is no meaning in the message!" The irony (or paradox) of such a claim is that they seem to need *that* message, or at least something similar to it, to convey that particular meaning. It seems an oversimplification, then, as neophytes and popular textbooks are prone to do, to suggest that, "meaning is in people rather than in messages." It makes it seem as if literacy never happened, as if there are no dictionaries. More people need to appreciate, deeply comprehend, how information is entailed within communication. Just as communication theory and context both require some kind of coded variety (some context of choice) to interpret and contextualize, all messages are interpretations that require further interpretation (some choice of context). Communication requires addressers and addressees engaging in acts of interpretation, but the meaning of any message—perceived or expressed—does not come from *either* us *or* from "the message." Rather, meaning comes from *both* us *and* the message (and the context too), and synergistically so.

Discourse—a socio-historical hermeneutic experience—offers so much more than merely one more choice from within the perceivable environment; it opens any context to dispute and redefinition and forms of translatability. Modern humans have been historically sentenced to a freedom from bonds of immediate perception. They have been released for the eidetic free play that includes denotatively entertaining subject/predicate relations. Discourse allows people to understand that individual persons are, *depending upon context and relevance,* just as much "citizens legally residing *in* a country," as "living, breathing organisms *on* the planet," as "places and moments *of* the self-aware cosmos."

What should be underscored is that the full meaning of any message (even an information theoretic one) depends upon the communicative context in which it occurs. Consider a simple statement such as "the cat is on the mat." If this is taken to be a factual assertion about a particular feline and a floor textile, we need extraverbal (intersemiotic) information to assess its veracity. But if the statement appears only on paper and is offered up merely as an illustration of a rhyming proposition in English, we have within the expression itself all that is needed for the assessment. Literacy, as is hopefully apparent, seems to be the source of many assumptions regarding "autonomous" or "context-free" information, and these very assumptions erroneously place information on equal par with communication.[47] Note as well that dictionaries have created uniform spelling for all words, bringing languages (and whole regions) together into nationalistic alignment, despite wide and unruly variance of pronunciation for any word, including regional pronunciations and individual affectations.[48]

The social reality that appears to us is shaped by *both* our prior experiences *and* our ideas about social reality. Moreover, when we consciously attend to aspects of the world, we easily find forms corresponding to our ideas but underestimate how our experiences, not just our ideas about those experiences, shape the overall nature of social reality. To Lanigan's highly perceptive "Figure 15. Phenomenology: The Form and Structure of Appearances",[49] we can add the insight from McLuhan: "Everybody experiences far more than he understands. Yet it is experience, rather than understanding, that influences behavior, especially in collective matters of media and technology, where the individual is almost inevitably unaware of their effects upon him."[50] The point here is that experiences with literacy—and with dictionaries and encyclopedias—have shaped not merely the ideas people have and the forms they see in the world, but have structured the appearances of the things themselves.[51]

I partly chose to write upon Lanigan's "Encyclopedic Dictionary" because both dictionaries and encyclopedias are artifacts of (and vital resources for) widespread literacy. They represent two dominant registers of how historical consciousness has corresponded, on the one hand, to increased capacity for poetic maneuvers and grammatical gymnastics (i.e., syntagmatic possibilities), and, on the other hand, to a widening and deepening of the "code" (i.e., paradigmatic possibilities). Dictionaries and encyclopedias solidify words and ideas; they turn them into institutions that move autonomously through public domains. They basically presuppose and exemplify the value of alphabetic literacy for making sediments of socio-historical consciousness available to detribalized self-educating denizens. People who read and write, who live in literate cultures, and especially those who study dictionaries and encyclopedias, have therein been opened to a particular kind of historical, hermeneutic sociality.

NOTES

1. Richard L. Lanigan, *Phenomenology of Communication: Merleau-Ponty's Thematics in Communicology and Semiology* (Pittsburgh, PA: Duquesne Press, 1988), 8.
2. Lanigan, *Phenomenology of Communication*, 62.
3. Lanigan, *Phenomenology of Communication*, 121.
4. First, please see works cited in the bibliography for some of the main places Richard's work has influenced mine. Second, I would like to offer a preemptive apology if, in any way, I am guilty of crucial omissions, oversimplifications, and/or misrepresentations. Given space limitation and limited understanding, I have tried, as best as I am able, to explicate, illustrate, and clarify without undue distortion. I would like to express thanks to Valerie V. Peterson for all of her thoughtful suggestions and support. I also wish to thank Chad Hansen for discussion and assistance during the final stages.
5. Richard L. Lanigan, *The Human Science of Communicology: A Phenomenology of Discourse in Foucault and Merleau-Ponty* (Pittsburgh, PA: Duquesne Press, 1992).
6. Here, the historical lens focuses upon the history of literacy and the development of literate technologies within literate societies. Arguably, the emotive, conative and phatic functions predate

the origin of language in the proper sense of the word, and the semiotic drift from animality to humanity occurred, over many thousands of years, with the rise of the poetic, referential, and metalingiustic functions. Moreover, these later adaptations were finely suited for alphabetic literacy. Relevant too is the degree to which modern sciences, especially linguistics, depended upon print literacy. But, now, today, as new media based in moving images and sounds claim dominance over the silent letter and written page, we can anticipate some backward slide to these earlier functions. Oversimplified for effect, one might say: if people were to have communication liquidated of denotative information, they would move toward being animals, and yet, if people were to have abundant information despite little to no communication, they would approach becoming robots.

7. Lanigan, *Human Science of Communicology*, 210.
8. Lanigan, *Human Science of Communicology*, 211.
9. Lanigan, "Information Theories," in *Theories and Models of Communication*, ed. Paul Cobley and Peter Schulz (Boston, MA: De Gruyter Mouton, 2013).
10. Lanigan, *Phenomenology of Communication*, 122.
11. McLuhan (*Understanding Media: Extensions of Man: Critical Edition*. Corte Madera, CA: Gingko Press, 2003) writes, "Language does for intelligence what the wheel does for the feet and the body. It enables them to move from thing to thing with greater ease and speed and ever less involvement" (113).
12. Lanigan, *Phenomenology of Communication*, 122.
13. Jürgen Ruesch and Gregory Bateson, *Communication: The Social Matrix of Psychiatry* (New York: W. W. Norton, 1951). Bateson writes:
    The existence of Gestalt processes in human thinking seems to be the circumstance which makes us believe that we are able to think about concrete objects, not merely about relationships. And this belief is further fortified by our use of language, in which substantives and verbs always stand for externally perceived Gestalten .... The same general truth—that all knowledge of external events is derived from the relationships between them—is recognizable in the fact that to achieve more accurate perception, a human being will always resort to change in the relationship between himself and the external object (173).
14. This is Langer's points when she suggests that primates apparently cannot think of one thing while only seeing something else in sensory experience. Without the eidetic economy funded through the development of denotative (symbolic) resources, "Out of sight, is out of mind." See Corey Anton, "Playing with Bateson: Denotation, Logical Types, and Analog and Digital Communication," *The American Journal of Semiotics* 19 (2003): 129–154.
15. Anton, "Playing," 129–154; also see Anthony Wilden, *System and Structure: Essays in Communication and Exchange* (London: Tavistock Publications, 1972).
16. Lanigan, *Human Science of Communicology*, 1–12.
17. Lanigan, *Human Science of Communicology*, 1–12.
18. Alfred Korzybski, *Manhood of Humanity: The Science and Art of Human Engineering* (Gloucestershire, UK: Dodo Press, 2008).
19. Holenstein (*Roman Jakobson's Approach to Language: Phenomenological Structuralism*, trans. Catherine Schelbert and Tarcisius Schelbert. Bloomington: Indiana University Press, 1976) writes, "As soon as the child is capable of a (diremic) construction, consisting of a subject and a predicate, he is also able to free himself from his respective hic et nunc. The child becomes aware that he can assign different activities to the same subject and different subjects to the same activity. And he begins playing with this possibility of contextual variations" (44).

20. Walker Percy, *The Message in the Bottle: How Queer Man Is, How Queer Language Is, and What One Has to Do with the Other* (New York: Farrar, Straus, and Giroux, 1954).
21. Susanne K. Langer writes, "It is absurd to suppose that the earliest symbols could be invented, they are merely Gestalten furnished to the senses of a creature ready to give them some diffuse meaning," in *Philosophy in a New Key: A Study in the Symbolism of Reason, Rite and Art* (New York: Mentor Books, 1942), 89.
22. Langer, *New Key*.
23. Holenstein, *Approach*.
24. Holenstein, *Approach*, writes, "The operation of both selection and combination presuppose an antecedent operation, the differentiation of signs, for which contrast functions as the base principle" (151). I take it Lanigan would prefer the word "apposition" to Holenstein's word "contrast." Note as well that forms of opposition within linguistic utterances (a differentiating inclusion "in abstentia" along the paradigmatic axis) are significantly different from digital opposition (disjunction) within mechanical information systems (an in presentia exclusion). Said simply, the semantic space of oppositional words is such that they phenomenologically invoke meaning through alluding to their opposite. This is quite distinct from the either presence or absence of a bit selected from a probability field.
25. Lanigan, *Human Science of Communicology*, 230.
26. Gregory Bateson, "A Theory of Play and Fantasy," in *Steps to an Ecology of Mind* (New York: Ballantine Books, 1972); Wilden, *System and Structure*; Anton, "Playing," 129–154. I have tried, in various other places to argue for a rather unorthodox revision of the ordering of the three kinds of signs: index, icon, and symbol. Admittedly, there are some ways in which index and icon cannot be separated except in imagination. But for purposes of many analyses, there is ample reason to suggest that indexes are the most primary, basal system of signs. Icons emerge out from and rest atop various other indexical signs, and symbols are the most abstract, emerging only after, atop, and between indexes and icons. As sheer mammalian organisms, we traffic in indexicality and iconicity; visual and auditory systems are indexical in ground and largely iconic in orientation. Nevertheless, the human being has been thoroughly made over in the logic of symbolic transformation (in presentational and discursive forms, as well as in redundancy features). Once one accepts that analogic communication is the larger set into which various subsets of analog and digital systems emerge, it is easier to show why indexicality must precede iconicity. Part of this is accomplished by understanding that any index, as an index, is actually a "sign-chain" rather than "a single sign" in isolation. One cannot specific the exact location of an indexical sign without introducing iconicity into the sign-chain. That is, for any symbol or icon actually employed, we also can partly identify the where and when of its employment (from indexes), but, for any sign systems which bear indexicality without yet iconicity or symbolicity, the precise "location" of the indexical sign-chain cannot be delimited with precision. We find, instead, variability relations of contiguity, pressure gradients, nutrient gradients, temperature gradients, magnitude ranges, distances with varied degrees of scope, etc.
27. Wilden, *System and Structure*.
28. Lanigan, *Phenomenology of Communication*, 197–202.
29. This is partly why Edward Hall's work (*Beyond Culture* [New York: Anchor Books, 1976]) is so important. Hall writes:
    Without context, the code is incomplete since it encompasses only part of the message. This should become clear if one remembers that the spoken language is an abstraction of an event that happened, might have happened, or is being planned …. The conceptual model I am using

takes into account not only what one takes in and screens out but what one does not know about a given system even though one has mastered that system. The two are not the same (77).

The later line Lanigan expands and develops greatly in his "Figure 15. Phenomenology: The Form and Structure of Appearances" (*Human Science of Communicology*, 208).

30. Langer, *New Key*, 113.
31. Lanigan, *Human Science of Communicology*, 231.
32. Lanigan, *Human Science of Communicology*, 231
33. Holenstein, *Approach*.
34. Bateson writes, "As soon as sufficient complexity is reached to permit of two or more levels of abstraction, the organism becomes able to treat abstractions of a higher level as though they were equivalent to abstractions of a lower level." (*Social Matrix*, 191)
35. Consider, for example, a statement such as: "A man ran down the street." The syntagmatic relations refer to the combination and contexture of these contiguous words. They create a context for themselves by their presence and syntactical relations. We now can imagine someone wishing to make a slight revision by selecting any one word and substituting it with a similar, nearly synonymous word. For example, someone could say, "A man dashed down the street," or perhaps "A man darted down the street." Such simple transformations reveal that what makes empirical expressions meaningful are all the currently absent words that could be substituted along the paradigmatic axis. As empirically absent, consciousness thus largely refers to the depth and range of the paradigmatic axis. Again: for any meaningful utterance, any intelligible use of language, the particular empirically present words remain funded by an ancient invisible (eidetic) bank, the code, the wealth of substitutable and similar elements absently haunting the paradigmatic axis.
36. Lanigan, *Human Science of Communicology*, 232 and also Holenstein, *Approach*, 145, 165.
37. Words empirically employed offer more than mere information. They incite action and often are an inseparable part of the action. For example, when parents ask a trouble-making teen, "Do you understand me?," the question, as direct and pointed at it is, overflows any simple or unequivocal meaning. On the one hand, it means: "Have you understood my expression?," but, on the other hand, it means, "Are you going to obey?" It is a command and a report, a multilevel message that makes the sense it does only by combination with actual situations, including both prior statements and the overall extra-verbal context.
38. Well beyond the scope of the present essay would be an exploration of the Lacanian categories of "real," "imaginary," and "symbolic." Future research might, respectively, explore three interrelated logics,
(1): [Real] Communication Theory Logic: Both/And: both "both/and" and "either/or." (e.g., Both man and woman and either man or woman; both light and dark and either light or dark).
(2): [Imaginary] Information Theory Logic: Either/Or: either "either/or" or "both/and." (e.g., Either man or woman or both man and woman; Either light or dark or both light and dark).
(3): [Symbolic] Transformational Theory Logic: And/Or: neither "both both/and and either/or" nor "either either/or or both/and." Rather: "'If and then either/or,' or 'if or then both/and.'" (e.g., If man and woman, then either man or woman, or if man or woman then both man and woman; if light and dark, then either light or dark, or if light or dark then both light and dark). In correspondence during the final stages, Richard suggested the formulation: "Both/Either: If 'both both/and and either/or', then 'either either/or or both/and.'" As much as his is cleaner, logically, and it helps to situate the symbolic between the Real and the Imaginary and also fortifies the argument for the indexical to the iconic, I would maintain some usefulness of the earlier formulations. The general point is that symbolic transformational logic underlies and /

or operates within the redundancy features of discourse. The Symbolic thus refers to possible transformations entertained at the intersection between the Real and the Imaginary. Redundancy features—semiotically as well as linguistically—seem to be characterized by: "if 'both/and' then, possibly, 'either/or,'" or "if 'either/or' then, possibly, 'both/and'" (see Holenstein, *Approach*, 138).

39. Holenstein, *Approach*, 44, 155.
40. Lanigan, *Phenomenology of Communication*, 118–133.
41. Corey Anton, "Early Western Writing, Sensory Modalities, and Modern Alphabetic Literacy: On the Origins of Representational Theorizing," in *Communication Uncovered: General Semantics and Media Ecology* (Fort Worth, TX: Institute of General Semantics, 2011), 93–112.
42. Maurice Merleau-Ponty, *The Prose of the World*, trans. John O'Neill (Evanston, IL: Northwestern University Press, 1973).
43. Walter J. Ong, *Orality and Literacy: The Technologizing of the Word* (London: Methuen, 1982); and also David R. Olson, *The World on Paper: The Conceptual and Cognitive Implications of Writing and Reading* (Great Britain: Oxford University, 1994).
44. Ong, *Orality*.
45. Eric A. Havelock, *Preface to Plato* (Cambridge: Cambridge University Press, 1963).
46. Richard L. Lanigan, "Communicology and the Mother of Civilization: The Semiotic Phenomenology of Human Embodiment as Cultural Media," *Korean Journal of Communication Studies* 20 (2012): 5–16.
47. Ong writes,
   Spoken utterance is addresses by a real, living person to another real, living person or real, living persons, at a specific time in a real setting which includes always more than mere words. Spoken words are always modifications of a total situation which is more than verbal. They never occur alone, in a context simply of words. (*Orality*, 101)
48. McLuhan, *Understanding Media*.
49. Lanigan, *Human Science of Communicology*, 208–209.
50. McLuhan, *Understanding Media*, 424.
51. Corey Anton, "Diachronic Phenomenology: A Methodological Thread within Media Ecology," *Explorations in Media Ecology: The Journal of the Media Ecology Association* 13 (2014): 3–30.

BIBLIOGRAPHY

Anton, Corey. "About Talk: The Category of Talk-Reflexive Words." *Semiotica* 121 (1998): 193–212.
Anton, Corey. "Agency and Efficacy in Interpersonal Communication: Particularity as Once-Occurrence and Non-Interchangeability." In *Communicology: The New Science of Embodied Discourse*, edited by Deborah Eicher-Catt and Isaac Catt, 81–101. Madison, NJ: Fairleigh Dickinson University Press, 2010.
Anton, Corey. "Comprehending Orders of Intensionality: An Adaptation of Laing, Phillipson, and Lee's 'Interpersonal Perception Method.'" *The Review of Communication* 15 (2015): 161–172.
Anton, Corey. "Diachronic Phenomenology: A Methodological Thread within Media Ecology." *Explorations in Media Ecology: The Journal of the Media Ecology Association* 13, (2014): 3–30.
Anton, Corey. "Early Western Writing, Sensory Modalities, and Modern Alphabetic Literacy: On the Origins of Representational Theorizing." In *Communication Uncovered: General Semantics and Media Ecology*. Fort Worth, TX: Institute of General Semantics, 2011.

Anton, Corey. "On the Nonlinearity of Human Communication: Insatiability, Context, Form." *The Atlantic Journal of Communication* 15 (2007): 79–102.

Anton, Corey. "Syntagmatic and Paradigmatic Synergism: Notes on Lanigan's 'Encyclopedic Dictionary,'" *The Atlantic Journal of Communication, 25* (2017): 48–63.

Anton, Corey. "Playing with Bateson: Denotation, Logical Types, and Analog and Digital Communication." *The American Journal of Semiotics* 19 (2003): 129–154.

Anton, Corey. "Terms for Talking about Information and Communication." *Information* 3 (2012): 351–371. Accessed August 3, 2015. http://www.mdpi.com/2078-2489/3/3/351

Bateson, Gregory. "The Message, 'This is Play.'" In *Group Processes*, edited by Bertram Schaffner. New York: Josiah Macy, Jr. Foundation, 1956.

Bateson, Gregory. "A Theory of Play and Fantasy." In *Steps to an Ecology of Mind*. New York: Ballantine Books, 1972.

Frazer, James G. *The Golden Bough*. New York: Macmillan Company, 1909.

Gass, William H. "On Talking to Oneself." In *Habitations of the Word*. New York: Simon and Shuster, 1985.

Gusdorf, Georg. *Speaking*. Translated by P. T. Brockelman. Evanston, IL: Northwestern University Press, 1965.

Hall, Edward T. *Beyond Culture*. New York: Anchor Books, 1976.

Hall, Edward T. *The Dance of Life*. New York: Anchor Books, 1983.

Havelock, Eric A. *The Muse Learns to Write: Reflections on Orality and Literacy from Antiquity to the Present*. New Haven, CT: Yale University Press, 1986.

Havelock, Eric A. *Preface to Plato*. Cambridge: Harvard University Press, 1963.

Holenstein, Elmar. *Roman Jakobson's Approach to Language: Phenomenological Structuralism*. Translated by Catherine Schelbert and Tarcisius Schelbert. Bloomington: Indiana University Press, 1976.

Korzybski, Alfred. *Manhood of Humanity: The Science and Art of Human Engineering*. Gloucestershire: Dodo Press, 2008.

Lanigan, Richard L. "Communicology and the Mother of Civilization: The Semiotic Phenomenology of Human Embodiment as Cultural Media." *Korean Journal of Communication Studies* 20 (2012): 5–16.

Lanigan, Richard L. *The Human Science of Communicology: A Phenomenology of Discourse in Foucault and Merleau-Ponty*. Pittsburgh, PA: Duquesne Press, 1992.

Lanigan, Richard L. "Information Theories." In *Theories and Models of Communication*, edited by Paul Cobley and Peter Schulz. Berlin/ Boston, MA: De Gruyter Mouton, 2013.

Lanigan, Richard L. *Phenomenology of Communication: Merleau-Ponty's Thematics in Communicology and Semiology*. Pittsburgh, PA: Duquesne Press, 1988.

Langer, Susanne K. *Philosophy in a New Key: A Study in the Symbolism of Reason, Rite and Art*. New York: Mentor Books, 1942.

Lévy-Bruhl, Lucien. *The Notebooks on Primitive Mentality*. Translated by Peter Riviére. New York: Harper & Row Publishers, 1975.

McLuhan, Marshall. *Understanding Media: Extensions of Man: Critical Edition*. Corte Madera, CA: Gingko Press, 2003.

Merleau-Ponty, Maurice. *Phenomenology of Perception*. Translated by Colin Smith. Atlantic Highlands, NJ: The Humanities Press, 1962.

Merleau-Ponty, Maurice. *The Prose of the World*. Translated by John O'Neill. Evanston, IL: Northwestern University Press, 1973.

Merleau-Ponty, Maurice. *The Visible and the Invisible*. Translated by Alphonso Lingis. Evanston, IL: Northwestern University Press, 1968.

Olson, David. *The World on Paper: The Conceptual and Cognitive Implications of Writing and Reading*. Great Britain: Oxford University, 1994.

Ong, Walter J. *Orality and Literacy: The Technologizing of the Word*. London: Methuen, 1982.

Percy, Walker. *The Message in the Bottle: How Queer Man Is, How Queer Language Is, and What One Has to Do with the Other*. New York: Farrar, Straus, and Giroux, 1954.

Ruesch, Jürgen, and Gregory Bateson. *Communication: The Social Matrix of Psychiatry*. New York: W. W. Norton, 1951.

Schrag, Calvin O. *Experience and Being: Prolegomena to a Future Ontology*. Evanston, IL: Northwestern University Press, 1969.

Wilden, Anthony. "Lacan and the Discourse of the Other." In *Speech and Language in Psychoanalysis*. Baltimore, MA: The John Hopkins University Press, 1968.

Wilden, Anthony. *The Rules Are No Game: The Strategy of Communication*. New York: Routledge & Kegan Paul, 1987.

Wilden, Anthony. *System and Structure: Essays in Communication and Exchange*. London: Tavistock Publications, 1972.

CHAPTER THREE

Communicability as Ground of Communicology

Impulses and Impediments

HORST RUTHROF

> The breakdown of communication [is] the absolute evil.[1]
> —Jürgen Habermas

Suppose resemblance relations rather than propositions are at the heart of human intentionality. After all, we imagine the past, present and future by means of mental projections. We even dream in terms of resemblance relations, however distorted. So if we take Aristotelian *homoiomata* (resemblance relations) as our starting point, the conditions of the very possibility of communication would include at least the following.

1. By definition, communication cannot be monadic; it presupposes interaction, that is, *social reciprocity*.
2. Human interaction is always complex as a result of the inevitable *ontic heteronomy* of acts of consciousness partaking as they do of *ideality, materiality,* and *intentionality*.
3. In human communication, verbal and nonverbal, two reciprocal conditions appear to be a *sine qua non*: *aboutness* and *voice*.
4. *Aboutness* is what communication points to, of which reference is a special case.
5. *Voice* always manifests itself in two forms, as marked or *explicit deixis* and unmarked or *implicit deixis*, demanding imaginative *reconstruction*.
6. Such reconstruction requires the mental projection of the other's intention via *introjection* and *intention-reading*.

7. Intention-reading involves the encompassing condition of *imaginability*. Without the continuous performance of the projection of *mental scenarios*, human communication could not get off the ground.
8. The inevitable methodological consequence of these preconditions of communication is a commitment for communicology to some form of *intersubjective mentalism*.

Together, these conditions establish *communicability* as the base line of communication and the central focus of *communicology*.

Communicability can be defined in a dual sense, as an ability of interacting persons to communicate and a social system of semiosis facilitating such interactions. The study of the former has benefitted as much from phenomenology as that of the latter has from semiotics. So it should not come as a surprise that in the meta-theoretical synthesis in Richard Lanigan's work from *Speech Act Phenomenology*[2] (1977) to his recent writings on communicology we see an intellectual trajectory stretching from the analysis of the minutiae of linguistic expressions to the broad concerns of the *Lebenswelt*, drawing on phenomenological and semiotic methodologies.[3] I do not however wish to retrace the evolution of Lanigan's contributions to communicology. Rather, I want to explore some of the *conditions* of communicability that I think are at the core of communicology. That there are *impediments* in the way of such an agenda is undeniable, some of which I will explore below. My main purpose however is to discuss a number of topics which communicology needs to address if it is to fulfil the agenda of a genuine human science. I end the chapter with three seminal impulses for such a science, Kant's poorly understood tools for dealing with *complex judgments*; some of the critical devices Charles Sanders Peirce left us for a *heterosemiotic* and *hypoiconic* analysis of communication; and the notion of the *ontic heteronomy* of complex entities, as proposed by the phenomenologist Roman Ingarden. My key concern here is how those impediments and positive impulses affect the theorisation of language.

IMPEDIMENTS TO COMMUNICOLOGY

The construction of communicology in the tradition of the *Geisteswissenschaften* faces certain hurdles that are in the way of a comprehensive portrayal of natural language. I start with Locke's *semantic privacy*, that is, his failure to reconcile private ideas with public discourse and his unsuccessful project of the generalisation of ideas. A partial solution to Locke's semantics can be found in Kant's theory of *schematization*, which makes linguistic meanings sharable without turning them into ideal entities. More decisively, semantic privacy can be socialized once we conceive of schematized linguistic meanings as *indirectly public* via pedagogy from the cradle to the grave.[4] Closer to the present, the study of language began to face some major impediments at the hands of Gottlob Frege in his initiation of analytical language philosophy. Frege's crucial move was the replacement of Aristotelian *homoiomata* by propositional formalisation, which launched a powerful paradigm that stretches from 1892 to current hyperintensional semantics.[5] Four steps are pivotal here: (1) Frege's collapse of natural language sense into formal sense; (2) the elimination of the role of *voice* in linguistic expressions; (3) the reduction of *Bedeutung* (meaning) to quantifiable reference; and (4) the elimination of *Vorstellung* (mental iconic projections) from linguistic meaning. Corrections of this paradigm need to argue the non-formal specificity of natural language *sense;* that *voice* is an indispensable ingredient of all linguistic expressions; that quantifiable reference is only a special case of *aboutness;* and that socially guided *Vorstellung* can be excised from linguistic meaning only at the expense of changing language into a formal sign system.[6] In the wake of Frege's revolution, and aided by Saussure's linguistic idealism, a conception of language evolved known as the *linguistic turn*. In its benign form, the linguistic turn holds that philosophical questions are problems of language; in its less benign version it claims that there is nothing *but* language. A serious consequence of the second claim is that perception, as the sum of nonverbal signification, can no longer be related to linguistic expressions and so provide a nonverbal ground for semantics. For now everything humans can experience is always already language, conceived either in formal terms or via radical arbitrariness. Corrections could be attempted via a Peircean heterosemiotic analysis that would re-embed language in nonverbal semiosis, by an alignment of language with the Husserlian *Lebenswelt*, or by a re-embodiment of the linguistic sign by *motivated signifieds*.[7] Yet the reconstitution of the *motivated signified* faces a major hurdle in Saussure's radical arbitrariness thesis, according to which *all* components of the linguistic sign are arbitrary.[8] A purely arbitrary (symbolic) description of natural language, however, inevitably plays into the hands of formal conceptions, a trend confirmed by talk of *mere* signifiers having semantic content by themselves. Radical arbitrariness is irreparable since it purges the *motivated signified* of its social dimension, together with its quasi-perceptual components.

An impediment arising out of the Saussurean emphasis on differential relations driving the dynamics of *langue* has been aptly summed up under the heading *syntactocentrism*.[9] According to this criticism, while the study of syntax tells us a great deal about the ordering principles of linguistic expressions, it cannot act as a foundation of language research. After all, without semantics our observations about how syntax does its regulative work could not get off the ground. One could say that in this sense, the entire syntactic apparatus of Chomsky begs the question of language in a big way. As Robbins Burling puts it more mildly, "while syntax certainly contributes to meaning, words do more."[10] Carnap then looks to have been right when he declared even semantics a derivative system, for "the basis for all of all linguistics" was "pragmatics."[11] Only the richest possible data bank of language, the phenomena of *instantiated expressions* will do as the basis of the study of verbal communication. Closely related to the bias of syntactocentrism is the popular assumption that sentences can have meaning by themselves. And yet neither sentence-types (e.g., NP—VP—PP) nor sentence-tokens (unuttered sentences) qualify as semantic entities for the simple reason that in them both *aboutness* and *voice* remain unrealized. It follows that only *utterances* can have meaning by virtue of their production of aboutness and voice as intentional facts, which renders the standard distinction between sentence meanings and utterance meanings defunct.[12] This, I think, is an incisive claim on behalf of communicology, for if it does not take the rich complexity of human interaction as its starting point, it has already conceded too much to reductive analyses.

Another hurdle to a "thick" description of verbal communication is the adherence to *semantic ideality* and *meaning identity*, a criticism that even applies to the early Husserl. Whenever Husserl attempts to illustrate ideality and identity for linguistic meaning he is forced to retreat to formal examples.[13] In natural language, they cannot be demonstrated, nor are they necessary. The notion of socially constrained meaning approximation will do. It would seem that the two concepts are remnants of the goals of avoiding psychologism and taking mathematisation as an appropriate methodological route for investigating complex human processes. Ironically, communicology here can glean support for a more fitting description of language from analytical philosophy. Realizing that strict analyticity could not possibly be a part of natural language, Quine proposed that we "lower our sights" to a concept of "domestic meaning" pragmatically viewed as Wittgensteinian "use."[14] If Quine is right, neither meaning ideality nor meaning identity can be candidates in a communicology oriented theory of language. Husserl, though, is not the only phenomenologist guilty of having sometimes succumbed to the demands of formal notions. In spite of his avowed commitment to the primacy of perception, at certain points in his writings Merleau-Ponty retreats to arguing perception as a "nascent logos" and natural language as an "incarnate logic", a "logic in contingency", all ultimately resting on "an essence beneath us", in short, on eidetic ideality.[15] This suggests a not entirely resolved tension between his avowed commitment to the reciprocity between perceptual corporeality and the world of things in the writings of a philosopher close to the heart of the human sciences.

Other theoretical positions far less easily attuned to the interests of communicology can be found in the broad paradigm of *externalism*. It will have to suffice here to single out one of its most popular examples, Wittgenstein's meaning as *use*. Attractive as this definition looks in the *Philosophical Investigations* as a radical turn away from the starkly propositional picture painted in the *Tractatus* and because it solves all kinds of problems of analytical semantics, meaning as *use* suffers from a serious flaw of the kind already identified in Frege: the banishment of *Vorstellung*.[16] And yet without mental iconic scenarios, the bulk of language would remain incomprehensible. After all, much of language use is about the world *in absentia*.[17] To make Wittgenstein's semantics compatible with communicology would necessitate recourse to a socially conceived, *intersubjective mentalism*. The *Vorstellungsklavier*, as he calls it, cannot be so easily dismissed.[18] Another much-applauded theorization of language is Jerry Fodor's *LoT*, the language of thought hypothesis. It consists in a brain based, computational symbol structure made up of propositional attitude expressions of the type S (subject; e.g. "I")—A (attitude phrase; e.g. "hope that")—P (hoped for state; e.g. "John likes me"), whereby content is provided by "atomic concepts."[19] The main charge that LoT faces is *infinite regress*. If language requires a prior language to function, why does the buck stop at LoT? Furthermore, Fodor's *homunculus* picture discards the relation between language and perception. But why must we substitute a propositional and computational second language in the brain for perception, a comprehensive sign system that can provide all the semantic anchors needed for natural language as a *social construct*? From the holistic perspective of communicology, at least two main corrections would be required to rescue LoT, the reincorporation of *nonverbal* intentional states and the social generation of concepts via *pedagogy*.

Two further candidates to be viewed with suspicion from the angle of communicology are cognitive science and language-brain research. The main shortcoming of cognitive linguistics is its continuing visual bias, especially in its two-dimensional concept of "mapping", a bias that blocks the way to a broad range of mental projections such as olfactory, gustatory, gravitational, and emotional readings. The correction here is to move to a more general level of abstraction in line with Kant's *schematism*, as in his concept of the *monogram*,[20] and Peircean *hypoiconicity*. Likewise, the notion of "neural concept" in the Lakoff School needs tweaking by reconnecting it with the all-important social facet of language.[21] Much the same criticism can be made of some recent biologically anchored work on language, as for instance Tecumseh Fitch's *The Evolution of Language*, in which the social dimension of speech is played down.[22] Lastly, in spite of its promise of placing language study on a scientific footing, current language-brain research has so far been underwhelming.[23] This may be less a failure of the specifics of such research as the result of a confusion of brain and mind. It is the mind rather than its biochemical base that tells us about language as a *social process*, the neglect of which must remain a serious limitation. Communicology is likely to benefit a good deal more from other avenues of research, to some of which I now turn.

PRINCIPLES OF COMMUNICABILITY

Aboutness and Voice

Communication did not arise out of language. Rather, language must have arisen out of nonverbal communication, whatever the specifics of this transformation. Furthermore, nonverbal communication must already have reached a high level of complexity when language gradually emerged. On this view, in opposition to structuralist accounts, the human capacity for verbal exchange needs to be premised on nonverbal preconditions. If we restore the premise of the evolutionary sequence from the nonverbal to the verbal, then *utterances* come first, logically and chronologically. This restoration reverses the tradition that hitches utterances to sentences as a pragmatic afterthought. And if utterances demand primacy, then the combination of *aboutness* and *voice* necessarily precedes the voiceless sentence, revealing it as a theoretical fiction. Where, then does this characteristic blend of *aboutness* and *voice* come from? It is a likely inheritance from pre-linguistic communication. While *aboutness* points us to what a linguistic expression is "saying", including the special case of Fregean reference, *voice* is short for the overall manner of the presentation of aboutness. In the nonverbal utterances of a smile, a greeting, or a stroking gesture *aboutness* and *voice* are intimately entailed. Likewise in language, except that our dominant discourses have neglected to elucidate this intricate relation.[24]

Since word sounds cannot act as a system of meaning constraint without motivated signifieds in a socially regulated system of nonverbal mental schematizations, our nonverbal differential system is likely to function as semantic coordination matrix. If so, then our nonverbal readings of the world act as a template of *semantic poly-angulation*, with perception providing a system of semantic anchors. Without such anchors, language would be a floating fiction. For mere differentiation is an insufficient condition of meaning. Humans require points of orientation in the actual world, either by perceptual grasp or its imaginary extension where perceptual evidence is unavailable. The socially organised store of our imaginable world here fulfils a vital function. In this respect, our nonverbal grasp *overdetermines* language, such that individual items of our linguistic expressions are semantically activated by a number of nonverbal projections. "There is a bushfire over there!" is overdetermined by perceptual, that is, visual, auditory, and olfactory readings as well as relevant scenarios stored in memory. In short, the arbitrary signifier "bushfire" is semantically *poly-angulated* by nonverbal realisations. In this relation, the phenomenal world always appears as abbreviated in verbal signification, while the threatening infinite description of phenomena is practically telescoped into manageability by language, within the boundaries of *sufficient semiosis*.[25] In this manner, nonverbal grasp stabilizes linguistic meanings semantically. Formal systems do not require such nonverbal, semantic stabilization; here axioms and definitional regulation suffice. Human linguistic communication, in sharp contrast, is anchored in culturally organised nonverbal signification and so reveals its dual grinding in animal perception and the social.

Implicit Deixis

By restricting *deixis* to the analysis of *marked* or *explicit deixis* in standard accounts, we lose comprehension of the all-pervasive *implicit deixis* that characterizes every single item of utterances.[26] The reduction of general deixis in linguistic expressions eliminates one of the indispensable components of natural language, *voice*. As the carrier of voice, *implicit deixis* can be viewed as the bulk of the submerged iceberg of general deixis with *explicit deixis* covering only what is immediately visible. Conceived in this manner, implicit deixis draws attention to the nuances of voice affecting all the components of an expression from function words to the Austinian *illocution*.[27] In order to be able to respond to communicative subtleties we must provide linguistic expressions with prosodic contours before we can settle for a transient meaning construction. The fact that all this occurs at camera shutter-speed must not blind us to the necessity of this basic interpretive procedure.[28] Once again, then, given the centrality of *voice* in linguistic communication, we cannot but concede that sentences do not mean by themselves; only utterances can have meaning. Nor will it do to shove utterances into the by-basket of socially enacted language. It is utterances rather than the illusion of unuttered sentences that must be placed at the core of semantics.

A special and critical kind of nonverbal utterance is *pointing*. In the gestures of pointing, aboutness and voice enter a unique relationship. Pointing directs our gaze to something another person has in mind, not only directing us towards a selected aboutness, Husserl's "exclusive directionality",[29] but also, by the manner of its performance, utterance intention. Yet far from regarding nonverbal pointing as a primitive and rudimentary form of communicating, recent research by Michael Tomasello has shown, convincingly in my view, that the gestures of pointing are a highly evolved form of meaning negotiation, involving interactive interpretation presupposing a highly developed stage of social reciprocity. In "Why Don't Apes Point?" Tomasello demonstrates a stark disparity between primate and human infants in the speed of acquisition of skills involved the performance of pointing.[30] While human children typically make rapid progress, the acquisition of the pointing ability amongst primates was observed to be slow and limited. On the evidence, then, it is likely that social reciprocity and the capacity for complex "intention-reading" must have been genetically sedimented in humans over a very long time of evolution.[31] Language has inherited this double message inherent in pointing in the form of what an utterance is *about* and the manner of its expression, that is, *voice*. In the social reality of linguistic exchange, the dialectic between the two components typically produce meaning nuances demanding considerable interpretive labour, a fact that needs to be acknowledged in our explanatory schemes. Much of this complexity has to do with the role played in communication by *imaginability*.

Imaginability

At the heart of the human sciences should be placed what humans do best: *imagining* things. And why should language somehow escape this fundamental human faculty? After all, if I cannot imagine what you are talking about, meaning fails. The crucial question then is what *sort* of imagining it is that occurs in linguistic communication and how precisely it does its work. Unfortunately, our dominant explications of language, by jettisoning *imaginability* from the agenda of investigation, have declared this very question illegitimate. But suppose we take the opposite route. By showing how much in language depends on the projection of mental scenarios at the level of the *motivated signified*, we should arrive at a *semantics of imaginability*.[32] The option of such an alternative approach can be found in Aristotle when he first describes language in terms of *homoiomata* (resemblance)[33] before proceeding to the perspective of propositions as a way of distinguishing between true and false statements. Indeed, the latter always requires the former as a precondition. *Aboutness* comes first. The same distinction can be observed in the two paths taken by Frege and Husserl. While both want to avoid psychologism and Frege opted radically for an approach via propositions, Husserl's meticulous descriptive approach led him to a component of language for which there is no room in the Fregean paradigm: *introjection*. Husserl introduces the concept of *introjection* as part of "intimation" in the sense of "acts which impart sense" and "acts that a hearer may introject into a speaker." This is so because linguistic exchange "demands a certain correlation among the mental acts mutually unfolded in intimation and in the receipt of such intimation, but not at all their exact resemblance."[34] To be sure, the tension between such mental, approximative resemblance relations and "exclusive directionality" and semantic exactitude remains unresolved throughout Husserl's writings. Yet his later vocabulary pertaining to the *Lebenswelt* suggests that had he had time to review his earlier semantics the logician's dream of exactitude, "identical sense" and the "ideal unities" of meanings in natural language would have been replaced by negotiated resemblance in his "type" and "typification."[35] This view finds support in such concepts as *appresentation,* and in the kinds of assumptions we cannot but make about alter egos.[36] Other relevant concepts are Husserl's ubiquitous use of *Vorstellung* as indispensable for "quasi-perceiving", "quasi-judging", "quasi-wishing", and other quasi-acts. Both the "reproductive consciousness" as "semblance acts" and its "productive" extension as "as-if-modification" depend on imaginability, and conspicuously so in "inactuality modification" and the "transforming fiction" of every "memorial as-if." For Husserl was never in doubt that "every experience has as its counterpart a phantasy (a re-presentation) corresponding to it."[37]

Just as does Michael Tomasello's more recent "intention-reading", Husserl's *introjection* relies heavily on our capacity to imagine *aboutness* and its modification by *voice*.[38] And since the vast bulk of linguistic utterances are about absent states of affairs, *imaginability* is a requisite component of linguistic communication. Furthermore, imaginability indicates not only a necessary faculty on the part of the language user but also a vital ingredient of language itself, namely that linguistic aboutness be *imaginable*. These two capacities reveal a key condition of natural language: mental *iconic* projection. In this sense, linguistic comprehension always involves nonverbal, interpretive reconstructive labour, suggestive of an account of linguistic meaning that is able to reconcile language and perception, such that the arbitrary signifiers of linguistic expressions are semantically activated by *motivated signifieds* made up of nonverbal, iconic, mental projections governed by concepts according to directionality, quality, quantity, and degree of schematisations under social guidance.[39] Meanings then would be individually instantiated but socially controlled by *pedagogy*, strictly conceived as *Abrichtung*.[40] From such a perspective, linguistic meanings can be conceived of as *indirectly public*. By reconciling invisible but socially controlled individual, mental linguistic meaning acts with public discourse and pedagogy, meaning is placed squarely in the arena of *social reciprocity*.

Social Reciprocity

Without paying attention to social reciprocity as methodological base line the theorisation of human communication goes astray from the very start. That this is so can be demonstrated by a critique of the various points of departure chosen by a diverse range of theories of *natural language*, as argued in section one above. Fundamental to the human sciences, then, is an acknowledgement of the role of social reciprocity. In this respect, communicology has been able to find succour in its two major support systems, phenomenology and semiotics, especially in its Peircean form. For more recent assistance we can draw on the work of Jürgen Habermas who argues a vital link between the Husserlian lifeworld with that of *communicative action*. It is of course no accident that Habermas here relies especially on Dilthey[41] for whom "the individual constantly experiences, thinks, and acts in a sphere of what is common." It is "*reciprocal* understanding" that "secures us the *Gemeinsamkeit* that exists among individuals." This commonality reveals itself in "the sameness of reason, sympathy in emotional life, and the *reciprocal* obligation in duties and rights." For Dilthey, the community is "the presupposition of understanding" and all "historical knowledge of the singular develops in a *reciprocal* relation to general truths." An important constituent of *Verstehen* for Dilthey is "empathy" conceived broadly, whether directed towards "a person or a work." As such, empathy involves "the transference of one's self into a given unity of expressions of life." Thus "reproduction or re-experiencing comes into being."[42]

In Habermas' pragmatics, every sentence "expresses unequivocally the intention of universal and unconstrained consensus."[43] Its fundamental orientation is "mutual *reciprocal* understanding," reflected in his triple division of the objectified world, our social world, and my subjective world. All three are based on social reciprocity, (1) on agreement in the scientific community; (2) on reciprocity amongst many; and (3) on social reciprocity as formative condition.[44] As a consequence, human self-awareness cannot be "inherent in the subject" but "is communicatively generated" and so pointing to "an intersubjective core."[45] In this sense, communicative understanding is a "universal condition" of *Verständigung*.[46] While this does not rule out deception in deliberately distorted communication, it makes it a negative derivative of the goal of reaching consensus. This is why for Habermas communicative action occurs when actors "harmonize their plans of action through internal means, committing themselves to pursuing their goals only on the condition of an agreement" about the communicative situation and prospective outcomes.[47] Such a commitment to social reciprocity continues to be a key concept in the *Geisteswissenschaften*.

Geisteswissenschaften

In the wake of Kant's *Critiques*, Wilhelm Dilthey undertook to set off the natural sciences from another "body of knowledge" that has "developed spontaneously out of the tasks of life itself, which is connected through the identity of its objects." He includes "such sciences as history, economics, legal and political science, the study of religion, of literature and poetry, of art and music, or philosophical worldviews and systems, and finally psychology."[48] To fully appreciate Dilthey's importance for communicology, it is instructive to compare his work with C.P. Snow's *Two Cultures and a Second Look*.[49] Snow draws an all too familiar and ultimately reductive demarcation between science as the sphere of the production of knowledge and the arts as a civilizing component of society, a source of subjective enjoyment and a kind of museum. Apart from more fundamental philosophical differences between British and Continental thought, Snow's popular picture of the arts is partly the reason why Dilthey's writings have not enjoyed the attention they deserve also in the Anglosphere. For Dilthey made a cogent case in favour of a methodological equilibrium between the natural sciences and rigorous investigations in the *Geisteswissenschaften*. A key characteristic that distinguishes the two approaches, according to Dilthey, is the contrast between the abstractive process aiming at uniformity in the natural sciences and the process in the human sciences of "translating back" our findings "into the fullness of life through a sort of transposition." In this process Dilthey's addresses "the connectedness of psychic life"; how "understanding penetrates into alien expressions of life." He contrasts nature which "we explain" with the psychic life "which we understand." Above all, he says, "what we have first is the experienced unity." And while abstraction cannot be abandoned in the cultural sciences, the difference is that "even in the most abstract sentences of the cultural sciences, the factual element that is represented in thoughts is *experience* and *understanding*." A crucial difference, then, between the natural and cultural sciences, is that "we understand ourselves and others by inserting our own experienced life into every form of expression of our own and others' lives." The *Geisteswissenschaften*, then, have their "own particular structure and laws", summed up by Dilthey in the categories of "*significance*" and "*development*." In his conception of the cultural present as always "filled with pasts and bears the future within itself",[50] Dilthey introduced into the human sciences a fundamental holistic orientation that sets them apart from natural science paradigms.

THREE SEMINAL IMPULSES

Complex Judgments

When Kant distinguishes between our bottom-up interpretive search for a not yet existing rule of judgment via *reflective reasoning* and the top-down interpretive frame allowing for meaning fulfilment via the stipulation of *teleological reasoning*, he is providing his successors with an innovative principle for complex judgments. Arguably, this is the most significant gift of the *Critique of Judgment* to secular hermeneutics, an opening gesture which however the tradition from Ast and Schleiermacher to Heidegger and Gadamer was never quite able to do justice to. The mechanism of reflective judgment is clear enough. It forges a bridge between puzzling particulars and a suitable interpretive frame "uniting particular experiences into a connected system", such that "the sum of objects of the senses" make sense under a stipulated quasi-causality.[51] As such, "the reflective power of judgment" subsumes surprising facts "under a law that is not yet given." Reflective reason, then, is no more than a "principle" for cases where "we are objectively at a complete loss" for a "concept of the object" that can be furnished only by a stipulated "principle covering the particular cases."[52] Thus Kant combines bottom-up interpretive search with top-down teleological speculation in the formation of complex judgments against the background of the interpretive community or *sensus communis*. This procedure proves appropriate not only to biological reasoning, Kant's immediate target, but also for handling the complexities of culture. While Kant's interpretive dialectic was designed to cope with judgments for which determining reason employing empirical concepts were ill suited,[53] hermeneutics fell back on the search for determinate meaning. Heidegger shrank Kant's open interpretive *helix* to the restrictive metaphor of the *hermeneutic circle*,[54] while Gadamer reintroduced "truth" which had been deliberately left aside in the *Third Critique*.[55]

A second fertile insight in Kant relevant to our topic is a method that allows us to heal the rift between *Vorstellung* and public discourse. By introducing the much maligned concept of *schematisation* in the *Critique of Pure Reason*, Kant was able to de-subjectivize intentionality.[56] In their generalised and schematized forms, mental projections become principles we can apply to *imaginability* as intersubjective entities, without which it is impossible to explain linguistic comprehension while at the same time avoiding the infinite regress threatened by words being cashed in by ever more words. If we want to exit the structuralist treadmill of mere differential relations of the lexicon and grasp meanings as nonverbal scenarios, the Kantian schematisation provides the ground for a rich analysis of verbal communication. It is in this spirit that Kant alerts his readers to the abstract principle of the "monogram" as the condition that "makes mental images possible" in the first place.[57] So it is no surprise that one of Kant's most astute readers, Charles Sanders Peirce, took up both Kantian innovations, reflective reason in his notion of *abduction* and schematization in his remarks on *hypoiconicity*.

Hypoiconicity

Amongst the many transformations of the Kantian machinery, such as abduction out of reflective and teleological reasoning, or iconicity from *Anschauung*, Peirce's abstraction of his tripartite concept of the *hypoicon* provides a fertile input into communicology. Following Kant's schematism chapter of the *Critique of Pure Reason*, Peirce subjected resemblance relation to a three-pronged analysis from image to diagram and metaphoric transposition.[58] Crucial for our purposes here is the second stage of the abstraction of iconicity, its *diagrammatic* form. In Peirce, the diagrammatical icon builds a bridge between full resemblance and empty symbolicity, the latter premised on the arbitrariness of terms and definitionally governed syntax, and so unaffected by subjectivity, culture, or history. Neither is symbolicity affected by the phenomenal infinite regress of *aboutness*, nor contaminated by the nuances of *voice*. As a result, formal languages and their applications yield univocal propositions, their very *raison d'être*. In sharp contrast, natural language is *heterosemiotic*, drawing as it does at the same time and of necessity on *symbolicity* (arbitrary signifiers, syntax), *indexicality* (inference; indirect iconicity), and *iconicity* (imaginability of resemblance). Peirce acknowledges this complexity when he writes that "every symbol must have, organically attached to it, its indices of reactions and its icons of qualities."[59] It is in the linguistic comprehension process where Peirce's *hypoicon* in its three versions of image, diagram, and metaphor proves its methodological fertility.[60] As diagrammatical schematisation, iconicity can be theorized as a component of language. We should also note here the *asymmetrical* triadic relation amongst

Peirce's sign types, symbol, index and icon. Whereas the symbol stands alone in its conventional arbitrariness, both index and icon partake of resemblance relations, the former indirectly (for instance the footprints in the snow guide us to *imagine* a fox schema), the latter directly (the arbitrary word sounds of *arbor, shu, Baum, and tree* can be grasped semantically only by exiting the verbal domain and activating our schematic grasp of a typical tree). Likewise *acrid, astringent, a soft touch* and so on. In natural language, the "logical interpretant"[61] is insufficient, lacking as it does meaning fulfilment by hypoiconicity.

Unlike cognitive linguistics, Peirce avoids the visual bias of cognitive "maps" by defining *hypoiconicity* at the level of generality inherited from Kant. By never letting go of iconicity even in his later writings, Peirce avoids any wholesale embrace of formalisation as ill suited to the description of communicability in the human domain. From his early insistence that "every assertion must contain an icon or a set of icons, or else must contain signs whose meaning is only explicable by icons"[62] to his much later assertion that "whenever we think, we have present to consciousness some feeling, image, conception, or other representation, which serves as a sign",[63] Peirce provides communicology with tools for handling the richness of human communication. Nor does his abstraction of subjective consciousness as quasi-mind in any way deny the carnal, visceral, spiritual and social nature of the inner world of personal signs.[64] By viewing society as "a sort of loosely compacted person",[65] while at the same time insisting on social reciprocity as the ground of individual semiosis,[66] Peirce rightly downgrades the merely subjective. In retaining iconicity in schematic form, Peirce's interpretant is well suited to account for the vital features of *aboutness* and *voice*, the latter profiting especially from Peirce's "emotional interpretant."[67] This applies to both relatively slow, interpretive meaning construction as it does to shutter-speed, habitual speech where comprehension is "unreflected."[68]

Long before Mikail Bakhtin placed dialogism at the centre of discourse, Peirce had turned reciprocity into a general semiotic principle: "Men and words reciprocally educate each other" in communication.[69] But whereas Bakhtin's theorization is firmly anchored in the verbal ground of *heteroglossia*, Peirce moves beyond the verbal and foregrounds iconicity. The signs so exchanged "excite in the mind of the receiver familiar images, pictures, or, we might almost say, dreams—that is reminiscences of sights, sounds, feelings, tastes, smells, or other sensations, now quite detached from the original circumstances of their first occurrence." This frees them "to be attached to new occasions. The deliverer is able to call up these images at will (with more or less effort) in his own mind; and he supposes the receiver can do the same."[70] In this way, Peirce offers a description of *hypoiconic appresentation* as a mandatory process underlying intersubjectivity. In a way, Peirce observes, we live in one another's brains.[71] Peirce terms such empathetic reciprocity "the natural judgments of the sensible heart."[72] What stabilizes these inferential constructions beyond the merely subjective is social reciprocity. For if "the content of consciousness, the entire phenomenal manifestation of mind, is a sign resulting from inference"[73] what is needed is the common ground of *"collateral experience."*[74] In the transformation of the symbolicity of word sounds into *hypoiconic interpretants*, "collateral experience" covers both our experience of language and our experience of the nonverbal part of the lifeworld. In Peirce, social reciprocity then is both ground and effect of human communication. A more recent but equally fruitful methodological impulse assisting in the exploration of human communication can be gleaned from Roman Ingarden's phenomenology of *ontic heteronomy*.

Ontic Heteronomy: Modes of Being and Existential Moments

Quine once neatly declared that "a curious thing about the ontological problem is its simplicity" because we can compress it into the question "What is there?" and provide the even shorter answer "everything."[75] This strikes us at least as counterintuitive when applied to human communication. That *it is there* we take for granted, but the way it exists is the big question brushed aside by Quine. To receive a more satisfying answer we have to move to the opposite philosophical register, one that addresses the *mode of being* of something and its characteristic *existential moments*. Precisely such an approach can be found in the magnum opus of the phenomenologist Roman Ingarden, arguably Husserl's closest disciple.[76] In four volumes and a total of some 1500 pages in *Der Streit um die Existenz der Welt*, Ingarden elaborates an ontology for objectivities that overtax the constraints of traditional ontology.[77] Ingarden identifies three modes of being: extra-temporal being, temporal being, and purely intentional being. He specifies their *existential moments* as follows. Extra-temporal or ideal being is characterized by the combination of *originality, autonomy, and non-actuality*, temporal or real being by *derivation, autonomy, and actuality;* and purely intentional being by *derivation, heteronomy, and non-actuality*. Intentional acts exist in the temporal mode and have directionality targeting an intentional object, which can have any mode of being, ideal, material, and purely intentional or can display ontic heteronomy, the typical mode of objectivities dealt with in communicology.

While the orthodoxy of ontological inquiry copes well with the ideality of definitions and the materiality of rocks, it fails to address what makes human phenomena complex. This is why a key notion in Ingarden's investigation is *ontic heteronomy*. Ingarden's writings are so very important to our topic in that almost anything addressed by communicology turns out to fall under ontic heteronomy in the sense that the processes we are trying to capture here display-varying degrees of materiality, ideality, and *intentionality*. Social systems, education, culture, and natural language are fundamentally heteronomous in terms of their *mode of being*. Language involves materiality in its word sounds and ideality in its syntax and, according to both Husserl and Ingarden, also its meanings.[78] At the same time, if we couldn't imagine what is being talked about we would have no comprehension. As such, language of necessity partakes of socially directed intentionality. In dealing with complex processes, Ingarden's introduction of the distinction between *mode of being* and *existential moments* is vital in allowing for a description of the acts we cannot but perform in constituting objectivities to the degree to which they involve intentionality, ideality and materiality.[79] The necessary conditions of utterances stipulated in the Introduction to this chapter were arrived at via Ingarden's methodological tools. In a similar vein, communicology can profit from this kind of ontology with respect to many of its core themes. While Ingarden's early and better know work was dedicated mainly to the demonstration of the ontic heteronomy of literary works and other art forms, his final volumes leaves this limitation behind by abstracting from specific ontic-epistemological relations a description of complex objectivities in general. This makes his contribution a major and so far neglected impulse for communicology.

CONCLUSION

By way of conclusion and in light of the three seminal impulses for communicability as ground of communicology provided by Kant, Peirce, and Ingarden, we are now in a position to address the pending question of how communicability might cope with "grasping the universally communicable".[80] Since neither formal identity nor immediate anchoring in the here and now of signification are appropriate principles for governing non-formal, highly abstract, "universal" communication, a special form of meaning generality seems to be needed to fit the bill. A combination of Kant's non-formal *pure reason* as a component of the dialectic between reflective and teleological reasoning may help meet this demand. Just as Kant's cognitive, human *pure* concepts of time and space are high-level generalities retaining traces of *resemblance*, so too can we conceive of what is communicably universal in non-formal contexts. Universal communicability in this sense remains tied to experience and so to culture. For Kant, the dialectic between reflective and teleological reasoning resulted in the instability of the subject-predicate relation, *stabilized* to a sufficient degree by recourse to the supplementary role of *sensus communis*. The parallel to this in Peirce's pragmatics is his definition of truth in non-formal sign relations as secured by community consensus, with universal truth as his limiting case of deferred, "ultimate" agreement.[81] And since in all non-formal sign exchange, *intentional* processes play a fundamental role, we need to place communicative universality in an enlarged ontology of the Ingardenian kind, beyond Quinean sets and particles. Communicative universality in this sense preserves resemblance relations at a high level of abstraction and, in reflecting community standards, must shift with cultural drift. Contrary to formal communicability, it must remain open-ended.

Humans are simultaneously perceptually-iconic, intentionally-indexical, and symbolic beings, their inferential capacities drawing on all three semiotic domains. Our dominant sign system, natural language, is the unique locus where all three processes are reflected and rendered socially efficient. This is displayed in the symbolicity of arbitrary word sounds and syntactic ideality, in the indirectly iconic inferences by which one thing can be employed intentionally to point to another, and in the indispensable hypoiconicity of the resemblance relations conveyed through linguistic meanings. As argued here, communicology is well placed to foster the exploration of those fundamental conditions by paying attention to the inseparability of *aboutness* and *voice*, the nuances of *implicit deixis*, the vital role of *imaginability*, and the formation of *complex judgments*, all of which can be coherently argued only against the rock bottom of *social reciprocity*. And since none of these can be described empirically without stipulating socially attuned mental processes, externalist and formal approaches provide insufficient tools for the analysis of human communicability. Instead, we are forced to take the methodological route of *introjection* in some form of a socially grounded *intersubjective mentalism*. This is why I have found the large synthesis proposed over many years in Richard Lanigan's communicology both congenial and inspiring. I dedicate this chapter to him for his achievements, and add my thanks for his generosity in judging my own writings.

NOTES

1. Jürgen Habermas on Karl Jaspers, in *Philosophical-Political Profiles* (London: Heinemann, 1983), 45.
2. Richard Lanigan, *Speech Act Phenomenology* (The Hague: Martinus Nijhoff, 1977).
3. E.g., Richard Lanigan, "Communicology," *Cultura International: Journal of Philosophy of Culture and Axiology* 4, no. 2 (2007): 212–216; "The Verbal and Nonverbal Codes of Communicology," in *Communicology: The New Science of Embodied Discourse*, ed. Isaac E. Catt and Deborah Eicher-Catt (Madison, NJ: Fairleigh Dickinson University Press, 2010), 102–128; "Communicology and Culturology: Semiotic Phenomenological Method in Applied Small Group Research," *The Public Journal of Semiotics* 4, no. 2 (2013): 71–103.
4. Horst Ruthrof, "Recycling Locke: Meaning as Indirectly Public," *Philosophy Today* 57, no. 1 (2013): 3–27.
5. Gottlob Frege, "On Sense and Reference," in *Translations from the Philosophical Writings of Gottlob Frege*, trans. Peter Geach and Max Black (Oxford: Blackwell, 1970), 56–78. On hyperintensional semantics see Marie Duzi, Bjorn Jespersen and Pavel Materna, *Procedural Semantics for Hyperintensional Logic: Foundations and Applications of Transparent Intensional Logic* (Dordrecht: Springer, 2010).
6. Horst Ruthrof, *Semantics and the Body: Meaning from Frege to the Postmodern* (Toronto: University of Toronto Press, 1997), 59–76.
7. Horst Ruthrof, "Semantics of Imaginability—Vorstellungssemantik: 13 Theses," *Review of Contemporary Philosophy* 10 (2011): 165–183.

8. Ferdinand de Saussure, *Cours de linguistique générale*, ed. and trans. Charles Bally, Albert Séchehaye, Albert Riedlinger, and Tullio de Mauro (Paris: Payot, 2005), 100.
9. Ray Jackendoff, *Foundations of Language: Brain, Meaning, Grammar, Evolution* (Oxford: Oxford University Press, 2002), 7–8.
10. Robbins Burling, *The Talking Ape: How Language Evolved* (Oxford: Oxford University Press, 2005), 4.
11. Rudolf Carnap, *Introduction to Semantics and the Formalisation of Logic* (Cambridge, MA: Harvard University Press, 1975), 13.
12. Horst Ruthrof, "Implicit Deixis," *Language Sciences* 47 (2015): 107–116, 108.
13. Horst Ruthrof, "Husserl's Semantics: Mending Husserl with Husserl," *Linguistic and Philosophical Investigations* 11 (2012): 11–41, 14–16.; *cf.* the defence of Husserl's ideality in Dorion Cairns, "The Ideality of Verbal Expressions," in *Phenomenology: Continuation and Criticism – Essays in Memory of Dorion Cairns*, ed. Fred Kersten and Richard Zaner (The Hague: Martinus Nijhoff, 1941), 239–250.
14. Willard van Ormond Quine, *Pursuit of Truth* (Cambridge, MA: Harvard University Press, 1993), 53–55.
15. Maurice Merleau-Ponty, *The Primacy of Perception and Other Essays* (Evanston, IL: Northwestern University Press, 1964), 25; *Signs*, trans. Richard McCleary (Evanston, IL: Northwestern University Press, 1964), 87–88; *The Visible and the Invisible*, trans. Alphonso Lingis (Evanston, IL: Northwestern University Press, 1968), 118. *Cf.* my remarks in The Body in Language (London: Cassell, 2000), 10–13.
16. Ludwig Wittgenstein, *Philosophical Investigations*, trans. G. E. M. Anscombe, P. M. S. Hacker and J. Schulte (Oxford: Blackwell, 2009), §6.
17. Horst Ruthrof, "A Critique of Meaning as Use," in *Language and Imaginability* (Newcastle upon Tyne: Cambridge Scholars Publishing, 2014), 101–120.
18. Wittgenstein, *Philosophical Investigations*, §6.
19. Jerry A. Fodor, *Lot 2: The Language of Thought Revisited* (Oxford: Oxford University Press, 2008).
20. Immanuel Kant, *The Critique of Pure Reason*, trans. Norman Kemp Smith (New York: St. Martin's Press, 1965), A142/B181.
21. Mark Johnson and George Lakoff, *Philosophy in the Flesh: The Embodied Mind and Its Challenge to Western Thought* (New York: Basic Books, 1999).
22. Tecumseh Fitch, *The Evolution of Language* (Cambridge: Cambridge University Press, 2010).
23. See for example the sober analysis in Friedemann Pulvermüller, "Brain-Language Research: Where Is the Progress?," *Biolinguistics* 4, nos. 2–3 (2010): 255–288.
24. The concept of illocution in speech act theory does not cover the nuances of voice addressed here.
25. Horst Ruthrof, "Sufficient Semiosis," *The American Journal of Semiotics* 31, nos. 1–2 (2015): 117–146.
26. Ruthrof, "Implicit Deixis," 107–116.
27. John Langshaw Austin, *How to Do Things with Words* (Oxford: Oxford University Press, 1962); *cf.* also John Searle, *Speech Acts: An Analysis in the Philosophy of Language* (Cambridge: Cambridge University Press, 1969) and "Indirect Speech Acts," in *Syntax and Semantics*, vol. 3, *Speech Acts*, ed. Peter Cole and Jerry Morgan (New York: Academic Press, 1975), 59–82.
28. Horst Ruthrof, "Shutter-Speed Meaning, Normativity, and Wittgenstein's Abrichtung," *Linguistic and Philosophical Investigations* 13 (2014): 33–54.
29. Edmund Husserl, *Logical Investigations*, trans. J. N. Finlay (London: Routledge and Kegan Paul, 1973), I, §13.

30. Michael Tomasello, "Why Don't Apes Point?," in *Roots of Human Sociality, Culture, Cognition and Interaction*, ed. Nick J. Enfield and Stephen C. Levinson (Oxford and New York: Berg, 2006), 506–524.
31. Michael Tomasello, *Origins of Human Communication* (Cambridge, MA: MIT Press, 2014).
32. Ruthrof, *Language and Imaginability*.
33. Aristotle, *De Interpretatione*, trans. John Lloyd Ackrill (Oxford: Oxford University Press, 2002), 1, 3–8, 16a.
34. Husserl, *Logical Investigations* I, §7.
35. Husserl, *Logical Investigations* I, §§ 13, 29.
36. Edmund Husserl, *Cartesian Meditations*, trans. Dorion Cairns (The Hague: Martinus Nijhoff, 1960), Meditation V.
37. Edmund Husserl, *Phantasy, Image Consciousness, and Memory (1898–1925)*, trans. John B. Brough, *Collected Works*, vol. 11, ed. Rudolph Bernet (Dordrecht: Springer, 2005), 413, 436, 709, 700, 707.
38. Michael Tomasello, *Constructing a Language: A Usage-Based Theory of Language Acquisition* (Cambridge, MA: Harvard University Press, 2003), 3–4.
39. Ruthrof, *Language and Imaginability*, 223–229.
40. Wittgenstein, *Philosophical Investigations*, §§ 5, 86, 129, 146, 151, 441, 630.
41. Jürgen Habermas, "Dilthey's Theory of Understanding Expression: Ego Identity and Linguistic Communication," in *Knowledge and Human Interests*, trans. Jeremy J. Shapiro (London: Heinemann, 1972), 140–160.
42. Wilhelm Dilthey, *Gesammelte Werke* (Göttingen: Vandenhoeck and Ruprecht, 1913–1967), 7.146 to 7.213–7.214; my emphasis.
43. Habermas, *Knowledge and Human Interests*, 314.
44. Jürgen Habermas, *Communication and the Evolution of Society* (London: Heinemann, 1979), 58, 68.
45. Jürgen Habermas, *Postmetaphysical Thinking*, trans. William M. Hohengarten (Cambridge: Polity Press, 1992), 177.
46. Habermas, *Communication and the Evolution of Society*, 1.
47. Jürgen Habermas, *Moral Consciousness and Communicative Action* (Cambridge: Polity Press, 1990), 134.
48. Dilthey, *Gesammelte Werke*, 7, 79–81.
49. C. P. Snow, *The Two Cultures and a Second Look* (Cambridge: Cambridge University Press, 1965).
50. Dilthey, *Gesammelte Werke*, 5,143 f.; 5,263; 7,84 ff.; 7,118; 7,232; 7,237.
51. Immanuel Kant, *Critique of Judgment*, trans. James C. Meredith (Oxford: Oxford University Press, 2007), § 61.
52. Kant, *Critique of Judgment*, §69.
53. Kant, *Critique of Pure Reason*, A727ff./B755ff.
54. Horst Ruthrof, *Pandora and Occam: On the Limits of Language and Literature* (Bloomington: Indiana University Press, 1992), 48–49, 56, 61.
55. Hans-Georg Gadamer, *Truth and Method* (London: Sheed and Ward, 1979); *Philosophical Hermeneutics*, trans. David E. Linge (Berkeley: University of California Press, 1976).
56. Kant, *Critique of Pure Reason*, A141ff./ B180ff.
57. Kant, *Critique of Pure Reason*, A142/B181.
58. Charles Sanders Peirce, *Writings of Charles S. Peirce: A Chronological Edition*, vol. 2, ed. Peirce Edition Project, 1867–1871 (Bloomington: Indiana University Press, 1984), EP 2.273.

59. Charles Sander Peirce, *Collected Papers of Charles Sanders Peirce, 1931–1966*, 8 vols., ed. Charles Hartshorne, Paul Weiss, and Arthur W. Burks (Cambridge, MA: Belknap Press, 1974), CP 5.119.
60. Peirce, EP 2.273.
61. Peirce, CP 5.467.
62. Peirce, CP 1.158.
63. Peirce, CP 5.283.
64. Peirce, CP 7.575 f.; CP 5.487.
65. Peirce, CP 5.421.
66. Peirce, CP 5.232; 5.249; 6.292; 6.295; 7.591.
67. Peirce, CP 5.475.
68. Peirce, CP 1.302 f.; 4.536; 8.328.
69. Peirce, CP 5.313.
70. Peirce, CP 3.433.
71. Peirce, CP 7.591.
72. Peirce, CP 6.292.
73. Peirce, CP 5.313.
74. Peirce, CP 8.314.
75. Willard van Ormond Quine, "On What there Is," in *From a Logical Point of View* (New York: Harper and Row, 1963), 1.
76. Barring the question of transcendental phenomenology.
77. Roman Ingarden, *Time and Modes of Being*, trans. Helen R. Michejda (Springfield, IL: Charles C. Thomas, 1964); *Der Streit um die Existenz der Welt: I Existentialontologie* (Tübingen: Max Niemeyer, 1964); *Der Streit um die Existenz der Welt: II/1 Formalontologie* (Tübingen: Max Niemeyer, 1965); *Der Streit um die Existenz der Welt: II/2 Formalontologie 2* (Tübingen: Max Niemeyer, 1965); *Über die Kausalstruktur der realen Welt: Der Streit um die Existenz der Welt III* (Tübingen: Max Niemeyer, 1974).
78. On this point I deviate from both Husserl and Ingarden; *cf.* Ruthrof, *Language and Imaginability*, 16–17, 25–26, 55–56, 90–91. The assumption of meaning ideality and meaning identity in natural language is an unnecessary and indemonstrable formal import rather than revealing necessary conditions.
79. On these premises I attempt a detailed characterization of language in "On the Mode of Being of Language", *Phenomenology and the Problem of Meaning in Human Life and History*, edited by Lubica Ucnik and Anita Williams, 215-244. Nordhausen: Traugott.
80. I gratefully acknowledge correspondence with Andrew R. Smith, who kindly drew my attention to this lacuna in my argument.
81. CP 8.112 f.; 3.432; EP 2.138; EP 1.138 f.; EP 1.114 f. For the most recent analysis of this aspect of Peirce's pragmatics, *cf.* Albert Atkin, *Peirce* (London: Routledge, 2016), 73–123.

BIBLIOGRAPHY

Aristotle. *De Interpretatione*. Translated by John Lloyd Ackrill. Oxford: Oxford University Press, 2002.
Atkin, Albert. *Peirce*. London: Routledge, 2016.
Austin, John Langshaw. *How to Do Things with Words*. Oxford: Oxford University Press, 1962.
Burling, Robbins. *The Talking Ape: How Language Evolved*. Oxford: Oxford University Press, 2005.

Cairns, Dorian. "The Ideality of Verbal Expressions." In *Phenomenology: Continuation and Criticism—Essays in Memory of Dorion Cairns*, edited by Fred Kersten and Richard Zaner, 239–250. The Hague: Martinus Nijhoff, 1941.

Carnap, Rudolf. *Introduction to Semantics and the Formalisation of Logic*. Cambridge, MA: Harvard University Press, 1975.

Dilthey, Wilhelm. *Gesammelte Werke*. Göttingen: Vandenhoeck and Ruprecht, 1913–1967.

Duzi, Marie, Bjorn Jespersen, and Pavel Materna. *Procedural Semantics for Hyperintensional Logic: Foundations and Applications of Transparent Intensional Logic*. Dordrecht: Springer, 2010.

Fitch, Tecumseh. *The Evolution of Language*. Cambridge: Cambridge University Press, 2010.

Fodor, Jerry A. *Lot 2: The Language of Thought Revisited*. Oxford: Oxford University Press, 2008.

Frege, Gottlob. "On Sense and Reference." In *Translations from the Philosophical Writings of Gottlob Frege*. Translated by Peter Geach and Max Black, 56–78. Oxford: Blackwell, 1970.

Gadamer, Hans-Georg. *Philosophical Hermeneutics*. Translated by David E. Linge. Berkeley: University of California Press, 1976.

Gadamer, Hans-Georg. *Truth and Method*. London: Sheed and Ward, 1979.

Habermas, Jürgen. *Communication and the Evolution of Society*. London: Heinemann, 1979.

Habermas, Jürgen. "Dilthey's Theory of Understanding Expression: Ego Identity and Linguistic Communication." In *Knowledge and Human Interests*. Translated by Jeremy J. Shapiro. London: Heinemann, 1972.

Habermas, Jürgen. *Knowledge and Human Interests*. London: Heinemann, 1972.

Habermas, Jürgen. *Moral Consciousness and Communicative Action*. Cambridge: Polity Press, 1990.

Habermas, Jürgen. *Philosophical-Political Profiles*. London: Heinemann, 1983.

Habermas, Jürgen. *Postmetaphysical Thinking*. Translated by William M. Hohengarten. Cambridge: Polity Press, 1992.

Husserl, Edmund. *Cartesian Meditations*. Translated by Dorion Cairns. The Hague: Martinus Nijhoff, 1960.

Husserl, Edmund. *Logical Investigations*. Translated by J. N. Finlay. London: Routledge and Kegan Paul, 1973.

Husserl, Edmund. *Phantasy, Image Consciousness, and Memory (1898–1925)*. Translated by John B. Brough, *Collected Works*, edited by Rudolph Bernet, vol. 11. Dordrecht: Springer, 2005.

Ingarden, Roman. *Der Streit um die Existenz der Welt: I Existentialontologie*. Tübingen: Max Niemeyer, 1964.

Ingarden, Roman. *Der Streit um die Existenz der Welt: II/1 Formalontologie*. Tübingen: Max Niemeyer, 1965.

Ingarden, Roman. *Der Streit um die Existenz der Welt: II/2 Formalontologie 2*. Tübingen: Max Niemeyer, 1965.

Ingarden, Roman. *Time and Modes of Being*. Translated by Helen R. Michejda. Springfield, IL: Charles C. Thomas, 1964.

Ingarden, Roman. *Über die Kausalstruktur der realen Welt: Der Streit um die Existenz der Welt III*. Tübingen: Max Niemeyer, 1974.

Jackendoff, Ray. *Foundations of Language: Brain, Meaning, Grammar, Evolution*. Oxford: Oxford University Press, 2002.

Johnson, Mark, and George Lakoff. *Philosophy in the Flesh: The Embodied Mind and Its Challenge to Western Thought*. New York: Basic Books, 1999.

Kant, Immanuel. *Critique of Judgment*. Translated by James C. Meredith. Oxford: Oxford University Press, 2007.

Kant, Immanuel. *The Critique of Pure Reason*. Translated by Norman Kemp Smith. New York: St. Martin's Press, 1965.
Lanigan, Richard. "Communicology." *Cultura International: Journal of Philosophy of Culture and Axiology* 4, no. 2 (2007): 212–216.
Lanigan, Richard. "Communicology and Culturology: Semiotic Phenomenological Method in Applied Small Group Research." *The Public Journal of Semiotics* 4, no. 2 (2013): 71–103.
Lanigan, Richard. *Speech Act Phenomenology*. The Hague: Martinus Nijhoff, 1977.
Lanigan, Richard. "The Verbal and Nonverbal Codes of Communicology." In *Communicology: The New Science of Embodied Discourse*, edited by Isaac E. Catt and Deborah Eicher-Catt, 102–128. Madison, NJ: Fairleigh Dickinson University Press, 2010.
Merleau-Ponty, Maurice. *The Primacy of Perception and Other Essays*. Evanston, IL: Northwestern University Press, 1964.
Merleau-Ponty, Maurice. *Signs*. Translated by Richard McCleary. Evanston, IL: Northwestern University Press, 1964.
Merleau-Ponty, Maurice. *The Visible and the Invisible*. Translated by Alphonso Lingis. Evanston, IL: Northwestern University Press, 1968.
Peirce, Charles Sanders. *Collected Papers of Charles Sanders Peirce, 1931–1966*. 8 vols, edited by Charles Hartshorne, Peter Weiss, and Arthur W. Burks. Cambridge, MA: Belknap Press, 1974. (CP)
Peirce, Charles Sanders. *Writings of Charles S. Peirce: A Chronological Edition*. Vol. 2, edited by Peirce Edition Project, 1867–1871. Bloomington: Indiana University Press, 1984. (EP)
Pulvermüller, Friedemann. "Brain-Language Research: Where Is the Progress?" *Biolinguistics* 4, no. 2–3 (2010): 255–288.
Quine, Willard van Ormond, "On What there Is." In *From a Logical Point of View*. New York: Harper and Row, 1963.
Quine, Willard van Ormond. *Pursuit of Truth*. Cambridge, MA: Harvard University Press, 1993.
Ruthrof, Horst. *The Body in Language*. London: Cassell, 2000.
Ruthrof, Horst. "Husserl's Semantics: Mending Husserl with Husserl." *Linguistic and Philosophical Investigations* 11 (2012): 11–41.
Ruthrof, Horst. "Implicit Deixis." *Language Sciences* 47 (2015): 107–116.
Ruthrof, Horst. *Language and Imaginability*. Newcastle upon Tyne: Cambridge Scholars Publications, 2014.
Ruthrof, Horst. "On the Mode of Being of Language." *Phenomenology and the Problem of Meaning in Human Life and History*. Ed. Lubica Ucnik and Anita Williams, 215-240. Nordhausen: Traugott, 2017.
Ruthrof, Horst. *Pandora and Occam: On the Limits of Language and Literature*. Bloomington: Indiana University Press, 1992.
Ruthrof, Horst. "Recycling Locke: Meaning as *Indirectly Public*." *Philosophy Today* 57, no. 1 (2013): 3–27.
Ruthrof, Horst. *Semantics and the Body: Meaning from Frege to the Postmodern*. Toronto: University of Toronto Press.
Ruthrof, Horst. "Semantics of Imaginability—*Vorstellungssemantik:* 13 Theses." *Review of Contemporary Philosophy* 10 (2011): 165–183.
Ruthrof, Horst. "Shutter-Speed Meaning, Normativity, and Wittgenstein's *Abrichtung*." *Linguistic and Philosophical Investigations* 13 (2014): 33–54.
Ruthrof, Horst. "Sufficient Semiosis." *The American Journal of Semiotics* 31, no. 1–2 (2015): 117–146.

Saussure, Ferdinand de. *Cours de linguistique générale*. Translated and edited by Charles Bally, Albert Séchehaye, Albert Riedlinger, and Tullio de Mauro. Paris: Payot, 2005.
Searle, John R. "Indirect Speech Acts." In *Syntax and Semantics*. Vol. 3 of *Speech Acts*, edited by Peter Cole and Jerry L. Morgan, 59–82. New York: Academic Press, 1975.
Searle, John R. *Speech Acts: An Analysis in the Philosophy of Language*. Cambridge: Cambridge University Press, 1969.
Snow, C. P. *The Two Cultures and a Second Look*. Cambridge: Cambridge University Press, 1965.
Tomasello, Michael. *Constructing a Language: A Usage-Based Theory of Language Acquisition*. Cambridge, MA: Harvard University Press, 2003.
Tomasello, Michael. *Origins of Human Communication*. Cambridge, MA: MIT Press, 2014.
Tomasello, Michael. "Why Don't Apes Point?" In *Roots of Human Sociality, Culture, Cognition and Interaction*, edited by Nick J. Enfield and Stephen C. Levinson, 506–524. Oxford: Berg, 2006.
Wittgenstein, Ludwig. *Philosophical Investigations*. Translated by G. E. M. Anscombe, P. M. S. Hacker, and J. Schulte. Oxford: Blackwell, 2009.

CHAPTER FOUR

The Human, the Family, and the *Vécu* of Semiotic Phenomenology

Lanigan's Communicology in the Context of Life Itself

FRANK MACKE

One of the things that I take to be most powerful about Richard Lanigan's work is the manner in which it positions the messiness and mystification of human experience in the scheme of both semiotics and phenomenology. Reflecting on the concept of the "icon" as a general problematic of cultural semiotics, Lanigan writes: "within the context of communication and culture the most visible icon is the conscious experience we have of a *child in the family*. There is no better person upon whom we can focus our attention to investigate the problematic of how communication and culture come to thematize one another in daily life."[1] Besides Lanigan, no one in the field that academia now recognizes as "communication studies" had ever considered the *lived* communicative experience (*vécu* is the preferred French term) of children and families (*other* than as behavioral abstractions) prior to the 1990s.

The lingering aspects of infantile attachment and childhood/adolescent adjustment now preoccupy me as I think through the directions of communicology as an academic field and as a modality of addressing human science issues. Lanigan's interpretation of Peirce's semiotics and Foucault's theory of discourse, particularly as it intertwines with his communicological interpretation of Margaret Mead's cultural theory of the family, enables thinking about the Self and Other—and what would appear, on the surface of things, to be relations of rational actors entailed in purposeful activity—to enter into new worlds of insight. It is this particular conceptualization that I will explore in this chapter.

Sixty years ago, two of America's preeminent sociologists, Talcott Parsons and Robert Bales, published a book on the function of the family, influenced by general systems theory, that colorfully described families as "'factories' which produce human personalities." The text, *Family: Socialization and Interaction Process*,[2] was recognized as a significant part of an effort of sociologists, psychologists, and psychiatrists to address the rising interest—perhaps, in some respects, a fascination—with the study of culture and human systems. Parsons developed a reputation for espousing a "structural/functionalist" approach to the study of society, forms and strategies of government, social institutions, and the various agencies and apparatuses of culture. Bales, a Harvard social psychologist, specialized in small group interaction. He eventually developed the SYMLOG (SYstematic MultiLevel Observation of Groups) method of group observation.[3]

Before we get too far in the analysis of this particular period in the development of human science theory, it is worth noting that the "systems" approach to the study of persons and culture—which many human scientists *now* are most inclined to conceptualize as a radical reconceptualization of Western assumptions of order, definition, and meaning (as for example, in the ecological thematics of Bateson or the integral thinking of Ervin László)—was taken by many theorists at the time as a logical extension of the prevailing modernist technocratic and mechanistic assumptions of scientific inquiry.[4] The appreciation for seeing *new* levels of connectedness and systemic integration in the patterns, structures, and institutes of society was, in fact, quite robust. As such, those espousing a structural-functionalist approach felt they had an important point of view to contribute to a new discourse in which new technologies and forms of information technology and communication were clearly changing social patterns, social life, and cultural understanding. In many ways, it comprised—for many—the first discursive means by which *culture* could be bracketed as a relative matter.

I mention the historical intellectual/academic transition of theoretical work on the topic of culture and systems because vestiges of structural-functionalism continued to pervade the application of systems thought for decades. Although it would seem to make good sense that social institutions and legal structures might serve as an important index of cultural expression and signification (and, in fact, for many social scientists the structures of social life continue to demand their primary focus), there are problems in attributing a delineated meaning to the most visible exponents of cultural architecture. In short, this was what Foucault's archaeological and genealogical projects sought to question.

More to the point, what we think we are looking at "as a structure" is only itself a mode of signification. At any given point, from the inception of a given delineation (taken, within a discursive field, as a "structure") to its mode of existence and expression over time, the structure and its delineation become saturated with projections. In a sense, when the character "Neo," in the popular science fiction film *The Matrix* learns "there is no spoon" as he observes the familiar object held before him, he is learning one of the most important and often forgotten lessons of both Husserlian phenomenology and Lacanian psychoanalytic theory. Simply, in a perceptual frame, there *will be* an object of perception. But that object has meaning *as function of mind*, not as a function of a disembodied existence.

SYSTEMS AND STRUCTURES, ICONS AND IMAGES

As systems theory, by way of its emergent rhetorical presence through normalized social science discourse as well as through its new voices in cultural anthropology (notably, Mead, Bateson, Sapir, and Edward T. Hall), enabled a broad platform for the analysis of culture and everyday life, one of the new areas of theoretical work and empirical investigation was the "family system." Deborah Weinstein closely examined the institutional and intellectual context of 20th century family systems research. Weinstein carefully addresses the formation of the GAP—namely, the Group for the Advancement of Psychiatry. She writes:

> The formation of the [GAP] was indicative of the trends shaping the formation of the field of family therapy. GAP was created in the spring of 1946 by psychiatrists who wanted to reorganize their national association, the American Psychiatric Association, in the wake of World War II (...) The experiences of the war would transform this professional landscape. World War II brought in many new, young practitioners who had served in the military medical corps as psychiatrists and who had been exposed to psychodynamic approaches to therapy. The war strengthened the environmental perspective on the causes of mental illness since a key message of the war experience was that the stress of combat induced breakdowns among soldiers without prior symptoms.[5]

As the Freudian, neo-Freudian and post-Freudian psychoanalytic modalities of clinical treatment were being transformed, some of the figures who became immediately prominent in the work of the GAP and who transformed the treatment of, eventually, a sizeable majority of persons entering into psychotherapeutic treatment were names many of us recognize as foundational in the study of communication.

Out of Stanford University Medical School (later to become known as the Palo Alto School) came Don Jackson, Virginia Satir, and Jay Haley. Gregory Bateson joined this group after their work on families had already begun. He had a tremendous influence, of course, on the research and dialogues that took place in Palo Alto (particularly in his framing of the double-bind), but, at the same time he is often given, maybe, a bit too much credit for the contributions of what came to be a critical mass of clinicians and scholars working in the San Francisco Bay area. On the East Coast, Nathan Ackerman, a New Yorker, often considered by many to be the "father of family psychotherapy," had a tremendous influence on clinical work and clinical training. He was publishing work on family and culture alongside Adorno, Jahoda, Horkheimer, and Frenkel-Brunswick. Eventually his work, as well as the growing ambitions of the GAP, came to influence the work of Salvador Minuchin, another New Yorker, and Murray Bowen, a psychiatrist at Georgetown Medical School. Minuchin and Bowen produced the most influential models of treating both troubled families and, importantly, individuals grasped as exponents of family systems in which habits of life and emotional coping are "learned," transmitted, and embodied.

It is impossible to understate how important the work of Minuchin and Bowen would prove to be, especially in the diagnosis and treatment of family-based disorders.[6] Simply, for family-centered therapists, the names of Bowen and Minuchin resonate with equivalent force to the names of Husserl and Heidegger in phenomenology. This is also to say, retrospectively (especially over the last decade or so), that the resistance, which some phenomenologists, philosophers, and cultural theorists express toward the work of Husserl and Heidegger, is comparable in some ways to the distance that a number of therapists are defining in their intellectual relationship to the legacies of Bowen and Minuchin.

Bowen and Minuchin took the work of the key psychoanalytic thinkers emerging from Europe (both the Freudians and the object-relations theorists) and adapted them to the immediate moments of emotional and psychological crisis as experienced by the persons they were both attempting to treat in post-WWII America. They both took a long look at the experiential bases of the family system. Certain invariables announced themselves: parents, children, grandparents—i.e., generational markers and legacies—as well as siblings, cousins, aunts, uncles, and the idiosyncratic codes by which aunts and uncles are ranked within a family network. They noted that aunts, uncles, and cousins define the boundaries of the family system as a psychological and communicative network—in other words, who gets to live as "family" (same) and who will reside outside the system (different). Bowen and Minuchin then thought through the logic of systems theory (which, at that point in the 20th century, had fully permeated the fundamental subject matter of human maturation and development,[7] but they avoided certain key critical phrases. They talked about maturation and development and about stages, but *without* talking about "stages of development". They talked about power within the family and between generations without talking about authority and the inherent power *of* generational authority.

The primary critical theme that has emerged over the years concerns the *structuralism* of Minuchin and Bowen. As such, the pragmatic direction of this criticism has been toward a strategy of family psychotherapeutic technique that has been called *post-structural* or *postmodern*.[8] The issue of "structuralism" has been one with which multiple modalities of human science theoretical work has had to come to terms with. The difficulty is with the *persistence* of structure, in other words with the persistence of the *object* that—unlike the clock in Dali's famous painting—does not melt or fade away but continues to function on terms of its own, or, at least, on terms that have not been sufficiently negotiated with its environment.

In Richard Lanigan's essay, "Star Trek: The Child and the Semiotic Phenomenology of Choosing a Family,"[9] the concept of how Peirce's concept of the icon functions within the family and, then, again within the culture is given an original and brilliant reading and interpretation. In this article, Lanigan talks about the child as an icon of the family and, implicitly, of the child (as an icon *representative* of the family) also serving as an icon of the culture as well. The family *is* an icon of a culture. We know this without hesitation because the family is an *institution* of a culture. The relationship is organic. The concept of the icon, here enters into human science conceptualizations of such an organic entity as a child within a family within a culture because an icon represents how we think of things, or rather, serves one of three ways we are given to think of things (i.e., as icon, index, or symbol).

Some of what I have described, in particular the inherently organic relationship of the child to the family, might seem to more fully satisfy the condition for indexicality. The difficulty here is that, at least with respect to the child, the indexicality only functions over a stretch of time, a stretch of time that cannot be experienced (or "seen") within a standard or normative framework of observation. When a person looks at a picture of a child and then views that same person as a fully-grown adult, an act of imagination (that is, an act of creative narrative functioning with a tincture of faith) is required to put the two objects into the framework of institutional organicity. One might look at the infant or childhood photograph of the adult we have grown to know and love and be led to say something like: "Wow, was that you?"—or "Yes, I can see your freckles, even back then." So, in practical discourse, as we consider invisible and, in so many ways, unknowable swaths of time, the relationship of the child to the adult is something *other* than indexical. We might say it is all a matter of "who you know." Or, better, it is all a matter of knowing and experiencing the linear narrative concept of the person.

In his essay, Lanigan is careful to consider iconicity in close connection with Pierce's unique rhetoric. Peirce writes: "an icon is a sign which refers to the object that it denotes merely by virtue of characters of its own, and, which it possesses, just the same, whether any such object actually exists or not."[10] It is important to note what is absent in Peirce's definition: *resemblance*. It is common for students gaining their introduction to semiotic theory to be taught that the "icon" is the sign of resemblance. In a technical sense, that would be correct—that is, as far as one maintains a careful eye on the full implication of what is meant by resemblance. *Resemblance*, grasped in terms of its etymology, suggests "likeness." That is, if something is *like* something else, it bears a *similarity* with that other thing—which, again, means that though it is indeed *different* from that other thing, there must be one or more ways in which those two things correspond. A similitude might be visual, it might be acoustic, it might be geometric, and it might be dramatic or strategic. In any case, the analog is built from the fundamental reality that the two things being compared are *not the same*. They are not the same but, at the same time, they bear some critical semiotic similarity that enables one to serve as *resemblant* of the other.

This concept of similitude and resemblance competes with a connotation of resemblance that has become increasingly persistent in the last half century, which is that of the photographic image. The photographic image is a mode of resemblance in which so many visual aspects of the object signified comport with its mode of representation that the observer forms little doubt that the object signified is the *same* as the object itself. A drawing might capture critical visual features calling forth the object to mind (and memory). The photo image, on the other hand, *seems* to capture *all* of key visual features of the object—producing an effect of, for all practical purposes, a visual *identity*. Interestingly, Peirce had initially used the term "copy" (and then, a bit later, "likeness") in place of the term "icon." The technological sense of "copy" as a *wholly identical* replication of the object was not a habituated part of the conceptual framework of 19th century discourse. Copy (from *copia*) literally means, via transcription or manufacture, to make abundant or copious. As such, the shift toward the term icon was, for Peirce, a recognition of the tropic play of signs. The icon was the mode of semiotic perception that enabled a representation of the *same* in the *different*. The resemblance of the icon to the object becomes a psychological matter of *sufficiency* rather than precise visual identity or structural congruence. Simply put, that which is iconic is in the mind of the beholder, not in the conformity of the sign to some sort of pattern.

The problem that is created by the pervasiveness of the camera as a preeminent mode of seeing is that resemblance and iconicity becomes a function of a technological *Augenblick*—of an opening and a closure of a lens that captures a scene of existence (*in the capacity of* "experience") as though it is always and has always been that way. Before the advent of photography, an *Augenblick*, as it is discussed in the work of Kierkegaard, constituted a "glance." It was an impression gained by way of the eye. It was a moment. It constituted *time* as grounded perceptual experience. It was something, therefore, conceptual. It was not intersubjectively empirical, not a snapshot in the sense we have come to know it through the intense, viral ways we have come to experience visual resemblance in our time.

As such, the problematic of the icon and the problematic of structure bear some significant parallels. It is my argument that the "structure" in the structuralism that post-structuralists subject to critique is, phenomenologically, a matter of image and similitude. More specifically, it is the persistence of a *particularity* of form and pattern that evokes the resistance in theory from the human scientist or as with the work of Bowen and Minuchin, the practicing therapist.

THE ICONOGRAPHY OF FAMILY LIFE AND THE AMBIGUITY OF NORMALITY

In the life of a culture, the structure of a family lends itself to iconicity. Patterns of comportment are reflected in multiple matters of discipline and relationality. We can see these patterns in terms of family boundaries and neighborliness, family size and inclusion, parental roles, child discipline, along with reflections of and resistances to expressions of broader cultural habits, trends, and manners. Lanigan, both in this essay and in many of his writings over the last several decades, has emphasized the primary cultural value orientations of egocentricity and sociocentricity when examining the dynamics and relational patterns of groups.[11] These orientations are also very much on display in the structure and comportment of families. One can view these orientations as much from the structural patterns of a family as from the choices made by family members.

Over the course of the last half-century, the saturation of televisual iconography in all matters of style and comportment has influenced the perception of family systems and their structural elements.[12] Rather than the perceptual experience that follows from observing other families first hand or by way of narrative (whether written or oral), we have the capacity to observe the order, structure, and comportment of a family system through the lenses and screens of video technology. We can perceive the structures of comportment (or behavior) that would be present in first hand observation, but we can also, if we care to look, perceive multiple family orders and systems simultaneously and superficially, drawing our gaze to aspects of image and structure rather than to details of choice or the nuances and hesitations of crisis.

As such, the experience of family has been guided by and tempered with narrative impressions of how families ought to function. When people comment on the strength or health of their own family system, they are (unless they have been detached from most forms of electronic communication, television, and film) basing their evaluations comparatively—which is to say: *iconically*. That is, they are examining the mode of resemblance of their family system and its images and representations of structure in terms of what they are *not*. Again, the icon is not a representation of identity, but a representation of *resemblance*. It is, again following Peirce, as a "sign which refers to the object that it denotes merely by virtue of characters of its own."[13] The "characters of its own," considered from a context of strategically emphasized family structures and images—particularly those that are functions of romanticized conceptions of virtue, redemption, or cultural excellence—constitute points of tension in the viewer's perceptual experience. They become features of sameness and difference as the viewer relates his or her own lived experience to the roles and expectations of the people circulating through the family system revealed in the narrative.

After a certain point a sense of normality begins to emerge. It is now entirely normal to spend hours of one's day watching characters in theatrical roles, both fictional and otherwise. People have been doing it for decades. Every character, even those who are isolated or companionless, will eventually be understood—if she or he is to be understood at all—in terms of her or his family background. Simply, family experience, beginning with one's parental relations, is how we assess the foundations of a person's personality, his or her temperament; in other words, his or her *persona* or narrative character—to wit: his or her Selfhood. The discourse of psychoanalytic theory and psychotherapy now pervades our talk about people and what they do, how they relate to one another, and what they seem to want.[14] Freud situated the primary architecture of consciousness in infancy and childhood, which is to say: mother, father, siblings, grandparents, boundaries, culture, and language.

In short, we watch television and think about our lives. We assess ourselves in terms of what we see. The sense of normality that we have come to employ as a measure of the relative functionality or dysfunctionality of our childhood and familial intimacies come not from our capacity to think through our habits—our sense of comfort with patterns and choices relative to what we say and how we talk with one another—but from looking at *other people's lives*. It is true that what we observe from looking at other people's lives is a sense of style. That is, we gain a sense of how other people live and talk. We find structure and habit as well as both conscious and unconscious rules at work, and we have no doubt taken note of these modes of engagement and embodiment, interconnection and relationality, for as long as we have lived in social clusters. But, as we think in terms of normality in the broad spectrum of televisual iconography, our modes of observation have shifted from a relational and communicological sense of style to a materialist, strategic, and structural sense of style as image and status.

As Foucault notes in *Omnes et Singulatim*, the early strategies of policing and statistics (as methods of "statism") deployed through the new science of governmentality during the 18th and 19th centuries sought knowledge of patterns and challenges in the body politic—people's ages, personal wealth, the nature of work, the level of agricultural yield, who was sick, who was destitute.[15] It was in the shift toward marketing strategies for the sale and distribution of surplus goods that a new self-consciousness of style began to pull consciousness toward not just iconic images of the other—employing status-consciousness and status-envy as a technique to drive ambitions of Selfhood—but toward iconic images of the *Self as an other*. That is, economic status, as reflected in bourgeois manners of speech and dress, began making persons aware of "who" they were and who they were not. The question of "how one was doing" (as when we ask one another: "how are you"?) became a relative matter. If not a matter of health and serenity, then one's status can quickly become a matter of economic, political, and cultural rank.

Since the dawn of the television era, even children become quite aware of how other families live. Because of the unique and intensely personal relations of parents with their children, what every child will commonly discover is that his or her life is different from the ones they watch on television. It is dissimilar not just because the person on television is *not* him or her, but because the mode of parenting is different, the home is different, the neighborhood is different, the school is different, and so forth. Children growing up in the early days of television measured their lives against the picket-fence idealisms and moral verisimilitudes of soothing black-and-white situation comedies and dramatic stories structured around comforting and familiar homilies.

As such, this set of experiences made it abundantly clear that a family can *itself* be an icon—both for the person within a culture and for the cultural system itself. This was evident even shortly after the turn of the century when the newspaper comic strip *Keeping Up with the Joneses* (begun in in 1913) depicted the psychology of social climbing in terms of envy and emulation.[16] Again, the particular instantiation of a family network serves as a recognizable representation of what a given family is and, then again, what it is not. The normalization of particular family styles, strategies, and structures, then, became intensified during the post-War period—a time when large-scale, multi-level television and print marketing strategies attempted to sell material signifiers and, for all intents and purposes, stylistic *copies* of the American dream in terms of automobiles, homes, home interiors, and appliances (of all sorts), as well as clothing and cosmetics. In the last several decades numerous cultural analyses have examined the iconography of the White, Protestant, affluent way of life that was celebrated and, then, projected onto the consumer psyche by studio executives, advertisers, and corporate interests in search of predictable large scale consumer markets.

THE NORMALITY OF THE FAMILY: FROZEN ICONS AND FLUID STRUCTURES

The concept of the child as an icon of a family system, which functions as both a thematic and problematic of Lanigan's essay, raises additional questions about what a family system is and how it functions psychologically, culturally, and communicologically. Again, the child can certainly function, within a limited range of possibility, as an *index* of a family. And a child can no doubt serve as a *symbol* of a family. The iconicity of the child, however, raises an interesting question concerning both identity (genetic and cultural) and difference. After all, the presence of the child is what makes a family a family in the first place. That is, two people who set up a household describe a *potential* family. They are a couple until a child is present. At least in terms of the consensus of literature in the fields of anthropology and family systems psychology, what produces a family is a lived, communicative connection between at least two generations.[17] Now, in most cases, the presence of the child connects multiple generations and, thus, calls for the history of the family, particularly as the grandparents psychologically re-live the childhood of the birth parents through the instance of the infant. As well, the child invokes the mythos of the family as it is imagined by the birth parents. The process of selecting a name, as well as deciding upon rituals of religious introduction (if any) and primary modalities of teaching and discipline, draw the expectant parents toward an imagined past and an imagined future. It is here that, in some cases, older, sociocentric traditions suggest ritual activities uniting multiple generations, both living and dead.

The child as infant signifies multiple imagined possibilities. The word "infant" literally means "not-speaking" or "before speech"—which means that the child, at that stage of its development, is, essentially a set of expanding and transforming projections accompanied by organically responsive volitional behavior occurring in the absence of intentional consciousness. Everything that the child does on its own volition, then, serves to modify and reconfigure these projections. At that point, the adult members of the family substitute, sometimes in quiet reflection and sometimes via talk, one projection and narrative horizon for another. It is not that the child is, iconically, now something different to itself than it had been before the possibility of a strength, a talent, or perhaps a difficulty seemingly revealed by way of its behavior. It is that the child is iconically a different representation to and for the family.

The fundamental reality is that the child matures beyond its infancy, grows out of its toddlerhood, and enters into a subjective Selfhood for which his or her own body becomes both the sign and vehicle of its desire. As Lanigan writes: "[W]e are reminded that abduction is always at work: a Rule plus a Result gives a Case (…) Not only is abduction at work, the formation of the icon is at stake."[18] And on this point Lanigan concludes: "The abduction process is clear: Birth is a Rule, life is a Result, and understanding is the Case."[19]

The logical relations here might seem deceptively simple. With respect to the child and her or his family, the icon and its object entails a relationship of presence and absence. The child is perpetually something that it is *not*, something that it has transcended and grown beyond, on one hand, or yet to become (but *not yet*) on the other. Moreover, the agency of the child (presence), as he or she becomes confident and capable of her or his talents and strengths, can only gain recognition for what it is when the voice and authority of the parent withdraws from the scene (absence).

But, as I have been arguing throughout this essay, what might *appear* to be the structure of the family, at any given moment is just a snapshot. As an image of lived-reality, the family is fluid and liquid. Identities and roles change continuously, especially in relationships that are both grounded and invested in intense intimacies. The deeper the structure, the more the organic system undergirds the communicology of generational influences and instruction, and is often elided in the focus on matters of identity and power. It is precisely this system that the child most fully represents iconically. What the child, irrespective of its gender, its culture, or its particular talents or challenges, represents is *time*.

The fundamental structure of the family is generational. Roles that flow from intergenerational tasks and dialogues, particularly with regard to the care of children and the aged, are expressions of culture, but at the same time the most significant influence for the transmission of culture is by way of intergenerational discourse. It is not as though the force of this influence, however, is without competition. Economic and market forces combined with remarkable technological changes have torn at the relationship between culture and intergenerational family intimacies for the last several decades in ways that could not have been foreseen by the family systems models that emerged in the years of the GAP. Whether we are talking about Margaret Mead's model of family and cultural transmission, the work of Nathan Ackerman, Bowen Minuchin, or the Palo Alto school, no one could have anticipated the rate of family atomization and nuclearization that would follow from the economic and demographic shifts of the last several decades. Simply, the likelihood of new or expectant parents to live within close proximity of intimate intergenerational support shrinks every year. The amount of time that parents have to spend with even early-developing children is limited by the loss of real wages that have occurred, not just since the market and banking disruptions over the last decade and a half, but from the movement of capital away from the middle and working class.

THE CHILD AS ICON AND GENERATIONAL TIME: THE FUTURE IS NOW

All of this is to say that the icon of the child as a representamen of the family has come to function differently than it did a century ago. Over the course of the last 50 years, educators and social critics have commented on the amount of time that children spend watching video screens of all sorts, a commitment of time that increasingly displaces not only reading and schoolwork, musical and artistic development, and healthy physical activity but time spent in face to face interactions with other children and grown-ups. Even for well-meaning parents, the video screens, even when carefully policed for content, serve to distract the child from the maieutic ambiguity inherent to conversation with others, particularly adults.

A shift from sociocentricity to egocentricity followed the American experience from the 19th century to the 20th century, and further shifts toward egocentricity (which we can observe in the trends toward social networking and high tech consumerism) now threaten the fabric of communal life.[20] Bernard Stiegler notes that "intergenerational conflict (…) is structurally necessary in order to become an adult."[21] He writes:

> This normal, necessary scene, however, in which the familial relationship becomes tense and then confrontational so that minors will be able to achieve their majority, has been short-circuited by the capture and diversion of individual, familial, and collective attention towards the objects and subjects of the mass media and through them, towards objects of consumption (…). This destroys the very thing that could found the desire of the social group as the circulation of desire between members of this group.[22]

Stiegler is concerned with a "liquidation of maturity" that arises, for whatever reason, in the course of a *withdrawal* from intergenerational struggle—the arguments from "authority" that parents have long maintained to assert their dominant position in the family and against which adolescents rebel in an effort to assert their confident, rational, adult Selfhoods. "Those 'parent-child relationships' that (…) are 'more relaxed' may in reality often be the very obstacle to becoming adult, being on the contrary part of the infantalization of parents themselves—who thus become 'friends' with their children."[23]

Another dimension of this analysis, which is not without irony, is that the particular family relations and intergenerational examples that Lanigan uses to illustrate his thematic come from a television program, *Star Trek: The Next Generation*. As such, the two particular cases that he uses are not only fictional, but exemplify characters representing a time that has not yet come to pass. What I find interesting in these two cases, along with their usefulness in illustrating Lanigan's concept of the child as icon, is that they each are projections of a cultural world that is moving beyond active, multiple layers of intergenerational contact. It is a world saturated with information and communication technology (like ours, but, of course more so) and which also explicates the lives of Starship inhabitants as, essentially, separated from the modes of cultural transmission that are enabled through regular contact with multiple generations of family. In one case, a child is mysteriously born to an unattached female officer. In the other, an early adolescent male is learning to adjust to the absence of his professional mother (the Starship's head physician), who has departed to her home planet for a new assignment.

Lanigan comments: "The *Star Trek* episode clearly agrees with Margaret Mead's characterization of a prefigurative culture. Such a culture has one rule: Adults learn from their children. In such a cultural situation, the new and unexpected is a normal expectation. Reality is defined as the future. To illustrate, Mead quotes the favorite slogan of the 1960s: 'The future is now!'"[24] If I have not as yet made this point clear, the episode to which Lanigan is referring initially aired in 1988—almost three decades ago. It aired during the last year of Ronald Reagan's second term of office, during a period of relative prosperity and middle-class affluence, and during a time of de-escalating rhetorical tension with the former Soviet Union. But it was also a time when patterns of social mobility were becoming synonymous with economic mobility, and that very same economic mobility was increasingly facilitated, especially among college educated workers, with geographic mobility. As such, upward mobility meant moving from one corporate office to another, from state to state, or at least from city to city. The two-career couple had increasingly become the norm for parents raising children, but they were also doing so at a geographic remove from intergenerational support systems.[25]

Three decades later, we are not on a starship exploring the heavens, but we have also very much continued in this pattern of family life—that is, if the young family is fortunate enough to have both parents gainfully employed appropriate to their level of education preparation. If anything, there is less time for the sort of intense, intimate, intergenerational contact that enables confident, mature growth to occur in the young person. As such, the world of both the child and the family has increasingly become more and more prefigurative. To quote Lanigan again: "The new and unexpected is a normal expectation. Reality is defined as the future (…). The Future is Now."[26]

David Lynch, the film director and screenwriter, who tends to think about families from the inside-out, once described a home as, uniquely, "a place where things can go wrong."[27] Given the atomization of 21st century family life, one can gain a sense of how isolated both family struggles and secrets have become. Lanigan is correct. The defining *moment* of the family, the abductive rule that establishes the existence of a family as being distinct from a house occupied by people (even people who care for one another) is captured in the child. As such, each child shares his or shadow with Laura Palmer, the tragic woman-child character motivating the mystery plotline of *Twin Peaks*—and it may be more true today than it was when the final episode of that series aired in 1991. "In their homes," Lynch maintains, "nobody's bothering them (…). People are well-placed for entering into a dream." And so, the lines that suggest the structure of American family life—that is, the structure that is given in the snapshot of "reality" that is, in truth, nothing more than an iconic "imaginary"—also suggest a dream landscape of the culture through which a family seeks its meaningful narrative. It is a dream that can turn dark in an instant, particularly when life is isolated and disconnected. As we have observed, especially through the economic collapses of the last decade and half, the so-called "American dream," like any hope of an economically-grounded, stable cultural existence, died hard because it was never just a "dream." It was a continuation of a set of threads, threads of language and ritual, weaving life histories, life lessons, and family memories into the Selfhood of the next generation. It was the continuation of a symbolic life, of *mythos* and *poiesis* and mystery that preoccupied our parents (and their parents before them)—which they could not quite explain to our satisfaction whenever we asked, and when they were able to find the time to attempt an answer.

These threads, these lines, these structures, these icons, these images never belonged to us. They do not belong to us now, but market capitalism along with the materialist foundations of the very rationality that isolates us from one another suggest that lines and boundaries can be indeed drawn and then secured with money and power. The *image* of the good life is not some sort of riddle to be solved by willing participants in a consumer-driven economy. Even by late adolescence, most young people have a very strong sense of what kind of place they want to call home and what kind things with which they would like to fill it up. Laura Palmer was not a victim of some aspect of poverty or addiction. She was the victim of a family secret, a secret hidden by snapshot images of normality, a normality suggested by all of the seemingly important structures positioned in their proper places. Like the two cases Lanigan explicates in his essay on *Star Trek*, her life is a fiction. She died on television, but the story remains as haunting now as it was over a quarter century ago. It is haunting because it reminds us of the dark side of unreflected iconography, particular when that dark side features a well-lit, stylishly appointed floor-plan of the good life.

NOTES

1. Richard L. Lanigan, "Star Trek: The Child and the Semiotic Phenomenology of Choosing a Family." In *Semiotics 1993*, ed. Robert S. Corrington and John Deely (New York: Peter Lang, 1996), 225.
2. Talcott Parsons and Robert F. Bales, *Family: Socialization and Interaction Process* (New York: Routledge, 1956).
3. See Parsons and Bales, *Family*.
4. Deborah F. Weinstein, "'Culture at Work: Family Therapy and the Culture Concept in Post-World War II America," *Journal of the History of the Behavioral Sciences* 40, no. 1 (Winter 2004): 23–46.
5. Weinstein, "Culture at Work," 26.
6. See Peter Titelman, *Differentiation of Self: Bowen Family Systems Theory Perspectives* (New York: Routledge, 2014). See also, Michael P. Nichols, *Family Therapy: Concepts and Methods*, 9th ed. (New York: Pearson, 2009).
7. See Robert B. Germain, "Self-concept and Self-esteem Reexamined," *Psychology in the Schools* 15, no. 3 (July 1978): 386–390.
8. See Nichols, *Family Therapy*.
9. Lanigan, "Star Trek," 226.
10. Charles S. Peirce, *The Collected Papers of Charles Sanders Peirce*, ed. Charles Hartshorne, Paul Weiss, and Arthur Burks. 8 Vols. (Cambridge, MA: Harvard University Press, 1931–35; 1958), 2.247.
11. Richard L. Lanigan, "Communicology and Culturology: Semiotic Phenomenological Method in Applied Small Group Research," *The Public Journal of Semiotics* 4, no. 2 (December, 2012): online @ pjos.org.

12. See Betty Farrell, *Family: The Making of an Idea, an Institution, and a Controversy in American Culture* (Boulder, CO: Westview Press, 1999).
13. Peirce, *Collected Papers*, 2.247.
14. See Ellen Herman, *The Romance of American Psychology: Political Culture in the Age of Experts* (Berkeley: University of California Press, 1996).
15. Michel Foucault, *Politics, Politics, Philosophy, Culture: Interviews and other Writings, 1977–1984*, ed. Lawrence D. Kritzman, trans. Alan Sheridan and others (New York: Routledge, 1988).
16. William Safire, "On Language: Up the Down Ladder," *New York Times*, November 15, 1998. Online @ nytimes.com.
17. See Elizabeth Carter and Monica McGoldrick, eds. *The Family Life Cycle: A Framework for Family Therapy* (New York: Gardner Press, 1980). See also Farrell, *Family*.
18. Lanigan, "Star Trek," 227.
19. Lanigan, "Star Trek," 227.
20. See Jonathan Crary, *24/7: Late Capitalism and the Ends of Sleep* (New York: Verso, 2014). See also Bernard Stiegler, *Taking Care of Youth and the Generations*, trans. Stephen Barker (Stanford, CA: Stanford University Press, 2010). See also Stiegler, *States of Shock: Stupidity and Knowledge in the 21st Century*, trans. Daniel Ross (New York: Polity Press, 2015).
21. Stiegler, *States of Shock*, 26
22. Stiegler, *States of Shock*, 26.
23. Stiegler, *States of Shock*, 26.
24. Lanigan, "Star Trek," 229.
25. See Jaber F. Gubrium and James A. Holstein, *Couples, Kids, and Family Life (Social Worlds from the Inside Out)* (New York: Oxford University Press, 2005).
26. Lanigan, "Star Trek," 228.
27. Lynch, in Chris Rodley, ed. *Lynch on Lynch* (New York: Faber and Faber, 1997), 10.

BIBLIOGRAPHY

Carter, Elizabeth, and Monica McGoldrick, eds. *The Family Life Cycle: A Framework for Family Therapy*. New York: Gardner Press, 1980.

Crary, Jonathan. *24/7: Late Capitalism and the Ends of Sleep*. New York: Verso, 2014.

Farrell, Betty. *Family: The Making of an Idea, an Institution, and a Controversy in American Culture*. Boulder, CO: Westview Press, 1999.

Foucault, Michel. *Politics, Politics, Philosophy, Culture: Interviews and other Writings, 1977–1984*. Edited by Lawrence D. Kritzman. Translated by Alan Sheridan and others. New York: Routledge, 1988.

Germain, Robert B. "Self-concept and Self-esteem Reexamined," *Psychology in the Schools*. 15, no. 3 (July 1978): 386–390.

Gubrium, Jaber F., and James A. Holstein, eds. *Couples, Kids, and Family Life (Social Worlds from the Inside Out)*. New York: Oxford University Press, 2005.

Herman, Ellen. *The Romance of American Psychology: Political Culture in the Age of Experts*. Berkeley: University of California Press, 1996.

Lanigan, Richard L. "Communicology and Culturology: Semiotic Phenomenological Method in Applied Small Group Research." *The Public Journal of Semiotics* 4, no. 2 (December 2012): online @ pjos.org.

Lanigan, Richard L. "Star Trek: The Child and the Semiotic Phenomenology of Choosing a Family." In *Semiotics 1993*, edited by Robert S. Corrington and John Deely. New York: Peter Lang, 1996.

Nichols, Michael P. *Family Therapy: Concepts and Methods*. 9th ed. New York: Pearson, 2009.

Parsons, Talcott, and Robert F. Bales. *Family: Socialization and Interaction Process*. New York: Routledge, 1956.

Peirce, Charles S. *The Collected Papers of Charles Sanders Peirce*. 8 vols. Edited by Charles Hartshorne, Paul Weiss, and Arthur Burks. Cambridge, MA: Harvard University Press, 1931–1935; 1958.

Rodley, Chris, ed. *Lynch on Lynch*. New York: Faber and Faber, 1997.

Safire, William. "On Language: Up the Down Ladder." *New York Times*, November 15, 1998. Online @ nytimes.com.

Stiegler, Bernard. *States of Shock: Stupidity and Knowledge in the 21st Century*. Translated by Daniel Ross. New York: Polity Press, 2015.

Stiegler, Bernard. *Taking Care of Youth and the Generations*. Translated by Stephen Barker. Stanford, CA: Stanford University Press, 2010.

Titelman, Peter. *Differentiation of Self: Bowen Family Systems Theory Perspectives*. New York: Routledge 2014.

Weinstein, Deborah F. "Culture at Work: Family Therapy and the Culture Concept in Post-World War II America." *Journal of the History of the Behavioral Sciences* 40, no. 1, (Winter 2004): 23–46.

SECTION TWO
Tropologic(s)

Tropologies

CHAPTER FIVE

Communicational Aspects in Experimental Phenomenological Studies on Cognition

Theory and Methodology

WILLIAM B. GOMES

Neo-Kantians of the Baden or Southwestern School, late 19th century, advanced the theory that knowledge differed by conceptual characteristics of their objects. They were concerned with the function of phenomenon (*capta*) and noumenon (*data*) to understand knowledge in its various forms and substances, as illustrated in the contrast between physics or biology with history or culture. This theoretical understanding led to two methodological views, being idiographic methods for the study of *capta* and nomothetic methods to the study of *data*. A century later, Richard Lanigan[1] in order to compare theory and methodology in the human sciences reaffirmed the difference, but reconfigured the relationship between objects and their conceptual characteristics. According to Lanigan, theory resides in the conjunction between an eidetic model (realization) and an empirical model (actualization). Thus, the eidetic model would be analytical (deduction, sufficiency) and critical (adduction, necessity); and the empirical model would be experimental (induction, actuality), and experiential (abduction, possibility). In turn, methodology would involve the combination and contrast between quantity (what is given) as the true condition method; and quality (what is taken) as a necessity and sufficient condition method.

Lanigan's epistemological view had anticipated what is now recognized in neuropsychology as first and third-person perspectives. The first-person brings back the experiential and subjective perception of a living experience, and the third-person allows standardized and shared observations for induced actions in predetermined situations. In the experimental phenomenological design, the experimenter him or herself lives both perspectives when he/she reverses the order of experience to the order of analysis, also being able to recognize the second-person perspective: that is the clear demarcation of a theory as consensual criteria of judgment. Thus, the experimental phenomenological methodology will attend the logic requirements of abduction (why experiential?), induction (why experimental?), deduction (why analytical?), and adduction (why critical?) that could be characterized as a hermeneutic circle. My argument is that Lanigan's writings bring in a metatheory that is indeed an epistemological guide for scientific investigation in general.

The chapter is organized in two parts. First, I will discuss the epistemological tension between idiographic and nomothetic methods in the psychological research tradition, taking cases from my university career in the field of psychology. I will argue that the two epistemologies may be applied to the same ontological object, depending on its nature and proprieties. Second, I will demonstrate how a progressive and systematic reversibility between *data* (what is given) and *capta* (what is taken) could offer a privileged position to look at the same object in different perspectives.

IDIOGRAPHIC AND NOMOTHETIC SCIENCES: THE CASE OF PSYCHOTHERAPEUTIC EFFECTIVENESS

In the 1960s, the field of psychology was dominated by an effervescent debate among its three major forces: behaviorism, psychoanalysis and humanism. I entered into this discussion with a humanistic background, which I had inherited from my psychology training in northeastern Brazil. I had favored Abraham Maslow's (1908–1970) opposition to all experimental psychology, meaning behaviorism; and to all concerns with human frailties, meaning psychoanalysis.

American humanistic psychology was described by Hilgard as a way to combine "a human significance of values which could conceivably have been studied by nomothetic methods, with holistic interest in personality change and psychotherapy according to unconventional methods, all largely idiographic."[2] The debate between the neo-Kantian methodological concepts of nomothetic (science for universal laws) and idiographic (science for uniqueness understanding) was introduced in humanistic psychology by Gordon Allport (1897–1967). However, these discussions and concerns did not promote or articulate empirical methods for idiographic descriptions or analysis.

Carl Rogers[3] (1902–1987), one of the first psychologists to be concerned with psychotherapeutic effectiveness using empirical methods, faced a serious dilemma between experimental and experiential values. For him, any fresh knowledge in therapy would come from the inner, total, organismic experience of therapists and clients, even that partially and imperfectly communicable. He was not against the rules of science, which he recognized to have contributed enormously to society and humanity, but science for him had an ethical implication, which could transform everything into an object, and it could lead to manipulation. For him, science ultimately would be controlled by the subjectivity of a person for good or for evil. Even so, he kept his optimism, envisioning that the conflict between experientialists and experimentalists would tend to disappear.

I had the opportunity to grasp the spirit of humanistic psychology from different perspectives. With Rogers, I lived an intense experiential workshop, a true immersion in a non-directive community for 15 days, exercising my authentic and empathic way of being.[4] With Barrett-Lennard, a former student of Rogers and mentor of my master's thesis,[5] I learned the psychometric dimension of humanistic psychology, applying his Relationship Inventory (BRLI) to family systems. The aim was to measure different aspects of family communicational styles, based on members' perception of empathy, regard, unconditional regard, and congruence. With Eugene Gendlin, a former student of Rogers who led him to existential phenomenology, I had a long interview about the phenomenological aspects of his experiential psychotherapy. In fact, my doctoral dissertation, under the direction of Richard Lanigan and Emil Spees, investigated Gendlin's theory and application of focusing; a therapeutic technique presented and justified as an applied version of the phenomenological epoché.[6]

In my studies and reflections, I struggled between the nomothetic research of Barrett-Lennard, the existential concerns of Gendlin, and the idiographic promises of Rogers. Rogers understood that a suggestive way to present the psychotherapeutic process could be as "a naturalist's observational, descriptive approach (...) and to draw forth those low-level inferences which seem most native to the material itself."[7] The psychotherapeutic process was described into seven phases and it could be followed taking as reference the changes in client's speech.[8] The phase development would not necessarily be gradual. The client, as Rogers would rather say, could start in any degree, and not necessarily reach the last stage. Therefore, the therapeutic effectiveness would be relative to the initial phase and treatment logical time. The sequence would be as follows: (1) the language is laconic as if refusing to communicate; (2) it addresses to externalities as if the personal problems belonging to others, (3) it becomes gradually relaxed and comes loaded with symbolic expressions, (4) it voices freely and fluently on feelings about Self; (5) it expresses and experiences actual feelings, referring to the present moment; (6) it assumes first person voice and the Self as Other tends to disappear; and (7) it refers to the immediate experience as fresh and new, rich in details and deep in reflections. However, the validation of the sentences that sustain these enunciations was based on a scale that could be confronted with statements taken from psychotherapy recordings. This comparison could estimate what stage was the psychotherapeutic process.[9]

Rogers' theoretical systematization, based on empirical evidences as showed mainly by psychometric measurements, was a research proposal in the 1950s.[10] However, his perplexities and questions seem to be how to do justice to the unique and reserved moment of the therapeutic encounter with its manifold facets: (1) the unveiling of the patient's inner life, (2) the capturing of the therapist's inner feelings about one's real insertion in that therapeutic encounter, and (3) the factuality of the communicational relation between therapist and client, as a verbal and corporal expression. In epistemological terms, he could count on materials and methods recognized for analysis in third-person perspective. Nevertheless, he was concerned with how to deal with the mutual factuality that is lived by the therapist and patient. The issue was about first-person perspective and the question was how to transform this communicational experience into recognized information.

In the history of humanistic psychology, Adrian Van Kaam (1920–2007) proposed a method that privileges the first-person perspective, in his phenomenological analysis for the experience of really feeling understood.[11] Later, the method was refined and widespread in the field of psychology by Amedeo Giorgi, representing the phenomenological psychology school of Duquesne University.[12] The approach was enriched with a semiotic phenomenological orientation, led by Tom Pace and Richard Lanigan, at Southern Illinois University—Carbondale, mostly applied to the study of communication. If the phenomenological tradition suggested a model of organizing the most varied materials for systematic reflection, the semiotic phenomenological tradition added the objective science of language as a structuring to the various manifestations of human perception and expression. With language, the human sciences were definitely rescuing their positive and real structure, which was already discovered and used by anthropologists and linguists.

This new model for empirical research went beyond the humanistic psychology, covering social and health sciences, and becoming known as qualitative research. Such advances resolved important epistemological issues about how to deal with human discourse in all its different forms, either in the objectivity of observation and in the tacit subjectivity of interpretation. However, the human cognitive processes as a combination of bodily sensory perception and rational logistic intellect should be considered by an epistemology able to deal with the interlaced levels of ontology. Ontological levels are always interconnected, even if addressed in their respective autonomies, which feature different scientific strata and diversity of expertise in areas of the same science. With elegance, Wiley[13] described these interconnected levels in two parts: (1) physical or not semiotic (physicochemical, biological), and (2) symbolic or semiotic (interactional, social organizational, cultural). Interestingly, human consciousness or self occupied the intersection space between these two great levels. Certainly, Lanigan would denominate this intersection as "the modern conjunction of the human intension (phenomenology) and human extension (semiotics)" that is "the human comportment and cultural behavior that we call communication."[14]

The terms nomothetic and idiographic are related to the discussion of Wilhelm Windelband (1848–1915) in regards to the mislead distinction between natural and human science. For him, the problem was not content, but method: "the same subjects can be the object of both a nomothetic and an idiographic investigation."[15] In the midst of the controversy was the new science of psychology, whose hope was to renew approaches for the humanities. Yet, psychological research was advancing by using the same procedures of natural sciences.

In fact, van Kaam conceived an anthropological psychology as "an open, personal, progressive integration of historical and contemporary psychological knowledge."[16] It would be a psychological science sufficiently foundational to integrate objectively, on a scientific basis, all validated findings and insights of the various theories and methods, covering both the subjective experiential and the objective experimental.

In that sense, Lanigan in his semiotic phenomenological metatheory offers a methodology in which *data* and *capta* are independent, yet juxtaposed. His insight into the enterprise of research in the human sciences was clearly stated in two levels: (1) what is theory, and (2) what is methodology. Theory is "the complete normative criteria for choosing or selecting contexts of judgment, a set of process rules."[17] It encompasses an eidetic dimension (realization model), by being analytical (deduction) and critical (adduction), and an empirical dimension (actualization model) by being experimental (inductive) and experiential (abductive). In turn, methodology expresses the complete normative context for making choices; a system for the constitution or production of results. Methodology entails both criteria: quantitative as a truth condition method; and qualitative as a necessary and sufficient condition method.

Semiotic phenomenology conception requires two metatheoretical assumptions.[18] The first is eidetic, i.e., an ideational or conceptual process is tested reflexively by building an empirical theory. The second is empirical, i.e., a performance or action is tested reflexively by building an eidetic theory. These assumptions combine the two common approaches to research, i.e., research-then-theory, and theory-then-research. In the research-then-theory approach, the facts reveal the object under investigation and are described as probabilistic generalizations or as exemplary types. In contrast, in the theory-then-research approach the postulates indicate which facts are relevant to research. In the combinatorial approach, the two approaches are united by looking at where the phenomenon is located and then proceed to the qualifying or quantifying.

This movement between qualifying and quantifying arose naturally in a series of studies that my research students and I conducted about "what is like to be in psychotherapy."[19] We started our empirical investigation interviewing ten psychology students that were, at that moment, attending psychotherapy. Among the mentioned psychotherapeutic treatments were psychodynamic psychotherapy, transactional analysis, bioenergetic analysis, and psychodrama. For this investigation, our thesis was that the quality of a psychological treatment is critically perceived and could be critically expressed in discourse. The interview focused on: (1) feelings and thoughts experiencing during therapy, (2) relationship with the therapists, and (3) expecting outcome.

We applied the systematic and systemic to the three semiotic phenomenological steps (description, reduction and interpretation). The description was constituted by native experiential expression in speech; and reduction was demarcated by analytical specification of relational (both/and function) and correlational (either/or function) speech hierarchies. This hierarchical ramification was indicated by the semiotic system (paradigmatic) and process (syntagmatic). Our phenomenological interpretation understood that: (1) psychotherapy was perceived as a positive experience, (2) patient's native language was fresh and personal, apart from theoretical language or justification, (3) psychotherapeutic contrasts between treatments were negligible, and (4) patients were aware to the process of change and impact of specific techniques.

Two years later,[20] we invited the same ten students to an interview about their psychological well-being and the perceived benefits of their psychological treatment. Eight of them attended our invitation. We recorded the interviews and repeated the same analytical procedure. The descriptions came out as a continuation of the first study. Thus, when the patient did not believe in the treatment efficiency, it ended dissatisfied; when the treatment was sought by intellectual curiosity, it ended up with a feeling of superficiality; when the treatment was moving loosely with apparent changes not discernible, it ended up with clear and positive changes; and when treatment seemed extraordinarily liberating of personal madness, it was not able to reverse madness to creative thought. Thus, the phenomenological first-person perspective leads to the rudeness of experience with its joys and disappointments, and raises the nuances of the process. However, the magnitude of the therapeutic effects was missing.

The third and final part of our research was characterized by a radical suspension of what we had learned so far. We critically interpreted the contradictory findings as not associated to treatment, but to students' intellectual interests about psychotherapy (abductive reasoning). So we decided to interview individuals who were not students of psychology or related fields about their retrospective experience in psychological treatments.[21] We adduced more than 20 interviews. At the same time, we asked 133 persons to respond to a widely used questionnaire in order to measure psychotherapy effectiveness (adductive reasoning). In this study we compared context of choice (interview) and choice of context (questionnaire), qualitative and quantitative inquiry, and the relation between *capta* (first person) and *data* (third person). The obtained results were those already expected. The greater number of participants increased information and redundancy, although communication and content remained the same. The statistical factor analysis brought back the numerical contextual specification as descriptive form, into four distinct magnitudes: (1) psychotherapy as a positive experience (15.9% of variance); (2) psychotherapy as a clarification of feelings and emotions (6.2% of variance); (3) psychotherapy as a place where one's wondering about the relationship between treatment and changes (5.15% of variance); and (4) psychotherapy as a vivid contact with present experience (bodily movements, gestures, silences, neutrality, lived changes, 4.5% of variance). After that, we correlated the four factors with variables usually compared in psychotherapeutic research: time in treatment, therapist training, weekly number of sessions, therapist's sex, and patient's sex. We found only a low negative correlation between time and satisfaction that means longer treatments less satisfaction ($r = -0.20$, $p < 0.01$).

The literature uses to argument that quantitative and qualitative methods complement each other.[22] However, how does this complementation work? We know that in the qualitative method, the choice is a combinatorial association among other possible choices, and that in the quantitative method the choice is an overlap between parties. In the studies mentioned above, the quantitative indicators pointed to the magnitude of emotional intensity and treatment effectiveness. In contrast, the qualitative descriptors contextualize aspects of emotions, defined contradictions of experience as how to convert experiential meaning to habitual speech, and delimited the magnitude of change, meaning that a great experiential satisfaction may refer to a small behavioral change. The point is that we could approach the same object (the retrospective experience of being in psychotherapy) both in an idiographic and nomothetic way, by describing exemplary types, and indicating probabilistic generalizations.

In the next session, we would like to explore a step forward (abductive reasoning): designing a phenomenological experiment where the same object could be accessed throughout different instruments and methodological criteria (adductive reasoning). The object has to be recognized along with its proper merits, as Lanigan recommends:

> Experimentation requires actuality as a standard of judgment. Actuality is the empirical presence/absence of a phenomenon, which validates the presence/absence of another phenomena. An experiment requires actuality as a function of probability as a standard of judgment, i. e., the empirical claim that the comparison holds true for this and subsequent cases.[23]

Therefore, the next session examines the same object with different methods and materials, to understand the internal/manifest conversation, as a reflexive manifestation.

INFORMATION AND COMMUNICATION INTERPLAY ON INTERNAL/MANIFEST CONVERSATION

In the mid-1990s, Norbert Wiley presented an attractive and controversial humanistic theory on the semiotic self.[24] He defined self as simply a human being, person, individual or agent, and semiotics as the human reflexive and dialogical capability of meaning. He explains this semiotic reflexive and dialogical activity by a concept of selfhood combining the theories of Peirce and Mead. Then, the conversation between I 'present' and ME 'past' (according to Peirce) together with the conversation between I 'present' and YOU 'future' (according to Mead) composed the Peirce-Mead triadic model of reflexive dialogue, where "I" talk with a "YOU" about a "ME." The interest here was to explore empirical ways to follow this reflexive process when audibly externalized. Wiley suggested some possibilities for research on internal/manifest conversation as an absent-minded person talking aloud, a sleep talking, or a children talking aloud. The interest here is to show how the practice of imaginary variations helped to create situations for the study of internal conversation. Therefore, the focus will be on the designs used in experimental phenomenology, including the perspective of first and third-person exemplified in two experiments.

First Experiment

Our first experiment is about internal conversation.[25] In this study, the experimental task was to perform the *Advanced Progressive Matrices*—the Raven test[26] by thinking aloud (inductive reasoning). Participants were 18 college students, aged between 19 and 34 years. All internal/manifest conversations were recorded and transcribed. Data was analyzed (deductive reasoning), following the three reflexive steps of description (researcher's close understanding), reduction (researcher's thematic selective specification) and interpretation (researcher's critical commentaries and appreciation).

Phenomenological description revealed a structure of internal/manifest conversation organized in three patterns: (1) visual description, in which they realized the missing part of the matrices (pictures) and how it could be completed by the suggested possible parts; (2) logical reasoning, in which they contrasted and compared parts that could be included or not; and (3) dialogue appreciation, in which they talk with themselves about the task, basically in linguistic forms. The linguistic forms were: (1) exclamation; (2) imperative; (3) question; (4) question-answer; (5) statement-question; (6) statement-negative; (7) question-statement; (8) question-negative. Example:

[The researcher leaves the room]. *Then, here we have (...) we have (...) hummm (...). Here we have a circle* [visual description]. *This flower, in fact, it stands far away of the circle* [logical reasoning]. *(...). What this wants to say? It wants to say that (...). Does it want to say what?* [dialogue appreciation] *Humm [cough] Humm (...).*

Phenomenological reduction specified for analysis the relation between context and reflexivity. Context was considered essential because it alone can establish the agreement-disagreement, statement-supplement, and question-answer relations that constitute a communicative dialogical relationship. The dialogues were characterized by two statement forms: (1) informational, when curtailing uncertainty, mainly by the discovery of a unnoted facet in the picture, and not requiring an active or immediate response; (2) communicational, when certainty was clear, in general, followed by immediate response of agreeing or changing the flow of thinking. By its turn, reflexivity took form and substance in the manifold and unique combinatory relations between time and space. In the internal/manifest conversation, time constitutes the flow of reflexivity as manifested in the semiotic dialogue of an 'I' (present) which talks to a 'You' (future), about a 'Me' (past). Space was the field where diachronic/monochromic and synchronic/polychromic interchanges made possible the continuous renovation in phenomenological horizons, that is the reversion between consciousness (if, what do I do?) and behavior (then, I do that.). Example:

> *Well. This one plus this one is equal to this. This one plus this one (...) equal to this. This one (...) plus this (...) It's gonna be (...) something with black in the middle. It would be five* [if, what do I do]. *Number five* [then, I do that]. *(...) But (...) No, stay calm! This one plus this one, equal to this. This one plus this one, equal to this if,* [what do I do]. *So, it would be just the number six* [then, I do that]. *(12M)*

Phenomenological interpretation highlighted the interplay between the inner dialogue and the following personal deliberation. This deliberation was reached by two combinatory simultaneous interchanges: Informational and communicational messages and time and space contraposition. The messages decode a type of choice, which define the nature of a context, if digital (context of choice) or analogical (choice of context). Time makes the flow of consciousness in a conversation (I-present talks to you-future, about me-past), and space makes possible contrasting views by decoding a choice as an action (changes in the position of you-future, revisions of me-past, and clarification of I-present). This conjunction between rules for decoding messages and rules for variation of voices support Wiley's semiotic triad of selfhood, because it explains the difficulties in decoding messages and keeping the focus to solve the problem.

Second Experiment

Our second experiment was a critical analysis of the first experiment, looking at alternative situations (adductive reasoning) to induce the occurrence of the same phenomenon in a different circumstance.[27] In fact, the performance of solving tasks by thinking aloud favors the alternation between reflective and ruminative thoughts, being reasoning that leads to outcomes, and reasoning that revolves around itself. The novelty was to introduce a psychometric measure, the Reflection and Rumination Questionnaire—RRQ.[28] The aim was to monitor the impact of reflection and rumination to the number of correct answers in the Raven test. In that experiment, we were interested in having both third and first-person perspectives. For third-person perspective, we used two measures: RRQ and Raven test. The RRQ is a 28 items Likert scale, with a good reliability score ($\alpha = 87$), where 14 sentences indicate reflection ("*I love to analyze why I do things*") and 14 sentences indicate rumination ("*My attention is frequently focused on aspects of myself I wish I would stop thinking about*"). The Raven test was used as a medium for the performance of thinking aloud. For the first-person perspective, we interviewed the participants after the application of psychometric measures. The short interview protocol was as following:

> *You initially responded to a questionnaire about ways you may usually think the routine of your life. Following, you completed a reasoning test by talking aloud to yourself. Now, I would like to ask you to describe what it was like for you to answer a psychological test talking aloud. Have you ever paid attention to these issues concerning talking aloud to yourself before? Do you usually talk like this in any specific situation in daily life? What about the questionnaire, did it made any sense for you? Would you like to say something to us about this research experience, any impression, suggestions?*

The experiment was conducted in two parts. For the first part, 23 college students, between the ages of 17–28 years, answered the RRQ and Raven test. For the second part (analytical novelty), we selected a small numbers of the same participants based in the following criteria: (1) longest time spent in Raven test (RT), (2) shortest time spent in RT, (3) largest number of emitted words doing RT, (4) smallest number of emitted words doing RT, (5) higher score in RT, (6) lower score in RT, (7) higher reflection score with lower rumination score in RRQ, and (8) higher rumination score with lower reflection score in RRQ. With this inclusion rule, we were preparing our analysis to reverse *data* into *capta*. In applying the Raven test, we proceeded in the same way as in the first experiment, recording and transcribing the internal/manifest conversation, but with a modifying procedure. We demarcated 10 minutes, between 5 and 15 minutes of application time, for detailed analysis of this selected small numbers of participants.

The analysis followed the order of the three semiotic phenomenological reflections, with some variations. The third and first-person perspectives received independent descriptions and reductions, converging to an integrated semiotic phenomenological interpretation at the end, which synthesizes our understanding of the experiment as a whole.

Third-person perspective

The *Phenomenological description* was furnished using a classificatory criterion, which included the conversational object, type of sentence, and statement form (Table 1). Figures 1 and 2 bring the internal/manifest conversation flow. The graphics contrast the number of correct answers provided to the Raven test (indicator of performance) and number of words (indicator of verbalizations). Redundancy between criteria occurred (RT = longest time spent and largest number of words) while the remaining seven cases were used for comparison.

As shown in Figures 1 and 2, each case indicates how intention is directed toward self or task in the internal/manifest conversation. Besides, it suggests greater or lesser incidence of reflection/rumination in conversation to the self. The correlation between rumination and performance was obviously negative (−0.239, $p < 001$). Statements concerning the task (verbal descriptions and logical reasoning related to the test) predominated among those who performed better on the test (participants 02, 11, 12, 15). The interesting point is that shift between focus to the self (*I'm not getting it*) or to environment (*what a cold room!*) occurred freely in the most unexpected moments.

Table 5.1: Classificatory Criteria of Statements for the Seven Cases Selected from the Study

Object	Type of sentence	Graphical Legend	Instance
Personal	Exclamation	+4	Communicative
	Personal questions	+3	Communicative
	Personal logical reasoning	+2	Informational
	Personal description	+1	Informational
Task	Description of the test	−1	Informational
	Test logical reasoning	−2	Informational
	Question concerning the test	−3	Communicative
	Imperatives	−4	Communicative

Source: Author

Phenomenological reduction selected for analysis the bi-dimensional structure of reflective action that is when conversation direct attention to the task or to oneself. This fluctuation between self and task was interpreted as analogous to the bi-dimensional sphere of pre-reflexivity and reflexivity. Husserl[29] defined the flow of consciousness in the bi-dimensionality of taking oneself as object (noetic analysis) and taking one's own experience as object (noematic analysis). The graphical dialogue, not only specified informational (either/or) and communicational (both/and) manifestations,[30] but also indicated the direction of intention. That is, the contents of internal/manifest conversation as self-consciousness or simply the semiotic self.[31]

Figure 5.1: Verbalizations of the Participants with High Scores on Raven Test

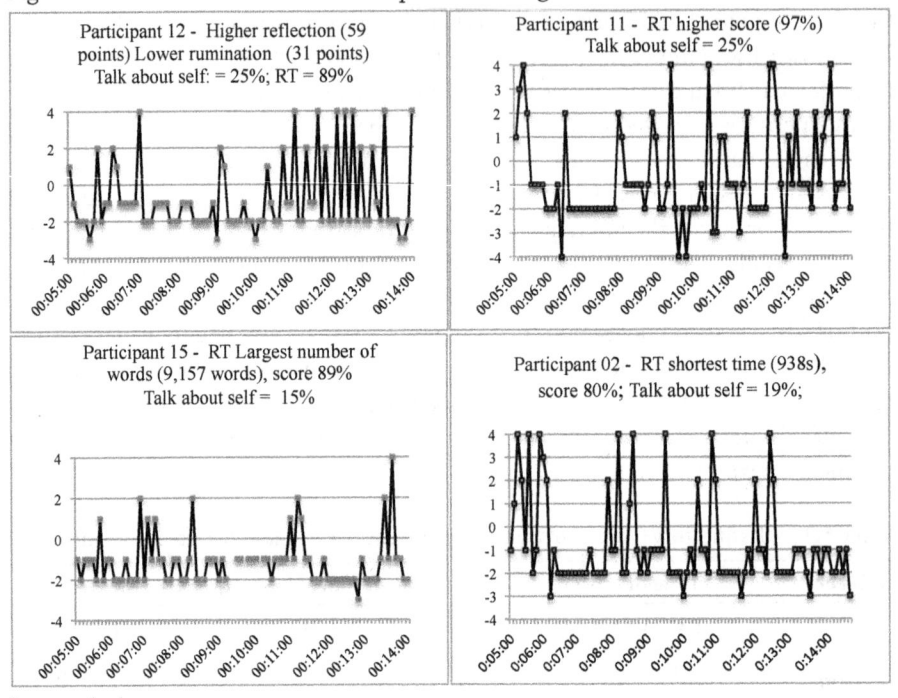

Source : Author

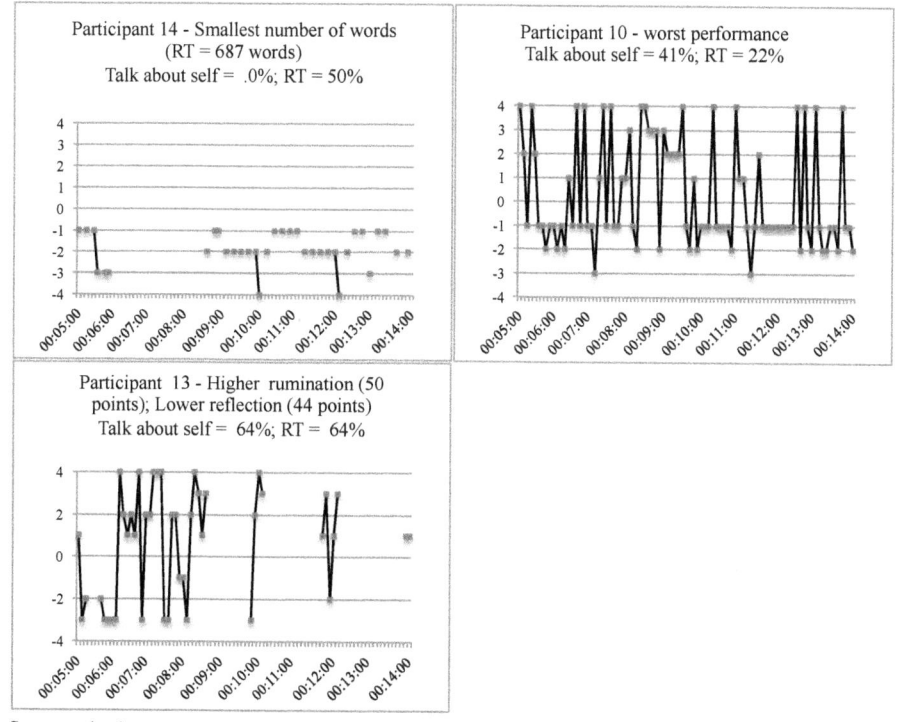

Figure 5.2: Verbalizations of the Participants with Low Scores on the Raven Test

[Figure showing three panels of verbalization plots for Participants 14, 10, and 13]

Participant 14 - Smallest number of words (RT = 687 words)
Talk about self = .0%; RT = 50%

Participant 10 - worst performance
Talk about self = 41%; RT = 22%

Participant 13 - Higher rumination (50 points); Lower reflection (44 points)
Talk about self = 64%; RT = 64%

Source : Author

Performance of participants in the measures compared: **P10** – Worst performance in talking about self (41%), 22% in the Raven test; **P13** – Higher rumination (50 points), Lower reflection (44 points), 64% of talking about self, score of 64% in the Raven test; **P14** – Smallest number of words (687), score of 50% in the Raven test, no talking about self.

First-person perspective

The *phenomenological description* for the first-person perspective was based on the interview's transcripts. Although participants referred to the estrangement of taking the Raven test thinking aloud, they evaluated the experience as interesting and instructive, leading to reflect on their own internal conversation. Following, the first person perspective about internal/manifest conversation is described in nine assertions. (1) It organizes thought to solve problems here and now. (2) It reassesses one's daily events. (3) It helps to proceed with logical reasoning when solving specific tasks. (4) It works as a rehearsal for situations when external dialogue is imminent. (5) It points out feelings and emotional aspects. (6) It is part of private life. (7) It is different from thought because it expresses things "beyond" thought. (8)

It can be an unwanted intrusion to be avoided because it may disrupt the solution of problems in everyday life. (9) When verbalized, inner speech goes through some kind of filter, where you do not always say what you actually think.

The *phenomenological reduction* redefined the nine descriptive assertions into three basic structures.

> Structure 1—Inner speech exceeds the system of signs used in external language, goes beyond thinking, and is preferentially expressed in privacy.
> Structure 2—Inner speech is experienced as a cognitive resource, organizing thought, both concrete and objective issues as to solve logical-mathematical problems for instance, and understanding and interpreting one's organismic felt meaning (naming feelings).
> Structure 3—Inner speech differs depending on temporal contexts, being an adjuvant tool in going back to issues from the past (as it involves reflections concerning memories), taking the immediate present (as it follows the resolution of problems that are presented to the individual in real time), or considering the future (as it reconciles ideas and the planning of events that will happen).

Semiotic phenomenological interpretation. The internal/manifest conversation was understood as a factual demonstration of an incisive reversible movement between perception and expression, making visible the progressive transition from conscious experience to experience of consciousness. The experiment was able to present the immediate, rich and rapid flow of thought with full semiotic freedom and its structural limits. By structural limits we mean the psychobiological, social, and cultural conjunction associated with individual cognitive and emotive styles. The boundaries of internal/manifest conversation arose with a bodily sense of what is seen and felt in, and what seems apparent but could take form and meaning.

This phenomenological experiment provided an overview of the various dimensions of internal conversation, whether related to content (internal or external), time (past, present and future), context (verbalize to other people or alone), and variations of evaluative character (whether it hinders or helps the individual). It provides a vivid demonstration of the Quadrilateral Discourse Model of Même et L'Autre.[32] The quadrilateral is constituted by combinations of Self (I-present, part) and Same (Me-past, substance) in relation to Other (You-future, whole) and Different (Me-attribute, different). Its dynamic is conversational where discourse and action are carried out from someone (I-present) to someone (You-future). The discourse is about Me (same/different) and takes the semiotic power to personal deliberations (presence/absence). The Self (I-present) is the one that speaks the different voices (reflexivity, rumination) and has the potential power to confront social structures, as synthesized by Bhaskar: "the causal power of social forms is mediated through social agency,"[33] which suggests the relevance of studying internal conversation as agential reflexivity.

The distinction between third and first person perspectives is able to demonstrate the manifestation of the phenomenon in its objectivity, within the limits of the internal/manifest conversation. This distinction is pointed out in our phenomenological reduction. The first-person perspective brought the particular experience of this crucial cognitive function that accompanies our day-to-day, clarifies our thoughts, our action plans, and assesses what we were able to accomplish. It highlights an inclusive relation among assertions recollected in various interviews. In contrast, the third-person perspective defined exclusive profiles that could describe different combinations for operational relations between reflexivity and rumination, with varying degrees of success in achieving results.

In this experiment, we reverted *data* into *capta* moving from experiencer to experienced, and from experienced to experiencer using different materials and procedures to enrich the experience in the objectivity, which was given as well as in the understanding that was taken. Thus, internal conversation may be defined as the expressivity of perception about things and oneself being part of the semiotic, reflective self, or simply the self. Internal conversation is a privileged means of recording communication that an individual has with him/herself and with others.

CONCLUSION

The concept of experimental phenomenology may be associated with the research tradition of Carl Stumpf (1848–1936), David Katz (1884–1953), James J. Gibson (1904–1939),[34] and has been a well-known approach among Italian experimental psychologists.[35] In the second half of the 20th century, Don Ihde,[36] a former professor at SIU-C, used the term for his creative and pedagogical introduction to phenomenological theory. Recently, experimental phenomenology is associated with the innovative research of Jean-Luc Petit, Shaun Gallagher, Jesper Brøsted Sørensen, and Daniel Schmicking.[37]

The objects approached in our experimental phenomenological laboratory could be situated in the border of experimental psychology and psychological intervention, specifically in the intersection between neuropsychology and behavior. This intercession gives prominence to the confluence of the great ontological spheres (physical or not semiotic/symbolic or semiotic). Therefore, human consciousness is constituted and defined as a holistic experience under the designation of embodiment. Its three core attributes are reflexivity (an identity manifested in the duality between perception and expression, or agent and action), reflectivity (an agent capable of exercising thought and judgment as action), and reversibility (the structural symmetrical possibility between agent and action, or perception and expression).[38] In that sense, internal conversation arises as a suggestive object for embodiment studies.

In the mid-20th century, the positivity of language resulting from studies on literature, linguistic and semiology emphasized the split between nomothetic and idiographic sciences. Phenomenology scholars have reviewed such a breach in order to combine both the perspectives of third and first-person.[39] The distinction between human sciences and humanities remains relevant for studies in aesthetics, rhetoric, law, hermeneutics, culture and history.

The possible connection or cautious balance between nomothetic and idiographic, or between natural sciences, and human and social sciences, is elegantly described by Lanigan[40] in his conjunctive distinction between: (1) realization and actualization models; and (2) synthetical and analytical methods. The experiments performed by our research group take into account the four phases of scientific work, namely, proposition of hypotheses, experimental design, quantitative and qualitative analysis, and critical experimental and conceptual follow up. The follow up includes performing new experiments with different methods and materials.[41] Lanigan, following Peirce, distinguished these four phases by reasoning modes, which called for abduction, induction, deduction, and adduction. Inductive and deductive reasoning composes the scientific method since its beginnings, respectively as quantitative and qualitative experimental judgment, and demonstrative inference. Abductive reasoning[42] is defined by Peirce as the provisional adoption of an explanatory hypothesis. Wirth[43] explains it as "the basis of interpretive code processing and of inventive code generation in the given context of understanding." In semiotic literature,[44] it is understood as a way that a good or bad choice is made to interpret data based on assumptions or hypotheses, which characterizes the hermeneutic circle. That reasoning is not necessarily explicit in the argument, but implicit in the interpretation. Lanigan defines abduction as experiential (possibility). I would add that it represents the phenomenological ethics in research since it should monitor the scientific work throughout its execution, capturing its surprises and favor its discoveries, mainly by free imagination. That is the road to formulate new hypotheses, create new materials and methods, and discharge disconcerting interpretations. Adduction is not a term defined in manuals of experimental design, but in theological and hermeneutics treatises.[45] Even so, I would say that adduction is a fundamental reasoning on sciences since it implies replication and theory testing or "adducing but few simple experiments" as would say Peirce,[46] which is a current practice in scientific laboratories.[47] That is the reason why Lanigan defines adduction as a necessity (critical). Adductive reasoning leads to certitude in science, building and criticizing knowledge through provisional truth. Therefore, an alleged phenomenon that I discovered should have existence in its own that we could call as phenomenological realism. In other words, it is a phenomenon in the world to be share by intersubjectivity (self-evident, apodictic, second-person perspective).[48] Finally, I would say that our experiments work with parts (quantitative) and attributes (qualitative) that are synthetically added into a whole or substance where provisional certainties are verified in a tense relation between both good and bad choices.

NOTES

1. Richard L. Lanigan, *Phenomenology of Communication: Merleau-Ponty's Thematics in Communicaology and Semiology* (Pittsburgh, PA: Duquesne University Press, 1988), 3–42; *The Human Science of Communicology* (Pittsburgh, PA: Duquesne University Press, 1992), 1–12, 197–236.
2. Ernest Hilgard, *Psychology in America: A Historical Survey* (San Diego: Harcourt Brace Javanovich, 1987), 790.
3. Carl R. Rogers, *On Becoming a Person* (Boston, MA: Houghton Mifflin, 1961), 199–224.
4. Rogers had visited Brazil in 1977, 1978, and 1983. On his first visit, the highlight was the large 15-day group meeting with 150 participants, held in a pleasant mountain farm in the state of Rio de Janeiro. See Eduardo P. Bandeira, *Carl Rogers on Brazil* (São Paulo: GRD Edições, 2012); and John Keith Wood, *Summer of Persons: A Logbook on the Person-Centered to Large Groups* (São Paulo: Via Lettera, 2013).
5. William B. Gomes, "The Communicational-Relational System in Two Forms of Family Group Composition" (master's thesis, Southern Illinois University, Carbondale, 1980).
6. William B. Gomes, "Experiential Psychotherapy and Semiotic Phenomenology: A Methodological Consideration of Eugene Gendlin's Theory and Application of Focusing" (PhD diss., Southern Illinois University, Carbondale, 1983).
7. Rogers, *On Becoming*, 125–159.
8. Rogers, *On Becoming*, 125–159.
9. Alan M. Walker, Richard A Rablen, and Carl R. Rogers, "Development of a Scale to Measure Process Changes in Psychotherapy," *Journal of Clinical Psychology* 16, no. 1 (1960): 79–85.
10. Rogers, *On Becoming*, 132–155
11. Adrian Van Kaam, "Phenomenological Analysis: Exemplified by a Study of the Experience of 'Really Feeling Understood,'" *Journal of Individual Psychology* 15 (1959): 66–72.
12. See the Series *"Duquesne Studies in Phenomenological Psychology"* published by Duquesne University Press, Pittsburgh, PA.
13. Norbert Wiley, *The Semiotic Self* (Chicago, IL: The University of Chicago Press, 1994), 59.
14. Richard L. Lanigan, "Capta versus Data: Method and Evidence in Communicology," *Human Studies* 17 (1994): 109.
15. Wilhelm Windelband, "Rectorial Address, Strasbourg, 1894" *History and Theory* (1980): 175.
16. Adrian van Kaam, *Existential Foundations of Psychology*, (New York: Lanham, 1966): xi–xii, 166.
17. Lanigan, *Human Science*, 211.
18. Lanigan, *Phenomenology*, 19.
19. William B. Gomes, Adriana C. Reck, and Christiane R. Ganzo, "A Experiência Retrospectiva de Estar em Psicoterapia: Um Estudo Empírico Fenomenológico" [The Experience of Being in Psychotherapy. An Empirical Phenomenological Study]. *Psicologia: Teoria e Pesquisa* 4, no. 3 (1988): 187–206.
20. William B. Gomes "A Experiência Retrospectiva de Estar em Psicoterapia: Um seguimento" [The Experience of Being in Psychotherapy: A Follow up], *Psicologia: Teoria e Pesquisa* 6 (1990): 87–105.

21. William B. Gomes, Adriana C. Reck, Alexandra A. Bianchi, and Christiane R. Ganzo, "O Uso de Descritores Qualitativos e Indicadores Quantitativos na Pesquisa em Psicoterapia" [Using Qualitative Describers and Quantitative Indicators in Psychotherapeutic Research], *Psicologia: Teoria e Pesquisa* 9 (1993): 415–434.
22. Kenneth W. Borland, "Qualitative and Quantitative Research: A Complementary Balance," *New Directions for Institutional Research* 112 (2001): 5–13; Charlene A. Yauch and Harold J. Steudel, "Complementary Use of Qualitative and Quantitative Cultural Assessment Methods," *Organizational Research Methods* 6 (2003): 465–481.
23. Lanigan, *Human Science*, 217.
24. Wiley, *Semiotic Self*, vii, 13–14; For the controversial debate see Vicent Colapietro, "Practice, Agency, & Sociality: An Orthogonal Reading of Classical Pragmatism," *International Journal for Dialogical Science* 1 (2006): 23–31, http://ijds.lemoyne.edu/index.html (accessed November 10, 2006).
25. Amanda C. DaSilveira, Mariane L. DeSouza, and William B. Gomes, "'Talking with My Buttons: The Ins and Outs on the Theoretical and Empirical Relations among Internal Conversation, Reflexivity, and the Self," *Estudos de Psicologia* 15 (2010): 223–231; Amanda C. DaSilveira and William B. Gomes, "Experiential Perspective of Inner Speech in a Problem-solving Context," *Paideia* 22 (2012): 43–52; Mariane L. DeSouza, Amanda C. DaSilveira and William B. Gomes, "Verbalized Inner Speech and the Expressiveness of Self-Consciousness," *Qualitative Research in Psychology* 5 (2008): 154–170.
26. John C. Raven, *Advanced Progressive Matrices, Sets I and II* (London: H. K. Lewis, 1962).
27. DaSilveira, DeSouza, and Gomes, "Experiential Perspective," 43–52.
28. Amanda C. DaSilveira, Mariane L. DeSouza, and William B. Gomes (2015) "Self-consciousness Concept and Assessment in Self-report Measures," *Frontiers in Psychology* 6 (2015): 930. Paul D. Trapnell and Jennifer D. Campbell, "Private Self-consciousness and the Five-Factor Model of Personality: Distinguishing Rumination from Reflection," *Journal of Personality Social Psychology* 76 (1999): 284–304. Cristian Zanon and Marco A. P. Teixeira, "Adaptação do Questionário de Ruminação e Reflexão (QRR) para Estudantes Universitários Brasileiros" [Adaptation of the Rumination and Reflection Questionnaire (RRQ) to Brazilian University Students], *Interação em Psicologia* 10 (2006): 75–82.
29. Edmund Husserl, *On the Phenomenology of the Consciousness of Internal Time (1893–1917)*, trans. John Barnett Brough (Dordrecht: Kluwer Academic Publishers, 1991), 85; Edmund Husserl, *Cartesian Meditations*, trans. Dorion Cairns (The Hague: Martinus Nijhoff Publishers, 1960): 36–37.
30. Lanigan, *Human Science*, 210–211.
31. Wiley, *Semiotic Self*, 1.
32. Lanigan, *Human Science*, 110; Richard L. Lanigan, "Human Embodiment: An Eidetic and Empirical Communicology of Phantom Limb," *Metodo: International Studies in Phenomenology and Philosophy*, 3 (2015): 279.
33. Roy Bhaskar, *The Possibility of Naturalism* (New York: Taylor & Francis e-Library, 2005), 28.
34. See Harry Heft, *Ecological Psychology in Context: James Gibson, Roger Barker, and the Legacy of William James* (Mahwah, NJ: Lawrence Erlbaum Associates Publishers, 2005).
35. See Liliana Albertazzi, ed., *Handbook of Experimental Phenomenology: Visual Perception of Shape, Space and Appearance* (New York: Wiley, 2013).
36. See, Don Ihde, *Experimental Phenomenology an Introduction* (New York: Paragon Book, 1979). See expanded new edition (Herndon, VA: Suny Press, 2012).

37. See Shaun Gallagher and Jesper Brøsted Sørensen "Experimenting with Phenomenology" *Consciousness and Cognition* 15 (2006): 119–134; Shaun Gallagher and Daniel Schmicking, eds., *Handbook of Phenomenology and Cognitive Science* (New York: Springer, 2010); Jean-Luc Petit, "Intention in Phenomenology and Neuroscience: Intentionalizing Kinesthesia as an Operator of Constitution," in *Naturalizing Intention in Action*, ed. Franck Grammont, Dorothée Legrand and Pierre Livet (Cambridge, MA: MIT Press, 2010): 269–292.
38. See Richard L. Lanigan, "Mind-Body Problem," in *Encyclopedia of Identity*, ed. Ronald L. Jackson II (Thousand Oaks, CA: Sage, 2010), 452.
39. An elucidative discussion about First, Second and Third Person Perspective is in Thomas Fuchs, "The Phenomenology and Development of Social Perspectives," *Phenomenology and the Cognitive Sciences* 12 (2013): 655–683.
40. Lanigan, *Human Science*, 207.
41. See Cassiano Terra Rodrigues, "The Method of Scientific Discovery in Peirce's Philosophy: Deduction, Induction, and Abduction." *Logica Universalis* 5, no. 1 (2011): 127–164.
42. Charles S. Peirce, *Collected Papers of Charles Sanders Peirce*, ed. Charles Harthorse, Paul Weiss (vols. 1–6), Arthur W. Burks (vols. 7–8) (Cambridge, MA: Harvard University Press). References are to the numbers of the volume and of the paragraph (1931–1958): 4.541
43. Uwe Wirth, "Abductive Reasoning in Peirce's and Davidson's Account of Interpretation." *Transactions of the Charles S. Peirce Society* 35, no. 1 (1999): 116.
44. Winfried Nöth, *Handbook of Semiotics* (Bloomington: Indiana University Press, 1990), 336–337.
45. See Avi Sion, "Adductive Logic in the Torah," in *Judaic Logic: A Formal Analysis of Biblical, Talmudic and Rabbinic Logic* (Geneva: Editions Slatkine, 1995), 23–35.
46. CP 6.567
47. See Keith E. Stanovich, *How to Think Straight about Psychology* (Boston, MA: Pearson, 2009), 105–166.
48. For example, Laura Galbusera and Lisa Fellin, "The Intersubjective Endeavor of Psychopathology Research: Methodological Reflections on a Second-person Perspective Approach," *Frontiers in Psychology* 5 (2014): 1150, doi: 10.3389/fpsyg.2014.01150.

BIBLIOGRAPHY

Albertazzi, Liliana, ed. *Handbook of Experimental Phenomenology: Visual Perception of Shape, Space and Appearance*. New York: Wiley, 2013.
Bandeira, Eduardo P. *Carl Rogers no Brasil* [Carl Rogers in Brazil]. São Paulo: GRD Edições, 2012.
Bhaskar, Roy. *The Possibility of Naturalism* (New York: Taylor & Francis e-Library, 2005).
Borland, Kenneth W. "Qualitative and Quantitative Research: A Complementary Balance." *New Directions for Institutional Research* 112 (2001): 5–13. doi:10.1002/ir.25.
Colapietro, Vicent. "Practice, Agency, & Sociality: An Orthogonal Reading of Classical Pragmatism." *International Journal for Dialogical Science* 1 (2006): 23–31. http://ijds.lemoyne.edu/index.html
DaSilveira, Amanda C., Mariane L. DeSouza, and William B. Gomes. "Self-consciousness Concept and Assessment in Self-report Measures." *Frontiers in Psychology* 6 (2015): 930. doi:10.3389/fpsyg.2015.00930.
DaSilveira, Amanda C., Mariane L. DeSouza, and William B. Gomes. "'Talking with my Buttons': The Ins and Outs on the Theoretical and Empirical Relations among Internal Conversation,

Reflexivity, and the Self." *Estudos de Psicologia* 15 (2010): 223–231. http://www.scielo.br/scielo.php?script=sci_abstract&pid=S0103-863X2012000100006&lng=en&nrm=iso&tlng=en

DaSilveira, Amanda C., and William B. Gomes. "Experiential Perspective of Inner Speech in a Problem-solving Context." *Paideia* 22 (2012): 43–52. http://www.scielo.br/pdf/paideia/v22n51/en_06.pdf

DeSouza, Mariane L, Amanda C. DaSilveira, and William B. Gomes. "Verbalized Inner Speech and the Expressiveness of Self-Consciousness." *Qualitative Research in Psychology* 5 (2008): 154–170. doi:10.1080/14780880701734511.

Fuchs, Thomas. "The Phenomenology and Development of Social Perspectives." *Phenomenology and the Cognitive Sciences* 12 (2013): 655–683. doi:10.1007/s11097-012-9267-x.

Galbusera, Laura, and Lisa Fellin. "The Intersubjective Endeavor of Psychopathology Research: Methodological Reflections on a Second-person Perspective Approach." *Frontiers in Psychology* 5 (2014): 1150. doi:10.3389/fpsyg.2014.01150.

Gallagher, Shaun, and Daniel Schmicking, eds. *Handbook of Phenomenology and Cognitive Science*. New York: Springer, 2010.

Gallagher, Shaun and Jesper Brøsted Sørensen. "Experimenting with Phenomenology." *Consciousness and Cognition* 15 (2006): 119–134. doi:10.1016/j.concog.2005.03.002.

Gomes, William B. "The Communicational-Relational System in Two Forms of Family Group Composition." Master's thesis, Southern Illinois University, Carbondale, 1980. Available from http://www.ufrgs.br/lafec/?page_id=14

Gomes, William B. "A Experiência Retrospectiva de Estar em Psicoterapia: Um Seguimento" [The Experience of Being in Psychotherapy: A Follow up]. *Psicologia: Teoria e Pesquisa*, 6 (1990): 87–105.

Gomes, William B. "Experiential Psychotherapy and Semiotic Phenomenology: A Methodological Consideration of Eugene Gendlin's Theory and Application of Focusing." PhD diss., Southern Illinois University—Carbondale, 1983. Available from http://www.ufrgs.br/museupsi/Intese.htm

Gomes, William B., Adriana C. Reck, Alexandra A. Bianchi, and Christiane R. Ganzo. "O Uso de Descritores Qualitativos e Indicadores Quantitativos na Pesquisa em Psicoterapia" [Using Qualitative Describers and Quantitative Indicators in Psychotherapeutic Research]. *Psicologia: Teoria e Pesquisa* 9 (1993): 415–434.

Gomes, William B., Adriana C. Reck and Christiane R. Ganzo. "A Experiência Retrospectiva de Estar em Psicoterapia: Um Estudo Empírico Fenomenológico" [The Experience of Being in Psychotherapy: An Empirical Phenomenological Study]. *Psicologia: Teoria e Pesquisa* 4, no. 3 (1988): 187–206.

Heft, Harry. *Ecological Psychology in Context: James Gibson, Roger Barker, and the Legacy of William James*. Mahwah, NJ: Lawrence Erlbaum Associates Publishers, 2005.

Hilgard, Ernest. *Psychology in America: A Historical Survey*. San Diego: Harcourt Brace Javanovich, 1987.

Husserl, Edmund. *Cartesian Meditations*. Translated by Dorion Cairns. The Hague: Martinus Nijhoff Publishers, 1960.

Husserl, Edmund. *On the Phenomenology of the Consciousness of Internal Time (1983–1917)*. Translated by John Barnett Brough. Dordrecht: Kluwer Academic Publishers, 1991.

Ihde, Don. *Experimental Phenomenology an Introduction*. New York: Paragon Book, 1979.

Lanigan, Richard L. "Capta versus Data: Method and Evidence in Communicology." *Human Studies* 17 (1994): 109–130.

Lanigan, Richard L. "Human Embodiment: An Eidetic and Empirical Communicology of Phantom Limb." *Metodo. International Studies in Phenomenology and Philosophy* 3 (2015): 257–284.

Lanigan, Richard L. *The Human Science of Communicology*. Pittsburgh, PA: Duquesne University Press, 1992.

Lanigan, Richard L. "Mind-Body Problem." In *Encyclopedia of Identity*, ed. Ronald L. Jackson II, vol. 1, 450–454. Thousand Oaks, CA: Sage Publications, 2010.

Lanigan, Richard L. *Phenomenology of Communication: Merleau-Ponty's Thematics in Communicaology and Semiology*. Pittsburgh, PA: Duquesne University Press, 1988.

Nöth, Winfried. *Handbook of Semiotics*. Bloomington: Indiana University Press, 1990.

Peirce, Charles S. *Collected Papers of Charles Sanders Peirce*. Edited by Charles Hartshorse and Paul Weiss (vols. 1–6), Arthur W. Burks (vols. 7–8). Cambridge, MA: Harvard University Press, 1931–1958.

Petit, Jean-Luc. "Intention in Phenomenology and Neuroscience: Intentionalizing Kinesthesia as an Operator of Constitution." In *Naturalizing Intention in Action*, ed. Franck Grammont, Dorothée Legrand, and Pierre Livet, 269–292. Cambridge, MA: MIT Press, 2010.

Raven, John C. *Advanced Progressive Matrices, Sets I and II*. London: H. K. Lewis, 1962.

Rodrigues, Cassiano Terra. "The Method of Scientific Discovery in Peirce's Philosophy: Deduction, Induction, and Abduction." *Logica Universalis* 5, no. 1 (2011): 127–164. doi:10.1007/s11787-011-0026-5.

Rogers, Carl. *On Becoming a Person*. Boston, MA: Houghton Mifflin, 1961.

Sion, Avi. *Judaic Logic: A Formal Analysis of Biblical, Talmudic and Rabbinic Logic*. Geneva: Editions Slatkine, 1995.

Stanovich, Keith E. *How to Think Straight about Psychology*. Boston, MA: Pearson, 2009.

Trapnell, Paul D., and Jennifer D. Campbell. "Private Self-consciousness and the Five-Factor Model of Personality: Distinguishing Rumination from Reflection." *Journal of Personality Social Psychology* 76 (1999): 284–304. doi:10.1037/0022–3514.76.2.284.

van Kaam, Adrian. *Existential Foundations of Psychology*. New York: Lanham, 1966, xi–xii, 166.

van Kaam, Adrian. "Phenomenological Analysis: Exemplified by a Study of the Experience of 'Really Feeling Understood.'" *Journal of Individual Psychology* 15 (1959): 66–72.

Walker, Alan M., Richard A. Rablen, and Carl R. Rogers. "Development of a Scale to Measure Process Changes in Psychothyerapy." *Journal of Clinical Psychology*, 16, no. 1 (1960): 79–85.

Wiley, Nobert. "Pragmatism and the Dialogical Self." *International Journal for Dialogical Science* 1 (2006): 5–21.

Wiley, Nobert. *The Semiotic Self*. Chicago, IL: The University of Chicago Press, 1994.

Windelband, Wilhelm. "Rectorial Address, Strasbourg, 1894." *History and Theory* 19, no. 2 (1980) 169–185. https://www2.southeastern.edu/Academics/Faculty/jbell/windelband.pdf

Wirth, Uwe. "Abductive Reasoning in Peirce's and Davidson's Account of Interpretation." *Transactions of the Charles S. Peirce Society* 35 (1999): 115–127.

Wood, John Keith. *Summer of Persons: A Logbook on the Person-Centered to Large Groups*. São Paulo: Via Lettera, 2013.

Yauch, Charlene A., and Harold J. Steudel. "Complementary Use of Qualitative and Quantitative Cultural Assessment Methods." *Organizational Research Methods* 6 (2003): 465–481. doi:10.1177/1094428103257362.

Zanon, Cristian, and Marco A. P. Teixeira. "Adaptação do Questionário de Ruminação e Reflexão (QRR) para Estudantes Universitários Brasileiros" [Adaptation of the rumination and reflection questionnaire (RRQ) to Brazilian university students]. *Interação em Psicologia* 10 (2006): 75–82. doi:10.5380/psi.v10i1.5771.

CHAPTER SIX

The Monstrosity of Adduction

IGOR E. KLYUKANOV

Scholars in communication still often assume as unproblematical knowledge that communication is a process. Isaac Catt calls this "The Message Mystique." He provides a short history of how the message reification occurred in a mainstream communications study conducted in the United States.[1] Many efforts have been made lately to overcome this mystique and suggest an alternative, more complex view of communication. Spearheading these efforts is communicology; a science that is grounded in consciousness and experience in its reflexive condition.[2]

In an embodied phenomenological experience, communication is irreducible to messages that contain meaning. Communication cannot be limited, as such; it is not only irreducible, it is limitless. When we talk about "the limits of communication," of what we are not, refuse to be, or are passable to,[3] it is important to remember that, no matter what mediums are used in this experience (including our very body), we can never capture meaning and turn it into a delimited message. Instead, "we probe, at best, the limits of our instruments."[4] The experience of communication is, first and foremost, always reaching towards and beyond its limits. In other words, "the limit of communication is precisely what gives rise to communication."[5] This nature of communication is best expressed by Charles S. Peirce who says that "you might as well pass a law that no man shall jump over the moon, it wouldn't forbid him to jump just as high as he possibly could."[6] Humans may never "jump over the moon," but they will never "stop trying to do so," which problematizes the idea that one cannot not communicate.

PARADOX

It is only through the "exposure to the limit", to use Jean-Luc Nancy's phrase, that we can become free.[7] This limit opens the subject to a shared experience with others. However, who those others may be, we may not know. Lee Thayer reminds us of Krishnamurti's words that the only real human freedom is freedom from the known, and "It is perhaps time that we ponder such paradoxes as this—as well as our unmitigated obsession with the means of communication."[8] Indeed, paradox, as something that challenges traditional logic, clearly seems to stretch our mind and must somehow be dealt with. Inded, it was to paradox that the 39th Annual Meeting of the Semiotic Society of America was dedicated (Seattle, WA, October 1–5, 2014). The theme of the meeting was formulated as follows: *Paradoxes of Life: Challenge—Determination—Resilience*. It was at that meeting that I presented a paper that forms the basis for the present chapter.[9]

Paradox is considered to be a part of the human condition, that is why we find paradox in so many proverbs and folk phrases, i.e., *common* expressions. Paradoxical statements seem to go against themselves in an infinitely circular manner. However, in a paradox, no choice needs to be made between two or more contradictions or opposing voices. Paradox includes and embraces seemingly irreconcilable ideas operating simultaneously. Unlike problems, a paradox is not solved; rather, it is resolved. If we look at the meanings of these two verbs—"to solve" and "to resolve"—we can note that the former suggests "dismissing, removing" something, while the latter—"loosening" something and "setting it free." The latter thus is more in line with the meaning of reconciling, which suggests "bringing something together." Therefore, in a paradox, two seemingly contradictory frames of reference are brought together based on some kind of *tertium*.

When the resolution of a seemingly self-contradictory statement occurs, it must be emphasized, within self-constructed frames of reference. When paradox is said to go against commonly held opinions or appearing contrary to received beliefs, it should be taken to mean *going away from, yet along with*, those beliefs; otherwise, it should be called an *anti*dox, not a "paradox." Here, our attention is clearly focused on Self. Perhaps that is why paradoxes are not scary phenomena. Often they are related to humor and wordplay. Aristotle, for example, said that "Good riddles are pleasing"[10] and Charles S. Peirce spoke favorably of jokes that make us wise. Both Aristotle and Peirce noted that paradox and riddles do not merely surprise and bewilder, but also teach us something. While Aristotle paid more attention to the riddle's impossible questions and the puzzling ways of speech, Peirce saw paradox as the necessary basis for the action of experience. What we learn from paradoxes explains why inconsistent ideas (i.e., those without practical value) generally disappear from circulation, while paradox as a self-contradictory statement continues to function in communication.

When we face paradox, a complex and recursive process takes place that begins with a suggestive and "extremely fallible insight" and results in a suggestion that "comes to us like a flash."[11] It's easy to identify this process through abduction. In fact, when Peirce speaks about abductive inference, he provides paradox as its paradigmatic case, using the example of Achilles and the tortoise. He writes: "[O]ur first premisses, the perceptual judgments, are to be regarded as an extreme case of abductive inferences from which they differ in being absolutely beyond criticism."[12] Abduction, says Peirce, "is not amenable to logical criticism" because such analysis "would be precisely analogous to that which the sophism of Achilles and the tortoise applies to the chase of the tortoise by Achilles, and it would fail to represent the real process for the same reason."[13] Abduction, therefore, is a way of understanding relations between disparate phenomena, such as in paradox, in light of which the phenomena would no longer appear surprising.

But, is paradox truly "an extreme case" of our perceptual judgments? Do we, with paradox, reach a limit beyond which there is nothing that is "amenable to logical criticism"? Is not there anything that is "better", so to speak, than "the best explanation"? Is communication only about working with what is given? Is communication only about being pleased with the result of figuring something out? What do we need to make of the nature of abduction that itself appears paradoxical? On the one hand, it "comes to us like a flash" and beyond any control, while, on the other hand, its "extremely fallible" insight is derived from phenomenological exploration and so must be a form of reasoning as a kind of controlled conduct. Let us not treat paradox as a law that forbids us to jump over the moon, as it were, and let us keep looking further.

ENTER THE MONSTER

The focus of abduction is on coming up with hypotheses, rather than testing or demonstrating them. Knowledge in all these cases is assumed to be unproblematic, i.e., treated as "presented experience" that must be hypothesized to the best explanation, tested, and demonstrated. Deduction, of course, is considered the culmination of the scientific method because it demonstrates the true knowledge. Yet, "one would do well to hear the root 'monstrum' in 'de-monstration.'"[14] Indeed, when we talk about experience as present, we should, above all, view it as pre-sent, or monstrated in "Monstration is the fact of showing that has already begun, but has not yet made sense."[15]

"Monster" is related not only to "monstrare" which means "to show", but also "monere" which means "to warn." Thus, "monstration" is also a divine omen, foreboding, and warning. In this respect, we can see monstrosity in "phenOMENology" as the study of anything that appears.

The word "monstrosity" in Greek is "teras", understood as "wonder", "marvel", and "divinity". A "teras" is a wondrous sign through which the divine shows itself in some manner. In other words, a "teras" is to be understood as the appearance of something (divine) in something else to which it does not properly or naturally belong (human). "Such showing must thus be understood in terms of excess, indeed in terms of eminent excess, of an access inhering in the very thing of which it is in excess. ... So understood, a monster is precisely the belonging together of a divine excess and the mundane thing through which such an excess shows itself."[16] And, it is this "belonging together", this connection, that we see, or fail to see.

The immediate presence of monstrosity takes us beyond paradox. No longer do we deal with what is humorous, playful, and pleasing to the mind. We now face something that is a divine omen and foreboding that can only be felt. It is something scary and truly anomalous, i.e., crossing boundaries and showing itself in unexpected ways, and thus difficult to classify. It is interesting to note that in China there is a special genre called *zhiguai* (Jer-Gwai), or anomaly accounts, which are tales written in literary Chinese that relate the appearance of category-busters such as pygmies and giants, fishes shaped like oxen, dragons, immortals, the dead returned to life, elusive jade maidens, and ferns that turn into worms. First recorded perhaps as early as the third century B.C.E., these narratives continued to be written until recent centuries, and even today the favorite bedtime reading of many allegedly secular (or "humanistic") Chinese intellectuals is said to be *Accounts of the Strange from the Studio of Leisure* (Liaozhai zhiyi); the 17th-century reworking of the genre by Pu Songling (1640–1715).[17] Because of the particular nature of paradox, and the universal nature of anomaly, the latter is a more serious beast. While paradox is more subject to being culturally determined, anomaly is truly inherent to the human condition. If we look at paradox, we usually find it in certain areas such as philosophy or literature. However, it can show itself anywhere—from biology to finance to music to geophysics to linguistics. One can even talk about Cosmic Anomaly (and not cosmic paradox).

Anomaly must be distinguished from both the abnormal and paranormal. Paranormal is something that is said to be beyond normal explanation yet still goes along with it, just as paralanguage is what accompanies language, i.e., goes along with it. As for abnormal, let's hear what Jacques Derrida says in one of his interviews: "A monster is always alive, let us not forget. Monsters are living beings. A monster is a species for which we do not have a name, *which does not mean that the species is abnormal*, namely the composition of hybridization of already known species. Simply, it shows itself [*elle se montre*]—that is what the word monster means—it shows itself in something that is not yet shown and that therefore looks like a hallucination, it strikes the eye, it frightens precisely because no anticipation had prepared one to identify this figure."[18] Such treatment of monstrosity goes all the way back to Aristotle who admitted that "even that which is contrary to Nature is in a certain sense according to Nature."[19] In other words, monstrosity appears as the sublime that "exceeds nature within nature."[20]

ADDUCTION

The immediate presence of monstrosity challenges our traditional logic and calls for a special kind of response. As mentioned earlier, we think of deduction as the culmination of the scientific method, which demonstrates the true knowledge (or "shows it completely" if we look at the meaning of the verb "to demonstrate") only if we fail to hear the root "monstrum" in "de-monstration." By the same token, abduction is "extremely fallible" because it's only a hypothesis: it can handle paradox, but not anomaly. We can never fully account for meaning, ever strange and elusive, and we can never show (or demonstrate) the truth completely, because monstrosity will monstrate (or show). We may like figuring out anything that is pleasing to the mind, such as humor and wordplay, but the joke seems to be on us. As Floyd Merrell puts it, "the world is an unfinished joke because we can't know the ultimate punch line."[21] Yet, we still can, and must, enjoy the joke without the ultimate punch line because as Kant begins the preface to the first edition of *Critique of Pure Reason*, "human reason has this peculiar fate in one species of its cognition that is burdened with questions which it cannot dismiss, since they are given to it as problems by the nature of reason itself, but which it also cannot answer, since they transcend every capacity of human reason."[22] Thus, we are not simply human—we are all too human.

In one of his lectures Peirce says: "the ground of deduction relates to symbols; that of induction to things; that of hypothesis to forms."[23] But, what would be the ground that relates to "the formless, mute, infant, and terrifying form of monstrosity"?[24] What would be the ground that is itself "the presentative condition", i.e., a "presentation [which] makes *re*presentation possible"?[25] It is known that in Peirce's discussions of the sign, "there are frequently shadows of possible fourth element," and that the concept of "ground," "may clearly be treated as a fourth sign constituent."[26] Similar to the shadow of a possible fourth element showing itself beyond the triadic framework in Peirce's discussions of the sign, there is something else present, or pre-sent, beyond abduction as supposedly "an extreme case" of our perceptual judgments. That is the ground of adduction.

As is well known, Peirce recognized three different types of reasoning. In a letter draft to Mario Calderoni he writes about abduction, deduction, and induction.[27] In a letter to Paul Carushe he writes: "Hypothesis, or, as I now term it, *retroduction.*"[28] Later on, he speaks about "Deduction, Induction, and *Retroduction*, or Hypothetic Inference."[29] Although Peirce used the term "adduction", he never seemed to clearly differentiate between hypothesis (read as abduction) and abduction (read as adduction).[30] In fact, adduction is different from deduction, induction, and abduction (or hypothetic inference, or retroduction).

Adduction, of course, "contrasts neatly with 'deduction.'"[31] Among other things, adduction does not conform to "the classical or Aristotelian/Scholastic theory of deductive entailment, sentential connectives, and monadic quantification."[32] Also, as Mark Blaug reminds us, "enormous confusion might be avoided if we could only enforce the linguistic usage of 'adduction' for nondemonstrative styles of reasoning vulgarly labeled 'induction.'" For example, it is common to encounter statements such as "all science is based on induction." It supposes that induction is the opposite of deduction and that these two are the only methods of logical thinking.[33] Blaug continues: "adduction is the nonlogical operation of leaping from the chaos that is the real world to a hunch or tentative conjecture."[34] This may sound similar to Peirce's definition of abduction, but here Richard Lanigan's careful, insightful, and sustained consideration of adduction is invaluable.[35] Lanigan shows how the "adductive claim is a sign relation by being universal and *a priori*."[36] He also shows where the main distinction lies between abduction and adduction: "the abductive logic means that in the same context (Rule), an internal comparison (Result) establishes the identity of two phenomena (Case); while the adductive logic means that in different contexts (Rule), an external comparison (Result) establishes the identity of two phenomena (Case)."[37] Adduction as a nondemonstrative style of reasoning which fits well with the nature of monstrosity: a monster is not really known through observation, rather, "the monster is known through its *effect*, its impact."[38] In other words, adduction does not demonstrate anything, but makes it possible. It calls on us so we can feel the effect of anomaly, and this is as close as one can get to the (limit of) phenomenology of experience.

AND THEN THERE WERE FOUR

Let us take the semiotic square as the framework for mapping out these four kinds of reasoning.

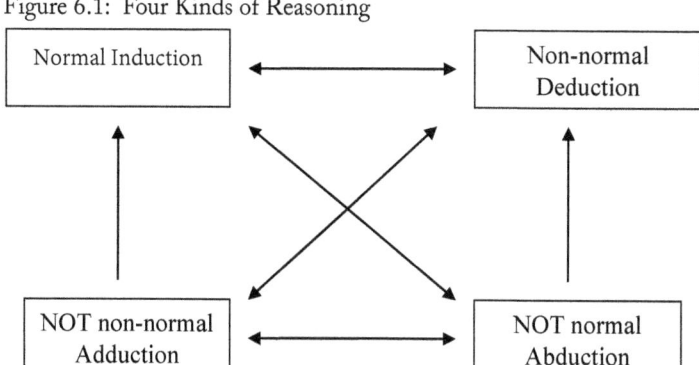

Figure 6.1: Four Kinds of Reasoning

```
┌─────────────────┐                    ┌─────────────────┐
│ Normal Induction│ ←───────────────→  │   Non-normal    │
│                 │                    │    Deduction    │
└─────────────────┘                    └─────────────────┘
         ↑            ↖       ↗              ↑
         │              ╲   ╱                │
         │               ╲ ╱                 │
         │               ╱ ╲                 │
         │              ╱   ╲                │
         ↓            ↙       ↘              ↓
┌─────────────────┐                    ┌─────────────────┐
│  NOT non-normal │ ←───────────────→  │   NOT normal    │
│    Adduction    │                    │    Abduction    │
└─────────────────┘                    └─────────────────┘
```
Source : Author

If we look at these forms of logic in terms of judgments, developed by Immanuel Kant and based on two dichotomies (a *priori*/*a posteriori* and *analytic*/*synthetic*), we can identify the following four positions:

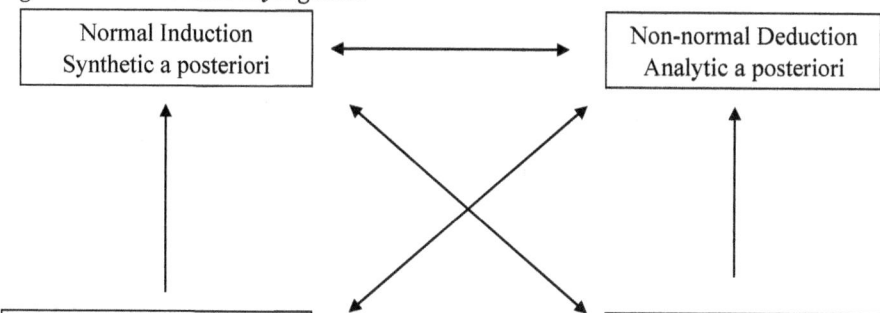

Figure 6.2: Four Forms of Judgment

```
┌──────────────────────┐              ┌──────────────────────┐
│  Normal Induction    │ ←──────────→ │ Non-normal Deduction │
│ Synthetic a posteriori│             │  Analytic a posteriori│
└──────────────────────┘              └──────────────────────┘
          ↑          ↖        ↗              ↑
          │            ╲    ╱                │
          │             ╲  ╱                 │
          │             ╱  ╲                 │
          │            ╱    ╲                │
          ↓          ↙        ↘              ↓
┌──────────────────────┐              ┌──────────────────────┐
│ NOT non-normal Adduction│ ←───────→ │  NOT normal Abduction │
│   Synthetic a priori    │           │    Analytic a priori  │
└──────────────────────┘              └──────────────────────┘
```
Source : Author

Here we will briefly look at only two positions of the square—analytic *a priori* and synthetic *a priori*.

Analytic *a priori* judgments are those that purely concern the properties of concepts alone and require no reference to anything beyond them. Every analytic *a priori* judgment can be seen as an attempt to figure out which predicate best fits the subject, or, to put it differently, is contained in the subject—just like the white beans from the bag in Peirce's well-known example.[39] Each attempt (as the best explanation) is based on habit. This way, abduction finds its justification in prag-maticism. Of course ultimately the experience must be tested. As Peirce puts it,

"Pragmaticism is simply the doctrine that the inductive method is the only essential to the ascertainment of the intellectual purport of any symbol."[40]

When Peirce speaks about abduction as "the only kind of reasoning which supplies new ideas," he says that it is "in this sense, synthetic."[41] However, the synthetic kind of reasoning that supplies new ideas applies better to adduction because adduction is a reasoning that moves by addition, and thus adduced judgments are amplicative, i.e., they amplify or add something new to what can be known simply by analyzing the concepts involved. Synthetic *a priori* judgments are presupposed by the very possibility of experience and apply only to the phenomenal realm, grounded upon truly transcendental ideas. Synthetic *a priori*, therefore, can be seen as "the bestest" explanation, albeit potentially even more fallible than abduction. And yet, analytic *a priori* (analyzing the concepts involved) can go only so far because at some point one must face the monster.

In other words, we must continue looking into the monstrous nature of adduction. We are terrified and repelled by monstrosity, but also drawn to it. Monsters haunt us "not because they represent an external threat ... but because they stir recognition within, a sense of our openness and vulnerability that western discourse insists on covering over."[42] That is why we would be better off using Derrida's concluding words in his essay *Structure, Sign and Play*, "we do not turn our eyes away in the face of the yet unnameable which is proclaiming itself ... under the species of the nonspecies."[43] In facing that challenge, we will, indeed, need determination and resilience. And yet, adduction is even a weaker kind of argument than abduction, and it has no force, especially "probative force". With adduction, we heed what is, perhaps, the main warning by monsters—always display something that is human, all-too-human: vulnerability, humility, care, faith, hope, and love.

Only this way, treading most lightly, can we enter the realm of the critical. Here is how Lanigan defines this realm: "CRITICAL = use of adductive logic [Rule + Result = Case (universal; *a priori*). In different contexts [Rule], an external comparison [Result] establishes the identity of two phenomena [Case]; criticism requires necessity (…) as a standard of judgment, i.e., the eidetic claim that the comparison holds true in all types of the case (universal; no exceptions, all tokens fit all types) and that the truth of the claim (tonality) is obvious before it is experienced (*a priori*)."[44]

Let us come back to Peirce's statement quoted earlier: "[O]ur first premisses, the perceptual judgments, are to be regarded as an extreme case of abductive inferences from which they differ in being absolutely beyond criticism."[45] At the same time, in his *Nomenclature and Divisions of Triadic Relations, as far as They Are Determined*, he writes: "The principles and analogies of Phenomenology enable us to describe, in a distant way, what the divisions of triadic relations must be. But until we have met with the different kinds of *a posteriori*, and have in that way been led to recognize their importance, the *a priori* descriptions mean little; not nothing at all, but little."[46] As we can see, our first premises, or abductive perceptual judgments, are "absolutely beyond criticism"; while, on the other hand, the *a priori* descriptions must still be open to criticism as they mean something—"little, but not nothing at all." I am reading this as Peirce the pragmaticist allows, albeit grudgingly, for some transcendental idealism: not nothing at all can be seen as something not non-normal, as synthetic *a priori*. For Peirce, the progress of science must come upon some ground where it is entitled to reflect. Kant, in his turn, speaks about the "transcendental ground of unity". It seems that Peirce, in his thinking, was reluctant to leave this Earth as it were, while Kant found (or, rather, founded) his ground not only in the moral law within him, but also the starry heaven above him. Following Kant and Peirce, Lanigan carries on their revolutionary fusion of transcendental idealism and empirical realism that showed itself to be so strange—monstrous, one might say. Similar to synthetic *a priori*, adduction is a creature that we can only be passable to and never able to grasp because it only monstrates continually receding from understanding. Since monstrosity is showing in both synthetic *a priori* and adduction, we're still grappling with the questions: "How is *a priori* synthetic knowledge possible?" and "What is the nature of adduction?"

CODA

Thus, the experience of communication always reaches towards and beyond its limits. And yet, "even when reason appears dialectical and reflective, knowing itself and its limits, it does not—some say cannot—know the limits of its knowledge of its limits,"[47] The "problem of reflection" (or, some might say, "the blessing of reflection") is that we can only see through the glass, darkly.

It is common to speak of "unlimited semiosis" following Umberto Eco's phrase: "Semiosis is unlimited and, through the series of interpretants, explains itself by itself (…)"[48] The focus here is clearly on Self and all the internal ways in which semiosis can be carried out through various meanings. It seems that treating semiosis as limitless, rather than unlimited, and shifts the emphasis beyond Self, which is more in line with the approach of semiotic phenomenology, as established in the discipline of communicology. Only by treating communication as irreducible and limitless can we stand outside of ourselves, as it were, i.e., "partake in the ecstasy (*ek-stasis*) of discovery."[49] While speaking of "unlimited semiosis", Eco notes that "there are at least two cases in which semiosis is confronted with something external to it. (…) The first case is that of indices. (…) The second case is due to the fact that every semiosic act is determined by a Dynamic Object (…)"[50] It is fair to say that the second case points toward the limitless: What is a Dynamic Object if not a monster—ever present and ever elusive—whom we can only feel by its effect but never capture?

Finally (or should it be "initially"?), a limit is not an end. As Nancy reminds us, "A meaning's end as extremity is at the same time its beginning. The end is the point from which meaning arises and to which it returns. In that sense, the end or limit is not a moment that is reached at the 'end' of a journey."[51] "Limit" is related to "limen" ("threshold"); in this light, communication is always a liminal experience. And, as we undergo communication, we experience the monstrosity of adduction—again, and again, and again. In this sense, "a human scientist is a 'perpetual beginner' (...) interrogating the construction of consciousness as such—in, through and as communication."[52] Richard Lanigan exemplifies such a human scientist of communication.

NOTES

1. Isaac E. Catt, "The Two Sciences of Communication in Philosophical Context," *Review of Communication* 14, nos. 3–4 (2014).
2. Richard L. Lanigan, *Phenomenology of Communication: Merleau-Ponty's Thematics in Communicology and Semiology* (Pittsburgh, PA: Duquesne University Press, 1988); *The Human Science of Communicology* (Pittsburgh, PA: Duquesne University Press, 1992); Isaac E. Catt and Deborah Eicher-Catt. *Communicology: The New Science of Embodied Discourse* (Madison, NJ: The Fairleigh Dickinson University, 2010).
3. Andrew R. Smith, "The Limits of Communication: Lyotard and Levinas on Otherness," in *Transgressing Discourses: Communication and the Voice of Other*, ed. Michael Huspek and Gary Radford. New York: State University of New York, 1997.
4. John D. Peters, "Space, Time, and Communication Theory," *Canadian Journal of Communication* 28 (2003): 409.
5. Pinchevski, Amit, *By Way of Interruption. Levinas and the Ethics of Communication* (Pittsburgh, PA: Duquesne University Press, 2005), 67.
6. Charles Sanders Peirce, *The Collected Papers of Charles Sanders Peirce*, vols. V and VI, *Pragmatism and Pragmaticism and Scientific Metaphysics*, ed. Charles Hartshorne and Paul Weiss, vol. 5 (Cambridge, MA: Harvard University Press, 1974), 356.
7. Charles Scott, *Living with Indifference* (Bloomington: Indiana University Press, 2007), 84.
8. Lee Thayer, "On the Limits of Communication: A Metaphilosophical Inquiry," *Philosophica* 6, no. 2, (1975): 107.
9. Igor Klyukanov, "Reflexivity and Transcendence Through Semiotic Analysis of Anomaly. Paradoxes of Life," *The 39 Annual Meeting of the Semiotic Society of America*. Seattle, WA, October 1–5, 2014.
10. Aristotle, *The Rhetoric of Aristotle*, trans. Sir Richard Claverhouse Jebb, ed. John Edwin Sandys (Introduction and with Supplementary notes) (Cambridge, England: The University Press, 1909), 173.
11. Peirce, *Collected Papers of Charles Sanders Peirce*, 181.
12. Peirce, *Collected Papers of Charles Sanders Peirce*, 181.
13. Peirce, *Collected Papers of Charles Sanders Peirce*, 182.
14. Shane Ewegen, Plato's Cratylus: The Comedy of Language (Bloomington: Indiana University Press, 2014), 193.

15. Garnet Butchart, "Haunting Past Images," *The American Journal of Semiotics* 30, nos. 1–2 (2014).
16. Ewegen, *Plato's Cratylus*, 106.
17. see: Stephen F. Teiser, "Strange Writing: Anomaly Accounts in Early Medieval China by Robert Ford Campany," *History of Religions* 39, no. 3 (2000).
18. Jacques Derrida, *Points…: Interviews, 1974–1994 (Meridian: Crossing Aesthetics)*, 1st ed. (Redwood City, CA: Stanford University Press, 1995), 386.
19. Aristotle, *The Works of Aristotle*. Translated into English under the Editorship of J. A. Smith and W. D. Ross. Vol. V. (Oxford, England: The Clarendon Press, 1912), 770b.
20. John Sallis, *Force of Imagination: The Sense of the Elemental* (Bloomington: Indiana University Press, 2000), 140.
21. Floyd Merrell, *Semiosis in the Postmodern Age* (West Lafayette, IN: Purdue University Press, 1999), 95.
22. Immanuel Kant, *Critique of Pure Reason*, A vii, NKS translation. (New York: St. Martin's Press, 1929), 7.
23. Charles Sanders Peirce, *Writings of Charles S. Peirce: A Chronological Edition*, vol. 1 (…), vol. 4, ed. Max H. Fisch *et al.* (Bloomington: Indiana University Press, 1982), 290.
24. Jacques Derrida, "Structure, Sign, and Play in the Discourse of the Human Sciences," in *A Postmodern Reader*, ed. Joseph Natoli and Linda Hutcheon (Albany: State University of New York Press, 1993), 293.
25. James J. Liszka, *A General Introduction to the Semiotic of Charles Sanders Peirce* (Bloomington: Indiana University Press, 1996), 117n7.
26. Lars Elleström, "Peirce and the Cenoscopic Science of Signs," *The American Journal of Semiotics* 30, nos. 1/2 (2014).
27. Charles Sanders Peirce, *Collected Papers of Charles Sanders Peirce*, vols. VII and VIII, *Science and Philosophy and Reviews, Correspondence and Bibliography*, ed. Arthur W. Burks, vol. 8 (Cambridge, MA: Harvard University Press), 209.
28. Peirce, *Collected Papers of Charles Sanders Peirce*, 227–228.
29. Peirce, *Collected Papers of Charles Sanders Peirce*, 385–388.
30. Lanigan, personal communication.
31. Max Black, *Margins of Precision: Essays in Logic and Language* (Ithaca, NY: Cornell University Press, 1970), 137.
32. Robert Hannah, *Kant and the Foundations of Analytic Philosophy* (Oxford: Clarendon Press, 2004), 15.
33. Mark Blaug, *The Methodology of Economics, or How Economists Explain* (Cambridge, UK: Cambridge University Press, 1992 [1980]), 17.
34. Blaug, *The Methodology of Economics*, 17.
35. Lanigan, *The Human Science of Communicology*.
36. Richard L. Lanigan, "From Enthymeme to Abduction: The Classical Law of Logic and the Postmodern Rule of Rhetoric," in *Recovering Pragmatism's Voice*, ed. Lenore Langsdorf and Andrew R. Smith (Albany: State University of New York Press, 1995), 63.
37. Lanigan, *The Human Science of Communicology*, 217.
38. Asa Simon Mittman, "Introduction: The Impact of Monsters and Monster Studies," in The Ashgate Research Companion to Monsters and the Monstrous, ed. Mittman Asa Simon and Peter J. Dendle (Farnham: Ashgate, 2012), 6.

39. Charles Sanders Peirce. *Collected Papers of Charles Sanders Peirce*, vols. I and II, *Principles of Philosophy and Elements of Logic*, ed. Charles Hartshorne and Paul Weiss, vol. II (Cambridge, MA: Harvard University Press, 1932), 623.
40. Peirce, *Collected Papers of Charles Sanders Peirce*, vol. 8, 209.
41. Peirce, *Collected Papers of Charles Sanders Peirce*, vol. 2, 777.
42. Margrit Shildrick, *Embodying the Monster: Encounters with the Vulnerable Self* (Thousand Oaks, CA: Sage, 2002), 81; cf. Donna Haraway, *Promises of Monsters: A Regenerative Politics for Inappropriate/d Others* (New York: Routledge, 1992).
43. Derrida, *Structure, Sign, and Play...*, 293.
44. Lanigan, *The Human Science of Communicology*, 217.
45. Peirce, *Collected Papers of Charles Sanders Peirce*, vol. 5, 181; emphasis added.
46. Charles S. Peirce, *The Essential Peirce: Selected Philosophical Writings, 1893–1913*, vol. 2, ed. Nathan Houser and Christian J. W. Kloesel (Cambridge, MA: Harvard University Press, 1998), 289; emphasis added.
47. Stephen Ross, *The Ring of Representation* (Albany: State University of New York Press, 1992), 8.
48. Umberto Eco, *The Limits of Interpretation*, First Midland Book ed. (Bloomington: Indiana University Press, 1994 [1990]), 38.
49. Frank J. Macke, "Intrapersonal Communicology: Reflection, Reflexivity, and Relational Consciousness in Embodied Subjectivity," in *Communicology: The New Science of Embodied Discourse*, ed. Isaac E. Catt and Deborah Eicher-Catt (Madison, NJ: The Fairleigh Dickinson University, 2010), 45.
50. Eco, *The Limits of Interpretation*, 38.
51. Francois Raffoul, "Translator's Preface," in *Nancy, Jean-Luc. The Gravity of Thought*, trans. F.Raffoul and G. Rocco (Atlantic Highlands, NJ: Humanities Press International, 1997), xiv.
52. Catt, "Two Sciences," 3.

BIBLIOGRAPHY

Aristotle. *The Rhetoric of Aristotle*. Translated by Sir Richard Claverhouse Jebb, edited with an introduction and with supplementary notes by John Edwin Sandys. Cambridge, England: The University Press, 1909.

Aristotle. *The Works of Aristotle*. Translated into English under the Editorship of J. A. Smith and W. D. Ross. Vol. V. Oxford, England: The Clarendon Press, 1912.

Black, Max. *Margins of Precision: Essays in Logic and Language*. Ithaca, NY: Cornell University Press, 1970.

Blaug, Mark. *The Methodology of Economics, or How Economists Explain*. Cambridge, UK: Cambridge University Press, 1992 (1980).

Butchart, Garnet. Haunting Past Images. *The American Journal of Semiotics* 30, nos. 1–2 (2014): 27–52.

Catt, Isaac E. "The Two Sciences of Communication in Philosophical Context." *Review of Communication* 14, nos. 3–4 (2014): 201–228.

Catt, Isaac E., and Deborah Eicher-Catt. *Communicology: The New Science of Embodied Discourse*. Madison, NJ: The Fairleigh Dickinson University, 2010.

Derrida, Jacques. *Points...: Interviews, 1974–1994 (Meridian: Crossing Aesthetics)*. 1st ed. Stanford, CA: Stanford University Press, 1995.

Derrida, Jacques. "Structure, Sign, and Play in the Discourse of the Human Sciences." In *A Postmodern Reader*, edited by Joseph Natoli and Linda Hutcheon, 223–242. Albany: State University of New York Press, 1993.
Eco, Umberto. *The Limits of Interpretation*. Bloomington: Indiana University Press, 1994 (1990).
Elleström, Lars. Peirce and the Cenoscopic Science of Signs. *The American Journal of Semiotics* 30, nos. 1/2 (2014): 83–138.
Ewegen, Shane. *Plato's Cratylus: The Comedy of Language*. Bloomington: Indiana University Press, 2014.
Hannah, Robert. *Kant and the Foundations of Analytic Philosophy*. Oxford: Clarendon Press, 2004.
Haraway, Donna. *Promises of Monsters: A Regenerative Politics for Inappropriate/d Others*. New York: Routledge, 1992.
Kant, Immanuel. *Critique of Pure Reason*. A vii, NKS translation. New York: St. Martin's Press, 1929.
Klyukanov, Igor. "Reflexivity and Transcendence Through Semiotic Analysis of Anomaly." *Paradoxes of Life. The 39 Annual Meeting of The Semiotic Society of America*. Seattle, WA, October 1–5, 2014.
Lanigan, Richard L. "From Enthymeme to Abduction: The Classical Law of Logic and the Postmodern Rule of Rhetoric." In *Recovering Pragmatism's Voice*, edited by Lenore Langsdorf and Andrew R. Smith, 49–70. Albany: State University of New York Press, 1995.
Lanigan, Richard L. *The Human Science of Communicology*. Pittsburgh, PA: Duquesne University Press, 1992.
Lanigan, Richard L. *Phenomenology of Communication: Merleau-Ponty's Thematics in Communicology and Semiology*. Pittsburgh, PA: Duquesne University Press, 1988.
Liszka, James J. *A General Introduction to the Semiotic of Charles Sanders Peirce*. Bloomington: Indiana University Press, 1996.
Macke, Frank J. "Intrapersonal Communicology: Reflection, Reflexivity, and Relational Consciousness in Embodied Subjectivity." In *Communicology: The New Science of Embodied Discourse*, edited by Isaac E. Catt and Deborah Eicher-Catt, 33–62. Madison, NJ: The Fairleigh Dickinson University, 2010.
Merrell, Floyd. *Semiosis in the Postmodern Age*. West Lafayette, IN: Purdue University Press, 1999.
Mittman, Asa Simon. "Introduction: The Impact of Monsters and Monster Studies." In *The Ashgate Research Companion to Monsters and the Monstrous*, edited by Mittman Asa Simon and Peter J. Dendle, 1–16. Farnham: Ashgate, 2012.
Peirce, Charles S. *The Collected Papers of Charles Sanders Peirce*, vols. I–VI, edited by Charles Hartshorne and Paul Weiss; vols. VII–VII edited by Arthur W. Burks. Cambridge, MA: Harvard University Press, 1931–1958.
Peirce, Charles S. *The Essential Peirce: Selected Philosophical Writings, 1893–1913*, vol. 2, edited by Nathan Houser and Christian J. W. Kloesel. Cambridge, MA: Harvard University Press, 1998.
Peirce, Charles S. *Writings of Charles S. Peirce: A Chronological Edition*, vol. 1 (…), vol. 4, edited by Max H. Fisch *et al*. Bloomington: Indiana University Press, 1982.
Peters, John D. "Space, Time, and Communication Theory." *Canadian Journal of Communication* 28 (2003): 397–411.
Pinchevski, Amit. *By Way of Interruption. Levinas and the Ethics of Communication*. Pittsburgh, PA: Duquesne University Press, 2005.
Raffoul, Francois. "Translator's Preface." In Nancy, Jean-Luc. *The Gravity of Thought*. Translated by F. Raffoul and G. Rocco. Atlantic Highlands, NJ: Humanities Press, 1997.
Ross, Stephen. *The Ring of Representation*. Albany: State University of New York Press, 1992.
Sallis, John. *Force of Imagination: The Sense of the Elemental*. Bloomington: Indiana University Press, 2000.

Scott, Charles. *Living with Indifference*. Bloomington: Indiana University Press, 2007.
Shildrick, Margrit. *Embodying the Monster: Encounters with the Vulnerable Self*. Thousand Oaks, CA: Sage, 2002.
Smith, Andrew R. "The Limits of Communication: Lyotard and Levinas on Otherness." In *Transgressing Discourses: Communication and the Voice of Other*, edited by Michael Huspek and Gary Radford, 329–351. New York: State University of New York Press, 1997.
Teiser, Stephen F. "Strange Writing: Anomaly Accounts in Early Medieval China by Robert Ford Campany." *History of Religions* 39, no. 3 (2000): 308–310.
Thayer, Lee. On the Limits of Communication: A Metaphilosophical Inquiry. *Philosophica* 6, no. 2 (1975): 99–111.

CHAPTER SEVEN

Is Martin Heidegger's Fourfold a Semiotic Square?

ALEXANDER KOZIN

The relationship between semiotics and phenomenology is hardly straightforward, although there exists a substantial body of evidence pointing to the inner-bound connection between the two modes of inquiry. A strong sense of semiotics can be found in E. Husserl's *Logical Investigations*, M. Merleau-Ponty's *Signs*, E. Levinas' *Totality and Infinity*, and J. Derrida's *Speech and Phenomena*.[1] Commonly, this sense is examined on the basis of such concepts as "language," "sign" and/or "system." In addition, both phenomenology and semiotics are interested in existence and being, word and meaning, world and experience, and other explicitly philosophical themes. It is from this intersecting perspective that I approach M. Heidegger's writings on language and literature, focusing on their specific contribution to semiotics.

In this regard, I wish to argue that not only Heidegger can be read semiotically, but that his phenomenological notion of *fourfold* is a semiotic model in both character and function and that it can rival a properly semiotic model called *semiotic square* constructed by linguist A.-J. Greimas.[2] Therefore, in this chapter I would like to suggest that we think about Heidegger's fourfold semiotically. The notion was referenced by Heidegger in a number of different works, most of which deal with the aesthetic dimension of the world, for example, his essays *The Thing* and *Building, Dwelling Thinking*.[3] Greimas' semiotic square also deals with poetics, although originally it was conceived with a much broader objective: to understand the semantic notion of meaning, or, to be more specific, the "world of signification."[4] My objective here is therefore to bring Heidegger's fourfold into the semiotic domain in order to see if it fits the general semiotic theory, and, co-extensively, if it could make a contribution to the methodological interface between the two modes of inquiry. In this scheme, the semiotic square would function as a conceptual link. The above task defines the composition of this article: in the beginning, after a brief historical overview, I introduce the basic parameters of Greimas' semiotic square. In the second part of the article, I proceed to investigate the fourfold. In the final part of the article, I apply Heidegger's model to Paul Bowles' novel *The Sheltering Sky*.[5]

THE SEMIOTIC SQUARE

A.-J. Greimas' most involved work on the semiotic square began in the early 1960s with his treatise *Structural Semantics*. The objective of this work was stated already in the subtitle of the monograph: *An Attempt at a Method*. The method implied here was not linguistic however, but semiological; that is, it was intended for the advancement of semiology, an emergent discipline of the study of the sign, or, as Saussure originally defined it, a "science that studies the life of signs within society."[6] One of the key contributions of *Structural Semantics* was the isolation of the structure of signification from its manifestation, allowing for an openness, which a phenomenologist might call "world." Working in close collaboration with Russian formalists (V. Propp, V. Shklovsky, Yu. Tynjanov) and French structuralists (L. Hjelmslev, R. Barthes, G. Demézil, C. Lévi-Strauss) helped Greimas expand the scope of semiology, albeit much in the structural direction. More importantly, his collaborative work brought him face-to-face with literature, the analyses of which allowed him to employ his most essential semiotic discoveries: isotopy, actantial models, and finally, the semiotic square.[7] V. Propp's influence on Greimas during the earlier period is obvious here: it is from Propp that Greimas understood that isotopy was a narrative unit and that its development was instigated by certain pre-set actions (he calls them "actants") performed by the figures pre-assigned to commit those very and not any other actions.[8] As important was the assignment to actants either a positive or negative valence, which endowed a narrative with the agonistic quality.

A linguist by training, Greimas presented his model in analytic terms, where the juxtaposition between the items would be retained as contradiction (negation) or stand in the relations of contrariety (opposition), for example "being" vs. "non-being." Negative terms are characterized by the absence of a common *seme* ("being" vs. "non-being"), while contrary relations are essentially antynomic. They also share the same seme (for example, "big" vs. "small," with the shared seme being "size"). In turn, complimentarity or implicature provide the terms with horizontal relations. In Greimas' own words, "basically, the square is a binary semic category, such as "black" vs. "white," whose terms are positioned in a relation of contrariety and therefore shall be considered as contradictory."[9] The contradictory terms can, in turn, enter a presupposition vis-à-vis the contrary term set off above it. The distinction between above and below is as important as the direction of analytical movement. Greimas presumed that this functional model represented "the elementary structure of signification designed to account for the first articulation of meaning within a semantic microuniverse."[10]

Figure 7.1: The Semiotic Square

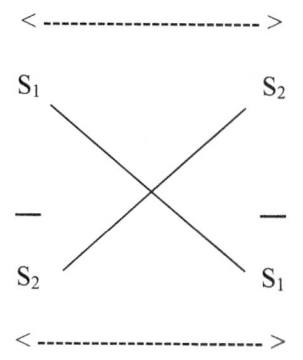

```
         < ----------------------- >
       S₁                       S₂


         —                       —


       S₂                       S₁
         < ----------------------- >
```

---------- > indicates presupposition and < ---------------- > indicates contradiction
Source : Author

However, even more important than the (a)positional distribution of terms was Greimas' realization that contrarieties allow for variations, which are indispensable for building the paradigmatic axis.[11] For example: the semantic continuum that opposes "large" to "small" includes multiple variations of both terms, with some of them presenting a strong contrariety (for example, "tiny" vs. "huge"). However, it is only when Greimas draws diagonal lines between the contradictory and contrariety terms that the model receives its generative potential: from a two-dimensional square, it becomes a three-dimensional figure.[12] This feature allows us to vary all the terms from any point, creating complex self-perpetuating models and with them whole micro-worlds, including literary worlds. When in motion, these words create a transformation that leads to a semiotic universe in the full sense. By "the full sense" I meant Yuri Lotman's definition of the worlds as a "semiosphere," which is "homogenous, asymmetrical, and singular at the same time."[13]

THE FOURFOLD

> "What is truth, that it can happen as, or even must happen as, art? How is it that art exists at all?"[14]

From this quote we can easily deduce both types of relations that assure the methodological proximity of *the fourfold* to *the semiotic square*. On the one hand, both

Heidegger and Greimas engage art as a path to truth, singling out the poetic context as a stimulus for both endeavours. In both cases, art embraces imagination and spirit and thus situates truth (meaning) in the symbolic realm, endowing it with the productive ambiguity at the highest level of associative generativity. Depending on whether art is examined in semiotic or phenomenological terms, the two approaches utilize different kinds of evidence to argue for both the existence of art and its effects. For example, Heidegger seeks truth in the constitution of art as a phenomenon of the world. He therefore asks, *What are the conditions for the creation and being of art?* Notably, for the semiotic connection, from the outset, Heidegger calls art *aistheton* or "that which is perceptible by sensations in the sense belonging to sensibility."[15]

In comparison, Greimas uses art to ask about the conditions of meaning, which is inalienable from the act of creation, as he considers it to be the key function of art. His key question therefore runs as follows: *What is the meaning of artistic work, any work, if we consider creation to be the main function of art?* The divergent accents in the two questions posed by the two scholars point to two non-coincident dialectical models of existence: while, by his model, Greimas offers us to discover the primary signification and associative synthesis which secure a self-generating universe of meaning, Heidegger asks us if the phenomenon of art is a true phenomenon and therefore can be in constitution of its own meaningful world. This kind of inquiry is justified by the inherent dynamism Heidegger espouses in his perspective on art as a work, which "is always a work even if it is something worked out, brought about, affected."[16] Thus, from the beginning, he approaches the fourfold from the genetic standpoint, which is a significant deviation from Greimas' static register.[17] At the same time, in contrast to the semiotic square, which proliferates outward, Heidegger views his fourfold as a closed system with the inwardly contained generativity. This also means that in order to examine the fourfold, one must unwrap rather than re-construct or re-cover it by trying to draw cohesion among and between positional relations. For Heidegger, "the work is a symbol,"[18] and, as such, it needs to be resolved in the form of *sumballein*, that is, semiotically.

The fourfold is simple oneness of the four. The four components are therefore neither replaceable nor exchangeable. They are earth, sky, divinities, and mortals. The distribution of the four components deals with Heidegger's understanding of them as pair-part symbols or allegories. For example, sky symbolizes divinities, while earth stands for mortals. In contrast to abstract mathematical symbols, which exist only within the rules of calculus, Heidegger's four "folds" are actual phenomena available to experience. Perhaps, they can be even called meta-phenomena, or even elementals or, as the ancient Greeks defined them, as mixed material/immaterial structures of existence. Similarly to the understanding of elementals in *Empedocles*, Heidegger approaches the four elemental folds as progressively joined domains; hence, his choice of the method: *techne*, which means, "bringing forth by means of unfolding."[19] Unfolding from this perspective is not a matter of analytical dissection but comes about as a result of a quest, which, for Heidegger, is a technical term that promotes his idea of hermeneutic analysis whose aim is the attainment of truth in the process of "undoing" the symbolic space.

Each domain, whether it connects to mortals or divinities, is a set place in the sense of the German notions of *Stellen*, *Gestalt*, and their Greek analogue *morphe*.[20] The relationship between and among the frames is stratified: immortals are preceded by sky, which is in turn preceded by mortals who originate from earth, which makes it the original domain and the first signification. The unfolding discloses the works of stratification starting with earth, therefore exposing the primary stratum of the original phenomenality. In other words, the unfolding is the clearing a way for the appearances that come through the open and become unconcealed. It is from this perspective that, for a phenomenologist, "bringing-forth" is both a symbolic quest and a creative activity. Unfolding is designed to bring us to truth (*aletheia*), which is a divine being for the Ancient Greeks. The encounter with this being discloses not just the meaning of the journey; it also shows the immortal who is associated with this meaning, as Heidegger describes it in his lecture course *Parmenides*. In either case, the journey begins with the most familiar: "the earth, the sheltering agent."[21]

The earth's ground is juxtaposed to the divine openness, the sky. The openness of earth itself is concealing, and it keeps things to itself. In contrast, sky is unconcealment. The earth grounds us, earth dwellers, in more than one way; defining and adjusting our biology and thus our relations to the hon-human world. It is also the ground on which we stand and walk and conduct our everyday affairs. We do so "naturally," writes Heidegger, thus drawing the border between the natural attitude and the phenomenological attitude. The division between the two calls us to begin the quest for truth by leaving earth, abandoning its shelter. The act of leaving should not be understood literally. "It is what opens up the world and keeps it abidingly in force."[22] Only when we learn how to suspend the natural attitude, albeit temporarily and never completely, opening up to sky, can we understand ourselves and the world of mortals. About their place, Heidegger writes, "mortals are in *the fourfold* by dwelling."[23] Mortals who dwell on earth are endowed with the task of protecting it. They preserve their dwelling by keeping and using it. Heidegger considers this task necessary for the preservation of all other folds.

Furthermore, sky completes the fourfold and the quest by "gathering of the bringing-forth."[24] It is the place where divinities dwell, where atmosphere is divine and where an encounter with a god or goddess never happens per chance (certain routes cannot be changed), and produces the disclosure of truth and its bearer as it were. In addition to gods and goddesses, sky is inhabited by the liminal characters called *daemons* who are the highest form of human emotionality. In Ancient Greek *daimôn* means "divine sign" that can be issued both to warn the person of an impending disaster and to lead him to it. In Plato's *Apology of Socrates*, Socrates refers to listening to the divine voice of a *daimonion* who functions as a guardian angel. Plato saw the main purpose of *daimonia* and *daimons* in the "interpreting and transporting human things to the gods and divine things to men; entreaties and sacrifices from below, and ordinances and requitals from above (...)"[25] With this focus on the divine and its *logos*, a brief analysis of *The Sheltering Sky* follows.

THE SHELTERING SKY

The mortals in Paul Bowles' novel are Port and Kit Moresby, two wealthy American travellers, who leave New York City in search for a place as far away from their home as possible. The remote places they visit are always chosen at random; the Americans are not searching for a different kind of humanity or culture. They are simply looking for whatever may happen, and it is this motivation that brings them to Morocco. On this journey for something extra-ordinary, they are accompanied by a sort of a family friend, Mr. Tunner, who is tagging along more so out of boredom than out of curiosity or any interest in the local exotics. He is the Other in the company of the Moresbys. Any land is only land for him, nothing more but the background for the ordinary. Being firmly attached to the earth, he is a quintessential tourist, an embodiment of the natural attitude. Unlike Kit and Port, who will be destroyed by their journey, he will never even have one.

It is at this juncture that I would like to ask, *How shall we understand the quest? What are the consequences of accomplishing it?* In order to answer these questions, in the next section, I would like to present an account of the journey undertaken by the protagonists of *The Sheltering Sky*.

Part 1

The first part of the novel is set up against the sedentary culture of a Moroccan Port. The environment there is still; it is difficult to detect movement of any kind, as if nothing of significance could possibly occur there. Kit explains this state by the melancholia of modernity: "The people of every country become like the people of any other country."[26] Port corrects her, pointing out at two radically different perspectives in apprehending the alien. One is that of the natural attitude; it comes from the home and is held by the earth. The other presupposes a quest, albeit without a point or destination. In the beginning of his journey, he explains the difference as follows: "the traveler goes to other countries and he may never return from his travels; a tourist always returns home, he cannot be lost."[27]

On the first day in the city, during a late night walk Port starts his quest by meeting a daemon who appears in front of him in the form of an Arab man, Smaïl, who, after much haggling takes Port to an empty tent where he asks his companion to wait until he finally returns with a beautiful young girl. The girl's name is Marhnia. Appropriately, Port does not understand Marhnia's speech, but the goddess could somehow communicate that she fell down to the earth to dance for ugly men. Meanwhile, far out there in the Sahara, where the sky meets the earth, there are beautiful men waiting for her.

The encounter with daemonic Marhnia, whom Port takes for a mortal, almost ends the quest; but instead, it begins it. The face of the goddess who danced for him would come up again and again, fueling his erotic desires, which slowly turn into an obsession, pushing him deeper into the alien land. The plans to leave Tangier are expedited. Due to some personal circumstances, Port and Kit go to Boussif in two different ways. Kit goes by a slow local train with Tunner, while Port chooses the company of the Lyles, the mother and the son, who travel in their own automobile, taking photographs and collecting information for travel agencies, or so they say. These figures shall also count as daemonic, their task being to take the mortals along the earth away from the earth and into the open.

On the train, overrun by boredom, guilt, and anxiety, Kit wanders away from Tunner only to encounter horrific images of raw and unpretentious humanity: a zombie like human mass of the natives in the third class carriage where men look at her without sympathy or antipathy, not even curiosity. "They all had the vacant expression on their faces as if a man who has just simply blown their nose."[28] For the locals who are bound to the earth irrevocably, she is invisible, as if she herself were a goddess. At the door, she sees a severed head of a sheep with glassy eyes and blue protruding tongue. Then, she meets the statuette-like leper on the platform, who keeps her standing there in horror until the ice rain chases her back into the first-class carriage and into the arms of Tunner, her temporary shelter, who "saves" her from the natives by getting her drunk on champagne and then taking advantage of her. However, for Kit their coitus meant little past a poignant reminder of her far-away home.

In Boussif, leaving the realm of the mortals behind, Port's consciousness starts taking a strange turn. The proximity of the sky makes him feel as if he is falling into a dark well a thousand miles deep; with a great difficulty he rises from the lower regions of his consciousness. When he does so, it is always with a sense of infinite sadness and repose. "The soul is the weariest part of the body," he keeps on saying until another daimon appears. In a local brothel he sees a dancing and singing girl of an uncanny grace: "The movements of the girl appeared graceful but of the impudence that verged on the comic."[29] In fact, transformed by the strident and wily sounds of the music, she appears daimonic. Her face is a mask of perfect proportion whose beauty accrues less from the configuration of features than from the meaning that is implicit in their expression—meaning or the withholding of it. After having realized that she is blind, with the unyielding obsession that verges on mania, Port tries to obtain the girl's company, as if recognizing that she can tell him more about his quest, its purpose and meaning; however, he is unable to reach her.

Part 2

The second chapter of the book moves the action, or rather the journey even deeper inside the Sahara. It is there that an impelling centrifugal force continues to drive Port to the ways of non-being. Breathing dust and feeling sharp stones underneath his feet, the chilling wind at night and the heaviness of the morning air symbolize the destiny that lies ahead. Trying to overcome the sense of ending, being supremely overwhelmed by the force of being that is not his, Port is looking for the path which is no longer there. "One said: another day, but always with the hidden knowledge that each day was unique and final, that there never would be a return, another time."[30] The sky, so welcoming in the beginning of the journey makes him avert his eyes. The sound of the wind replaces the sound of human voices. The voices of the locals, discordant and abject, seems to have only one purpose: to imitate the wind, while their eyes reflect nothing else but the sky.

Soon, the typhoid, which has been pushing him slowly over the edge, brings his consciousness to its final image: "the spots of raw bright blood on the earth. Blood on excrement. The supreme moment, high above the desert, when the two elements, blood and excrement, long kept apart, merge. A black star appears. Reach out, pierce the final fabric of the sheltering sky, take repose."[31] For Port, the journey is over: the earth is taking him back.

Part 3

The last chapter of the novel describes the transformation of Kit. This time, it is Kit's story, a story about her being in Port's possession, physically, materially, and symbolically, and not only as a body but also as an inalienable part of his self. Without Port and his impossible maps, his obsession with moving; her sense of herself can barely go beyond short intervals of time that had no history and no story, only images. After his death, torn from the earth, she stalls, reaching the brink of the sky, waiting for guidance. Her encounters with mortals brings about "a new horror, connected with sunlight, dust."[32] Now, finally free from her husband's dominant rationality, she receives a chance to finally live by her omens. However, there is no need for that because she becomes an omen of herself to herself. This mystical auto-affection erases the former edge of her stable being. Her elation about being absolutely free is in fact the symptom of madness that immortals gave her as truth.

After Kit escapes from the French barracks into the desert night, she refuses to look at the past. The past itself becomes a distant blur, not even a dream. The death of Port becomes indistinct, indefinable. She feels renewed. Tuning out her self-reflection allows Kit to assume a different and new sense of being. Appropriately, her new Self emerges in the liminality of the dusk. It is at that time that the desert appears most mysterious; it alters perception: the sense of distance lapses, and each small detail acquires an immense significance. Things come into focus as if on their own, without the assistance of the background or an interpretation. Existence is brought out by the confluence of earth and sky: "The journey must continue,"[33] she says to herself as if the sense of movement symbolizes her new freedom and, with it, the authority of the traveler. When several hours later Kit joins a passing caravan, headed by young and handsome Belqassim, she is sure of only one thing: she is not dead. The motions of the camels reminds her of being alive. All else appears secondary. She has found her truth.

When Belqassim takes Kit to his house and, after having locked her up, uses her as a sex slave, it hardly seems inappropriate for Kit. She is deeply enthralled by the tenderness of the young master. She accepts him as she accepted all her transformation: unequivocally. The alien inside herself stirs like an animal; she is the herdsman's favorite sheep, as she likes to think about herself. She is his property. He is her truth. Her earlier celebration of freedom reaches its pinnacle in a celebration of its abnegation. The erotic state of animality is taking a hold on her stronger and stronger, letting her transcend her own being and be absorbed into his. Her only sense of herself at this point is wholly irrational sensuality, without purpose, determination, or will. The elements around her change as well. No longer ominous, fragmented, they erase the separation between earth and sky. The entire sky appears to her as a white metal dome, the symbol of heaven full of beautiful men who sit around waiting for her to dance for them. She becomes fully erotic and knows of no other way of being any longer.

After countless days in the house of Belqassim, when the endless monotony of the world gets broken one night by the incessant beating of the drums, she escapes. Her wiles lead her out into the cold moonlight night. Yet, by now, the encounter with truth changes her completely and irrevocably. Even after she is told that the French authorities and Mr. Turner managed to track her down and that a plane is sent from Tangier to pick her up, she, the creature of the sky, barely cares. The last memory of Kit when she boards the plane is the violent blue sky. Like a great overpowering light it destroys everything in her mind, paralyzes her. Liberation, relief, an opportunity of coming home, all that pass right by her. Someone else once said that the sky could hide the night behind it, sheltering the person beneath from the horror that lied above. Now that she is getting back, her anxiety returns: "At any moment the rip in the sky would occur, the edges would fly back, and the giant maw will be revealed."[34] There is nothing that can make it otherwise. She disappears by putting herself on a crowded street car and rides on it through the entire city until the end of the line.

CONCLUSION

In this chapter I argued that Heidegger's *fourfold* should be considered as the primal condition for the emergence and the existence of art. The attempted argument was made on semiotic grounds vis-à-vis Greimas' *semiotic square* so that Heidegger's suggested contribution to semiotics could be validated and his symbolic analysis could be compatible with semiotic terms. Among the most significant findings of the chapter I consider the fact that, judging by its composition and function, the fourfold generates a symbolic meaning which is primal to language and whose morphology is capable of accommodating such primordial phenomena as the elementals which are gathered as a singular whole or a model. While the semiotic square appears as a geometrical figure, which allows for the infinite generation of the self and its self-directed meanings, the fourfold refers to the world which is founded on the disclosive dimensions of experience. The four domains—earth and sky, mortals, and divinities—form a relational model based on a "quest", which is the model's key function and the basic operation of any empirical analysis. Importantly, Heidegger's quest does not tend toward a resolution of any kind, but rather leans on ambiguity in order for the world to disclose its own meaning. Thus, in the case of *The Sheltering Sky*, the windy path taken by mortals Port and Kit leads them to Eros, a divinity responsible for the disclosure of the fourfold in the novel by becoming its symbolic pinnacle. For the reasons unknown, Eros becomes responsible for killing Port and for driving Kit to madness. These are the truths, which Heidegger's fourfold helps disclose, and, although this is not sufficient to claim the existence of Heidegger's semiotics as a discrete strand of inquiry, I consider the findings indicative enough as to encourage furthering our attention to the semiotic potential of Heidegger's work.

NOTES

1. Edmund Husserl, *Logical Investigations*, vols. 1–2, trans. J. N. Findlay (London: Routledge, 2001); Maurice Merleau-Ponty, *Signs*, trans. Richard McCleary (Evanston, IL: Northwestern University Press, 1964); Emmanuel Levinas, *Totality and Infinity*, trans. Alfonso Lingis (Pittsburgh, PA: Duquesne University Press, 1969); Jacques Derrida, *Speech and Phenomena*, trans. David B. Allison (Evanston, IL: Northwestern University Press, 1973). A similarly strong sense of phenomenology can be identified with such semioticians as Richard Lanigan, *The Human Science of Communicology. A Phenomenology of Discourse in Foucault and Merleau-Ponty* (Pittsburgh, PA: Duquesne University Press, 1992); Richard Lanigan, *Phenomenology of Communication. Merleau-Ponty's Thematics in Communicology and Phenomenology* (Pittsburgh, PA: Duquesne University Press, 1988); Eero Tarasti, *Existential Semiotics* (Bloomington: Indiana University Press, 2000); Thomas Sebeok, *Global Semiotics* (Bloomington: Indiana University Press, 2001).
2. For the duration of the text I leave both operational terms unmarked unless a special emphasis is required.
3. Martin Heidegger, "The Thing," in *Poetry, Language, Thought*, trans. Albert Hofstadter (New York: Harper & Row, 1971), 161–184; "Building Dwelling Thinking," in *Poetry, Language, Thought*, 141–160.
4. Algirdas-Julien Greimas, *Structural Semantics: Attempt at a Method*, trans. Daniele McDowell, Ronald Schleifer, and Alan Velie (Lincoln: University of Nebraska Press, 1983), 3.
5. Paul Bowles, *The Sheltering Sky* (London: Penguin, 1947).

6. Ferdinand de Saussure, *Course in General Linguistics*, trans. Wade Baskin (New York: Mc-Graw-Hill Book, 1959), 16.
7. For practical applications of Greimas' semiotics to literature, see Algirdas-Julien Greimas, *Maupassant. La sémiotique du texte exercices pratiques* [*Maupassant. Practical exercises in text semiotics*] (Paris: Editions du Seuil, 1976).
8. Vladimir Propp, *On Comism and Laughter*, trans. Louis A. Wagner (Toronto: University of Toronto Press, 2009).
9. Greimas, *Structural Semantics*, 67.
10. Algirdas-Julien Greimas, *On Meaning. Selected Writings in Semiotic Theory*, trans. Paul J. Perron and Frank H. Collins (Minneapolis: University of Minnesota Press, 1987), 65–66.
11. Roman Jakobson's distinction between the syntagmatic and paradigmatic axes in relation to metaphor and metonymy should be pertinent here as well (see his *Language in Literature*, ed. Krystina Pomorska (Cambridge, MA: Harvard University Press, 1987), 109–114.
12. For other representations of the semiotic square I suggest that we consult Richard Lanigan's scheme of Michel Foucault's quadrilateral model of discourse (see his *The Human Science of Communicology*, 92), as well as James Clifford's semiotic square of cultural authenticity (see his "On Collecting Art and Culture," in *The Cultural Studies Reader*, ed. Simon During (London: Routledge, 1993), 57–76, 63.
13. Yuri Lotman, *Внутри мыслящих миров* [Inside the thinking worlds] (Moscow: Languages of the Russian Culture, 1996), 175.
14. Heidegger, *Poetry, Language, Thought*, 55.
15. Heidegger, *Poetry, Language, Thought*, 25.
16. Heidegger, *Poetry, Language, Thought*, 55.
17. The dsitinction is Husserlian. With it, Husserl separates two distinctly different ways of approaching the world: as origin and as structure (see his "On Static and Genetic Phenomenological Method," in *The Analysis Concerning Active and Passive Synthesis. Lectures on Transcendental Logic*, trans. Anthony J. Steinbock (The Hague: Kluwer Academic Publisher, 2001), 605–634.
18. Heidegger, *Poetry, Language, Thought*, 19.
19. Heidegger, *Poetry, Language, Thought*, 57.
20. Heidegger, *Poetry, Language, Thought*, 162.
21. Heidegger, *Poetry, Language, Thought*, 41.
22. Heidegger, *Poetry, Language, Thought*, 43.
23. Heidegger, *Poetry, Language, Thought*, 148; author's italics.
24. Heidegger, *Poetry, Language, Thought*, 83.
25. Plato, *Complete Works*, ed. and trans. James Cooper (Indianapolis: Hackett, 1997), 202e.
26. Bowles, *The Sheltering Sky*, 12.
27. Bowles, *The Sheltering Sky*, 11.
28. Bowles, *The Sheltering Sky*, 65.
29. Bowles, *The Sheltering Sky*, 108.
30. Bowles, *The Sheltering Sky*, 104.
31. Bowles, *The Sheltering Sky*, 188.
32. Bowles, *The Sheltering Sky*, 156.
33. Bowles, *The Sheltering Sky*, 212.
34. Bowles, *The Sheltering Sky*, 231.

BIBLIOGRAPHY

Bowles, Paul. *The Sheltering Sky*. London: Penguin, 1947.

Clifford, James. "On Collecting Art and Culture." In *The Cultural Studies Reader*, edited by Simon During, 57–76. London: Routledge, 1993.

Derrida, Jacques. *Speech and Phenomena*. Translated by David B. Allison. Evanston, IL: Northwestern University Press, 1973.

Greimas, Algirdas-Julien. *Maupassant. La sémiotique du texte exercices pratiques* [Maupassant. Practical exercises in text semiotics]. Paris: Editions du Seuil, 1976.

Greimas, Algirdas-Julien. *On Meaning. Selected Writings in Semiotic Theory*. Translated by Paul J. Perron and Frank H. Collins. Minneapolis: University of Minnesota Press, 1987.

Greimas, Algirdas-Julien. *Structural Semantics: Attempt at a Method*. Translated by Daniele McDowell, Ronald Schleifer, and Alan Velie. Lincoln: University of Nebraska Press, 1983.

Heidegger, Martin. *Poetry, Language, Thought*. Translated by Albert Hofstadter. New York: Harper & Row, 1971.

Husserl, Edmund. *Logical Investigations*, vols. 1–2. Translated by J. N. Findlay. London: Routledge, 2001.

Husserl, Edmund. "On Static and Genetic Phenomenological Method." In *The Analysis Concerning Active and Passive Synthesis. Lectures on Transcendental Logic*. Translated by Anthony J. Steinbock, 605–634. The Hague: Kluwer Academic Publisher, 2001.

Jakobson, Roman. *Language in Literature*. Edited by Krystina Pomorska. Cambridge, MA: Harvard University Press, 1987.

Lanigan, Richard. *The Human Science of Communicology. A Phenomenology of Discourse in Foucault and Merleau-Ponty*. Pittsburgh, PA: Duquesne University Press, 1992.

Lanigan, Richard. *Phenomenology of Communication. Merleau-Ponty's Thematics in Communicology and Phenomenology*. Pittsburgh, PA: Duquesne University Press, 1988.

Levinas, Emmanuel. *Totality and Infinity*. Translated by Alfonso Lingis. Pittsburgh, PA: Duquesne University Press, 1969.

Lotman, Yuri. *Внутри мыслящих миров* [Inside the thinking worlds]. Moscow: Languages of the Russian Culture, 1996.

Merleau-Ponty, Maurice. *Signs*. Translated by Richard McCleary. Evanston, IL: Northwestern University Press, 1964.

Plato. *Complete Works*. Translated and edited by James Cooper. Indianapolis: Hackett, 1997.

Propp, Vladimir. *On Comism and Laughter*. Translated by Louis A. Wagner. Toronto: University of Toronto Press, 2009.

Saussure, Ferdinand de. *Course in General Linguistics*. Translated by Wade Baskin. New York: McGraw-Hill Book, 1959.

Sebeok, Thomas. *Global Semiotics*. Bloomington: Indiana University Press, 2001.

Tarasti, Eero. *Existential Semiotics*. Bloomington: Indiana University Press, 2000.

CHAPTER EIGHT

Communicology and the Practice of Coding in Qualitative Communication Research

ERIC E. PETERSON AND KRISTIN M. LANGELLIER

Coding, as a research practice, is receiving increased attention in the human sciences as witnessed by burgeoning discussions on the topic in research handbooks, textbooks, and manuals. Part of this increased attention is due to the growth in qualitative inquiry and the demands for rigorous methods of conducting systematic observation and analysis. Another contributing factor is the emphasis on coding approaches in forms of qualitative inquiry and analysis, such as Grounded Theory. And, of course, there is the continued influence of quantitative research practices as well as the importation of quantitative procedures made possible by the advent of computer-assisted qualitative data analysis software (CAQDAS) and the emphasis on "mixed methods." But what is a code? What is coding as a research practice? What theoretical assumptions does this research practice make about the study of communication?

For Saldaña, "a code in qualitative inquiry is most often a word or a short phrase that symbolically assigns a summative, salient, essence-capturing, and/or evocative attribute for a portion of language-based or visual data."[1] Therefore, "to codify is to arrange things in a systematic order, to make something part of a system or classification, to categorize."[2] In a similar way, Charmaz states, "coding means categorizing segments of data with a short name that simultaneously summarizes and accounts for each piece of data. Your codes show how you select, separate, and sort data to begin an analytic accounting of them."[3] Lindlof and Taylor emphasize practical concerns in their discussion of coding: "at some point—usually after a rich data set has begun to build up—researchers recognize the need to create categories. *Category* is a covering term for an array of general phenomena: concepts, constructs, themes, and other types of 'bins' in which to put items that are similar. *Categorization* refers to the analytic process of sorting units of data with respect to properties that they have in common."[4]

These three quotations suggest that coding is primarily positioned as a procedural concern with how to sort, categorize, and order data. This emphasis on procedural training does not clarify the theoretical basis for coding as a research practice. For example, what do researchers take as an object of analysis suitable for coding? Is it the conscious experiences of interviews, of audio or video recordings, and/or of transcripts? If transcripts are selected as the object of analysis, to take one option, then what kind(s) of transcription are subjected to coding? Furthermore, how does a researcher know what the "bins" are into which discourse is to be "sorted?" What criteria, or sets of criteria, form the basis for making judgments about both what constitutes the kinds of "bins" to be used and what falls within them? How does a researcher know if these judgments about sorting, categorizing, and ordering are right? These questions indicate that research involves choices about the context of inquiry and choices about how communication is to be conceptualized (whether as information, conscious experience, and/or event, for example), how best to inscribe and document it, how to do so rigorously, and with what consequences. In brief, the practice of coding raises questions about ontology, epistemology, logic, and axiology in qualitative communication research.[5]

Eco points out that "code" is a messy, contested concept in theorizing about communication.[6] Eco attributes some of this confusion to the rhetorical convention of using "code" to name both a system of elements organized by rules—what he calls an "s-code"—and a rule coupling items from one system with items of another system or systems. Eco reserves the name "code" for the latter phenomenon. He argues that an s-code, or code as a system, "deserves theoretical attention only when it is inserted within a significant or communicational framework."[7] Following Eco's distinction, we discuss the practice of coding in qualitative communication research as syntactic, semantic, and pragmatic systems of elements (that is, as s-codes) before taking up coding as a rule coupling elements from those systems within a theory of communicational acts. At the conclusion of each section on syntactic, semantic, and pragmatic systems (s-codes), we briefly describe an example selected from our own empirical research to illustrate alternatives to coding based in the human science tradition of communicology.[8]

In order to illustrate our arguments regarding the practice of coding in qualitative communication research, we make use of a readily accessible example from Lindlof and Taylor's popular textbook on *Qualitative Communication Research*.[9] The example is taken from Lindlof's own research on image management in national political campaigns. It appears in the textbook as part of Lindlof and Taylor's discussion of "Qualitative Data Analysis" in the chapter on "Sensemaking: Qualitative

Data Analysis and Interpretation." As such, it is but one of a series of examples used throughout the textbook to illustrate a variety of research practices. We selected this specific example for its brevity and because it provides the codes themselves, an excerpt of the interview transcript on which those codes are based, and a brief description of the rationale for coding. We would like to emphasize that our use of this example is necessarily selective and partial in that it neglects the larger context of research decisions about Lindlof's project and analysis that would be discussed in publications that document the research itself. Given these cautions, this example has the benefit of illuminating problematic aspects of coding practices in general and, at the same time, avoids conflating them with possible concerns about computer-assisted qualitative data analysis software.

A SYSTEM OF SYNTACTIC ELEMENTS

Indexical Marking

One of the most obvious and common uses of coding is as a system of syntactic elements that functions to mark or point to a specific portion of the communication event. The goal here is to assist the researcher in easily locating a specific excerpt of discourse. The elements of the system are not necessarily connected with the "content" of the interview—just that they serve as a set of signals organized by internal combinatory rules. A common example is the creation of a "tag" to aid in retrieving segments of discourse from interview tapes or transcripts. Thus, a coding of "G3:52" would index the interview according to the order in which it occurs: where "G" stands for the seventh interview in a series of interviews and "3:52" is a time stamp indicating a segment located at 3:52 minutes into the interview. In the Lindlof and Taylor transcript example (set apart in a text box in the textbook), the excerpt is marked with "SG" to indicate the initials of the interviewee's name (or pseudonym), and thereby creates a way to distinguish different interviews by speaker. Codes, as Lindlof and Taylor point out, "have a more mechanical purpose. They are used to mark the units of text from fieldnotes, transcripts, documents, and audio-visual materials, which permit the researcher to sort, retrieve, link, and display data. Codes are in fact indispensable tools for handling the 'office' function of data analysis."[10] The focus here is on efficiency, standardization, and control of the recall, manipulation, and display of the communication event.

Punctuation

When researchers move to select elements of experience and to separate them as segments of communication, they engage in punctuation. That is, they *locate* segments or units of communication as utterances, words, phrases, lines, turns, sentences, and so on. Hammersley argues that "one traditional way of conceptualizing this issue is to say that we need to 'cut nature at the joints': in other words, our categories must mark out those types of phenomena that are different from one another in significant and relevant ways."[11] The difficulty for the researcher comes in distinguishing what counts as meaningful or significant in the communication event—not a problem of "the naming of the parts," as Wilden describes it, but of distinguishing such "parts" in the first place out of the continuity of lived experience.[12] Does a researcher "cut" the lived experience of communication at the "joint" of pauses in speech, for instance? Lindlof and Taylor engage in punctuation when they use codes, as they describe it, "to mark the islands, archipelagos, and other landmasses of meaningful data from the surrounding sea of raw, uncoded data."[13] In a similar way, the research practices concerning transcription involve organizing syntactic elements into a system of rules that are used to guide the challenge of "punctuating" the flow of interaction into a readable text.[14]

For our first example of an alternative to coding from the tradition of communicology, we point to our essay on the politics of personal narrative methodology.[15] In that essay, we explore some implications of indexing and punctuating specific portions of an interview with a breast cancer survivor, taken from a larger study of breast cancer storytelling.[16] Rhea's interview (with Kristin) constructs a narrative of getting her mastectomy scar tattooed with an image of Victorian flowers after her second episode of breast cancer. In her storytelling of her family members' reactions to the tattoo, we compare and contrast two ways to locate and segment the continuity of this lived experience—in Hammersley's words, two ways to "cut nature at the joints" from the rough transcription. A first way, which we indexed as "There's Nothing There," focused on how the storytelling built to a memorable, quotable punchline of one son's reported speech ("there's nothing there"), constituting an identifiable, self-contained item that was stylized, dramatized, and repeated by the narrator, and that was distinguishable from surrounding talk and extractable by researchers. A second way situated the lived experience within its local occasioning in the surrounding talk; in this case, a segment detailing a series of reactions (from female relatives, medical personnel, her husband) to Rhea's tattoo as well as the interviewer's co-constructing responses. This second punctuation, which we indexed with another narrative quotation as "The Boys Wanted to See It," embeds the "There's Nothing There" segment and makes explicit the narrator's anxieties about exposing the tattoo to her sons.

As we consider the politics of selecting one or the other of these segmentations as the object of analysis—the implications of "cutting it this way or that way"—we discuss issues in communicative mode, or text-context relations; competing theories of narrative identity, and questions about interviewer-interviewee relations. Understood within the communicology tradition, indexing and punctuating reveal that the practice of coding *produces* experience and narrative as well as producing knowledge about experience and narrative. In other words, locating an experience, story, or event is both a textualizing move and, simultaneously, a contextualizing move. Thus, it is misleading to reduce coding to a problem in how to locate meanings as a kind of content in pre-given data. For this reason, communicology focuses on describing the system of understanding and memory in embodied discourse—that is, a concern to articulate how both content and context are constituted as such in conscious experience and in the practice of research.

A SYSTEM OF SEMANTIC ELEMENTS

Labeling

When researchers move from punctuating discourse to naming it, they shift from a system of syntactic elements to a system of semantic elements. For example, Lindlof and Taylor point out that researchers can "code the data for standard demographic categories (e.g., sex, race, age, occupation, education, religion); institutional labels (e.g., manager, profit, loss, curriculum); and other descriptive, 'precoded' topics in wide use."[17] In this instance, the researcher mimics the positivist procedures of quantitative analysis by labeling a segment of discourse with a nominal variable, such as labeling a portion of speech as originating in a speaker coded as male or female. Another example of labeling can be seen in Doctorow's use of "hashtags" (#tag) to organize his research notes, a practice borrowed from the social networking platform Twitter.[18]

One consequence of such coding practices is that analysis tends to focus on nouns and objects rather than relations in locating and formulating labels. For example, in the Lindlof and Taylor excerpt, "You get in it for the experience" becomes "Political Experience" and "You get in it to be able to manage yourself under very stressful circumstances" becomes "Testing Oneself." The analyst drops pronouns and verbs (such as "You are" and "You can") to create labels rather than use other *in vivo* formulations such as "advance is given a lot of leeway" or "it allows you to express your creative abilities" or "there's no room for failure." What happens in coding the discourse in this way is that the predominant pattern of ordering relations (pronoun + verb + phrase/action or attribution) is obscured. As Lanigan asks, "what language is the research using as an empirical activity?"[19] Consider the following schematic arrangement we created of phrases taken from Lindlof and Taylor's transcription excerpt[20]:

You	are	witness to the inner workings of government
		witness to what happens behind the scenes
		given general guidelines

		given certain rules to follow
		given this much time
You	interact	with them
You	have	a close interaction with a candidate
You	do	advance
You	start	with a blank slate or blank canvas
You	can	take those guidelines
		kind of paint the picture
		kind of connect the dots
You	get	in it for the experience
		in it to be able to manage yourself
nobody	gets	into it for the money

This arrangement of the transcript suggests that the discourse orders subjective agency in a particular pattern of relations, a pattern that is left behind by labels based on nouns and objects. The problem for the researcher is that, as Lanigan points out, "English *grammar* dictates a very specific subject-predicate *logic* in analysis wherein typologies of meaning are pre-given [data] and it is impossible to distinguish between code signification (syntactics) and message meaning (semantics)."[21]

Common Sense Categorization

Another way to reduce the ambiguity of lived experience in communication is to adopt "commonsense" meanings of language in the creation of codes. According to Lindlof and Taylor, "these are low-inference categories because they denote concrete, common-sense items. Such categories require fewer decision rules for coders to apply, because there are only a few obvious ways in which they appear in the data. While many of these low-inference categories will be found in the content of a respondent's speech, or in the actions described in fieldnotes, you can also code for the *topic* of the text."[22] What Lindlof and Taylor refer to as "topic" might be described as the general or commonsense meaning of a word or phrase rather than the part of an utterance that is emphasized through vocal intonation, or by the grammatical structure of a sentence. But how common are these commonsense meanings? For whom are these coding decisions "obvious?"

Consider the segments "witness to what happens behind the scenes" and "witness to the inner workings of government" that are initially coded as "Close to the Action" in Lindlof and Taylor's example. In this case, "witness to x" is used as a label taken from the discourse to both name and represent it. It relies upon an understanding of "witness" in the sense of a firsthand account ("You interact with them") where being present to the inner workings of government and to what happens behind the scenes yields privileged access—that is, "firsthand" rather than "secondhand" experience. But "witness" also suggests different types of moral engagement:

for example, "witness" in the sense of "being present to" differs from "witness" in the sense of offering testimony (as in legal and religious contexts), which differs from offering testimony of political injustice (as in "bearing witness" in a public or civic context). In a similar way, the meaning of "having a close interaction with a candidate" is not the same as "being close to a candidate"—whether that is meant as political, personal, or emotional engagement with a candidate. The coding of "witness to x" as "Close to Political Backstage" thus serves a double function, both of which are semantically problematic. First, it emphasizes "proximity" as a "low inference category" for the commonsense meaning of "closeness" but without distinguishing related meanings, such as "intimacy" or "emotional closeness" (to focus on affect), or "insider knowledge" (to focus on cognition), or "privileged access" (to focus on conation). Second, the use of "close to" as a label makes it possible to group the code "Close to Political Backstage" with the code "Close to Candidates," even though their respective meanings must be conflated in order to do so. Taken together, these problems suggest that the emphasis on "low inference descriptors" in qualitative communication research fails as a *reliable and rigorous* basis for generating codes and analytic categories because they assume the taken-for-granted knowledge they purport to describe.

Sorting Subjects

A third element in the semantic system concerns the positioning of the subject. In the Lindlof and Taylor excerpt, the positioning of the subject works in at least two ways. First, the discourse positions the *subject as an addressee* by referring to common knowledge shared by addressees in general, in expressions where "you know" (second person plural) refers to what everyone knows at the same time, that it marks ambiguous discourse that requires further interpretive effort by a specific addressee (second person singular) in such phrases as "You know, for people who are goal oriented" and "You know, advance never pays well." Second, the discourse displaces the speaker by positioning the *subject as a character* in the use of a second-person rather than a first-person narrative of experience. That is, the discourse positions "witnessing" as something "you are" rather than something "I do" or "I act as." The use of second-person rather than first-person or third-person pronouns is strategic: it positions the subject as ambiguous in a speaking position that retains the authority of personal experience found in first-person accounts yet moves it closer to the neutrality and objectivity found in third-person accounts. As a result, the system of semantic elements works to position the speaker as authoritative without sounding arrogant or conceited.

For our second example of empirical research in the communicology tradition, we turn to part of our analysis of family storytelling (in *Storytelling in Daily Life*) where we take up semiotic pheonomenology as a methodology to explore how narrative orders a semantic system of elements.[23] We argue that storytelling, as a communication practice, involves both how families perform stories of experience and how storytelling forms families within, between, and over generations. As a participatory practice of doing family, storytelling forms a system of relationships among narrators and characters, storytellers and audiences; including the researchers. Rather than view family storytelling as a canon of story-texts that circulate within "the family," we take the position that family storytelling is an evolving cultural formation—of making stories and doing family dispersed in time and space among multiple participating members. Neither "the family" nor "storytelling" can be taken as self-evident, pre-given entities or activities. Taking and making stories of family experience involves *ordering* discourse, that is, semantic relations that make sense of lived experience and create family and family sensibilities. The communication focus on ordering discourse considers *how* participants order content and context to make family stories, *how* participation is ordered in telling and listening and storing family stories, and *how* storytelling forms family identities and small group cultures. In communicology, family is the subject, medium, and outcome of storytelling.[24] To illustrate the communicological approach in our analysis, we traced how the experience of "the sewing sandwiches" by one Franco American family in Maine emerges in a semantic system.[25]

As content-ordering, family stories are made and performed more than found and labeled by nouns, objects, and topics. Content is formed in struggles to understand the meanings and sensibilities of events, activities, and identities. In this research exemplar, two male cousins in their 70s, Alain and Gerald, the spouse of one of the cousins, and the researcher (Kristin) sit at a kitchen table in a small town in central Maine and talk about the family sewing circle, an activity of women witnessed by the cousins from upstairs through grates in the floor when they were children. The participants collectively recall the sewing circles, with some disagreements, ongoing modifications, gaps in knowledge and memory, and occasional innovations: who inside and outside the family was in the sewing circle, what lunches were made and what went into the sandwiches, and when was French interspersed with English? At one point Gerald's spouse leaves her kitchen work and joins everyone at the table to describe details of the food preparation. The memories unfold among participants, and we hear that the women always saved sandwiches for the men and children, and that now Alain makes them for his grandchildren and calls them "sewing sandwiches" even though they are no longer associated with sewing circle meetings. As content is ordered into the meanings and senses of family, information is transformed to communication as saying supplements doing and as doing the work of storytelling supplements saying something about family. What may have been missed or considered minor by researchers moves to family significance.

Task-ordering—the labor of telling and listening and remembering and keeping—is the interactional work that families do to create and maintain productive internal and external relations as family stories evolve in changing environments. In our analysis, we explore the elements of task allocation that routinize storytelling by generation and gender with a range of creative variations in how that work gets done. This is shown in Alain's retrieval and transformation of the family women's sewing circles to his grandchildren's sewing sandwiches, and varieties of co-narrations by spouses, siblings, "sides," "lines," and alliances with "outsiders." Thus, family storytelling orders possibilities for identity and agency in discourse: opening and closing boundaries of who is and can/cannot be in the family circle of the "we," of the families "like us" or "like them," of the enfamilied and the individualized "I's." Rather than sorting subjects and taking family identity as self-evident or pre-given, communicology interrogates how making and marking internal and external boundaries forms local models for subjective agency and family identity across generations in the specific, historical formations of Franco American families in Maine that we studied. Analysis of ordering content, tasks, and identities can access the "hows" of verbs and relations in semantics obscured by the "whats" of commensense nouns, objects, and topics.

A SYSTEM OF PRAGMATIC ELEMENTS

Answering Questions

As suggested by the positioning of the subject as an element in a semantic system, the addressee's discourse is an answer to a question. Lindlof and Taylor describe their example in this way: "SG responds to a question Tom has asked about what attracts him so much to advance work that he, a professional man with a family, keeps coming back to this life on the road for one election cycle after another."[26] As such, the interviewee's response functions as an element in a pragmatic system, that is, it does something as part of the interview situation that goes beyond a narrative account of experience. In her discussion of "giving an account of oneself," Butler argues that "the moment the story is addressed to someone, it assumes a rhetorical dimension that is not reducible to a narrative function. It presumes that someone, and it seeks to recruit and act upon that someone."[27] In this case, the "answer" can be interpreted as working strategically to redirect potential criticism away from the interviewee as someone who takes time away from family to work in advance. Or, the answer can be interpreted as a defense for accepting a poor salary. Or, it can be interpreted as a moral claim that casts advance as a form of witnessing. In all of these variations, the focus is on what the discourse does and not merely on what it is about. When coding situates discourse as the semantic content of "an answer" and not more than that, it neglects the ways that discourse works to act upon multiple audiences—the "someones" who are both present and absent. This effort is what Eco refers to as the ideological labor of code switching: "In order to avoid openly acknowledging the contradictory nature of the Global Semantic System (...) ideological discourse must *switch* from one code to another without making the process evident."[28] In this case, discourse switches from a semantic system where an "answer" constitutes the "datum's primary content and essence"[29] to a pragmatic system where "answering a question" recruits and acts upon the interviewer and other possible "someones."

Asking Questions

Just as answering a question functions strategically, so too does the act of asking questions. Charmaz argues that by creating codes, researchers "try to understand our participants' standpoints and situations, as well as their actions within the setting (...). We create our codes by defining what we see in the data."[30] In Lindlof and Taylor's example, the code "ATTRACTIONS OF ADVANCE" is a label given to the answer. However, the question also contains that answer: "Tom has asked about what attracts him [SG] so much to advance work."[31] Indeed, the category of "ATTRACTIONS OF ADVANCE" is described by Lindlof and Taylor as one of "the open codes created by Tom that relate to his question."[32] In this way, the act of asking questions, rather than the act of answering them, functions to order the discourse and guides the creation of codes. Why is the interviewer so interested in advance work? What is the nature of his attraction? Is advance work a kind of gravity well, romantic suitor, or carnival ride to "attract" such attention? Why is the researcher trying to get access to inside information on advance work? To claim that a particular label codes the answer is to ignore the question that informs the answer it requests or invites. In this sense, SG's responses can be seen as replicating or mirroring the form of Tom's question. That is, Tom wants to know what goes on behind the scenes in advance work, so SG complies and describes what happens behind the scenes. The question locates the interviewer in a pragmatic system as a witness to the interviewee's act of answering which is itself a description of acting as witness in advance work. The act of coding is therefore only another step in this infinite regress: the coder acts as witness to the interviewer's witness of the interviewee's witness of advance work.

Doing an Interview as a Collaborative Practice

To focus on the strategic functions of answering and asking questions demonstrates that "doing an interview" is a practical accomplishment for both interviewer and interviewee. As Lindlof and Taylor recognize, "there is a lot going on here—much more, it turned out, than just responding to Tom's question."[33] Eco describes this pragmatic system by focusing on the joint labor necessary to articulate and interpret content. He writes, "there is labor performed by both the sender and the addressee to articulate and interpret sentences whose content must be correctly established and detected."[34] To approach interview discourse as "raw, uncoded data" neglects the pragmatic system by which the interviewer and interviewee work together to articulate and interpret content. As Silverman emphasizes, "'coding' is not the preserve of research scientists. In some sense, researchers, like all of us, 'code' what they hear and see in the world around them. Moreover, this 'coding' has been shown to be mutual and interactive."[35] The research interview, in other words, is always already coded; the interviewer and interviewee rely on and mobilize shared syntactic, semantic, and pragmatic systems in order to participate in the interview.

For our final empirical research example, we point to the analysis of an interview with a Somali immigrant in Maine.[36] This analysis focuses on one phrase spoken in the interview, the speech act "if you ask," and how it reveals the mutual and interactive "coding" that takes place among interview participants. The phrase emerges in an interview with Caaliya (a pseudonym), a young Somali woman. The interview was one part of a collaborative, community-based participatory project among researchers, Somali students, and community members.[37] "If you ask" constitutes what Lanigan calls a "revelatory phrase" in that it illuminates the pragmatic system of elements in the research interview from the perspective of communicology.[38] To build on the point Butler makes about account giving (cited above), in the moment of saying "if you ask," Caailya gives an account of herself that is not reducible to its narrative function but presumes its addressee or *that someone* ("you") and seeks to recruit and act upon these listeners, both present and absent. The interview is not only a pragmatic system of embodied and co-constructed discourse but also a problematic one. "If you ask" and "if you ask me" are strategic moves in the intersubjective mesh of answering and asking questions within a larger context of unequal social relations.

Somali immigrants such as Caaliya narrate in a culture of alterity and hypervisibility. "If you ask" refers to the (unasked) question about Caaliya's wearing a *hijab*, a potential sign of women's oppression in the U.S. The phrase points out the conditions of the interview: that the listeners (Kristin is among them) are non-Somali and non-Muslim and non-refugees; and Caaliya positions her identity by responding to her own question. "If you ask" may mean something like "you should ask or want to ask because I want to answer" or "you are implicitly asking and I must answer" or other possibilities. The variation "if you ask me" arises when Caaliya introduces the topic of female genital mutilation in response to the follow-up interviewer question, "Can you give us an example of what would be culture versus religion?" The possible meanings of "if you ask me" in this instance may be something like "this is what I believe about it" (a strong opinion), "I think this way but it's just my opinion" (a minimized stance), "it's a problem but not for me" (dismissal of a controversy), and "I've stated my position on this and won't say more" (termination of a topic)—among other possibilities. In every case it displays pragmatic relations in the joint labor of the research interview to articulate and interpret content and to create and contest codes that guide the talk and listening.

The revelatory phrase "if you ask" illuminates pragmatic complexities of answering and asking questions in the research interview and troubles the understanding of codes as something researchers find in a text. If the interview itself is a collaborative practice of coding, then how does that practice relate to coding practiced by researchers in analysis? How does the practical accomplishment of "doing an interview" relate to the practical accomplishment of "coding an interview?"[39] In the next section, we move from a consideration of coding in what Eco calls a Theory of Codes to coding in a Theory of Communicational Acts in order to clarify how the practice of coding raises methodological issues of ontology, epistemology, logic, and axiology.

A RULE COUPLING ELEMENTS FROM SYNTACTIC, SEMANTIC, AND PRAGMATIC SYSTEMS: CODING AND INVENTION IN A THEORY OF COMMUNICATIONAL ACTS

Coding and Ontology

According to Eco, in a Theory of Codes a code organizes the "stuff" of "experience" by correlating produced units in a syntactic system (as expression) with interpreted units in a semantic system (as content).[40] By contrast, in a Theory of Communicational Acts, the pragmatic processes of communication make it possible to discover a particular relation of addressee and addresser engaged in discourse.[41] The researcher, from the perspective of a Theory of Communication Acts, is faced with a paradoxical situation—much like the situation of painter in front of a canvas that Eco describes—where she or he must work to understand and express the content of discourse "that is neither coded nor divided into precise units. It has to be *invented.*"[42] Working in the absence of given codes, the painter in Eco's example "has a fairly clear idea of *what* he would like to 'say', but he does not know *how* to say it; and he cannot know *how* to do so until he has discovered *precisely what* to say (...). Thus the painter (...) has to propose a new way of coding."[43] Such invention demonstrates that, as Catt summarizes, "communication is no mere exchange; it is an experience. Where meaning emerges, the experience is shared consciousness: my expressions become your perceptions, my perceptions become your expressions, and inversely, your expressions become my perceptions and your perceptions become my expressions."[44] Invention in research is a process of mapping, as Eco suggests, but where both the territory and the map are emergent, partial, fragmentary, and dispersed.

What does the researcher take to be the lived phenomena under investigation? What is the object of analysis in coding? Is it the researcher's conscious experience of the interview for which a recording or a transcript serves as an aide to memory? Is it the perception of an audio-recording or a transcript for which multiple listenings and readings is the expression to be analyzed? To conceptualize coding as the categorization of information privileges the system of semantic elements over both the system of pragmatic elements and the system of syntactic elements. Furthermore, it obscures the place of the researcher as an embodied participant and the act of research itself as a communication event.

Coding and Epistemology

The focus on invention raises the epistemological issue of how the researcher knows what is going on in communication. As practiced in qualitative communication research, coding functions as a process of *defining* "what the data are about" rather than a process of *describing* meaning. For example, Charmaz claims that "through coding, you *define* what is happening in the data and begin to grapple with what it means."[45] Thus, she continues, "we define what we see as significant in the data and describe what we think is happening. Coding consists of this initial, shorthand defining and labeling; it results from a grounded theorist's actions and understandings."[46] What is the goal of research and analysis here? Does definition lead to description or does description lead to definition? To what extent are they reversible and reflexive? The emphasis on defining and labeling knowledge before moving to understand meaning raises the issue of interpretation as practiced in the human sciences. Traditionally, the focus of interpretation is on explication rather than translation; that is, definition emerges from description rather than vice versa. As Dreyfus describes it, interpretation is best understood as an ontological problem in the context of shared bodily practices rather than an epistemological problem of how to represent knowledge. He argues that we understand when we come to share "know how" and discriminations rather than arriving at agreements about what is true—what he calls the difference between "finding one's way" and "cracking a code."[47] Therefore, coding is more than a choice of how to represent or categorize a collection of messages; it is the discovery of a way to get a "better grip" on the situation or, following Eco, a way of moving in a multileveled discourse or aesthetic text.

Coding and Logic

Part of our difficulty in clarifying how coding works in qualitative communication research is the coincidence of two types of ambiguity. First, as the previous discussion of ontology and epistemology suggest there is ambiguity because qualitative research encompasses both the coding practiced by participants in the interview and the coding practiced by researchers in analysis. The ambiguity this creates is meaningful because coding in the order of experience is *appositional* to coding in the order of analysis.[48] That is, the position of the researcher is doubled—the researcher has access to both situations of coding in consciousness and uses that ambiguity to position the interview experience in relation to the experience of analysis. Typically, the analysis (the second position) is taken as making sense of the interview (the first position).

A second type of ambiguity concerns how the researcher moves between what Lanigan, drawing on phenomenological traditions of human science research, calls the order of experience and the order of analysis. An issue here is the logic for "combining the experiencer (researcher) with the activity of experiencing (researching) the phenomenon being experienced (what is researched)."[49] An example of this ambiguity can be seen in Saldaña's description of coding. He writes, "When we reflect on a passage of data to decipher its core meaning, we are *de*coding; when we determine its appropriate code and label it, we are *en*coding. For ease of reference throughout this manual, *coding* will be the sole term used. Simply understand that coding is the transitional process between data collection and more extensive data analysis."[50] Saldaña's solution to the ambiguity of coding, in brief, conflates encoding and decoding by ignoring the directionality of what he calls "the transitional process." In this case, Saldaña assumes that the order of experience and the order of analysis are parallel forms of logic. This assumption replicates the logic employed in positivistic and postpositivistic social science where experience is simply that which is given prior to analysis. This formulation implies that all researchers are the same (that is, "objective" in their coding) and will therefore analyze the same experience (decoding) in the same way (encoding). Or, as Lanigan states: "The researcher is simply researching what is researched, but we have mysteriously put aside the question of how."[51]

If, however, the goal of research is *understanding*, then the researcher begins with her or his consciousness of the phenomenon in order to discover that which is taken as evidence for analysis. In other words, rather than replicating the order of experience in the order of analysis, the researcher reverses it to generate a description of the phenomenon. The researcher begins with her or his experience of *what is researched* (encoding) to discover the activity of *researching* (decoding) as a rule of judgment employed by the *researcher* (coding). Lanigan emphasizes that "only by starting with the OE [order of experience] and reversing it as the OA [order of analysis] can the researcher be guaranteed of both accuracy and abstraction in description."[52] Thus, the ambiguity of coding is meaningful and productive for the researcher in order to understand *how* the interviewee and interviewer communicate and not just *what* they are talking about.

Coding and Axiology

We have taken a critical position in this analysis in order to trouble the practice of coding in qualitative communication research. In doing so, we have "overcoded" the analysis by moving among elements in syntactic, semantic, and pragmatic systems to clarify the theoretical possibilities for coding in research. As such, our critical position and advocacy of communicology is "motivated." As Eco remarks,

> Everybody who wants to know something wants to know it in order to do something. If he claims that he wants to know it only in order "to know" and not in order "to do" it means that he wants to know it in order to do nothing, which is in fact a surreptitious way of doing something, i.e. leaving the world just as it is (or as his approach assumes that it ought to be) (…). If semiotics is a theory, then it should be a theory that permits a continuous critical intervention in semiotic phenomena. Since people speak, to explain why and how they speak cannot help but determine their future way of speaking.[53]

In this way, to clarify the practice of coding can help to determine future possibilities for qualitative communication research and suggest the importance of theoretically-based methodologies in communicology.

NOTES

1. Johnny Saldaña, *The Coding Manual for Qualitative Researchers* (Thousand Oaks, CA: Sage, 2009), 3.
2. Saldaña, *Coding*, 8.
3. Kathy Charmaz, *Constructing Grounded Theory: A Practical Guide Through Qualitative Analysis* (Thousand Oaks, CA: Sage, 2006), 43.
4. Thomas R. Lindlof and Bryan C. Taylor, *Qualitative Communication Research Methods*, 3rd ed. (Thousand Oaks, CA: Sage, 2011), 246.
5. We adopt this organization from Richard L. Lanigan, *The Human Science of Communicology: A Phenomenology of Discourse in Foucault and Merleau-Ponty* (Pittsburgh, PA: Duquesne University Press, 1992).
6. Umberto Eco, *A Theory of Semiotics* (Bloomington: Indiana University Press, 1976).
7. Eco, *Semiotics*, 38.
8. For examples of this tradition, see Lanigan, *Human Science of Communicology*; and Deborah Eicher-Catt and Isaac E. Catt, *Communicology: The New Science of Embodied Discourse* (Cranbury, NJ: Associated University Presses, 2010).
9. Lindlof and Taylor, *Qualitative*.
10. Lindlof and Taylor, *Qualitative*, 248.
11. Martyn Hammersley, *Questioning Qualitative Inquiry: Critical Essays* (Thousand Oaks, CA: Sage, 2008), 51.
12. Anthony Wilden, *The Rules Are No Game: The Strategy of Communication* (New York: Routledge & Kegan Paul, 1987).
13. Lindlof and Taylor, *Qualitative*, 248.

14. For a discussion of the implications of punctuation in transcription, see Martyn Hammersley, "Reproducing or Constructing: Some Questions about Transcription in Social Research," *Qualitative Research* 10 (2010): 553–569.
15. Eric E. Peterson and Kristin M. Langellier, "The Politics of Personal Narrative Methodology," *Text and Performance Quarterly* 17 (1997): 135–152.
16. See Kristin M. Langellier and Claire F. Sullivan, "Breast Talk in Breast Cancer Narratives," *Qualitative Health Research* 8 (1998): 76–94; and Kristin M. Langellier, "'You're Marked': Breast Cancer, Tattoo, and the Narrative Performance of Identity," in *Narrative and Identity: Studies in Autobiography, Self and Culture*, ed. Donal Carbaugh and Jens Brockmeier (Amsterdam: John Benjamins, 2001), 145–184.
17. Lindlof and Taylor, *Qualitative*, 247.
18. For example, see Cory Doctorow, "Extreme Geek," in *Context: Further Selected Essays on Productivity, Creativity, Parenting, and Politics in the 21st Century* (San Francisco, CA: Tachyon Publications, 2011), 18–20.
19. Richard L. Lanigan, "Communicology and Culturology: Semiotic Phenomenological Method in Applied Small Group Research," *The Public Journal of Semiotics* 4, no. 2 (2013): 84.
20. Lindlof and Taylor, *Qualitative*, 253.
21. Lanigan, "Communicology and Culturology," 84; brackets and parentheses in the original.
22. Lindlof and Taylor, *Qualitative*, 247.
23. Kristin M. Langellier and Eric E. Peterson, *Storytelling in Daily Life: Performing Narrative* (Philadelphia, PA: Temple University Press, 2004).
24. For a related discussion of family as a small group medium, see Lanigan, "Communicology and Culturology."
25. Kristin M. Langellier and Eric E. Peterson, "Narrative Performance Theory: Telling Stories, Doing Family," in *Engaging Theories in Family Communication: Multiple Perspectives*, ed. Dawn O. Braithwaite and Leslie A. Baxter (Thousand Oaks, CA: Sage, 2006), 99–114.
26. Lindlof and Taylor, *Qualitative*, 252.
27. Judith Butler, *Giving an Account of Oneself* (New York: Fordham University Press, 2005), 63.
28. Eco, *Semiotics*, 155.
29. Saldaña, *Coding*, 3.
30. Charmaz, *Constructing*, 46.
31. Lindlof and Taylor, *Qualitative*, 252.
32. Lindlof and Taylor, *Qualitative*, 253.
33. Lindlof and Taylor, *Qualitative*, 253.
34. Eco, *Semiotics*, 155.
35. David Silverman, *Interpreting Qualitative Data: Methods for Analyzing Talk, Text and Interaction*, 5th ed. (Thousand Oaks, CA: Sage, 2015), 439.
36. Kristin M. Langellier, "'If You Ask': Troubling Narrative Interviews," *Departures in Critical Qualitative Research* 3 (2014): 442–456.
37. See Kristin M. Langellier, "Performing Somali Identity in the Diaspora: 'Wherever I Go I Know Who I Am,'" *Cultural Studies* 24 (2010): 66–94; and Kim Huisman, Mazie Hough, Kristin M. Langellier, and Carol Toner, eds., *Somalis in Maine: Crossing Cultural Currents* (Berkeley, CA: North Atlantic Press, 2011).
38. For a discussion of revelatory phrases, see Lanigan, "Communicology and Culturology."

39. William Housley and Robin James Smith, "Telling the CAQDAS Code: Membership Categorization and the Accomplishment of 'Coding Rules' in Research Team Talk," *Discourse Studies* 13 (2011): 417–434.
40. Eco, *Semiotics*, 52.
41. For a discussion of this point, see Roman Jakobson, "Linguistics and Communication Theory," in *Selected Writings II: Word and Language* (The Hague: Mouton, 1971), 570–579.
42. Eco, *Semiotics*, 188.
43. Eco, *Semiotics*, 188.
44. Issac E. Catt, "The Signifying World between Ineffability and Intelligibility: Body as Sign in Communicology," *Review of Communication* 11 (2011): 122–144.
45. Charmaz, *Constructing*, 46.
46. Charmaz, *Constructing*, 47.
47. Hubert L. Dreyfus, "Holism and Hermeneutics," *Review of Metaphysics* 34 (1980): 2–23.
48. Richard L. Lanigan, "Capta versus Data: Method and Evidence in Communicology," *Human Studies* 17 (1994): 109–130.
49. Lanigan, "Capta," 112.
50. Saldaña, *Coding*, 4.
51. Lanigan, "Capta," 113.
52. Lanigan, "Capta," 113.
53. Eco, *Semiotics*, 29.

BIBLIOGRAPHY

Butler, Judith. *Giving an Account of Oneself*. New York: Fordham University Press, 2005.
Catt, Isaac E. "The Signifying World Between Ineffability and Intelligibility: Body as Sign in Communicology." *Review of Communication* 11 (2011): 122–144.
Charmaz, Kathy. *Constructing Grounded Theory: A Practical Guide Through Qualitative Analysis*. Thousand Oaks, CA: Sage, 2006.
Doctorow, Cory. "Extreme Geek." In *Context: Further Selected Essays on Productivity, Creativity, Parenting, and Politics in the 21st Century*, 18–20. San Francisco, CA: Tachyon Publications, 2011.
Dreyfus, Hubert L. "Holism and Hermeneutics." *Review of Metaphysics* 34 (1980): 3–23.
Eco, Umberto. *A Theory of Semiotics*. Bloomington: Indiana University Press, 1976.
Eicher-Catt, Deborah, and Isaac E. Catt, eds. *Communicology: The New Science of Embodied Discourse*. Cranbury, NJ: Associated University Presses, 2010.
Hammersley, Martyn. *Questioning Qualitative Inquiry: Critical Essays*. Thousand Oaks, CA: Sage, 2008.
Hammersley, Martyn. "Reproducing or Constructing: Some Questions about Transcription in Social Research." *Qualitative Research* 10 (2010): 553–569.
Housley, William, and Robin James Smith. "Telling the CAQDAS Code: Membership Categorization and the Accomplishment of 'Coding Rules' in Research Team Talk." *Discourse Studies* 13 (2011): 417–434.
Huisman, Kim, Mazie Hough, Kristin M. Langellier, and Carol Toner, eds. *Somalis in Maine: Crossing Cultural Currents*. Berkeley, CA: North Atlantic, 2011.
Jakobson, Roman. "Linguistics and Communication Theory." *Selected Writings II. Word and Language*, 570–579. The Hague: Mouton, 1971.

Langellier, Kristin M. "'If You Ask:' Troubling Narrative Interviews." *Departures in Critical Qualitative Research* 3 (2014): 442–456.

Langellier, Kristin M. "Performing Somali Identity in the Diaspora: 'Wherever I Go I Know Who I Am.'" *Cultural Studies* 24 (2010): 66–94.

Langellier, Kristin M. "'You're Marked:' Breast Cancer, Tattoo, and the Narrative Performance of Identity." In *Narrative and Identity: Studies in Autobiography, Self and Culture*, edited by Donal Carbaugh and Jens Brockmeier, 145–184. Amsterdam: John Benjamins, 2001.

Langellier, Kristin M., and Eric E. Peterson. "Narrative Performance Theory: Telling Stories, Doing Family." In *Engaging Theories in Family Communication: Multiple Perspectives*, edited by Dawn O. Braithwaite and Leslie A. Baxter, 99–114. Thousand Oaks, CA: Sage, 2006.

Langellier, Kristin M., and Eric E. Peterson. *Storytelling in Daily Life: Performing Narrative.* Philadelphia, PA: Temple University, 2004.

Langellier, Kristin M., and Claire F. Sullivan. "Breast Talk in Breast Cancer Narratives." *Qualitative Health Research* 8 (1998): 76–94.

Lanigan, Richard L. "Capta versus Data: Method and Evidence in Communicology." *Human Studies* 17 (1994): 109–130.

Lanigan, Richard L. "Communicology and Culturology: Semiotic Phenomenological Method in Applied Small Group Research." *The Public Journal of Semiotics* 4, no. 2 (2013): 71–103.

Lanigan, Richard L. *The Human Science of Communicology: A Phenomenology of Discourse in Foucault and Merleau-Ponty*. Pittsburgh, PA: Duquesne University Press, 1992.

Lindlof, Thomas R., and Bryan C. Taylor. *Qualitative Communication Research Methods*. 3rd ed. Thousand Oaks, CA: Sage, 2011.

Peterson, Eric E., and Kristin M. Langellier. "The Politics of Personal Narrative Methodology." *Text and Performance Quarterly* 17 (1997): 135–152.

Saldaña, Johnny. *The Coding Manual for Qualitative Researchers*. Thousand Oaks, CA: Sage, 2009.

Silverman, David. *Interpreting Qualitative Data: Methods for Analyzing Talk, Text and Interaction*. 5th ed. Thousand Oaks, CA: Sage, 2015.

Wilden, Anthony. *The Rules Are No Game: The Strategy of Communication*. New York: Routledge & Kegan Paul, 1987.

SECTION THREE

Trans/formations

CHAPTER NINE

Emmanuel Levinas

The Turning of Semioethics

RONALD C. ARNETT, SUSAN MANCINO, AND HANNAH KAROLAK

Levinas's understanding of ethics as first philosophy counters the priority of the communicative subject with the importance of the Other.[1] Levinas's project contends with an "originative I," which seeks escape from responsibility for the Other. Levinas's ethical alternative is a "derivative I" called forth into responsibility by the Other and an immemorial ethical echo. His ethics project hinges on one principal sign—the face of the Other, which eschews literal visual representation. In contrast, the face is a presentation of the inarticulable alterity of the Other, which rhetoric eclipses and totalizes. In *Totality and Infinity*, Levinas asserts that rhetoric obscures the Other with "linguistic illusion," which is an absence of truth.[2] This essay recognizes Levinas's dismissal of rhetoric in that it reduces signification to a sign game void of meaning. The semiotic interplay of the face of the Other as sign and an understanding of rhetoric not aligned with Levinas centers this communicological investigation of signification via the particular and ethics.

Richard L. Lanigan's pioneering conception of communicology involves embodied experience of human discourse through human science inquiry responsive to the interchange of description, reduction, and interpretation.[3] Part I of this essay, "Particularity of Embodied Conceptual Insight," structures examination of communicology through a reflexive engagement of description, reduction, and interpretation. Part II, "Description of Levinas's Project: Ethical Signification Beyond the Verse," interprets Levinas's insight on "beyond the verse," then identifies and reviews seminal articles that examine the relationship between and among semiotics and rhetoric, concluding with Levinas's notion of signification. Part III,

"Reduction of Levinas's Project: Semioethics and Rhetorical Demand," reduces Levinas's performative ethics project to semioethics and rhetorical demand, both of which are interpreted and reduced to central components that describe the functions of Levinas's project. Part IV, "Interpretation of Levinas's Project: Ethics and the Derivative I," provides concluding remarks on our interpretation of the role of rhetoric and semioethics in Levinas's performative understanding of ethics as first philosophy.

This essay is attentive to the particularity of the human experience, ever cognizant of ambiguity. This essay centers on two questions: (1) how do semiotics inform Levinas's conception of face as sign? and (2) how does the immemorial ethical echo recast Levinas's critique of rhetoric? We now turn to an experiential understanding of description, reduction, and interpretation as a guide for examining the distinctiveness of Levinas's project related to a communicology of semiotics and rhetoric.

PARTICULARITY OF EMBODIED CONCEPTUAL INSIGHT

Lanigan situates communicology within human discourse, naming qualitative methods, interpretive approaches, and narrative as central to the human sciences in the illumination of particularity of human perception within embodied experience.[4] Human sciences, within the scope of communicology, center on performative practices composed of embodied experiences that serve as "valid" research sources.[5] This action is in contrast to the universalizing implications of the social sciences. Lanigan's communicology differentiates human science from social science, with the former seeking to understand particularity and the latter propelled by universal generalizability of findings. For Lanigan, communicology embraces semiotic phenomenology as an exemplar of understanding communicative experience that "begins empirically at the point of human meaning, self-expressed and self-perceived in the *person*".[6] Isaac E. Catt refers to semiotic phenomenology as a paradigmatic exemplar that combines the study of signs and sign systems with conscious experience. Communicology explicates the distinctiveness of human meaning-making through three embodied practices: (1) description, (2) reduction, and (3) interpretation.[7]

The first practice, description, provides an initial account of a phenomenon via three subsections: description[8] ("human awareness of *what* a phenomenon is"), reduction ("a fundamental account of *how* a description has meaning"), and interpretation ("*why* a meaning is manifest by the analysis of a given description").[9] The second step, reduction, offers a "second reflection and analysis," repeating the process of description, reduction, and interpretation outlined above to render a definition of a "necessary condition (e.g., a typology)" of the subject matter that is "merely a sufficient condition under description (e.g., a token)".[10] The final step, interpretation, again repeats the described process of description, reduction, and interpretation in a "concrete application" of a combined examination of first act of description and second act of reduction.[11] As indicated above, throughout communicological analysis, there is an ongoing interplay among description, reduction, and interpretation, which sediment communicology within an embodied experience of human discourse.

Lanigan explains that these three acts of description, reduction, and interpretation when combined with "the semiotic view of meaning as constituted in coded signs (signifiers/signifieds)" contour communicology.[12] These three processes are both interdependent and simultaneously distinct. As understood by Lanigan, this theoretical framework is reordered when the theory moves into a methodology. Conventional social sciences assume that the order of analysis outlined in the theoretical framework above is identical to the order of experience. However, in communicology's commitment to uncovering particular embodied experiences, there is a recognition that the order of experience moves inversely from the order of analysis.[13] Lanigan summarizes the interdependency of communicology in the following reflexive understanding of communicative experience:

1. Description (Thematizing the)
    a. Interpretation (of the)
    b. Reduction (of the)
    c. Description (of the Sign[s])
2. Reduction (Abstracting the)
    d. Interpretation (of the)
    e. Reduction (of the)
    f. Description (of the Signifier[s])
3. Interpretation (Explicating the)
    g. Interpretation (of the)
    h. Reduction (of the)
    i. Description (of the Signified[s])[14]

Each step of description, reduction, and interpretation inherently involves the presence of description, reduction, and interpretation. These meaning-making functions are co-present at each level of analysis in recognition of persons as "creators and beholders of meaning"[15] engaged in embodied analysis of human discourse. Communicology yields pragmatic and theoretical application, as seen through the work of fellow communicologists, such as Jacqueline Martinez, Deborah Eicher-Catt, and Isaac Catt.

Martinez states that the combined study of semiotics and phenomenology transfers from signs and codes to semiosis—"ongoing action of signs".[16] Semiotic phenomenology recognizes human consciousness as embodied within a physical environment situated among other human consciousnesses.[17] For Martinez, the projects of Roman Jakobson (1896–1982) and Maurice Merleau-Ponty (1908–1961) lay the groundwork for communicology's semiotic phenomenology. While Ferdinand de Saussure (1857–1913) moved the study of language into the field of human communication with an emphasis on culture, consciousness, and experience, the insights of Jakobson and Merleau-Ponty joined diachrony and synchrony "with a phenomenological emphasis into a dialectical relationship." This move resisted understanding structure as "an abstract and absent concept like grammar" Instead, their work understood structure as present and concrete, emerging from a particular "speaking subject".[18] An understanding of the speaking subject as a sign-system recognizes that language is not an object, but rather a "gesture" of meaning expressed pre-consciously.[19] Jakobson and particularly Merleau-Ponty argue that one must embody codes in order to study them. They acknowledge the temporal subjective value of linguistic data that profiles communicology's experiential examination of the particular.

Martinez recounts communicology as a practical process of meaning discovery. The first step, description, allows researchers to "back track" an embodied interpretation of phenomena in order to expose a reduction from which an experience is thematized in a description. The second step, reduction, reminds us that we rely on our "already thematized (interpreted) understanding of experience" as we move through the human science of communicology, allowing one to practice "abstraction" as a process that privileges parts of the description and then reorganizes those parts within a multiplicity of interconnections. Thus, the process of reduction allows us to remain aware of presupposed meanings. The third step, interpretation, explicates interpretive understanding that leads to abstraction described in the essential characteristics of the investigated phenomenon.[20] This engagement does not eliminate the subject, but rather makes the subject's distinct interpretation the primary focus. Martinez's pragmatic application of communicology is reflective of Eicher-Catt and Catt's theoretical engagement of communicology.

Eicher-Catt and Catt conceptualize communicology as "the science of embodied discourse."[21] Communicology, characterized as a "reflexive methodology" of semiotic phenomenology, is distinct in its "refusal (...) [to embrace] the dominant Logos of discourse"[22]; it announces in the social sciences an acceptance of a "holistic" embrace of communication understood within lived and embodied experience.[23] The "event" of communication understood as a *"possibility,"* rather than a "probability," emerges "in signs and [is] actualized by the body."[24] Eicher-Catt and Catt work from the following assumption: "Everything experienced is by means of a sign, and inversely, there are no signs outside real or imagined experience."[25] Meaning, however, is not inherent in signs or in the person; it is "hidden" in normative conventions.[26] Communicology explores the *"existential* ground" of subjectivity with an embodied semiotic understanding of wholeness attentive to the particularity of the experience of communication.[27]

This essay understands Levinas's ethics as tied to particularity of the experience of communication through an embodied encounter with the face of the Other that initiates a turn toward an immemorial ethical echo that returns one to obligation to and for the particular Other as a "derivative I" charged with responsibility without universal assurance about the correct form of ethical action. This essay examines Levinas's project of ethics as first philosophy via two central themes in communication: semiotics and rhetoric. These coordinates guide our communicological analysis of the lived communicative experience of Levinas's performative engagement with the phenomena of ethics.

DESCRIPTION OF LEVINAS'S PROJECT: ETHICAL SIGNIFICATION *BEYOND THE VERSE*

The descriptive phase of Lanigan's communicology commences with an interpretation of the experience, a reduction of the experience, and finally a description of the signs that give insight, clarity, and coordinates for explicating the consciousness of the event—in this case Levinas's project as first philosophy. Our description of Levinas's project acknowledges the importance of signification beyond the verse—in the practicality of everyday life. In this section three descriptive acts emerge: (1) an interpretation of Levinas's project that yields ethical signification beyond the verse; (2) a reduction to significant essays examining the relationship between Levinas's project, semiotics and rhetoric; and (3) a description of the ongoing significance of this scholarship. This essay follows the otherwise than conventional movement from description to interpretation announced by Lanigan. Lanigan's insights seem particularly relevant to Levinas's ethics as first philosophy in that his work is otherwise conventional within the Western conception of philosophy. We begin our description of Levinas's project by turning to *Beyond the Verse*, which announces the importance of examining semiotics and rhetoric in Levinas's project as a hermeneutic key to understanding both the experience of Saying, the dwelling of signification, and the pragmatic importance of the Said. We then reduce our description to key essays that examine semiotics and rhetoric in Levinas's project, describing the ongoing significance of this scholarship.

Interpreting Ethical Signification Beyond the Verse

The manner in which Levinas presents *Beyond the Verse* introduces the importance of both semiotics and rhetoric in signification, as he emphasizes that one cannot control or possess meaning. Meaning-making and signification in Levinas, rests in the ambiguity of the Saying. To understand signification, one must attend to living expression within an ongoing communicative context of "surplus of meaning"[28] that carries a "prophetic essence."[29] This sense of meaning is beyond the control of the interpreter; it is beyond the verse itself, and is met within an ethical context of attentive "dis-inter-estedness."[30] The interpreter must cease imposing meaning and attend to the emerging significance of an experience tied to a given historical moment.

Levinas acknowledges ethics tied to the personal as the first step toward the act of possession and control of a house of totality. On the contrary, infinity lives within multiplicity and ethically driven disinterest where a surplus of meaning demands a political ingress for attentiveness to the Other. The quintessential reason for this perspective of hermeneutic generosity is propelled by a pragmatic recognition that one cannot control or stop infinity, which houses a surplus of meaning. "Surplus" is the defining feature of a reality inclusive of all, both Palestinians and Jews, in Israel.[31] Surplus of meaning requires outreach beyond our comfort to a point of upsetting our narrow and contrived worldviews. "It should not be forgotten that *my* lonely family and *my* people, despite the possessive pronouns, are my 'others,' like strangers, and demand justice and protection."[32] Ethical surplus moves one toward Otherness with acknowledgment that possession and control of meaning is a Sartrian act of "bad faith" that requires lying to oneself.[33]

Levinas submits that fidelity to God is an ethical surplus beyond naming. Such surplus is suggested by R. Ishmael's contention that if a person studied the whole of the Torah day and night, one must then "find a time that is neither day nor night and learn then Greek wisdom."[34] Levinas offers a yes to difference that is demanding. Semiotics beyond the verse take the reader/listener into a critique of rhetoric and the limits of "eloquence" propelled by "flattery" and "charm."[35] Levinas worried about a rhetoric that panders to the excessive hopes and fears of an audience. He rejects the contriving of surplus meaning, which is fundamentally different from an immemorial ethical surplus of meaning that is before and beyond the text.

Levinas contends that such a view of rhetoric invites "cities of refuge" composed of multiple laws and restrictions that yield everyday acts of hypocrisy.[36] He argues that such places are not a Jerusalem propelled by genuine faith, where "students [are] engaged in the study of Torah!"[37] Such study nourishes surplus of meaning in daily interaction and in engagement with the text. Beyond the verse, for Levinas, finds meaning in study without ignoring contradictions that form our lives together. A rhetoric of perfection moves to totality with an emphasis on pristine images. For Levinas, the meanings of the faith live in interspaces of each city of refuge that acknowledges "deep contradictions."[38]

Continuing with the theme of surplus, Levinas counters both political and faith-based views of totality. The power of the Torah reminds one to pray for the State, even Rome at its height.[39] The task of the Torah is to announce a covenant of multiplicity that demands acknowledgement of the infinity of Otherness. Levinas cites the Rabbi's contention that for each Israelite there are multiple "covenants."[40] For Levinas, the meaning beyond the verse is responsibility for the Other and for the Other's responsibility—a covenant beyond immediacy. This responsibility for the Other has implications for a communicative covenant with Others. One is responsible for both the Said and the "not Said," which together drive the meaning of the communicative interaction. In the ambiguity of the moment, one finds meaning within silence called forth by mercy and responsibility for those not present—the ethical praxis of a surplus of meaning.

Levinas functions otherwise than the convention of totality, suggesting that a world of meaning is lost when identity and significance emerge with undue clarity. He contends against words uttered with too much praise, enthusiasm, and undue assurance; such action is contrary to the semiotic tradition of Jewish hermeneutics. There is pluralism within the interpretive process of the faith that paradoxically informs "the unity of the Revelation."[41] This pluralism of meaning eschews unflinching clarity and defies arrogance and possession. The "fear of God" demands distance that resists thematization.[42] Possession finds a counter through recognition of dis-interest and surplus that is always "present," but is "without beginning at all."[43] The self, as interpreter, responds to unknown forces before the moment and is at the mercy of contextual forces that include the unseen and the unknown. Levinas attends to "a beyond being, resistant to thematization and origin—something preceding the originary: beyond non-being—an authority that orders my neighbor for me as a face."[44] Possession tied to undue clarity of naming, invites totalization to no longer be responsive to uniqueness.

Countering possession is the pragmatic consequence of revelation situated within multiple meanings. Levinas reminds readers of Psalm 62:11: "Once God has spoken; twice have I heard this," is the signification of "innumerable meanings."[45] The notion of the revelatory lives in the meeting of everyday existence on its own terms. In this meeting, one hears a voice of faith that requires one to "sober up" and pay attention to existence, whether or not one approves of such a reality, "a sobering up that is 'always' deeper and, in this sense, the spirituality of the spirit in obedience."[46] Revelation is central to the image of God, in that God is nameless; the unnamable has a "beginning," but no "ending."[47] Faithful metaphors of meaning and significance attend to beginning traces that assure no endings. The beginning is immemorial and forever; such is of the image of God.

Levinas rejected interpretive possession that functions as a form of hermeneutic imperialism. He sought history not tied to the imperialism of Caesar nor to the "eloquence of a careless moralism."[48] Levinas calls for a move from idolatrous politics to a concern for meeting existence in the name of a God that is beyond naming and lives in the prophetic voices of an immemorial past and in ongoing existence. For Levinas, this concern of an immemorial past and existence defines what it means to be a Jew in modernity—a history contrary to the West and the vestiges of assimilation from the West. "For as long as this confusion lasts, we will not have overcome the temptation of assimilation."[49] The hermeneutic key for Levinas is recognition that meaning is ultimately beyond the verse and one's comprehension;

yet, the human task is responsibility to temporally discern. Signification is for understanding, not possession.

Levinas's emphasis on ethical signification begins with the recognition of the face of the Other as sign that prompts an immemorial rhetorical demand of obligation and responsibility. Signification beyond the verse points toward two central Levinasian coordinates: semioethics and rhetoric.

Reduction to Semiotics and Rhetoric as Otherwise than Convention

We continue our description as we review scholarly essays that examine semiotics that acknowledge the face of the Other as signs that open opportunity for transcendence. Face as sign, in Levinas, moves one from an immemorial ethical echo back to a particular Other. Next, essays in rhetoric examine Levinas's project in a manner otherwise than his dismissal of rhetoric. Levinas's semioethical conception of the human face as interruption serves as a rhetorical mandate to attend to an immemorial ethical echo. This subsection's reduction of the semiotic interpretation of Levinas's project leads us to reclaim rhetoric as otherwise than convention. With *ensemble*, semiotics and rhetoric point toward signification that yields an ethical bridge of responsibility to and for the Other.

Semioethics. The work of Augusto Ponzio and Susan Petrilli explore the semiotic interpretation of Levinas's project. Together, these scholars have published over a dozen scholarly books on semiotics, with Ponzio authoring five books on Levinas. Ponzio introduced Levinas to Italy. He was the first scholar to edit and translate Levinas's original works into Italian. Petrilli, the seventh Thomas A. Sebeok fellow of the Semiotics Society of America, along with Ponzio, explores the interplay of semiotics, ethics, and human communication. Together, they are credited with the development of "semioethics."

Petrilli and Ponzio acknowledge that substitution—the-one-for-the-Other—is the juncture that separates Levinas's project from Western ontology. Following the insights of Thomas A. Sebeok (1920–2001), Petrilli writes that all "human sign behavior" connects to language. For Petrilli, this ongoing sign behavior of human language—semiosis—is not without ethical impact.[50] Particularly, Petrilli turns to the work of Levinas, who posits an understanding of human semiosis that is "otherwise than being." Petrilli writes that for Levinas, though humans are capable of language and, therefore, semiotic animals, human behavior is not reducible to ontology, being, or communication. Rather, persons have the capacity for otherness, which, for Levinas, is substitution. Ponzio's work extends the conversation about substitution in Levinas with the introduction of existential semiotics and signification founded "in the relation with the other".[51] Levinas's relation with the Other is neither Martin Heidegger's "being-with" nor Jean-Paul Sartre's "being-for." Rather, for Levinas, the Other is "*étranger*"—the absolutely Other, who is necessary for the identity of the self.[52]

Levinas's project, understood through semioethics, assumes a descriptive reduction centered upon recognition of the face, an impersonal attentiveness to an ethical command, and a comprehensive œurve that explicates the importance of the Other without a return to an original self. This tracing of the face of the Other as the fulcrum of semioethical signification announces the power of a visual optic that is rhetorically augmented by an audio ethic. The face as sign acts as the fulcrum of signification in Levinas's project that moves one into the second pillar of descriptive reduction—rhetoric rather than convention.

Rhetoric, our descriptive reduction, thus far, announces the performative phenomenon prompted by the face as sign that initiates a rhetorical interruption that is otherwise than convention in the form of "I am my brother's keeper." This immemorial ethical echo intimately connects to the recognition of the face of the Other. This immemorial ethical echo operates as a form of rhetoric filled with signification rather than conventional rhetoric motivated by impulses to possess or persuade. We acknowledge Levinas's well-documented critique of rhetoric as articulated by Susan Shapiro. Shapiro points to Levinas's "earliest and best-known treatment of rhetoric" in *Totality and Infinity* in which he ties rhetoric to "propaganda, flattery, [and] diplomacy."[53] She explains that for Levinas, conventional rhetoric "always refer[s] within—but never beyond—totality."[54] Levinas criticizes the "deceptiveness" of rhetoric as articulated by Plato in *Gorgias*, *Phaedrus*, and *Republic*. Levinas's concern with rhetoric lies within its "function [to persuade] in the absence of all truth" as it "imitates" ethical discourse while minimizing appearances from reality. Rhetoric is a sign game void of signification.[55] Signification emerges in one-being-for-the-Other, secured in one's ability to meaningfully respond to the face of the Other.[56] Conventional rhetoric fails to prompt signification. It eclipses the face, thereby, bypassing the audio immemorial obligation; a rhetoric rather than convention.

Shapiro asserts that Levinas's later works locate rhetoric in "ethical proximity" that counters conventional understandings of persuasion tied to an aesthetics of eloquence.[57] Orthodox rhetoric in the form of eloquence "absorb[s] the Saying in the Said" by confronting the Other rather than accepting responsibility.[58] Rhetoric emerges through the prophetic; the "Saying of the Saying (without the Said)" of the "Here I am."[59] Shapiro argues that rhetoric allows the prophetic to transcend to proximity.[60] The rhetoric of the immemorial ethical echo commands that one move to a particular Other, held hostage and charged with responsibility for that particular person. Recognition of the rhetorical dimensions of the immemorial ethical echo frame a 2005 special issue of *Philosophy and Rhetoric*. The remainder of this subsection details the importance of that collection.

The issue begins with Diane Perpich, who observes that despite the fervent critique of rhetoric. Levinas employs rhetorical dimensions in his conception of the face of the Other as a non-literal expression of that which cannot be represented. Levinas's view of language as emerging in the "distance" between the same and the Other invites "transcendence" where the Other represents an "obligation" to speak.[61] Perpich asks, if the ethical relationship is accomplished through language "outside of" and "overcoming" rhetoric, then how can we understand his early accounts of invocation that suggest that all discourse accomplishes ethical relationships?[62] Perpich argues that Levinas's representation of the face serves as a non-literal "rhetorical trope" that "represents the impossibility of its own self-representation."[63] According to Perpich, rhetoric as otherwise than convention announces the ambiguity of the face in an alterity that resists reification.

Bettina Bergo follows by examining ambiguity of the face through preconsciousness in Levinas's performative phenomenon, which she writes is a "form of presyntheic phenomenology."[64] For Levinas, one encounters the face of the Other in preconsciousness that is lost at the moment of reflection. Bergo notes the paradox of preconsciousness—as one communicates, one must reflect. This reflective process of rhetoric and philosophy disrupts the meaning and power of Saying, the preconscious being-for-the-other that is a Saying before the Said. For Levinas, meaning prior to logos emerges when one-is-for-the-other in an ethical act of signification. Bergo points to a rhetorical demand of ethical Saying before the Said, which permits the-one-being-for-the-other.

Oona Eisenstadt builds upon Bergo's essay with attentiveness to the ethical trace of Saying in the Said through the metaphors of Greek and Hebrew. Eisenstadt explains that Levinas understands Greek as an "ontological mode seeking to describe the whole."[65] Conversely, Levinas understands Hebrew as "the dialogical mode that is never complete and preserves dissent."[66] Eisenstadt associates Greek with the Same, politics, the Said, and totality; on the other hand, Hebrew is associated with the Other, ethics, the Saying, and infinity.[67] Derrida argues that neither concept (Greek or Jew) operates in "pure form," leaving both Greekjew and Jewgreek. The former "focus[es] on the building of totalizing orders" and the latter works "to particularize universals, to break syntheses, to live in ruptured totalities, to call the judgment of history into question."[68] Despite juxtapositions, Levinas insists that justice requires a unity of contraries where the rhetorical trace of Saying infuses the Said with ethical meaning.

Claire Elise Katz textures the unity of contraries with consideration of Levinas's Jewish texts through an examination of Scripture references in his philosophical works. Katz explains that Levinas's quoting of Biblical references serves a purpose similar to his quoting of Shakespeare, Tolstoy, and Dostoyevsky.[69] Katz explains that these works "express the same concerns that occupy philosophy" but do so without articulating a "philosophical argument."[70] The frequency of biblical references "blurs" philosophical boundaries. For Katz, references to Scripture are both rhetorical and pedagogical.[71] The rabbinic midrash allows the written word to signify more than it says with the text, "ask[ing] to be interpreted."[72] Katz describes the midrash as "interdependent, interconnected, and intersubjective," working toward an "ethical end."[73] For Levinas, "the holy voice of God" is alterity.[74] God's voice commands responsibility to and for the Other with ethics understood as religion.[75] Katz concludes that Levinas's use of scripture is not "proof," but rather "illustration."[76] Levinas's Jewish works are a source of signification in his philosophical corpus. The signification is derivative of the alterity within the voice of God, who interrupts with a rhetorical demand, "I am my brother's keeper," obligating one without clarity of response.

James Hatley concludes this special edition by reviewing four books that explore the relationship between Levinas's philosophy and Judaism.[77] Hatley points to four authors, Eisenstadt, Adam Zachary, Katz, and Robert Gibbs, who attend to the Jewish context as a background for understanding Levinas's ethics project and his philosophical writings. Hatley emphasizes that much remains lost when one attempts to understand Levinas's philosophy without attentiveness to his Jewish commitments. This attentiveness moves one beyond the verse and is inclusive of a rhetorical trace in the face of the Other that makes signification possible.

Describing Levinas's Project of Ethical Signification

We conclude this first step in reflexive understanding of communicative experience with a stress on semioethics and rhetoric as key to signification. The performative phenomenon of encountering the face of the Other reveals signification as a meeting point of rhetoric and semiotics in Levinas's ethics project. Our description began with an interpretive acknowledgement of Levinas's project beyond the verse, followed by a reduction to semioethical and rhetorical considerations, which culminate in a description of signification "in the form of a despite-me, for-another."[78] Levinas explains that our ethical responsibility to and for the Other is the fulcrum point from which signification occurs. It is only through the losing of oneself to and for the Other that the self ignites in meaningful response to a particular Other.

Levinas understands signification as prior to essence and identity in "the glory of transcendence"[79] in the act of substitution—the-one-for-the-other—that derivatively makes one responsible for a particular Other. Signification occurs within the Saying and within the trace of the Saying in the Said. Signification via Saying is an interruption of the Said. Levinas suggests that signification is not fusion with the Other or a totalizing into the Same or an absorption into the Other. Signification emerges in the act of obligation to the Other.

Phenomenology uncovers preoriginary signification, or meaning without appearance.

Levinas argues that signification involves "the whole gravity of the body extirpated from its *conatus*" in the substitution of one-for-the-other.[80] Relationships made meaningful from signification are not formal but informed by a general signification that exists before and beyond essence. This signification provides an opening for transcendence to the particular. Levinas announces the emergence of signification in the trace of a Saying within the Said. "Signification is witness ... intelligibility before the light."[81] Levinas's primary project rests in the idea that ethics precedes being—the face of the other calls one to consciousness. To ignore the trace of the Saying in the Said is the archetype of Western philosophy that overlooks a conception of phenomenology that attends to an essence that "signifies on the basis of an ascription of meaning that devolves from the-one-for-the-other, the signifyingness of signification."[82] Responsibility to and for the Other is beyond being, dwelling in an origin of signification.[83]

Levinas explains that when one-is-*for*-the-other, the one becomes a signification without opportunity for escape from responsibility. The ethical mandate of responsibility marks the point of origin for signification before being, which gives birth to transcendence.[84] For Levinas, signification is the possibility for transcendence; the existence of God rests in the ambiguity of signification as the potential for transcendence. Signification does not arise out of controlled configuration.[85] If signification is limited to an ends and means virtue structure, it would have to be akin to language in a grammar structure. Significance is a surplus and gratuity outside of "any preestablished system."[86] Levinas associates signification with the-one-for-the-other with the proximity that substitutes one and another.

Signification dwells not in the particular but within the trace of an immemorial ethic that begins with the particular. Levinas explains that this performative command permits signification to emerge before and beyond human origins or interpretations. Access to signification emerges through this trace of the Saying. Signification, for Levinas, has an impersonal quality and is contrary to consciousness, choice, and/or commitment.[87]

Responsibility for the Other is not a product of personal relationships, but rather a derivative response of the-one-for-the-other via signification situated within "non-indifference."[88] Signification creates meaning in its response to the Other as derivative of the immemorial command for responsibility. Signification is the "I" "disengaged as unique."[89] In signification, for Levinas, it is the particularity of the Other that becomes meaningful and unique. The one is understood as meaningful in derivativeness from the Other and in the substitution and transcendence from one-for-the-other. Levinas understands that the signification of Saying often rests within the Said of books, traditions, sciences, poetry, and conversations. Levinas points toward a conceptualization of the performative phenomenon as surplus of Saying, signification, and meaning that recognizes a particular Other. Signification in its origin engages alterity, proximity, responsibility, and substitution.[90] Signification in the Saying and the trace of Saying within the Said announces meaning discerned without our control and sense of will. Signification of Saying emerges in the phenomena of the face as a sign in semioethics and rhetoric otherwise than convention. The next section reduces Levinas's project in an interpretation, reduction, and description of the terms semioethics and rhetoric.

REDUCTION OF LEVINAS'S PROJECT: SEMIOETHICS AND RHETORICAL DEMAND

The reductive phase, for Lanigan, begins with interpretation of the experience, then reduces the description to key issues, which are then exemplified in the description of principle signifiers of one's consciousness of the experience—in this case, Levinas's kinship with semioethics and rhetoric. This section commences with brief interpretive comments on the connections between and among Levinas's project, semioethics, and rhetorical demand. Examination of the kinship between Levinas and semiotics originates with recognition of face as sign. Substitution announces semioethics as derivative of an encounter with the face of the Other, characterized by impersonality and lack of reciprocity. Encounter of the face as sign situates signification at the meeting point of semiotics and rhetoric through an interruption of the immemorial ethical echo. Despite Levinas's critique that rhetoric obscures signification, it is in an otherwise than convention description of Levinas's conception of rhetoric that one finds signification. Description of rhetoric as emergent forms a semiotic interpretation of Levinas's ethics project, recognizing meaning-making via signification inclusive of the face as sign and immemorial ethical echo as rhetorical mandate. From this semiotic recognition of the call as a rhetorical mandate, we move to a reduction that identifies central coordinates for semioethics and rhetorical demand from the Other. Within these reductions, we include descriptions that align signification with semioethics (the face of the Other) and rhetorical demand (immemorial ethical echo) originating from the Other in Levinas's project.

Semioethics

We highlight five coordinates explicated by Petrilli and Ponzio's work essential to understanding the interplay between and among semiotics and Levinas's philosophical corpus: (1) semioethics,[91] (2) the face of the Other (3) the impersonal (4) œuvre and (5) signification. This descriptive reduction renders further insight into the larger description of face as sign that prompts the rhetoric of an immemorial ethical echo.

1. *Semioethics*—Petrilli and Ponzio's approach to semiotics is responsive to humans belonging to the lifeworld in a "detotalizing" manner in that one is continually responsive to the Other.[92] Specifically for Petrilli, individuals are

born into sign systems that are before the individual and are constitutive of the life network.[93] As a part of the sign network, the human self, as a semiotic animal, has the "unique capacity for responsibility towards life, for caring for life in its joyous and dialogical multiplicity," which makes the human self also a "semioethical animal."[94] Petrilli extends semioethics with a connection to existential semiotics. She understands semioethics as "connected to our capacity for creative awareness of the other, the assumption of responsibility for the other, [and] accountability or answerability, which presupposes the global condition of interrelated and intercorporeal dialogical otherness to which we are all subject biosemiocally as living organisms."[95] For Petrilli and Ponzio, Levinas's ethics project is semiotic within the realm of the semioethical, which announces the signification of the face of the Other.

2. *Face*—The face begins substitution for Petrilli and Ponzio. Petrilli and Ponzio acknowledge that the semiotic significance of Levinas's project begins with the face of the Other, attends to an immemorial ethical call, and then responds to a particular Other.[96] The face as sign in Levinas constitutes recognition of one's powerlessness. The face as sign holds one hostage as it exposes obligation to alterity. The face as sign begins in substitution prior to identity and consciousness. While the face begins the relationship between Levinas and semiotics, the signification of semioethics is dependent upon an impersonal response to the Other.[97]

3. *Impersonal*—Ponzio notes that an ethical sense of consciousness opens to the Other in an impersonal and disinterested manner: "Non-indifference for the other, that is, responsibility without alibis for the other, is openness toward the other than being."[98] Pre-consciousness removes the totalizing choice of ethical response from the "I"; yet Ponzio notes that this loss of freedom is an opening for transcendence—a nonintentional and pre-reflective consciousness that constitutes ethics as first philosophy. For Ponzio, pre-reflective consciousness characterized as "ethical sense" is not consciousness in a cognitive sense.[99] Petrilli explores the pre-reflective nature of responsibility through Levinas's use of "il y a," which constitutes an "impersonal happening."[100] Responsibility to and for the Other is derivative of the impersonality of semioethics as it is the impersonality of Levinas's ethics that allows one to attend to the particularity of the Other.

4. *œuvre*—Ponzio begins with acknowledgement of the Other in Levinas as that which "the totality of being and of thought can neither embrace nor encompass."[101] Levinas's *œuvre* defines the movement toward the Other without possibility of a return to the original self. Levinas's entire project revolves around responsibility emerging from semioethical commands. Ponzio explains that for Levinas, the movement towards an Other without a return to the "original I" transforms the relationship between self and other from

"same/other" to "I/other" with the former belonging to the realm of totality and the latter recognizing the human present in sociality.[102] The *œurve* in Levinas's project is an explication of substitution, being-for-the-Other, which opens the possibility for signification.

5. *Signification*—Petrilli and Ponzio connect infinity to existential semiotics, which they characterize as "*a priori* conditions for the flourishing of signs viewed in terms of 'becoming' rather than being."[103] Petrilli argues that Levinas's work is reflective of a relationship between semiotics, philosophy of language, ontology, and metaphysics.[104] For Petrilli, Levinas's pre-intentional response to the Other invokes, not a feeling of nothingness, but an attentiveness to an ethical demand that requires a unique answer.

Rhetoric

1. *Alterity*—Levinas's project begins with alterity and recognition that "I" cannot and must not possess the Other. Levinas rejects conventional rhetoric in its attempt to control the Other through flattery and propaganda that eclipses the face by disregarding alterity. Instead, Levinas's project positions "me" as a hostage responsible to and for a particular Other. This recognition, prompted by the alterity of a face as Other, ignites a rhetorical mandate that commands my response. Levinas's rhetoric otherwise than convention emerges in the Saying power of the immemorial ethical echo that moves one toward alterity, the face of the Other.

2. *Saying and Said*—Levinas's project hinges on the interplay of Saying and Said. The immemorial ethical echo that serves as rhetorical mandate emerges in a "pre-original saying" before and beyond time.[105] This Saying commands that I am responsible for the particular face that stands before me without "limit or measure",[106] moving me toward the Other through obligation of response to an ethical trace within a Said. The Said "absorbs" the Saying in word, name, and phenomenon.[107] The Said forms a vocabulary of the "already said" that makes possible identification and rediscovery of what is "inscribed in memory."[108] The Saying depends upon the enactment of a Said that moves one to accept responsibility. Saying requires me to respond to the alterity of the Other within the scope of a particular Said. Levinas's rhetoric otherwise than convention, however, requires that this particular Said respond with the maintenance of a trace of Saying.

3. *Trace*—For Levinas, Saying moves "beyond" the Said in one's "proximity" with another,[109] but it is the Said that houses a trace of Saying. While the Saying offers the rhetorical mandate—I am my brother's keeper—and the Said obligates one in responsibility to a particular other, it is the trace that

brings forth the reply: "Here I am." Conventional rhetoric destroys the Saying in the Said as it ignores the alterity of the face in an attempt to totalize the Other. Levinas's ethics project and a rhetoric understood as otherwise than convention depends upon the trace of Saying in the Said. The trace manifests in the response "Here I am," which contains recognition of the Saying of a rhetorical mandate that emerges in the Said of a particular response to the face of the Other.

4. *Derivative Response*—The Said that contains the trace of Saying offers a derivative response called forth by the immemorial rhetorical mandate of ethical responsibility. This call emerges in response to the Saying and cannot be demanded. Rather than derivative, the totalizing attempts of conventional rhetoric are originative responses characterized by either the rejection of responsibility for the Other or the imposition of an action upon the Other. Levinas's otherwise than convention rhetoric recognizes the derivative response of "Here I am," which maintains the trace of Saying in the Said, when one emerges in responsibility through the immemorial ethical echo—I am my brother's keeper. It is the derivative response of "Here I am," attentive to a rhetoric otherwise than convention, that makes possible the substitution of one-being-for-the-other in signification.

5. *Signification*—Signification, for Levinas, occurs within his performative ethics project when one-is-being-for-the-other. Signification requires a derivative response to the rhetorical mandate of "Here I am" that maintains the trace of Saying in the Said, as I am obligated to accept responsibility for the Other in his or her alterity. Levinas's critique of conventional rhetoric occurs as it eclipses the alterity of the face of the Other and denies recognition of the Saying and Said. Such action destroys the trace of Saying in an originative response, and is void of signification. Rhetoric otherwise than convention through the immemorial ethical echo and the trace of Saying in the "Here I am" allows one-to-be-for-another within an immemorial sense of signification.

Within our reduction, this section first interpreted the components central to Levinas's ethics project: (1) the semioethics of the optics in the impersonal recognition of the face of the Other; and (2) the rhetorical mandate otherwise than convention within the audio ethic obligating one to be responsible for a particular other. We then reduced semioethics and the rhetorical mandate to five coordinates that define their significance with Levinas's project. Following the identification of each coordinate, descriptive material contextualized the importance and function of each coordinate within the larger project of Levinas's performative ethics.

INTERPRETATION OF LEVINAS'S PROJECT: ETHICS AND THE DERIVATIVE I

In the interpretive phase, one interprets the signifiers followed by a further reduction of the conscious experience of these signifiers, which are then described and explicated as fundamental signifiers—in this case interpretation of signification of Levinas's project that dwells with unending obligation and responsibility. Interpretation of Levinas's project centers on two basic terms, one repetitively used by Levinas and another, one repetitively questioned by Levinas. These two terms, semioethics and rhetoric, explicate a signification that is beyond and prior to a given meeting, signification beyond the verse. The interplay of semioethics and rhetoric otherwise than convention provides the coordinates for Levinas's performative ethics. Ethics performed is derivative of and constituted by the face as sign and recognition of the rhetorical ethical echo, I am my brother's keeper.

Reduction to semioethics and rhetoric otherwise than convention announces the transformation of an originative I into a derivative I. Encountering the face as sign which then refers one back to a rhetorical ethical mandate charges one with a responsibility and an obligation for the Other than is unending and particular.

Described, the derivative I embraces the face of the Other as a sign. This is a movement of semioethics at work. This sign moves a person to an immemorial ethical echo that operates as a rhetorical demand charging one with responsibility to and for the Other. Levinas's work offers both expectation and irony. Expectation presupposes that a philosophy centered on ethics as first philosophy would take the notion of ethics as fundamental. Irony arises in that Levinas's dismissal of rhetoric is in contrast to his own project. For the immemorial echo that charges one with responsibility is an archaic rhetorical command that offers no code or assurance. Signification resides in both cases, however, beyond the face and beyond the rhetorical demand. Signification for Levinas resides in an unending obligation of responsibility to and for another. This signification emerges in the doing of responsibility inclusive of an ethical optic and an audio rhetorical demand of unending responsibility to and for the Other.

NOTES

1. Claire E. Katz, "Levinas—Between Philosophy and Rhetoric: The 'Teaching' of Levinas's Scriptural References," *Philosophy and Rhetoric* 38, no. 2 (2005).
2. Emmanuel Levinas, *Totality and Infinity: An Essay on Exteriority* (Pittsburgh, PA: Duquesne University Press, 1969). Original work published 1961: 70–71, 241.
3. Richard L. Lanigan, *The Human Science of Communicology: A Phenomenology of Discourse in Foucault and Merleau-Ponty* (Pittsburgh, PA: Duquesne University, 1992).
4. Lanigan, *Human Science of Communicology*, 1.

5. Lanigan, *Human Science of Communicology*, 2.
6. Lanigan, *Human Science of Communicology*, 30.
7. Isaac E. Catt, "The Signifying World between Ineffability and Intelligibility: Body as Sign in Communicology," *Review of Communication* 11, no. 2 (2011).
8. Lanigan uses both description and depiction as terms for the first act. For clarity and consistency, we use only description in this essay.
9. Lanigan, *Human Science of Communicology*, 17.
10. Lanigan, *Human Science of Communicology*.
11. Lanigan, *Human Science of Communicology*.
12. Lanigan, *Human Science of Communicology*, 30.
13. Lanigan, *Human Science of Communicology*, 112.
14. This outlined understanding of communicative experience appears in Lanigan, *Human Science of Communicology*, 21.
15. Lanigan, *Human Science of Communicology*, 31.
16. Jacqueline M. Martinez, *Communicative Sexuality: A Communicology of Sexual Experience* (Plymouth, UK: Lexington Books, 2011), 98.
17. Martinez, *Communicative Sexuality*, 97.
18. Martinez, *Communicative Sexuality*, 58.
19. Martinez, *Communicative Sexuality*, 61–62.
20. Martinez, *Communicative Sexuality*, 103.
21. Isaac E. Catt and Deborah Eicher-Catt, "Pierce and Cassirer, 'Life' and 'Spirit': A Communicology of Religion," *Journal of Communication & Religion* 36, no. 2 (2013), 81.
22. Catt and Eicher-Catt, "Pierce and Cassirer."
23. Isaac E. Catt and Deborah Eicher-Catt, eds., *Communicology: The New Science of Embodied Discourse* (Madison, NJ: Fairleigh Dickinson University Press, 2010), 17.
24. Catt and Eicher-Catt, "Pierce and Cassirer," 81; *Communicology*, 20.
25. Catt and Eicher-Catt, "Pierce and Cassirer," 81.
26. Catt and Eicher-Catt, "Pierce and Cassirer," 81.
27. Catt and Eicher-Catt, *Communicology*, 17.
28. Emmanuel Levinas, *Beyond the Verse: Talmudic Readings and Lectures* (London: The Athlone Press, 1994.), xiii. Original work published 1982.
29. Levinas, *Beyond the Verse*, xv.
30. Levinas, *Beyond the Verse*.
31. Levinas, *Beyond the Verse*, xiii.
32. Levinas, *Beyond the Verse*, xx.
33. Jean-Paul Sartre, *Being and Nothingness: The Principal Test of Modern Existentialism* (New York: Washington Square Press, 1992). Original work published 1943.
34. Levinas, *Beyond the Verse*, 26.
35. Levinas, *Beyond the Verse*, 27.
36. Levinas, *Beyond the Verse*, 34.
37. Levinas, *Beyond the Verse*, 50.
38. Levinas, *Beyond the Verse*, 51.
39. Levinas, *Beyond the Verse*, 66.
40. Levinas, *Beyond the Verse*, 83.
41. Levinas, *Beyond the Verse*, 101.
42. Levinas, *Beyond the Verse*, 85.

43. Levinas, *Beyond the Verse*, 126.
44. Levinas, *Beyond the Verse*.
45. Levinas, *Beyond the Verse*, 130.
46. Levinas, *Beyond the Verse*, 146–147.
47. Levinas, *Beyond the Verse*, 161.
48. Levinas, *Beyond the Verse*, 181.
49. Levinas, *Beyond the Verse*, 193.
50. Susan Petrilli, "On Communication: Contributions to the Human Sciences and to Humanism from Semiotics Understood as Semioethics," *The American Journal of Semiotics* 24, no. 4 (2008).
51. Augusto Ponzio, "Signification and Alterity in Emmanuel Levinas," *Semiotica* 171, no. 1 (2008): 117.
52. Ponzio, "Signification and Alterity," 118.
53. Susan E. Shapiro, "Rhetoric, Ideology, and Idolatry in the Writings of Emmanuel Levinas," in *Rhetorical Invention and Religious Inquiry: New Perspectives*, ed. Walter Jost and Wendy Olmsted (New Haven, CT: Yale University Press, 2000), 256, 254–278.
54. Shapiro, "Rhetoric, Ideology, and Idolatry," 255.
55. Shapiro, "Rhetoric, Ideology, and Idolatry," 257.
56. Shapiro, "Rhetoric, Ideology, and Idolatry," 259.
57. Shapiro, "Rhetoric, Ideology, and Idolatry," 262.
58. Shapiro, "Rhetoric, Ideology, and Idolatry," 265.
59. Shapiro, "Rhetoric, Ideology, and Idolatry," 265–267.
60. Shapiro, "Rhetoric, Ideology, and Idolatry," 271.
61. Diane Perpich, "Figurative Language and the 'Face' in Levinas's Philosophy," *Philosophy and Rhetoric* 38, no. 2 (2005), 113.
62. Perpich, "Figurative Language," 115.
63. Perpich, "Figurative Language," 117, 120.
64. Bettina Bergo, "What is Levinas Doing? Phenomenology and the Rhetoric of an Ethical Unconscious," *Philosophy and Rhetoric* 38, no. 2 (2005), 123.
65. Oona Eisenstadt, "Levinas versus Levinas: Hebrew, Greek, and Linguistic Justice," *Philosophy and Rhetoric* 38, no. 2 (2005), 145.
66. Eisenstadt, "Levinas versus Levinas," 145.
67. Eisenstadt, "Levinas versus Levinas," 145–146.
68. Eisenstadt, "Levinas versus Levinas," 146–148.
69. Katz, "Levinas," 159.
70. Katz, "Levinas."
71. Katz, "Levinas," 160.
72. Katz, "Levinas," 161.
73. Katz, "Levinas," 163.
74. Katz, "Levinas," 161.
75. Katz, "Levinas," 165, 169.
76. Katz, "Levinas," 171.
77. James Hatley, "Generations: Levinas in the Jewish Context," *Philosophy and Rhetoric* 38, no. 2 (2005).
78. Emmanuel Levinas, *Otherwise than Being: Or Beyond Essence* (Pittsburgh, PA: Duquesne University Press, 1999), 11. Original work published 1981.
79. Levinas, *Otherwise than Being*, 13.

80. Levinas, *Otherwise than Being*, 72.
81. Levinas, *Otherwise than Being*, 77–78.
82. Levinas, *Otherwise than Being*, 78.
83. Levinas, *Otherwise than Being*, 90.
84. Levinas, *Otherwise than Being*, 94.
85. Levinas, *Otherwise than Being*, 95.
86. Levinas, *Otherwise than Being*, 96–97.
87. Levinas, *Otherwise than Being*, 138.
88. Levinas, *Otherwise than Being*.
89. Levinas, *Otherwise than Being*, 139.
90. Levinas, *Otherwise than Being*, 184.
91. Michael Eskin continues a discussion of semiotic theory tied to Levinas's ethics with a basic assumption—Levinas's ethics is a counter to the Western intellectual tradition. Eskin stresses the notion of "semethics" as a necessary lexicon understanding the interplay of semiotics and Levinas's ethics. The term semethics aligns Levinas's conceptualization of ethics as both descriptive and prescriptive. See Michael Eskin, "A Language before Words: Levinas's Ethics as a Semiotic Problem," *Semiotica* 129, no. 1–4 (2000): 29–50.
92. Susan Petrilli and Augusto Ponzio, "Transcendence and Alterity: On life, Communication, and Subjectivity," *Semiotica* 184, no. 1 (2011): 235.
93. Susan Petrilli, "Identity, Freedom, and Answerability in the Global World: A Semiotic Approach," *Semiotica* 171, no. 1/4 (2008), 101.
94. Petrilli, "Identity, Freedom, and Answerability," 103.
95. Petrilli, "Identity, Freedom, and Answerability."
96. Petrilli and Ponzio, "Transcendence and Alterity."
97. Alexander Kozin explores the semiotic influence on Levinas's philosophical project through three essays: "The Sign of the Other: On the Semiotic of Emmanuel Levinas's Phenomenology," (2004); "In the Face of the Other: Between Goffman and Levinas," (2009); and "The Return of Phenomenological Semiotics to Translation Studies: A Contribution of Emmanuel Levinas, (2007)" Kozin particularly examines Levinas's face of the other as a sign.
98. Ponzio, "Signification and Alterity," 122.
99. Ponzio, "Signification and Alterity," 121.
100. Susan Petrilli, "Semiotic Phenomenology of Predicative Judgment," *The American Journal of Semiotics* 24, no. 4 (2008), 161.
101. Ponzio, "Signification and Alterity," 118.
102. Ponzio, "Signification and Alterity," 119.
103. Petrilli and Ponzio, "Transcendence and Alterity," 230.
104. Petrilli, "Semiotic Phenomenology," 160.
105. Levinas, *Otherwise than Being*, 5–6.
106. Levinas, *Otherwise than Being*, 47.
107. Levinas, *Otherwise than Being*, 37.
108. Levinas, *Otherwise than Being*, 36–37.
109. Levinas, *Otherwise than Being*, 5, 37.

BIBLIOGRAPHY

Arnett, Ronald C. *Communication Ethics in Dark Times: Hannah Arendt's Rhetoric of Warning and Hope.* Carbondale: Southern Illinois University Press, 2013.

Bergo, Bettina. "What is Levinas Doing? Phenomenology and the Rhetoric of an Ethical Unconscious." *Philosophy and Rhetoric* 38, no. 2 (2005): 122–144.

Catt, Isaac E. "The Signifying World between Ineffability and Intelligibility: Body as Sign in Communicology." *Review of Communication* 11, no. 2 (2011): 122–144.

Catt, Isaac E., and Deborah Eicher-Catt, eds. *Communicology: The New Science of Embodied Discourse.* Madison, NJ: Fairleigh Dickinson University Press, 2010.

Catt, Isaac E., and Deborah Eicher-Catt. "Pierce and Cassirer, 'Life' and 'Spirit': A Communicology of Religion." *Journal of Communication & Religion* 36, no. 2 (2013): 72–106.

Eisenstadt, Oona. "Levinas versus Levinas: Hebrew, Greek, and Linguistic Justice." *Philosophy and Rhetoric* 38, no. 2 (2005): 145–158.

Eskin, Michael. "A Language before Words: Levinas's Ethics as a Semiotic Problem." *Semiotica* 129, no. 1–4 (2000): 29–50.

Hatley, James. "Generations: Levinas in the Jewish Context." *Philosophy and Rhetoric* 38, no. 2 (2005): 173–189.

Katz, Claire E. "Levinas—Between Philosophy and Rhetoric: The 'Teaching' of Levinas's Scriptural References." *Philosophy and Rhetoric* 38, no. 2 (2005): 159–172.

Lanigan, Richard L. *The Human Science of Communicology: A Phenomenology of Discourse in Foucault and Merleau-Ponty.* Pittsburgh, PA: Duquesne University, 1992.

Levinas, Emmanuel. *Beyond the Verse: Talmudic Readings and Lectures.* London: The Athlone Press, 1994. Original work published 1982.

Levinas, Emmanuel. *Otherwise than Being: Or Beyond Essence.* Pittsburgh, PA: Duquesne University Press, 1999. Original work published 1981.

Levinas, Emmanuel. *Totality and Infinity: An Essay on Exteriority.* Pittsburgh, PA: Duquesne University Press, 1969. Original work published 1961.

Martinez, Jacqueline. M. *Communicative Sexuality: A Communicology of Sexual Experience.* Plymouth, UK: Lexington Books, 2011.

Perpich, Diane. "Figurative Language and the 'Face' in Levinas's Philosophy." *Philosophy and Rhetoric* 38, no. 2 (2005): 103–121.

Petrilli, Susan. "Identity, Freedom, and Answerability in the Global World: A Semiotic Approach." *Semiotica* 171, no. 1/4 (2008): 97–114.

Petrilli, Susan. "On Communication: Contributions to the Human Sciences and to Humanism from Semiotics Understood as Semioethics." *The American Journal of Semiotics* 24, no. 4 (2008): 193–236.

Petrilli, Susan. "Semiotic Phenomenology of Predicative Judgment." *The American Journal of Semiotics* 24, no. 4 (2008): 159–192.

Petrilli, Susan, and Augusto Ponzio. "Transcendence and Alterity: On life, Communication, and Subjectivity." *Semiotica* 184, no. 1 (2011): 229–250.

Ponzio, Augusto. "Signification and Alterity in Emmanuel Levinas." *Semiotica* 171, no. 1 (2008): 115–130.

Sartre, Jean-Paul. *Being and Nothingness: The Principal Test of Modern Existentialism.* New York: Washington Square Press, 1992. Original work published 1943.

Shapiro, Susan E. "Rhetoric, Ideology, and Idolatry in the Writings of Emmanuel Levinas." In *Rhetorical Invention and Religious Inquiry: New Perspectives*, edited by Walter Jost and Wendy Olmsted, 254–278. New Haven, CT: Yale University Press, 2000.

CHAPTER TEN

Mental Health in the Communication Matrix

A Semiotic Phenomenology of Depression Medicine

ISAAC E. CATT

Communicologists recognize a history to their field of study that may differ substantially from that which is typically rendered in mainstream American communication studies.[1] In this alternative story, philosophy, psychiatry, and the study of communication have common historic origins that are unknown, repressed or perhaps irrelevant to the social science of information transmission. As I have noted, human science may be considered a practical, "living philosophy" in the sense advocated by John Dewey.[2] This pragmatist perspective is reciprocally informed by the phenomenology of the lifeworld as European philosophy and psychiatry merge in the history of American communicology. Thus, when philosophy bumps up against the real world it may become a human science. In particular, Richard L. Lanigan's communicological assessment is that perception and expression are the reversible and reflexive logic foundations of the human sciences. Lanigan is, of course, a major interpreter of Maurice Merleau-Ponty who presaged this strong claim in the "Preface" to the *Phenomenology of Perception* where he concludes that: "All forms of knowledge are supported by a 'ground' of postulations, and ultimately upon our communication with the world as the first establishing of rationality."[3] It would be hard to overestimate the implications of this idea. In this chapter I shall take his claim seriously and expose some of its import in the interface of psychiatry and communicology.

I have explored some of these implications in recent expositions on mental health, particularly today's paradigm exemplar of psychiatry, depressive mood disorder.[4] Ultimately, my discussions of depression and its treatment are all about re-focusing on the person as a living body whose existence (*hexis*) encounters experience (*habitus*) in the communication matrix. Each moment of this encounter is fraught with possibility and risk, as the body is in the chiasm of flesh in Merleau-Ponty's sense of it, and is opened up to the world of others. Indeed, flesh is the tissue of the world.

At no time will I deny the legitimacy of the suffering that many people endure in anxiety, apprehension, isolation, alienation, and existential despair. It is my intent to provide a clearing for greater understanding of depression medicine, of what it presumes about lived-consciousness and communicative relationships, and to thereby increase the likelihood of informed choices. Above all, in this fourth paper on the topic, I again seek to return communication to its proper place; front and center in discussions of mental health. Additionally, I dare to hope that communicology and psychiatry could re-commence dialogue as compatible human sciences capable of mutually informing and influencing each other.

Health communication is a well-ensconced sub-discipline of the mainstream communication studies discipline, but it predominately *presupposes* communication in its message-centered approach. As might be anticipated, health communication is a relative newcomer to the field and arrives with its own theories, an analogue to all the new categories and divisions of communication studies each of which fractionalizes the theoretical terrain. Communicology, on the other hand, already covers the full range of discourse: intrapersonal communicology, interpersonal communicology, social communicology and cultural communicology.[5] Issues of health arise at every level. Jürgen Ruesch reminded us more than a half century ago, however, that these levels are conceptual tools, so we must always remember that "individual, interpersonal, group, and cultural events occur simultaneously in reality."[6]

Now, the levels are not contexts, as they have too often been portrayed in communication studies. Rather, the levels are a dependent hierarchy, as stressed by Gregory Bateson, writing with Ruesch nearly 70 years ago.[7] Contexts are produced at each level on horizontal planes that intersect the vertical structure. Perhaps semioticians will recognize this through the lens of paradigms and syntagms, selections and combinations. In this dependent hierarchy, each rung of ascension becomes an environment for the preceding rung, and the former is a moment of stability, of presumed existence carried forward into worldly experience. Experience builds on presumed existence, expression in semiotic systems is increasingly codified, then becomes perception on which existential ground further expressions ensue. This is effectively what C. S. Peirce named the Interpretant (realm of the symbolic or "womb of the future"), Dewey discussed as dispositions of habits, Merleau-Ponty elaborated as predispositions of embodiment, and Pierre Bourdieu explicates as habitus. Bourdieu explicitly identifies a dialectical movement of habitus/hexis that is comprehensible only through the structuralist-constructivist combinatory logic of semiotic phenomenology.[8]

Speaking, consisting of the synthetic and synchronous movement of the perception-expression doublet, is, then, the advent of consciousness to being. At another level, the analogue holds as speaking implies listening, and inversely. Consciousness is grounded in a presupposition of actualization and realization through perception and expression. Or, with this background in mind we simply say that consciousness is originarily (continuously, not once and for all) constituted in, through, and as communication.

There is a certain ecology that is presupposed and maintained in the relative synchronization of existence and experience through perception and expression, the phenomenal grounds of communication and culture in speaking. This is what is meant by Lanigan's many discussions of reversibility, though it is important to understand that the reversal is never complete.[9] This ecology is contingent and may be disrupted by many things including congenital defects, injuries, deaths of loved ones, traumatic events of natural or human-made disaster, atrocities committed against individuals and populations, afflictions of bad parents, economic disparities, everyday injuries and slights, and also by how we theorize and treat persons who experience threats to their existence, even when it is difficult to rationalize the reality of the experience.

Bernard Stiegler's philosophy of *pharmacology* is helpful in this regard. Not coincidentally, his book on this topic is entitled *What Makes Life Worth Living?* That life is deemed worth living is a *feeling*, but it is connected to an "economic and spiritual crisis of our time" that affects the whole "earth ark;" the *pharmakon* arrives as a "question of care, and of its condition;" as semiotic stability encounters phenomenological change, and reversibly, both possibility and risk ensue, that is "[t]he *pharmakon* is at once," Stiegler explains, "what *enables* care to be taken and that *of which* care must be taken—in the sense that it is necessary to *pay attention*: its power is *curative to the immeasurable extent ... that it is also destructive*."[10]

As existence opens to experience it assumes a sense of being, of identity and selfhood, of habitus. Simultaneously, however, this openness to *possibilities* also assumes *risk*. Experience presupposes infinite *capacity* of existence, and existence desires, indeed requires the risk so as to *construct* life, to make it worth living.

Now, if, or more likely when the ecology I describe is disturbed, mental health is threatened. By degree, experience then ceases to affirm existence. Existence comes to have a tenuous hold on reality, is aware of its declining resonance of voice, and ruminates, the awareness of awareness continuously recycled in experience. Experience is no longer reliable for positive reports on the stability and taken-for-grantedness of habits of mind and action. Existence is no longer validated by experience. Experience can no longer count on the capacities of existence. In short, the body-lived and the lived-body are destabilized as habitus and hexis conflict and pose a problem of felt disembodiment. This asynchrony of expression and perception is a lost "ground" of postulations as depicted by Merleau-Ponty or a natural logic of "foundations" as described by Lanigan. It is an unhealthy communicative relationship with the social world, and it is depressing (I use the word "depressing" here in the commonsense of the term, not in the psychiatric sense).

In this situation, now rendered mundane by major depression disorder, the most widely diagnosed malady of our time, and by the widespread use of antidepressants by millions of people, life worth living is questioned. David Karp captures the problem quite well, by suggesting that drug consumption is now naturalized as the way of modern life. Consequently, he states, "the line between normal life pain and genuine pathology has become seriously blurred. The effort to secure personal happiness has become a social mandate, if not a moral obligation."[11] This obligation is not without its critics, but it also has strong supporters. Psychiatrist Peter Kramer is prominent among the latter.

THE KING OF PROZAC AND THE PRINCESS

Kramer is most famous for his best selling work in 1993, *Listening to Prozac* in which he extols the virtues of drugs that enable melancholic people to overcome deflated self-concepts, recover the "real" selves they are meant to be, and change their passivity to activity.[12] In the more than two decades following publication of this book, abundant research has promulgated the myth of a chemical cure for depression. Most new drugs coming onto the market are of the "me too" variety, perhaps different in chemical make-up, but serving a common goal of righting supposed imbalances of, for example, serotonin. Several experimental approaches are always underway, even so, the treatments proceed on the basis of the psychology of the individual and the brain remains almost the exclusive focus of research. Virtually all funded activity is under the umbrella of the medical model. Regardless of the new approach, depression is nearly comprehensively considered a "disease," which is to say a pathological condition of the body. Even though pharmaceutical companies have backed off from their former explicit claims of cure from correcting imbalances, the myth survives in medical practices and in the opinions of most of the public. On more than one occasion the Food and Drug Administration (FDA) scolded the companies for marketing the chemical imbalance hypothesis, but their campaign to create this myth was far too successful to be easily retracted. As a result very little treatment is conducted in psychotherapy by comparison to drug prescriptions. The research is all about the pills and whether they successfully make more "good" chemicals available in the brain.

In a two step process, an inference is made from the pill's efficacy that depression disorder is relieved, and from this relief a second inference follows the *ex juvantibus* logic to claim that antidepressant medicine resolves a brain disease. Concomitant with this, a massive rhetorical campaign by the pharmaceutical industry continues to sell the public, the medical field and the FDA on the science behind antidepressants. Against the almost insurmountable odds of this deeply entrenched and impossibly well-financed establishment there has also been a backlash grounded in research that critically examines the science purporting to show the curative effects of SSRIs (serotonin reuptake inhibitors such as Prozac and Zoloft) and like medicines. This ever-growing body of literature questions the philosophic basis and ethical implications of the medical model of mental "disease," exposes the politicization of psychiatry by the medical turn, and draws attention to the long history of undue influence and corruption on the part of the pharmaceutical companies that produce and market the drugs. Perhaps it is a sort of proof of the potency of the criticism that leads to Kramer's 2016 book, *Ordinarily Well: The Case for Antidepressants*.[13] Jonathan Rosen's sympathetic review of this book in *The Atlantic* is aptly titled, "The Assault on Antidepressants," because it enthusiastically endorses and supports Kramer's defensive posture regarding antidepressants.[14] Rosen begins the book review in a most unusual way, and I shall follow his path. His personal narrative is as follows:

> Several years ago, in the middle of reading volume five of *The Princess Diaries* to our elder daughter, my wife came to a passage about a dog who is so anxious when left alone that he licks himself until his hair falls out. The royal veterinarian has prescribed Prozac, but the young princess thinks the dog's real problem is that it lives with her grandmother: "If I had to live with Grand-mère, I would totally lick off all my hair." Our daughter was curious about the medication, which she had never heard of. "Wouldn't it be wonderful," she said, "if there was something like that for people?"[15]

Sometimes a whole philosophy of the subject belies a simple, brief and seemingly innocuous narrative. Rosen follows up with an interpretation of the story, first noting of course that such a drug exists. Then he tacitly chastises critics who probably would not give the dog the Prozac that it obviously needs and moreover would broadcast the absurd view that such life-changing medications are a "fairy-tale invention." Rosen goes on to describe Kramer's careful and sensitive work to prove the efficacy of antidepressants through analysis of the research studies supporting the medical model and as a refutation of critics who have questioned the widespread prescription of the drugs, mostly for everything but psychiatrically diagnosed depression. Following Kramer's model in the book, Rosen weaves pathos for the depressed with appeals to medical science. He is clearly an admirer of Kramer and of biologically based psychiatry, though he and Kramer both graciously yield some minimal space for psychotherapy.

Of course, when confronted with the choice of drug versus psychotherapy, doctors, some patients and most certainly health insurance companies, have a strong preference for the prescription pad. Efficiency, not profusion of alternatives rules the day, and the discourse is marked from the beginning by the silent but encompassing semiotic frame of "evidence based" or "precision medicine." The psychiatrist sees the problem as pathology of the body, but even granting the legitimacy of this exclusive contextualization, by far the greatest number of prescriptions is written not for psychiatrically diagnosed depressed patients but rather for those who have convinced other health professionals that their sadness is, in fact, a disorder. And, the patients themselves are persuaded by mass media marketing to think of themselves as victims of a brain disease caused by chemical imbalances. This can be described as "epistemic pathology," again, lost "ground" or "foundations" for rationality. Discourse with the world is problematic. To better understand this situation we may turn to communicology.

A fundamental lesson of semiotic phenomenology is that the constraints of discourse are subtle and all the more powerful because of it. Epistemic pathology, as described by psychiatrist and phenomenologist Michael Ratcliffe, is a way of residing in the world through culturally inherited but dubious habits.[16] The incorporation of epistemic pathology[17] is not limited to scholarly endeavors or even to thought processes; it goes deeper than this. The pathology he describes is a "natural attitude" in the phenomenological sense that it presupposes but ignores the originary ecological human condition in which we find ourselves already inserted into the world. In communicology, we know this as a communicative interrelationship of reversibility.

Lanigan explains that "[c]ommunication is the name for the reversible relationship between an organism (person) and its environment (lived-world), both of which exist in a mutual context or Environment," and he further specifies that:

> At its most sophisticated level this relationship is one of language (langage). Language is, of course, an analogue system in which semantics (capta), syntactics (data), and pragmatics (acta), are constituent parts (a code), each relating to the other as a matter of degree.[18]

Knowing must somehow account for the *feelings of being* that precede the analysis of emotion and the diagnosis of mental disorders. Ratcliffe's thesis is in part that feeling precedes *mood*, whether considered in Martin Heidegger's existential sense or in the psychiatric sense of mood *disorder*. This is quite consistent with the combinatory logic of semiotic phenomenology, which holds that ontology and epistemology are inextricably intertwined. The roots of depression lie in these originary relations, and it would seem that sound treatment would then commence with an account of them.[19] Ratcliffe employs phenomenology in a fresh description of the conscious experience of being depressed. Particularly as described by Lanigan, phenomenological methodology is directly suited to analysis of such an experience and the natural attitude that now takes medical treatment for granted.[20] Perhaps more than anything else this paradigm of communicology imposes the discipline of an open mind through reflection on the reversibility of human existence and experience as reflexively perceived and expressed by the lived-body and the body-lived. The rigor of this approach provides a means by which we can begin to see the meanings that inhere in the actualization of being and the realization of oneself as a speaking being.

Returning, then, to Rosen's opening, we may notice that the things immediately before us are sometimes the most difficult to see, a testament to the distance that often inheres between feelings of being and emotions, between existence and experience, and in asynchronous perception and expression, the origins of disembodiment as described here. In congruence with Kramer and other bio-psychiatrists, Rosen is uninterested in meaning, whether existentially rooted in communication or deconstructed in philosophy. The only question is what works, but what works is taken as a certainty, that is, as an unambiguous resolution of a problem. This is, on my account, the fundamental illusion of psychologism and biologism, which is to say that *the problem orientation is the problem*. Kramer appeals to medical practicality, not to a philosophy of pragmatism. As is well known, the *Diagnostic and Statistical Manual of Mental Disorders (DSM)* was invented for the express purpose of terminating theory in psychiatry. The illness, now semiotically codified as a disease, is presumed understood in its entirety. All that is lacking is brain research, which amounts to tests for chemical efficacy. Kramer is explicit regarding depression, stating that "theories of illness and recovery remain unchanged," and his theme is therefore simple: "the main question [and thesis of his new book] is whether antidepressants work."[21] This is not the main question, it is actually the *only* question deemed relevant within the medical paradigm. If a doctor's prescription alleviates a problem, even by repressing it, further analysis is unnecessary; it is presumed that the problem was caused by a deficit of what the medicine provided. By analogy, if I am thirsty and drink a beer, it could be presumed that I had a deficit of Pilsner Urquell in my system.

Quite a contrast is provided by a willingness to question depression experience from a phenomenological point of view. Ratcliffe writes:

> (...) the empirical study of depression cannot proceed in ignorance of the relevant phenomenology (...). If we rely on cursory and superficial symptom descriptions, rather than on more discriminating phenomenological analyses of depression, this is exactly what we will face. The point applies equally well to all of the different evolutionary, genetic, developmental, and neurobiological stories that might be told about depression. Insofar as we lack a clear description of what it is that we seek to account for, the various competing or seemingly competing hypotheses cannot be satisfactorily assessed.[22]

Rosen hears only the expression of interest in Prozac, not listening to what the princess says. He is not unlike most of us who from time to time forget that *capta* (that which is taken in perception) is intervolved with *data* (that which is given in expression) in *acta* (that which is done verbally and nonverbally).[23] Perception is a level of consciousness distinguishable but inseparable from expression. Perception is already expression; an important lesson of which is that hearing is not identical with listening. Hearing may be framed or codified by listening habitus and thus attends to what the body wants, not necessarily what the body needs. To understand mental illness requires interrogation of its full complexity as a cultural-social-personal issue. Essential to this is recognition that we are creatures of desire, not of needs. We need what we do not desire, prominently exposure of our presumptive habits of mind and action. We desire what we do not need, unlimited existential possibility without the constraint of experiential risk. The result is paralysis. Prozac seems to fix the paralysis by enabling a false *épochè*, a reduction not to self-reflection on habitus/hexis dialectics, but to the benefits of unreflective productivity. The passivity of depression is replaced by *employability*. Prozac represses the encounter of an actual hexis with a real habitus. The body's lifeworld is endlessly deferred as a question that must be answered: *What makes life worth living?*

In phenomenology intentionality is structured as a reflexive arc, objects of perception are mediated by semiosis, sign action in discourse. This means that humans are inherently signifying creatures of a unique kind, capable of time-binding in space, similar to Alfred Korzybski's description of it, but in a more sophisticated synthetic phenomenological way as depicted by Peirce.[24] As cultural and social beings we are primarily motivated by desires that may not align, certainly, with what is required. To heed the call of the world is to attend to it, to draw outlines of identities, demarcating figures from ground, thereby rendering the latter less visible, and by default less valuable.

Let us look again. What does the dog lack such that s/he becomes a canine narcissist? The anxiety (or is it depression?) is explained in the passage. The dog is alone and suffers disconnection from others. It is this above all else that characterizes depression. Sadness results from lost feelings of being that arise from a deficiency of existential communication. Rosen presumes that the dog is not already on Prozac, but we do not know whether the medical treatment has commenced. We only know that a veterinary doctor has prescribed Prozac. It may be that the condition of disconnection continues even under a chemical regimen. We know that these drugs are only about 38–40% effective for humans. I am at a loss to explain the diagnosis of dogs, cats or dolphins with depression, as it seems to me the clearest case possible of a category error: anthropomorphism. Animals can most certainly express what we humans perceive to be sadness. However, only in a mechanistic world of psychologism and biologism can we venture that this sadness is a mood disorder originating in the chemistry of a dog's brain, which will be alleviated by a drug designed for the human brain. It may be ventured instead that the dog is just as described, lonely for affection and suffering from disconnection, lost communication.

We also know that the drug's effectiveness is determined for the most part by a placebo effect, suggesting that the dog might do better once someone shows care and affection for it.[25] The doctor's attention and care for the animal may be the real key; perhaps the veterinarian will pet the dog. On the other hand, perhaps the dog needs Abilify, Rexultis or Risperdal, meta-antidepressants prescribed upon the failure of a standard antidepressant to provide relief. We know that the rate of relapse into illness is far greater for those who take the drugs than for those who are not on them. Based on considerable analysis of the available evidence many critics of antidepressants would say that the drug does not cure the dog, because it makes an object of the dog's "self," as opposed to connecting the dog to the others who are absent and have become a severe depravity in the dog's world. The dog, we may say, is disembodied. Effectively the dog is forced to pet itself.

What does the princess say? What is her analysis? She is a good semiotician and observes what the dog lacks. In addition, her diagnosis is empathetic and she shows involvement with her world. Her lay psychiatric opinion is grounded in her phenomenological relation to the dog and to the semiotic object of the dog's desire. She clearly states that she too would be in the dog's state, and would be forced to compensate for feelings of disconnection by turning inward if she had to live in the situation that the dog endures. And, what is this circumstance, the dog's world? Is it a brain disease? Is it the lack of an antidepressant effect on the brain that will prove the chemical imbalance hypothesis by *ex post facto* logic? There is no evidence of a brain disease, unless perhaps we want to make up a protocol consisting of a statistical correlation between canine behavioral patterns and the tardily applied medicine. Of course, we cannot ask the dog to answer questions on the Hamilton depression scale such as whether it has been getting enough sleep, questions concerning the duration of feeling despondent, suicidal thoughts, and so forth. There may be a sense of urgency, because the dog is after all losing its hair, which protects the animal from the elements. But what of the communicative aspects of the dog's life with people, notably the grand mother? Prozac does not fix the problem of disconnection by connecting the dog to the desired affection of the other. Kramer does not focus on communication, on the contrary, he refers to antidepressants as his "cotherapists;" "they're the good cop to my bad," he elaborates.[26] The princess observes that the real problem is interpersonal communication, but then she falls back on the default mechanism of culture—"Wouldn't it be wonderful" if we could take a pill and our problems of communication with others would just disappear.

Now, before reading Rosen's review with its idiosyncratic opening I had no knowledge of *The Princess Diaries* phenomenon, nor do I desire now to pursue this too far. However, as it turns out, it is interesting that the author of the books is known for interjecting elements of contemporary culture into her storyline, sometimes to the dismay of readers who may regard this tendency as a distraction from the adolescent fantasy theme. Also, it is of note that in volume nine of the series Mia Thermopolis, the adolescent female protagonist, succumbs to her parents' pressure to seek therapeutic help for her melancholy. Certainly, it is a recognized danger to prescribe antidepressants to children. Kramer is aware of this, and moderates his enthusiasm to say that:

> I worry a great deal about an area of practice I have little access to, the treatment of children. My impression is that antidepressants work unreliably in children and carry serious risks—known ones and, more frighteningly, unknown ones hinted at by our knowledge about the vulnerability of the developing brain.[27]

As is well known, the brain matures on average in the years 19 to 24. The consequences of giving the drugs to teens are well proven to induce violence, suicidal ideation, and the completion of suicides. Nonetheless, parents commonly accept the chemical myth and frequently send their children off to college, drugs in hand, as a preventive strategy for stress and anxiety. It is estimated that up to 50% of college students in the United States are on antidepressants.[28] In this environment, the idea of allowing students to carry firearms on university campuses, now accepted practice in some states of the union... well, I leave it to my reader to decide.

Even while accepting the severe problems of clinical studies, Kramer sticks to his theme, suggesting that the evidence is good enough, adequacy of proof an imagined deficit of serotonin sufficient to prescribe. He seems to explicitly endorse drugs for prevention within this context, as follows:

> It's true that psychiatrists are agnostic priests. We are aware that the Pharma trials are shameful, ethically and scientifically. We are aware that our understanding of medications is incomplete. We feel obliged to protect our patients from unknown harms—not demonstrated but imaginable.[29]

Of course, if Mia is like most women in America, she will grow up to be twice as likely than her male friends to have depression disorder. No one knows why. This certainly limits the medical model claim that it is a matter of brain chemistry, because there is no proof that the female brain is intrinsically more susceptible to chemical imbalances than the male brain. Karp reports that, "if, as studies routinely show, women suffer from depression twice as often as men, it strains credibility to believe that such a finding can be accounted for by biological differences alone."[30] As Mia reaches the age range of 40 to 59 she may well join 25% of other female Americans who are on antidepressants. If her husband dies, she has only a few weeks for normal grieving, after which her despondency will be considered a brain disease and she can get antidepressants to dull the pain of loss.[31] This, too, weakens the disease model hypothesis. If Mia were from another culture that has radically different customs and semiotic systems of expression for sadness, it would be a matter of indifference to western psychiatry, because the medical model does not and cannot account for culture as an intrinsic part of human consciousness. This subscription to the idea of a universal consciousness, a consciousness that occurs completely and absolutely outside the world in which it resides, is perhaps the most fatal flaw in the disease model of depression. Contrary to this, I have argued that culture, in fact, inheres in consciousness. Culture is the epistemic, semiotic habitus phenomenologically expressed by the ontological body.[32]

So, could it be that the dog's condition is an analogue code through which we may witness the danger of meaningless human relations? According to Princess Mia it is the dog's relationship with her grand mother that drives the animal mad, and she plainly sees that it could be her, not just the dog who suffers alienation and loneliness. She imagines licking her own hair from her body, which, from a critical standpoint could be interpreted as a metaphor for drug induced legitimized disconnection. Would taking a pill make communication better? Prozac is a cultural reference in the story to our tendency to see sadness through the semiotic code of antidepressants. However, the efficient quick fix of a pill seems a fantasy of its own, a repression of the problem at hand, a diversion even. It appears as an adolescent wish in the story told by the daughter: "Wouldn't it be wonderful" *if*... but if the drug *did what*? Stop the neurotic behavior, end the loneliness, cure the anxieties of depression, or make us feel better for having imposed a scientifically rationalized solution? The statement seems to suggest that the pill is a magic bullet cure. The association of the medicine with the reality of unhealthy relations seems stretched though, a leap of imagination, a "what if" that is an eccentric solution for a deeper issue of existential communication.

Of course, the drug remedy absolves the patient and the doctor of responsibility where the person of Mia might be concerned. The animal lives, as Jakob von Uexkull would say, in a dog's world, the semiotic sphere specific to its biological class.[33] Mia belongs to *homo sapiens sapiens*, a far younger species but having the unique talent of symbolicity, the capability of creating and using advanced, perhaps infinite, signifying capabilities pertaining to the reflexivity of consciousness and experience. She may be relieved to know that sadness is not her fault; that it results from nothing she has done. Moreover, she has little to do, save take the medicine and maintain the regimen. No corrections need be made in her life progress and situation. There is no obligatory self-narrative such as might be expressed in psychotherapy; exposure of the triumphs and travails of personal history is unnecessary. No new self-insights through reflection are required. Revelations are not the stuff of medicinal co-therapy. Having captured her supposed essential self, Mia can escape or delay personality change.

Sometimes psychotherapy is recommended to accompany drugs. A real life co-therapist in the present flesh of an embodied person might not help though. No one locked into the medical model wants to ask an important question: Who exactly is being rendered therapy once the patient is drugged? Is it the melancholic patient initially encountered or a personality created by chemical changes to the brain? How will the doctor evaluate the patient's responses? How will either the patient or the doctor know whether the depression is cured so long as the patient is intoxicated? Mia might know under sedation that her emotional world is sealed off, reduced in its capacity to experience the feelings of being that connect her originarily to the world in general and to other people. As Kramer admits, the drugs mute apprehension. Mute is the right word. Millions of people are on a train without a stop. As Kramer admits,

> [m]ost Americans taking antidepressants have been on them for two years or more—30 percent for five years or more. This extended use creates intimate relationships with these medicines, for better and for worse. Patients live unhappily, with side effects such as diminished sex drive, and contentedly with a sense of security long absent in their lives.[34]

A life devoid of Eros is frequently passed over in the literature, as though this is a small thing to give up. Mia on drugs may never know the libidinal pleasures of emotional love in its physical expression.

A taciturn Mia might come to the question of: "Is it me or the my meds?" The doctor, as I have mentioned, will not know either. This is a common experiential but not existential crisis that occurs with those who live under the intoxication of antidepressants.[35] The possibility of a genuine existential crisis is ruled out of court by the medicine. Experience is absolved of reflexivity with existence. Calmness creates a sense of security and perhaps confidence. There is no way to know whether patients are still depressed or whether they would have gotten better without the medicine. The risk of being a lifelong "patient" defined by antidepressants is quite real. Patients fear going off the medicine, and should not absent the supervision of a medical professional. The fear is warranted, because suicide or its ideation among other tragic consequences may occur. This is euphemistically called "discontinuation syndrome,"[36] which is assumed in the medical literature to bring a patient back to the depressed condition and thus to once again affirm the drug's efficacy. The only solution may be to continue on antidepressants indefinitely. In reality, the ostensible syndrome is drug withdrawal from an intoxicated state. Of course, Mia could very well be susceptible to violence and suicide on the pill; as I have mentioned, the risks of adolescent consumption of antidepressants are well known and often tragic.

Rosen is caught up in the semiotic code and may not see the frame he has imposed. Even fundamental questions are not asked such as whether the dog is giving itself pleasure; rather, the pathology is almost a conditioned response once the word Prozac is mentioned. What is the motive of the doctor who has prescribed the medicine, the good of the dog or the satisfaction of the observer-owner? Did the doctor relieve the animal's suffering or the observer's?

Is it possible that Rosen does not read this story as a metaphor, that he does not see it as a cautionary tale, the moral of which is that it is the princess who is at risk?

POSSIBILITY AND RISK IN THE COMMUNICATION MATRIX

Concluding this endeavor requires a partial recursion to the beginning where I described the philosophy of consciousness and human science that converge in communicology's paradigm exemplar as semiotic phenomenology. The place of communication in discussions of depression and antidepressants becomes increasingly clear. What have we accepted and what have we left unexplored? Karp answers the first part of the question: "In the end, nearly everyone comes to favor biochemically deterministic theories of depression's cause." This, he ruminates, is "partly a result of their gradual commitment to a medical version of reality."[37] As to the second part of the question, communicology responds: Reality has no preference for its many alternative interpretations. A teachable moment for Rosen's daughter could well include the idea that *"finding oneself in the world* is a phenomenological achievement, one that is fragile and changeable."[38] There is an anticipated stability in everyday life that I mentioned at the beginning of this endeavor. It is the province of the habitus where dispositions are really predispositions; yet, I hasten to add that the habitus is artfully employed. The aesthetic is ambiguous, though not necessarily paradoxical, as cultural customs in-form action in signifying processes, even while the body uniquely expresses the built reality of feelings of being, as hexis. The world is not initially an object of analysis, but it is interpreted. Interpretations are ordinarily flexible and ever changing. Recall that with reference to Stiegler's concept of the *pharmakon* I raised the question of "what makes life worth living." In depression, there is a "poignant awareness of life as finite and meaningless."[39] Ratcliffe explains:

> (…) a sense of any activity's being worthwhile tacitly depends on the possibility of its infinite teleological development. This is incompatible with the extinction of every human accomplishment, something one accepts as inevitable in properly grasping the nature of mortality. There is a felt realization that everything we do will ultimately leave no trace upon the universe.[40]

In other words, in melancholy expression and perception are asynchronous, if not at odds. The fundamental discursive relation with the world is rendered problematic. Or, in Bourdieu's terms, the ecology of hexis and habitus can no longer be presumed.

There are paradoxes to be considered in making an informed choice about psychotherapy or antidepressants. Of course, a patient could choose both but the latter will inevitably transcend the former as the most expedient alternative. This is the prevailing *Weltanschauung* that we have constructed. I said early on that the problem orientation of psychiatry is itself the problem. Psychiatry represses interpretation of illness by naming it a disease. Kramer welcomes the medical model; phenomenology interrogates its presuppositions. Rosen's daughter could be alerted to the perils of observing contents while ignoring the frame. Ratcliffe elaborates:

> The reality of this world, it is maintained, can be wholly captured by the deliverances of empirical science. It is a world of matter, to be understood in mechanistic terms and manipulated accordingly, people themselves being increasingly included in this mechanistic scheme of things. The fact that we belong to the world in a way that is presupposed by any such conception is not merely something that goes unacknowledged. It is *denied*, by the insistence that a particular set of epistemic practices, which concerns itself only with the actual, is able in principle to tell us *everything* there is to know about the world. The outcome of this insistence is a form of what I earlier referred to as "epistemic pathology," where the world we live in is ignored altogether and replaced by an abstract, meaningless realm.[41]

There are two conditions that have concerned me, both of which abstract us from normal, lived ambiguity. Karp succinctly describes the first one: the central premise of depression is "the need to withdraw and the distress of isolation."[42] Remembering that the dog's need to withdraw in Mia's world is a metaphor for human possibility and risk, we may certainly conclude that communication is at issue. Indeed, Karp names the central theme of depression; it is discontentment with communication, disconnection from the social world. This theme occurs in every phenomenological account, including that of Ratcliffe. He concludes his insightful work on the phenomenology of depression by arguing that problematic communication is "absolutely central" to experiences of depression.[43]

The second condition, however, is that all phenomenological accounts of experiences of being on antidepressants include as a central theme that *the medicine disconnects* the patient from empathetic contact with other people. My previous synthesis of several studies is worth repeating here:

> Now intoxicated by the drugs, patients may feel better, though it is typical that they worry about their reliance on the drugs and fear going off them. In a state of stupefaction, their emotions are leveled out. They are now disconnected by means of chemicals; intoxication is substituted for social isolation and disconnection. On analogy with alcohol or several illicit drugs the suffering person is now a victim deprived of volition in any meaningful sense, a medical "patient" whose obligations to the world of others are short-circuited by treatment of a postulated alien element in the brain. Interpersonal "others are anonymous," "empathy with them unnecessary," "feeling untouchable," "disengaged," "detached," "not responsible," "a passive observer of events," "not too high and not too low," "lacking in depth," "the dial turned down," "no feel for feelings," "unmoved by others," "distanced from events," "not needing anything," "no sexual desire," "lost sense of agency" and "unable to reach out to others," the victim-patient is now in a self-satisfied disconnected world. These revelatory phrases are signifiers of unresolved loss of communication as described by patients on antidepressants.[44]

Ratcliffe again reminds us that "Impaired interpersonal relations are not an 'effect' of depression experiences but absolutely central to them. So it is a mistake to suggest, as the *DSM* does, that depression is merely 'accompanied' by "impairment in social, occupational, or other areas of functioning" and "in *all* cases," Ratcliffe declares, "there is a sense of disconnection from the interpersonal world [emphasis mine]."[45]

It is a paradox that antidepressant medicine replicates the very thing that produces the depressed experience. Communication is the essence of what is lost in melancholia and communication is repressed under the regime of depression medicine. The source of depression is what Thomas Fuchs calls "desynchronization" and I have named here "asynchronization of perception and expression."[46] Fuchs focuses attention on time in relations. Here I have focused on the other (discourse) as medium of expression and the body as channel of perception. In communicological terms, a paradox is a double-bind, a *perceived* forced choice, but there is a way to step outside the frame. Stiegler's *pharmacology* exposes a space not of possibility or risk, but rather, the locus of their intersection. The *pharmakon*, he notes, is always "composed of two contrary sides," "at *once* good and evil, at *once* a remedy and a poison (...)"[47]

Communication is not to be idealized. It is not an alternative magic bullet cure. We must accept its twin sides. Communication may prevent or enable narcissism, deter passivity or rationalize it, preclude or express apathy, deepen an interpersonal relationship or dissolve it, and ultimately involve us in the world or alienate us from it. As such, communication is the essential pharmakon relevant to mental health. Perhaps it is wise, then, to heed Stiegler's warning that the pharmakon "*enables* care to be taken," but it is also, and at the same time, "that *of which* care must be taken."[48] My presumptive being is exposed and put at risk in every contact I make with another person, even while my possibilities are expanded. We must each decide whether the possibilities of human dialogue in everyday life or in therapy are worth the candle. Such decisions as this require imagination.

Failures of imagination abound. I prefer to imagine communication as the originary anti-depressant to which we may always return for nourishment, regardless of the consequences. I did not raise a daughter, but I believe I have taught my sons, and trust that they will extend the lesson to my grandchildren, that communication makes life worth living. I understand, as does Lanigan and Merleau-Ponty before him, that I am in an ecological relationship with my world. I do not doubt the health of my conviction that communication provides the existential-experiential ground for my very being.

NOTES

1. Isaac E. Catt, "The Two Sciences of Communication in Philosophical Context," *The Review of Communication* 14, no. 3–4 (2014). This article complements a history authored by Richard L. Lanigan, "Husserl's Phenomenology in America (USA): The Human Science Legacy of Wilbur Marshall Urban and the Yale School of Communicology," *Shutzian Research* 3 (2011).

2. Isaac E. Catt, "Communicology and Human Conduct: An Essay Dedicated to Max," *Semiotica: International Journal / Revue de l'Association Internationale de Sémiotique*, (2015): 204: 341–60.
3. Richard L. Lanigan, "Communicology Paradigms of Self and Person: The Perspectives Model of Interpersonal Communication as the Logic Foundation of Human Science" (paper presented at The First Communicology Institute Colloquium, "The Cultural Matrix of Communicology," at Eastern Washington University, Cheney, WA, May 19, 2014); Maurice Merleau-Ponty, *Phenomenology of Perception*, trans. Donald A. Landes (London: Routledge, 2012/1945), lxxxv.
4. Isaac E. Catt, "Communicology, Antidepressants and Employability: A Critique of the Pathologization of Precarity," in *Hyperprecarity*, ed. Rolf Dieter-Hepp and Robert Reisenger (Europäischer Hochschulverlag, Bremen: Oxford, 2017); Isaac E. Catt, "Communicology and the Ethics of Selfhood Under the Regime of Antidepressant Medicine," in *Philosophy of Communication Ethics*, ed. Ronald C. Arnett and Pat Arneson (Madison, NJ: Fairleigh Dickinson University Press, 2014), 285–302; Isaac E. Catt, "Communicology and the Worldview of Antidepressant Medicine," *The American Journal of Semiotics* 28, no. 1–2 (2012): 81–103.
5. Deborah Eicher-Catt and Isaac E. Catt, eds., *Communicology: The New Science of Embodied Discourse* (Madison, NJ: Fairleigh Dickinson University Press, 2010).
6. Jürgen Ruesch, *Semiotics and Human Relations* (The Hague: Mouton, 1972/1953), 68.
7. Jürgen Ruesch and Gregory Bateson, *Communication: The Social Matrix of Psychiatry* (New York: Norton, 1951).
8. Isaac E. Catt, "Pierre Bourdieu's Semiotic Legacy: A Theory of Communicative Agency," *The American Journal of Semiotics* 22, no. 1–4 (2006): 31–54.
9. Sally Fisher, "Social Ecology and the Flesh," in *Merleau-Ponty and Environmental Philosophy*, ed. Suzanne L. Cataldi and William S. Hamrick (Albany: SUNY, 2007), 206
10. Bernard Stiegler, *What Makes Life Worth Living? On Pharmacology*, trans. Daniel Ross (Malden, MA: Polity Press, 2013/2010), 4–5.
11. David A. Karp, *Is It Me or My Meds?* (Cambridge, MA: Harvard University Press, 2006), 16.
12. Peter Kramer, *Listening to Prozac* (New York: Viking, 1993).
13. Peter Kramer, *Ordinarily Well: The Case for Antidepressants* (New York: Farrar, Straus and Giroux, 2016).
14. Jonathan Rosen, "The Assault on Antidepressants," review of *Ordinarily Well: The Case for Antidepressants*, by Peter Kramer, *The Atlantic*, July/August Issue. http://www.theatlantic.com/magazine/archive/2016/07.
15. The diaries belong to a series of books authored by Meg Cabot and chronicle the life of a young girl. It is my understanding that Disney made a movie based on the stories. I leave it to my feminist friends whose scholarly analysis of the stories might reveal much more than I am able to cover in this brief essay.
16. Michael Ratcliffe, *Feelings of Being* (New York: Oxford University Press, 2008).
17. This is a term used by Matthew Ratcliffe to designate the underlying feelings of being that are ignored and presumed in much discourse, especially in psychiatry. See *Feelings of Being*, reprinted 2011.
18. Richard L. Lanigan, *Phenomenology of Communication: Merleau-Ponty's Thematics in Communicology and Semiology* (Pittsburgh, PA: Duquesne University Press, 1988), 11; Lanigan references James M. Edie's essay, "Can Grammar Be Thought?," in *Patterns of the Lifeworld*, ed. J. M. Edie and others (Evanston, IL: Northwestern University Press, 1970).
19. Michael Ratcliffe, *Experiences of Depression* (New York: Oxford University Press, 2015).

20. See Lanigan, *Phenomenology of Communication*; Also see *The Human Science of Communicology: A Phenomenology of Discourse in Foucault and Merleau-Ponty* (Pittsburgh, PA: Duquesne University Press, 1992) and numerous other works spanning the time period of 1969 to the present day.
21. Kramer, *Ordinarily Well*, xxi.
22. Ratcliffe, *Experiences of Depression*, 267.
23. Richard L. Lanigan has described this many times and many places. Perhaps the clearest statement is "Capta versus Data: Method and Evidence in Communicology," *Human Studies* 17 (1994): 109–130. For examples applying this methodology, see Eicher-Catt and Catt, *Communicology*.
24. Isaac E. Catt, "Korzybski and Charles Sanders Peirce," in *Korzybski and...*, ed. Corey Anton and Lance Strate (New York: Institute of General Semantics, 2012), 69–99.
25. Irving Kirsch, *The Emperor's New Clothes* (New York: Basic Books, 2010).
26. Kramer, *Ordinarily Well*, 189.
27. Kramer, *Ordinarily Well*, 228.
28. R. Kadison, "Getting an Edge: Use of Stimulants and Antidepressants in College," *New England Journal of Medicine* 353, no. 11 (2005): 1089–1091.
29. Kramer, *Ordinarily Well*, 214.
30. David A. Karp, *Speaking of Sadness* (New York: Oxford University Press, 1996), 80.
31. Catt, "Communicology and the Worldview"; Also see Catt, "Communicology and the Ethics."
32. Isaac E. Catt, "Culture in the Conscious Experience of Communication," *Journal of Communication, Ethics, Religion and Culture*, Special Issue on Communicology and Culture, 48, no. 2 (Spring 2013): 99–119.
33. Any number of works by bio-semioticians reference von Uexkull's theory of the Umwelt. See for example Thomas A. Sebeok, *Global Semiotics* (Bloomington: Indiana University Press, 2001).
34. Kramer, *Ordinarily Well*, 199.
35. Karp, *Is It Me or My Meds?*; See also, Katherine Sharpe, *Coming of Age on Zoloft* (New York: HarperCollins, 2012).
36. Kramer, *Ordinarily Well*, 202.
37. Karp, *Speaking of Sadness*, 31.
38. Ratcliffe, *Experiences of Depression*, 268.
39. Ratcliffe, *Experiences of Depression*, 270.
40. Ratcliffe, *Experiences of Depression*, 271.
41. Ratcliffe, *Feelings of Being*, 289–290.
42. Karp, *Speaking of Sadness*, 34.
43. Ratcliffe, *Experiences of Depression*, 280.
44. Catt, "Communicology and the Ethics."
45. Ratcliffe, *Experiences of Depression*, 218.
46. Thomas Fuchs, "Melancholia as a Desynchronization: Towards a Psychopathology of Interpersonal Time," *Psychopathology* 34 (2001): 179–186.
47. Stiegler, *What Makes Life Worth Living?*, 10.
48. Stiegler, *What Makes Life Worth Living?*, 4.

BIBLIOGRAPHY

Catt, Isaac E. "Communicology, Antidepressants and Employability: A Critique of the Pathologization of Precarity." In *Hyperprecarity*, edited by Rolf Dieter-Hepp and Robert Reisenger. Europäischer Hochschulverlag, Bremen: Oxford, 2017

Catt, Isaac E. "Communicology and the Ethics of Selfhood Under the Regime of Antidepressant Medicine." In *Philosophy of Communication Ethics*, edited by Ronald C. Arnett and Pat Arneson, 285–304. Madison, NJ: Fairleigh Dickinson University Press, 2014.

Catt, Isaac E. "Communicology and Human Conduct: An Essay Dedicated to Max." *Semiotica: International Journal/Revue de l'Association Internationale de Sémiotique* 204 (2015): 341–360.

Catt, Isaac E. "Communicology and the Worldview of Antidepressant Medicine." *The American Journal of Semiotics* 28, no. 1–2, (2012): 81–103.

Catt, Isaac E. "Culture in the Conscious Experience of Communication." Special Issue on Communicology and Culture, *Journal of Communication, Ethics, Religion and Culture*, 48, no. 2, Spring (2013): 99–119.

Catt, Isaac E. "Korzybski and Charles Sanders Peirce." In *Korzybski and ...*, edited by Corey Anton and Lance Strate, 69–99. New York: Institute of General Semantics, 2012.

Catt, Isaac E. "Pierre Bourdieu's Semiotic Legacy: A Theory of Communicative Agency." *The American Journal of Semiotics* 22, nos. 1–4 (2006): 31–54.

Catt, Isaac E. "The Two Sciences of Communication in Philosophical Context." *The Review of Communication* 14, nos. 3–4 (2014): 201–228.

Edie, James M. "Can Grammar Be Thought?" In *Patterns of the Lifeworld*, edited by J. M. Edie and others. Evanston, IL: Northwestern University Press, 1970.

Eicher-Catt, Deborah, and Isaac E. Catt, eds. *Communicology: The New Science of Embodied Discourse*. Madison, NJ: Fairleigh Dickinson University Press, 2010.

Fisher, Sally. "Social Ecology and the Flesh." In *Merleau-Ponty and Environmental Philosophy*, edited by Suzanne L. Cataldi and William S. Hamrick, 203–215. Albany: SUNY, 2007.

Fuchs, Thomas. "Melancholia as a Desynchronization: Towards a Psychopathology of Interpersonal Time." *Psychopathology* 34 (2001): 179–186.

Kadison, R. "Getting an Edge: Use of Stimulants and Antidepressants in College." *New England Journal of Medicine* 353, no. 11 (2005): 1089–1091.

Karp, David A. *Is It Me or My Meds?* Cambridge, MA: Harvard University Press, 2006.

Karp, David A. *Speaking of Sadness*. New York: Oxford University Press, 1996.

Kirsch, Irving. *The Emperor's New Clothes*. New York: Basic Books, 2010.

Kramer, Peter. *Listening to Prozac*. New York: Viking, 1993.

Kramer, Peter. *Ordinarily Well: The Case for Antidepressants*. New York: Farrar, Straus and Giroux, 2016.

Lanigan, Richard L. "Capta versus Data: Method and Evidence in Communicology." *Human Studies* 17 (1994): 109–130.

Lanigan, Richard L. "Communicology Paradigms of Self and Person: The Perspectives Model of Interpersonal Communication as the Logic Foundation of Human Science." Paper presented at The First Communicology Institute Colloquium on the "The Cultural Matrix of Communicology" at Eastern Washington University, Cheney, WA, May 19, 2014.

Lanigan, Richard L. *The Human Science of Communicology: A Phenomenology of Discourse in Foucault and Merleau-Ponty*. Pittsburgh, PA: Duquesne University Press, 1992.

Lanigan, Richard L. "Husserl's Phenomenology in America (USA): The Human Science Legacy of Wilbur Marshall Urban and the Yale School of Communicology." *Shutzian Research* 3 (2011): 203–217.

Lanigan, Richard L. *Phenomenology of Communication: Merleau-Ponty's Thematics in Communicology and Semiology*. Pittsburgh, PA: Duquesne University Press, 1988.

Merleau-Ponty, Maurice. *Phenomenology of Perception*. Translated by Donald A. Landes. London: Routledge, 2012/1945.

Ratcliffe, Michael. *Experiences of Depression*. New York: Oxford University Press, 2015.

Ratcliffe, Michael. *Feelings of Being*. New York: Oxford University Press, 2008.

Rosen, Jonathan. "The Assault on Antidepressants." Review of *Ordinarily Well: The Case for Antidepressants*, by Peter Kramer. *The Atlantic*, July/August Issue. http://www.theatlantic.com/magazine/archive/2016/07.

Ruesch, Jürgen. *Semiotics and Human Relations*. The Hague: Mouton, 1972/1953.

Ruesch, Jürgen, and Gregory Bateson. *Communication: The Social Matrix of Psychiatry*. New York: Norton, 1951.

Sebeok, Thomas. *Global Semiotics*. Bloomington: Indiana University Press, 2001.

Sharpe, Katherine. *Coming of Age on Zoloft*. New York: HarperCollins, 2012.

Stiegler, Bernard. *What Makes Life Worth Living? On Pharmacology*. Translated by Daniel Ross. Malden, MA: Polity Press, 2013/2010.

CHAPTER ELEVEN

Decolonial Phenomenological Practice

Communicology Across the Cultural and Political Borders of the North-South and West-East Divides

JACQUELINE M. MARTINEZ

Communicology presents itself as a scholarly and research practice that has the capacity to interrogate the very conditions though which the specificity of thought and action become possible. The promise of this kind of scholarly and research practice is that it has the capacity to carry the value of what is essentially humane within concrete human worlds that often are not humane. Capacity, however, is not actuality[1] and an understanding of this difference allows for thinking that can engage the reflective, reflexive and reversible conditions in which the particularity of *this* actuality becomes manifest in the immediacy of our communicative engagement with others and the world.

The significance of these conditions—reflectivity, reflexivity, and reversibility—is that they constitute the very terrain over which the difference between capacity, and actuality may be discerned. Such discernment, however, is subject to the conditions in which it is engaged, which means that to have engaged a study based in descriptions of the dynamic and synergistic relationships (among reflectivity, reflexivity, and reversibility) is not in and of itself adequate as a basis for judgment as to the accuracy of our assertions made. This is particularly true in cases where we attempt to depict the actuality of experience as it is lived in the immediacy of our communicative engagements. The inevitable inadequacy of our descriptions is tied inexorably to the problem of *perspective*. It is, in fact, our very humanity, engaged humanely, that situates us within this inexorable problem of perspective.

The problem of perspective is, among other things, a problem of how we understand lived-experience. In one sense, lived-experience falls within the domain[2] of the person. No one other than me can articulate my lived-experience. In another sense, however, the very fact that I *articulate* my lived-experience locates me within systems of articulation whereby my articulations can never be in a direct or isomorphic relationship to lived-experience itself; neither can they be simply my own. Other domains of human interrelatedness intervene even in my most privately felt experience, and this is why we cannot presume the adequacy of a person's account even of her or his own experience. On this point it is crucial to keep in mind that "adequacy" is different from "true" or "false." To recognize that my own or someone's descriptions of lived-experience are not adequate as representations is to recognize the essential existential fact that human existence always exceeds what is graspable in any moment or in articulation. Our "arrival" at total "truth" is always just beyond, and any presumption otherwise compromises our ability to engage what is most humane about the human world.

In the work that follows I shall explicate this thesis through the theory and logic of communicology within the discursive contexts of North-South and West-East interrelations. The geographical significance of North-South and West-East interrelations lies in the historical deployment of Euro-Modernity as the standard bearer of reason and rationality.[3] This historical deployment of Euro-Modernity has meant that the North and the West have been constructed as the universal center from which all of human thought emerges. This mentality is at the root of historical colonialism and the neo-colonialism that persists to this day. It is no coincidence that 15th Century emergence of Euro-Modernity occurs within colonialist projects. Essential to this colonialist project is the dehumanization of people and cultures located on the American, African and Asian continents.[4] Euro-modernity is a "western supremacist ideology" that sustains the idea that "the West deserves to control and lead the world."[5] My effort in the present work is to focus on the decolonial project in Latin American thought as exemplified in Enrique Dussel's *Ethics of Liberation in the Age of Globalization and Exclusion*,[6] in order to demonstrate how a cultural communicology as exemplified in the work of Richard Lanigan's can also serve the decolonial project. Dussel's focus is on the North-South interrelation and Lanigan focus is on the West-East interrelation.[7] I take the work of Dussel as an exemplar of the decolonial project in order to show convergences with Lanigan's communicological approach to West-East interrelations.

ENRIQUE DUSSEL AND RICHARD LANIGAN

Enrique Dussel is a Latin American philosopher whose scholarship is dedicated to decolonial projects. His formal education includes "an undergraduate degree in Philosophy (from the Universidad Nacional de Cuyo/National University of Cuyo in Mendoza, Argentina), a Doctorate from the Complutense University of Madrid, a Doctorate in History from the Sorbonne in Paris, and an undergraduate degree in Theology obtained through studies in Paris and Münster."[8] Dussel's extensive study within Western philosophy included "a turn toward Marxism and liberation theology, and the development of the comprehensive articulation of a philosophy of liberation."[9] Although Dussel dedicated much time to the study of Western philosophy, his life and work are hardly defined by such study. His life has also been shaped significantly by "political activism, repression and exile from a military dictatorship."[10]

Dussel writes with an explicit intent to analyze and therefore usurp the longstanding proliferation of Eurocentric colonialist thought that has been and continues to be essential to the project of Euro-modernity (and, often, postmodernity as well). His purpose is to usurp centuries of Eurocentric thought that presents itself—and all of its deeply seated prejudices—as simply neutral, objective, and correct. Dussels's overall project is to reclaim "important foundations of [philosophy] that lay outside its acknowledged geographical domain."[11]

Richard Lanigan is a U.S. American scholar whose formal education includes an undergraduate and Master's degree from the University of New Mexico, and a Doctorate from Southern Illinois University. Lanigan is a direct descendant of the "Yale School of Communicology."[12] The Yale School of Communicology is distinguished by the unique bringing together of philosophy and linguistics in the works of Wilber Marshall Urban, Ernst Cassirer, Edward Sapir, and their graduate students Benjamin Lee Whorf and Hubert Griggs Alexander. Alexander went on to teach at the University of New Mexico, where Lanigan became his student. Over the course of his career Lanigan has brought to full fruition the communicology initiated by the Yale School of Communicology.

At this point in the discussion, caution must be raised: In taking the work of Lanigan, a U.S. American[13] scholar who by all appearances occupies a position easily within the center of Eurocentricity, to show how it can serve the purposes of Modernity's Other, one runs the risk of reinforcing the long standing tradition of interpreting Latin American and Africana thinkers in terms of a Eurocentric tradition. Lewis Gordon refers to this as the "problem of subordinated theoretical identity,"[14] wherein non-European thinkers are identified in terms of those European scholars they studied with or whose scholarship they use. There is a strong tendency to identify Latin American or African philosophers, for example, as "followers" of European philosophers, to reduce "their thought to the [European] thinkers they study."[15] Such a dynamic rarely occurs when European scholars study or comment upon the work of Latin American or Africana scholars.

Consider also that although Dussel is very well versed in the European (analytic and continental) philosophical tradition, that tradition has never been sufficient for his own projects. His dedication to thought and dialogue emerged from daily life experiences of suspicion, threat, and violence that few who live unproblematically within Eurocentric thought have to confront. To set the goal of illustrating how Lanigan's work helps further the decolonialist goals found in the work of Dussel and others, makes it easy for those engaging Lanigan's work to claim a solidarity or alliance with figures like Dussel without ever having engaged his work; or, having engaged his work, subordinating it to the perspectives and presuppositions carried within the Eurocentricity of one's own thought. I am very wary of producing a work that suggests that it is possible to pursue the same decolonial goals and achieve the same insights as Latin American and Africana thinkers by using semiotic phenomenology, or taking a communicological approach without ever having sought thought from a perspective other than a Eurocentric one. In fact, I shall argue that taking up the perspective of cultural communicology requires, at minimum, a bracketing of the Eurocentric tradition within which the mainstream of US American scholars and researchers work.

A second caution is also required in that Lanigan writes with a primarily interest in *scientific inquiry* in the Peircian sense. The problem here is that the concept of "scientific" is often conflated with positivism and a goal of a "scientific validity" that portends to discover apodictic certainty. This positivist orientation and claim of "scientific validity" has been essential to Euro-modernity's racist, hegemonic and genocidal projects. In contradistinction, Lanigan's dedication to scientific inquiry is a commitment to inquiry that requires a *radical engagement* with the human being situated within the immediacy of dynamically alive and living worlds, or systems of interrelations, continuously unfolding as human beings communicate. This kind of commitment of scientific inquiry to radical engagement is central to Lanigan's explications of communicology and its methodological cognate of semiotic phenomenology.

These points of caution return me to the thesis above—namely, that capacity is not actuality. Grasping this difference and then, more importantly, adequately assessing which is which, is a problem that any *human science* worth its name must take as its most essential commitment. There is, therefore a recursive aspect to the present project. The task of demonstrating theoretical convergences within the three discursive contexts I've selected is the most obvious goal. But these "theoretical convergences" themselves point to a problematic that cannot be adequately addressed by a straightforward lining up of ideas.[16] Something more happens as ideas get lined up and that something more must be accounted for in the work itself. This accounting, and the logic through which that accounting precedes, constitutes reflexive, reflective, and reversible sets of interrelations that must then become the very *stuff* of the inquiry.

The theoretical center point of my explication of Dussel and Lanigan is C.S. Peirce's concept of the "interpretant." The interpretant is the "practice category of the sign" and as such it functions as a "sign of symbols,"[17] or at the "meta-level of perspective."[18] For Peirce, the interpretant is inherently phenomenological in that as the "practice category of the sign" it is always embodied and motivated (rather than arbitrary, as in Saussure). As a result, the interpretant makes it possible to engage in the reflective, reflexive and reversible characteristics of consciousness. Cultural communicology retains a commitment to Peirce's notion of scientific inquiry wherein our inquiries become heuristically concerned with "fostering *intelligence*, pragmatically understood,"[19] so that intelligence consists "in acting so that one's deeds are concentrated upon a result."[20] This requirement is *not* one that can be met by mere acclimation. It must be discerned in the practice of interrelationships and demonstrated in the work thusly performed. How exactly that performance is demonstrated is a major point toward which the present work is directed.

I turn now to a discussion of Euro-Modernity and coloniality. This discussion sets the historical and theoretical context (that is, Eurocentric) in which the decolonial project is situated. I use the historical example of Junipero Serra, the 18th century Spanish missionary who founded 9 of the 21 missions in California, to illustrate the function of the interpretant in recognizing the difference between capacity and actuality and how that recognition allows us to interrogate the particularity of *this* actuality as it becomes manifest in the immediacy of our communicative engagement with others and the world.

Following this discussion, I turn specifically to the work of Dussel. This leads me back to the focus on perspective, and allows me to consider how Lanigan's work is complementary to the decolonial project. I shall feature Lanigan's explication of West-East reality (2015) as a way to direct our focus toward *cultural perspective* that moves us through the phenomenological aspect of lived-experience and into the semiotic condition of our human interrelatedness within the specificities of time and place, history and location. I conclude by returning again to the caution raised above, which requires that the worked produced here be taken again through a critical evaluation of position and context within the legacies of Eurocentrism and colonialilty as they remain at work particularly within the U.S. American academy.

THE 15TH CENTURY FOUNDING OF MODERNITY AND THE VIOLENCE OF COLONIALISM AS IT EXTENDS INTO THE 21ST CENTURY

The violence of colonialism manifests in many ways. As a communication system, colonialism delimits possibilities for human recognition and understanding. Cultures and institutions also function by delimiting possibilities for human recognition and understanding, although not all cultures or institutions perpetuate the violence and dehumanization that are perpetrated in the colonial situation. In all cases, however, it is the *communicative interrelationships* that give structure to culture and institutions such that these delimitations give concrete form to the perceptual capacities of persons who function within them; perceptual capacities are essentially linked to the material and concrete practices that sustain the dehumanizations of the colonial situation. The fact that these delimitations and the structuring of the perceptual capacities of persons do not necessarily result in a colonialist orientation or the dehumanization of those who think, feel, live, or communicate within them, identifies an important point of inquiry—namely, what makes the difference? In other words, even within the most fully encompassing systems of dehumanization, there are those who see through it or beyond it, who recognize their own humanity despite the preponderance of evidence constructed by the colonizing situation (i.e., reality) that says otherwise. Recognizing one's humanity, despite existing within communicative systems that deny that status, is an achievement at the fullest possible level of *humanity*.

What makes the delimitations of culture and institution into dehumanization is a totalizing semiotic that functions at the level of the Peircian interpretant. When a culture, institution, or person denies the fact that delimitations are essential to its perspective, it asserts its own perspective as universal. This denial of delimitations are relevant when they function at the level of *practice*, in a recurring pattern of sign usage that sustains a meta-perspective in which the particularity of their own perspective retains a holistic and unquestioned commitment. This creates a *totalizing semiotic* that becomes cemented as an abstraction that simultaneously reaches deeply into the most immediately communicative aspects of experience and consciousness. These cemented abstractions then become social reality—i.e., a sociality that dominates all other possible manifestations.

This idea that something becomes cemented in abstraction is a stronger way of asserting what phenomenologists commonly refer to as "sedimentation."[21] The sedimentation of meanings, or the deeply entrenched structures of language and other semiotic systems, point to a layer of pre-conscious and unreflected upon dispositions, habits, or tendencies toward action that carry us within a "natural attitude" of everyday life. As much as phenomenologists seek to interrogate the taken-for-granted presumptions that constitute the "natural attitude," this effort can never be presumed to effective or adequate. The effort itself must always be *judged* for its level of adequacy. To focus on a totalizing semiotic that becomes cemented in an abstraction that simultaneously reaches deeply into the most concrete aspects of experience and consciousness, is to move beyond an individualistic phenomenology and into a semiotic or cultural phenomenology that has the capacity to interrogate the delimitations that constitute the perspective that fails to see itself as a perspective.

Consider Pope Francis' 2015 conferral of sainthood upon Junipero Serra—the 18th century Spanish missionary who founded 9 of the 21 missions in California. This is an excellent example of the failure to see a perspective as a *perspective* in a case where such a failure hides the violence it perpetuates from that perspective itself. It allows us to see how the specificity of the interpretant –as it retains fixity despite its dynamic and open capacity–functions as a totalizing semiotic that sustains the violence of colonialism. This point was clearly recognized by the descendants of those who were the objects of the Spanish colonization of Alta America, much of which was presided over by Serra himself. Olin Tezcatlipoca, director of the Mexia Movement, which promotes indigenous rights, described his organization's protest to the conferral of sainthood to Serra in this way: "Our protest is to tell the Pope that by canonizing Junipero Serra, they want to canonize colonialism, they want to canonize white supremacy and they want to canonize the genocide of our people. And that is an immoral act."[22] Survivors of cultures that have been the object of colonialism retain a time-boundedness to their culture and its history that Pope Francis' canonization of Serra fails to recognize.[23] This time-boundedness gives today's members of the Mexia Movement the capacity to see beyond the totalizing perspective that allows Pope Francis to gloss over or deny the violence of colonialism—enabled and promoted by Serra—over those where the objects of the 18th century colonial regimes. The conferral of sainthood upon Serra upholds a colonialist perspective that hides from view the violence and inhumanity of 18th century colonialism as it extends into the 21st century.

During his time as "father president of the California missions,"[24] Serra was keenly aware of the violence enacted, primarily by the Spanish soldiers attached to the missions, against the Amerindians. In letters, reports, and personal appeals, Serra documented this violence by arguing that "repeated attacks against women and summary reprisals against men who dared to interfere undermined the efforts of the priests to attract Amerindians to the missions and to Christianity."[25] Serra's greatest concern was not for the actual lives and ways of living of the Amerindian women and men who were subjected to violent degradations. Rather, he was concerned that "the despicable actions of the soldiers were severely retarding the spiritual and material conquest of California."[26] With specific regard to sexual violence Serra wrote that the soldiers were "guilty of the most heinous crimes, killing the men to take their wives."[27] One wonders which is more heinous: murder or sexual slavery; or, is it the breaking of the patriarchal marriage that makes this the "most heinous crime"?

In 1772 Sera wrote a report entitled, "Report of the General Conditions and Needs of the Missions: Thirty-Two Suggestions for Improving the Government of the Missions."[28] Regarding the sexual violence perpetrated by the soldiers, Serra's recommendation was that the key military commander "should be removed and that Spaniards who married Indian women should be rewarded."[29] For Serra, the essential link between sexual violence and conquest is ostensibly ameliorated by the sanctity of marriage. The actual violence and degradation enacted against the Amerindian women themselves is seen as only an impediment to the goal of a Christianization that is also a cultural genocide, rather than as a material human harm that requires redress for the one against whom that harm was leveled. The delimited and fixed interpretant that remains fully in place here is the righteousness of Christianization coupled with the proprietary nature of women's sexual and reproductive body. Serra's many reports reveal his *capacity* to see the sexual violence perpetrated against Amerindian women, yet what becomes *actualized* within the context of this capacity is a retention of the very logic (i.e., thinking) that gave rise to the license for such violence in the first place.

Serra presented himself as benevolent, and his concern about violence enacted against the Amerindians by the Spanish soldiers concealed the actuality of the material and human harm perpetrated in lock step with the cultural genocide (Christianization) that he was undertaking. His benevolence is itself violence rooted in the presumption of a spiritual righteousness and superiority over those he sought to Christianize. At the level of the human being, the effect is that colonialism seeks the *destruction of the capacities* of those whom it takes as its objects of domination—for the Amerindians there was no mistaking the actualities that would follow from the colonial governance and clearly recognized its destructive intent. It was precisely this capacity for seeing that the colonialists sought to kill by asserting their own cultural dispositions as the essential and only possible standard for what is human. Serra's benevolence therefore requires a category of "less than human" that enables him to have "concern" to bring the Amerindians into his notion of human. This basic assertion functions within a semiotic linkage—as an interpretant—that remains firmly in place across contexts of time, place and circumstance. The righteousness of Serra's cause—the Christianization the Amerindians—delimits his perceptual capacities such that even while he saw Amerindians being brutalized in the most concrete and material ways, he still failed or declined to recognize the inherent linkage between that concrete brutality, the violence of the cultural genocide he presided over, and the fact that it was the limitations of his own perceptual capacities that facilitated both.

The fact of Serra's elevation to sainthood by Pope Francis in 2015 reveals the power of colonialist thought to dominate far beyond the end of colonialism proper. It glosses over the countless atrocities perpetrated in its name, and which have been sustained across centuries to this very day. The Pope's conferral of sainthood on Serra sustains a Eurocentric colonialism in which the cultural and material violence of colonialism is hidden, denied, justified and otherwise sustained. The totalizing semiotic retains its power at the level of the interpretant such that one can elevate Serra to Sainthood despite his province over a period of cultural genocide and the most violent of social and interpersonal relations.

ENRIQUE DUSSEL'S PHILOSOPHY AND ETHICS OF LIBERATION: COMMUNICOLOGICAL CONVERGENCES

Overturning this totalizing semiotic of European thought is central to the Latin American decolonial project. An important aspect of Dussel's decolonial project is to think and see from the "underside of modernity."[30] This is a complex project that involves bringing the perspective of those living and thinking from within "Third World realities to the center of critical thought"[31] in ways that reveal the neocolonialist delimitations of Eurocentric thought and practice. Thinking from within "Third World realities," however, involves much more than identifying persons with a specific biographical and geographical history—although the specificity of biography and geography are always relevant to the capacities for thinking as they emerge in the intersubjective world of human beings communicating. Rather than presume the relevance of biography and geography, thinking from the perspective of Euro-Modernity's Other must also involve taking account of one's capacity to see the perspective from which one's thinking and seeing emerges. This is, in fact, a necessary, though not sufficient, condition of Enrique Dussel's treatise on the *Ethics of Liberation in the Age of Globalization and Exclusion*.

Taking account of one's capacity to see the perspective from which one's thinking and seeing emerges is necessary because absent the capacity to see one's perspective as such it is impossible to place that perspective within a context, which then makes it impossible to identify an alternative context from which other perspectives can also exist. Even the capacity to place one's perspective within a context, however, is still inadequate unless one also can identify the specific ways in which *conditions of practical and material harm* are perpetrated within that context.[32] This is why Dussel insists that any ethics of liberation must engage the perspective of the "victim." As Dussel puts it,

> My hope is that Ethics of Liberation could provide these movements [of political struggle] with some guidance as to critical criteria and principles for the unfolding of the praxis of liberation from the perspective of the victims, as they confront the effects of oppressive norms, acts, microstructures, institutions, or ethical systems in the context of everyday life.[33]

Dussel's "critical criteria and principles" are, however, "nonproceduralist in character [and] grounded in daily life and the dominant models prevalent in that context, and which seeks to encompass the nonintentional negative effects (the production of victims) resulting from every kind of autonomously organized and regulated structure."[34]

A full articulation of Dussel's ethics of liberation is beyond the scope of the present work; however, a focus on Dussel's specific engagement with C. S. Peirce, which occurs in his effort to establish a "foundation of ethics," allows me to explicate key features of a cultural communicology within Dussel's ethics of liberation. This is a project that Dussel himself endorses when he describes his ethics of liberation as being "informed by the motivations similar to those of pragmatism,"[35] and suggests, "that a dialogue in the near future between pragmatism and the philosophy of liberation would be extremely fertile."[36]

Dussel correctly points out that Peirce's philosophy is a "philosophy of mediation—of *Betweeness*—in which the immediate is never given to us since it is always mediated."[37] The interpretant is key to the inescapability of mediation. Dussel characterizes his "grounding of an ethics of liberation" as traversing three *moments*: (1) "the ethical-material moment of content," (2) "the moral-formal, procedural moment of intersubjective and communicative moral validity that is fulfilled in the symmetry of the affected participants" and (3) "the ethical-processual moment of possible feasibility."[38] Each of these three moments—of content, intersubjective validity, and feasibility—carry an "ethical" or "moral" modifier. For Dussel, this ethical or moral modifier serves as a reminder that there are ethical and moral implications in each of these moments; he is not suggesting that his "foundation of ethics" offers an *a priori* standard from which to guide inquiry or behavior. Rather, as Dussel puts it, "the 'foundation,' paradoxically, has to be deepened in direct proportion to what is to be built on top of it."[39] For Dussel, the effort to develop an ethics or behave ethically requires the traversing of "moments."

Thus, for Dussel the priority is less in creating an "explicit theoretical normative capacity," but rather to "play a strategically necessary role in another dimension, which is especially important in collaborative learning processes where critical consciousness can be developed as part of the political, economic, and social organizing efforts of new emerging social movements in civil society."[40] By eschewing the goal of creating an "explicit theoretical normative capacity," Dussel points to "another dimension" that features "critical consciousness" connected to the political, economic and social *capacities of communities*. What makes new social movements emerge is a new capacity for seeing and communicating that alters the delimitations of perspective that were previously unrecognized as such. Most importantly, however, these new perspectives cannot be anticipated or established prior to the very processes (processual engagement) involved in collaborative learning—i.e., they must be a radical inquiry.

This point is very much in keeping with communicology's insistence on "rhetorical ethic" over "ethical rhetoric"[41]; rhetorical engagement—embodied speech and speaking—always precedes judgment about it. In this way, judgment is always contingent and provisional because it is always dependent upon the immediacies (moments) of our human engagements; our effort to establish a foundation of ethics, in other words, requires a *good ambiguity* wherein "rhetoric as speaking refers to ethics as human values."[42] Discerning how this "referring" occurs, what becomes actual within this "referring," and how we account for such "referring" requires the communicological turn wherein we traverse the reflective, reflexive and reversible capacities of consciousness.

Peirce's interpretant is extremely valuable for the project of traversing the reflective, reflexive and reversible capacities of consciousness that does not function with a particular and explicit content that serves as an ethical imperative. As Dussel points out, "it is not possible to operate from the immediate [because] every form of knowledge and action finds itself already determined by the mediation (Thirdness): mediation of the knowing of an object by the intersubjectivity of interpreters as an agreement (through a sign as representamen)."[43] It is precisely through this representamen, that we can grasp the *semiotic facticity of thought*—that is, thought has always been understood as embodied and therefore much more than a matter of conscious experience. As the "practice category of the sign" the interpretant functions as a "sign of symbols."[44] Thus, for Dussel the level of the immediate, or of the "moment," is recognized as beyond our grasp because we are always first in the grasp of mediation or Thirdness. We are therefore resigned to "the knowing of an object by the intersubjectivity of interpreters as an agreement."[45]

It is on this point, however, that communicology diverges from Dussel's reasoning. This divergence is due largely to the fact that in his discussion of North American pragmatics, Dussel treats the work of C. S. Peirce and William James as if their work is consonant with each other. Thus, Dussel's describes his second "moment" across which the foundation of ethics must traverse as "the moral-formal, procedural moment of intersubjective and communicative moral validity that is fulfilled in the symmetry of the affected participants."[46] Dussel relies on the notion of "intersubjective validity" that is very much in keeping with the traditional social science notion of consciously and explicitly identified and agreed upon referents shared by a group of interpreters (i.e., scientific community, critical social sciences, etc.).[47] In fact, Dussel asserts that the fundamental intuitions of pragmatism can be fully subsumed by an ethics of liberation but with a difference: if pragmatism thinks preferentially from the experience of a scientific community (...) and from North American *common sense*, the ethics of liberation thinks primarily from the experience of the practical-political community, from the critical social sciences (its critique of global political economy, for example), and from the oppressed or excluded of the periphery, as well as those in the center.[48]

Communicology, in contrast, does not think preferentially from the experience of a scientific community, nor does it feature "intersubjective validity" as a key point in its radical inquiry. Rather, communicology is interested in the intersubjective understanding—or, more precisely, the intersubjectively shared structures and processes through which conscious experience (i.e., the individual self, self-identity, perceptual capacities) becomes possible in the first place. It is a matter of the shared semiotic structures—always dynamically processual—in which the "irreducible triadicity"[49] of semiosis continues unabatedly. The shared presumptions of a "community," scientific or otherwise, are precisely what communicology seeks to interrogate so as to ascertain how those very presuppositions come to become the taken-for-granted and thus the re-created actuality of lives being lived. Dussel is correct to point out that we are always bound to mediation and thus can never arrive at a "pure" Firstness or "moment" in which we can discern how all of our imbrications in our social, cultural, historical and communicative world are at work; however, the very fact that we are imbricated in these complex interrelations that are our world and our perspective within it, gives us access, not to a "pure" Firstness, but to those interrelations within which both our perceptual capacities are structured, and the actualities of our concrete reality of experience (i.e., as they are expressed and perceived).

This communicological divergence from Dussel's "foundation of ethics" is not contrary to Dussel's overall project. This is because for Dussel, "the freedom of the Other (...) is always a quasi-unconditionality with reference or 'relative' to a context, a world, a concrete reality, or a feasibility." In other words, "the Other is understood as being the other woman/man: a human being, an ethical subject, whose visage is conceived of as the epiphany of living human reality in bodily form (corporeality)."[50] It is precisely this visage, or perspective, that communicology recognizes as having a capacity for realization (epiphany) that can become a radical point of contact with our very intersubjectively imbued experience within immediacy of our communicative engagements. Given this aspect of communicology—and the fact that it is a discipline clearly born and developed within a North American context—it is possible to question Dussel's claim that "pragmatism could not discover the phenomenon of Eurocentrism because it interpreted the United States as the full Western fulfillment of Europe—in the long path from the East toward the West of universal culture, just as Hegel had conceived it. It did not take as if its departure point were the periphery; the dominated, the excluded, the poor, women, or the races discriminated against."[51] The history of pragmatism writ-large supports Dussel's claim. However, I am suggesting that a Peircian-centric pragmatism informed by communicology is not only capable of discovering phenomena that, like Eurocentrism, fail to see the totalizing tendencies in its own perspective, but is successful only to the degree it does.

THE DECOLONIAL PROJECT OF CULTURAL COMMUNICOLOGY: UNDERSTANDING CULTURAL DIFFERENCE AT THE LEVEL OF PERCEPTUAL CAPACITY

The decolonial effort undertaken in Dussel's ethics of liberation requires that we think from the "perspective of the victims, *as they confront* the effects of oppressive norms, acts, microstructures, institutions, or ethical systems in the context of everyday life" [emphasis added].[52] Dussel's concern is to expose the "dominant models" prevalent in the daily life context in order to understand how "autonomously organized and regulated" structures produce victims. Such a production is a "nonintentional negative effect" of those very structures at work in the "dominant models" prevalent in the daily life context.[53] Dussel is correct in asserting that Peirce did not take as his departure point in the development of his semiotics, "the periphery, the dominated, the excluded, the poor, women, the races discriminated against."[54] There is, however, an unidentified problem in Dussel's formulation: who exactly counts as "victims" and how do we make such a determination? The geographical boundaries of North-South and East-West are clearly relevant, but are certainly inadequate as a basis for assessing the total aspect of a person's "daily life context." As general categories, "the poor," "women," "the races discriminated against" accurately depict those who are likely to be "victims" of the dominant structures and systems. On the other hand, when it comes to the "lived context" of poor people, women, or members of racial categories that are discriminated against, one cannot conclude that all persons are identically positioned as "victims." It is also possible (perhaps inevitable) that there are those positioned within a clearly recognizable general category of "victim" who nonetheless adopt the thinking of the dominant system and therefore make victims of those who share their position within the daily life context and systems in which that context is situated.[55]

To attend to the daily life context of persons confronting the material effects (especially those that cause material harm) of the structures and systems in which they are situated is precisely the task of Peirce's notion of scientific inquiry wherein our inquiries become heuristically concerned with "fostering *intelligence*, pragmatically understood,"[56] so that intelligence consists "in acting so that one's deeds are concentrated upon a result."[57] The communicological commitment to the Peircian notion of scientific inquiry is a basis for Lanigan's communicological analysis at the cultural level. A "critical part" of such an analysis is an "understanding of the dynamic spiral of perspectives constituting the logic of exchange" between communicators.[58] Attending to this dynamic spiral of perspectives is precisely what gives communicology its potential as a *radical inquiry*—that is, an inquiry that does not take its own perspective for granted and inquires as to how the difference between capacity and actuality are manifest in the immediacy of our communicative interrelations.

In order to bring the current analysis to a close, I would like to make one final point regarding the "how" of attending to this "dynamic spiral of perspectives." It is a point worthy of much fuller explication than I provide here, but it illustrates the thesis I've been pursuing throughout this work—namely, how communicology can serve the interests of the decolonial project. In order to attend to the "how" of the "dynamic spiral of perspectives," it is essential that the idea of "perspective" not be reduced to the presumptions retained within the egocentricity of the cultures of Euro-modernity. The problem with such a reduction is, of course, the fact that the colonialism that Dussel and other decolonial scholars seek to usurp is deeply egocentric in its perceptual capacity at the level of culture.

Egocentricity and sociocentricity are commonly recognized as the two primary cultural orientations governing our perceptual capacities at the level of culture.

Not as commonly recognized, however, is the fact that egocentricity exists within sociocentric cultures and sociocentricity exists within egocentric cultures—which is not the same thing as saying that the sociocentricity that exists within egocentric cultures is the same as it exists in sociocentric cultures. Nor is the egocentricity that exists in sociocentric cultures the same as it exists in egocentric cultures. This is why it is possible to fully recognize the differences between egocentricity and sociocentricity yet still in our embodied human interrelations have perceptual capacities governed exclusively by one or the other. It is, in other words, in the facticity of our embodied interrelations that we take a perspective at the preconscious level of habit or disposition toward action—and the abstractions (i.e., norms of egocentric or sociocentric perspective) carried therein become actual in the concrete immediacy of human beings communicating. Consider Lanigan's characterization of egocentricity and sociocentricity—each quoted at length for conceptual precision. In the egocentric culture:

> Each person is viewed as a unique individual with distinguishing personal characteristics, the most notable of which is the belief in a Non-Place Community, e.g. a member of a profession (teacher, doctor, etc.) where community is artificially constructed. In short, western, occidental cultures are for the most part egocentric in nature. Note, however that sociocentric groups live within the larger egocentric culture. The egocentric cultural cosmology is one of infinite world resources available to the local community. This is a typical American (U.S.A.) attitude and belief. If one person uses up a share of the whole, another person assumes an equal share is available in this whole or in another whole to be found somewhere else (unfortunately, the share usually belongs to some "not-self" other—person, country, etc.). Such an attitude is a form of the American cultural value of *equity*: the belief that each individual has a right to obtain what s/he expects as a "fair share" of the object in question. Note that a "fair share" is often *more* than "equal share" (= cultural value of *equality*).[59]

In contrast, sociocentric cultures

> are marked by the fact that they are group centered. The culture as a whole considers each person as a unit in the system; a part of the whole identified with a Place Community, e.g., a family, a village, etc. In cosmology terms, the sociocentric culture believes in finite resources available to the local community within the world community as a finite whole. There is a fixed amount of everything. If one person uses up a share, the other person has just lost an equal share of the resource. This is a situation in which there is a negative conception of cultural equity, i.e., there is an expectation that a person may lose more than an equal share (which is perceived as "unfair") (…). In short, sociocentric culture is Eastern, and oriental for the most part. Recall, however, that egocentric groups live within the larger sociocentric culture.[60]

Perhaps it is the case that the egocentric cosmology will always tend to dominate the sociocentric cosmology precisely because when egocentricity governs our perceptual capacities at the level of culture we will always seek our "fair share," which we presume cannot harm others because we live in a world of infinite resources. The sociocentric cosmology has no such presumption about infinite resources and thus has the capacity to perceive the material effects of the demand for "equal share." Consider also, that the "Non Place community" governing egocentric identities also removes one from the immediacy of our interrelations within the context of our daily life. In contrast, the "Place community" of sociocentric cultures entail a continuous recognition of location, and this continuous recognition of location is also an essential aspect of the decolonial project that recognizes the location of Euro-Modernity and eurocentricity in the North and the West. In short, the sociocentric cosmology is more greatly committed to the concrete and material realities that have a practical effect (in the Peircian sense) within the context of daily life. And this is why Lanigan argues that

> the perspective Other in a Group is a better starting place for understanding consciousness experience in the human world where embodiment is a combinatory, curvilinear and cyclical process, rather than a causal one. Husserl's epochē needs to be applied to the very mindset of Western culture, or as Merleau-Ponty has commented, the first methodological task of an embodied philosophy as a human science is a "phenomenology of phenomenology." To this research agenda, I add the requirement that such a recursive phenomenology much be guided by a logic grounded in a semiotic.[61]

CONCLUSION: PERSPECTIVE AND PRESUMPTIONS

I began this work with a caution about presuming that work produced by a "mainstream" U.S. American scholar comfortably situated within Euro-Modernity that could be used in the service of decolonial projects. As the points of this analysis have shown, however, the question of how and where Eurocentric thoughts perpetuates its exclusion of its Other is much more complex than identifying social labels or locating a person within the broad swath of geography or history. The present author excluded, Lanigan's work is not typically circulated among scholars working in the United States who focus on issues of racism, sexism, heterosexism, colonialism, etc. Nor does Lanigan cite those authors who might be considered at the leading edge of such studies in the United States. Yet, there is a powerful confluence of interests between Lanigan and these scholars and their interests—and it is one that the present analysis has aimed to show.

I have emphasized throughout the present work that Lanigan's commitment is to a radically scientific inquiry. Such an inquiry requires that we traverse the reflective, reflexive and reversible terrain of consciousness in order to discover the terms and conditions in which capacity becomes actuality. I have emphasized this point in order to hold true to the essential existential fact of human existence— namely, the value of recognizing that human existence always exceeds our ability to grasp what is present in any given moment of perception or understanding. This point is, I think, essential to any project of liberation, and particularly to any project that portends an ethics of liberation. The work of Enrique Dussel, particularly his "paradoxical" foundation of ethics, also, I believe, embraces this essential existential fact of human existence.

Throughout the present work I have moved cautiously in suggesting that taking up the work of Lanigan or of communicology contributes to the decolonial project. Despite the fact that my purpose has been precisely to demonstrate that communicology in fact does contribute to the decolonial project, I have cited the problem of "subordinated theoretical identity."[62] The problem of perspective, however, is inescapable and complex. This is as true for the social worlds and people we study as it is for ourselves. Thus I conclude present work by highlighting the fact that despite appearances to the contrary, Richard Lanigan is not simply located within eurocentricity nor a product of "mainstream" U.S. American culture. Richard was born and raised in New Mexico, with a family history dating back to the building of the Santa Fe Railroad in the 1870s. As Richard himself puts it,

> my family history is intimately tied to the Navajo and Apache cultures and their legacy with Spanish history. All this to say, when I was in the Catholic primary and secondary schools at Albuquerque, the student body was about equally divided among those who spoke English, Spanish, and Navajo. The experience of two Sociocentric cultures dominated my worldview.[63]

The problem of perspective implicates each one of us, and knowing our own history of place and culture aids us in the effort to accurately discern the point of practice wherein humanity is degraded.

NOTES

1. "Capacity" and "actuality" are technical terms. Capacity, or capability, refers to "what can be thought by a person." It is "the process of constituting a subject/object of consciousness." In contrast, actuality, or actualization, is "what can be lived by a person." It is "the process of constituting a subject/object of experience." Richard Lanigan, *The Human Science of Communicology: A Phenomenology of Discourse in Foucault and Merleau-Ponty* (Pittsburgh, PA: Duquesne University Press, 1992), 213.
2. For a full explication of "domain" in the sense I am using it here, see Richard Lanigan, "The Postmodern Ground of Communicology: Subverting the Forgetfulness of Rationality in Language," *The American Journal of Semiotics* 11 (1194[1998]): 5–21; "Semiotic Confusion in the Phenomenology of Perception: West Meets East, One Actuality Becomes Two Realities," *Chinese Semiotic Studies* 11 (2015): 227–262.
3. Linda Martín Alcoff,, "Philosophy, the Conquest, and the Meaning of Modernity: A commentary on 'Anti-Cartesian Mediations: On the Origin of the Philosophical Anti-Discourse of Modernity' by Enrique Dussel," *Human Architecture: Journal of the Sociology of Self-Knowledge* XI (2013): 57–66.

4. For a fuller explication of this point see Walter D. Mignolo, *Local Histories/Global Design: Coloniality, Subaltern Knowledges and Border Thinking* (Trenton, NJ: Princeton University Press, 2012); Lewis R. Gordon, "Shifting the Geography of Reason in an Age of Disciplinary Decadence," *Transmodernity: Journal of Peripheral Cultural Production of the Luso-Hispanic World* 1 (2011): 95–103. For a discussion of this point related specifically to Husserl see Lewis R. Gordon, *Fanon and the Crisis of European Man: An Essay of Philosophy and the Human Sciences* (New York: Routledge, 1995).
5. Alcoff, "Philosophy."
6. Enrique Dussel, *Ethics of Liberation in the Age of Globalization and Exclusion* (Durham, NC: Duke University Press, 2013).
7. Lanigan, "Semiotic Confusion"; Lanigan, "The Logic of Phenomena: Semiotic Structures of West and East in Communicology and Culture," *Chinese Semiotic Studies* 6 (2012): 39–77.
8. Enrique Dussel, http://enriquedussel.com/Home_en.html (accessed June 29, 2016).
9. Linda Martín Alcoff and Eduardo Mendieta, eds., introduction to *Thinking from the Underside of History: Enrique Dussel's Philosophy of Liberation* (Lanham, MD: Rowman and Littlefield Publishers), 2. See also Michael Barber, *Ethical Hermeneutics: Rationality in Enrique Dussel's Philosophy of Liberation.* New York: Fordham University Press, 1998.
10. Alcoff and Mendieta, introduction, 1.
11. Alcoff, "Philosophy"; Gordon, "Shifting the Geography," 97.
12. Richard L. Lanigan, "Husserl's Phenomenology in America (USA): The Human Science Legacy of Wibur Marshall Urban and the Yale School of Communicology," *Schutzian Research—A Yearbook of Life-Worldly Phenomenology and Qualitative Social Science* 3 (2011): 203–217; "Philosophy of Communicology: 'Discourse Which Expresses Itself is Communication,'" *Review of Communication* 15, no. 4 (2015): 349–358.
13. Here I am aligning U.S. American with European in the sense of the centricities of dominant scholarship. U.S. American scholarship emerges in continuity with Modernity and the Enlightenment (for a discussion of the post World War II emergence of the United States as the inheritor of the global imperialist project see, Edward W. Said, *Orientalism* [New York: Vintage Books, 1979]). At the same time, however, there are important currents within U.S. American scholarship that de-center it from its European heritage—specifically scholarship that emerges from Native-American, African-American, Asian-American and Mestizo communities. There is a unique and often unseen element of Lanigan's work with regard to this de-centering of Eurocentrism, and that point shall be developed when I focus specifically on the decolonial project of cultural communicology.
14. Lewis R. Gordon, *What Fanon Said: A Philosophical Introduction to His Life and Thought* (New York: Fordham University Press, 2015), 5.
15. Gordon, *What Fanon Said*, 5.
16. Those of us who have studied under Lanigan, or dedicated significant time to studying his work, are very familiar with the impressive and comprehensive way in which he "lines up" thought across a broad array of figures—e.g., Husserl-Merleau-Ponty-Peirce, Cassirer-Bühler-Benveniste, etc. This "lining up" is, in my view, at the heart of Richard's pedagogical effort. Each "lining up" suggests important points for continuing study and any competent use of Lanigan's work requires attending to this lining up of concepts. But over the nearly 30 years that I have been studying Richard's work, I have come to the opinion that the most important contribution of Richard's work is its concrete application within the world of human beings communicating. Thus, the

quality of each new theoretical insight gained through the study of his work is best measured by its applicability to the concrete immediacy of human beings communicating.
17. Lanigan, *Human Science*, 162. For a full discussion of Peirce's interpretant in a communicological analysis see Jacqueline M. Martinez, "Semiotic Phenomenology and Intercultural Communication Scholarship: Meeting the Challenge of Racial, Ethnic, and Cultural Difference," *Western Journal of Communication* 70 (2006): 299–303.
18. Richard L. Lanigan, "Semiotic Paradigms of Self and Person: The Perspective Model of Communicology as the Logic Foundation of Human Science," *Language and Semiotic Study* 1 (2015): 113.
19. Vincent M. Colapietro, "Immediacy, Opposition, and Mediation: Peirce on Irreducible Aspects of the Communicative Process," in *Recovering Pragmatism's Voice: The Classical Tradition, Rorty, and the Philosophy of Communication*, ed. Lenore Landgdorf and Andrew R. Smith (New York: State University of New York Press, 1995), 25.
20. Charles Sanders Peirce quoted in Colapietro, "Immediacy," 25.
21. For a full explication of "sedimentation," particularly in relation to language, see Maurice Merleau-Ponty, "On the Phenomenology of Language," in *Signs*, trans. Richard C. McCleary (Chicago, IL: Northwestern University Press, 1964), 84–97.
22. "Saint Junipero Serra—a halo stained with blood?," September 18, 2015, http://www.reuters.com/article/us-pope-usa-serra-idUSKCN0RI0Z520150918 (accessed July 6, 2016).
23. For a discussion of time-boundedness, see Richard, L. Lanigan, "Time Binding: The Conjunction of Semiotics and Communicology," *Cruzeiro Semiotico*, 22–25 (1995): 325–336.
24. Antonia I. Castañeda, "Sexual Violence in the Politics and Policies of Conquest: Amerindian Women and the Spanish Conquest of Alta California," in *Building with Our Hands: New Directions in Chicana Studies*, ed. Adela De La Torre and Beatríz M. Pesquera (Berkeley: University of California Press, 1993), 15.
25. Castañeda, "Sexual Violence," 19.
26. Castañeda, "Sexual Violence," 15.
27. Castañeda, "Sexual Violence," 16.
28. Castañeda, "Sexual Violence," 19.
29. Castañeda, "Sexual Violence," 20.
30. Alcoff and Mendieta, introduction, 1.
31. Alcoff and Mendieta, introduction, 1.
32. This essential insight has been arguably one of the most important contributions of Chicana feminists Cherríe Moraga and Gloria Anzaldúa. See Cherríe Moraga, "La Güera," in *This Bridge Called My Back: Writings by Radical Women of Color*, ed. Cherríe Moraga and Gloria Anzaldúa (New York: Kitchen Table: Women of Color Press), 29. See also Gloria Anzaldúa, *Borderlands/La Frontera: The New Mestiza*. San Francisco: Aunt Lute Foundation, 1987; and Jacqueline M. Martinez, *Phenomenology of Chicana Experience and Identity: Communication and Transformation in Praxis* (Lanham, MD: Rowman and Littlefiled Press, 2000).
33. Dussel, *Ethics*, xviii.
34. Dussel, *Ethics*, xvii.
35. Dussel, *Ethics*, 160.
36. Dussel, *Ethics*, 166.
37. Dussel, *Ethics*, 161.
38. Dussel, *Ethics* 159.
39. Dussel, *Ethics*, 158.

40. Dussel, *Ethics*, xix.
41. Richard L. Lanigan, *Phenomenology of Communication: Merleau-Ponty's Thematicx in Communicology and Semiology* (Pittsburgh, PA: Duquesne University Press, 1988), 3.
42. As distinct from a bad ambiguity, see Lanigan, *Phenomenology*, 4–7.
43. Dussel, *Ethics*, 162.
44. Lanigan, *Human Science*, 162.
45. Dussel, *Ethics*, 162.
46. Dussel, *Ethics*, 159.
47. Paul D. Reynolds, *A Primer in Theory Construction: An A&B Classic Edition* (New York: Routledge, 2006).
48. Dussel, *Ethics*, 166.
49. John Deely, *Basics of Semiotics* (Bloomington: Indiana University Press, 1990).
50. Dussel, *Ethics*, xxii.
51. Dussel, *Ethics*, 166
52. Dussel, *Ethics*, xviii.
53. Dussel, *Ethics*, xviii.
54. Dussel, *Ethics*, 166.
55. This is the problematic brilliantly explicated by Frantz Fanon, *Black Skin, White Masks* (New York: Grove Weidenfeld, 1967), 83–108.
56. Colapietro, "Immediacy."
57. Charles Sanders Peirce quoted in Colapietro, "Immediacy," 25.
58. Lanigan "Logic of Phenomena," 44.
59. Lanigan, "Logic of Phenomena," 50–51.
60. Lanigan, "Logic of Phenomena," 53.
61. Lanigan, "Logic of Phenomena," 71.
62. Gordon, *What Fanon Said*, 5.
63. Richard L. Lanigan, "Familiar Frustration: The Japanese Encounter with Navajo (Diné) 'Code Talkers' in World War II," in *Languages in Contact 2011*, ed. Zdzisław Wasik and Piotr P. Chruszczewski (Wrocław: Philological of Higher Education Publishing, 2012), 47–69, 66.

BIBLIOGRAPHY

Alcoff, Linda Martín. "Philosophy, the Conquest, and the Meaning of Modernity: A Commentary on 'Anti-Cartesian Mediations: On the Origin of the Philosophical Anti-Discourse of Modernity' by Enrique Dussel." *Human Architecture: Journal of the Sociology of Self-Knowledge* XI (2013): 57–66.
Alcoff, Linda Martín, and Mendieta, Eduardo, eds. *Thinking from the Underside of History: Enrique Dussel's Philosophy of Liberation*. Lanham, MD: Rowman and Littlefield Press, 2000.
Anzaldúa, Gloria. *Borderlands/La Frontera: The New Mestiza*. San Francisco, CA: Aunt Lute Foundation, 1987.
Barber, Michael. *Ethical Hermeneutics: Rationality in Enrique Dussel's Philosophy of Liberation*. New York: Fordham University Press, 1998.
Castañeda, Antonia I. "Sexual Violence in the Politics and Policies of Conquest: Amerindian Women and the Spanish Conquest of Alta California." In *Building with our Hands: New Directions in Chicana Scholarship*, edited by Adela de la Torre and Beatríz M. Pesquera, 15–33. Berkeley: University of California Press, 1993.

Colapietro, Vincent M. "Immediacy, Opposition, and Mediation: Peirce on Irreducible Aspects of the Communicative Process." In *Recovering Pragmatism's Voice: The Classical Tradition, Rorty, and the Philosophy of Communication*, edited by Lenore Landgdorf and Andrew R. Smith, 23–48. New York: State University of New York Press, 1995.

Deely, John. *Basics of Semiotics*. Bloomington: Indiana University Press, 1990.

Dussel, Enrique. *Ethics of Liberation in the Age of Globalization and Exclusion*. Durham, NC: Duke University Press, 2013.

Fanon, Frantz. *Black Skin, White Masks*. New York: Grove Weidenfeld, 1967.

Gordon, Lewis R. *Fanon and the Crisis of European Man: An Essay of Philosophy and the Human Sciences*. New York: Routledge, 1995.

Gordon, Lewis R. "Shifting the Geography of Reason in an Age of Disciplinary Decadence." *Transmodernity: Journal of Peripheral Cultural Production of the Luso-Hispanic World* 1 (2011): 95–103.

Gordon, Lewis R. *What Fanon Said: A Philosophical Introduction to His Life and Thought*. New York: Fordham University Press, 2015.

Lanigan, Richard L. "Familiar Frustration: The Japanese Encounter with Navajo (Diné) 'Code Talkers' in World War II." In *Languages in Contact 2011*, edited by Zdzisław Wasik and Piotr P. Chruszczewski, 47–69. Wrocław: Philological of Higher Education Publishing, 2012.

Lanigan, Richard L. *The Human Science of Communicology: A Phenomenology of Discourse in Foucault and Merleau-Ponty*. Pittsburgh, PA: Duquesne University Press, 1992.

Lanigan, Richard L. "Husserl's Phenomenology in America (USA): The Human Science Legacy of Wibur Marshall Urban and the Yale School of Communicology." *Schutzian Research—A Yearbook of Lif-Worldly Phenomenology and Qualitative Social Science* 3 (2011): 203–217.

Lanigan, Richard L. "The Logic of Phenomena: Semiotic Structures of West and East in Communicology and Culture." *Chinese Semiotic Studies* 6 (2012): 39–77.

Lanigan, Richard L. *Phenomenology of Communication: Merleau-Ponty's Thematics in Communicology and Semiology*. Pittsburgh, PA: Duquesne University Press, 1988.

Lanigan, Richard L. "Philosophy of Communicology: 'Discourse Which Expresses Itself is Communication.'" *Review of Communication* 15, no. 4 (2015): 349–358.

Lanigan, Richard L. "The Postmodern Ground of Communicology: Subverting the Forgetfulness of Rationality in Language." *The American Journal of Semiotics* 11 (1994 [1998]): 5–21.

Lanigan, Richard L. "Semiotic Confusion in the Phenomenology of Perception: West Meets East, One Actuality Becomes Two Realities." *Chinese Semiotic Studies* 11 (2015): 227–262.

Lanigan, Richard L. "Semiotic Paradigms of Self and Person: The Perspective Model of Communicology as the Logic Foundation of Human Science." *Language and Semiotic Study* 1 (2015): 113.

Lanigan, Richard L. "Time Binding: The Conjunction of Semiotics and Communicology." *Cruzeiro Semiotico* 22–25 (1995): 325–336.

Martinez, Jacqueline M. *Phenomenology of Chicana Experience and Identity: Communication and Transformation in Praxis*. Lanham, MD: Rowman and Littlefield Press, 2000.

Martinez, Jacqueline M. "Semiotic Phenomenology and Intercultural Communication Scholarship: Meeting the Challenge of Racial, Ethnic, and Cultural Difference." *Western Journal of Communication* 70 (2006): 292–310.

Merleau-Ponty, Maurice. "On the Phenomenology of Language." In *Signs*. Translated by Richard C. McCleary, 84–97. Chicago, IL: Northwestern University Press, 1964.

Mignolo, Walter D. *Local Histories/Global Design: Coloniality, Subaltern Knowledges and Border Thinking*. Trenton, NJ: Princeton University Press, 2012

Moraga, Cherríe. "La Güera." In *This Bridge Called My Back: Writings by Radical Women of Color*, edited by Cherríe Moraga and Gloria Anzaldúa, 27–34. New York: Kitchen Table: Women of Color Press, 1981.

Reynolds, Paul D. A *Primer in Theory Construction: An A&B Classic Edition*. New York: Routledge, 2006.

Said, Edward W. *Orientalism*. New York: Vintage Books, 1979.

CHAPTER TWELVE

In the Context of Communicology

Issues of Technical Risk Communication About Sustainability

HONG WANG

Husserl once distinguished between intentionality of act, which is that of our judgments and those occasions when we voluntarily take up a position; and operative intentionality, or that which produces the natural and antepredicative unity of the world and our lives.[1] In semiotics, it is the distinction between the sign that takes on a linguistic form and the sign that entails bodily performance of action. The first kind is exemplified in something like "I ate an apple", a string of words which may refer to a physiological act in the lived-through world of the subject "I." The second type finds its examples in the human act of putting an apple into the mouth, chewing and swallowing it so as to satisfy "my" quest for thirst or hunger. On the surface, type one differs from type two in the expressive form: one resorts to linguistic means while the other to the coordination of the human body. The difference speaks to the long-time philosophical disputes over the mind and the body. Contemporary semiotic study does not fully appreciate the distinction, not to mention the practical significance of such a distinction.[2] According to Saussure and his school of thoughts, signs are related and distinctive due to their structural composition. An act, or rather the notion of an act, becomes the Signified that may find its representation in the Signifier. As a natural consequence, the human act is not much of an interest for investigation with this tradition. Peirce's logical investigation of signs moved beyond the dyadic tradition when he proposed that triadic relation as something that stands for something to someone in some aspect or capacity. He and his school of semiosis extend their research interest into "action, or influence, which is, or involves, a cooperation of three subjects, such as a sign, its object, and its interpretant, this tri-relative influence not being in any way resolvable into actions between pairs."[3] With the element of the human actor into the investigation, the emphasis is somehow still attached to intellectual understanding of meaning. If we accept Peirce's idea that "we [human beings] think only in signs"[4] does it mean that we only act in signs, too? In other words, how exactly do a sign, its object, and its interpretant, coordinate to constitute an action? Would such coordination necessarily prompt a bodily action?

The above questions are critically important in the global effort for environmental sustainability. Aldo Leopold (1887–1948), an American scientist and environmentalist, offered the following view to rally people in the joint effort: "If the public were told how much harm ensues from unwise land-use, it would mend its way. This was once my credo, and I think still is a fairly accurate definition of what is called 'conservation education.'"[5] In essence Leopold was suggesting that talking about the problem would lead to behavior change in people. This motto is adopted by the US Environmental Protection Agency (EPA) in reference to what Cox calls the "technical risk communication." There, technical data about environmental or health risks (provided by scientists, experts, and/or authorities) are translated for public consumption. Its ultimate goal is "to inform, change, and assure."[6] Similar environmental education is taking place in the United States at institutional levels, and in the media. There is no denying that such effort has helped more people become aware of environmental problems. Evidence reveals that a large proportion of the public in various regions express verbal commitment to the environment, whereas participation in environmentally-supportive behavior rarely mirrors the strength of this stated commitment. In some cases an individual may hold environmental values, and yet other priorities such as safety or financial security may take precedence over environmentally-supportive behavior.[7] In fact, little has changed in people's actual natural resource consumption that steadily aggravates the existing problems of our eco-system. According to Twenge, Campbell, and Freeman's comparative study of generational differences, a steep decline is revealed in concern for the natural environment. The study found that three times more people in their 20s and 30s make less effort to practice personal sustainability techniques verses that of older generations.[8] Such discrepancy presents a strong call for us to explore the relationship between sign of thoughts and sign of action.

In this chapter, I take the belief that discourse on environmental problems cannot automatically translate into proper action to solve the problems because the body with which we act has a tendency to act in defiance of our conscious thought, so as to achieve a "maximum gripping"[9] on the world in which the body lives. From a communicative perceptive, information is a series of signs that project themselves as pre-existing objects for the conscious experiences of the public whereas interpretation is a process of sign dismantlement and reconstruction, mediated by embodiment. To explore the conditions in which information *may* coincide with an action, I place this study in a communicative situation. To be more specific, I will be using the EPA website as an example by looking into the semiotic features of its presentation regarding "zero nature."[10] I will then examine the intentional arc or embodied conditions of the general public who live in this complex interplay of the different worlds wherein meanings have to be personally sought after. In the final section I shall discuss how the technical risk communication fails its purpose from the perspective of communicology. I conclude that the performance of an action is a step away from conscious recognition of the need for that action, with an explanation of how embodied intentional arc presents a big challenge in performing environmental sustainability. Communication, rather than information transmission, will better prepare the public for living a sustainable life.

EDUCATION ON "ZERO-NATURE"

The Environmental Protection Agency of the United States' mission is to "teach people about the environment." It hosts its official website (epa.gov) as a platform to share information and facilitate environmental education.

One-way of reading the website content is to divide its front page into three major parts from top to bottom. The top third of the page displays four major components of related information, arranged horizontally from the left to the right: (1) issues of environmental problems; (2) science and technology as the backbone of solutions; (3) laws and regulations that guarantee the implementation of the right measures; and (4) a description of the structure and functions of the organization. The central part of the front page is up-to-date environmental news and images (pictures and video clips/slide shows) that reinforce the seriousness of problems in verbal discourse, and blogs and Twitter pages that encourage the readers' participation. The lower portion of the front page lists attainable goals for one to strive in relation to the environment. Nearly all the items on this front page are clickable; i.e., they serve as indexes for further information if the reader decides to explore.

Semiotically speaking, the EPA works on the concept of a perfect nature in saying, "The aggregate of the powers and properties of all things take place without the agency, or without the voluntary and intentional agency, of man."[11] Such nature corresponds to what Kull would label as "zero nature," or a nature without human beings. In that self-sustained and self-governed system, things exist for a reason, and beings are pre-programmed in perfect harmony. A change of their location is "trashing" and concentrating a "pollution," or that of chemical combination "intoxication." The absence of the proper number of trees becomes "deforestation," and the advance of a sandy earth, "desertification."

In the section "Learn the issues," a natural change to become an environmental concern needs to satisfy two criteria at the same time: (1) the change in nature is due to human intervention, and (2) the change has (potential) negative impact on human beings. Therefore, a volcano eruption does not count, even though it may release harmful gases and heavy metals into the environment; it is simply "spectacular and beautiful."[12] Honeybees alone would not be a problem unless their number reduction affects honey production or the fertilization of crops that directly relates to our well beings. The "land and cleanup" example is more illustrative of the two criteria, where it states the necessary "cleanup actions at sites where oil or hazardous chemicals have been or may be released into the environment."[13] The earth has been storing the solar heat residues in petroleum and other fossil energy forms for millions of years. It becomes an environmental problem when the oil is transported to a new location for human use, while presenting itself as a health and safety threat to us; thus the need for cleanups.

Deviation from its "natural" status is bad, but the semiotic chain reaction as depicted on the EPA website can be more serious. By "semiotic chain" I mean a process of sign-making in which the meaning is realized in terms of different, yet linked texts. The EPA example states, "[W]hen the water in our rivers, lakes, and oceans becomes polluted [with the release of untreated sewage from a manufacturing plant, for instance], the effects can be far reaching. It can endanger wildlife, make our drinking water unsafe and threaten the waters where we swim and fish."[14] The semiotic chains are troubling, not because of the strings of signs that are arranged together in a cause-effect manner, but because of the chain effect that presumably happens *in nature*. A loss of one natural element may trigger a semiosis that consequently hurts human beings through global warming, animal extinction, application of pesticides, waste, etc.

Yet chain reaction is, on the other hand, a "natural" phenomenon; a fundamental feature of all existence. According to the EPA, trees breathe in CO_2 and breathe out O_2, which becomes vital for sea creatures, and in return provides food for bigger animals. Zero nature does not allow absolute waste since every sign finds its proper place for every other sign. The tragedy with human intervention is that the signs we produce do NOT fit back into the nature's system. Nature rejects the signs we produce and throws them back at us. To "decompose" and re-enter the natural system will take a long time, if it is at all possible.

However, we can be part of the solution too. The EPA assures us of that. Right next to "learn the issues" is a section titled "Science and Technology" where scientific research and technological development are presented in a very positive light. They discover the truth in zero nature, and they present varied possibilities for our action. For instance, when mosquitos bite, we tend to kill them with spray. However, science presents other options such as draining and filling temporary pools of water with dirt, or keeping swimming pool water treated and circulating so as to remove Mosquito Habitats, or to use structural barriers by making sure window and door screens are in good working order.[15] In other words, we do not have to simply kill it off when a sign is identified as a cause to human discomfort. If the whole community faces, say an "urban heat island" phenomenon, people can, instead of installing more powerful air conditioners, mitigate the heat by increasing tree and vegetative cover, or installing green roofs (also called "rooftop gardens" or "eco-roofs").[16] Science and technology reveals to us which options go along with nature better, thus producing less harmful consequences.

The EPA seems to have recognized the limits of ordinary people's abilities to explore nature. After all, we do not see nor do we much care about the microforms of life in the ocean. An individual cannot possibly walk from a central Pennsylvania town to the North Pole to witness global warming effects. In a semiotic sense, the EPA, through the channel of science and technology, plays with signifiers that are sensible for the general public to process. For instance, greenhouse emission hides from our sight (not as visible as dark smokes from factory chimneys), stops short before our ears (not audible as the deafening sounds of low-altitude flying air planes), and evades other senses (not smelly or sluggish as smog). So the EPA informs us via science that "[m]any greenhouse gases occur naturally in the atmosphere, such as carbon dioxide, methane, water vapor, and nitrous oxide, while others are synthetic .... While gases such as carbon dioxide occur naturally in the atmosphere, through our interference with the carbon cycle (through burning forest lands, or mining and burning coal), we artificially move carbon from solid storage to its gaseous state, thereby increasing atmospheric concentrations."[17] Thanks to modern instruments, we can "see" the hazardous gas in images that magnify the particles that are usually elusive from our naked eyes.

In a similar fashion, the science and technology section of the EPA website brings what lies underground before our eyes, the far-away close for our inspection, and the past into the present. It verifies the existence of that which eludes our sensible perceptions; it is not imaginary or illusionary but real, having both ontological and existential truth. With rules of exclusion (paradigmatic relations) and of inclusion (syntagmatic relations), they project with assured accuracy signs of survival for the future, which in turn can influence what we should do now. Science and technology are thus both the solution to our current environmental problems and the fundamental guideline for taking the right action.

To complete the description of the top third of the EPA front page, laws and regulations are listed according to topics. So are the Agency's major functions that reinforce laws and implement policies to those that are identified as being responsible for the so-called bad "human interventions."

Recall that the EPA follows what Cox would term as a technical risk communication model to inform, assure, and change. If reading the top third of its website proceeds from left to right, as American/English readers normally read, the semiosis effect generated would look something like Figure 12.1, which is an expansion of Peirce's model of sign[18]:

Figure 12.1: Technical Risk Communication Model as Semiosis of a Peircean Sign

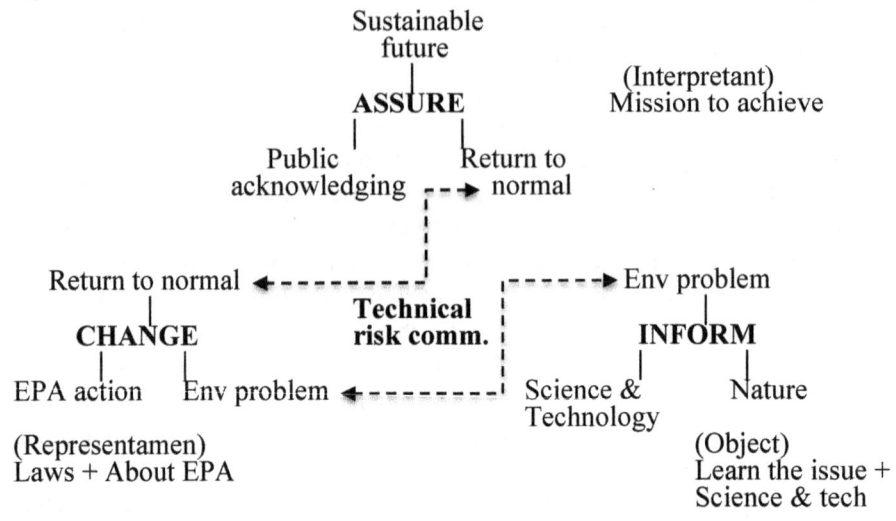

```
                    Sustainable
                      future
                        |                   (Interpretant)
                     ASSURE                 Mission to achieve
                        |
              Public          Return to
          acknowledging  ---→ normal
                              |
                              |
  Return to normal ←----------'   ,-----→ Env problem
        |                 Technical |         |
      CHANGE              risk comm.|       INFORM
        |        |                  |         |
   EPA action   Env problem ←-------' Science &    Nature
                                      Technology

  (Representamen)                              (Object)
  Laws + About EPA                             Learn the issue +
                                               Science & tech
```

Source: Author

That is, nature in its zero-touched state is or has become problematic (environmental problems) thanks to scientific discoveries. The identified environmental problems are and will be corrected through EPA's law enforcement so that the polluted nature is returned to its normal state. With such environmental quality change, the future will be sustainable, to the relief and recognition of the public, or so are they assured.

There are a few problems with such an information model, the first of which is representation. While the information on the website is committed to reliable and truthful scientific research about the zero nature, the "reality of nature" is by no means automatically meaningful. According to Lotman, everything about nature is a nonsemiotic phenomenon until they are incorporated into semiotization in *human recognition*.[19] In other words, zero nature needs to become signified and to be expressed by signifiers, in recognizable forms, just like what is done on the EPA website. And yet, once nature is represented in signs, it instantly transports out of itself; it moves into the human-intervened worlds, as Kull would remind us, wherein the representative means take meaning into their own hands, whatever the zero nature may be.

For the majority of the time, the signifiers chosen for the website content are the English language. As soon as something is defined in linguistic signs, it means reducing the continuous to a digital statement that categorizes. In other words, language allows us to deal with a moment apart from its necessary complement of other elements and its whole. As Sokolowski pointed out, because we can refer to a moment by itself, without mentioning its associated moments, we can begin to think that this moment can exist by itself; that it can become a concretum.[20] Therefore, in this linguistic world, or the 3rd nature in Kull's terminology, the continuum of integration and interrelatedness of all creatures are instantly divided in the categories of, say, polar bears and micro forms, of a process into fragments. They are then labeled either as endangered or as safe, according to arbitrary cutting lines. The population growth follows either J-cruve or S-curve (and the word "curve" suggests steady and gradual deviation, which means the possible elimination of the unfitting numbers or phenomena); a natural form of energy is either renewable or nonrenewable; what we can do is to either recycle or waste. The "natural facts" get frozen in the statements, at least temporarily.

Apart from the general representational problems associated with language (or langage in Saussurean term), the EPA faces the challenge of translating scientific discourse for laymen folks. Such translation would require a set of codes that open to different interpretation possibilities. Just as Eco pointed out, "The hiatus between 'scientific' certitude and 'social' certitude constitutes the difference between scientific hypotheses and laws, on the one hand, and semiotic codes, on the other. The necessity of scientific evidence has little in common with the necessity of semiotic evidence. The semiotic plausibility is based on social habits, whereas the scientific plausibility is based on other criteria of verifiability."[21] The code problem will be further discussed in the following section.

By definition, representation is partial. It will not be able to bring out the full identity of the thing represented since a sign stands in *some* aspect or capacity for a thing. Therefore, it leaves room for our consciousness to play hide-and-seek, to shift between figure and ground, and to attend to the past as present or the present as the future.

Critical as representation is, a more pressing issue for the author of this paper would be the assumed link between information and action change. There is no denying that the EPA does acknowledge the role of the public. Its goal is "[b]y 2030, the GREEN POWER PLAN will reduce carbon emissions from power plants by 32% below 2005 levels" (as cited at the bottom third section of the EPA front page); this is mediated by the mid-third section calling for public particiption through its blog and twitter functions, and direct engagement in "your community." Its display of the public's role may be summarized in Figure 12.2.

Figure 12.2: Assumed Link Between "Inform" and "Change"

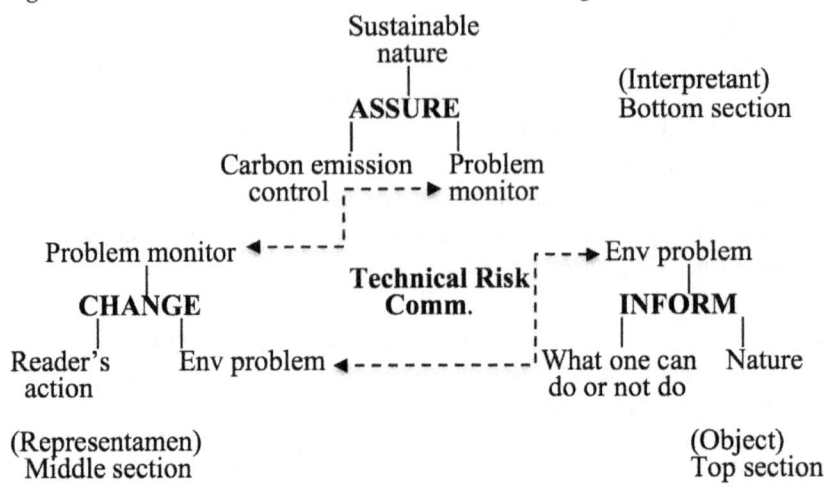

```
                         Sustainable
                           nature
                             |                    (Interpretant)
                          ASSURE                  Bottom section
                     |         |
         Carbon emission     Problem
            control  ┌ ─ ─ ─ ▶ monitor
                     ╎
                     ╎
Problem monitor ◀ ─ ─┘           ┌ ─ ▶ Env problem
        |              Technical Risk╎           |
     CHANGE               Comm.      ╎        INFORM
        |                   |        ╎           |
    Reader's            Env problem ◀╌╌╌╌╌ What one can    Nature
    action                                  do or not do

  (Representamen)                                (Object)
   Middle section                               Top section
```

Source : Author

Similar in their semiotic composition, Figure 12.2 differs from Figure 12.1 in one big way—the communication actors. In Figure 12.2, the public is intended as first the receiver of the EPA information, and then the performer of change, including changing its own behavior pertaining to environmental consumption. To accomplish this, the person who reads the website in a top-down fashion will need to internalize environmental problems by learning about the issues; externalizing such awareness by following blogs and twitter news, and learning about local environment conditions. Please notice the difference between the immediate and dynamic interpretants, as Peirce elaborates: "In regard to the Interpretant we have [...] to distinguish, in the first place, the Immediate Interpretant, which is the interpretant as it is revealed in the right understanding of the Sign itself, and is ordinarily called the meaning of the sign; while in the second place, we have to take note of the Dynamical Interpretant which is the actual effect which the Sign, as a Sign, really determines."[22] For the EPA, cognition (Representamen) of environmental problems (Object) naturally leads to the right action (Immediate Interpretant). However, such an assumption begs an investigation of two sets of questions: (1) Under what conditions does the body act; how does the mind and body interact in one's lived-through world such that, for example, the knowledge that fertilizers may cause environmental problems, stops one from applying fertilizers on their lawn? (2) Why should individuals respond to EPA's expectation when they are not identified as responsible for the existing problems; how does education/communication create a personal sense of action? These two sets of questions guide the discussion of the following two sections.

THE PHENOMENAL WORLD THAT CONDITIONS MEANING MAKING

In the development of semiotic theories, signs are not "natural;" as they have an expression plane and a content plane, the combination of which makes the whole. However, the force that binds the expression to the content has never been sufficiently clarified. Usually it is referred to as a "conventional" force, or a social/cultural force; that is, because the combination already exists. Thanks to the existing force, it emerges as a sign or an object for consciousness.[23] In the context of this discussion, the EPA states that "overexposure to ultraviolet (UV) radiation from the sun can result in a painful sunburn. It can also lead to more serious health problems, including skin cancer, premature aging of the skin, cataracts and other eye damage, and immune system suppression."[24] The text links the notion of "sunshine/sunbathing" (the words as signifier) to the idea of "health risks" (the concept as signified), thus warning the public to avoid excessive bodily exposure to it. Sunshine becomes a sign of danger thanks to the powerful EPA statement, which is further backed up by hard science. Traditional semiotic theory says little about the person who has to internalize the relation between the expression and content, so as to intend it as a sign. After all, it is the person who can will a brute thing into an object (therefore a sign); be it sun radiation, a legendary Santa Claus, or a scientific discourse about global warming. The very fact that "[m]ore than 3.5 million new cases of skin cancer are diagnosed annually"[25] testifies to the power of the sign-perceiver. In contrast to Saussure, the semiotic tradition inaugurated by C. S. Peirce recognizes the person, stressing that for something to be a sign, it must involve a person who takes it as such. But to him, the person is a logical person, someone who is invested with reasoning (presumably Western style reasoning). The sign or a new sign, therefore, comes as a consequence of rationality, or rational thinking. Again in the sun's example above, people may accept the authority and rationality of EPA's statement, but they may not have taken recommended actions, a discrepancy that needs accounting for. I now turn to the concepts of intentionality and intentional arc related to the personal power of sign making.

To a great extent, the study of signs is that of conscious experience that signs induce as well as are operated in—appearances of signs, or signs as they appear in our experience, or the ways we experience signs—thus the meanings signs have in our experience. The sign study has to address, in Smith's words, "the meaning things [signs] have in our experience, notably, the significance of objects, events, tools, the flow of time, the self, and others, as these things arise and are experienced in our 'life-world.'"[26] Two issues in phenomenology that are specifically important in the understanding of semiosis include intentionality and intentional arc. According to Husserl, intentionality refers to the directedness of experience toward things in the world; it is the power of minds to be about, to represent, or to stand for, things, properties, and states of affairs.[27] In other words, intentionality refers to a mental state; it is the phenomenon of "aboutness."[28] It concerns itself with why a given thing shows up for us in the way it did and calls us to act in certain ways while other things do not. Phenomenology denies the sole existence of signness in the object. As Grillo explained, it is not the object that makes an act intentional "but rather *an immanent feature of the act itself*, which gives it its '*directness*', thereby making it *intentional*."[29] Science stands as a sign of hope because we, the sign users, allow our mind to be directed toward that proposition and accept it as valid.

The concept of intentionality does not deny social conventions. If anything, it emphasizes on the investigation of social normality that conditions individual mental directedness. However, this mental directedness is not, nor should it be, rendered as the starting point of phenomenological investigation; the body that enables the given individual's mental activities and directedness calls for a serious study too. As Merleau-Ponty argued, intentionality, instead of being a mere property of the subject's conscious acts, characterizes the behavior of an embodied subject. In his words, the lived body "is our general medium for having a world … It is the origin of the rest, expressive movement itself, that which causes them to begin to exist as things, under our hands and eyes."[30] For instance, to be able to see something on a table, one needs to adjust one's body in such a way that the object is distinguishable. The body cannot be too far or too close to the thing; it needs to create an "oriented space." "[W]hen I say that an object is on a table, I always mentally put myself either in the table or in the object, and I apply to them a category which theoretically fits the relationship of my body to external objects."[31] Thus said, the concept of intentional arc draws us to the grounds that enable conditions of the possibility of intentionality because it gives experience its meaning.

Intentional arc, also known as corporal intentionality, refers to "the tight connection between the agent and the world, viz. that, as the agent acquires skills, these skills are 'stored', not as representations in the mind, but as more and more refined dispositions to respond to the solicitations of more and more refined perceptions of the current situation."[32] It includes embodiment, bodily skills, cultural context, language and other social practices, social background, and contextual aspects of intentional activities. The concept helps us to understand the need to go beyond either the mental activities (characterized by signs) or physical activities (characterized by "intuitions"), and appreciate the meaning associated with and arose from that interplay of the body, the mind, and the world. After all, the world would not take on any semiotic significance to a mind without a body or to a body without a mind. But this body is a situated body, a body that lives in and through this phenomenological world "where the paths of my various experiences intersect, and also where my own and other people intersect and engage each other in like gears."[33]

The concept of intentionality directs us to pay close attention to "positioning, directionality, ultimately, behavioral manner,"[34] where the concept of intentional arc urges us to anchor intentionality in the lived-in and lived-through world. Let me now explore the intentional arc of the general public that EPA's information targets at. I argue that their embodied habits do *not* secure the "natural" connection between environmental problems as a sign and sustainability performing act as the immediate Interpretant of that sign. As a matter of fact, if anything, our intention towards nature is more likely to be directed away from it due to the intentional arc being nurtured in consumerism, money-mediation, and tele-presence that makes up for bodily limits. The tangled relation of the body, the world, and intended phenomenon requires that I first arbitrarily treat them as if they were separable and then put them back together. I begin with the "world" that attributes to the intentional arc.

As the United States has grown to become a culture of consumerism for individuals living in and through this society, Nature is almost totally engulfed in commercialization; it is experienced vicariously in varied forms of human products. Instead of going into nature for a living, we live in this mediation of products. When we are hungry, we almost never turn directly to nature for food; we do not climb trees for ripe fruits, or to hunt for meat. We go to grocery stores instead. In other words, resource shortage and nature-related crises are softened and reduced to a level that easily escapes our consciousness of lived experience. Commodities strip nature of all experienced qualities, as Neil Evernden would argue, leaving us "with an unrecognizable abstraction" which is beyond our initial appreciation for it.[35] They lead to direct gratification of the bodily sense that requires the experiencer's attention. Statements such as global warming loses its meaning and its call to us as we stay indoors away from the brute force of nature. On the other side of the coin, Nature does not have the chance to present its (limited) resources directly to the individuals. We may experience environmental problems as if they were supply problems, which are within human control, and do not require the need for individual change of their behavior/way of living.

So, the consumerist lived experience is an experience not of Nature per se, but a nature mediated by cultural/human products. Such a material phenomenon is yet further mediated via money, the powerful mega-sign that wraps up nearly our entire living experience. In fact, "the use of money creates particular kinds of experiences based upon a semiotic code that establishes the symbolic meaning of money".[36]

As a sign, money turns a thing (usually material thing like water or labor, though sometimes non-material like idea or imagination) into a commodity via three aspects: its use value, its exchange value, and its symbolic value. According to Baudrillard, exchange value to use value is what the signifier to the signified[37]:

$$\text{Exchange value} = Sr$$
$$\text{Use value} = Sd$$

In a consumerist society like the U.S. where consumption becomes the end for itself, a commodity is both exchange value and use value, though "use value and signified do not have the same weight as exchange value and signifier respectively."[38] That is, when the exchange value of a product is lost, its use value is gone, for the consumer. And the normal place for such is the dumpster—there will be no semiotic place for that product. We carry such view into our perception of the environment. It may very well be that nature, or parts and moments of nature, is easily discharged simply because they do not present obvious exchange value at the time. For instance, what can a piece of wetland provide in exchange—it is saturated land, consisting of marshes or swamps? Who would want it when it cannot be used for house building or direct tourism? For over a century, wetlands are either converted into big dumpsters for polluted matters or "developed" so as to add its exchange value. Consequently "[h]alf of the world's wetlands have disappeared since 1900," according to World Wildlife Fund's estimate.[39] Recently our attention is drawn to it because they are found to be "diverse, productive *ecosystems* of ecological and economic value."[40]

Dyer moves further to the symbolic dimension of money as a sign. He says that once money is viewed semiotically, "medium of exchange function becomes its most elemental social function. (…) By re-presenting objects and experiences as comparable containers of exchange value, money symbolically transforms life and, thus, mediates our understanding of it."[41] It mediates our understanding in such a way that when massive pieces of wetlands (including the Passaic, Hackensack, Rahway, Raritan, Saddle and Delaware River watersheds in Maryland) are polluted, Garden Homes, the company responsible for the pollution, was asked, "to pay a $225,000 penalty."[42] This money amount is not enough to buy a 2015 Ferrari FF, or even a third of what is needed to buy a Bulgari Magsonic Sonnerie Tourbillon watch. If a car is affordable, so would be "that piece of nature" since they both can be mediated as equivalent through money. Husserl reminded us that the intentionality of an act (its being *directed toward* something) depends entirely upon an "immanent feature of the act itself," that is, having a component of "noematic sense" such that the *intentional relation* holding between the act and its object would still hold even if there were *no object* at all corresponding to what is intended in the act.[43] When we put a price tag on things, and when everything and every aspect of life is price tagged, we automatically attend to equations, regardless of what is at either end of a given equation. It is in such a light that Marx's remarks would make perfect sense of money "that which mediates my life for me (…) [and] mediates the existence of other people for me."[44] Money fosters the ground for our intentionality to be directed to what we can have easy access to, and to the absence of what we are denied, which constitutes the process of motivated searching till the need is met. It not only represents, but also masks and buries relations that cannot or should not be measured in money.

Bodily limits often confine us, determining to what degree and in what capacity we synthesize a signifier with the signified, and how one sign connects to others.

Biologically we are limited to experience environmental problems in certain ways. For instance, we do not "hear" the cry of creatures affected by fertilizers. We do not "feel" the subtle change of the global temperature over a span of a 100 years. And we tend to treat such absence as non-existent. On the one hand, our bodily ability may be culturally trained—anyway, we can differentiate subtle variations of musical notes in a concert, and have little problem detecting distinctive sounds in a language familiar to us. Some of our natural abilities and skills are sharpened in order to prepare us to get what Merleau-Ponty would call "maximum gripping." On the other hand, the limiting abilities of the human body is partially "made up" by the ever increasing "tele-presence." The moment we turn on the TV, the moment we open a book, the moment we flip open an iPhone, the moment we google with our laptop—our contemporary life is full of such moments, wherein the meaning of signs are presented to us in a pre-determined manner. They provide diverse ways of making signs and attaching sign chains, and they can be at odds with each other in meaning. Just as the EPA is showing evidences of human responsibility for global warming, others are equally forceful in presenting opposing facts and views.[45] The situated body allows itself to be open to the competing discourses and to varied meaning presentations; often after reflections, attuning the self to what it judges as sensible and significant.

The bodily limits determine if something is too small (for our sight or body) in the micro world, or it is too far away (that the body can not reach) in the cosmo world; the cause and effect of an event that is not visible within our memory or discernable during our life time. In a very important way, the realization that one has a body with limited capacity makes the environmental problem enormous, too big to overcome, by the specific individual. Personal effort would be meaningless if a whole river is black with pollution, or if the earth temperature rises.

In sum, the body provides the starting point to enter the world, to have a world, and to create a world. Living-in-the-world trains us and prepares us with certain conditions. It positions us in such way that we form a habit-body that in turn directs the mind to combine signifiers with signifieds, to act in a way that fits that habit. Please be reminded that the intentional arc is not static, though it does imply inertia of life experience with a tendency to "be directed beyond" by reflective intentionality. It is constantly challenged by life moments when an "unfitting phenomenon" occurs, or in other words, when the intention meets resistance. It is therefore open to adjusting its "due" course moment by moment when each moment is granted as meaningful by communication.

COMMUNICATION AND SEMIOTIC PHENOMENOLOGY

In laying the groundwork of communicology as an interdisciplinary study of human science, Lanigan spoke of semiotic phenomenology as a communication paradigm and as "communicology". This means that as a phenomenon, the study is attributed to and motivated by comparable models of human science studies, namely: (1) a discursive model of being human; (2) a human model of discourse; (3) a normative logic in communicological theory; and (4) a normative logic in communicological praxis. That is, when approaching a meaning making phenomenon, or human discourse in a broad sense, we need to take the investigation into its situated context wherein the discursive phenomenon is treated as the converging result of speech spoken and speech speaking; as the self is similar to and distinctively different from others within the speech community, as the body encompasses the mind and mind encompasses the body, and as action entailed is in body orientation and mental representation.[46] The independence and interdependence of person, discourse, and world contextualizes each other to such a degree that it would be noncommunicological to treat them without synthetic reflection and synergic reflexivity.

In the context of semiotic phenomenology, we see three major problems in the EPA technical approach to environmental sustainability: its indistinctive treatment of Addresser as Addressee, its resorting to certain codes that diverge from the public effort, and its failing to recognize the intentional arc of the body through which the expected behavior realizes.

Research suggests that in an idealized communication model, the Addressee is expected to reconstruct what the Addresser is trying to say by restoring its original matrix of syntagmatic and paradigmatic relations that the Addresser may have at the time—the availability of choices, the context that choices were made, his/her interpretation of/understanding of the social/cultural codes that served as judgment for the right or wrong of his/her choice making, etc. In a practical sense, we hardly actualize communication in such a way, if at all. Life phenomena may be arranged differently according to paradigmatic and syntagmatic relation. Therefore, the context within which the Addresser (EPA) has created an opportunity for the Addressee (the general public) to make a meaningful choice may become problematic for the Addressee, who has to make a choice based on the context they started with. That is why the major function of interaction is not for the participants to follow along in each other's texts, but to find contact points, which then would serve as a springboard for a new multidimensional network of meaning.

One of the dilemmas the EPA faces with its technical approach is that it has to resort to certain codes in order to enable public understanding of the issues. However, in so doing, it reinforces the codes that the public needs to give up in order to make sustainable practice meaningful. The term "code" here is used by Jakobson's to refer to apperception and social language (langue) that consists of (1) linguistic form, (2) language as supraindividual, social endowment, and (3) the unifying, centripetal aspect of language that forms a synchronic/syntagmatic relation with other components. The term forms an opposing pair with a "message" which is defined as an expression or speaking (parole) that consists of (1) linguistic utterance; (2) language as individual, private property; and (3) the individualizing, centrifugal aspect of language that forms diachronic/paradigmatic relations with other.[47] The EPA messages in both verbal and non-verbal forms reveal a certain type of relationship between "nature" and "mankind." The code embedded in the messages may help people with different views form a new vision, especially when it assumes authority and scientific validity. However, since a code guides the use of symbols in re-presenting some aspect of reality to an interpreter in a particular way, it may get reinforced in operation, such as measuring "nature" with money. For instance, the environment, and its products and off-sets are represented in terms of money on the EPA website: "The report shows that global action on climate change will significantly benefit Americans by saving lives and avoiding costly damages across the U.S. economy" (…) "In 2100 mitigation is projected to result in cost savings of $4.2–$7.4 billion associated with avoided road maintenance (…) the estimated damages to coastal property from sea level rise and storm surge in the contiguous U.S. are $5.0 trillion through 2100 in a future without emission reductions. When cost-effective adaptation along the coast is included, the estimated damages are reduced to $810 billion."[48] In essence, such code specifies "nature" and "man" as competitive forces—either nature or man, with the latter prioritized. So the website calls for buying more human products to combat man-made problems. The codes reinforce the rational ground to keep the public's intentional arc as status quo.

The study on intentional arc suggests that our living experience is such that the maximum gripping that the body posits and orients stops short of going beyond intellectual awareness and the effort to exercise the body. Merleau-Ponty states, "To act is to place oneself for a moment in an imaginary situation, to find satisfaction in changing one's 'setting' (…) Will presupposes a field of possibilities among which I choose."[49] Contemporary research in social psychology suggests, "that we are likely not only to think ourselves into a way of acting but also to act ourselves into a way of thinking."[50] The EPA information model fails to recognize the motivating power of intentional arc of the body, and its tendency for maximum gripping. On its website what has been structurally absent is the lack of environment-friendly practices (in terms of what people actually do) and personal engagement. Recall the verbs used in the goal statements: "understand," "learn about," "appreciate," and "critically evaluate." They all point to the cognitive state of the mind: you listen to scientific facts; you make the right associations; you come to "see" the relationships between cause and effects, problems and consequences; and you challenge different views as unscientific, incorrect, and possibly immoral. It is essentially a language-mediated experience that has no room for related behaviors. The problem is, phenomenology has put behind the Cartesian era when "I think, therefore I am" to move into a time wherein "I think, therefore I am a verb."[51] If learning creates particular conceptions of reality as it should and if living is sign activity, as Sebeok would argue, then learning needs to contribute to one's living by interpreting the related signs and by invoking practical activities that come from such interpretation.

To be sure, informing is necessary in the sense of creating awareness. However, EPA information provides one way of seeing things. For the EPA, it is the one and only truth. From its perspective, the immediate Interpretant is the only sensible action for the public is to do what it recommends. Their linear certainty, once received and incorporated into the lived world of the public (Addressees in Jakobson's communication term), becomes just *one* of the many possibilities. It is deconstructed, re-positioned, and put in parallel relation with other possibilities like their daily concerns of the body and mind for the public.

If the EPA is to synthesize and coordinate the public effort for sustainability in a significant way, its dichotomic discourse about zero nature and culture needs to be changed. As many scholars such as Hornborg,[52] Cox,[53] and Killingsworth[54] would argue, nature and culture are not mutually exclusive domains or essences, but sedimentations of semiotic processes at different levels of integration. The EPA does not need to abandon the distinction, but has to acknowledge them through the discourse; as referring merely to "aspects" or "dimensions" of living systems rather than to partitioned "segments" of reality. When seen as aspects of integrated wholes rather than entities in their own right, "the opposite poles of such analytical dichotomies should not be treated as standing in some kind of causal relationship to each other."[55] In addition, "Everything is both manufactured and natural in man (...) Already the mere presence of a living being transforms the physical world, bringing to view here 'food', a 'hiding place', and giving 'stimuli' a sense which they have not hitherto possessed."[56]

For the practicality of communication, if the dichotomy of culture and nature has to be preserved, at least new codes should be created in which the public shifts its perspective about their relation to the pair. That is, instead of arranging discourse to the effect of human being as the creator and provider (with its products) for human existence, the EPA may need to foreground the nature's role as the Giver. This means putting nature as the agent, as a dynamic sign in-itself whose call needs to be answered. It also means re-doing the narration by what we human beings would lose if nature stopped giving and appealing.

CONCLUSION

Communication is a process where the process reveals itself to be the condition for the normal course of a more comprehensive process. It does not change bodily habits and its performance, but provides a perspective and rationality for the intentional body to pause, reflect, and re-position itself. It moves beyond what is immediately present, aiming at phenomena of greater significance in the long run. In phenomenological terms, the ultimate goal of environmental education should aim at "the joining of the experience, as an object for consciousness, and consciousness as an object of consciousness [of environmental problems]."[57]

NOTES

1. See Maurice Merleau-Ponty, *Phenomenology of Perception*, trans. Colin Smith (London: Routledge, 2002), 497–499.
2. Umberto Eco, *Semiotics and the Philosophy of Language* (Bloomington: Indiana University Press, 1984), 33–42.
3. Charles Sanders Peirce, *Pragmatism and Pragmaticism*, vol. 5 of *Collected Papers of Charles Sanders Peirce*, ed. Charles Hartshorne and Paul Weiss (Cambridge, MA: Harvard University Press. 1965), 332.
4. Peirce, *Elements of Logic*, vol. 2 of *Collected Papers of Charles Sanders Peirce*, 169.
5. Susan L. Flader, *Thinking Like a Mountain: Aldo Leopold and the Evolution of an Ecological Attitude* (Columbia: University of Missouri Press, 1974), 206.
6. J. Robert Cox, *Environmental Communication and the Public Sphere*, 3rd ed. (Los Angeles, CA: Sage Publications, 2013), 359–361.
7. Emily Huddart Kennedy *et al.*, "Why We Don't 'Walk the Talk': Understanding the Environmental Values/Behaviour Gap in Canada," *Human Ecology Review* 16, no. 2 (2009): 151.
8. Jean M. Twenge, W. Keith Campbell, and Elise C. Freeman, "Generational Differences in Young Adults' Life Goals, Concern for Others, and Civic Orientation, 1966–2009," *Journal of Personality and Social Psychology* 102, no. 5 (2012): 1045–1062, doi: 10.1037/a0027408.
9. Merleau-Ponty, *Phenomenology of Perception*, 155–157.
10. Kalevi Kull, "Semiotic Ecology: Different Natures in the Semiosphere," *Sign Systems Studies* 26 (1998): 354–356. There, Kull proposed the concept of different worlds pertaining to nature—nature with humans and without. According to him, when nature is free from human influence and remains to itself, it is considered absolute zero nature. This zero nature becomes "environment" with human beings in perspective: First nature—the nature as we see, identify, describe and interpret it; Second nature—the nature which we have materially interpreted; and Third nature, which is a virtual nature, as it exists in art and science.
11. Mark Sagoff, "On the Value of Natural Ecosystems: The Catskills Parable," the website of EPA, http://yosemite.epa.gov/sab/sabcvpess.nsf/2a890dc663b46bc685256d63006ac3aa/9a8590d7380 2c75085256f9d00485e36/$file/catskills%20parable.pdf.
12. V. Yu Kirianov, "Environmental Impacts of Volcanic Eruptions in Natural and Human Induced Hazards," *Encyclopedia of Life Support Systems* (EOLSS), developed under the auspices of the UNESCO, 2010, http://www.eolss.net/sample-chapters/c12/E1-07-01-08.pdf.
13. "Basic Information about Cleanups," http://www2.epa.gov/cleanups/basic-information-about-cleanups.
14. "Learn about Water," http://www2.epa.gov/learn-issues/learn-about-water.
15. "Tips to Prevent Mosquito Bites," http://www2.epa.gov/insect-repellents/tips-prevent-mosquito-bites.
16. "Urban Heat Island Mitigation," http://www.epa.gov/heatisld/mitigation/index.htm.
17. "Greenhouse Gases," https://www.ncdc.noaa.gov/monitoring-references/faq/greenhouse-gases.php.

18. Floyd Merrell, "Charles Sanders Peirce's Concept of the Sign," in *The Routledge Companion to Semiotics and Linguistics*, ed. Paul Cobley (London: Routledge, 2001), 28–39.
19. Yuri Lotman, *Universe of the Mind: A Semiotic Theory of Culture*, trans. Ann Shukman (Bloomington: Indiana University Press, 1990), 131–142.
20. Robert Sokolowski, *Introduction to phenomenology* (Cambridge: Cambridge University Press, 2000), 24.
21. Eco, *Semiotics and the Philosophy of Language*, 38–43.
22. Peirce, *The Simplest Mathmatics*, vol. 4 of *Collected Papers of Charles Sanders Peirce*, 422.
23. Ferdinand de Saussure, *Course in General Linguistics*, ed. Charles Bally and Albert Sechehaye, trans. Wade Baskin (New York: McGraw-Hill, 1959), 67–69.
24. "Action Steps for Sun Safety," http://www2.epa.gov/sunwise/action-steps-sun-safety.
25. "Action Steps for Sun Safety."
26. Smith David Woodruff, "Phenomenology," in *The Stanford Encyclopedia of Philosophy*, s.v. http://plato.stanford.edu/archives/win2013/entries/phenomenology/.
27. Pierre Jacob, "Intentionality," in *The Stanford Encyclopedia of Philosophy*, s.v. http://plato.stanford.edu/archives/win2014/entries/intentionality/.
28. Alex Byrne, "Intentionality," in *Philosophy of Science: An Encyclopedia*, s.v. ed. J. Pfeifer and S. Sarkar (Routledge, 2006).
29. Eric Grillo, "The Conception of Intentionality in Phenomenology and Pragmatics," *Phenomenology World-Wide: Foundations—Expanding Dynamics—Life-Engagements: A Guide for Research and Study*, ed. Anna-Teresa Tymieniecka (Boston, MA: Kluwer Academic Publishers, 2003), 553.
30. Merleau-Ponty, *Phenomenology of Perception*, 169.
31. Merleau-Ponty, *Phenomenology of Perception*, 117.
32. Hubert L. Dreyfus, "The Current Relevance of Merleau-Ponty's Phenomenology of Embodiment," *The Electronic Journal of Analytic Philosophy* 4 (1996), http://ejap.louisiana.edu/EJAP/1996.spring/dreyfus.1996.spring.html.
33. Merleau-Ponty, *Phenomenology of Perception*, 20–22.
34. Iordanis Marcoulatos, "Merleau-Ponty and Bourdieu on Embodied Significance," *Journal for the Theory of Social Behaviour* 31, no. 1 (2001): 5, doi:10.1111/1468-5914.00144.
35. Charles Brown and Ted Toadvine, eds., *Eco-Phenomenology: Back to the Earth Itself* (New York: SUNY Press, 2003), xiv–xv.
36. Alan W. Dyer, "Making Semiotic Sense of Money as a Medium of Exchange," *Journal of Economic Issues* 23, no. 2 (1989): 505.
37. Jean Baudrillard, *For a Critique of the Political Economy of the Sign*, trans. Charles Levin (St. Louis: Telos Press, 1981), 123–129.
38. Baudrillard, *For a Critique*, 137.
39. "Threats to Wetland," http://wwf.panda.org/about_our_earth/about_freshwater/intro/threats/. The fact is also confirmed at http://www.epa.gov/reg3esd1/wetlands/.
40. "Ecology of Wetland Ecosystems: Water, Substrate, and Life," http://www.nature.com/scitable/knowledge/library/ecology-of-wetland-ecosystems-water-substrate-and-17059765.
41. Dyer, "Making Semiotic Sense of Money," 505.
42. EPA News release "New Jersey Developer to Pay Civil Penalty for Stormwater Violations and Preserve Wetlands," http://yosemite.epa.gov/opa/admpress.nsf/0/79b11506ef504ff685257e54005c7747.
43. Grillo, "Conception of Intentionality," 555–556.
44. As quoted in Dyer, "Making Semiotic Sense of Money," 505.

45. James Gerken, "More Americans Trust Fox News than Obama on Climate Change, Poll Finds," *The Huffington Post*, April 2, 2015.
46. Richard L. Lanigan, *The Human Science of Communicology: A Phenomenology of Discourse in Foucault and Merleau-Ponty* (Pittsburg, PA: Duquesne University Press, 1992), 3–12.
47. Lanigan, *Human Science of Communicology*, 233.
48. EPA Report: "Climate Change in the U.S.—Benefits of Global Action," http://www2.epa.gov/cira/climate-action-benefits-key-findings.
49. Merleau-Ponty, *Phenomenology of Perception*, 56–88.
50. David Myers and Steven Spencer, *Social Psychology*, 3rd ed. (Toronto: McGraw-Hill Ryerson, 2006), 116.
51. Thomas A. Sebeok, "A Semiotic Perspective on Sciences," in *I Think I Am a Verb: More Contributions to the Doctrine of Signs* (New York: Plenum Pub Corp, 1986), 17–44.
52. Alf Hornborg, "Vital Signs: An Ecosemiotic Perspective on the Human Ecology of Amazonia," *Sign Systems Studies* 29, no. 1 (2001): 121–152.
53. Cox, *Environmental Communication*, 20–26.
54. M. Jimmie Killingsworth, "A Phenomenological Perspective on Ethical Duty in Environmental Communication," *Environmental Communication* 1, no. 1 (2007): 58–63, doi:10.1080/17524030701334243.
55. Hornborg, "Vital Signs," 126.
56. Merleau-Ponty, *Phenomenology of Perception*, 220.
57. Richard L. Lanigan, *Phenomenology of Communication: Merleau-Ponty's Thematics in Communicology and Semiology* (Pittsburg, PA: Duquesne University Press, 1988), 8.

BIBLIOGRAPHY

Baudrillard, Jean. *For a Critique of the Political Economy of the Sign*. Translated by Charles Levin. St. Louis: Telos Press, 1981.

Brown, Charles S., and Ted Toadvine, eds. *Eco-Phenomenology: Back to the Earth Itself*. New York: SUNY Press, 2003.

Buckley, Jessica. "Re-storing the Earth: A Phenomenological Study of Living Sustainably." *Phenomenology and Practice* 7, no. 2 (2013): 19–40.

Byrne, Alex. "Intentionality." In *Philosophy of Science: An Encyclopedia*, edited by J. Pfeifer and S. Sarkar. New York: Routledge, 2006.

Coward, Rosalind, and John Ellis. *Language and Materialism: Developments in Semiology and the Theory of the Subject*. London: Routledge and Kegan Paul, 1977.

Cox, J. Robert. *Environmental Communication and the Public Sphere*. 3rd ed. Los Angeles, CA: Sage Publications, 2013.

Dreyfus, Hubert L. "The Current Relevance of Merleau-Ponty's Phenomenology of Embodiment." *The Electronic Journal of Analytic Philosophy* 4 (1996). http://ejap.louisiana.edu/EJAP/1996.spring/dreyfus.1996.spring.html.

Dyer, Alan W. "Making Semiotic Sense of Money as a Medium of Exchange." *Journal of Economic Issues* 23, no. 2 (1989): 503–510.

Eco, Umberto. *Semiotics and the Philosophy of Language*. Bloomington: Indiana University Press, 1984.

Flader, Susan L. *Thinking Like a Mountain: Aldo Leopold and the Evolution of an Ecological Attitude toward Deer, Wolves, and Forests*. Columbia: University of Missouri Press, 1974.

Grillo, Eric. "The Conception of Intentionality in Phenomenology and Pragmatics." In *Phenomenology World-Wide: Foundations—Expanding Dynamics—Life-Engagements: A Guide for Research and Study*, edited by Anna-Teresa Tymieniecka, 553–561. Boston, MA: Kluwer Academic Publishers, 2003.

Hornborg, Alf. "Vital Signs: An Ecosemiotic Perspective on The Human Ecology of Amazonia." *Sign Systems Studies* 29, no. 1 (2001): 121–152.

Ihde, Don. *Experimental phenomenology: An introduction*. Albany: SUNY Press, 1986.

Jacob, Pierre. "Intentionality." In *The Stanford Encyclopedia of Philosophy*, edited by Edward N. Zalta et al. Winter ed. CA: Stanford University, 2014. http://plato.stanford.edu/archives/win2014/entries/intentionality/

Jakobson, Roman. "Language in Relation to Other Communication Systems." In *Selected Writings*. Vol. 2 of *Word and Language*, 570–579. The Hague: Mouton, 1971.

Kennedy, Emily Huddart, Thomas M. Beckley, Bonita L. Mcfarlane, and Solange Nadeau. "Why We Don't 'Walk the Talk': Understanding the Environmental Values/Behaviour Gap in Canada." *Human Ecology Review* 16, no. 2 (2009): 151–160.

Killingsworth, M. Jimmie. "A Phenomenological Perspective on Ethical Duty in Environmental Communication." *Environmental Communication* 1, no. 1 (2007): 58–63. doi:10.1080/17524030701334243.

Kirianov, V. Yu. "Environmental Impacts of Volcanic Eruptions in Natural and Human Induced Hazards." In *Encyclopedia of Life Support Systems* (EOLSS), developed under the auspices of the UNESCO. Paris: Eolss Publishers, 2010. http://www.eolss.net/sample-chapters/c12/E1-07-01-08.pdf.

Kozin, Alexander. "The Sign of the Other: On the Semiotic of Emmanuel Levinas's Phenomenology." *Semiotica* 156, no. 1 (2004): 235–249.

Kull, Kalevi. "Semiotic Ecology: Different Natures in the Semiosphere." *Sign Systems Studies* 26 (1998): 344–371.

Lanigan, Richard L. *The Human Science of Communicology: A Phenomenology of Discourse in Foucault and Merleau-Ponty*. Pittsburg, PA: Duquesne University Press, 1992.

Lanigan, Richard L. *Phenomenology of Communication: Merleau-Ponty's Thematics in Communicology and Semiology*. Pittsburg, PA: Duquesne University Press, 1988.

Lotman, Yuri M. *Universe of the Mind: A Semiotic Theory of Culture*. Translated by Ann Shukman. Bloomington: Indiana University Press, 1990.

Marcoulatos, Iordanis. "Merleau-ponty and Bourdieu on Embodied Significance." *Journal for the Theory of Social Behaviour* 31, no. 1 (2001): 1–27. doi:10.1111/1468-5914.00144.

Merleau-Ponty, Maurice. *Phenomenology of Perception*. Translated by Collin Smith. London: Routledge, 2002.

Merrell, Floyd. "Charles Sanders Peirce's Concept of the Sign." In *The Routledge Companion to Semiotics and Linguistics*, edited by Paul Cobley, 28–39. London: Routledge, 2001.

Myers, David G., and Steven J. Spencer. "Chapter 4: Behaviour and Attitudes." In *Social Psychology*. 3rd ed. Toronto: McGraw-Hill Ryerson, 2006.

Peirce, Charles S. *The Collected Papers of Charles Sanders Peirce*. Edited by Charles Hartshorne and Paul Weiss. Vols. 2, 4, and 5. Cambridge, MA: Harvard University Press, 1965.

Saussure, Ferdinand de. *Course in General Linguistics*. Edited by Charles Bally and Albert Sechehaye and translated by Wade Baskin. New York: McGraw-Hill, 1959.

Sebeok, Thomas A. *I Think I Am a Verb: More Contributions to the Doctrine of Signs*. New York: Plenum Pub Corp, 1986.

Seif, Farouk Y. "Mutual Mimesis of Nature and Culture: A Representational Perspective for Eco-Cultural Metamorphosis." *Sign Systems Studies* 38, no. 1/4 (2010): 242–269.

Smith, David Woodruff. "Phenomenology." In *The Stanford Encyclopedia of Philosophy*, edited by Edward N. Zalta *et al.* Winter ed. 2013. http://plato.stanford.edu/archives/win2013/entries/phenomenology/.

Sokolowski, Robert. *Introduction to Phenomenology*. Cambridge: Cambridge University Press, 2000.

Twenge, Jean M., W. Keith Campbell, and Elise C. Freeman. "Generational Differences in Young Adults' Life Goals, Concern for Others, and Civic Orientation, 1966–2009." *Journal of Personality and Social Psychology* 102, no. 5 (2012): 1045–1062. doi:10.1037/a0027408.

SECTION FOUR

Voicing Bodies/ Embodying Voices

CHAPTER THIRTEEN

Authoring Life Writing as a Technology of the Self

A Communicological Perspective on the Concept of Voice

DEBORAH EICHER-CATT

Ever since feminists embraced the practice French theorist Helen Cixous called "women's ecriture," the performance of writing (especially autobiographical or life writing) has become associated with women's attempts to overcome oppressive socio-political circumstances. After all, Cixous declared that women's writing is an important rhetorical practice by which we can "put [ourselves] into the text—as into the world and into history—by [our] own movement."[1] As a common code of representation, historically life writing for women became an acceptable and viable rhetorical means of activating our "right to speak" or a way of "finding our voice" within structures of domination that do not serve us. And, given that early feminist voices were literally barred from public or oral forums, it is understandable then that "women's ecriture" became an essential, rhetorical means by which discontentment and outrage could be expressed and recorded. As feminist critic Carolyn Heilbrun, author of the best-selling book, *Writing a Woman's Life* notes about women poets in particular, "… women poets … can now be seen to have transformed the auto-biographies of women's lives, to have expressed, and suffered for expressing, what women had not earlier been allowed to say."[2]

In his later writings, where he advocates we theoretically re-evaluate what it means to "care for oneself," Michel Foucault identifies a range of rhetorical and behavioral practices he calls "technologies of self."[3] Self or life writing, he says, is one such technology.[4] Fashioned as a means of resituating ourselves within socio-political relations and consequently affecting our understanding of our own capabilities to impact the world, Foucault claims that such practices "enable us to separate out, from the contingency that has made us what we are, the possibility of no longer being, doing, or thinking what we are, do, or think."[5] Thus, as a particularly dominant socio-cultural code for women, the technology of self known as life writing is closely associated with our commonsense understanding of voice. Considered more broadly in social discourse, we typically use the term voice rather loosely—marking its interchangeable form depending upon whether the practice we are focusing upon is speaking *or* writing. Regardless of its form, most feminists nowadays would agree that voice is an integral aspect of a woman's sense of agency and efficacy in the world.

Given their significance as cultural signs and their apparent pragmatic functions in social discourse, I contend that a more careful examination of the phenomenological practice of life writing and the semiotic contours of voice are warranted. Currently, for example, the practice of life writing is almost exclusively positioned theoretically as only a linguistic phenomenon. Similarly, the concept of voice is used rather loosely by feminists and associated with only expression (whether oral or written) with little consideration of its perceptive or participatory components as a combinatory practice of discourse. I suggest that, without more sophisticated, theoretical treatments of voice and life writing as rhetorical practices of discourse (which implies both expression and perception as communicative elements), we inevitably diminish their capacities to effect social relations in productive ways. More important, without examining and understanding life writing and voice as technologies of the self, as Foucault outlines, we do not recognize the ramifications of our limited thinking nor can we, as feminists, experience their emancipatory potential as discursive practices. As we shall see, interpreting life writing and voice as technologies of the self that play out reflexively within discursive practices, provides us with richer insights about their semiotic contours and how they function phenomenologically to affect personal and social change.

In what follows, I offer a Communicological perspective to life writing as an issue of voice. I draw heavily from the Communicological work of Richard L. Lanigan, in particular his insightful interpretation of Foucault's writings on rhetoric.[6] Based upon Foucault's semiotic and phenomenological work concerning the oppositions/appositions of language and discourse, I argue that the real potential that inheres in feminist voice as life writing lies in the dialectical relation played out between practical discourse and discursive practices. After an explication of this important communicative dialect from a Communicological perspective, I contend that only by viewing voice as the combinatory logic(s) of expression and perception, language and discourse, praxis and poeisis, can we move beyond a limited understanding of voice from merely the writer or sender perspective. We discover that when viewed as a discursive practice (and not merely a practice of discourse), voice enacts its true authorship, thereby demonstrating its transformative potential for self and others. Only then, I suggest, can life writing become the powerful technology of the self that feminists claim it to be.

THE LIFE WRITING AND WRITING LIFE DIALECTIC: "VOICE" AS AN EMERGENT DISCURSIVE PHENOMENON

To begin, I explore the distinctions (opposition) and simultaneous relationships (apposition) between writing and speaking. I believe it is within their dialectical relations that we begin to appreciate life writing as a *discursive*, i.e., as a participatory accomplishment of both writing and speaking, and reading and listening. It is within this dialectical, tropological relation that the thematic of voice frames our pursuits. As Lanigan informs us, Foucault offers insight in this regard. (Refer to Table 13.1 below for the following discussion.)

Responding to Nietzsche's explination of Aristotle's distinction between writing (*lexis graphike*) and speaking (*lexis agonistike*), Foucault unpacks this nagging philosophical question. As Lanigan reminds us,[7] by looking at the distinction between writing and speaking, we discover "the classic distinction between communication and expression, i.e., the cognitive function of signification [which is expression] versus the affective function of meaning that must combine as the conative function of discourse [communication]." As such, we begin to understand what French semioticians and phenomenologists Maurice Merleau-Ponty and Michel Foucault identified as the classic distinction between *parole parlee* or *enunciation* (spoken speech = language) and *parole parlante* or *enonce* (speaking speech = rhetoric/discourse). In his writings Foucault, of course, aligns rhetoric or speaking speech with discourse in his attempts to move past rhetoric's historically-narrow usage as mere verbal, expressive persuasion about some *a priori* condition. For Foucault, speaking speech is thus communicative—accomplished through participation of addresser and addressee in the constitution of meaning.

Table 13.1: Foucault's Semiotic and Phenomenological Oppositions/Appositions of Language and Discourse

Writing	Speaking
lexis graphike	*lexis agonistike*
speech spoken	speaking speech
parole parlee	*parole parlante*
	(Merleau-Ponty)
enunciation	*enonce* (Foucault)
language	discourse

Writing	Speaking
expression	perception
semiotics	Phenomenology
writer	reader
writer	author (Foucault)
practical discourse	discursive practice (Foucault)
life writing	writing life
voiceless name	nameless voice (Foucault)

Source : Author

According to Lanigan,[8] while preserving the distinction between writing (language) and speaking (discourse), Foucault takes issue with Nietzsche's association of writing as a mere practical expression (language is rhetoric) of one's opinion (*doxa*). Instead, in writings such as the *Order of Things*, Foucault advocates that we should view rhetoric not as a mere linguistic device of expression but also as a discursive practice that necessarily establishes epistemes (or knowledge formations) through *lexis agonistike* (or the participatory practice of debate or speaking).[9] Through the lens offered by Foucault's writings, we can begin to see how language and discourse play out as a combinatory, reversible, and reflexive logic within any communicative process and event. We start to appreciate, in other words, the complexity of the communication process in our everyday lives as we move effortlessly (and often unwittingly) between the reflexive and reversible poles of spoken speech in its referential/linguistic functions to speaking speech in its discursive, participatory functions where structures of power are instituted or transformed.

Applying this distinction to our topic of life writing, we discover that when we theoretically reduce life writing to only its narrow rendition as a mere linguistic or verbal accomplishment as expression of a writer, we are viewing it as *parole parlee* or spoken speech. Life writing is thought to merely conjure or represent past ideas or actions. Unfortunately, this perspective is easy for us to adopt especially when we think of diary writing or autobiographies. Furthermore, as the feminist scholarship of Smith and Watson exemplify,[10] most literature in the field of feminist studies on life writing refers to the process of writing in this way—naming it "life writing" as if the practice is able to capture the qualities of someone's life already lived. Hence, such a theoretical position advocates viewing it as a *practical discourse* for women to use to try to accomplish voice. Furthermore, this theoretical position promotes viewing the autobiographical subject as predating expression and experience.[11]

While this theoretical position is not without its descriptive merits, I suggest that the current scholarship in this area is pointing us in a different direction. We learn from Smith and Watson, after all, that it is through *discursive* means that the autobiographical subject actually emerges within discourse and action. So, following Foucault, I think when we theoretically position life writing as a *discursive practice*, we honor it as speaking speech (*parole parlante*). When it comes to life writing, I suggest in my own work that we call such discursive practices "writing life" so as to acknowledge the ways in which subjects may institute or position themselves relative to the discursive relations they experience and perceive—taking into account the whole of relations of which they are a part. Feminists Smith and Watson also appear to emulate such thinking when they contend, "subjects know themselves in language because *experience is discursive*, embedded in the languages of everyday life and the knowledge produced at everyday sites."[12]

More important, I claim that it is within this dialectic of life writing and writing life that our communicative gestures are activated as they simultaneously demonstrate our particular politics at that point in time. Thus, I interpret Foucault's technologies of the self as more than representations of spoken speech as some feminist have unfortunately done. Technologies of the self are not merely "life writing" in other words. Technologies of the self are activated within the dialectical relation of language (speech spoken) *and* discourse (speaking speech) as communicative accomplishments of writer/reader—speaker/audience. So, technologies of the self are also speaking speech or "writing life." As my discussion proceeds, we find that the reversibility of this dialectic is the discursive function that truly "authorizes" our relations with self and others as communicative beings.

Once we understand this important distinction and reversibility between spoken speech and speaking speech in its ironic combinatory movement between language and discourse, we can begin to unpack life writing as a semiotic process and phenomenological event. According to Lanigan's reading of Foucault, through this distinction we identify "Foucault's concern with the contest between *practical discourse* as a semiotic formation and *discourse practices* as a phenomenological transformation."[13] Spoken speech (verbal expression in language) highlights the semiotic elements of the writing process. This is because semiotics is the study of representational processes in *language* that mark distinctions and differences within cultural sign systems. In contrast, speaking speech (perception in discourse) highlights writing's phenomenological entailments as combinatory logic—these sign processes must become embodied events of affectual awareness for self and others. As we know from the works of Merleau-Ponty, phenomenology honors the immediate experience of speaking as an embodied event in its primacy of perception.[14]

When these oppositional and appositional structures are brought to bear on the issue of "voice," there are theoretical extensions we can now make about its nature and scope. Above all, we find that voice inheres within this dialectical movement of language and discourse. This means that it is not something a writer or a speaker *possesses* as a personal linguistic instrument of power. As Foucault suggests, at the very least we discover that spoken speech only signifies a "voiceless name."[15] That is, our speech is easily over-determined by the cultural signs and codes (semiotic markers) within the representational system of language we employ. Because of this, ironically the very quality and agential powers of voice that we want to attribute to it are severely diminished. In its use as a *practical discourse* of life writing, it is possible that we may exhibit some semblance of agency as we have come to know it—but it is an agency defined solely be a representational system not of our own making. It is also an agency that is severely diminished by the over-determination of the expressive or emotive qualities of the speech act without its corresponding evocative functions. This insight should give feminists (and any other minority group) pause.

To the contrary, we find that speaking speech represents for Foucault the "nameless voice," because it "accentuates our abilities to exercise our phenomenological and semiotic freedoms (...) [as] our 'names' [are] eclipsed by our embodied voices."[16] It is through the latter's dialectical relation with the former, that we find the *authorization* we need to inaugurate true personal and cultural transformation and change as a function of voice. So ironically, when we narrowly perceive self writing as only "life writing," its agential qualities are actually reduced by its very association with a "voiceless name." In contrast, when we perceive self writing as "writing life," we begin to announce its power as truly a "nameless voice." Understood as a "nameless voice" in dialectical relation with a "voiceless name," self writing has the potential to carry the weight of agency we desire—the power to not only emote but also to evoke attitudes, values, and sentiments that are personally and socially productive.

In this way, contrary to what some feminists have advocated about Foucault and his supposed under-developed theory of agency,[17] we discover that he actually views agency as an integral aspect within the combinatory logic of discursive practices and practical discourse. For it is *within* a rhetorical frame (viewed as discourse) that Foucault acknowledges a subject's birth and his/her possibilities for re-positioning (or agency) within the wider network of socio-political relations. Therefore, in terms of the feminist construct of voice, I suggest it is best conceptualized as a *mediated* phenomenon between spoken speech and speaking speech, between expression and perception, between life writing and writing life, and between a writer and reader, an author and audience. The activation and emergence of voice are thoroughly steeped within this ever-evolving contest or *agon* of language and discourse through its semiotic processes and phenomenological events as a communication phenomenon. The same, of course, holds true for Foucault's notion of technologies of the self and particularly his concept of *parrhesia* or truth telling accounts of oneself he describes as "fearless speech."[18] Fearless speech is not enacted as a result of audience abandonment; to the contrary, fearless speech is so designated because of the presence of the auditor and the perceived risk the auditor's position instantiates.

At this point in my discussion, I want to highlight the important distinction that Foucault also makes between a "writer" and an "author."[19] For it is also in this distinction that we find the subtle power inherent within the life writing process as a whole and its ultimate connection to voice that can be truly transformational for both speaker and listener.

AUTHORING LIFE WRITING AS A TECHNOLOGY OF THE SELF

Surprisingly, feminist theorists Smith and Watson in their book, *Reading Autobiography*, do not emphasize the concept of the "death of the author" in their literature review.[20] To me, the concept of the "author" is a logical extension of the notion of agency, a topic they do give considerable attention to. Of course, Roland Barthes' now famous 1968 essay, "The Author is Dead" problematizes the positionality of the author and raises concerns about the agential qualities he/she may activate within the life writing process.[21] Barthes' proclamation caused quite a stir within literary circles as poststructuralist thought increased in momentum during this time period. Particularly problematic for feminists, especially in the immediate wake of his proclamation, was the fact that the disappearance of the author signaled the possible silencing of women's voice within the discourse of modernity, a voice that feminists had just fought long and hard to legitimize. So often in the feminist literature you will see the construct of voice directly linked with the concept of the writer or author. After all as Foucault rightly suggests, in modernity we were concerned with such questions as: "Who is the real author? Have we proof of his/her authenticity and originality? What has the author revealed of his/her most profound self in his/her language?"[22] But as feminists soon realized, the death of the author as the natural or presumed authority over a work held promise for feminist theorizing on subjectivity. This is because it meant privileging the *acts* of writing and textuality as potential vehicles of agency for women, creating the discursive sites where subjectivity might emerge.[23]

However, Foucault is quick to point out in his 1969 essay, "What is an Author?" that the theoretical issues and definitions surrounding an author, a work, and the writing process itself are often confused or conflated. In our attempts to replace the privileged position of the writer or author with either the work (as in the case of Barthes) or the writing process (*ecriture*) itself (as in the case of Cixous), he claims that we merely "suppress the real meaning of his [*sic*, author's] disappearance."[24] Instead, Foucault attempts to re-position the issues surrounding the author, the work, and the writing process by asking the important question: Does the author/writer have to assume the role of a dead man[*sic*] for us to appreciate the acts of writing and the texts so produced? According to Lanigan, by grappling with this question Foucault extends Barthes' theoretical exploration by attempting to reconcile what he believes is a misleading trend in poststructuralist thought.[25] As such, Foucault examines the now taken-for-granted assumptions we hold about how to replace the privileged position of the author. I briefly address each one of these assumptions below.

The first theoretical position Foucault analyzes is our understanding of what constitutes a "work." He claims that we do not, at present, have an adequate theory of the work. Through examples given, he advocates that a work cannot be simply a "curious unity" linked to those products of writing attached to one individual/author. This is because the boundaries of these curious unities are, indeed, rather slippery; furthermore, distinctions (and ownership) often blur. As a consequence and contrary to Barthes' position, he says, "it is not enough to declare that we should do without the writer (author) and study the work itself. The word *work* and the unity that it designates are probably as problematic as the status of the author's individuality."[26] According to Foucault, such a theoretical move only employs a logic of substitution (valorizing the work over the author) that proves to be unproductive.

The second way we think we are replacing the privileged position of the author concerns our theoretical understandings of the writing (*ecriture*) process itself. He argues that we have "transpose[d] the empirical characteristics of the author into a transcendental anonymity ... giving writing a primal status" affirming its function as critical/creative or even as a religious or sacred act.[27] So, in elevating the status of writing, he thinks we run "the risk of maintaining the author's privileges under the protection of writing's *a priori* status."[28] Again, he is concerned that we are only employing a logic of substitution, in this case granting privilege to writing (*ecriture*)—to the abandonment of the relationships between the author, the work produced, and the reader. Ironically, by privileging the writing process and abandoning the writer/author, we reduce writings' status within the wider network of socio-political relations. Unfortunately, writing becomes, he theorizes, capitalistic, consumerist, and without substance and style. Similar to Barthes' position, Foucault thus sees that "writing" and "authoring" can signify very different categories of experience and agency.[29] For example, Barthes identifies how mere "writers" transform thoughts (or consciousness) into merchandise and calls "writers" (not authors) mere cybernetic machines.[30] So, in analyzing Barthes' 1968 essay, Foucault is examining just how we should understand writing as a potential site of agency and "authority" without valorizing the author, the work, or the writing process itself within our investigations. As Foucault says, it is not enough to echo the "empty affirmation that the author has disappeared ... instead, we must locate the *space* left empty by the author's disappearance, follow the distribution of gaps and breaches, and watch for the openings that this disappearance uncovers."[31]

With that proclamation, Foucault reverses our modernist conceptualizations of the author, along with the work and the writing process, with their focus on questions such as: Who is the author and what claim to originality and authority does he/she hold? Instead, in terms of the author he claims that "the author is not an indefinite source of significations which fill a work; the author does not precede the work."[32] Instead, he moves us theoretically from the modern focus on language to the postmodern problematic of discourse. Viewing these topics from the vantage point of discourse, we discover that the author, the work, writing, and reading are held in socio-political relation as *functions* of discursive practices that are, altogether, participatory. This theoretical reversal announces a completely different set of postmodern questions he thinks we should we be asking. As Lanigan's reading of Foucault outlines, such questions begin primarily to announce the interrelationships of the author, a work, writing, and the reader as semiotic and phenomenological boundary setting enactments.[33] According to Foucault, questions that arise from postmodern theorizing are: What are the modes of existence of this discourse? Where does it come from? How is it circulated? Who controls it? What placements are determined for possible subjects? Who can fulfill these diverse functions of the subject?

So for Foucault, writing (as *ecriture*) is not merely a modern, consumerist, linguistic practice of *langue* that any person might do. Writing within a modernist understanding only re-produces sedimented discourse in its production by a "writer"—in the valorization of the name. This condition is what I have identified earlier as a "life writing" perspective and exemplifies speech spoken as an example of a *practical discourse* that is used for instrumental gain. Instead, Foucault views writing (*ecriture*) as a special case of *discursive practice*. Viewing writing through a discursive lens recognizes its socio-political dimensions. Likewise from this perspective, an author does not precede the text, as is the case with a writer. Instead, an author emerges within the speaking/writing process of *enonce* or *parole parlante* with an audience/reader. Thus, an author, as a special case of *parole parlante*, functions within discursive practices to interrupt or impede the free flow "of cancerous and dangerous proliferation of significations … the free circulation, the free manipulation, the free composition, decomposition, and recomposition of fiction."[34] The latter condition is generated, of course, by the works of a mere writer. Conversely, defining the author in terms of an "author function." Foucault claims that it "does not refer, purely and simply, to an actual individual insofar as it simultaneously gives rise to a variety of egos and to a series of subjective positions that individuals of any class may come to occupy"[35] within the participatory enactment. Thus, the writer is someone who becomes "subject to" a discourse rather than "subject of" discourse, as is the case with an author. In other words, the postmodern author (and not writer) becomes an "author of the self," a new self that is possibilized within the process of *ecriture* only through a participatory enactment of writing/reading. So, with Foucault, we come to realize in the case of the postmodern author that, "I am the author of my Self, the subject of my consciousness to which I am subjected."[36] Based upon this reading of Foucault (through a Communicological lens provided by Lanigan), we must conclude that not all writing (including life writing) is actually "authored" in Foucault's sense of the term. Some texts are merely written—emotive expressions of sentiments and beliefs. So, we might ask: How should we characterize a discourse that contains an author function?

Foucault outlines four different characteristics that make a particular form of writing as a discursive practice "authored."[37] *First*, discourses have an author function if they are thought to be transgressive or at least there is a critical component to the appearance of an author. Here Foucault is focusing on how works that are authored are fraught with some degree of existential risk—given the socio-political field in which they emerge—paying homage to the importance of the audience or reader. Consequently this produces Foucault's attraction to the concept of *parrhesia*, i.e., fearless speech. *Second*, Foucault stipulates that the author function does not characterize all discourses in the same way. In other words, there is not universality to the way the function works. This helps to specify their variance in appearance, from literary texts to scientific ones. Again, Foucault is specifying that the socio-political field helps to shape a discursive practice (writing/ecriture) as meeting the condition of being authored or merely written. *Third*, the author function "does not develop spontaneously, as the attribution of a discourse to an individual. It is, rather, the result of a complex operation that constructs a certain rational being that we call author."[38] He goes on to say that there are "rules of author construction" that also vary socially and historically. So, an aspect of the construction of a given author should not be linked to an individual's deep motive or any internal creative power he/she might possess; Foucault calls such attributions mere psychological "projections." Instead, how we construct our sense of what an author is varies depending upon changing and shifting socio-political constraints/rules that are at play within a given matrix of discursive relations at a given place in time. *Fourth*, he says, "All discourses endowed with the author function do possess [a] plurality of the self."[39] Here he is specifying that all discourses that are authored and not merely written are open to problematizing the very self that narrates and the self that reads by virtue of their evocative characteristics. Authored discourses can "give rise simultaneously to several selves, to several subjects—positions that can be occupied by different classes of individuals"[40] based upon their poetic functions. In sum, writing (*ecriture*) that is authorized in this sense is one that has transformative potential for the writer/author *and* the reader.

The important theoretical thread that I want to tease out from the above discussion is that, as we theorize the practice of life writing, Foucault has given us an insightful mechanism for making necessary distinctions about life writing (in its generic sense) and the authoring of life writing (in its generative sense). As feminist researchers we need to resist the temptation to merely lump all of life writing into one generic category, as if all writings contain author functions as Foucault describes. All life writing does not automatically meet the criteria of being a technology of the self or exhibit the author function, for the writing would have to meet the criteria he set forth.

In addition, reading with Foucault, we begin to appreciate that "the author is therefore the ideological figure by which one marks the manner in which we fear the proliferation of meaning"[41] that is not our own—a meaning produced by a mere writer. As a function of discursive practices, the author for Foucault, then, serves to reduce the "great danger with which fiction threatens our world"[42] by critically assessing the writing practice and establishing the limits of the fact/fiction dialectical movement of a text so produced. Hence he reverses our typical taken-for-granted assumptions about the author as the "genial creator of a work in which he[*sic*] deposits, with infinite wealth and generosity, an inexhaustible world of significations."[43] As we now understand, this condition designates merely a writer. Instead, Foucault is specifying that an author "is a certain functional principle by which, in our culture, one limits, excludes, and chooses; in short, by which one impedes the free circulation (...)" of discourse.[44]

CONCLUSION

In sum, I argue that by focusing on only the *writer's* linguistic choices of expression (as voice) in our theorizing about life writing we severely reduce our understanding of writing to a narrow question about its effectiveness as an example of a *practical discourse*.[45] Instead (and thinking with Foucault), I suggest that our theorizing on women's life writing will be served better if we honor the tropological space created inevitably between a writer/author (expression) and reader (perception). It is within this communicative space where technologies of the self are activated as combinatory logics of *discursive practices* that *possibilize* author functions, as Foucault claims.[46] Acknowledging the dynamic elements at play within the life writing/writing life process, a Communicological perspective, as promoted by Richard Lanigan, thus helps to flesh out the agonistic struggle always at the heart of this important reversible and reflexive semiotic phenomenological relationship. In order to bring a communication focus to the process of life writing (as opposed to merely viewing it as an object of linguistic expression), theoretically we must explicate this agonistic relationship between writing and speaking, speech spoken (*parole parlee*) and speaking speech (*parole parlante*), life writing and writing life as a semiotic embodied activity of discourse.

My project on reading my father's diary entries and writing my honest responses to those entries—which brings together in apposition on the oppositional nature of life writing (my father's) and writing life (my own),[47] seeks to demonstrate this very *agon* of discourse and action. Rather than accepting the dominant or generic world view provided by my father's entries regarding our familial relations, I want to reveal the generative qualities *possibilized* in my writing life. In doing so, I hope to expose the author function of writing life as an issue of voice. I am fully aware that my success in "finding" my voice in this project, however, will be determined not by my assessment alone. My voice will be co-constituted by my reader's evocative responses to what I articulate.

So theoretically we can now conclude that voice functions similarly to Foucault's idea of the author function. Viewed from this enhanced theoretical perspective, life writing can achieve the status of a technology of the self where a voice may emerge. As we can see, voice does not express or achieve power in itself as expression. Instead, voice announces transformative capabilities that are only fully realized through the participatory enactment within the author/reader dialectic. It is my assumption, therefore, that my discourse (writing) concerning our father-daughter relationship will not authorize a voice—unless it evokes a response that also proves transformative in some way for my reader. Finding my voice means finding the other's and vice versa in a possible shared code of meaning. It is within this space of communicative praxis and poiesis that together we instantiate the authorial voice that both sustains and transforms our understandings of self and other. Voice is thus a *communicative* phenomenon that may emerge within discursive practices as we seek to authorize technologies of the self.

NOTES

1. Helen Cixous, "The Laugh of the Medusa," *Signs: Journal of Women in Culture and Society* 1, no. 4 (1976): 875.
2. Carolyn Heilbrun, *Writing a Woman's Life* (New York: W.W. Norton), 60.
3. Michel Foucault, "Technologies of the Self," in *Technologies of the Self: A Seminar with Michel Foucault*, ed. Luther H. Martin, Huck Gutman, and Patrick H. Hutton (Amherst: University of Massachusetts Press, 1988).
4. Michel Foucault, "Self Writing," in *Michel Foucault: Ethics, Subjectivity and Truth*, ed. Paul Rabinow (New York: New Press, 1994).
5. Michel Foucault, "What is Enlightenment?," in *Foucault Reader*, ed. Paul Rabinow (New York: Pantheon Books, 1984), 46.
6. Richard L. Lanigan, "Foucault's Science of Rhetoric: The Contest between Practical Discourse and Discursive Practice," *Symploke* 4, nos. 1–2 (1996).
7. Lanigan, "Foucault's Science," 189–190.
8. Lanigan, "Foucault's Science," 191.
9. Michel Foucault, *The Order of Things: An Archaeology of the Human Sciences* (New York: Vintage Books, 1973).
10. Sidone Smith and Julia Watson, *Women, Autobiography, Theory: A Reader* (Madison: University of Wisconsin Press, 1998).
11. Sidone Smith and Julia Watson, *A Guide for Interpreting Life Narratives: Reading Autobiography* (Minneapolis: University of Minnesota Press, 2010), 31.
12. Smith and Watson, *Guide for Interpreting Life Narratives*, 32.
13. Lanigan, "Foucault's Science," 190.

14. Maurice Merleau-Ponty, *Phenomenology of Perception*, trans. Colin Smith (New York: Humanities Press, 1962[1945]).
15. Richard L. Lanigan, "The Voiceless Name and the Nameless Voice: Foucault's Phenomenology of Discourse," in *The Human Science of Communicology: A Phenomenology of Discourse in Foucault and Merleau-Ponty* (Pittsburgh, PA: Duquesne University Press, 1992), 155–177.
16. Deborah Eicher-Catt, "Recovering the Voice of Embodied Dialogue," *International Journal of Communication* 20, no. 1 (2010): 130.
17. See for example Jean Grimshaw, "Practices of Freedom," in *Up Against Foucault: Explorations of Some Tensions between Foucault and Feminism* (New York: Routledge, 1993), 51–72 and Lois McNay, *Foucault and Feminism: Power, Gender and the Self* (Boston, MA: Northeastern University Press, 1992).
18. Michel Foucault, *Fearless Speech*, ed. Joseph Pearson (Los Angeles: Semiotext(e), 2001).
19. Michel Foucault, "What is an Author?," in *Foucault Reader*, ed. Paul Rabinow (New York: Pantheon Books, 1984), 101–120.
20. Perhaps they conclude that it is a topic long since interrogated by post-structuralists. As I aim to show, following Foucault, we can reach a different conclusion. As he suggests, the "author" per se is not dead, but the writer should be.
21. Roland Barthes, "The Author is Dead," in *The Rustle of Language* (New York: Hill and Wang, 1968), 49–55.
22. Foucault, "What is an Author?," 119.
23. We have the French feminists who are concerned with writing such as Helen Cixous, "Laugh of the Medusa"; Luce Irigary, *Elemental Passions*, trans. Joanne Collie and Judith Still (New York: Routledge, 1992); and Julie Kristeva, *Revolution in Poetic Language*, trans. Margaret Waller (New York: Columbia University Press, 1984) as Continental examples. We also have classic examples of writing as a form of life revision from the likes of Adrienne Rich, *Of Woman Born: Motherhood as Experience and Institution* (New York: Norton, 1976).
24. Foucault, "What is an Author?," 103.
25. For a thorough discussion of Foucault's revisioning project, see Richard L. Lanigan, "The Postmodern Author: Foucault on Fiction and the Fiction of Foucault," *The American Journal of Semiotics* 17, no. 1 (2001).
26. Foucault, "What is an Author?," 104.
27. Foucault, "What is an Author?," 104.
28. Foucault, "What is an Author?," 105.
29. For an insightful discussion on Barthes and his distinctions between authors and writers (made in a 1960's essay), refer to Lanigan, "Postmodern Author," 253–271.
30. Lanigan, "Postmodern Author," 254.
31. Foucault, "What is an Author?," 105, italics mine.
32. Foucault, "What is an Author?," 118–119.
33. Lanigan, "Foucault's Science of Rhetoric."
34. Foucault, "What is an Author?," 118–119.
35. Foucault, "What is an Author?," 113.
36. Lanigan, "Postmodern Author," 263.
37. Foucault, "What is an Author?," 124–130.
38. Foucault, "What is an Author?," 110.
39. Foucault, "What is an Author?," 112.
40. Foucault, "What is an Author?," 113.

41. Foucault, "What is an Author?," 119.
42. Foucault, "What is an Author?," 118.
43. Foucault, "What is an Author?," 118.
44. Foucault, "What is an Author?," 119.
45. Lanigan, "Foucault's Science of Rhetoric."
46. Lanigan, "Foucault's Science of Rhetoric."
47. Deborah Eicher-Catt, "Writing Life as Voice: An Archaeology of a Father-Daughter Love" (paper presented at the meeting of the International Communicology Institute, Duquesne University, Pittsburgh, PA, July 2013).

BIBLIOGRAPHY

Barthes, Roland. *The Rustle of Language*, 49–55, New York: Hill and Wang, 1968.
Cixous, Helen. "The Laugh of the Medusa." *Signs: Journal of Women in Culture and Society* 1, no. 4 (1976): 875–893.
Eicher-Catt, Deborah. "Recovering the Voice of Embodied Dialogue: Edward Sapir's Contribution to Communicology." *International Journal of Communication* 20, no. 1 (2010): 9–33.
Eicher-Catt, Deborah. "Writing Life as Voice: An Archaeology of a Father-Daughter Love." Paper presented at the meeting of the International Communicology Institute, Duquesne University, Pittsburgh, PA, July 2013.
Foucault, Michel. *Fearless Speech*. Edited by Joseph Pearson. Los Angeles, CA: Semiotext(e), 2001.
Foucault, Michel. *The Order of Things: An Archeology of the Human Sciences*. New York: Vintage Books, 1973.
Foucault, Michel. "Self Writing." In *Michel Foucault: Ethics, Subjectivity and Truth*, edited by Paul Rabinow, 209–222. New York: New Press, 1994.
Foucault, Michel. "Technologies of the Self." In *Technologies of the Self: A Seminar with Michel Foucault*, edited by Luther H. Martin, Huck Gutman, and Patrick H. Hutton, 16–49. Amherst: The University of Massachusetts Press, 1988.
Foucault, Michel. "What is an Author?" In *Foucault Reader*, edited by Paul Rabinow, 101–120. New York: Pantheon Books, 1984.
Foucault, Michel. "What is Enlightenment?" In *Foucault Reader*, edited by Paul Rabinow, 32–50. New York: Pantheon Books, 1984.
Grimshaw, Jean. "Practices of Freedom." In *Up Against Foucault: Explorations of Some Tensions Between Foucault and Feminism*, edited by Caroline Ramazanoglu, 51–72, New York: Routledge, 1993.
Heilbrun, Carolyn. *Writing a Woman's Life*. New York: W.W. Norton, 1988.
Irigary, Luce. *Elemental Passions*. Translated by Joanne Collie and Judith Still. New York: Routledge, 1992.
Kristeva, Julia. *Revolution in Poetic Language*. Translated by Margaret Waller. New York: Columbia University Press, 1984.
Lanigan, Richard L. "Foucault's Science of Rhetoric: The Contest between Practical Discourse and Discursive Practice." *Symploke* 4, no. 1–2 (1996): 189–202.
Lanigan, Richard L. "The Postmodern Author: Foucault on Fiction and the Fiction of Foucault." *The American Journal of Semiotics* 17, no. 1 (2001): 253–271.
Lanigan, Richard L. *The Human Science of Communicology: A Phenomenology of Discourse in Foucault and Merleau-Ponty*. Pittsburgh, PA: Duquesne University Press, 1992.

McNay, Lois. *Foucault and Feminism: Power, Gender and the Self.* Boston, MA: Northeastern University Press, 1992.

Merleau-Ponty, Maurice. *Phenomenology of Perception.* Translated by Colin Smith. New York: Humanities Press, 1962. (Original work published in 1945).

Rich, Adrienne. *Of Woman Born: Motherhood as Experience and Institution.* New York: W.W. Norton, 1976.

Smith, Sidone and Julia Watson. *A Guide for Interpreting Life Narratives: Reading Autobiography.* Minneapolis: University of Minnesota Press, 2010.

Smith, Sidone and Julia Watson. *Women, Autobiography, Theory: A Reader.* Madison: University of Wisconsin Press, 1998.

CHAPTER FOURTEEN

Communicative Possibilities in/of a Glance

PAT ARNESON

I have long enjoyed watching people—looking at them and noticing their everyday gestures—whether I am sitting, walking, or even driving. For example, I recall driving through a small town in western Pennsylvania. The speed limit was 30 miles an hour. I was also in a school zone but school was out for the summer. I was focusing on the road, the speed limit sign, my speedometer reading, and traffic. I found my attention drawn out my window to the left where a person was walking on the sidewalk next to the school. She was a gray-haired woman wearing a smart blue-and-white vertically striped shirt-dress with a red belt and a navy sweater, pushing a small black walker/cart. She was alone. I saw the school building behind her, and even though I was looking at her, I noticed the large brick wall. I still think about her, wonder about her story, and in some ways imagine myself in her.

In this essay, I consider philosophical differences between *gaze* and *glance*. *Gaze* has been the dominant term used in philosophical discussions. Particular attention is paid to gaze in the works of Jean-Paul Sartre, Michel Foucault, and Jacques Lacan. Edward S. Casey's work examines *glance*. I address the role of one's attentiveness in glancing with particular attention to visual and mental glancing. I briefly discuss communicology and consider how work in intrapersonal communicology provides an alternative understanding of glance.

GAZE

The range in meaning of the verb *to see* is so broad that a thesaurus may contain 50 or more synonyms, including both *gaze* and *glance*. While each word involves the act of visual perception, the terms gaze and glance have philosophically come to mean differently. The term gaze has received primary attention in the literature. The alienating and objectifying power of the gaze is a central theme in the work of Jean-Paul Sartre,[1] Michel Foucault,[2] and Jacques Lacan.[3]

Jean-Paul Sartre's emphasis on the gaze is included in *Being and Nothingness: An Essay on Phenomenological Ontology*, first published in 1943. In discussing what he means by the *being* of a phenomenon, Sartre makes a binary distinction between unconscious being or being-in-itself (*l'être-en-soi*) and conscious being or being-for-itself (*l'être-pour-soi*).[4] Being *in*-itself is concrete thereby lacking the ability to change, and is unaware of itself. Being *for*-itself is aware of its own consciousness and is therefore incomplete. "[B]eing in-itself *is* what it is ... [being for-itself] *has to be* what it is."[5] For Sartre, one's undetermined nature defines a person. She is forced to create herself from nothingness.

In a section of *Being and Nothingness* entitled "The Look," Sartre explores the ways an individual being for-itself relates to another person. He explains that "the modalities of the Other's presence to me is *object-ness*."[6] One apprehends another person as both an object and at the same time as a person, a person-as-object. Sartre argues that a person becomes aware of herself only when she is confronted with the gaze ("being-seen-by-another"[7]) of another person. Not until one is aware of being watched does she become aware of her own presence. The gaze of the other is objectifying in the sense that when one gazes at a person, for example, checking out a library book, she sees that person as simply (objectively) a patron of the library. In the reciprocation of a gaze, a sense of community arises between Us-objects.[8]

When one perceives herself to be an object of another person's gaze, she objectifies herself in the same way she is being objectified by the other. This objectification robs people of their inherent freedom and deprives a person as an existence being for-itself. Instead, one falsely self-identifies as a being in-itself. People as being for-itself have an undetermined nature; freedom allows for the possibility of change. Without freedom to change, being for-itself cannot exist. "To be free is to-be-free-to-do, and it is to-be-free-in-the-world."[9] For Sartre, the gaze is the locus of the relation between a person and that which surrounds her.

Michel Foucault is probably best known for his inquiries into the nature of power and the manners in which power functions, particularly in social institutions. Foucault examines *le regard* in his work *The Birth of the Clinic: An Archeology of Medical Perception* first published in 1963. Alan Sheridan, translator of Foucault's work, recognizes that many French terms, including *le regard* have no normal equivalent in English.[10] While translated as gaze, the term *regard* can mean look, observe, glimpse—none of which contain the abstract connotations in the French word *regard*. As Foucault used the term, he implied that the object of knowledge and the knower are constructed. Early medical practitioners greatly depended on the visibility of a patient's symptoms. Foucault explained that the gaze creates a mind-body dualism that separates the patient's body from her person (identity).

In the section of *The Birth of the Clinic* titled "Seeing and Knowing," Foucault extended his discussion of the medical or examining gaze, which separates a person's body from her identity (personhood). The gaze is a means for effectively disembodying a person. The person becomes a medical *case*, an object that is examined within a particular branch of knowledge (power). His analyses of the body are intermixed with power interests; a person potentially becomes a target for manipulation by others. In this way, the gaze becomes a tool of power, a means by which to dominate another person. By objectifying a vulnerable patient through the gaze, a physician can do violence to the patient. The individual becomes an object for scientific investigation, subjected to various procedures.

The work of Sartre and Foucault chronologically preceded the writing of French psychoanalyst and psychiatrist Jacques Lacan. However, Lacan's 1973 work *Four Fundamental Concepts of Psycho-analysis* brought the term *gaze* to public attention. In the second section of that work "Of the Gaze as *Objet Petit a*," Lacan discussed transference, one of the four fundamental concepts of psychoanalysis addressed in the work.

For Lacan, the body is both subject and object. As such, one sees and is seen; one observes and may be observed. A gaze places the person (subject) under observation, which results in the person experiencing oneself as an object that is seen by another person. This viewing alienates people from themselves, causing the subject to identify with self as an object. Lacan noted that desire disorganizes one's field of perception; the gaze coordinates one's desire. In being reduced to the object of another person's desire, a person's full subjectivity is denied and she is alienated from herself. The gaze is not just visible (a function of the eye) but is *omnivoyeur*—"I see from a certain point, but I am being seen from everywhere."[11]

An anxious state potentially arises with an awareness that one is being viewed by others. Lacan argued that a person loses a degree of autonomy when she realizes that she is a visible object. This corresponds to the mirror stage in Lacan's theory, in which a child encounters a mirror and realizes that she has an external appearance. Extending beyond a mirror, one's awareness of any object may induce an awareness of being an object. At first one has a sense that she is in control of her gaze. When she realizes that another person can look back at her, she is reminded of her own incompleteness (a gaze "reflects our own nothingness"[12]). In the gaze a split occurs in the subject during the relational encounter.[13]

The writings of Sartre, Foucault, and Lacan provide information on gaze, which Casey differentiates from glance.[14] David Kleinberg-Levin offers a brief synopsis of differences between gaze and glance: "Whereas the gaze has been taken to represent the epistemic paradigm of knowledge and truth, the glance has been either taken for granted, included without any specific recognition in perceptual theories, or regarded as too insignificant to serve experience in any significant way."[15] Casey shows how a glance figures in one's orientation within the life-world.

Casey, a Distinguished Professor in the Department of Philosophy at Stony Brook University in New York, describes himself as "a phenomenologist with special interests in aesthetics who has been influenced by psychoanalysis and poststructuralism."[16] He has been credited with differentiating archetypal psychology from other psychological theories; he explains that an image is a way of seeing rather than as something seen.[17] Casey's book *The World at a Glance* is the first extensive philosophical investigation of glance. The work is divided into four parts: Approximating to the Glance, Glancing Earlier and Farther Afield, Getting Inside the Glance, and Praxis of the Glance.

In comparing gaze and glance, Casey asserts that the glance encourages thought that attends to becoming instead of being, transience instead of constant presence, brevity instead of permanence, and particularity instead of syntheses. He writes, "If the gaze promotes contemplation and passive receptivity, the glance is a force of subversion, sudden, spontaneous, unpredictable, unruly: 'the glance is the force of becoming in the field of vision.'"[18] The next section examines Casey's work on glance in greater detail.

GLANCE

The German term *Erfahrung* is often translated into English as *experience*. Attentiveness is integral to experience. Edmund Husserl noted, "All genuine activity is carried out in the scope of attentiveness."[19] William James wrote, "My experience is what I agree to attend to."[20] When one glances, she attends to something. Casey asserts that one may engage in visual as well as mental glancing.

Glancing is one of the fundamental ways in which attending occurs; according to Casey the two are "coterminous acts."[21] Glancing is a mode of attending—and attending often proceeds by glances. One should not make the mistake of thinking that glancing is a quick superficial action and that attending is slow and deliberate. Attending is often interspersed with momentary glances. Those momentary glances thicken attending. Casey asserts that there is a thickness to a glance that is more insightful and telling than has been previously recognized.[22]

In his understanding of a glance, Casey identified three modalities of visual attention: central attending, attending-away, and identifying in attending.[23] Central attending is visually focusing on something, wherein one's eye maintains a continuous steady regard. Attending-away maintains one's eye focus but there is an attentional shift, wherein one looks away without actually looking away. When identifying in attending, in attending, one looks away from the first content of attention and toward something else. The act is cognitive in nature, one shifts from detecting a particular noise to identifying that the noise is generated by a barking dog.[24] While a glance "can figure in" any of these moments of visual attention, a glance is not necessarily present in any of the three moments.[25] For Casey, an attentional shift precedes one's glancing at the something of interest.

An attention shift accompanies a person's glancing at a specific location of interest. Attention forges its own path, and the trajectory of that path is often not predictable. There is an element of freedom in attentional consciousness. But however free it may be, attention is elicited by items of potential interest in the visual field. The effort a person extends to pay attention is work that strives to keep one's attentional focus as open as possible. "What is held open is not just the future course of one's attentive experience but the material to which attention is paid: e.g., states of mind, unconscious fantasies, archetypes, felt bodily senses."[26] Heidegger refers to this as "the openness of this open": "truth can only be what it is (...) when and as long as it establishes itself in its open."[27] Openness in attending may bring-forth truth in the act of glancing.

Casey recognizes that one may attend to experience in visual glancing and mental glancing. He identifies two forms of visual glancing: glancing around and concerted glancing. Casey draws from Edmund Husserl's discussion of the polythetic character of *Blick*, its capacity to attend to several things at once,[28] to explain what he means by glancing around. When one glances around, she notices what is going on, but not in a concerted or focused way. Her attention is not directed to any particular thing in her environment and she is not scanning with any intent or in a directed way. When glancing around, one's attention is more or less equally distributed toward the setting in which she finds herself.[29] Visual attention to experience is primary.

In contrast to glancing around, Casey discusses concerted glancing. In *concerted glancing* one glances intently within her field of mental activity. A person singles out certain items in her visual field and draws them into her "active mind."[30] The mind illuminates the thing either for its own sake or in comparison to something else in the field. In concerted glancing, "the visual field is no longer bifurcated into foreground (what one is focusing on) area and background (either perceptual or mental) but more adequately characterized as heterogeneous."[31] Concerted glancing is still primarily visual but may shift into remembering, thinking, or supposing.[32]

Concerted glancing opens the possibility for mental glancing, another way of attending to the life-world. While visual glancing is the optical act of observing things situated in one's external environment, mental glancing can occur entirely inside oneself ("my mind"[33]). Drawing from Husserl, Casey considers "the mental look" (*die geistige Blick*).[34] "Within the twilight world of the mind (...) the only light is that cast by the mental glance. The rays are no longer exclusively or literally, visual in character; part of their polythetic character is their polyaesthetic enactment: the real possibility that they can be realized in several sensory modalities."[35] In mental glancing, various sensory modalities can glance including smell, touch, taste, and hearing.

The glance takes on fluidly crazy-quilt spontaneity. Glancing allows one to take in matters of interest while also allowing subtleties and wholistic aspects to come into focus for the person. Attention prompts one to glance (and a glance prompts one's attention) while drawing upon the multiplicities that are present in one's mind. Yet, Casey explains that the diverse multiplicities do not necessarily result in a feeling of confusion because a person is in a situation of complex consciousness. Casey notes that interpretive complexity may emerge due to several factors including elusiveness/evanescence, braidedness, edgelessness, and self-illumination. While prompting complexity, each factor is also important in reducing potential anxiety. He identifies a form of glancing that regards and corresponds to each of these four factors.[36]

First, objects of inner attention are *elusive* (holding a "phantom-like character") and exhibit *evanescence*, having a tendency to disappear almost as soon as they appear. Casey offers erotic fantasies or traumatic memories as examples of elusiveness/evanescence. He writes, "we have little choice but to attend to them since they dominate the psychic space altogether."[37] This corresponds to *glancing-after*. "To glance-after is to *follow* what eludes the seizure of any straightforward understanding. Glancing-after is a gentle looking that fits into the path of what eludes us. For example, the thoughts that follow my eyes as they trace the outline of fast-moving clouds."[38] Attentional glancing-after is characterized by following after what has appeared in one's mind, we glance-after what we have experienced.

Second, objects in a person's inner attention are *braided*. In one's busy life she is often directed outside herself in taking up daily tasks. In this busy-ness one's mental life insinuates itself in a manner that is continuous and unpredictable. A random thought or hope or memory may intervene at any time. A person's ordinary perception is "deeply intertwined (braided) with the mind's coming and going in the midst of everyday engagements: such braidedness at once alleviates and complicates our experience in the life-world."[39] The factor of braidedness is associated with *glancing-at*. We glance-at what spontaneously comes to our awareness. The directed awareness of glancing-at discerns connections between emergent phenomena and becomes interbraided with them in one's understanding.[40]

Third, the *edgeless* quality of the glance may diminish an overwhelming sense of complexity. "The inward domain of the mind constitutes a world without edges: everything presented is just that thing (or that event, or that object) not hidden by some other thing (or event, or object, etc.)."[41] Objects of attention move into and through the mental and physical world. For example, my glancing includes the computer screen, a deer walking by the window, Lyme disease in the deer population, a green chair on the deck, the oldness yet functionality of that chair, the greenness of the recliner in which I am sitting, and so forth. "We have no choice but to take the inner world *on its own terms*."[42] This corresponds to *glancing-through* the edgeless attentional world. Casey notes that "[w]hen edges vanish, an important source of resistance disappears, leaving me free to glance through what I think, imagine, or remember at my own pace and as I wish (…). [T]he inward domain of the mind constitutes a world without edges."[43] Glancing-through allows one to access the edgeless quality of attention that traverses external and internal glancing.

Fourth, the attentional world in a mental glance is *self-illuminated*. A mental glance has a special luminescence. The illumination is neither visual nor is it the world's light entering from outside oneself. "This is a third form of light, one that begins and ends within the mind."[44] The illumination is attendant to and present in mental attention itself. This self-illumination is associated with a form of glancing Casey calls *glancing-into*. When one glances-into, she considers the contents of her mind by examining what is already present there, "fully revealed in an edgeless self-lit realm." When attending to one's experience one makes associations to "that which is arrayed on the surface of my own mind, set forth in the light of my own mentation."[45] Glancing-into is a means for accessing the self-illuminated world of one's mind.

Glancing-after, glancing-at, glancing-through, and glancing-into provide a means for managing the complexities that arise in one's lived-experience. Each of these four features emerge in the inner attentional world that psychotherapists call *mind*. Casey adds two additional ways in which a person enacts a glance to manage complexities: glancing-in-depth and glancing-along. Both visual and mental glancing are joined in these two forms of glance.

When one glances-in-depth, she glances at surfaces, but interprets them as surfaces-in-depth. One does not strive to see their other side, but "to linger in their ambience—to sense what is happening on the surface itself. This sense is felt in opening from vision into other sensory modalities such as touch or smell—or using a different system, such as words."[46] In glancing-in-depth "it is as if we have finally come to terms with our own state of mind by rejoining it through body (…). We glance into the depth to experience more than we can experience in mind alone."[47] In this sense, one opens from vision to other sensory modalities to gain greater understanding.

Glancing-along is also introduced as a form of glance. Casey draws on the ideas of *going along* (e.g., with what someone suggests, with a hypothetical idea, with what is appropriate in a given situation) and *alongside* (to align oneself with something or beside something) to illustrate this type of glance. When someone pays close attention to something, she draws herself near to it. This can occur by glancing along the surface to navigate the object, event, idea, or so forth by her mental look.[48]

In so doing one recognizes an object as it is perceived rather than framing it within a predetermined understanding of the item.

Casey acknowledges that glancing in everyday life is not as neat and tidy as his typology would suggest. He addresses the interpenetration of gaze and glance, offering an example of Buddhist meditation (a "disposition of mind"[49]). He acknowledges that the hegemonic gaze and the freedom of glance collaborate in "moments of creative combination which, however counterintuitive they may appear to be."[50] Gaze and glance are coterminous with one another.

This brief consideration of attending in Casey's works on glance raises some questions from a communicological perspective. His approach seems to draw more heavily from his psychoanalytic influences than from phenomenology and does not address how communication plays in glancing. A semiotic phenomenological orientation opens the fullness available in one's freedom as she is communicatively engaged in the lived-world.

COMMUNICOLOGY

Richard L. Lanigan, working within the context of a philosophy of the human (or moral) sciences, has articulated a theory and methodology of semiotic phenomenology. The semiotic phenomenological approach he advances, communicology, is a science of human discourse in all of its forms, including human gesture and speech.[51] Communicologists "interrogate the reversible, reciprocal, and reflexive nature of the 'expressive and perceptive body' (...) [that is] the essential point of mediation between us and the cultural signs and codes of disorder under which we inescapably live."[52] One's corporeal body provides an axis for orienting a person in her life-world.

In communicology there are several complex interpenetrating communicative networks, including an intrapersonal (self) domain, interpersonal (self-other) domain, social (group-organizational) domain, and cultural (intergroup) domain. Each "foregrounds aspects of how we come to consciousness as embodied subjectivities, braiding in multiple possibilities of interpretive agency."[53] These networks are not distinct from one another in everyday life.

Martin Heidegger asserts that a person is always-already fundamentally connected with her lived-world.[54] One's experiences are interpreted perceptions of the lived-body.[55] Messages are intersubjectively created in a communicological approach to an event of intrapersonal communication. In communicology "neither 'messages' nor 'mind' are things."[56] An experience of intrapersonal communication is about how a person semiotically relates to her world. Given that the subject of this investigation is *glance*, this section emphasizes the perceptual component of communicology.

One's body, her flesh, is the fundamental substantive agent for any and all of her perceptions (visual, tactile, auditory, taste, olfactory). Following Merleau-Ponty, "inside and outside are inseparable."[57] The experience of communication participates in the ecstasy (*ek-stasis*) of discovery. A moment of discovery can take on a life of its own: "it is that vital instant in which the body becomes flesh."[58] Rather than feeling surprise as a reaction to something external to oneself observed in glancing, one communicatively *experiences* fresh associations.

In contact with one's lived-world, conjecture becomes a fundamental aspect of the communicative moment. Macke suggests the metaphor of a "strange situation" as significant to the phenomenology of intrapersonal communication.[59] Perceptual contact is essential to experience; to make sense of a strange situation "we have to be able to take note of objects that gain illumination in our fields of perception."[60] Communication has a meaning for someone insofar as she experiences a meaning. A strange situation tests a person's attachment to what she has determined holds consequential meaning in her life. My perception and interpreted meaning of that perception in any given moment "is my body's articulation of my will."[61] The poiētic entailments of one's will are expressed in language.

Language is an analogue system in which semantics (*capta*), syntactics (*data*), and pragmatics (*acta*) synergistically relate to each other as parts (*a code*) of communication. A communicological examination follows Merleau-Ponty's philosophic analysis of perception, working within and between themes of phenomenological description, phenomenological reduction, and phenomenological interpretation. The adjective *phenomenological* draws attention to the communication as occurring in conscious experience (*capta*).[62] As conscious beings, people are engaged in the communicative activity of perception and expression.

In phenomenological analysis Merleau-Ponty stresses "the importance of semiotics in the description of phenomena, the importance of structural analysis in defining (reducing) phenomena, and the importance of hermeneutic principles for the interpretation of phenomena."[63] He emphasizes "the reversible, reflexive, and reflective relations between perception and expression."[64] Rather than distinguishing between verbal and nonverbal systems of communication, communicologists consider only a semiotic system of meaning.[65] A communicological perspective understands glance not primarily as a psychological experience, but rather as a communicative event.

CONSIDERING AN EVENT OF GLANCING

Let us return to the event provided in the opening to this essay: I was driving through a small town in western Pennsylvania. The speed limit was 30 miles an hour. I was also in a school zone, but school was out for the summer. I was focusing on the road, the speed limit sign, my speedometer reading, and traffic.

Phenomenological Description names "the reversible relationship between an *organism* (person) and its *environment* (lived-world), both of which exist in a mutual context."[66] A person and her lived-world are related in language. She experiences the content of communication as a perception of (or consciousness of) what is expressed by herself or another person. "Phenomena become meaningful when experienced-as-lived, experienced-as-signs, rather than as conceived, as sensed symbols."[67] Meaning functions in one's everyday life to orient a person in her life-world.

In the event of glancing, I found my attention drawn out the car window toward the left. I noticed a person walking on the sidewalk next to the school. I saw a gray-haired woman wearing a smart blue-and-white vertically striped shirt-dress with a red belt and a navy sweater. She was pushing a black walker/cart. She was alone. I saw the school behind her, and even though I was looking at the woman, I was also aware of the large tan brick wall.

Given that phenomenological description, reduction, and interpretation are synergistic, each appears within the other areas. Description thematizes an Interpretation of the Reduction of the Description of the sign. In my example, I am drawn to focus on the sign that is a wholistic figure of the woman. Another person may be drawn to consider the construction of the building or the cart with a basket attached to it. The second phase of analysis emphasizes Reduction.

In Phenomenological Reduction, one specifies the structure of a phenomenon ("the phenomenological reduction of the essential *Gestalt*"[68]). An interpreter goes "beyond the superficial designation of essential structural relationships to the existential structure of meaning."[69] One must consciously bracket one's experience (phenomenological *epoche*) to do so. This allows one to analyze the experience absent (as much as possible) the influence of one's personal lived-experience. "In particular, investigators should suspend their analytic, philosophic, sensual, and other prejudices or predispositions as to the nature of perception or the phenomena to be perceived."[70] One is then able to reduce the essential structures of phenomena to existential phenomena.

In the event of glancing, I discerned certain features. The woman was smartly dressed, perhaps doing errands, and appeared old enough to be retired. My apperception was of a woman who embodied a certain generic image: "healthy older person," "attractive," "walking with purpose." Simultaneously I saw her singularity against stereotypes: she did not appear "elderly," she had no "difficulty moving," and did not seem "tired."

The three themes of Description, Reduction, and Interpretation work together, appearing in one another. Reduction abstracts the Interpretation of the Reduction of the Description of the Signifier. In my example, the wholistic figure of the woman signifies particular qualities to me. She is healthy, attractive, and purposeful. The third stage of analysis emphasizes Interpretation.

In Phenomenological Interpretation one is "concerned with pure intentionality devoid of consciousness and absent from the structural phenomena that are hidebound to the preconscious as sign-to-signification."[71] Interpretation progresses beyond bracketed experience to arrive at thetic intentionality or existential meaning, the preconscious perception of self prior to the perception of stimuli that is taken as meaningful. "Existential meaning is the knowledge base from which 'I' realize that 'I am able to' or 'I can' perceive and express."[72] In Interpretation, one considers the meaning or value contained in the perceptual experience of the glance.

In the example, the woman was walking alone in the late morning on a sunny summer day. I began to think about (not just imagine) where she was going—moving from the downtown area to a residential area, perhaps going home after getting some groceries from the stores I just passed. I took a side-wise glance imagining myself in her place. She moved herself with a healthy ease and had a cheerful look about her. I shifted in my seat and an invisible smile overcame me. A warm, pleasant sensation rose through my chest. I felt my posture shift to emulate her. (She reminded me of Mrs. Thacker: poised, calm, gentle strength.) My neck stretched to elongate. A feeling of confidence increased in me. My being was refreshed. I returned my eyes to the road and did not glance back. Now outside my visual range, she continues to inspire a sense of goodness. I recall her posture, her appearance, and her gait.

Description, Reduction, and Interpretation are interwoven. Interpretation explicates the Interpretation of the Reduction of the Description of the Signified. In my example, the woman's presence inspired me to strive to be like her, both in the immediate present and portending me into a similar future. Another person may not even notice, or much less be affected by the woman with a cart, but her presence was/is significant to me. This strange situation is a reminder that life is an ongoing creation in which I have some element of control.

In his writing, Merleau-Ponty asserted "the more energetic our intention to see the things themselves, the more the appearances by which they are expressed and the words by which we express them will be interposed between the things and us."[73] His work considered the nature of Being "by examining the lived-encounters of perceptive and expressive *signs* that are experienced as communication."[74] This example offers an analysis of glance with particular attention to the perceptual component of communicology, revealing the manner in which signs shape one's world.

CONCLUSION

This essay considered how communication occurs in a glance. While *gaze* has been considered within the works of Sartre, Foucault, and Lacan, glance has been examined less frequently in scholarly investigations. Casey recognizes glancing as a mode of attending to one's experience; a person attends to what is of interest to her. He outlines three modalities of visual attention (central attending, attending-away, and identifying in attending) and discusses both visual (external) glancing and mental (internal) glancing as they work separately and together in one's experience. He asserts that although complexities may arise in glancing, one may not necessarily become disconcerted. The qualities of elusiveness/evanescence, braidedness, edgelessness, and self-illumination of inner attention alleviate potential anxiety.

A communicological perspective understands glance as interwoven with expressivity. Drawing upon Lanigan's writings on communicology, an interrogation of glance is offered. The approach wholistically considers how one semiotically relates to her world. In a communicological analysis, themes of phenomenological description, reduction, and interpretation are interwoven to discern the meaning of a perceived sign. The meaning of a sign becomes part of one's interpretive understanding and influences how one responds to other signs within the semiotic system.

An event of glancing at a woman walking exemplified the difference between a communicological approach to glance as distinct from other writings on gaze and glance. Hegemonic objectifications, present in understandings of gaze, are not present. Communicology does not speak of messages or mind, or inside and outside. Further, no bifurcation of visual and mental glancing exists. Illumination occurs in one's field of perception, rather than in mental glancing. Visual and mental glancing are united in one's communicative orientation in one's lived-world. A person's bodily orientation shapes perception as she attends to various features in the phenomenal field. One becomes aware of fresh connections to the world and considers how one's life may be enriched by those associations. These aspects of glance are opened differently depending on the approach one takes toward *glancing*.

Glance plays a significant role in one's everyday life. Each event of glancing—whether toward a woman walking, a person reading, or a gardener readying the soil for winter after a dry autumn—phenomenologically orients a person in her life-world. One's being-in-the-world *is* her communicative life.

NOTES

1. Jean-Paul Sartre, *Being and Nothingness: An Essay in Phenomenological Ontology*, trans. Hazel E. Barnes (New York: Washington Square Press, 1992).

2. Michel Foucault, *The Birth of the Clinic: An Archaeology of Medical Perception*, trans. Alan M. Sheridan (New York: Routledge, 1989); *The Order of Things: An Archaeology of the Human Sciences*, trans. Alan Sheridan (New York: Vintage, 1973).
3. Jacques Lacan, *Four Fundamental Concepts of Psychoanalysis*, ed. Jacques-Alain Miller, trans. Alan Sheridan (New York: W. W. Norton, 1998).
4. Sartre, *Being and Nothingness*, 25.
5. Sartre, *Being and Nothingness*, 28.
6. Sartre, *Being and Nothingness*, 253.
7. Sartre, *Being and Nothingness*, 257.
8. Hazel E. Barnes, translator's introduction to *Being and Nothingness: An Essay in Phenomenological Ontology*, by Jean-Paul Sartre (New York: Washington Square Press, 1992), xxxi. See also Sartre, *Being and Nothingness*, 512 ff.
9. Sartre, *Being and Nothingness*, 650.
10. Alan Sheridan, translator's note to *The Birth of the Clinic: An Archaeology of Medical Perception*, by Michel Foucault (New York: Routledge, 1989), vii.
11. Roberto Harari, *Lacan's Four Fundamental Concepts of Psychoanalysis: An Introduction*, trans. Judith Filc (New York: Other Press), 110.
12. Lacan, *Four Fundamental Concepts*, 92.
13. Lacan, *Four Fundamental Concepts*, 69.
14. Edward S. Casey, *The World at a Glance* (Bloomington: Indiana University Press, 2007); "The World at a Glance," in *Chiasms: Merleau-Ponty's Notion of Flesh*, ed. Fred Evans and Leonard Lawlor (Albany: SUNY Press, 1999), 147–164; "Attending and Glancing," *Continental Philosophy Review* 37 (2004): 83–126; "The Ethics of the Glance," in *Calvin O. Schrag and the Task of Philosophy after Postmodernity*, ed. Martin Beck Matuštík and William L. McBride (Evanston, IL: Northwestern University Press, 2002), 91–115.
15. David Kleinberg-Levin, review of *The World at a Glance*, by Edward S. Casey, *Hyperion: On the Future of Aesthetics* 4 (2009): 135.
16. Casey, "Ethics of the Glance," 91.
17. Casey, Edward S. "Toward an Archetypal Imagination," *Spring: An Annual of Archetypal Psychology and Jungian Thought* (1974): 1–32; James Hillman, *Archetypal Psychology: A Brief Account* (Dallas, TX: Spring Publications, 1985).
18. Casey, *World at a Glance*, 163.
19. Edmund Husserl, *Analyses Concerning Passive and Active Synthesis: Lectures on Transcendental Logic* (Dordrecht: Springer Science+Business Media, 2001), 276.
20. William James, *The Principles of Psychology*, vol. 1 (New York: Henry Holt and Company, 1890), 402.
21. Casey, "Attending and Glancing," 84; *World at a Glance*, 299–335.
22. Casey, "Attending and Glancing," 84.
23. Casey, *World at a Glance*, 305–306.
24. Casey, "Attending and Glancing," 88.
25. Casey, "Attending and Glancing," 89.
26. Casey, "Attending and Glancing," 104–105.
27. Martin Heidegger, *Off the Beaten Track*, ed. and trans. Julian Young and Kenneth Haynes (New York: Cambridge University Press, 2002), 36.

28. Edmund Husserl, *Ideas Pertaining to a Pure Phenomenology and to a Phenomenological Philosophy. First Book: General Introduction to a Pure Phenomenology*, trans. F. Kersten (Boston, MA: Martinus Nijhoff Publishers, 1983), quoted in Casey, *World at a Glance*, 313.
29. Casey, "Attending and Glancing," 93; *World at a Glance*, 299–335.
30. Casey, "Attending and Glancing," 94.
31. Casey, "Attending and Glancing," 94.
32. Casey, "Attending and Glancing."
33. Casey, "Attending and Glancing," 93.
34. Casey, "Attending and Glancing," 92; *World at a Glance*, 313.
35. Casey, "Attending and Glancing," 94–95.
36. Casey, "Attending and Glancing," 314–321.
37. Casey, "Attending and Glancing," 95.
38. Casey, "Attending and Glancing," 97.
39. Casey, "Attending and Glancing," 96.
40. Casey, "Attending and Glancing," 97–98.
41. Casey, "Attending and Glancing," 96.
42. Casey, "Attending and Glancing."
43. Casey, "Attending and Glancing," 98.
44. Casey, "Attending and Glancing," 97.
45. Casey, "Attending and Glancing," 98.
46. Casey, "Attending and Glancing," 105.
47. Casey, "Attending and Glancing."
48. Casey, "Attending and Glancing," 106.
49. Casey, "Attending and Glancing," 102.
50. Casey, "Attending and Glancing."
51. Richard L. Lanigan, *The Human Science of Communicology: A Phenomenology of Discourse in Foucault and Merleau-Ponty* (Pittsburgh, PA: Duquesne University Press, 1992); *Speaking and Semiology: Maurice Merleau-Ponty's Phenomenological Theory of Existential Communication* (New York: Mouton de Gruyter, 1991); *Phenomenology of Communication: Merleau Ponty's Thematics in Communicology and Semiology* (Pittsburgh, PA: Duquesne University Press, 1988).
52. Isaac E. Catt and Deborah Eicher-Catt, "Communicology: A Reflexive Human Science," in *Communicology: The New Science of Embodied Discourse*, ed. Deborah Eicher-Catt and Isaac E. Catt (Madison, NJ: Fairleigh Dickinson University Press, 2010), 17.
53. Frank J. Macke, "Intrapersonal Communicology: Reflection, Reflexivity, and Relational Consciousness in Embodied Subjectivity," in *Communicology: The New Science of Embodied Discourse*, ed. Deborah Eicher-Catt and Isaac E. Catt (Madison, NJ: Fairleigh Dickinson University Press, 2010), 37.
54. Peg Birmingham, "Heidegger and Arendt: The Birth of Political Action and Speech," in *Heidegger and Practical Philosophy*, ed. François Raffoul and David Pettigrew (Albany: SUNY Press, 2002), 197.
55. Maurice Merleau-Ponty, *Phenomenology of Perception*, trans. Colin Smith (New York: Routledge and Kegan Paul, 1962), 169.
56. Macke, "Intrapersonal Communicology," 35.
57. Merleau-Ponty, *Phenomenology of Perception*, 407.
58. Macke, "Intrapersonal Communicology," 45.
59. Macke, "Intrapersonal Communicology," 48–51.

60. Macke, "Intrapersonal Communicology," 51.
61. Maurice Merleau-Ponty, *The Visible and the Invisible*, ed. Claude Lefort, trans. Alphonso Lingis (Evanston, IL: Northwestern University Press, 1968), 225, quoted in Macke, "Intrapersonal Communicology," 52.
62. Lanigan, *Phenomenology of Communication*, 11. A phenomenological approach to Description, Reduction, and Interpretation is designated in text with capital letters on the term.
63. Richard L. Lanigan, "Communicology: The French Tradition in Human Science," in *Perspectives on Philosophy of Communication*, ed. Pat Arneson (West Lafayette, IN: Purdue University Press, 2007), 178.
64. Lanigan, *Phenomenology of Communication*, 15.
65. Lanigan, *Phenomenology of Communication*.
66. Lanigan, *Phenomenology of Communication*, 12.
67. Lanigan, *Phenomenology of Communication*, 47.
68. Lanigan, *Phenomenology of Communication*.
69. Lanigan, *Phenomenology of Communication*, 48.
70. Lanigan, *Phenomenology of Communication*.
71. Lanigan, *Phenomenology of Communication*, 49.
72. Lanigan, *Phenomenology of Communication*.
73. Maurice Merleau-Ponty, *The Structure of Behavior* (Boston, MA: Beacon Press, 1963), 20, quoted in Lanigan, *Phenomenology of Communication*, 45.
74. Merleau-Ponty, *Structure of Behavior*.

BIBLIOGRAPHY

Barnes, Hazel E. Translator's introduction to *Being and Nothingness: An Essay in Phenomenological Ontology*, by Jean-Paul Sartre, viii–xliv. New York: Washington Square Press, 1992.

Birmingham, Peg. "Heidegger and Arendt: The Birth of Political Action and Speech." In *Heidegger and Practical Philosophy*, edited by François Raffoul and David Pettigrew, 191-202. Albany: SUNY Press, 2002.

Casey, Edward S. "Attending and Glancing." *Continental Philosophy Review* 37 (2004): 83–126.

Casey, Edward S. "The Ethics of the Glance." In *Calvin O. Schrag and the Task of Philosophy after Postmodernity*, edited by Martin Beck Matuštík and William L. McBride, 91–115. Evanston, IL: Northwestern University Press, 2002.

Casey, Edward S. "Toward an Archetypal Imagination." *Spring: An Annual of Archetypal Psychology and Jungian Thought* 28 (1974): 1–32.

Casey, Edward S. "The World at a Glance." In *Chiasms: Merleau-Ponty's Notion of Flesh*, edited by Fred Evans and Leonard Lawlor, 147–164. Albany: SUNY Press, 1999.

Casey, Edward S. *The World at a Glance*. Bloomington: Indiana University Press, 2007.

Catt, Isaac E., and Deborah Eicher-Catt. "Communicology: A Reflexive Human Science." In *Communicology: The New Science of Embodied Discourse*, edited by Deborah Eicher-Catt and Isaac E. Catt, 15–29. Madison, NJ: Fairleigh Dickinson University Press, 2010.

Foucault, Michel. *The Birth of the Clinic: An Archaeology of Medical Perception*. Translated by Alan M. Sheridan. New York: Routledge, 1989.

Foucault, Michel. *The Order of Things: An Archaeology of the Human Sciences*. Translated by Alan M. Sheridan. New York: Vintage, 1973.

Harari, Roberto. *Lacan's Four Fundamental Concepts of Psychoanalysis: An Introduction*. Translated by Judith Filc. New York: Other Press, 2004.
Heidegger, Martin. *Off the Beaten Track*. Translated and edited by Julian Young and Kenneth Haynes. New York: Cambridge University Press, 2002.
Hillman, James. *Archetypal Psychology: A Brief Account*. Dallas, TX: Spring Publications, 1985.
Husserl, Edmund. *Analyses Concerning Passive and Active Synthesis: Lectures on Transcendental Logic*. Dordrecht: Springer Science+Business Media, 2001.
Husserl, Edmund. *Ideas Pertaining to a Pure Phenomenology and to a Phenomenological Philosophy. First Book: General Introduction to a Pure Phenomenology*. Translated by F. Kersten. Boston, MA: Martinus Nijhoff Publishers, 1983.
James, William. *The Principles of Psychology*. Vol. 1. New York: Henry Holt and Company, 1890.
Kleinberg-Levin, David. "Review of *The World at a Glance*, by Edward S. Casey". *Hyperion: On the Future of Aesthetics* 4 (2009): 132–140.
Lacan, Jacques. *Four Fundamental Concepts of Psychoanalysis*. Edited by Jacques-Alain Miller. Translated by Alan Sheridan. New York: W. W. Norton, 1998.
Lanigan, Richard L. "Communicology: The French Tradition in Human Science." In *Perspectives on Philosophy of Communication*, edited by Pat Arneson, 168–184. West Lafayette, IN: Purdue University Press, 2007.
Lanigan, Richard L. *The Human Science of Communicology: A Phenomenology of Discourse in Foucault and Merleau-Ponty*. Pittsburgh, PA: Duquesne University Press, 1992.
Lanigan, Richard L. *Phenomenology of Communication: Merleau Ponty's Thematics in Communicology and Semiology*. Pittsburgh, PA: Duquesne University Press, 1988.
Lanigan, Richard L. *Speaking and Semiology: Maurice Merleau-Ponty's Phenomenological Theory of Existential Communication*. New York: Mouton de Gruyter, 1991.
Macke, Frank J. "Intrapersonal Communicology: Reflection, Reflexivity, and Relational Consciousness in Embodied Subjectivity." In *Communicology: The New Science of Embodied Discourse*, edited by Deborah Eicher-Catt and Isaac E. Catt, 33–62. Madison, NJ: Fairleigh Dickinson University Press, 2010.
Merleau-Ponty, Maurice. *Phenomenology of Perception*. Translated by Colin Smith. New York: Routledge and Kegan Paul, 1962.
Merleau-Ponty, Maurice. *The Structure of Behavior*. Boston, MA: Beacon Press, 1963.
Merleau-Ponty, Maurice. *The Visible and the Invisible*. Edited by Claude Lefort. Translated by Alphonso Lingis. Evanston, IL: Northwestern University Press, 1968.
Sartre, Jean-Paul. *Being and Nothingness: An Essay in Phenomenological Ontology*. Translated by Hazel E. Barnes. New York: Washington Square Press, 1992.
Sheridan, Alan. Translator's Note to *The Birth of the Clinic: An Archaeology of Medical Perception*, by Michel Foucault, vii. New York: Routledge, 1989.

CHAPTER FIFTEEN

Laban and Lanigan

Shall We Dance?

MAUREEN CONNOLLY AND TOM D. CRAIG

In *The Structure of Behavior*, Maurice Merleau-Ponty (1963) attacked the atomistic and associational elements of prevailing learning theories. By introducing the notion of *gestalt*, or form; Merleau-Ponty argued that the whole of a system is not decomposable to a sum of isolated parts, but rather is defined by total processes in which the parts may be indiscernible from each other and where change in one part of the system affects *both* the system as a whole *and* all other parts. Rather than looking for the individual or physical event, the situation as a whole must be considered because physical events are always integrated into larger, structural processes. Sadly, contemporary learners experiencing learning frequently experience it in irrelevant, meaningless, disembodied and coercive (or, worse, abusive) fashion—regardless of the holistic character of its psychomotor, cognitive or affective domains. Yet, according to Merleau-Ponty's prescient wisdom, it does not have to be this way. The "problem" of experiencing embodied coercion in educational contexts, especially when the context is attempting to subordinate particular forms of bodily expressivity to other expressive forms (such as speech and/or text and/or "appropriate" emotional responses and/or "mature" movement patterns), is that the act of learning itself becomes the site of embodied oppression, and subsequent expressive modes will be constructed by and given over from a body that has experienced its own abjection, usually with accompanying physical violence, surveillance and stigma. Thus this meaning-making body has to be accounted for, or honored—if you will—in any description of its expressivity. Acknowledging the whole lived experience of learning and meaning in our research calls for better forms of description and better forms of engagement with expressive bodies.

When Maureen began experimenting with the connections between semiotics and choreology over a decade ago, she recognized a variety of embodied convergences across phenomenology, semiotics and Laban movement theory. She realized that other expressive forms like mime and ballet, ballroom and jazz dance, while interpretively functional and animated by story and emotion, melody and rhythm; were still closely related to more literal re-presentation and not yet discerning of the deeper eidetics of expression of culture and code inscribed on and in the body, and the normative logics of language and other expressive modalities. She recognized that a *semiotic choreology* was needed to implicate the body, opening a pathway to expression of this unavoidable tension between body and world, signs and disclosures of a different kind. What such a semiotic choreology makes possible is the implication of the body of the person attempting to formulate meaning, and the tethering of that meaning-making to the body's expressive and reflexive potentialities. The body remembers.

In this paper, we will use examples of bodily expressive movement in everyday life as a site for a semiotic phenomenological elucidation blending of Rudolf Laban's movement analysis with Richard Lanigan's embedded tripartite methodology of description, reduction, and interpretation. In so doing, we hope to disclose cultural norms and inscriptions, the body as socially volatile sign, and the sign system/s that hold these together.[1] In effect, we are going to offer a semiotic choreological exploration of an embodied poetics of practice. What this means is that we will be weaving a semiotic phenomenological description (using Lanigan's tripartite approach) with a Laban movement analysis while acknowledging the necessity of both being embedded within a cultural context that also informs the bodily-expressive examples that are the focus of the analysis. For this paper we will be exploring the movement experience of "pressing", a basic effort action that combines *time, weight, space* and *flow* and that also carries and expresses cultural norms and inscriptions. We will describe and examine pressing in basic and more elaborated forms, and, hopefully, engage the reader in its embodied intricacies and complexities. First, we will provide some background on the contexts and concepts that inform this endeavour.

THEORETICAL AND METHODOLOGICAL INFLUENCES

Maureen works within a complex blending of a number of theoretical and methodological frameworks of body, expression and culture. She identifies as a semiotic phenomenologist that is heavily influenced by the theoretical work of Merleau-Ponty[2] and Lanigan[3] and the ongoing, applied semiotic phenomenological work she does with her research partner and frequent co-author, Tom Craig.[4] Maureen also acknowledges her own orientation toward ideology critique and post-colonial deliberations, as well as years of training in Laban-based Movement Education, overlaid upon three decades of training and practice within physical education and adapted physical activity with the neurological, biomechanical, and motor control frameworks therein. Tom brings his own prior training in discourse analysis and phenomenology to an ongoing exploration of the felt sense of religious experience, and the lived relations of disability and stressed embodiment. Discovering the theoretical convergences of expressive body and cultural codes in the research methodology of Communicology while working with Lanigan (as doctoral student and research assistant) in the 1990s, Tom has continued to explore the inextricable relation of discourse and practice disclosing, misdirecting, shaping, and intertwining the socially volatile body.

In its most naively articulated form, phenomenology is the study of lived experiences or meaning structures as they reveal themselves to an embodied consciousness. Phenomenologists attempt to suspend the "natural attitude" or already assumed "truths" or "givens" about the everyday world. With this bracketing technique (i.e., the placing of one's so-called "certainties" in brackets) phenomenologists try to explicate the eidetics of phenomena typically taken for granted in habitual experiences of reality. In this way, the eidetic features or layers of meaning structures might be missed because of presumption or assumption that can be perceived and clarified. A common method used within this reductive aspect of phenomenological analysis is free imaginative variations, whereby the understanding of phenomena is pushed to its extreme limits of existential possibility. This allows phenomenologists to consider features and interpretations that might be dismissed as preposterous by the constraints of more traditional approaches.

Further, since consciousness is necessarily embodied, the body understood phenomenologically can be seen in its constitution as subject/object. This serves to highlight the tension between *having* and *being* a body.[5] Merleau-Ponty's[6] groundbreaking study developed a conception of human embodiment which attempted to transcend mind-body dualism. He grounded perception in the experienced and experiencing body. The world as perceived through the body was, for Merleau-Ponty, the ground level of all knowledge, for it is through the body that people gain access to the world. Human perception of everyday reality depends upon a "lived body"[7] which is a body that simultaneously experiences and creates the human world of experience. This expresses the essential ambiguity of human embodiment as both personal and impersonal, objective and subjective, social/cultural and natural. In the process of inquiry, phenomenologists work though a recursive and embodied process of description, reduction and interpretation all the while taking into account the "*Lieb*"—animated living through the experiential body (body-for-itself) and "Körper", the objective exterior institutionalized body (the body-in-itself).[8]

Invoking the *semiotic* aspect of semiotic phenomenology means locating the lived body within the codes and signs of a given culture. The body is located at the nexus of lived experience and culture, hence constituting a portal and a site for disclosure, as well as an experience. Lanigan's[9] semiotic phenomenological analysis adds a cultural dimension to the aforementioned phenomenological process of description, reduction and interpretation. It considers the norms and inscriptions of a culture, the body as sign and the sign systems which hold these together. This analysis necessitates a semiotic and phenomenological examination of the contexts—large and small—which constitute culture and which constrain choices. Lanigan encourages a meta-cognitive strategy, a *"choice of context"*, wherein interpretive options may be chosen as opposed to presumed within pre-determined *"contexts of choice"* (where choices or interpretations are always already given within the context). This is an especially helpful framework for studying disability, pain, high-level performance, new learning, and other forms of stressed embodiment, which are typically considered within already established contexts. It is also a more culturally and contingency-sensitive approach which acknowledges the complex ways in which typical and/or atypical bodies, as "carnal property",[10] are culturally produced and productive.

Given their propensity for disclosing cultural norms and inscriptions, semiotic phenomenological approaches are politically post-colonial in their ideology critique and also resonate with infusion- and inclusion-based and cultural/social minority perspective approaches.[11] In addition, they allow for an interrogation of tokenistic and/or ableist driven efforts at integration/assimilation at all costs, approaches which are coming under critique from an increased presence of Critical Disability Studies scholars and theorists.

MOVEMENT EDUCATION

When it comes to observing movement—especially idiosyncratic habits of body—"seeing it" means more than simply looking. Laban Movement Analysis (LMA) offers a non-mechanistic, adaptable, body-friendly approach to observing human movement across contexts and ability levels. Developed by the Austro-Hungarian dancer, choreographer, and movement theorist Rudolf Laban, movement education thematic analysis has been used in performance, competition, rehabilitation, training, and workplace settings since the 1930's. The beauty of this analytic method is that it provides a framework for observation, a language for description, a notation system for preserving the movement, and a logic for therapeutic, and/or pedagogic intervention.

The framework is a deceptively simple matrix of existential themes of movement: BODY, SPACE, QUALITY, and RELATION. Within each of these thematics are features or components that allow for more detailed and individualized breakdown of the over-arching theme. For example, within a consideration of BODY, one would engage in a deeper consideration of shape, function, body part responsibilities, symmetry and asymmetry, weight transfer, balance, locomotion, and gesture, among others. A consideration of SPACE would compel examination of personal and general use of and awareness of space, directions, pathways, levels, near and far extensions, planes of movement, and so forth. If one observed a mover (over time and across context) avoiding or demonstrating distress in the low level, for example, one could, from this observation-based profile, anticipate the long term developmental, strategic, and neurological effects of this avoidance, and plan an appropriate intervention. This type of movement profiling allows a teacher, coach or therapist to observe a mover over time and across contexts using the features and components of each theme to develop a "movement fingerprint," such that not only dominant patterns become apparent, but also missing features become apparent. Here, one can plan interventions, use the dominant patterns to facilitate the interventions, and then do a follow-up profile to assess the effect of the intervention on the movement repertoire. Since movement education language is conceptual and non-pejorative, it can be used in any situation with any mover of any movement capacity. The movement profile, developed out of Laban movement education analysis, can function as a pedagogic, evaluative, pre-post comparative, training, and therapeutic tool. It complements other measurement modalities, and can be easily taught to coaches, parents, teachers, and other interested professionals.

There are resonances between this type of attuned observation and description, and Lanigan's embedded recursive methodology.[12] Indeed, the LMA described above applies the basic steps of a semiotic phenomenological analysis, that is,

1. Description (observing for/re-presenting a sense of the whole, identifying literal elements, key movements and idiosyncratic gestures, summarizing patterns and salience, and attending to detail particularity),
2. Reduction (further explaining patterns, salience, revelatory comportment/s and connections across the situated particularities), and
3. Interpretation (critically comparing the consolidated essential features to existing research and contextualizing the features within and over against the research question).

Further, this robust complementarity exemplifies the introductory paragraphs' claims about the integrative, interdependent and inseparable intersectionality of the parts and wholes of learning. Learning is an important context for this paper since the examples of pressing that we explore are necessarily embedded in learning experiences, as are habits of body of all humans immersed in their various culturally normative functional and expressive modes.

THE READER'S ENCOUNTER WITH PRESSING

Semiotic choreology is an approach Maureen developed for exploration and analysis of cultural phenomena through the expressive body. She believes it offers a means to engage with the problems embodied people experience in ongoing ways in ableist, productivist, dis-embodied cultures. Using Laban's[13] movement existentials of body, space, quality and relation, in combination with a semiotic phenomenological analysis, she can describe and (sometimes) physically enact how thematized and spontaneous movement sequences can disclose and deepen meaning with/in textual and other expressive modalities. Such poetizing need not be limited to written or spoken word, and meaning can reside in a felt sense, known and expressed carnally and made accessible for a broad range of embodiments and forms of meaning-making.

In Laban's movement analysis and pedagogy, the effort qualities of movement constitute the "how" of a movement's intentionality. Quality of movement includes a consideration of *Time* (on a spectrum of sustained to sudden, or fast to slow, or of long or short duration), *Weight* (on a spectrum of firm or fine, heavy or light), *Space* (on a spectrum of direct or indirect forms of linearity or circularity), and *Flow* (on a spectrum of bound or free). Pressing is a basic effort action, combining sustained time, firm weight, direct/linear space and bound flow. You can experience pressing by pushing your flat hands against each other, or pushing against a heavy or immovable object; or two partners pushing against each other's hands, and so forth. When Maureen wants students to experience a "felt sense" of coercion, she engages them in pressing activities, solo, partner and group. One such effective activity is a group of four students performing group pressing; that is, resisting as if something heavy were being forced on top of them or applying pressure as if they were forcing something or someone down into the ground. This activity helps them feel the undeniable participation of their bodies in these acts of resisting or applying force. Everyday learning in even mundane movement patterns contains many examples of pressing—e.g., lifting and lowering of objects and people with some measure of control, moving objects or people out of one's way, cooking, cleaning, playing, dancing, etc. The embodiment of pressing calls on the bodies of the doers and observers not only to witness but also to experience the dominating power of sustained pushing and pulling, demanding and resisting, coercion and derision.

Stillness as a movement concept is usually explored within the existential category of *Body*, oft-times in conjunction with motion, and frequently in the exploration of pressing, in those moments when one is in between the effects of pushing and being pushed, of pushing back or yielding. Students work on moving into and out of motion and stillness. In Laban's movement work, stillness is not simply "not moving", but is as much a presence of tension and anticipation as it is a holding in abeyance of motion or as a hovering that precedes motion, a barely perceptible leaning or inclination of the body. In the dance example that follows, the presentation of stillness is manifest in coiled tension in contrast to more languid styles of embodying stillness and motion. The dance we explore, Tango, achieves these nuances of and within stillness through subtle shifts in weight and posture so that when the dancers move, both dancers and observers are simultaneously jolted and relieved, grateful for the chance to exhale. And, in intersected and interdependent resonance, the dance discloses itself; one cannot tell the dancers from the dance.

INVITATION TO THE DANCE

We invite you to journey with us into the heart of Tango, the most amazing and disturbing postmodern dance, the perfect hybrid of death and desire, and the elusive rhythm haunting the psychic space. Maureen will acquaint you with several concepts associated with touch dancing—Tango in particular. We will then—in an ongoing way—relate these dance concepts to the semiotic, phenomenological, and post-colonial themes we are exploring in a particular movement thematic: pressing.

We begin with the footwork and body positions which present as deceptively simple. As Maureen speaks and walks you through the space and shape of the dance, imagine yourself as the lead and the respond. Try not to fall into the heterosexist binary gender categories often associated with touch dancing. You can both lead and respond; for this dance to work, you must. In all touch dancing, the movement of the partners depends on the functional tension they create by posture, hand and arm position, and coordinated pushing and pulling against each other.

Try this very safe exercise with someone near you: with each of you with one open hand, place your palms together. Exert no active tension. Simply let them rest against each other. In a moment, you will take turns pushing. The person being pushed will not resist the push. Be pushed. The person doing the pushing exerts moderate tension against your partner's hand. Try to decide who will push first and when you will switch roles without speaking. Use eye contact and subtle head, facial and postural cues. Go ahead. Now, exert tension against each other's hands; meet each other's push. Decide who will "lead" in a simple up and down, circular, and/or forward and back pattern. Then switch. Again, do this without speaking. This hand-to-hand exercise is a progression that many movement and somatic educators use to prepare learners for learning the more complicated, and often intimidating, footwork and body postures associated with touch dancing.

Footwork in dance is learned through the basic step. Each dance has its own distinctive basic step—a series of step-like weight transfers constrained by rhythm and sequence. This basic step is constant as the means of travel. The Tango "basic" is step, step, step side, step together, with the rhythmic timing of slow, slow, slow, quick. The body position is partners facing each other in a tight ballroom hold, very close, faces turned deliberately away from each other, the chase and avoidance of the gaze being one of the more erotic and seductive components of Tango. The steps are mirror images of each other. The costumes are flamboyant and outrageous. The bodies of the dancers are displayed, flaunted. The postures and movements are dramatic and excessive. The erotic and destructive drives barely contained. The fury and sadness of the dance demanding, exhausting, exciting, and frightening in what it lays bare and where it can take you. Historically, Tango emerged as a dance of exile and remembrance and involved the partners who were available, typically males who longed for a felt sense of a particular cultural rhythm and pace. It has evolved into a form that is as challenging as it is fluid, as elusive and subtle as it is dramatic and bold.

REFLECTION ON ACTION

We have just engaged in a simple deconstruction of several myths about touch dancing in general and Tango in particular that: (a) that a good lead makes a dance happen and all the partner has to do is "follow"; as you have felt, pushing against a soft hand does not create a functional pattern; as Maureen's former ballroom master would say, "the woman is not a stick shift"; (b) leading and following are a fluid interplay of dominance and subordination; as you have felt, it is the reciprocity of push that makes movement in an direction possible; (c) patterns of movement unfold naturally and effortlessly, that negotiation and decision-making are not an explicit part of the experience; as you have felt, it is very difficult to "know" intuitively what is being signaled unless the cues already have been established as representing something intersubjectively significant. True, long time dance partners develop a sense of each other's bodies and expressions, but Maureen can assure you, it does not begin that way; and (d) *following* is the appropriate response to leading. We use "respond" rather than follow because it more closely represents the dynamic. One could also use "initiate: respond" or "move: respond". Leading and following reflect neither the embodied nor the attitudinal intentions and possibilities.

We frequently use dance exercises to disclose other mythologies—that a good leader (or cultural icon or prophet or priest) is all one needs to allow a socio-political agenda to unfold, and all the participants (or citizens) need to do is follow; that communication is effortless and transparent, that negotiation is unnecessary for understanding and for moving together; and that dominance and subordination are "natural" states of give and take—not really the oppression of a less privileged group by a more privileged group with the means to inscribe and enforce those inscriptions. Following this line of reasoning to its conclusion would lead to the collapse of Tango as a dance following its collision with the wall! There is nowhere to go once the limit- horizon has made itself painfully obvious. How can dominance and subordination be repackaged so it entices as exotic and compelling? Once your body has "felt" the difference, you are implicated heuristically and politically in ways that make safe havens of "neutrality" almost impossible. Tethered by one's embodied implicature, trial and process are difficult to avoid.

Maureen's experiences in dance have provided her with a "body of evidence" which demonstrates how facile and unhelpful dichotomous categorizations can be when one is considering discourses of gender, leadership and political change. Maureen's body transgresses what Kristeva calls the "one law—the one sublimating transcendent guarantor of the ideal interests of the community and its correlate call for 'an increasingly purified community discipline.'"[14] She is too muscular to be feminine, too graceful to be male, too physically hybrid to dance ballet. Thankfully, ballroom dance, with all its constraints was plastic and variable enough for the many improbable bodies who dance, Maureen's included. Likewise, Tom's experiences of high level sport activity and "orphan" disease diagnoses provide similar evidence of unbearable liminality, of impressive proficiency in competitive tennis and then significantly disabled in episodic phases of debilitation and disbelieved in his embodied expressions of pain and unmanageability. Here we see the unhelpful application of the necessity of having to choose between an "either/or" proposition and a "both/and" proposition. Lanigan's insistence on *both* "both/and" *and* "either/or" allows for different possibilities, different analyses, and different understandings.

Power differentials grounded in social construction of embodied intersectionality, like gender and disability, are at the heart of much critical unpacking of texts and movement; however, it is not enough for a critical reading (be it phenomenological, semiotic or post-colonial) of any embodied expression to take up gender, gender relations, disability, hegemonic normalcy and the lived experience of being embodied (male, female, abled, disabled, both, neither, or in process) as a singular emphasis. Gender, disability, lived relation, and embodiment exist within a swirling multiplicity of locations, textures, and intersections, and as critical reflexive readers, we aim to acknowledge the intersections, borders, and complexities across gender, ethnicity, class, race, sexual, and bodily orientation.

Polarizing portrayals of embodiment breed the bitter repercussions of transgressing the "One Law—the One, Sublimating, Transcendent Guarantor of portrayal" and its correlate call for "an increasingly purified community discipline."[15] These embodied transgressions have consequences of stigma, disenfranchisement, dismissal and dehumanization. Tango is political; movement is political; bodies are socially volatile. Much can be learned about parts and wholes through engagement with movement forms and their analysis.

REFLECTION IN ACTION

You have experienced your own felt sense of functional tension; you have experienced the complex interplay of footwork, body posture and movement through space, the illusion of spontaneous fluidity made possible only through intricate, deliberate, and motivated choreography; and you have unpacked mythologies of transparency, effortlessness, and neutrality. Political change is intricately intertwined with illusions of blame, forgiveness and reward blended with the false promises of romance, loyalty and security. Thus camouflaged, colonial, hierarchical, heterosexist, classist, and ableist norms and inscriptions are insidiously, invisibly enacted and re-enforced in *unproblematized* constructions of evil and good, prosperity and depravity, love and betrayal, *jouissance* and despair. Recognizing both the seductive and threatening power of transgression, dominant and normative structures of control create their own places of *mythos* and escape, which constitute an insidiously inscribed law of their own. Systems of oppression can be architectural, physical, social, sexual, attitudinal, psychical, as well as violent, exploitative, manipulative, persuasive, degrading, consultative, reciprocal, or illusory combinations of all of these. They are seldom, if ever, neutral or effortless and, if engaged from those borderlands between thought and sensation, seldom transparent. How do we learn to see what is happening to bodies and their functional and expressive forms?

CONCLUSION

The female protagonist from the infamous 1972 film, "Last Tango in Paris", comments to the male protagonist that "this is pathetic" as they visit and view Tango performances in a remarkable scene. Shortly thereafter, she kills him. Desire, passion, suspicion, jealousy, anger, betrayal. Promises of progress and conformity, the seduction of security and sanctioned *jouissance*, the consequences of transgression; these form the contexts of choice and constitute the sign systems that disallow expressive bodies to become visible as signs of embodied oppression. Lanigan's recursive analysis methodology offers the possibility of a constitution of a choice of context buttressed by an acceptance of the celebratory ambiguity of *both* "either/or *and* both/and" options. Laban's carnally grounded analytic methodology offers the possibility of deep attunement to and wonder about expressive bodies in cultural semiosis. The body of this type of deep engagement is not bound by absurd binaries, and neither is it condemned to unbearable liminality. It is a political sign, and perhaps its own form of sign system, *in process*, *on trial*, yielding and resisting, sick and well, joyful and depraved, already autopoetic. This body may be the means by which comportment attunes to contexts of choice and offers alternatives.

We have offered this paper as an example of a blending of Lanigan and Laban and the analyses made possible by their resonances and complementarities. We used a basic effort concept of pressing to lead you into a deeper consideration of forms of coercion and oppression and the unavoidable implicature of bodies in that project. And we have walked you through an experience with Tango. We would like to finish with a few comments on Tango: Consider Tango as that borderland dance, a site of ongoing recursion and recall simultaneously riding and pushing structure and reciprocal tension; pursuing the ever-elusive resonant connection, the ongoing act of hope; acknowledging the dangerous confusion of proximity with intimacy; pathetic only if the despair of betrayal constructs an abject and unbearable darkness, and an avoidance of the risks of being bodies in refrain, moving beyond the limits of space and time.[16]

NOTES

1. Richard Lanigan, *Phenomenology of Communication: Merleau-Ponty's Thematics in Communicology and Semiology* (Pittsburgh, PA: Duquesne University Press, 1988), 105, 148. See Lanigan, *Phenomenology of Communication*. For a summary of Lanigan's methodology as a reflective, reflexive, and reversible discovery-disclosure process of choice and context, see Thomas D. Craig, "Disrupting the Disembodied Status Quo" (PhD diss., Carbondale, IL: Southern Illinois University, 1997), 50–54.
2. Maurice Merleau-Ponty, *Phenomenology of Perception*, trans. Donald A. Landes (New York: Routledge, 2012).
3. Lanigan, *Phenomenology of Communication*.
4. Merleau-Ponty, *Phenomenology of Perception*; Lanigan, *Phenomenology of Communication*; Maureen Connolly and Thomas D. Craig, "Stressed Embodiment: Doing Phenomenology in the Wild," *Human Studies* 25 (2002): 451–462; Maureen Connolly and Thomas D. Craig, "Theory and Method in the Human Sciences," A book review essay. [Amedeo Giorgi, *The Descriptive Phenomenological Method in Psychology: A Modified Husserlian Approach* (Pittsburgh, PA: Duquesne University Press, 2009)], *Schutzian Research. Special Issue: Phenomenology of the Human Sciences* 3 (2011): 251–257. Guest Editor: Richard L. Lanigan; Thomas D. Craig and Maureen Connolly, "Biblical Apocalypso in Zechariah and the Moulin Rouge" (paper presented at the Society for Biblical Literature Conference, Atlanta, GA, November 20–23, 2003).
5. Kevin Paterson and Bill Hughes. "Disability Studies and Phenomenology: The Carnal Politics of Everyday Life," *Disability and Society* 14, no. 5 (1999): 597–610.
6. Merleau-Ponty,*Phenomenology of Perception*.
7. Gillian A. Bendelow and Simon J. Williams. "Transcending the Dualisms: Towards a Sociology of Pain," *Sociology of Health and Illness* 17 (1995): 139–155.
8. Bendelow and Williams, Transcending the Dualisms.
9. Lanigan, *Phenomenology of Communication*; Richard Lanigan, *The Human Science of Communicology: A Phenomenology of Discourse in Foucault and Merleau-Ponty* (Pittsburgh, PA: Duquesne University Press, 1992).
10. Paterson and Hughes, "Disability Studies and Phenomenology."
11. Claudine Sherrill, "Least Restrictive Environments and Total Inclusion Philosophies: Critical Analysis," *Palaestra* 10, no. 3 (1994): 25–35. Claudine Sherrill and T. Williams, "Disability and Sport: Psychosocial Perspectives on Inclusion, Integration, and Participation," *Sport Science Review* 4, no. 1 (1996): 42–64.
12. Richard Lanigan, *Semiotic Phenomenology of Rhetoric: Eidetic Practice in Henry Grattan's Discourse on Tolerance* (Washington, DC: Center for Advanced Research in Phenomenology and

University Press of America, 1984); Lanigan, *Phenomenology of Communication; Human Science of Communicology*, continues to summarize his semiotic phenomenology methodology as a recursive process of description, reduction, and interpretation in which each component entails interpretation, reduction, and description. For a recent explication and clarification of this methodology applied to "semiotic paradigms of self and person," see Lanigan, *Semiotic Phenomenology of Rhetoric*; *Phenomenology of Communication; Human Science of Communicology*; "Semiotic Paradigms of Self and Person: The Perspectives Model of Communicology as the Logic Foundation of Human Science," *Language and Semiotic Studies* [China], 1, no. 1 (Spring 2015): 106–112.

13. Rudolph Laban organized much of his thinking about movement forms under his original conceptualization of a system of description known as Choreutics. Laban's work is well articulated in Vera Maletic, *Body—Space—Expression: The Development of Rudolf Laban's Movement and Dance Concepts* (Berlin: Mouton de Gruyter, 1987).
14. Toril Moi, *The Kristeva Reader* (New York: Columbia, 1986), 141.
15. Moi, *Kristeva*, 141.
16. We have taken up this notion of the liminal dance in the borderlands of exile in a joint project on "apocalypso" in the biblical book of Zechariah and the contemporary film, Moulin Rouge (2001), both of which offer performances of celebration of underground identity across evocatively choreographed bodies and an overstated sensuous ideal of desire and discharge (i.e., *jouissance*).

BIBLIOGRAPHY

Bendelow, Gillian A., and Simon J. Williams. "Transcending the Dualisms: Towards a Sociology of Pain." *Sociology of Health and Illness* 17 (1995): 139–155.

Connolly, Maureen. "Bikini Bytes: A Communicology of Front Stage and Back Stage Performances at Competitive Body-Building Events." *The American Journal of Semiotics* 17, no. 4 (2001/2003): 229–246.

Connolly, Maureen. "Semiotic Choreology–Links to Embodiment." International Communicology Institute Symposium, University of Bemidji, Bemidji, Minnesota. July, 2004.

Connolly, Maureen, and Thomas D. Craig. "Stressed Embodiment: Doing Phenomenology in the Wild." *Human Studies* 25 (2002): 451–462.

Connolly, Maureen, and Thomas D. Craig. "Theory and Method in the Human Sciences." A book review essay with Maureen Connolly" [Amedeo Giorgi, *The Descriptive Phenomenological Method in Psychology: A Modified Husserlian Approach*. Pittsburgh, PA: Duquesne University Press, 2009]. *Schutzian Research. Special Issue: Phenomenology of the Human Sciences* 3 (2011): 251–257. Guest Editor: Richard L. Lanigan.

Craig, Thomas D. "Disrupting the Disembodied Status Quo." PhD diss., Southern Illinois University, 1997.

Craig, Thomas D., and Maureen Connolly. "Biblical Apocalypso in Zechariah and the Moulin Rouge." Paper presented at the Society for Biblical Literature Conference. Atlanta, GA. November 20–23, 2003.

Kristeva, Julia. "About Chinese Women." In *The Kristeva Reader*, edited by Toril Moi, translated by Seán Hand, 138–159. New York: Columbia, 1986.

Lanigan, Richard. *The Human Science of Communicology: A Phenomenology of Discourse in Foucault and Merleau-Ponty*. Pittsburgh, PA: Duquesne University Press, 1992.

Lanigan, Richard. *Phenomenology of Communication: Merleau-Ponty's Thematics in Communicology and Semiology*. Pittsburgh, PA: Duquesne University Press, 1988.

Lanigan, Richard. "Semiotic Paradigms of Self and Person: The Perspectives Model of Communicology as the Logic Foundation of Human Science." *Language and Semiotic Studies* [China], 1, no. 1 (Spring 2015): 106–112.

Lanigan, Richard. *Semiotic Phenomenology of Rhetoric: Eidetic Practice in Henry Grattan's Discourse on Tolerance*. Washington, DC: Center for Advanced Research in Phenomenology and University Press of America, 1984.

Maletic, Vera. *Body-Space—Expression: The Development of Rudolf Laban's Movement and Dance Concepts*. Berlin: Mouton de Gruyter, 1987.

Merleau-Ponty, Maurice. *Phenomenology of Perception*, trans. Colin Smith. New Jersey: The Humanities Press. 1962. [Translation of *Phénoménologie de la perception* (Paris: Gallimard, 1945)].

Merleau-Ponty, Maurice. *The Structure of Behavior*. Boston, MA: Beacon Press, 1963. [Translation of *La Structure du comportement* (Paris: Presses Universitaires de France, 1942)].

Moi, Toril, ed., *The Kristeva Reader*. New York: Columbia, 1986.

Paterson, Kevin, and Bill Hughes. "Disability Studies and Phenomenology: The Carnal Politics of Everyday Life." *Disability and Society* 14, no. 5 (1999): 597–610.

Sherrill, Claudine. "Least Restrictive Environments and Total Inclusion Philosophies: Critical Analysis." *Palaestra* 10, no. 3 (1994): 25–35.

Sherrill, Claudine, and T. Williams. "Disability and Sport: Psychosocial Perspectives on Inclusion, Integration, and Participation." *Sport Science Review* 4, no. 1 (1996): 42–64.

CHAPTER SIXTEEN

Lexis Agonistic and Lexis Graphike

Translation from Library Document to Museum Monument

THADDEUS MARTIN

In his 1887 *Gemeinschaft and Gesellschaft* (translated as *Community and Society*), Ferdinand Tönnies anticipated Foucault's apposition between the library and the museum. *Gemeinschaft*, often translated as "community," refers to collectives based on family and neighborhood bonds and ensuing feelings of togetherness. *Gesellschaft*, often translated as "society," references collectives that are sustained by an instrumental goal. Tönnies divides the *Gesellschaft* into two parts: "non-place communities" are communities of emotion, of times remembered, such as museums and monuments. By contrast, "place communities" are communities of location, of places remembered; such as libraries and documents.[1]

In the third book, Chapter 12 of his *Rhetoric*, Aristotle asserted an apposition between *lexis agonistike*, or performative style, and *lexis graphike*, or written style. Written style, according to Aristotle, is more finished and precise, but that it is not appropriate for all venues; the performative style, by contrast, is more dramatic. Therefore, Aristotle advised the use of *lexis graphike* for venues, such as the courtroom and of *lexis agonistike*, for venues such as a speech for the general public.[2]

Both the Vietnam Memorial (VM) and Independence Rock (IR) are sites for inscription, and specifically for inscription of names. Placing these two well-known icons in apposition creates an inscription contest (*lexis agonistike*) through which the phenomenology of reversibility, reflexivity, and reflection become present for the embodied viewer.[3] The conjunction of the Subject/Author in a combinatory of logic of inclusion requires we return to the text as an interstices of relationships between discourse and practice, not as an artifact, but as an "(...) act of initiation that constitutes discursive practice".[4] The author function is a discursive formation (message as code) derived from the *subject function* as discursive transformation (code as message).[5]

Richard Lanigan associates the voiceless name (Asyndeton) with the Library and Foucault's document of the nameless voice (Prosopopoeia) with the Museum and Foucault's monument.[6] The Asyndeton is a rhetorical device in which conjunctions are deliberately omitted, as in *"veni, vidi, vici"* (I came, I saw, I conquered). In the university as library, massive amounts of information (documents) exist and but there is no one there to tell you how to put it together, you can just keep searching the catalogues endlessly, like a man trying to understand the universe by reading the dictionary. Prosopopoeia is a rhetorical device in which a speaker or writer communicates by speaking as another person, object, or even deity. Thus in the asylum, the "insane" are silenced by the diagnoses which name them, forever monuments to the various diagnoses of and names for madness.

VM and IR are also Tönniesian *Gesellschaft* (aspects of society), but are they non-place communities of emotion, i.e., times remembered (museums/monuments) or place communities of location, i.e., places remembered (libraries/documents? As we shall see, the answer is perhaps more complicated. The changing status of Independence Rock through history will be seen to exemplify a progression of the document (Library, *lexis agonistike*), becoming the monument (Museum, *lexis graphike*). The spatial location of the pioneers' embodiment in the signature (or trace) is renamed as a temporal transposition by the rationality of the museum.

INSCRIPTION CONTEST

Vietnam Veterans Memorial

The Vietnam Veterans Memorial consists of two walls of black granite, each some 247 feet long and 10 ½ feet high, arranged in a corner configuration. On these walls the names of the dead are inscribed. This artifact was commissioned by the U.S. government specifically as a memorial, i.e., as it is meant by the state as a monument. It is the state that controls this monument: they control access to it, for example, and are responsible for its maintenance.

The Vietnam Memorial is an excellent example for the exploration of modernist and postmodern authorship. From a modernist perspective, who is the "author" of a piece of art? The artist, of course. Maya Lin is the de facto "author" who created this artifact, and we will see in a moment how through this work she ingeniously co-opts the normative subject placement. But from a postmodern perspective, the Vietnam Memorial instantiates a code, a semiotic structure, through which embodied viewers can take various subject positions and embody various subject functions, such as memory, memorialization, and hermeneutic self-, other-, collective- interpretations.

In postmodern authorship, the semiotic function of the Author is conjoined with the semiotic function of the Subject in authentic discourse as *énoncé*, which has been enunciated or expressed. Lanigan notes,

> The dimensions of "spatial dispersion" containing the *subject discourse* [writer] domain of sedimented discourse (*énonciation*) are intersected by those dimensions of "temporal deployment" situating authentic *author discourse (énoncé)*. In such a matrix, the Self is in a condition of *Le Même et L'Autre*, which is to say, the Self is both the Same Self and a Different Other in discourse.[7]

In Lanigan's description we may be reminded of Derrida's notion of *différence* as both to differ (separation of identity) and to defer (separation in time). As Roland Barthes noted in "Authors and Writers," "(…) the author dialecticizes himself, he does not dialecticize the world."[8] Barthes' choice of the term, "dialecticize," is itself a double entendre: the Author/Subject function is both a dialectic tension and its own dialect, or manner of speaking. We might even say that the Author/Subject creates a dialect.

Barthes' says that the author would like to dialecticize the world, to discuss the truth of various opinions, to inquire into its contradictions and arrive at solutions. Instead, the author dialecticizes him/herself; we might say *they split themselves*, by this act of writing, into a bastard type, an author-writer who by his own actions institutionalizes his subjectivity and, by extension, intersubjectivity for all involved. In this institutionalization, which is the text, we achieve the death of the writer-author, and as you read this text you achieve the birth of the writer-scriptor. As I read these words I have just written, I also become the postmodern author, both the reader and the scriptor. I will present parts of this paper aloud; I will verbalize this discourse, as though I was the voice in your head. In doing so I seek to thematize authentic discourse, *énoncé* as *écriture;* to incarnate a me that is not I but is not you. I will embody a voice that speaks from the possible modes of existence of this discourse, from a nowhere which is now here; to incarnate a me that is not I but is not you, embracing the text as both message and code.

As I gaze at the Vietnam Memorial, I read the words, the names of the dead. This Derridian grammar etched in stone, the trace or signature is there, and the precondition of my self-authorship. I did not write these words, or place them in the stone just so, but I bring them to life by reading them. A voice speaks in my mind, and it both is and is not mine.

I see my reflection in the burnished sheen of the granite, and the image both is and is not me. I know that I am not my image; but in a more powerful sense, I am not the same me as I encounter these names; as what Jaspers would call an *Existenzen* or Heidegger called *Dasein*, I have a Being-towards-death, and as I am confronted by more than 58,000 of these names I observe (and my reflection provides an empirical reminder) myself being confronted.

The sculptor, Maya Lin, is known for her integration of sight, sound, and touch into her pieces. As she herself notes,

> As for me, the first time I visited the memorial after it was completed I found myself searching out the name of a friend's father and touching it. It was strange to realize that I was another visitor and I was reacting to it as I had designed it.[9]

In addition, her memorials seem to be designed to fade away over time, as the events they commemorate slowly disappear.

> In two of her projects, the "Civil Rights Memorial" (1987–89) in Montgomery Alabama, and "The Women's Table" (1990–93) in New Haven Connecticut, water rises up out of the stone and floats along the surface of the rock. Inviting to the touch, the water in these works leaves a physical trace on those who venture to feel the names and numbers inscribed on stone tables. Lin's use of water also predicts the demise of the memorial itself, as centuries of running water will eventually soften the stone, turning it back into earth.[10]

The Vietnam Veteran's Memorial is therefore meant to be touched, and this touch, this trace of embodiment, is meant to slowly wear away the material from which it was made. This fact is in direct conflict with the interests of the state.

Let us summarize possible functions of the subject embodied in the tissue of signs which is this artifact. The monument is mean to be touched, and people do touch it. Whose presence do you feel, however, when you touch this memorial? If it is the presence of the artist, then Maya Lin has failed in her endeavor, for in the assertion of such brute authorship, those whom the memorial was created to make us remember would be subsumed, covered over, displaced, and forgotten. But the monument is polished, and as you touch the monument you also see your own reflection. By etching the names of the dead in the very granite of the wall and by polishing the stone to a reflective finish, the artist/author attempts her own sublimation. Yet this sublimation fails to evoke the dead themselves, who remain mute, voiceless names, lost in history except for those who already knew them. What then is invoked by the artist's sublimation?

As I explore the memorial, *I feel what I am reading*, and what I am reading is the names of the dead. In the somatic experience of touching that language, I am synecdochetically touching them (rhetorical trope in which a part is used for the whole or a whole is used for a part); language speaks in my mind, as the voice of the narrator, and in my hands, the presence of the dead (a present absence), and in my vision, as I and the dead parade slowly and tragically by each other, meeting in the hallucination of the burnished stone. Language speaks the words of the dead; each soldier seems to come forth, come forward, and speak his name, and I touch him across the years. The somatic experience itself engenders the imagination: I animate, I corporealize an imaginative other whom I have never met.

Yet the voices of the Vietnam Memorial begin to speak in unison, or become monotone over time. As I feel and read these names, the voices of these individuals unknown to me blend into one as they come forward, each reciting the same litany, the same slow march of death. Voices only become particularized when I know them, so if I come across a name, I know the character of the voice; the voice changes to become that of the person I remember. With this recognition face, a simulacrum, comes to me out of the dark, and I know him.

By way of summary, recall Husserl's pronouncement that "subjectivity is intersubjectivity." In his *Greek Voices of Discourse and Epistemology Explicated in French Discourse,* Lanigan provides an intertextuality between French Communicology's *Le Même et L'Autre* (Self/Other//Same/Different) and the ancient Greek voices of *Mythos/Logos//Mystos/Magikos*.[11] The Self is the voice within the mind, or *mythos*. Other is the voice outside the mind, or *logos*. Same is the voice of silence (being Mute), or Greek *mystos*. Different is the voice of practice, or Greek *magikos*.

We can see the play of these voices in the postmodern authorship in the Vietnam Memorial. The visual reflection, my image in VM, provides an indexical clue to how we should trace the voices. The Self is the *mythos* of the voice inside the mind. The counterpoint to this are the names of the dead, the Other who confronts me as voice outside the mind, and the two together produce a discourse (someone communicating to someone else about something). These are the conditions of subjectivity. Subjectivity becomes intersubjectivity where the self/other of *mythos/logos* is confronted by *mystos* and *magikos*. We do not read the names of the dead out loud; rather, the voice inside the mind is confronted by the voice of silence (*mystos*) as we are mute before the edifice. Touch becomes the voice of practice, a *magikos* of embodiment through which we become scriptors/authors of a different self, an experience of consciousness that makes us conscious of experience.

Independence Rock

Independence Rock is a gigantic granite boulder approximately 130 feet high, 1900 feet long, and 850 feet wide, for a total area of 170 acres. It is located in the middle of the high plains grasslands 55 miles Southwest of Casper, Wyoming. In 1841 the Belgian Jesuit Priest, Pierre Jean De Smet, named the rock "The Register of the Desert." This name is telling for our analysis:

> When the pioneer priest, Pierre Jean De Smet, saw the rock in 1841, he found "the hieroglyphics of Indian warriors" and "the names of all the travelers who have passed by are there to be read, written in coarse characters." Other sojourners called it the backbone of the universe, but De Smet dubbed the rock "the great register of the desert."[12]

The site became a landmark for the pioneers traveling the Old Oregon Trail on the way to California. What interests me in this landmark from a Communicological and semiotic standpoint is that those pioneers who made it to this edifice in Wyoming would etch their names and usually the date into the rock to signify their progress and survival thus far. As the rock became a National Historic Landmark, various plaques, signs, and other boundaries (such as barbed wire) as well as various directives placed by the State regulate how we approach, behave, think and do not think about Independence Rock. These regulative boundaries structure our discourse (someone communicating to someone else about something).

Independence Rock of course immediately brings to mind questions of authorship, legitimation, and institutionalization. The authorship problematic/thematic provides an important perspective in understanding Foucault's famous apposition of the metaphors of the library and the museum. As Lanigan notes in *The Postmodern Author: Foucault on Fiction and the Fiction of Foucault*, Roland Barthes incisive discussions first of authors and writers (1960), and later on the death of the author and replacement by the scriptor (1968) set the stage for Foucault's 1969 essay, *What is an Author?* In this essay, Foucault famously distances himself from such questions as the "who" of the author, his authenticity, and the fidelity of his self-representation, replacing them with the rhetorical questions: "What are the modes of existence of this discourse? Where does it come from; how is it circulated; who controls it? What placements are determined for possible subjects? Who can fulfill these diverse functions of the subject?"[13]

Independence Rock became a state park in 1879. The name, "Great Register of the Desert," remains a secondary name by which it is known and is referenced in their official brochures and on the Wyoming State Parks website. The term, "register," is a wonderful Freudian slip. A register has several meanings, including: an official record (such as a marriage register or a ship's register), an entry in such a register (record of a particular marriage or death), the display or manifestation of a particular instrument (register of an oscilloscope), and the particular range or part of a voice or instrument.

In the case of Independence Rock, no artist designed it—there was no particular intent on the part of any "artist." The State notes for us that Independence Rock is constantly being "damaged" by the wind and by lichen and that the signatures will eventually disappear. Such things mark the rock as an historical site, a human artifact despite its existence as an object of nature. When a rock is not a human artifact or a state park, lichen simply grows on it and the wind causes "erosion."

Several park billboards ask visitors not to etch/carve their own names into the rock or to otherwise "deface" the rock or the signatures thereon. I found this particularly interesting, a wonderful contradiction: the same act that in the past made Independence Rock a site of historical significance (etching/carving/scratching one's name into the stone) destroys its historical significance if performed in the present!

Again, let us now turn our attention to the possible functions of the subject embodied in the tissue of signs that is this artifact. Independence Rock is too big to perceive all at once, and signatures exists on all surfaces of the rock, not just on one side intended for display. I bodily traverse the distance to the other; I make a journey around and over the rock to meet those who journeyed around and over the mountains. My journey is indexical to or symbolic of their journey.

I am not allowed to touch the signatures on it, but am reduced merely to seeing them. Yet these are actual signatures, not the engravings of an artist in standardized font of a certain size and shape. As signatures, these artifacts reflect more empirically the signatory's embodiment. The voices of Independence Rock sustain their independence long into the experience.

Museum and Library

Independence Rock and the Vietnam Veterans Memorial have both been mislabeled by the state. The state sees Independence Rock as a library, a collection of voiceless names whose existence is to be protected into antiquity. Independence Rock is preserved as a Library, a massive historical document of all figures from a particular historical period who passed by and left their signatures. For whom do the names etched, carved, and inked on the surface of Independence Rock have meaning? Certainly not for the individuals who made the marks, as they are now all dead. The names have meaning for us as (postmodern) authors: we become other selves when reading them. These signatures are traces of embodiment, left by the scriptor/writer. If these are embodied, it is we as readers who embody them. Independence Rock is not a collection of voiceless names, but rather the possibility of the nameless voice: one's own voice, embodying the lives of those who came before, our predecessors, to borrow a term from Alfred Schutz. Thus, Independence Rock is meant to be a library, but is actually a museum.

By the same token, the Vietnam Veterans Memorial is meant to be a museum, but is really a library. If it is full of nameless voices, and these voices exist eidetically in the embodiment of the individuals who go there. The voiceless names chiseled into the granite wall retain only a technical historical significance once those who remember these veterans, those with whom these individuals were consociates or, minimally, contemporaries, (to borrow again from Schutz), are gone. The Vietnam Veterans Memorial becomes a museum only by being touched by persons whose embodiment (nameless voice) enacts the image of life. In the terminology of the early Martin Heidegger, the Vietnam Veterans Memorial is an artifact whose function is to throw Dasein back upon its own authenticity in its being towards death.

In the case of the Vietnam memorial, the artist has artfully crafted the eidetic demise of the artifact into the work itself by designing it to be touched and thereby, slowly worn out. Most likely, after being touched for another 100 to 200 years, there will be a park service sign saying something like, "please do not touch the wall, the marble is wearing out." This situation currently exists for Independence Rock, except the embodiment is now empirical as the rock slowly fades away, like our bodies. The embodiment of Independence Rock was once eidetic, before the rock was not worn out: here is a space into which you may insert the empirical evidence of your having been here.

Thus for Independence Rock it seems to me we have a progression of document (*lexis graphike*) to monument (*lexis agonistike*), i.e., the Library becoming the monument Museum. For the Vietnam Veterans Memorial, we have a progression of monument (*lexis agonistike*), to document (*lexis graphike*), i.e., the Museum becoming the Library. The solution to the problem of Independence Rock, from a practical standpoint, has already been explored by the Vatican. The Vatican's solution has been to allow people to purchase a brick and have their names engraved on it. The bricks are then used as a path to or around the artifact (such as a statue). A place for a signature is very important and cannot be stopped by any act of the state. The signature is an embodied nameless voice (museum)—a signature will speak of its author, will assert its author—it is part of being human. The very existence of Independence Rock demonstrates this facticity.

SIGNATURE VS. SOUVENIR

The park service for Independence Rock is partially correct in the sense that folks just cannot go around scratching their names over other names. Independence Rock is an embodied voiceless name (library). Scratching your name over another's is graffiti or, from the Italian, "graffito," the singular form of the term literally meaning, "little scratch." The lack of embodiment engendered by such action is actually anonymous, marked by no signature or, more precisely, a "signature" that is meant to be anything but an identification of its originator. Therefore the signature as graffito is truly under erasure. It is a repression of the name in a violent dialectic. While the original signatures on Independence Rock were arguably produced on a semiotically innocent, tabula rasa surface, as the wagon trains of pioneers across Wyoming were replaced by actual trains and finally automobiles, new signatures became graffiti. In general, the dialectics of historical preservation and graffiti entail an escalation pattern. It begins with signs forbidding graffiti and touching the rock. So people scratch their names into the signs instead. Eventually, the park rangers post a "do not deface the signs" sign; the voiceless names mark the sign with bullet holes or scratch marks or paint; a new sign goes up with a penalty noted for defacing it, and the cycle continues.

Echoing Heidegger, Barthes and Foucault assign authorship to temporality where the museum/asylum consists of things/people in some time, but without a place. They assign writing/speaking to spatiality where the library/university consists of things/people in their place. In the realm of public space, this has all in a certain sense been anticipated by Ferdinand Tönnies in his division of the *Gesellschaft* into non-place communities (communities of emotion, of times remembered, such as museums and monuments) and place communities (community of location, places remembered, such as libraries and documents). Authorship by signature allows the two places of the *Gesellschaft* to exist in apposition. Graffito makes the places exist in opposition; allowing everyone to purchase a brick and sign it harkens to the French invention of the "souvenir," something your buy or keep to remind you of an event as participation on culture:

> It is not the souvenir as an object that is prioritized in this series but its sign as a vestige of cultural memory dislodged from history and resuscitated through mass production. As an element of modern tourism, the souvenir is a testimony of the traveler's experience, carried away as evidence of someone's participation in a cultural heritage. It is not the object per se that is meaningful; rather it is the object's capacity to resurrect a memory of both an experience and a culture that gives it value ... (T)he object is an empty container of cultural memory, but its trace remains a cultural specter in in the void. In its emptiness, it is prime for myth to be re-inscribed within the language of the form and with it, a revivication of cultural memory.[14]

The souvenir functions as time by signature, i.e., I know I have been there already as I hold it my hand. The time remembered is embodied in an artifact.

The question we have been implicitly asking throughout this paper is really: why are the signatures of the pioneers venerated artifacts of history, whereas the signatures of those who came after Independence Rock's status as National Historic Landmark considered graffiti? The signatures of the pioneers are marked (marked and unmarked terms in Jakobson's, following Trubetzkoy's, sense) as innocent symbols by the legitimacy of the state. Yet we can see dynamics of guilt and innocence in both the Vietnam Memorial and Independence Rock. The Vietnam Memorial often engenders survivor's guilt for those who served but returned, and a kind of generational guilt for those who were too young or too old to have served there. In the case of Independence Rock, those signatures added later are not innocent symbols; they bear the guilt of vandalism. Of course, the *méconnaissance* of this marking is in its failure to similarly legitimize the hieroglyphics of Native Americans, which pre-dated those of the American pioneers. The Native American hieroglyphs pre-date the signatures of the pioneers, but are so under erasure as to be almost invisible.

So from a Native American perspective on history, perhaps the signatures of the pioneers are as lacking in innocence as the graffiti forbidden by the state.

NOTES

1. Ferdinand Tönnies, *Community and Society*, trans. Charles Loomis (Mineola, NY: Dover Publications, 2002), 33.
2. Aristotle, *Rhetoric and Poetics of Aristotle*, trans. W. Rhys Roberts (New York: McGraw-Hill, 1984), 159.
3. Richard Lanigan, "Foucault's Science of Rhetoric: The Contest between Practical Discourse and Discursive Practice," *Symplokē, Special Issue: Rhetoric and the Human Sciences* 4, nos. 1–2 (1996): 191.
4. Richard Lanigan, "The Postmodern Author: Foucault on Fiction and the Fiction of Foucault," *The American Journal of Semiotics* 17, no. 1 (2001): 262.
5. Lanigan, "Foucault's Science of Rhetoric," 193; Thaddeus Martin, "A Semiotic Phenomenology of the Will-To-Communicate in the Philosophy of Karl Jaspers" (PhD diss., Southern Illinois University, Carbondale, 1992).
6. Lanigan, "Foucault's Science of Rhetoric," 197.
7. Lanigan, "Postmodern Author," 257.
8. Roland Barthes, "Authors and Writers," in *Critical Essays*, trans. Richard Howard (Evanston, IL: Northwestern University Press, 1960), 146.
9. Maya Lin, "Making the Memorial," *The New York Review of Books*, November 2, 2002.
10. Marie Conn and Therese McGuire, *Not Etched in Stone: Essays on Ritual Memory, Soul, and Society* (Lanham, MD: University Press of America, 2007), 1–2.
11. Richard Lanigan, "Greek Voices of Discourse and Epistemology Explicated in French Discourse," *Academia.edu*, https://siucarbondale.academia.edu(accessed April 9, 2016).
12. Will Bagley, "Independence Rock," Wyoming Historical Society, http://www.wyohistory.org/essays/independence-rock (accessed April 9, 2016).
13. Lanigan, "Postmodern Author," 255–256.
14. Rosemary O'Neill, *Art and Visual Culture on the French Riviera, 1956–1971: The Ecole de Nice* (Burlington, NJ: Ashgate, 2012), 71.

BIBLIOGRAPHY

Aristotle. *The Rhetoric and Poetics of Aristotle*. Translated by W. Rhys Roberts. New York: McGraw-Hill, 1984.

Bagley, Will. "Independence Rock." Wyoming Historical Society. Accessed April 9, 2016. http://www.wyohistory.org/essays/independence-rock.

Barthes, Roland. "The Author is Dead." In *The Rustle of Language*. Translated by Richard Howard, 49–55. New York: Hill and Wang, 1968.

Barthes, Roland. "Authors and Writers." In *Critical Essays*. Translated by Richard Howard, 143–150. Evanston, IL: Northwestern University Press, 1960.

Conn, Marie, and McGuire, Therese. *Not Etched in Stone: Essays on Ritual Memory, Soul, and Society.* Lanham, MD: University Press of America, 2007.
Foucault, Michel. "What is an Author?" In *Language, Counter-Memory, Practice: Selected Essays and Interviews.* Translated by Donald Bouchard, 113–138. Ithaca, NY: Cornell University Press, 1969.
Lanigan, Richard. "Foucault's Science of Rhetoric: The Contest between Practical Discourse and Discursive Practice." *Symplokē, Special Issue: Rhetoric and the Human Sciences* 4, nos. 1–2 (1996): 190–202.
Lanigan, Richard. "Greek Voices of Discourse and Epistemology Explicated in French Discourse." Adademia.edu. Accessed April 9, 2016. https://siucarbondale.academia.edu/ https://siucarbondale. academia.edu/RichardLanigan/HANDCHARTS-&-RESEARCHTEACHING-AIDS RichardLanigan/HANDCHARTS-&-RESEARCH—TEACHING-AIDS
Lanigan, Richard. *The Human Science of Communicology: A Phenomenology of Discourse in Foucault and Merleau-Ponty.* Pittsburgh, PA: Duquesne University Press, 1992.
Lanigan, Richard. "The Postmodern Author: Foucault on Fiction and the Fiction of Foucault." *The American Journal of Semiotics* 17, no. 1 (2001): 253–271.
Lanigan, Richard. "Semiotic Paradigms of Self and Person: The Perspectives Mode of Communicology as the Logic Foundation of Human Science." *Language and Semiotic Studies* [China], 1, no. 1 (2015): 106–129.
Lin, Maya. "Making the Memorial." *The New York Review of Books*, November 2, 2000.
Martin, Thaddeus. "Schizoanalysis in Pink Floyd's The Wall." Paper presented at the annual meeting of the Semiotic Circle of California, Berkeley, California, January 26, 2008.
Martin, Thaddeus. "A Semiotic Phenomenology of the Will-To-Communicate in the Philosophy of Karl Jaspers." PhD diss., Southern Illinois University, Carbondale, 1992.
O'Neill, Rosemary. *Art and Visual Culture on the French Riviera, 1956–1971: The Ecole de Nice.* Burlington, NJ: Ashgate, 2012.
Tönnies, Ferdinand. *Community and Society.* Translated by Charles Loomis. Mineola, NY: Dover Publications, 1988.

SECTION FIVE
Horizons of Communicability

CHAPTER SEVENTEEN

The Subject at Hand

VINCENT COLAPIETRO

> Some [signs] address themselves to us, so that we fully apprehend them [as signs]. But it is a paralyzed reason that does not acknowledge others that are not directly addressed to us, and that does not suppose still others of which we know nothing definitely.[1]
> —Charles S. Peirce

Whatever else signs are, they are means of communication. But since this encompasses reflexive communication (the self in dialogue with itself), signs are no less instruments of thought. Whatever else communication is, it is a process in which the power of λόγος to disclose a world and constitute a subject capable of exploring the depths, details, and dimensions of this world manifests itself. Whatever else Richard L. Lanigan has contributed to a wide range of important topics (and he has unquestionably contributed a great deal), his contribution, as the very word *communicology* attests, bears directly upon the power of λoγoς to accomplish this. In this endeavor, he draws significantly upon Charles S. Peirce's theory of signs (or semeiotic), also the resources of phenomenology (as these have been provided not only by Peirce but also Maurice Merleau-Ponty). In it, he has committed himself to doing the fullest justice possible to the relevant phenomena, above all, the phenomenon of λoγoς itself.

To some extent, however, this phenomenon is a self-effacing phenomenon. Its very power to disclose the world and constitute a subject capable of exploring the world, including the means by which such exploration is alone possible, tends to deflect attention away from itself. But, then, once the reflexive turn has been made—once the power of signs is acknowledged—there emerges the tendency to become increasingly skeptical about our claims regarding reality. Reality becomes "reality," the scare quotes being symptomatic of a loss of confidence in our ability to encounter or know anything "outside of our own consciousness." We seem to be imprisoned in our own minds, without any possibility of escape, enshrouded in a miasma of signs, without any chance of seeing through their occlusions and obfuscations. With the aid of Peirce, Merleau-Ponty, and other theorists, Lanigan compellingly argues that this is not at all the case. Put positively, he gives both signs and reality their due. On this occasion, then, I want to celebrate his achievement (in particular, this facet of his achievement) by joining him in this undertaking. While my efforts have been informed by Lanigan's writings, I will not track in detail my indebtedness to his work. Rather I will draw upon the resources of Peirce to make a point still insufficiently appreciated by most thinkers today, though one Lanigan deeply appreciates. A celebration of Richard Lanigan will accordingly take, in this essay, the form of what for him and me has proven to be so central to our work—a retrieval, explication, and elaboration of Charles Peirce. Let me begin with our shared vision of the human animal.[2]

Human beings are unquestionably sign-using organisms, but so are countless other species of animals and arguably plants.[3] On countless occasions, we consciously and deliberately address our utterances and gestures to other human beings, but also to other animals (think here of a greeting or command one might direct toward a dog).[4] So, too, other persons address us. Hence, it seems, at least at the outset, more accurate to say that some signs are deliberately or intentionally addressed to us than to claim that some signs address themselves to us.[5] However expressed, there are situations in which we fully apprehend some perceptible configuration *as* a sign directed toward us (including the growl and pose of a dog or the swooping and cawing of a bird). In fact, the general intention of actors in doing so might be even more readily apprehended than the specific import of their utterance (e.g., someone might be angrily shouting at us for reasons and even in a language escaping our comprehension, but there is little doubt that anger—whatever its justification or occasion—is being directed at us).[6] Even a suppressed reaction can betray a resolute intention, allowing another to read what we have desired to conceal. What is left unsaid might indeed sound more loudly than what is said, signs decidedly *not* addressed to us (the furtive glance, the blushing face) might cancel the import of those that *are* addressed to us.

Of anyone who would try, R. W. Emerson contends in "Literary Ethics," "Hide his thoughts? Hide the sun and the moon. They will publish themselves to the universe. Thought is all light. (…) It will speak, though you were dumb. It will flow out of your actions, your manners, your face (…)"[7] He insists, "Don't *say* things: What you *are* stands over you the while and thunders so that I cannot hear what you say to the contrary."[8] In "Spiritual Laws," Emerson employs hyperbole when he claims,

"If you would not be known to do a thing, never do it; a man may play the fool in the drifts of the desert, but every grain of sand shall seem to see. (...) Confucius exclaimed,— 'How can a man be concealed? How can a man be concealed?'"[9] There is however no exaggeration in either the claim that we communicate far more than we consciously intend or the claim that what we resolutely intend to keep hidden works in both subtle and crude ways to publish itself to the universe.

Apart from intention or consciousness, then, we are caught up in processes of communication, ones in which the latent meaning of certain perceptible signs not infrequently calls into question the manifest meaning of other such signs. The participants in even a deliberately undertaken conversation with a definite focus are often not cognizant of the levels and dimensions of meaning operative in their seemingly simple exchange. While this is frequently the case, the process of such an exchange might provide the theorist for a model (if not *the* model) of semiosis or sign-activity.[10] At any rate, Charles S. Peirce found in this process such a model.[11]

The implications of this model are profound. Two especially call for our attention at the outset. The first concerns what I am disposed to call *implicated agency*,[12] the second concerns what (not simply who) counts as an agent in a process of communication.[13] That is, the participants in this process are both implicated agents and more various than the rational agents who seem to be the only ones responsible for initiating, sustaining, and concluding communicative exchanges. The very agency of the participants is not a transcendental condition of a purely formal capacity, but rather an emergent function of a historically situated actor. In short, it is a manifest instance of *implicated* agency. While any agent is implicated in countless situations, the identity of that agent is to some degree bound up with each of the situations in which s/he is implicated.

Moreover, what is being discussed or debated (the subject at hand) exerts itself in ways that imply it has a force and status of its own, apart from the desires and designs of those who according to common sense seem to be the only communicative agents imaginable. In other words, rational agents (personal beings bearing such proper names as *Richard Lanigan* or *Andrew Smith*) are in a sense inseparable from the communicative processes and practices in which they are from the origin of their lives implicated: their very being is bound up with these processes and practices, in sum, with communication. In addition, reality in the apparently modest form of the subject at hand (*whatever* is being discussed by these agents) is not so much inert, amorphous stuff to be shaped in any way one or another of the interlocutors can get away with.[14] These considerations point to a less elevated conception of our power and sovereignty, conjoined to a more exalted understanding of the subject at hand.

OPEN-ENDED, SELF-TRANSFORMATIVE EXCHANGES

Let us return to the example of a conversation and, after highlighting several of its most salient characteristics, prescind[15] from the distinctive features of a deliberate exchange between (or among) rational agents. Our *experience* of the exchange of signs—the give-and-take of communication—is at the basis of any viable theory of signs or account of communication. It is not only our point of departure but also the site to which we must return, time and again, to ascertain whether we know what we are talking about. Whatever abstractions we make have their validity only in reference to the processes from which they are derived and to which they are applicable. What we are talking about indeed exerts itself, however unobtrusively, in our discourses. In our conversations the addresser (or "utterer") and addressee (or "interpreter") exchange roles, and these two roles seem to be essential to any process involving meaning. As I hope becomes ultimately clear, however, the paradox is that, in Peirce's account, the object of semiosis takes the place of the utterer, while at the highest level of generality the utterer vanishes altogether. In a conversation, a speaker or utterer is the source from which signs issue. To a great extent, they issue from an improvisational spontaneity but nonetheless there tends to be a retrospective endorsement of a large bulk of the ordinary speaker's extemporaneous utterances. What further complicates the situation is that the object, as the quasi-utterer, might need to be seen not so much as the initiator of, but a constraint on, an ongoing processes encompassing within itself unrealized possibilities of self-criticism and self-control.[16]

"The action of a sign generally takes place," Peirce observes, "between two parties, the utterer and the interpreter," but he immediately notes that these parties "need not be persons, for a chameleon and many kinds of insects and even plants make their living by uttering signs, and lying signs, at that."[17] For the purpose of this paper, however, my concern is primarily with our species. That purpose is to probe the question, who (or what) are the parties to an exchange of signs? I am using the word *party* here in a strong sense. It designates whatever possesses the power to make a contribution to the exchange. In other words, it designates nothing less than a quasi-agent.

There can be no doubt that *we* utter and interpret signs. Moreover, we institute and modify them, create and try to proscribe them. Quite apart from intention or awareness, we are expressive beings. Our expressivity is inextricably interwoven with our sociality (e.g., an infant spontaneously cries and others take the sounds, tears, and gestures to be expressions of distress or discomfort). We are however also communicative agents: by design and with resolve, we strive to make ourselves understood and to comprehend the expressions, verbal and otherwise, of others. Our humanity is bound up with our ability to utter and interpret a range of signs. Our intelligence is itself intelligible only in reference to this ability.[18] Our agency is efficacious and indeed significant only insofar as it embodies and expresses itself in intelligible exertions, interpretable endeavors.[19] The pattern of drawing and expelling breath is no more involuntary or continuous than are the most rudimentary forms of human signifying. Put the other way around, signifying is as much a part of our being as is breathing. Unquestionably, we are sign-using and symbol-making animals. Our capacity to use and improvise signs and specifically symbols is rooted in innate dispositions or instinctual tendencies. Given our constitution, we cannot help tracing out the practical implications of what arrests our variable attention (this growling animal *means* danger, that broken fence *signifies* the possibility of escape; this stern glance means disapproval; that gentle laugh tolerant acceptance of one's idiomatic fallibility, one's tendency to make just this kind of mistake!).[20]

This is so obviously true that one of the most important features of our reliance on signs is likely to escape our notice. We unreflectively take our reliance on signs to be, in effect, *their* reliance on us: objects and events are elevated to the status of signs as the result of our ingenuity and effort. We confer this status on objects and events; apart from our conferral, nothing is significant.[21] Or so the story goes. But consider for a moment the alternative, one difficult for many of us even to comprehend. It is of course a commonplace that beauty is in the eye of the beholder, so much so that many of my students cannot imagine any other locus. To suggest that beauty is also in the form of the beheld is commonly met with knee-jerk rejection. Without eyes, seeing would be impossible. But, without light, not only seeing but eyes themselves would be impossible. There is a sense in which light called into being the very organs by which it can be apprehended. The evolution of the eye is testimony to the seemingly miraculous power of light to transform tactile sensitivity into distant receptors. The immediacy of contact receptors (the sense of touch requires direct contact with the sensed object) is richly supplemented by the freedom of distance receptors and, beyond these, symbolic resources (above all, the capacity to conceive by means of symbols of the remote and the absent, what no longer is actual and what is not yet so). Unlike touch and taste, hearing and seeing operate at a remove from their objects, if often only a slight distance. In contrast to less complex organisms, more complex ones:

> (…) have distance receptors and a structure in which activators and effectors are allied to distance even more extensively than to contact receptors. What is done in response to things near-by is so tied to what is done in response to what is far away, that a higher organism acts with reference to a spread-out environment as a single situation. We find also in all these higher organisms that what is done is conditioned by consequences of prior activities; we find the fact of learning or habit-formation. In consequence, an organism acts with reference to a time-spread, a serial order of events, as a unit, just as it does in reference to a unified spatial variety. Thus an environment both extensive and enduring is immediately implicated in present behavior. Operatively speaking, the remote and the past are "in" behavior making it what it is.[22]

Put otherwise, present behavior is implicated in a world far beyond the immediate confines of tactile experience. It is implicated in nothing less than a world, not merely *this* environment or even the totality of *Umwelten*.

The distant object, fleetingly glimpsed, no less than a tactile sensation, intensely felt, readily conveys significance. Moreover, the merely symbolized object, no matter how vaguely or elusively conjured by us,[23] can possess a degree of stability sufficient to orient nothing less than our lives.[24] Whatever functions as a sign does so, to some extent, by virtue of its own *agency* (Ransdell). In other words, signs do not depend completely on us, however much some signs are manifestly—and mainly—our handiwork. Objects and events arrest our attention, solicit our concern, and prompt our efforts to make sense of their character, appearance, or numerous other facets of themselves.[25] Our agency is bound up with our capacity to utter and interpret signs, so much so that the very being of anything as a sign is often taken to be utterly dependent on the exercise of our agency. Such an exalted view of human agency might be identified as Promethean humanism. Apart from its designation, countless theorists try to convince us that objects and events are, in themselves, meaningless. They contend that we invest them with significance.

As should be clear by now, the purpose of this paper is to challenge this presumption. To repeat the thesis of this essay, then, the signs on which we rely possess *an agency of their own*. Signs are inherently dynamic: they are in effect actors in the drama of meaning unfolding and, in the course of doing so, generating conflicts—indeed, crises—of signification. Charles S. Peirce is quite explicit about this (see, e.g. MS 634 [September 16, 1909], p. 22). He does not hesitate to speak of the *agency of signs*. This implies that our use of signs draws upon the energy and trajectories of processes tracing their origin to forces and factors other than our own consciousness and even purposes. These signs are not simply tools we use: they are, in some manner and measure, agents with which we collaborate. In this as in all other contexts, then, our sovereignty is limited, our power circumscribed. We are caught up in processes and practices for the most part not initiated or instituted by us or any other human agency, collective or "individual."

Even the overwhelming bulk of our linguistic signs do not depend upon the inaugural acts of the *contemporary* community of linguistically competent individuals. We are for the most part inheritors, not initiators or innovators.[26] Words mean for us, here and now, what they have come to mean ordinarily over the tangled course of a long history, though of course we contribute, mostly unwittingly, to their *ongoing* evolution. So, they mean what have come to mean *and* what they are at pressing coming to mean.[27] The growth of words and other symbols is in certain respects a self-development.[28] There is no transcendental subject or external sovereign directing the course of this development from on high. Rather symbols *evolve*, though they do so in the context of other processes, so there are innumerable, ubiquitous constraints on the self-development of any symbol. But these constraints are in many cases *enabling*, not necessarily oppositional or stultifying. No living being can survive outside of a minimally congenial environment. This is as true of symbols as it is of symbol-using/making animals.

So many theorists today imagine that consciousness or culture endows signs and symbols with significance. The radical implications of the Peircean approach are still not yet as widely and fully appreciated as they need to be. No implication of his approach is of greater importance than this one. Reality is a party to any discourse about it (Middelthon). If you and I are conversing about something, that about which we are talking is one of the participants in the exchange. That *about* which we are conversing is, in effect, something *with* which we are conversing. It has nothing less than the status of (to use Peirce's expression) a *quasi-utterer* or *quasi-interpreter*: it is as though the *Fach* were, in some way, a *Du* (or *Tu*).

Contrast here the positions of Peirce and Mikhail Bakhtin. In "Discourse in the Novel," Bakhtin asserts:

> Mathematical and natural sciences do not acknowledge discourse as a subject in its own right. In scientific activity, one must, of course, deal with another's discourse—the words of predecessors, the judgments of critics, majority opinion and so forth; one must deal with various forms of transmitting and interpreting another's word … but all this remains a mere operational necessity and does not affect the subject matter of the science, into whose composition the speaker and his discourse do not, of course, enter.[29]

On this account, the subject of discourse (that about which scientists are speaking and writing) is ultimately separable from discourse as such. In a claim very close to the one made by Jürgen Habermas in *Knowledge and Human Interest*, Bakhtin insists, the "entire methodological apparatus of the mathematical and natural sciences is directed toward mastery over *mute objects, brute things*, that do not reveal themselves in words, that do not *comment on themselves*."[30]

For our purpose, the most salient point is not his stress on the drive toward mastery over such objects, but his characterization of these objects as mute. There is muteness and muteness.[31] Of course, he would readily grant (at least, I imagine Bakhtin would unhesitantly concede) mathematical and natural objects *do* reveal themselves in signs, just not verbal or discursive ones. But the burden of this passage is to drive a wedge between the objects with which such sciences are preoccupied and those with which the humanities or *Geistwissenschaften* are concerned[32] (see Rorty's "Texts and Lumps"). "In the humanities—as distinct from [or in contrast to] the natural and mathematical sciences—there arises," he observes, "the specific task of establishing, transmitting and interpreting the *words* of others."[33] What is true of the humanities in general is manifestly true of philosophy in particular: "And of course in the philosophical disciplines," Bakhtin immediately adds, "the speaking person and his discourse is the fundamental object of investigation."[34]

Hence, in the humanities, mastery over mute objects gives way to communication with expressive beings.

There are, without question, crucial distinctions to be drawn among just these discourses, but the Peircean cannot help but wonder if (as they are drawn by Bakhtin) they fall in the right places and, moreover, if false notes are not sounded with one or more of Bakhtin's most emphatic claims (most of all, his claim regarding the muteness of objects). It is certainly true that physical objects do not comment upon themselves *in words*. It is however far from evident that they are essentially mute in every sense. They neither disclose themselves in words nor comment on the manner in which they do disclose themselves, again, in words (if indeed they *do*). But the signs by which anything makes its existence known (to be precise, the *indexical* signs by which such things more or less emphatically proclaim themselves), in addition, those by which it ineluctably reveal themselves, in some manner and measure, suggest that such objects (while often being verbally mute) are semiotically articulate.

Our linguistic signs are massively dependent on causal relationships securing a formally semiotic relationship between indices and their objects. In turn, causal relationships involving purely physical objects are themselves indicative of a play of forces. For certain purposes, we can set in stark contrast a world of purely mechanical forces and one of complexly interwoven signs. But the world in which we live is not divided so sharply along these lines. Many words function indexically, just as many events generate of their own accord a sequence of signs. Hence, our world (not the one depicted by our theoretical imaginations, but that *inhabited* by our embodied intelligence) is rather one in which our effective use of language is inseparably bound up with causal relationships of objects and events, also one in which the observable effects of causes are instinctively interpreted as signs of some putatively actual being.

Richard Rorty's voice might be joined to Mikhail Bakhtin in pronouncing the world to be mute. "The world," he insists in *Contingency, Irony, and Solidarity* (Cambridge, 1989), "does not speak. We do."[35] What he adds is very important for our purpose: "The world can, once we have programmed ourselves with a language, cause us to hold beliefs. But it cannot propose a language for us to speak. Only other human beings can do that."[36] Much like Bakhtin, then, Rorty draws an extremely sharp distinction between the realm of causality and that of language, between the world investigated by the natural sciences and that encountered in human discourse. As a literary theorist, Bakhtin is desirous to give literary texts and, more generally, human utterance their due, just as a cultural critic Rorty is committed to giving human vocabularies their transfigurative power. The web of causal relationships is effectively separated from that of linguistic signs, save for objects and events in the world having the power to cause to hold certain beliefs and, by implication, to abandon other beliefs. Also (again, to some extent like Bakhtin), Rorty pays attention almost exclusively to linguistic signs. Mute objects, brute things, simply by virtue of their physical impact can indeed force or prompt human beings to alter their beliefs. But the dualism implicit in such a view is as radical and stultifying as anything put in place by Descartes, Hume, or Kant. Bakhtin's dialogism implies he is, in general, closer to Peirce than Rorty, but we fail to appreciate just how radical Peirce's own dialogism is if we fail to appreciate that the natural world *as approached by natural science* has the status of a partner in a dialogue. Bakhtin does not appear to go this far and Rorty emphatically rejects this position.[37]

Peirce notes an irony in how others tend to respond to his logic, i.e., his theory of signs. What is needed, above all, in the first instance is a "definition of a sign (…) which no more refers to human thought than does the definition of a line as the place which a particle occupies, part by part, during a lapse of line."[38] Just as we can conceive of a line in complete abstraction from the motion of that which leaves a line as a trace of its movement, so we can, in the first instance, conceive a sign in complete abstraction from the operations of mind. But "a good many people who tell themselves that they hold anthropomorphism in reprobation will nevertheless opine (though not in these terms) that I am not anthropomorphic enough in my account of logic as a theory of signs and in describing sign without making any explicit allusion to the human mind."[39] (*NEM*, IV, 313). Indeed, his logic is a curious mix of anti-psychologism and pro-anthropomorphism (without being in the least anthropocentric!).

For our purpose, it is especially important to recall what Peirce claims regarding a line of bricks knocking one another over sequentially as might a line of dominoes.

> A line of bricks stands on end upon a floor, each facing the next one on the line. An end one is tilted so as to fall over upon the next one; and so on until they all successively fall. The mechanical statement of the phenomenon is that a portion of the sum of the energy of motion that each brick had at the instant its centre of gravity was directly over its supporting edge, added to the energy of its fall is transformed into an energy of motion of the next brick. Now I assert no more than this, *but less*, since I do not say whether it was mechanical energy, or what it was that was communicated, when, applying my definition of a Sign, I assert (as I do) that each brick is a Sign (namely, an Index), to the successive bricks of the line, of the original effect produced on the first brick. I freely concede that there is an anthropomorphic constituent in that statement; but there is none that is not equally present in the mechanical statement, since this [by implication, at least,] asserts all that the other form [of statement] asserts. Until you see this, you do not grasp the meaning that I attach to the word "sign."[40]

This sequence of events is a physical phenomenon. But it is equally a semiotic phenomenon. Peirce's use of the word *sign* is indeed bound up in conceiving this phenomenon as semiotic (to repeat, unless you see this, you will not grasp what he means by *sign*).

Three points especially need to be stressed here. First, the mechanistic statement is no less metaphorical than the anthropomorphic one (if we happen to be enamored of metaphors derived from the realm of machines, that might say more about us than the phenomena being described mechanistically). Second, the semeiotic description of the phenomenon in question (the line of bricks falling one after the other) is less metaphysically loaded than the mechanistic one. In other words, the semeiotic description begs fewer fundamental questions than does the mechanistic one—or so Peirce claims in this passage. What are we to make of Peirce's claim here? The specific mode of causality operative in this sequence of events calls for greater justification than the specific type of semiosis exhibited in this sequence. We are closer to a purely phenomenological level when we describe the phenomenon semeiotically than when we describe it mechanistically. The causal and the semeiotic are conjoined in indexicality, but the specific mode of causality needs to be discovered in a way that the indexical functioning of signs does not. Somewhat paradoxically, the significance of *this* (whatever this might be) seizes our attention, simply by its self-assertion or self-insistence, even when we are at a loss with respect to the *significance* of this. Something commands or coerces our attention and, simply in doing so, mobilizes our sense of salience and our instinct to render meaningful what so emphatically asserts itself in our experience. There is indeed something instinctive or innate in our reliance on the index, just as there is in our drive to make sense of things and events.

This drive however is often taken to involve making of things and events something they are not (in a word, meaningful). The operation of this drive is less like the realization of a potentiality than the imposition of order upon chaos, of purely human forms on inherently amorphous stuff. In elevating us to this level of sovereignty, however, we have effectively cut ourselves off from reality. The way out is, in part, to craft a vision in which objects and occurrences are allowed to speak for themselves. Better put, it is to *acknowledge* the extent to which they not only *do* speak for themselves but also the degree to which *we* (at least, by implication) take them to disclose themselves to us. Put most simply, the way out is to reject the characterization of objects as mute. Articulation is a process into which we are initiated by the grace of forces other than ourselves, above all, perceptible objects in their intelligible relationships to one another and to us. In response to the charge that such a characterization entails anthropomorphism, we ought to be unabashed in our defense of the propriety of our reliance on metaphor,[41] and of our deployment of metaphors drawn from the activities of humans.

Insofar as we imagine that reality is, in our discourses, at our beck and call, that there are no limits to our capacity to conceal or distort what we are speaking or writing about (insofar as this is the case), the limitless sovereignty of the modern subject is still in place. Peirce's theory of signs entails nothing less than regicide, for it requires beheading just this sovereign. While walking down the street or groping in the dark, reality unquestionably has the capacity to trip us up. Even in our discourses (however seemingly insular they might seem to be), reality arguably possesses this power. The secondness of the obdurate objects and the perceptible events so prominent in our engagement with the world, the irreducible otherness of those brute Seconds, is a pivotal feature of our discursive exchanges as much as of our physical existence: they are, after all, affairs around which much turns. Even so, we resist fully acknowledging that reality has the power to trip us up nearly as much in the give and take of our discursive exchanges as in the rough and tumble of our everyday actions (e.g., walking down the stairs, climbing up a tree, or pulling down a book from a shelf).

Going back to at least Plato, power (in part) defines reality. Whatever else we might mean by *reality*, we must mean that which has the power to exert (or assert) itself in some fashion and degree, in some context, so that it makes a difference to beings other than itself.[42] Anything that would prove itself to be utterly negligible in every conceivable context—anything that would not make *any* difference anywhere—would be a candidate for nothingness.

Whatever two or more people are talking about, even whatever a solitary person happens to be considering, is a party to the interpersonal exchange or even the solitary reflection. The reason for this is nothing recondite. Whenever anyone is engaged in a dialogue (and, at bottom, our innermost and most private reflections are dialogical), there are discoverable traces of a potentially disruptive reality. As already noted, our very attempts to conceal or misrepresent reality, unwittingly or indirectly, pay homage to its presence and power. Even when we are animated by a desire to do justice to reality, ironically, we ordinarily occlude or distort to some extent what we desire to disclose. Despite our mendacity or obtuseness, reality will out, in some manner and measure. But, despite our painstaking care, rigorous procedures, and nobler passions, reality in its fullness will elude us!

The *subject* is, in one of its principal meanings, an object, being that about which we are talking. But it signifies no less a subject in one of the primary meanings of that word, since it is in effect able to object (to force us to recoil from our attributions or ascriptions to it).[43] The expression serving as my title ("Subjects at Hand") is of course ambiguous. It might mean the topic about which we are conversing *or* (by a slight stretch) the subjects, as already constituted, who are ordinarily identified as the sole actors in a communicative exchange. I intend this ambiguity and, indeed, possibilities beyond these two meanings. The subjects at hand who are caught up in an exchange have, to some extent, consolidated identities and truly fluid ones. The most densely sedimented habits can become unsettled, the seemingly most rigidly fixed identity altered, though many authors today make too much of this (habits are after all—habits; as such, they tend not to be easily modifiable). Even so, the power of *Logos* is nowhere more apparent than in its role in accomplishing just this. Who I in my singularity actually am at this moment lends itself to the task of carrying the exchange forward. But I, as just this recognizable singularity (*this* person partly identifiable by *these* tendencies and habits), am, time and again, exposed to the risk—or, better, benefited by the opportunity—of becoming other than I have been. The subjects at hand, the sign-using actors engaged in conversation, are in some measure at the disposal of a power that they can hardly, if at all, identify, and when these subjects can identify this power they can do so only in a crude, glancing, and superficial manner. The form-generating, open-ended processes in and through which the identity of reality no less than the identities of the inquirers is shaped, misshaped, and reshaped—these processes—demand our recognition.

A realist might be defined as someone who is willing, in some contexts, to remove the scare quotes from the word *reality* and its rough equivalents. Even so, the realist need not be portrayed as an utterly benighted figure. In the case of the Peircean realists, we know that what practically counts as reality is never anything more what some fallible individual or community takes *to be* reality. But we also know, as Peirce puts it, that when we "distinguish between absolute truth and what we do not doubt" (slightly modified), we do so "*only* in the abstract, and in a Pickwickian, sense" (emphasis added). What we do not doubt is, for us, virtually, absolute truth, whatever our verbal qualifications and rhetorical poses. The two things that enable us to draw the distinction between what we do not doubt and absolute truth, albeit only abstractly, are: (1) the nature of our "individual" selves as agents who can question that which we are inclined to accept and (2) our circle of society as "a sort of loosely compacted person, in some respects of higher rank than the person of the individual organism."[44] That is, the dialogical nature of the self and (in certain respects) the personal status of the community enable us to conceive what we do not actually doubt might nonetheless be erroneous.

This is a historical judgment made in the course of an ongoing history. Too little is made of this, especially by traditional defenders of realism, who are inclined to take thick historicism (the kind of historicism exemplified by, say, Hegel and Peirce) to be a form of historical relativism. Moreover, this judgment is a formally fallibilist conception of reality, so understood: what practically counts for us as reality is intrinsically tied to what might be overturned in the course of our experience. The affirmation of reality is qualified by an abiding awareness of our ineradicable fallibility (there is, in particular, no method we might institute that would eliminate the very possibility of error). Hence, such a realist may conceive reality as other than what this or that individual or community happens to take to be the case. We might in principle be mistaken. But, at present, there are instances in which there is no specific, practical reason to doubt that our understanding is, in practice, adequate for the purpose at hand. What so counts as reality is, for us, practically speaking, emphatically or unquestionably real.

The infant is thrust into a world completely transcending *its* understanding. (There is arguably wisdom in the German usage of *id* to designate the infant at the earliest stages of development.) Its lack of control over itself matches its lack of comprehension of the world into which it has been thrown. From the beginning, its life is a struggle to make sense out of what is going on, a struggle inseparably tied to that of winning control over the movement of its own limbs. The very distinction between somatic and extra-somatic events and objects is one drawn in the course of experience. In addition, the distinction between the two can never be an absolutely sharp one. By the very nature of the case, it implies a fuzzy boundary. The distinction between the inner and outer world is nevertheless crucial. The inability to draw it is a hallmark of insanity, as is the incapacity to revise the boundary indicative of at least stupidity, if not fanaticism.

"A sign cannot even be false without being a sign and so far as it is a sign it must be true."[45] A mistaken or deceptive sign trades on its ability to take the interpreter in, to render that agent a dupe. It can do so only insofar as it functions as a sign and, moreover, as a sign of some specific object. In this sense, "it must be true"; that is, it must in some respects be true in order to be false! But the classes of signs, identifiable as symbols, are not simply the handiwork of humans. "A symbol is," Peirce insists, "an embryonic reality endowed with power of growth into the very truth, the very entelechy of reality."[46] A symbol is in its own right a reality, but one possessing the power to disclose facets or dimensions of realities other than itself. Of course, Peirce is keenly aware of how implausible such a claim must sound. He goes so far as to acknowledge this claim cannot but appear "mystical and mysterious because we insist on remaining blind to what is plain." And what he contends is plain or manifest is that "there can be no reality which has not the life of a symbol"[47]

In order to help us see how this might be the case, let's return to Peirce's explanation of what he means by a *perfect sign*. He asks us:

> Consider then the aggregate formed by a sign and all the signs which its occurrence carries with it. This aggregate will itself be a sign [just as book or library or literature is, in a sense, a sign]; and we may call it a *perfect* sign, in the sense that it involves the present existence of no other sign except such as are ingredients of itself. Now no perfect sign is in a statical [or inert] condition: you might as well suppose a portion of matter to remain at rest during a thousandth of a second, or any other long interval of time. The only signs which are tolerably fixed are non-existent abstractions. We cannot deny that such a sign is real; only its mode of reality is not that active [or dynamic] kind which we call existence [or actuality]. The existent acts [its being—more precisely, its mode of being—*is* its activity or actuality], and whatever acts changes, and, indeed, changes by virtue of acting.[48]

What Peirce goes on to say regarding a perfect sign is even more relevant to our principal concerns. "Every real ingredient of the perfect sign is," he suggests, "aging, its energy of action upon the interpretant is running low, its sharp edges are wearing down, its outlines becoming indefinite."[49] However, this tendency is counterbalanced by another. For "the perfect sign is perpetually being acted upon by its object, from which it is perpetually receiving the accretions of new signs, which bring it fresh energy, and also kindle that energy that it already had, but which had lain [or been rendered] dormant."[50] Intimately connected to this tendency, there is the irrepressible spontaneity of the perfect sign: "the perfect sign never ceases to undergo changes of the kind we rather drolly call *spontaneous*, that is, they happen *sua sponte* [of its own accord] but not by *its* will."[51] What such signs manifest are nothing less than "phenomena of growth." Among other things, this implies that such signs are quasi-minds and, as such, "have, like everything else, their own special qualities of susceptibility to determination."[52]

Elsewhere in this manuscript, Peirce characterizes "an ordinary conversation" as "a wonderfully perfect kind of sign-functioning."[53] Reality has a way of inserting itself in the flow of such a conversation. Our mendacity and obtuseness tend to be no match for its wiliness and insistence. This must strike most readers as incredibly sanguine and naïve. But human history offers countless examples of human beings being tripped up and found out, despite their steadfast resolve and ingenious cunning, by reality acting spontaneously (i.e., of its own accord).

It has been no part of my purpose to deny the intelligent agency of human sign-users. While much might go on behind our backs (more precisely, behind the backs of our conscious selves), our conscious agency is not an illusory affair. But we inevitably rely on conspirators, often unacknowledged and hence unappreciated ones, in our efforts to make sense of our world and our lives. Our relationship to these conspirators is exceedingly complex, our purposes only partly overlapping with the trajectories and promptings of these quasi-minds. Our cognitive successes are collaborative accomplishments and our collaborators are hardly limited to other human beings. Whatever turns out to be the subject at hand also turns out to have a hand in the course of any discourse about it, at least when the exchanges making up this discourse are sustained over a significant length of time and, as a result of this duration, tend to be inclusive of a growing number of interlocutors.

Whether truth crushed to earth will rise[54] again, the possibility of crushing truth with impunity—simply the power to forestall indefinitely the discovery or disclosure of truth—turns out, time and again, to prove more than liars, dissemblers, dogmatists, and other enemies of the truth can effect. Whether or not they are destined in the long run to fail, they court exposure the longer they fail humbly and courageously to give reality its due. Here as in so many other respects, we tend to exaggerate, often quite wildly, our own power to denigrate, if not outright to deny, the power of beings other than ourselves. Whatever the subject at hand, neither truth nor humanity is served by such denigration or denial. The promptings and pressures of reality are omnipresent, however attenuated and mediated they characteristically are. Of course, we unquestionably can resist or ignore them, at least in the short run. Our capacity for evasion has as great a reach as does our capacity for denial. Even so, reality proves itself to be an incomparable antagonist to human shiftiness. A steadfast resolve to acknowledge the *force majeure* of enveloping reality is, accordingly, the most prudent course of human conduct. Beyond this, it is an ennobling, because transformative, ideal.[55] "Instead of waiting for experience to come at untoward times," the intelligent person deliberately adopts an experimental approach: that person provokes experience "when it can do no harm and changes the government of his internal world accordingly."[56] But such a person adopts such a stance not only on narrowly prudential grounds (to be able intelligently to anticipate unfortunate or favorable outcomes),[57] but also for ennobling reasons (to sustain a dialogue with reality in which both the possibilities of reality and those of inquirers are more fully realized than the self-delusions of a baseless sovereignty would allow).

CONCLUSION

"Man is," Justus Buchler suggests in *Nature and Judgment*, "born in a state of natural debt, being antecedently committed to the execution or furtherance of acts that will largely determine his individual existence."[58] This is nowhere more apparent than in the execution and furtherance of acts of communication. We are, for the most part, the inheritors, not the initiators, of the conversations in which we are caught up and, indeed, the ones by which we lay effective claim to our communicative competencies. This "natural debt" imposes not so much an impossible burden as countless opportunities for unlimited growth. In seizing these opportunities, we are indeed related to endless things beyond our consciousness. In turn, they relate themselves to us but the accent here falls on an active sense of relating. The relationships in question do not simply obtain; rather they are forged, sustained, intensified, widened, and deepened, by one or another of the relata. To suggest that in many instances they are forged is likely misleading, since this suggestion can all too easily be taken to imply that we begin with disparate events and objects, the work of the mind being that of conjoining them. This is, in my judgment, not ordinarily the case. Continua are as much (if not more) the presupposition as the result of our actions and endeavors. From first to last any human being "discharges obligations. He is obliged to sustain or alter, master or tolerant, what he becomes and what he encounters."[59]

I would have thought that, even more than *pragmaticism*, the word *communicology* would be safe from kidnappers![60] And I would have been wrong! It has been taken up by a far from insignificant number of responsible scholars. Whatever one might feel about the word, that toward which it points is critical. It however might seem pleonastic, since the logos of communication is, after all, the logos of logos. But there is nothing redundant here. There is rather simply the acknowledgment of the inherent and ineluctable drive toward reflexivity (what William James in a different context called intelligent intelligence). Indeed, intelligence can be intelligently or, alas, stupidly deployed. As Richard Lanigan has demonstrated in his work (1992), communicology ultimately promises nothing less than an account in which the very λόγος of κοινωνία is, insofar as this is possible, made manifest. Any form of community however ultimately presupposes nothing less than "continuity of being."[61] The possibility of communication is rooted in such continuity, while the necessity for us to address one another is entangled in the innumerable forms of irreducible otherness. But, if we take seriously the *reality* of communication, then we are at least nudged toward acknowledging the continuity of our being. For Peirce, this practically means that we should "abjure the metaphysics of wickedness,"[62] at the heart of which is the conviction that "I am altogether myself, and not at all you." First of all, it is crucial to realize that "your neighbors are, in a measure, yourself, and in far greater measure than, without deep studies in psychology, you would believe;" second, it is no less critical to acknowledge that "*all* men who resemble you and are in analogous circumstances are, in a measure, yourself, though not quite in the same way in which your neighbors are."[63] The realization or acknowledgment of this of course does not eliminate the distance between us, though the extent to which near and far, neighboring and distant, and other spatial metaphors distort our understanding of the relationships involved in communication requires critical attention.

The various forms of community in which λόγος resounds and indeed by which they are constituted are both "always already" in place and "ever not yet" realized. There *is*, in place, continuity of being. But there is, at present (*whatever* present we happen to inhabit), the becoming of greater continuity, at least the possibility of such becoming. This makes, on the one side, the work of memory and acknowledgment vital to all of these forms of community and, on the other side, imagination and hope no less vital. Indeed, λόγος must call upon all of the Muses, not only Clio but also those luring us to the disciplined cultivation of artistic imagination. In the most rudimentary exchange of signs, the most commonplace instance of communication, we are caught up in the potentially creative tension between the "always already" community of being in which our lives our rooted and the "ever not yet" becoming of a community (a community more worthy of the names that it invokes than historically it has proven to be).

In his opposition to Richard Rorty, Michel Foucault draws the distinction too sharply. He takes Rorty to appeal to a community antecedent to the act of questioning, while he is only comfortable identifying with others as a consequence of critique. But the "we" subsequent to questioning and critique is only possible because there is, in however inchoate and unacknowledged a form, some "we" already in place.

But we have inherited the roles of initiators and innovators, just as we stand in traditions of interrogation and critique (not least of all, a vibrant tradition of ceaseless criticism of everything existing, i.e., of anything traditional). In our various modes of inheritance, appropriation, and transformation of these roles and traditions, the λόγος of communication is dramatically evident. This entails that λόγος must always at certain critical junctures assume the form of μῦθος. A story must be told about how an argument obtained in the course of debate its strictly logical force, how a previously implausible claim won for itself a widening circle of responsible advocates, how a term of denigration became transformed into one of aspiration.

The story of λόγος is, among other things, one in which the dramatic encounter with otherness shatters inherited frameworks and traditional images. It is accordingly one in which the task of communicating across various kinds of divides is taken up anew (see, e.g., Smith). It is, moreover, one in which the reality enveloping those who take up this task works to render itself audible. It is, finally, a task in which failure is inevitable but illuminating, at least potentially illuminating. The most exalted form of λόγος thus turns out to be the most humble form—the capacity to learn from our mistakes and misunderstandings. As much as anything else, this depends upon breaking out of the circle of our own ideas, most of all, the excessively narrow circle of our inherited ideas, and discerning the not yet intelligible manner in which reality itself is addressing us. Reality is more than "reality," more than our conceptualizations or anticipations of it. It is not an exaggeration to claim that λόγος is not only the capacity to communicate with one another but also the capacity to envision ourselves always already in communication with some facet of reality. Of course, such a vision would be incomplete if we did not also stress that, regarding just this facet of reality, we are ever not yet in a position to make final or definitive claims. Approximation must be the fabric out of which our philosophy, especially our philosophy of communication, is woven.[64] Of course, "there is a world of difference between fallible knowledge and no knowledge,"[65] just as there is such a difference between fragmentary or partial knowledge and absolute or complete knowledge. The modern problematic of knowing reality is symptomatic of a deracinated sensibility. A sensibility rooted in nature, history, and language is simply not disposed to doubt the very possibility of knowledge, however much it readily admits the inescapable inadequacy of inherited frameworks. Such a deeply root sensibility reveals itself not least of all by its nuanced receptivity to experiential reality, reality as it discloses itself in the course of our experience. It accords reality the status of an interlocutor. The subject at hand, whatever that subject might be, is no lifeless plaything of an allegedly sovereign subject. It is rather a living presence in an ongoing dialogue. Peirce knew that, to modern ears, this must sound like "stark madness, or mysticism, or something equally devoid of reason and good sense."[66] So much the worse for modern ears, those possessed by thinkers who imagine themselves to begin by being completely cut off from reality and, despite this ontological rupture, imagine it is possible to institute the means by which to bridge this divide between mind and reality. As a theorist who has so deeply and imaginatively drawn upon Charles Peirce, John Dewey, Maurice Merleau-Ponty, and others to eradicate this image, the multifaceted contribution of Richard L. Lanigan[67] (in a sense, the subject at hand) encompasses the abiding need to acknowledge experiential reality in its full force. Hence, I have, in focusing on this topic, tried to honor him by exploring, in my own manner, an important facet of that singular contribution. In being little more than notes for a phenomenology of communication (if indeed it is more than a set of such notes), this essay has in effect joined him in probing the depths of "that wonderfully perfect kind of sign-functioning"— "an ordinary conversation." In such an exchange of signs, there are always more than two partners. In sometimes brutally intrusive but more often imperceptibly subtle ways, the subject at hand asserts itself, intrudes upon the attributions and impositions of human utterers, but also gently guides and continually animates the course of the conversation. No doubt, those who are familiar with the writings of Richard will discern the numerous places where he has made his illuminating presence felt.

NOTES

1. Charles S Peirce, *New Elements of Mathematics*, vol. IV (*NEM* IV), ed. Carolyn Eisele (Atlantic Highlands, NJ: Humanities Press, 1976), 299.
2. The extent to which our thought overlaps and the points at which they diverge can be discerned by comparing and contrasting Lanigan's "The Two Senses of a Phenomenology of the *Weltanschauung*," *The American Journal of Semiotics* 28, no. 1/2(2012): 63–72, and my "In Behalf of the World," 129–147.
3. "Even plants," Peirce insists, "make their living ... by uttering signs."
4. For an insight into Peirce's relationship to his poodle Zola, see Charles S. Peirce, *The Essential Peirce*, vol. 2, ed. Peirce Edition Project (Bloomington: Indiana University Press, 1998), 467–468. Also see Douglas Anderson, "Peirce's Horse: A Sympathetic and Semeiotic Bond," in *Animal Pragmatism*, ed. Erin McKenna and Andrew Light (Bloomington: Indiana University Press, 2004), 86–96.
5. Of course, a person might intentionally address another individual without being explicitly or vividly conscious of the intention to do. That is, an intention, one unqualifiedly and unhesitantly acknowledged upon being asked, can be implicit in an act without issuing from a conscious resolve. One can imagine an individual acting on an explicit resolution (e.g., "If the opportunity arises, I will speak to Josephine"). But one can as easily imagine a person purposefully speaking to another person without the act of doing so being one issuing from such a resolution. It would in most circumstances nonetheless be purposive or deliberate.
6. Virginia Woolf, *A Room of One's Own* (San Diego: Harcourt Brace Jovanovich, 1989), 5–6.
7. Ralph Waldo Emerson, "Literary Ethics" in *Nature: Addresses and Lectures* (Boston, MA: Houghton, Mifflin, 1849.), 129.
8. Ralph Waldo Emerson, "Social Aims" in *Letters and Social Aims* (Boston, MA: Houghton, Mifflin, 1892), 95. "It is," he asserts in this essay, "the law of our constitution that every change in our experience instantly indicates itself on our countenance and carriage, as the lapse of time tells itself on the face of a clock. We may be too obtuse to read it, but the record is there" (83).
9. Ralph Waldo Emerson, "Spiritual Laws" in *Essays: First and Second Series*. Boston: Houghton, Mifflin.
10. See especially Max H. Fisch, *Peirce, Semeiotic, and Pragmatism* (Bloomington: Indiana University Press, 1986), 370; also Joseph Ransdell, "Another Interpretation of Peirce's Semiotic," *Transactions*

of the *Charles S. Peirce Society* 12, no. 2 (Spring 1976): 97–110; Mats Bergman, *Peirce's Philosophy of Communication* (London: Continuum, 2009), 93–94.

11. In *Peirce, Semeiotic, and Pragmatism*, Fisch rightly notes: "Peirce began where most of us begin, with a model, which taken by itself, would suggest too narrow a definition of [*semiosis* or sign-activity]; namely, the model of conversation between two competent speakers of the same natural language – say, English" (357). *Cf.* Ransdell, "Another Interpretation," 97–108. To go to the horse's own mouth, see Peirce, *Essential Peirce*, 403–404.

12. I derive this expression partly from John Dewey. In an article on "The Terms 'Conscious' and 'Consciousness,'" he notes: "That of being 'conscious *to* one's self': having the witness to something within one's self. This is naturally said especially of one's own innocence, guilt, frailties, etc., that is of personal activities and traits, where the individual has peculiar or unique evidence not available to others. 'Being so conscious unto my selfe of my great weaknesse' (Usher, 1620). Here is a distinctively personal adaptation of the social, or joint, use. The agent is, so to speak, reduplicated. In one capacity, he does certain things; in another, he is cognizant of these goings-on. A connecting link between 1 and 2 is found in a sense (obsolete like 1) where conscious means 'privy to,' a cognizant accomplice of, – usually, a guilty knowledge. It is worth considering whether 'self-consciousness,' in both the moral and the philosophic sense, does not involve this distinction and relation between the self doing and the self reflecting upon its past or future (anticipated) doings to see what sort of an agent is implicated; and whether, in short, many of the difficulties of self-consciousness as a 'subject-object' relation are not due to a failure to keep in mind that it establishes connection between a practical and a cognitional attitude, not between two cognitional terms." This is reprinted in *The Middle Works of John Dewey*, vol. 3, ed. Jo Ann Boydston (Carbondale: SIU Press, 1977), 79–80 (*MW* 3, 79–80). In an even earlier essay ("Social and Moral Interpretations in Mental Development"), Dewey wrote of the situation in which a child is being initiated into morality by an elder: "the 'other' personality is not the source of moral law, but simply the mediator who, through deeper insight and greater power of interpretation and expression, reveals to the child the reality of the situation, the organized action, in which as agent he is *implicated*. The moral law is the law of this situation, and the moral self is the one which organizes its various powers into unity through functioning them in reference to the situation" (*EW* 5, 421; emphasis added). *The Early Writings of John Dewey*, vol. 5, ed. Jo Ann Boydston (Carbondale: SIU Press, 2008).

13. More than a decade ago, the anthropologist Anne-Lise Middelthon suggested this idea to me. A dialogue is, she observed, triadic in that two people are talking about something and what is being talked about finds a way of exerting an influence of its own. Initially, I failed to grasp either most basic meaning of this suggestion or its fundamental importance. I doubt that I have done justice to it here, but in the time since she first suggested this to me I have become convinced that this idea is not only deeply Peircean but also fundamentally right.

14. This is obviously an allusion to Richard Rorty's suggestion, in *Philosophy and the Mirror of Nature* (Princeton, NJ: Princeton University Press, 1979), that truth is "what your contemporaries let you get away with" (176).

15. As Peirce uses the term, *precission* (the verb *prescind* being obviously a cognate of this word) is that mode of abstraction in which we consider some facet or aspect of a thing or event in abstraction from other facets or aspects (e.g., the dynamics of a family apart from the neighborhood in which it resides). The form of functioning characteristic of semiosis is discerned only by attending to certain features of observable processes in abstraction from other features. In brief, it is discerned by means of precission. *Precissive* abstraction is to be distinguished from hypostatic *abstraction*.

See T. L. Short, "Hypostatic Abstraction in the Empirical Sciences," *Grazer Philosophische Studien*, 32 (1988): 51–68, and "Hypostatic Abstraction in Self-Consciousness," in *The Rule of Reason: The Philosophy of Charles Sanders Peirce*, ed. Jacqueline Brunning and Paul Forster (Toronto: University of Toronto Press, 1997), 289–308; also J. Jay Zeman, "Peirce on Abstraction," in *The Relevance of Charles Peirce* (La Salle, IL: Monist Library of Philosophy, 1983), 292–311.

16. See Vincent Colapietro, "Toward a Pragmatic Conception of Practical Identity," *Transactions of the Charles S. Peirce Society* 42, no. 2 (2006): 173–205; also T. L. Short, *Peirce's Theory of Signs* (Cambridge: Cambridge University Press, 2007).

17. MS 318, variant 17; quoted in Colapietro 1989, 22. The action of a sign entails, as it turns out, the agency of that sign. Signs are actors in the unfolding dramas of incipient meaning, as often as not, dramas of self-correction (ones wherein a mistake or misunderstanding not only comes to light but also forces modifications, often profound ones, in the way one is to go on.

18. Umberto Eco, *A Theory of Semiotics* (Bloomington: Indiana University Press, 1976).

19. In "Being, Immediacy, and Articulation," *The Review of Metaphysics* 24, no. 4 (1971): 593–613, John E. Smith compellingly argues for the need to recognize *insistence* and *persistence* as traits of any being whatsoever. In this essay, I am simply developing an important implication of this suggestion. In this same essay, he shows how all action is an instance of expression and, in turn, all expression itself an enactment or the result of an exertion. So, my conception of agency is also an elaboration of insights put forth by Smith here and indeed elsewhere.

20. John Dewey, *Experience and Nature*, vol. 1 of *The Later Works of John Dewey* (Carbondale: SIU Press, 1988), 142. Hereafter cited as *LW* 1.

21. In contrast to Nietzsche, we might identify *nihilism* with the tendency to take objects and events apart from us to be devoid of meaning and value.

22. Dewey, *LW* 1, 213.

23. See, e.g., Charles S. Peirce. *The Collected Papers of Charles Sanders Peirce*, vols. 1–6, ed. Charles Hartshorne and Paul Weiss, vols. 7 and 8, ed. Arthur W. Burks (Cambridge, MA: Belknap Press of Harvard University Press, 1931–1958), *CP* 3.433.

24. Generally, "ordinary words in the bulk of languages are assertory. They assert as soon as they are in any way attached to any object. If you write GLASS upon a case, you will be understood to mean that the case contains glass. It seems certainly the truest statement for most languages to say that a *symbol* is a conventional sign which being attached to an object signifies that that object has certain characters. But a symbol, in itself, is a mere dream; it does not show what it is talking about. It needs to be connected with its object. For that purpose, an *index* is indispensable" (*CP* 4.56). He adds: "A *meaning* is the associations of a word with images, its dream exciting power" (*CP* 4.56.). It is however important to note that, in strictest terms, a symbol is a sign based upon a disposition, not necessarily a convention. For there are, in Peirce's judgment at least, natural symbols (ones rooted in innate dispositions, e.g., the tendency of a deer to interpret certain sounds as signifying the proximity of a predator).

25. See, e.g., Dewey, *LW* 1, 141–143.

26. Justus Buchler, *Nature and Judgment* (New York: Columbia University Press, 1955), 3.

27. Above all, we need to look, Peirce advises, to "the *history* of words, not their *etymology*," since this history is "the key to their meanings, especially for a word saturated with the idea of progress as science is" Wiener, Philip W. (ed.). *Charles S. Peirce: Selected Writings* (NY: Dover, 1958), 403.

28. *Cf.* Peirce, *CP* 4.10.

29. Mikhail Bakhtin, *The Dialogical Imagination: Four Essays by M. M. Bakhtin*, trans. Caryl Emerson and Michael Holquist (Austin: University of Texas Press, 1981), 351.

30. Bakhtin, Dialogical Imagination, 351
31. Bakhtin's critique of what we would call *scientism* is, in fact, very close to Peirce's critique of what he called nominalism and positivism. In many, perhaps most, fundamental respects, he is closer to Peirce than Rorty. But there is one important respect in which Bakhtin is closer to Rorty than Peirce and this is what I want to stress here (though for those unfamiliar with these authors this clearly runs the risk of misleading characterizations). Physical objects as studied by physical scientists are, for Peirce, not mute, whereas they are, for Bakhtin and Rorty. I am indebted to Andrew Smith for his criticism of an earlier attempt at triangulation among these three thinkers.
32. There is certainly an irony in the fact that, regarding the distinction between the natural and the human sciences, Bakhtin's position is far more nuanced than Rorty's, but Rorty in such essays as "Texts and Lumps" refrains from drawing a categorically sharp distinction between the two domains. Rorty's essay was first published in *New Literary History* 17, no. 1 (1985): 1–16, then reprinted in Rorty's *Philosophical Papers*, vol. 1 (Cambridge: Cambridge University Press, 1990), 78–92.
33. Bakhtin, Dialogical Imagination, 351 (emphasis added).
34. Bakhtin, Dialogical Imagination, 351
35. Richard Rorty, *Contingency, Irony, and Solidarity* (Cambridge: Cambridge University Press, 1989), 6. *Cf.* Karsten Harries, "Metaphor and Transcendence," *Critical Inquiry* 5, no. 1 (Autumn 1978): 73–90; reprinted in Harries, "Metaphor and Transcendence," in *On Metaphor*, ed. Sheldon Sacks (Chicago: University of Chicago Press, 1979), 71–88. Harries is as emphatic in claiming the world itself speaks as Rorty is in denying this.
36. Rorty, *Contingency, Irony, and Solidarity*.
37. Given his importance for the task of theorizing communication, it is not irrelevant here to recall that Jürgen Habermas actually attributes to Peirce the view he (Peirce) rejects. See *Knowledge and Human Interests*, trans. Jeremy J. Shapiro (Boston, MA: Beacon Press, 1972), Chapters 5 and 6; also "Peirce and Communication," in *Peirce and Contemporary Thought*, ed. Kenneth Laine Ketner (New York: Fordham University Press, 1994), pp. 243–266. See also Klaus Oehler's "A Response to Habermas," in this volume, 467–471. What Habermas inexplicably misses and Oehler so astutely discerns is Peirce's *tuism*, (as defined by Peirce in 1891 in the *Century Dictionary*) "the doctrine that all thought is addressed to a second person, or to one's future self as to a second person." This definition is quoted in Max H. Fisch's Introduction to volume 1 of the *Writings of Charles S. Peirce: A Chronological Edition* (Bloomington: Indiana University Press, 1982), xxix.
38. Peirce, *NEM*, IV, 20.
39. Peirce, *NEM*, IV, 313.
40. Peirce, *NEM*, IV, 313–314.
41. *Cf.* Max Black, *Models and Metaphors: Studies in Language and Philosophy* (Ithaca, NY: Cornell University Press, 1962); also Buchler, *Nature and Judgment*.
42. See my "Marking Distinctions and Making Differences: Being as Dialectic," *Journal of Speculative Philosophy* 10, no. 1 (1996): 1–18; reprinted in *Being and Dialectic: Metaphysics as Cultural Presence*, ed. William Desmond (Albany: SUNY Press, 2000), 37–56.
43. Dewey, *LW* 1, 184.
44. Peirce, *Collected Papers* (*CP* 5.421); also in *Essential Peirce*, vol. 2, ed Peirce Edition Project (*EP* 2, 338).
45. Peirce, *NEM* IV, 262.
46. Peirce, *NEM* IV, 262. It is certainly not incidental or insignificant that *entelechy* is a term borrowed from Aristotle's writings, at least in the sense in which Peirce is using it here. There is

a *telos* immanent in semiosis. This is not antecedently fixed, once and for all, except possibly at the highest level of generality. It is rather a dramatic instance of what Peirce calls *developmental teleology*, a process in which historically novel ends emerge and evolve. See "The Law of Mind" in *Collected Papers of Charles Sanders Peirce*, vol. 6, ed. Hartshorne and Weiss (CP 6.156); also in *The Essential Peirce*, vol. 1, ed. Nathan Houser and Christian Kloesel (Bloomington: Indiana University Press, 1992), 331.

47. Peirce, *NEM* IV, 262.
48. Peirce, *The Essential Peirce*, vol. 2, 545, note 25.
49. Peirce, *The Essential Peirce*, 545.
50. Peirce, *The Essential Peirce*, 545.
51. Peirce, *The Essential Peirce*, 545.
52. Peirce, *The Essential Peirce*, 545 (slightly modified).
53. Peirce, *EP* 2, 391.
54. Peirce was very fond of these lines in William Cullen Bryant's poem "The Battle-Field": "Truth, crushed to earth, shall rise again;/The eternal years of God are hers;/But Error, wounded, writhes in pain,/And dies among his worshipers." See *The Essential Peirce*, vol 1, p. 378, note 21.
55. Peirce, *Charles Sanders Peirce: Contributions to The Nation: Part One: 1869–1883*, ed. Kenneth Laine Ketner and James Edward Cook (Lubbock: Texas Tech University Press, 1975), 188–189. Quoted in Colapietro, *Peirce's Approach to the Self* (1989), 95–97.
56. Peirce, *EP* 2, 2, 370.
57. In *The Quest for Certainty* (1929) – that is, *The Later Works of John Dewey*, vol. 4, ed. Jo Ann Boydston (Carbondale: SIU Press, 2008) – Dewey not only brings this point into sharp focus but also connects it to our capacity for symbolization. "By means of symbols, whether gestures, words, or more elaborate constructions," he insists, "we can act without acting. That is we perform experiments by means of symbols which have results which are themselves only symbolized, and which do not therefore commit us to actual or existential consequences. If a man starts a fire or insults a rival, effects follow; the die is cast. But if he rehearses the act in symbols in privacy, he can anticipate and appreciate its result. Then he can act or not act overtly on the basis of what is anticipated and is not there in fact. The invention or discovery of symbols is doubtless by far the single greatest event in the history of man. Without them, no intellectual advance is possible; with them, there is no limit set to intellectual development except inherent stupidity" (*LW* 4, 121).
58. Buchler, *Nature and Judgment*, 3.
59. Buchler, *Nature and Judgment*, 3.
60. Peirce, *EP* 2, 335.
61. "All communication from mind to mind is," Peirce insists, "through *continuity of being*" (*CP* 7.572; emphasis added).
62. Peirce, *CP* 7.571; slightly modified.
63. Peirce, *CP* 7.571
64. Peirce, *CP* 1.404.
65. Peirce, *CP* 1.37.
66. Peirce, MS 290, 58; quoted in Colapietro, *Peirce's Approach to the Self*, 113.
67. The better word here is *power*, at least if we are trying to be faithful to Peirce. What the pragmaticist adores "is *power*; not the sham power of brute force, which even in its own specialty of spoiling things, secures slight results; but the creative power of reasonableness, which subdues all other powers" (*CP* 5.520; Colapietro, *Peirce's Approach to the Self*, 92).

BIBLIOGRAPHY

Anderson, Douglas R. "Peirce's Horse: A Sympathetic and Semeiotic Bond." In *Animal Pragmatism*, edited by Erin McKenna and Andrew Light, 86–96. Bloomington: Indiana University Press, 2004.

Bakhtin, Mikhail. *The Dialogic Imagination: Four Essays by M. M. Bakhtin*. Edited by Caryl Emerson and Michael Holquist. Austin: University of Texas Press, 1981.

Bergman, Mats. *Peirce's Philosophy of Communication*. London: Continuum, 2009.

Black, Max. *Models and Metaphors: Studies in Language and Philosophy*. Ithaca, NY: Cornell University Press, 1962.

Buchler, Justus. *Nature and Judgment*. Ithaca, NY: Columbia University Press, 1955.

Colapietro, Vincent. "In Behalf of the World." *The American Journal of Semiotics* 28, no. 1/2(2012): 129–147.

Colapietro, Vincent. "Marking Distinctions and Making Differences: Being *as* Dialectic." In *Being and Dialectic: Metaphysics as Cultural Presence*, edited by William Desmond, 37–56. Albany, NY: SUNY Press, 2000.. Originally published in *Journal of Speculative Philosophy* 10, no. 1 (1996): 1–18.

Colapietro, Vincent. *Peirce's Approach tot eh Self*. Albany: SUNY Press, 1989. "Signification and Interpretation," 2003.

Colapietro, Vincent. "Toward a Pragmatic Conception of Practical Identity." *Transactions of the Charles S. Peirce Society* 42, no. 2 (2006): 193–205.

Dewey, John. *Experience and Nature*. Vol. 1 of *The Later Works of John Dewey*. Edited by Jo Ann Boydston. Carbondale, IL: SIU Press, 1925. Cited as *LW* 1.

Dewey, John. *The Quest for Certainty. The Later Works of John Dewey*, vol. 4. Edited by Jo Ann Boydston. Carbondale, IL: SIU Press, 1988 [1929]. Cited as *LW* 4.

Eco, Umberto. *A Theory of Semiotics*. Bloomington: Indiana University Press, 1976.

Emerson, Ralph Waldo. *Essays: First Series*. Boston, MA: Houghton, Mifflin, 1968.

Emerson, Ralph Waldo. *Letters and Social Aims*. Boston, MA: Houghton, Mifflin, 1892.

Emerson, Ralph Waldo. *Nature: Addresses and Lectures*. Boston, MA: Houghton, Mifflin, 1883.

Emerson, Ralph Waldo. "Spiritual Laws." In *Essays: First and Second Series*, 93–120. Boston: Houghton, Mifflin, 1981.

Fisch, Max H. *Peirce, Semeiotic, and Pragmatism*. Edited by Kenneth Laine Ketner and Christian J. W. Kloesel. Bloomington: Indiana University Press, 1986.

Habermas, Jürgen. *Knowledge and Human Interests*. Translated by Jeremy J. Shapiro. Boston, MA: Beacon Press, 1971.

Habermas, Jürgen. "Peirce and Communication." In *Peirce and Contemporary Thought*. Edited by Kenneth Laine Ketner, 243–266. New York: Fordham University Press, 1994.

Harries, Karsten. "Metaphor and Transcendence." *Critical Inquiry* 5, no. 1 (Autumn 1978): 73–90.

Harries, Karsten. "Metaphors and Transcendence." In *On Metaphor*, edited by Sheldon Sacks, 71–88. Chicago: University of Chicago Press, 1979.

Langer, Susanne K. *Philosophy in a New Key*. 3rd ed. Cambridge, MA: Harvard University Press, 1996.

Lanigan, Richard. "The Two Senses of a Phenomenology of *Weltanschauung*." *The American Journal of Semiotics* 28, no. 1/2 (2012): 63–73.

Oehler, Klaus. "A Response to Habermas." In *Peirce and Contemporary Thought*, edited by Kenneth Laine Ketner, 467–471. New York: Fordham University Press, 1994.

Peirce, Charles S. *Charles Sanders Peirce: Contributions to the Nation: Part One: 1869–1883*. Edited by Kenneth Laine Ketner and James Edward Cook. Lubbock: Texas Tech University Press, 1975.

Peirce, Charles S. *The Collected Papers of Charles Sanders Peirce*, vols. 1–6. Edited by Charles Hartshorne and Paul Weiss, vols. 7 and 8. Edited by Arthur W. Burks. Cambridge, MA: Belknap Press of Harvard University Press, 1931–1958.

Peirce, Charles S. *The Essential Peirce*. Edited by the Peirce Edition Project. Bloomington: Indiana University Press, 1998.

Peirce, Charles S. *The New Elements of Mathematics of Charles S. Peirce*, vol. IV. Edited by Carolyn Eisele. Atlantic Highlands, NJ: Humanities Press, 1976. Cited as *NEM* IV.

Ransdell, Joseph. "Another Interpretation of Peirce's Semiotic." *Transactions of the Charles S. Peirce Society* 15, no. 2 (1976): 97–110.

Ransdell, Joseph. "Semiotic and Linguistics." In *The Signifying Animal: The Grammar of Language and Experience*, edited by Irmengard Rauch and Gerald F. Carr, 135–185. Bloomington: Indiana University Press, 1980.

Rorty, Richard. *Contingency, Irony, and Solidarity*. Cambridge: Cambridge University Press, 1989.

Rorty, Richard. "Lumps and Texts." *New Literary History* 17, no. 1 (1985): 1–16.

Rorty, Richard. *Objectivity, Relativism, and Truth* [*Philosophical Papers*, volume 1]. Cambridge: Cambridge University Press, 1991.

Rorty, Richard. *Philosophy and the Mirror of Nature*. Princeton: Princeton University Press, 1979.

Short, T. L. "Hypostatic Abstraction in Self-Consciousness." In *The Rule of Reason: ThePhilosophy of Charles Sanders Peirce*, edited by Jacqueline Brunning and Paul Forster, 289–308. Toronto: University of Toronto Press, 1997.

Short, T. L. "Hypostatic Abstraction in the Empirical Sciences." *Grazer Philosophische Studien* 32 (1988): 51–68.

Short, T. L. *Peirce's Theory of Signs*. Cambridge: Cambridge University Press, 2007.

Smith, John E. "Being, Immediacy, and Articulation." *The Review of Metaphysics* 24, no. 4(1971): 593–613.

Smith, John E. *Reason and God: Encounters of Philosophy and Religion*. New Haven, CT: Yale University Press, 1961.

Woolf, Virginia. *A Room of One's Own*. San Diego: Harcourt Brace Jovanovich, 1989.

Zeeman, J. Jay. "Peirce on Abstraction." In *The Relevance of Peirce*, edited by Eugene Freeman, 293–311. La Salle, IL: The Monist Library of Philosophy, 1983.

CHAPTER EIGHTEEN

Being in Speech

Inferentialism, Historicism, and Metaphysics of Intentionality

JASON HANNAN

What does it mean to possess the power of speech? What separates a talking parrot from a person? Why do we not count our pets as one of us, even if they reliably respond to certain vocal commands? Why do we not treat computers as interlocutors, even though we make use of language to interact with them? When we distinguish ourselves from other beings and entities—animal and machine—who are "we" and why do "we" take ourselves to be different from "them"? What exactly are the relevant criteria of demarcation by which we recognize each other as members of the community of "us" and "we"?

It is easy to say that "we" are different or special because we possess the power of speech. It is likewise easy to illustrate that difference through examples of "us" and "them." However, being explicit about what this power entails is a much more challenging task. If we set our focus either too narrowly or too broadly, we are liable to reach conclusions that strike us as intuitively wrong, theoretically deficient, or wholly misleading. If, for example, speech is understood merely as a matter of being able to exercise our vocal chords in such a way as to utter words and sentences, then surely parrots should be counted as speakers. Yet, we do not treat parrots as speakers or persons. Similarly, if speech is, by definition, a specifically human faculty, then we would, by that same definition, have to rule out the possibility of non-human animals and machines capable of speech. That, too, strikes us as problematic. After all, what if some breeding group of non-human primates were to develop the ability to speak? What if we were to succeed in creating artificial intelligence? What if we were to discover an intelligent form of alien life? These are very real possibilities, though their probability is a different matter. That they can be entertained as real possibilities at all is sufficient to appreciate why conceptualizing speech in anthropocentric terms is ultimately disappointing: we would need some way to describe what it is that hypothetical non-human speakers and persons would need to possess without reducing them to our human biology. How, then, should we understand the power of speech, if not as a faculty defined in human terms?

The thought of Robert Brandom is devoted to providing a philosophical conception of the power of speech. Introducing Brandom to an audience of outsiders is no minor challenge. Brandom is very much a philosopher's philosopher—someone to whom professional philosophers turn for original insights into very basic and traditional questions in philosophy. It can take some time, and in some cases years, just to wrap one's head around Brandom's complex system. So, what I hope to do in this chapter is to give a very basic idea of what he's about. Unlike pragmatist figures like Richard Rorty or Richard Bernstein, Brandom remains largely unheard of in communication studies. And unfortunately, his writings may appear formidably dense and technical, making him even less likely to find an audience outside of his home territory.

Brandom had three main teachers at Princeton: Richard Rorty, Donald Davidson, and David Lewis. From Rorty and Davidson, Brandom inherited a certain radical philosophical outlook, and from Lewis, a love of technical complexity and conceptual precision. Together, the two styles combine to create an original and exciting philosophical orientation. Perhaps the best way, though, to appreciate Brandom's thought is by comparing him to the classical figures of American pragmatism. One of the many strands that bind the classical figures together is their indebtedness to Hegel. This indebtedness is most obvious in the cases of Dewey and Mead, less so in that of Peirce, and only indirectly in the case of James. Nonetheless, their key Hegelian orientation lies in their rejection of old dualisms like subject and object, and mind and body, and a shift towards the social, the practical, the historical, and the organic. Thus, instead of understanding mind and body as separate entities to be explained in separate terms, the kind of explanatory strategy that typically results in explanatory failure, they posited a single organic system interacting with its surrounding environment.

However, because the classical figures saw the human organism as just one biological organism among others, they stressed the continuities between the human and the non-human—our contemporary non-human cousins and our prehistoric hominid ancestors. In emphasizing this continuity, they effectively dissolved the distinctions between the human world and the natural world. Instead, they saw just one world, inhabited by human and non-human alike, a world just as Darwin conceived it.

Although Brandom has no wish whatsoever to revive any notion, religious or humanistic, of an essential human uniqueness or metaphysical importance, he nonetheless affirms that there is a valid distinction to be drawn between the natural and something else. This distinction concerns *discursive capacity*. Brandom's entire project revolves around Hegel's insight that the ability to ask and to answer "Why?" questions—that is, to be suitably caught up in social practices in which *reasons* may be given for what one says or does—"transforms merely *natural* creatures into distinctively *cultural* ones".[1] And because discursive creatures are caught up in a discursive space, their "*history* plays a role that *nature* plays for non-discursive creatures."[2] So that, if you were to ask why it is that birds fly south in the winter, the question will be very different from asking why it is that we celebrate holidays, stand during national anthems, or oppose child labor. In each of these latter cases, there is a certain historical chain of reasons behind our decision to act the way we do, a historical chain that Hegel, and others following him, calls a tradition.

Again, Brandom has no interest in preserving any hard and fast distinctions between the human and the non-human. His focus, rather, is on the difference between the discursive and the non-discursive: what it is to possess the capacity for speech, as opposed to, say, a well-trained dog which more or less reliably responds to certain vocal sounds, or a parrot that says, "Polly want a cracker". In this respect, Brandom's philosophical project may be understood as a systematic theory of this discursive capacity, as well as of the implications of possessing it—a capacity that, in principle, is open to non-human animals, intelligent alien life, and artificially intelligent machines.

The difference between discursive and non-discursive creatures is the difference between the capacity for *sapience* and that of mere *sentience*. On this view, merely sentient creatures are those with a certain awareness of their surrounding environment: of the presence and distance of physical objects, of the location of food and the means to it, or of imminent danger. Sapient creatures, on the other hand, are those with an awareness of their discursive environment—of the complex network of reasons that animate the speech and action of those who similarly inhabit that environment. To be a sapient creature is thus to be able to see what a merely sentient creature cannot see.

The title of Brandom's *magnum opus* is *Making it Explicit*. The idea of making something explicit is taken from Hegel's description of expressive rationality in his *Science of Logic*. This idea can be understood as "making what is implicit in practice explicit in principle."[3] So, if I were to ask, for example, why you consistently object to my conduct, I am asking for the *reason* behind your objection. Perhaps you find my conduct elitist, or racist, or sexist, or homophobic. When we articulate a reason in this way, we are making explicit a principle that implicitly guides what we say and do, a commitment we may not have thought explicitly about before. Making something explicit means we can now talk about it. We have an awareness of it. We've brought it under our spotlight, so to speak, and can now analyze it. And, with enough time, we may realize that this commitment-turned-principle has itself been guided by a further, deeper commitment, one which itself may in turn be made explicit. In this way, we would have achieved an awareness of some aspect of our earlier awareness. And this ongoing process of making it explicit means an ever-increasing awareness. This is not just a description of what ordinary people do in everyday life. According to Brandom, making it explicit is the very stuff of the philosophical enterprise.

It is on this core idea of making it explicit that Brandom's entire philosophical system revolves, a system that includes a semantic theory, a theory of communication, a theory of norms and normativity, a theory of action, a theory of truth and objectivity, a theory of mind, and, ultimately, a theory of rationality. A superficial reading of Brandom may lead one to believe that he is merely another technical analytic philosopher of little or no value to a critically engaged discipline like rhetoric and communication studies. This impression, however, would be very gravely mistaken. For one thing, there is a tension between Brandom's thought and the basic thrust of analytic philosophy, since he rejects its traditional aims and methods, even if he retains a commitment to answering many of its traditional questions. Second, quite unlike his analytic colleagues, most of whom have an incurable hatred of Continental thought, Brandom's work happily crosses the Analytic-Continental divide and draws from both traditions. His heroes include Spinoza, Leibniz, Hegel, Frege, Heidegger, and Wittgenstein.[4] Third, and most importantly, Brandom's system offers the conceptual tools for social and political critique. In what follows, I discuss two such examples.

CONCEPTS, SELVES, AND HISTORY

The first example concerns the recognitive basis of selves and concepts. In *Tales of the Mighty Dead: Historical Essays in the Metaphysics of Intentionality*, Brandom provides a pragmatist reading of Hegel's conceptual idealism. He investigates not only the meaning of concepts, but also their normative power: why it is that concepts exert a certain power and authority over us. We, for example, take accusations of sexism and racism seriously. We do not, however, take accusations of "elbowism" or "hairism" seriously. Why not?

Brandom's first order of business is to draw a careful distinction between Hegel and Kant on the normative character of concepts. As Kant rightly showed, judgments can be the targets of critical evaluation. We can evaluate a judgment to be correct or incorrect, including our judgment about judgments. This is one of the principal distinctions between sapient and sentient beings: sapient beings can be held responsible for what they do and say. But this raises a fundamental question: where do we locate the standards of judgment? How do we know that a particular judgment is correct or incorrect, including our judgments about judgments? Kant held the view that these standards are derived through transcendental means. They are to be found in a noumenal realm above the messy and imperfect world of everyday life and practice. Because these standards derive from the noumenal realm, they are fixed, timeless, and unchanging. Unlike worldly standards, which change with time, the standards derived from the noumenal realm are impervious to time and history. Kant's view was that we select from a stock of standards from the noumenal realm and apply them to the practical sphere. If we get it wrong, then it's our fault, not the fault of the standard. We then simply apply a different standard until we get it right. Hence, moral judgments, such as *sexism* and *racism* have a singular and unchanging meaning. As normative beings that apply judgments to particulars, we lack the power to shape or influence the meaning of those standards. They are fixed for all time. This makes sense in light of Kant's overall philosophical project, which eliminates individual arbitrariness from the realm of moral and empirical judgment.

But as Brandom reminds us, Hegel departs from Kant in his explanation of conceptual normativity. According to Hegel, it's not just that we select and apply standards to particulars. Rather, we also have the power to determine the content of those standards by applying them to unprecedented particulars. Hegel regards Kant's treatment of standards and concepts as essentially inorganic. By contrast, Hegel insists that standards and concepts are living entities, subject like all other life to development over the course of history. For Hegel, standards and concepts are therefore determined, not by the transcendental realm, but rather by actual conceptual practice. What, then, is the difference that makes the difference between Hegel and Kant?

Brandom holds the view that, if we want to understand Hegel's philosophy of the concept, we need to understand first the mutual authority and reciprocal recognition on which they're based. This authority and recognition come in three distinct parts: social, inferential, and historical. Concepts come into being the same way that selves come into being: they arise through reciprocal recognition. On this view, understanding the nature of the self is the key to understanding the nature of concepts. The self only arises through other selves. It requires recognition by other selves. When recognition is mutual, the self is fully synthesized. The self then secures membership in a community of selves. There is another key part of selfhood, though. To be a self is to be a creature of normativity, "a locus of commitment and responsibility."[5] Freedom is not the absence of norms. Rather, freedom is only achieved through commitment and responsibility. Acting according to norms to which one is committed in practice is to follow rational authority. By contrast, acting according to norms to which one is not committed in practice is to follow non-rational force.

Norms, however, are not to be found in the noumenal realm. On the contrary, norms are synthesized through acts of mutual recognition. A community without norms is not a truly free community. Only through the synthesis of norms can a community be free. These norms indicate social relationships of independence and dependence. To endorse a norm is to elect to follow it independently. But in following a socially synthesized norm, one is then allowing oneself to be held accountable by those who also follow that norm, thereby being dependent upon their judgments. Both the content and power of norms are thus rooted in mutual, social recognition. We can now see the similarity between concepts and the self: since both are governed by norms, both are grounded in the social. Without the social, neither concepts nor the self could have any existence at all.

The second part concerns the inferential dimension of language use. Following Kant, Hegel holds that norms are nothing more than concepts. Hence, as Brandom argues, they both regard "talk of norms and talk of concepts" as "alternatives for addressing one fundamental common phenomenon."[6] But there's a big difference. Hegel sees the meaning of concepts as determined by their role within inferential relationships. Such relationships come in two types: mediate and determinate negation. The meaning of a concept is determined in part by the mediating role it plays between the premise and conclusion of an inference. For example:

> Racism is an injustice.
> Injustice is intolerable.
> ∴ Racism is intolerable.

In this inference, *injustice* is the middle term that links racism to intolerability. The meaning of concept of *injustice* is thus determined partly through inferences linking it to other concepts, like *racism* and *intolerability*. On the other hand, determinate negation occurs when one concept negates another. For example, if inequality is an injustice, then inequality cannot be just. If only justice is tolerable, then injustice cannot be tolerated. When seen together, these two types of inferential relationships not only give concepts their meaning, but also determine the norms by which they can be applied as judgments.

These inferential relationships reveal two types of authority that determine the content of concepts: universals and particulars. First, concepts have abstract relationships to each other. When I assert that inequality is an injustice, I help to determine the meaning of both inequality and injustice. But as pure abstractions, these ideas are meaningless. They need to be applied to real life situations to have actual meaning. When I apply the concept of injustice to a particular circumstance, such as a case of police brutality against a racial minority, I'm applying a universal to a particular to help make sense of that circumstance. But the nature of the circumstance can be such as to demand that the concept be applied. The particular therefore calls out, as it were, for that universal to be applied. Universals and particulars exert power over each other.

We therefore have two types of judgments: mediate and immediate. Mediate judgments are the result of abstract relationships. Consider the following example:

"It has been found that law enforcement in the US is racist. Therefore, the US suffers from injustice." On the other hand, we can directly apply universal concepts to particular circumstances to make immediate judgments: "Law enforcement in the US is racist." Of course, the application of a universal concept to a particular circumstance is never a straightforward affair. Sometimes, we disagree about whether a universal applies to a particular. For example: "Killing animals for food is an injustice." While some might agree that killing animals for food is indeed an injustice, not everyone would follow them in this application of the concept of injustice. We therefore struggle for recognition of the appropriateness of applying a concept to a particular circumstance. That struggle, that conflict, is what enables the meaning of a concept to evolve.

The third dimension is *historical*. The application and negotiation of concepts is not merely a synchronic process within a given discourse community; it is also a diachronic process spanning multiple generations over time. The way in which reciprocal recognition determines the meaning and authority of concepts over time is through the authority that past and future applications exercise over each other. Because the application of concepts requires some historical precedent to be meaningful and intelligible, past applications establish the boundaries or parameters that distinguish legitimate from illegitimate future applications. However, past applications may not be entirely compatible with one another. Hence, the need to evaluate past applications to differentiate legitimate from illegitimate past applications. Thus, past and future applications hold each other accountable.

But does the relationship between past and present not introduce the problem of asymmetrical authority? If the past is to be evaluated by the future, then who holds the future accountable? Doesn't the future then enjoy the last and final word? Well, no, not exactly. We need to ask, at which *point* in the future? Any future generation evaluating the past will subsequently be held accountable by a later generation. Each point in the future is subject to judgment by a later point in the future. This means that the process of making judgments and then evaluating those judgments (making judgments about judgments) has no ultimate end. The process is open-ended and indeterminate.

The evolutionary history of the idea of equality serves as a powerful case in point. When Jefferson declared that all men are created equal, which relied on earlier applications of the concept of equality, applications that provided his declaration with meaning. As such, this did not mean that the concept of equality applied to literally all men, and certainly not to all people, but rather only to privileged white Anglo-Saxon men like himself. The idea of equality evolved over the course of time to include all white men generally, then to include black men, and eventually to include women. The concept then continued to evolve to include LGBTQ individuals and people with disabilities. There is now a fierce debate underway, led by animal rights activists, over whether to extend the idea of equality to animals. We can therefore see that a moral concept that was initially limited to a very narrow class of people has evolved and grown to include a much broader range, not only of people, but now increasingly of non-human beings.

The history of the idea of equality is instructive. We can clearly see how it developed over time through the process of negotiation. New applications of the concept managed, through social struggle, to secure social recognition. Following Hegel, Brandom holds that by studying the history of public discourse, we can uncover hidden principles that guided our use of those concepts all along. Identifying them, bringing them into the light, giving them a name is what Brandom calls "making it explicit." So, we can understand the objection to Jefferson's concept of equality as the charge of elitism. We can understand the objection to the subsequent version as the charge of racism, the third objection as that of sexism, and so on. Each of these objections is based on the principle that arbitrarily excluding people from the domain of equality is wrong.

Equality therefore has no essential or unchanging meaning. It is a concept that has evolved over the course of history through the process of struggle, negotiation, and recognition. Through this process, we have come to recognize different types of discrimination that violate the principle of equality: elitism/classism, racism, sexism, homophobia, ableism, speciesism, etc. According to Brandom, it is not just in the historical process that concepts find their meaning. It is in the historical process that selves come into and sustain their being.

DEMOCRACY AS TRADITION

Jeffrey Stout has demonstrated the enormous value of Brandom's thought for ethical and political theory. Stout is arguably one of the most provocative and politically important scholars in the field of religious studies. His work is devoted to the study of ethics in pluralistic democracies. A central concern for Stout is the problem of relativism. Specifically, he worries about the implications of relativism for communication and democratic discourse. This concern was first addressed in his book, *Ethics After Babel: The Languages of Morals and their Discontents*, a detailed study of the challenge that moral and cultural diversity presents to modern liberal democracies. Like others before him, Stout uses the Biblical story of Babel as a powerful metaphor for our present time. He sees modern democracies as suffering from two related types of internal division, moral and linguistic. Stout poses the problem as follows: if we lack a universal moral language by which to make sense of each other's utterances, and if we lack universal standards of truth and justification, then are not, in effect, fated to become a latter-day version of Babel, marked by a chaos of moral tongues?

Ethics After Babel can be read as a kind of extended conversation with Alasdair MacIntyre, whose controversial 1981 book, *After Virtue*, leveled a merciless critique of the state of moral discourse in modern liberal democracies. In addition to challenging MacIntyre, Stout also took up the relativist challenge, represented by such figures as David Wong and Gilbert Harman. It is often claimed that nobody would actually admit to being a relativist. But this popular myth isn't actually true. There are indeed some who would happily identify as relativists, albeit in a qualified, moderate form, Wong and Harman being two salient examples. What are the practical implications of being a relativist about which Stout worries so much? The answer is that relativism undermines the possibility of a rational politics by making choice between different political standpoints purely arbitrary. Relativism is, of course, a very complicated and heated topic, not least because relativism can be formulated through multiple and sometimes incompatible theses. Stout never intended to provide a final and definitive rebuttal to moral or linguistic relativism. He did, however, make a forceful case that relativism should not be seen as the final and definitive word on the possibility of moral discourse in a pluralistic world.

In *Democracy and Tradition* (2004), Stout continues his project by raising the philosophical sophistication of his original argument. While he remains within a broadly pragmatist framework, he now relies on Brandom's thought to bolster his argument. He advances a vigorous and impassioned political theory of democracy, one that compares in its originality and complexity to the political theories of John Rawls and Jürgen Habermas. What is the core to Stout's theory of democracy? Like Habermas, the core is a conception of communication and public deliberation, conceived as the language game of giving and asking for reasons, an idea with philosophical roots in Wittgenstein and Sellars. Set against Locke's transportation model of communication, Brandom's inferentialist approach to language conceives of communication as the practice of navigating through the utterances of one's interlocutor. On this view, meaning isn't transported from one mind to another. Rather, we hear another's utterances, we create a map of those utterances, and continually work to make sense of what the other is saying, leaving each utterance open to reinterpretation in the light of a new map or picture of the larger web of utterances. On this view, concepts lack fixed and unchanging meanings. Rather, their meanings are constantly negotiated and developed through the practice of discourse. Brandom also departs from Kuhn and Feyerabend, who insist that incommensurability rules out the possibility of common reference to objects in the world. Brandom holds that different inferential systems, despite lacking a common foundation, can still be used to refer to common objects in the world. In so doing, Brandom upholds a referential dimension to discursive practice while rejecting the representationalism characteristic of so much of analytic philosophy. The upshot of this model is a view of communication that allows for a working, imperfect understanding of each other's webs of belief.

Stout relies upon Brandom's model to propose a theory of deliberative democracy as an alternative to the so-called "new traditionalists," a category in which Stout places such figures as Alasdair MacIntyre, Stanley Hauerwas, and John Milbank. Stout contends that the new traditionalists, with their valorizing of tradition and their rejection of a universal morality, end up denying a rational, deliberative politics. Stout advances the view that the absence of a universal morality does not logically conclude with the rejection of democratic deliberation. Relying on Brandom's navigation model, he defends a conception of communication and linguistic ability shared by all speakers. He further contends that a universal morality is unnecessary for mutual accountability. Turning to Rawls, he holds the view that immanent criticism can do a perfectly fine job of putting each other's moral and political claims to the test. Immanent criticism, however flawed and imperfect, is sufficient for rational public deliberation.

Against his neo-traditionalist rivals, Stout sets out in *Democracy and Tradition* to uphold a vision of democracy as a bona fide tradition. This goal is driven by two basic reasons, theoretical and practical. The first has to do with the very idea of rationality. Despite his strong disagreements with MacIntyre, Stout acknowledges that rationality is a decidedly historical phenomenon, bound like other phenomena by time, culture, and history. MacIntyre is, of course, derivative in this respect, having drawn this idea from the thought of Hans-Georg Gadamer and Michael Polanyi. To endorse this historicist conception of rationality is to reject any and all appeals to rationality as such, a supposedly timeless, transcultural, and ahistorical space of reasons. The historicist argument holds that our moral and political reasoning inevitably hits a limit in the form of time-bound and historically particular premises. MacIntyre goes so far as to assert that the pretension to tradition-independent reasons and premises is little more than the imposition of one's culturally idiosyncratic values upon others. The best we can ever hope for is a social universe marked by creative contest between traditions. To play this game honestly, it is therefore necessary to acknowledge the tradition(s) on which our moral arguments are based.

The political reason behind Stout's project concerns the threat to the culture of democracy by the new traditionalists, a threat that regards democracy as incurably biased towards tradition and that demands the abandonment of tradition as a prerequisite for participation in democratic politics. Stout therefore formulates a theory of democracy *as tradition* to show his new-traditionalist rivals that democratic citizenship does not demand the abandonment of tradition. More to the point, there is no reason to withdraw from the public culture of democracy and seek refuge within the safe and comfortable confines of some supposedly pure and protected tradition. Stout adamantly rejects the idea of democracy as a bland, lifeless, and utterly procedural system devoid of the markers of inspiring traditions: heroes, saints, epic sagas, and virtues. Democratic citizenship is perfectly compatible with communal identity and commitment. It allows for the retention of one's moral identity. It does not demand that we speak through an artificial and procedural idiom. On the contrary, democracy can be seen, indeed must be seen, as a living, organic tradition, inspired by democratic heroes, shaped by democratic narratives, guided by democratic virtues, and striving for democratic ideals. Stout beautifully illustrates democracy's status as a tradition through moving accounts of such democratic figures as Ralph Waldo Emerson, Walt Whitman, Ralph Ellison, and James Baldwin. What these great figures have in common is their contributions to a democratic discourse whose conceptual structure Stout describes through Brandom's theoretical model. By turning to Brandom, Stout is thus able to make explicit dimensions of democratic culture entirely overlooked by his neo-traditionalist colleagues. He moreover demonstrates that being in speech is a fundamentally democratic mode of being.

HISTORICISM AND PHENOMENOLOGY: TWO PARADIGMS FOR POSTHUMANISM

In this final section, I would like to explore the promise of two different paradigms for a posthumanist ethics and politics. But why posthumanism? The answer concerns the disturbing character of our contemporary condition. We are now living in what scientists have called the sixth extinction: a period of unprecedented destruction of the natural world, driven by anthropogenic activity. At a rapidly increasing rate, we are losing countless animal and plant species to human overpopulation, industrial agriculture, industrial fishing, deforestation, and air, water, and land pollution. The legacy of modern humanism, with its focus upon the human to the exclusion of the non-human, is a distinct blindness to the suffering we inflict upon nature. We have erected all manner of false ideas to justify our domination over nature. We imagine ourselves to be special because we possess the capacity for speech, because we are toolmakers, because have rituals and traditions, and because we have complex codes of morality—all secular versions of the ancient belief that we were created in God's image. We take our supposed superiority over nature as the moral foundation to justify factory farming. We use it to justify animal testing for medicine and cosmetics. We imprison wild animals in zoos and force them to perform in circuses for our entertainment. We raze ancient forests to make way for cash crops, thereby depleting one of the planet's natural carbon sinks. Among ecologically minded activists, politicians, and academics, there is a growing consensus that we badly need a new way of thinking about our place in the world and our relationship to nature. In this respect, posthumanism is not another academic fashion, but rather a timely and urgent project for acting responsibly toward nature and reversing the worst of our human excesses. Fortunately, we can turn to two distinct philosophical traditions for conceptual tools for formulating a posthumanist approach to ethics and politics.

The first of these traditions is Brandom's version of historicism, as recounted above. In developing a theory of rationality grounded in the social practice of giving and asking for reasons, Brandom takes care not to define sapience in human terms or humanity in sapient terms. Brandom's categories of rationality and intentionality are not, in principle, limited to human beings. His theory allows for the possibility of non-human creatures of speech, both animal and machine. Indeed, by elevating rationality and intentionality to supreme importance, the very category of the human is of decidedly secondary importance in Brandom's order of philosophical concern. The type of being in whom Brandom invests so much interest is similar to the being that Heidegger designates as Dasein—a discursive being so immersed in everyday social and linguistic practices that the implicit principles that guide those practices become the ground of its conscious existence. For Brandom, as for Heidegger, what follows from the capacity for speech is not universal human rights, but rather implicit normative commitments, which can be made explicit through interpersonal reasoning. These normative commitments can become the basis for contingent rights—rights for humans, for animals, and for the planet—but they are the result of the social practice of giving and asking for reasons. Rights are the outcome of communication, not prior to it. Just as we can demand rights for ourselves, we can demand rights for those who cannot demand them for themselves. The upshot of Brandom's philosophy is a theoretical foundation for a pluralism of rights, a foundation that consists, not of human free will or human dignity, but of intersubjective recognition. Rather than a humanistic conception of human rights over nature, historicism enables *responsibility* toward nature through the recognition of the suffering of non-human beings. Through the communicative practice of giving and asking for reasons, Brandom's historicism offers a paradigm for a posthumanist ethics and politics.

Can the same be said of phenomenology? The answer is complicated by the fact that phenomenology can lend itself to both humanism and posthumanism. The thought of Richard Lanigan is an example of the first. Lanigan's lifelong project has been the development of the discipline of communicology, which he defines as the science of human communication. This science is indebted to the two principal historical figures of phenomenology, namely, Edmund Husserl and Maurice Merleau-Ponty. Lanigan takes Husserl's dictum that "subjectivity is intersubjectivity" and Merleau-Ponty's principle that "the body is our general medium for having a world" to be the twin axioms of communicology.[7] Lanigan does also draw from other key theorists, such as Charles Peirce, Martin Heidegger, Roman Jakobson, and Michel Foucault, but Husserl and Merleau-Ponty can be said to be his central theorists.

So, how does Lanigan understand phenomenology? Referencing the history of philosophy, Lanigan insists that a semiotically inflected phenomenology is "the most promising approach to understanding the scope of human conscious experience."[8] Lanigan sees phenomenology as providing the answer to the longstanding problem of mind-body dualism in philosophy and science alike. By understanding the nature of human consciousness, we can account for the link between expression and perception. The twin foundations of Husserl (intersubjectivity) and Merleau-Ponty (embodiment) form the answer to the mind-body problem. But in pursuing this line of argument, Lanigan makes an anthropocentric claim, which thus accounts for the humanistic focus of his philosophical project. As he puts it, "Human beings, *unlike animals and machines*, function on three simultaneous levels of consciousness that integrate the expression and perception of (1) Affect or emotion, (2) Cognition or thought, and (3) Conation or purposeful action."[9] Lanigan thus sets humanity apart from the non-human world. By relegating animals outside the scope of his multilevel conception of human consciousness, Lanigan not only affirms the traditional hierarchy of man over beast, but also excludes the non-human from his scope of philosophical concern. Hence, his focus on human communication, human consciousness, and human experience. The practical applications of his thought invariably concern human subjects, as for example his illuminating discussion of phantom limbs.[10]

This is not, of course, to dismiss the enormous value of Lanigan's work for shedding light on the nature of human experience. It is, however, to point out a limitation, one that might be overcome by rethinking phenomenology in more expansive terms. How, then, might phenomenology lend itself to a posthumanist outlook? Here, I think the rise of object-oriented ontology offers the greatest promise for reorienting phenomenology in a posthumanist direction. Recent theorists, such as Graham Harman, Ian Bogost, and Levi Bryant, have developed an object-oriented ontology that decenters the human and reconceptualizes the relationship between the human and the non-human in non-hierarchical terms.[11] The relevant distinction is that object-oriented ontologists reject any argument about human uniqueness, especially with respect to consciousness, and this for the simple reason that we simply do not have access to the phenomenal experience of non-human beings—animal, machine, and otherwise. Object-oriented ontologists therefore regard objects of whatever kind, both animate and inanimate, as possessing a uniqueness and integrity that cannot be understood reductively by their relationship to us. We can *treat* certain objects as possessing or lacking intentionality. This does not mean that they do or do not possess intentionality. From the standpoint of object-oriented ontology, any definitive claim that non-human objects lack our cognitive capacities is a non-starter.

Object-oriented ontology works through the general paradigm of phenomenology, but draws from systems theorists such as Jakob von Uexküll and Niklas Luhmann, whose theories of embodiment pave the way for a radical perspectivism. And it is here that phenomenology offers real promise for a posthumanist ethics and politics, for what humans and non-humans share is embodiment in the physical world. In so far as we take up three-dimensional space, we will necessary perceive and experience the world from a certain finitude and situatedness, limited not only by our spatio-temporal location, but also by our physical and chemical composition—biology, in the case of human and non-animals; technology, in the case of machines. Each of us apprehends the world through such a perspective. Each of us attempts to communicate through that perspective. This necessarily limits what we can say with confidence about other beings, both non-human and even human. Thomas Nagel, for example, has famously argued we cannot possibly claim to know what it is like to be a bat. No matter how advanced our scientific understanding of bats, we can never step into the mind and body of a bat to know what it is like to be one. But the implications of this argument extend to other human beings, as well. If we cannot know what it is like to be some non-human being, why should we think we know what it is like to be a human being from another culture or even one from our own culture? Doesn't our embodiment and inescapable situatedness undermine any confident claim to a universal human experience? Thus, if we adopt the radical perspectivism demanded by an object-oriented ontology, thereby demoting our perspective in status and importance, we find ourselves called upon to consider the perspectives of both, non-human beings and even our fellow human beings as something at once embodied, yet to some degree beyond our experience. We might know that another creature experiences pain, but we will likely never know what it is *like* to experience that pain. That we can both endure pain brings us together; that we cannot know each other's pain sets us apart. Object-oriented ontology thus clarifies our powers and our limitations in knowing each other. These powers and limitations warrant, not rights and entitlements, but rather responsibility toward other perspectives. In recognizing our inability to know what it is like to be another object, whether human or non-human, we simultaneously recognize an implicit responsibility toward that object, the same responsibility we feel toward ourselves as embodied beings that have needs and face dangers. Far from resulting in an ethical relativism, a phenomenology of objects would result in a more compassionate world.

I would like to suggest that Lanigan's lifelong interest in the interpretation of human experience can easily be extended to the interpretation of *non*-human experience. His project has all the tools set in place for examining objects through the prism of phenomenology. Just as Brandom's historicism can underwrite an ethics and politics of responsibility toward nature, Lanigan's model of a semiotically inflected phenomenology is ideally suited for the interpretation of non-human suffering, thereby similarly underwriting an ethics and politics of responsibility. In decentering the human and restructuring the relationship between humans and non-humans in non-hierarchical terms, a semiotically inflected phenomenology of objects can help craft a posthumanist politics.

One final word of caution is necessary. In the appendices to Lanigan's *The Human Science of Communicology*, he includes a review of the French ethnologist Lucien Lévy-Bruhl's 1910 book *Les Fonction Mentales Dans Les Sociétés Inférieures*, which was translated into English in 1926 and euphemistically titled *How Natives Think*.[12] Lévy-Bruhl divides humanity into two types of "minds;" the first he terms "native," "prelogical," and "primitive" minds. These are the "minds" of certain non-European peoples, who, according to Lévy-Bruhl, see all objects, both human and non-human, in supernatural terms. Thus, they see life and spirit in inanimate objects, such as mountains, clouds, and trees. What Lévy-Bruhl has in mind is something like animism, though it is unclear which cultures he would classify as animist. In contrast to "primitive" minds, Lévy-Bruhl describes "Western" and "logical" minds as those that see life in living organisms only. In keeping with the Darwinian spirit of his day, Lévy-Bruhl argues for an evolutionary teleology according to which "primitive" minds evolve over time into "civilized" minds. He does express sympathy for "primitive" minds, albeit from an armchair perspective, and criticism of "Western" minds, albeit to a very limited degree. He suggests that we can turn to "primitive" minds to learn how to appreciate the world around us through what he calls the "Law of Participation," in which both human and non-human, animate and inanimate, beings might participate with each other through shared experience. Notwithstanding this limited sympathy for non-European peoples, Lévy-Bruhl's hierarchy of humankind, with Europeans on top and non-Europeans at the bottom, is the sort of thing that makes 21st century readers cringe with horror. Yet, Lanigan suggests that Lévy-Bruhl can serve as a basis for the human science of communicology.

While Lanigan's brand of phenomenology can serve as a paradigm for a posthumanist ethics and politics, I would strongly argue against the use of so curiously antiquated a figure as Lucien Lévy-Bruhl for any purpose other than as an example of how *not* to conduct humanistic inquiry. Although Lanigan does not explicitly invoke an object-oriented ontology in his review of *How Natives Think*, the temptation to draw from Lévy-Bruhl for such a purpose would be seriously misguided, for it would entail endorsing arguments, premises, and categories from Lévy-Bruhl's hierarchical division of humanity, which no serious reader could possibly accept, and would beg more questions than it could possibly answer. Any attempt to draw from non-European cultures for a posthumanist ontology should proceed entirely outside of the racist lens of a Eurocentric ethnology.

NOTES

1. Italo Testa, "Hegelian Pragmatism and Social Emancipation: An Interview with Robert Brandom," *Constellations* 10, no. 1 (2003): 554–570.
2. Testa, "Hegelian Pragmatism and Social Emancipation," 555.

3. Testa, "Hegelian Pragmatism and Social Emancipation," 555.
4. Robert Brandom, *Tales of the Mighty Dead: Historical Essays in the Metaphysics of Intentionality* (Cambridge, MA: Harvard University Press, 2002).
5. Brandom, *Tales of the Mighty Dead*, 53–54.
6. Brandom, *Tales of the Mighty Dead*, 223.
7. Richard Lanigan, "Human Embodiment: An Eidetic and Empirical Communicology of Phantom Limb," *Methodo: International Studies in Phenomenology and Philosophy* 3, no. 1 (2015): 257–287.
8. Brandom, *Tales of the Mighty Dead*, 258.
9. Richard Lanigan, "Mind-Body Problem," in *Encyclopedia of Identity*, ed. R. L. Jackson. (Thousand Oaks, CA: Sage, 2010), 450–454. emphasis added.
10. Lanigan, "Human Embodiment."
11. Graham Harman, *Tool-Being: Heidegger and the Metaphysics of Objects* (Peru, IL: Open Court, 2002); Ian Bogost, *Alien Phenomenology, Or What It's Like to Be a Thing* (Minneapolis: University of Minnesota Press, 2012); and Levi Bryant, *The Democracy of Objects* (London: Open Humanities Press, 2011).
12. Richard L. Lanigan, "Appendix A: Lévi-Bruhl and the Human Science 'Law of Participation.'" *The Human Science of Communicology: A Phenomenology of Discourse in Foucault and Merleau-Ponty* (Pittsburgh, PA: Duquesne University Press, 1992), 191.

BIBLIOGRAPHY

Bogost, Ian. *Alien Phenomenology, or What It's Like to Be a Thing*. Minneapolis: University of Minnesota Press, 2012.

Brandom, Robert. *Making it Explicit: Reasoning, Representing, and Discursive Commitment*. Cambridge, MA: Harvard University Press, 1994.

Brandom, Robert. *Tales of the Mighty Dead: Historical Essays in the Metaphysics of Intentionality*. Cambridge, MA: Harvard University Press, 2002.

Bryant, Levi. *The Democracy of Objects*. London: Open Humanities Press, 2011.

Harman, Graham. *Tool-Being: Heidegger and the Metaphysics of Objects*. Peru, IL: Open Court, 2002.

Hegel, George Wilhelm Friedrich. *The Science of Logic*. Translated by George Di Giovanni. Cambridge: Cambridge University Press, 2015.

Krebs, Angelika."Discourse Ethics and Nature." *Environmental Values* 6, no. 3 (1997): 269–279.

Lanigan, Richard L. "Appendix A: Lévi-Bruhl and the Human Science 'Law of Participation.'" In *The Human Science of Communicology: A Phenomenology of Discourse in Foucault and Merleau-Ponty*, 191. Pittsburgh, PA: Duquesne University Press, 1992.

Lanigan, Richard. "Human Embodiment: An Eidetic and Empirical Communicology of Phantom Limb." *Methodo: International Studies in Phenomenology and Philosophy* 3, no. 1 (2015): 257–287.

Lanigan, Richard. "Mind-Body Problem." In *Encyclopedia of Identity*, edited by R. L. Jackson, 450–454. Thousand Oaks, CA: Sage, 2010.

MacIntyre, Alasdair. *After Virtue: A Study in Moral Theory*. Notre Dame, IN: University of Notre Dame Press, 1981.

Stout, Jeffrey. *Democracy and Tradition*. Princeton, NJ: Princeton University Press, 2004.

Stout, Jeffrey.*Ethics After Babel: The Languages of Morals and Their Discontents*. Princeton, NJ: Princeton University Press, 1988.

Testa, Italo."Hegelian Pragmatism and Social Emancipation: An Interview with Robert Brandom." *Constellations* 10, no. 4 (2003): 554–570.

Wolfe, Cary. *Animal Rites: American Culture, the Discourse of Species, and Posthumanist Theory*. Chicago, IL: University of Chicago Press, 2004.

Wolfe, Cary. *Humans and Other Animals in a Biopolitical Frame*. Chicago, IL: University of Chicago Press, 2012.

Wolfe, Cary. *What is Posthumanism?* Minneapolis: University of Minnesota Press, 2010.

CHAPTER NINETEEN

The Theory of Perfective Drift

JOHAN SIEBERS

> Again, perfection is a notion which haunts human imagination.
> It cannot be ignored. But its naïve attachment to the realm of
> forms is entirely without justification.[1]
> —Alfred North Whitehead

The theory of which I aim to sketch a basic outline here has to be understood as a philosophical theory of communication. Our first task, then, will be to clarify what sets a philosophical theory of communication apart from other communication theories. It is here that the contemporary scholar feels deep gratitude towards the work of Richard Lanigan. For he has, over many years and in many publications, drawn our attention like few others to the specifically philosophical aspects of communication as a concept and as a phenomenon. In particular, I wish to refer here to his seminal explorations in the philosophy of Merleau-Ponty.[2] Any reading of Merleau-Ponty's mature philosophical writings cannot fail to give us the strong impression that questions of communication were central to his investigations, but it is the contribution of Lanigan, and others, to have shown just how central the theme of communication is to Merleau-Ponty's embodied phenomenology of relationality and expression are; and more so to have begun to make this phenomenological approach fruitful for the whole field of communication studies.

In an early publication on this topic, Lanigan highlighted the dialectical relation that exists between perception and expression in Merleau-Ponty's phenomenology.[3] These functions are, as it were, two sides of the same coin, what Lanigan calls the *synergic function of intentionality*. Both perception and expression are characterized by what I would like to call a reaching-out, a real relating or communicating, that creates and pervades the togetherness or synergy of being. Perception is then understood as a relation of signs that connect subject and object while expression is understood as the synthesis of a sign system and its use in concrete occasions of the projection of a self into a world that surrounds it. This process, the process of speech, then has two modalities, an existential and an empirical one. Lanigan shows how both interpersonal communication as well as intrapersonal communication can be understood along the lines of the mutual dependency of perception and expression. The point to note here is that perception and expression are understood as ontological factors. They are the way in which being is constituted in its nature as a dialectical going-together of unity and plurality, of one and many. Because perception and expression are, in Lanigan's interpretation of Merleau-Ponty, the two sides of the single process that we call communication, we begin to see that communication has a much more fundamental role to play in philosophy than we often think. To put in a slightly laconic formulation: *the point is not to understand communication as a mode of being, but to understand being as communication.* I would like to expand on the leads that Lanigan's work gives us to develop such an understanding in a bit more detail.

The profound depth of the connection between communication and the specific nature of philosophical thought has been explored, albeit implicitly, by Merleau-Ponty in his beautiful and arresting inaugural lecture, *In Praise of Philosophy*.[4] As true beginning always comes in the fullness of time, it is perhaps fitting in this Festschrift to use this text, which marks the beginning of a professorial career at the Collège de France, as a starting point to clarify the nature of philosophical thinking. It will be particularly apt to do so, as it will turn out that the theory of perfective drift requires the kind of viewpoint Merleau-Ponty develops in order to be understood correctly.

The lecture investigates the function of the philosopher; by giving a critical assessment of those that held the philosophy chair at the Collège de France earlier, Merleau-Ponty articulates his own view of what the task of philosophy consists in. The lecture ends in a eulogy of philosophy in the form of a eulogy of its patron saint, Socrates. It is clear that for Socrates, philosophy exists in communication; its home is the living and open conversation between people, seeking understanding collectively in the knowledge that they don't know. But this is just the first aspect of the obviously communicative dimension of philosophy. For Merleau-Ponty shows that the particular position that Socrates assumes, and makes available to all of us, is not just that of acknowledging that truth has to be found and legitimized in a collective investigation, but that of someone who has taken possession of him- or herself as a speaker, as someone who expresses to others in order to understand. The philosopher stands for that part of ourselves where we experience our existence, and indeed that of the world, as not understood, but as perhaps, waveringly, provisionally; open to being understood. The philosopher stands for that part of ourselves which Merleau-Ponty describes in terms of a negative, an openness in being, or indeed "a weakness in the heart of being": over against the solidity of religion, theology, history and discourse, with their modes of explanation, the philosopher is aware of the radical individuality of her existence in which no other ground for assent to any of the claims of religion, science, politics or history can be found that one that has been established in "a turn toward the personal conversation that develops within us and that we are;" philosophy "investigates the power of expression which other symbolic complexes merely exercise."[5] This makes the philosopher, "the human being who awakens and speaks," the unwelcome guest he or she is in the company of those who insist on certainty, dogma and convention.[6]

It is clear from these formulations that Merleau-Ponty invites his readers to an existentialist view of philosophy. In philosophy we grasp our own existence as finite, but as related to others and to being, in ways that remain open, to be clarified and explored and above all, to be given a place in the way we live and think. Philosophy does not seek explanations—for how, as Merleau-Ponty asks himself, can a weakness in the heart of being explain anything?—Rather, it seeks to put us in a certain position; vis-à-vis ourselves, the others and truth, a position that involves an inversion or conversion from our normal positions, in which we play along, or act out, our implication in the various symbolic complexes. Philosophy does not demolish those—Socrates was faithful to Athens to the very last—but it puts them in a different light by articulating our relation to them, as individual persons, as those beings who express themselves and by expression seek understanding. The philosophical position is, thus, for Merleau-Ponty not one of pleading one's cause or of challenging, not one of seeking to contribute to the solidity of existing discourse, but to speak in such a way that freedom. This point of openness shows itself in the theories the philosophical practice develops. Here lies the function of the philosopher. He concludes: "the mystery of philosophy (and of expression) consists in this, that sometimes life is the same, for oneself, the others and the true. These are the moments that justify philosophy. For the philosopher only these matter."[7] We can conclude that the, or at least a, task of philosophy is to make available to us, in understanding and action, expression as lived, related and relating reality, here and now.

Such a task for thought does not coincide with science, or religion, or art, or politics. Perhaps it contributes something to all these pursuits, but it is not the same. The difference has already been indicated by speaking of a conversion that is required of our normal modes of consciousness. Philosophy, in the function we have highlighted here, is not conceptual, not deductive or inductive but rather indicative. Its reflections, mediated as they are by language, logic and conceptualization, point imperfectly to something immediate, an intuitive grasp of ourselves as both related to and distinct from others and caught up in a continuous flux in which the fleeting moment is the primary locus of an elusive truth and an experienced ignorance, the mirror-image of a question we find in each lived fleeting moment and indeed in the world itself. It seems that all philosophies circle, in one way or another, around such a nearly inexpressible intuition, even if they differ greatly in how they theorize, conceptualise and articulate it. But they have the permanent dual function of pointing out the intuition and then articulating it as best they can, a process which, if it goes well, strengthens both sides rather than only one at the expense of the other. I claim that we can read Merleau-Ponty's eulogy of philosophy as a way of showing the irreducibility of this level of intuition for all our attempts at understanding, at speaking truth and at living together, and at safeguarding it precisely in and by its detailed articulation. This is the view of the nature of philosophical theories to which the theory of perfective drift that I develop in outline here subscribes, and which it therefore also applies to itself. This theory does not have many explicit precursors, but the idea of perfective drift combines some of the intuitions of classical metaphysics with a view of communication as a creative process aimed at understanding and meaning making, but not at annexation or incorporation of the other. As such it recognizes precursors in Burke's analysis of religious language as the language of perfection, which formed the basis of his general notion of rhetoric as a perfecting, purifying and identifying effort and, in the wake of this idea, by William Booth's ameliorative view of rhetoric as put down in his *The Rhetoric of Rhetoric*. There Booth quotes Burke: "I never think of 'communication' without thinking of its ultimate perfection, named in such words as 'community' and 'communion.'"[8] Booth makes an explicit connection between rhetoric as ameliorative communication and the religious perspective of the world as imperfect or *broken*. He also suggests, in a rhetorical analysis of the relation between religion and science, that the shared recognition of imperfection is the common ground that makes a communication between religion and science possible.[9] The theory of perfective drift is not unconnected to these religious roots of the idea of perfection, as they form such an important part of classical metaphysics as well—it suffices here to only mention Aristotle's idea of the unmoved mover to illustrate this point. Nevertheless, I claim that the notion of perfective drift does not require a theistic context in order to be understood or meaningful.

What, then, is the guiding intuition of the theory of perfective drift, and how does it seek to articulate, and investigate this intuition? Probably the shortest way to say it is that the theory conceptualizes communication as the linchpin connecting a classical view of being and its "perfections"—unity, truth and goodness—with a processual ontology for which being is becoming.

The traditional perfections are trans-categorical predicates and are therefore, like the concept of being, necessarily analogical in their application. They articulate what is given with any being at all, insofar as it is. Although such articulation is possible—indeed the whole of classical metaphysics was such an articulation—the only appeal here is to the intuition that there are three of such traditional perfections of being. Firstly, all being is one—it is a unity and is itself one within a manifold of beings that somehow displays solidarity. Secondly, all being is true—all being is either itself "true" in an ontological sense (which could mean intelligible) or it is a something that makes a true proposition (about it) true. Thirdly, all being is good—all being participates in perfection, usually as being perfectible. In classical philosophy the "transcendentals" were thought of, onto-theologically, as having their pinnacle in a highest being, God, or "being itself", in which they were realized perfectly. But for all other spheres of being the trans-categorical predicates are also perfections, albeit in a different way, namely as aspects that are inexhaustibly and infinitely capable and in need of further development, both in reality and in our understanding of them (we see this notion of perfection also in contemporary perfectionist ethics).[10] It is not the case that the perspective of the transcendental predicates of being has simply been abandoned with Kant, as facile histories of philosophy sometimes suggest, rather the structure of the transcendentals finds its way into the relation between Kant's three critiques, and from there on continues, sometimes nearly unrecognizably, in contemporary philosophy, as has been shown in great detail recently by Aertsen.[11] Here we only use the basic and lasting intuition, so aptly expressed by Plato as "the desire and pursuit of the whole" (*Symposium* 193a).[12]

But we don't find this wholeness in a static, formal perception of an eternally unchanging reality in which we imperfectly participate and which exists somewhere else, fully determined and formed. We find it in the living moment, the position of the philosopher, the Socratic position. It exists only in the flow of mutual interpenetration that we experience within and around us as the unstoppable movement of reality itself. We find it in the river of becoming, into which we can't step twice, and where sense, as Merleau-Ponty says, is always "sense-in-the-making", in which truth "lasts only a single moment", and in which "life can renew itself as it simply follows its course."[13] In other words, it is only in the existential now, a moment beyond what has become and which therefore is a transgressive movement into the future or the new, that being "is"; being is its becoming, it is a flux that we miss when we try to dissect it with static concepts, and yet it exists in its articulation or expression, it is in each transgressive now, which is an explication of the implicit wholeness of being.[14]

These brief indications are meant to give an initial idea of what "perfective drift" means. The communicative act is conceptualized by the theory as an ontological and transcendental (in the classical sense) moment of self-expression and communication, an active moment of relating to others that provides the space, as it were, for the wholeness of being, which remains implicit in order to become explicit. The theory thus articulates an ontological dimension of overflowing or ecstatic being that is generic to what it means to be and it sees this not as an overflowing into nothingness but as a creative seeking out of relatedness to others.

What does the theory say to those, and contemporary philosophy is full of them, who deny such intuitions of wholeness or see them as having been overcome since philosophy declared the end of metaphysics? We would point out that there is no implication here of a traditional vision of a harmony or great chain of being. There is an idea of harmony only in the root sense of a "joining", which remains shot through with negativity and difference and finite momentariness. There is the further suggestion that the whole, or one, is only manifest in the way the many actually relate to each other and so when seen as a theory of the one and the many, the theory of perfective drift accords equal status to both, with the see-saw of actuality tipping over the latter side. But, on the positive side, the theory is compatible with the view of the relation between universality and communication that lies at the basis of Whitehead's process metaphysics, according to which universality is defined in terms of communication (what doesn't communicate is unknown). Rather than the other way around, the nature of communication determines the nature of the relation between unity and plurality.[15] Finally, in less strictly philosophical but more cultural terms, a reflection on and nuanced theory of wholeness seems to be more urgent in terms of philosophy's contribution to developing the conceptual resources, ideas and visions necessary for the world today than a further prolonged insistence on fragmentation. It is precisely the power, and aim, of the theory of perfective drift to find a new way of understanding the nature of the complementarity of pairs such as universal-particular, truth-appearance, community-individual, and one-many.

With these preliminary remarks about the nature of philosophical thinking in general and some of the commitments of the theory of perfective drift in particular, we will now turn to a sketch of the theory itself.

The theory of perfective drift brings together two lines of thought: one, the ontology of possibility and process; especially as it has taken shape in the utopian philosophy of Ernst Bloch and the work by others that is based on his ideas and takes them further; and two, communication theory as schematized by Robert Craig as the idea that conceptualization of communication is inherently pluralistic and geared towards explicating and critiquing what communicators "always already" understand by communication, in various contexts and practices.[16] In Craig's 1999 charting of the area of communication theory he mentions the possibility of new types of communication theory arising on the basis of hitherto neglected, but clearly present, self-understandings of communicators in the act of communication. One of these aspects is the self-organizing and novelty-creating dimension of communication, the subtle and yet pervasive moment within the communicative act where I as communicator somehow move beyond myself and find the next word—and find myself. We have tried above to indicate it and to show that this moment is intrinsically related to the function of philosophy, and so has to be understood using a philosophical approach. It is a moment in which something that was not yet there finds its way into present being, the realization of a possibility. But I can only engage in this creative way with communication if I am enveloped or implicated (literally: "folded into") in the communicative act with a basic attitude of hope: that the next word can be found, that I can say what I have to say, that I may, even, be understood, that something—be it truth, be it understanding, be it misunderstanding and falsity—comes from this, my self-expression. I can also only engage in this creative way with communication if I don't already quite know what I am going to say, if my communication is more than a pre-orchestrated mode of coordination, or if I can open up to the curious aspect of consciousness which Bloch called the not-yet conscious in contrast to the no-longer conscious that we have learnt so much about from Freud. The not-yet conscious, the forward-looking, transgressive threshold of consciousness, is given in hunches, daydreams, pre-appearances of all kinds, longings, wishing, and what might be but is not yet. "Longing is the only honest characteristic of all people", Bloch writes in the introduction to his *The Principle of Hope*, and we could add that, like life, it is no characteristic at all since it is the very sign of, and sail into, novelty, not tradition.[17] Our desire gives a clue as to the possibility of creativity, and as communication consists in the renewal of relatedness from moment to moment, as communication, at least the dimension we are concerned to conceptualize, consists in the creation of the new as a fundamental layer of existence itself, we have to look to desire to understand communication. So, while it is possible to look at communication from the point of view of system homeostasis (but even that is a goal and as such a to and fro between no-longer and not-yet), here our concern is the other aspect: that of transgression.

The rhetorical tradition has always known about the close link between communication and desire, in a more or less instrumentalizing fashion, as fashions in rhetoric have waxed and waned. Plato's *Phaedrus*—with its double-decker structure of a discourse about rhetoric as the leading of souls and erotic love as the luring of souls, both finding their consummation in the philosophical life of Socrates in which speech is more central than writing, the life we explored above—leaves no doubt as to the close relation between matters of communication and the erotic itself. Kenneth Burke's *Grammar of Motives* and *Rhetoric of Motives* can be seen as a rhetorical theory that links motivation, so closely connected to desire, to the structure of the communicative act.[18] Without a motivation to influence and persuade there can be no meaning at all, according to Burke. Even the most formal semantic operation takes place against a dramatic background of drive and purpose. "Wherever there is *persuasion*, there is *rhetoric*, and wherever there is *meaning*, there is *persuasion*".[19] The goal of persuasion is, for Burke, identification. We can see the process of identification as an orientation on a not-yet, which might be, whether we are dealing with identification with self (self-expression), relation with others (community; separation) or identification by mystification (his term for what he calls "perfection").

For communication to move in the realm of the not-yet, of motivation and desire (itself, recall, the realm of being as becoming), it has to contain within itself a distance to the massive identity of the present. There can be, in other words, no communication with a moment of negativity that is built into the communicative act itself. Again, this is not a new insight and we have seen how it almost defines the position of consciousness having taken, to whatever measure possible, possession of itself in its ignorance, the position of the philosopher. Burke held that negativity is a "product of human symbol systems", that the symbol itself is a paradoxical unity of identity and difference, the opening up of a gap in reality itself, but only with an eye to crossing it. The symbol both "is" and "is not" what it signifies.[20] For Burke this quality of the symbol puts the human being at a distance from him- or herself, and opens up the need or desire for identification. Here we have the basic insight into the nature of "motivation" and its many shadings that Burke offers us. We can see how the gap between symbol and symbolized only exists when there is a drive to overcome it, and that the drive only exists because of the proleptic identification of symbolic activity with what it symbolizes. Without the drive, the signifying act could not even arise. It is only because word and object have something to do with each other, in one way or another achieve an identity, that meaning can arise in the first place. This is what it means to say that where there is meaning, there is persuasion. Burke sums his point up in his all-famous words "man is rotten with perfection". The negative inscribes itself into our being as the lack that is co-originary with the drive to perfection, to becoming whole. The metaphor of rot is aptly chosen as the negative is not reducible to an organic category and yet pervades the organic wholeness of the embodied individual. The rot of perfection in the embodied individual, this is another way of saying "spirit" or "soul", not as the form of the body (Aristotle) but as its incompleteness. But also Aristotle understood rot: for in his philosophy the soul as the form of the finite living body is the urge to become infinite, the imitation of the divine.

There is an impossibility about this aim at identification. Identification is given as a goal with the nature of symbolic activity itself and rendered concrete in imaginative constructions and practices that are themselves only possible on the basis of the availability of symbols, but if identification were ever reached, symbolic activity—and hence communication and consciousness—would cease. On the view we have articulated about becoming as fundamental to being, we might even say that in such a situation being would cease—an absurd conclusion. We can say: identification is a limit notion of communication, and with that of being. The sanity of a symbol-wielding animal might consist in coming to terms with both the necessity of the drive for identification and the impossibility of satisfying this drive. Such an animal might come to the mystical insight that its nature as a symbolic creature *is*, in the final instance, its identity: that it *is* this "gap" in the real, that it *is* the movement of the negative: an *is* that is crossed out as self-identity right from the start. It might then experience a moment of enlightenment, after which it might become possible for this animal to live as what it is: creative, transgressive, expressive advance into novelty, in relation to an implicit whole to which it relates and gives a place in the same act as with which it distances itself from it. This perspective would imply an ethics of what we might call a "purification of desire", along the lines of Burke's suggestion that rhetoric and communicative action are purifications of war, which changes our attitude towards our desires and which, by widening our perspective of the dynamics of the relation between self, other and wholeness, might be able to put us in a free relation to our desires, where we do not have to deny them but also are not consumed by them in a narrow, egocentric fashion in which they have more control over us than we over them. But, as other lines of thought indicated here, this point cannot be elaborated now.

Burke was very clear about the ontic regionality of negativity. Nature did not partake in it. For him, only the human world is constituted by the triad symbol-identification-perfection. Nature is what it is and as it is. This view implies that language is not part of nature, that this very statement says something about nature that nature itself has no dealing with at all: the opposition nature-human is absolute and not open to mediation. Burke displays here a lingering commitment positivism, one which the theory of perfective drift resolutely breaks with. It sees nature, this self-contained "other" of symbolic activity, as itself an imaginative or virtual construction, a pre-appearance of identity as coinciding with oneself and as such as a pole of the process of realization that is always, not just in the human realm, a process of communication and relation, of setting up and traversing the gap of the negative, of living into the unknown possible new. "Nature" means then either what is self-identical because it is dead and past, or the image of a union of opposites in which life lives and moves and yet is what it is: this is the conceptual structure at the base of most religious, mystical and utopian visions of perfection, the wolf lying down with the lamb and not eating it, a world in which we can be at home.

We can clarify and give further structure to the theory of perfective drift by listing several claims that it makes, although it is not possible here to provide exhaustive justifications for each of them. Some of them we have already implicitly discussed.

1. The best way to understand, at the ontological level, the process of realization, is to understand it as communication. Thus, the theory of perfective drift generalizes communication into a universal, speculative ontological concept. To be means to relate to others, to be for others. This relating is

not something static or formal nor an emanation, but a truly new, creative movement of going out of oneself, an ontological abundance.
2. Communication cannot be understood in abstraction from the mutually dependent notions of drive, negativity, perfection and the not-yet; the subjunctive is an ontologically more fundamental category than the indicative.[21]
3. The general drive towards perfection is no guarantee that its aim will be realized, but the possibility that it will cannot be ruled out: this transforms the *drive* into a *drift*: the universe is set on a course, which may yet be thwarted but has not been thwarted yet. There is a positive orientation within the process of realization, a "principle of hope" that is more than an add-on, rather it is constitutive of the very process of being. Our individual creative and communicative acts take place against the background of this positive orientation.
4. The frontier of communication is always a transgression, a danger and a possible rescue, a "sail into the other world" (Bloch).[22] It is the Socratic place of ignorance.

Now "perfective drift" does not mean "things are getting better all the time", we are cruising steadily onwards to a point Omega.[23] Often things do not get better, at least not visibly so; the tendency to solve the problem of evil by arguing that the evil in the world is good for something is far from the theory of perfective drift. Catastrophe is always possible and often real and its negativity can be bottomless. Suffering is universal. Hope is often misguided and if not that, nearly always disappointed. Roadmaps of what this "better" would consist in are not available; if they were, we would have to be suspicious of them. The nature of the new itself precludes such facile teleology. But we have to go even further: the universe itself may die a slow entropic death, while being long-forgotten because no mind will be there to care or lament its demise. Death is the foreseeable horizon of our individual lives, mine and yours; a limit we cannot claim to understand and which only a facetious grin or hypocritical smile can call into doubt. And yet, *the fact that things are this way*, shows, *ex negativo*, that it might be otherwise, and better. We could think of this "might be better" as an escapist fantasy fed on denial and anxiety; something like this Erich Fromm had in mind when speaking of humanity's tendency to want to escape freedom: a vision that looks to be alive but is actually dead, unchanging. However, the fact that hope is given with the very structure of the symbolic act, and the fact that the symbolic act universalizes itself because every "other" that it sets up as laying outside of it is already part of the symbolic act (its nature is transgression), indicate that this "might be better" is part of the very fabric of being itself (being is perfective). In this way we can understand Bloch's idea that the world has a dream of itself as connected to Whitehead's idea cited above, that, in philosophy universality defined by communication is universality enough.

One consequence of this line of argument is that reality is filled with symbols, that it has a symbolic side by which it pre-empts itself, as it were. Bloch called this category of the real "real symbol" (*Realsymbol*), and traced it back to cabbalistic thought and to Jakob Boehme's idea of *signatura rerum*, and his book by that name, in which things are seen as signs, and vice versa. A theory of real symbols can be developed, which would be part of understanding the cultural matrix of communicology, a theme that is so central to much of Lanigan's work: (T)he symbolic communicates itself to its expression solely from the perspective of its object content, differentiates the individual symbols from the perspective of the objectively real material, whose variously situated content of cloakedness, content of factual identity they respectively depict as this cloaked and factually identical aspect. And it is solely this depictiveness of a *real cipher*, of a *real symbol*, which finally lends symbols their genuineness.[24]

Perfective drift exhibits the two elements Bloch identifies in reality as process, *tendency* towards identity and the *latency* or "cloakedness" of this identity: we do not know what it is, and also the world itself does not know where it is headed. But perfective drift is also a profoundly communicative phenomenon because it is through and through symbolic. It exists only in the moment of relating, both as the moment of the self-relation or reflection in taking possession of the self, the Socratic moment, as well as the moment of the creation of the new in the relation between self and other.

On the basis of this understanding of the real symbol, a critical theory of culture and communication can be developed that would help us to understand the history and future of cultural formations and communicative practices such as religion, politics, art, social and legal institutions and science. The real symbol, understood on the basis of the theory of perfective drift, can in this way provide a matrix for a form of communicology that allows us to explore perfective drift as it precipitates in communicative cultures and practices as well as institutions aimed at increasing understanding and communicative exchange free from structures of domination or violence. But the cultural domain conceived of as a *matrix*, a temporarily fixed set of communicative coordinates and symbolic practices, is part of a much wider, ontological, *flux* of symbolization, like a vortex that forms on the surface of a flowing river and dissolves back into the general flow before long. This flux is the sphere of the constitution of the communicating subjects, awakening and speaking.

One of the structural features of the field of communication theory as identified by Craig is its dialogical-dialectical coherence.[25] Different communication theories speak to each other, provide corrections and illuminations of each other in a way that is inherently pluralistic but also ameliorative. The "dialogue" different theories have with each other should help each of them further along, as well as helping our understanding of communication further along. For the theory of perfective drift two developments present themselves, which we will briefly discuss: (a) it will prove illuminating to explore the possibilities of creating a communication model of perfective drift and (b) the centrality of dialogue to the field of communication theory as a whole creates an opportunity for the theory of perfective drift, for which the Socratic communicative exchange is so important, as we have seen, to contribute to a better understanding of what dialogical-dialectical coherence is.

I would like to suggest in particular that Dance's helical model of communication can be connected in an illuminating way to the theory of perfective drift.[26]

Figure 19.1 A Helical Model of Communication [Based on Dance (1967)]

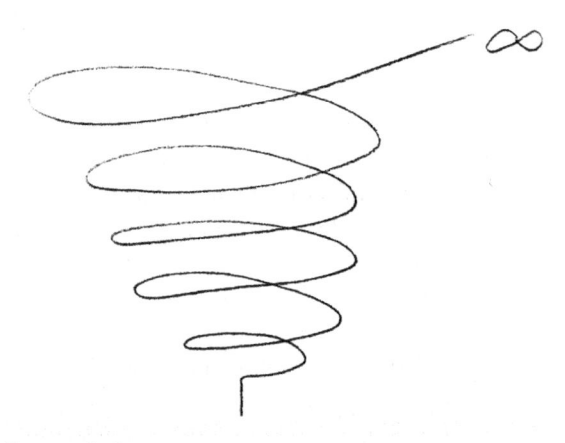

Source : Author

First of all, concerning its status as a model: the model is simply an image, and therefore it can be interpreted in many different ways. We might say that it acts as an allegory or analogy for communication, by which different aspects of the phenomenon of communication can be articulated in different ways; it is not a linear or simple representation and that is not its purpose. Properly speaking, the temptation to see a model such as this as a metaphor that illustrates a literal statement of the nature of communication which still eludes us, is I think wrong. The metaphorical, the poly-interpretable, analogical image *precedes* the literal meaning statement. Metaphors are not possible on the basis of literal signification, it is rather the other way around. Seeing x as y is simply another form of the basic symbolic act, something that cannot be reduced to a literal assignment or naming that would order a space of understanding. Definitions come always last. The model is therefore quite philosophical: it shows something that is present in many different ways and yet is similar in all cases. It is interesting to note here that in this way the medial affordance of the difference between image and word can be used to express the distinction between what Wittgenstein called saying, and showing.[27] Logical structure, for Wittgenstein, cannot be said or articulated, it can only be shown as the structure that is present in all saying. Although Wittgenstein apparently himself held that a philosopher admits that he does not know what he is saying when he takes recourse to drawing images or diagrams,[28] he did so himself when discussing the nature of "seeing as", and showing (because it cannot adequately be said) the impossibility of a mediation between forms of "seeing as" that would lead us from one to the other, while at the same time making it clear that we recognise it is the same image that we see now as this, now as that[29]:

Figure 19.2 The Play of Perception

Open Source: [Based on Joseph Jastrow, *Fact and Fable in Psychology* (London: MacMillan, 1901), 295]

(On a more charitable reading of "not knowing" as a philosophical virtue, we might even rescue Wittgenstein's philosopher "who admits he does not know" and—draws a picture.)

So, part of the theory of perfective drift is to claim that there is a certain kind of knowledge that we may call analogical, which cannot be reduced to other kinds of knowing, which is characterized by poly-interpretability and that we need to acknowledge this type of knowledge is relevant to communication (we will see below how Dance's model can be read in this way). If this is correct, it provides a new contribution to communication theory as a field, not so much in its contents, but in its epistemological status, especially as far as the nature of the coherence of the field is concerned. More specifically, the theory of perfective drift provides an embedding of Craig's multiverse of communication theories, in other words the dialogical-dialectical coherence of the field of communication theory points towards the theory of perfective drift. Dialogical-dialectical coherence is dialogical in that it refers to concrete subjects engaged in communication and in the process of understanding communication; it is dialectical in that the relatedness of different theories is not external but internal, and the coherence is itself analogical and creative, never unambiguous or final. "Coherence" emphasizes the realization that different ways of conceptualizing communication need each other, while yet not being reducible to each other, and that they need each other as elements of communication theory seen as metadiscursive practice: the different communication theories are as many different forms of "seeing communication as", held together by the analogical nature of perfective drift. Perhaps Craig had the Hegelian concept of a concrete universal in mind, a universal which exists in its various manifestations, which all add to the content of the universal, while not being merely instances of it. He rightly avoids an essentialist as well as a nominalist reading of the concept of communication. But dialogical-dialectical coherence requires a tendency within communication to even come off the ground, which the concrete universal itself cannot provide. Craig therefore relies on Carey's ritual model, to provide him with a working definition of the purpose of communication as the grounding of the constitutive meta-model. But this is a bit of a stop-gap as it does not sit well with the obvious one-sidedness (which is not a defect) of Carey's ritual model which after all is much more one of the available theories or conceptualisations than an articulation of the ground of their togetherness.

Interestingly, Craig recognizes that after Dance's model speculation about defining communication stopped, only be taken up again, but in a pragmatic and community-oriented way, by Carey's work in the 1980s.[30] The theory of perfective drift, by understanding itself as an explicitly analogical theory, can make it clear how Dance's model can be used in a richer way than as a mere definition and can provide a more comprehensive "meta-model" of communication than Carey's, which was never intended as a constitutive meta-model in the first place. The theory of perfective drift, with its ontological understanding of communication (and hence community) as flux can also provide an ontological embedding of Carey's ritual model, which tends to be more of a matrix model (see the discussion of this distinction above).

Secondly, Dance's model envisages communication as moving between singularity and infinity. It transgresses the boundaries of linearity, because the relation between the singular and the infinite is not one of instantiation or mere augmentation and adding up, what Hegel called *bad infinity*. There is an ontological difference between the singular point or moment of existence and infinity, and yet we can say that the singular contains the infinite within itself as much as the other way around: this is a key insight of what we have called the Socratic position. The helix is an image of metamorphosis between these two poles: how the infinite contracts into a singular instance, and how the singular instance becomes infinite. The process of becoming is a dialectical pulse, it moves in concentric but widening, or narrowing, circles, back and forth between these two poles.

Figure 19.3 Yin and Yang

Open Source: [adapted from https://en.wikipedia.org/wiki/File:Yin_yang.svg; retrieved 21 February 2017]

Thirdly, on the basis of this dialectic we can see the usefulness of the model. It can be applied to a wide range of communicative phenomena, from dialogues and the development of self-consciousness to rumours, stories, political and mass media communication, speech acts, institutionalization, conflict and misunderstanding, and many others. In each case the model provides a way of articulating the dimension of communication that is properly philosophical, that is analogical and has to do with the "awakening and speaking" of the subject that Merleau-Ponty talks about. The model is speculative: it manifests a general feature of communication that is realized differently in different instances of communication and allows us because of that to challenge any reductive understanding of communication. Fourthly, the model visualises the joint but counter-posed centrifugal and centripetal dimensions of communication (Bakhtin). Meaning strives to fixed, singular identity on one hand; on the other it strives towards an infinite widening out. In our theory, we can say that this striving represents the Janus-face of perfective drift: the communicative process strives towards identity, in the sense of becoming singular, and it strives towards totality. Again, we see the proximity to strands in mystical thinking, in this case the relation to the Greek thought of "hen kai pan", "one and all". In different, but related, senses, the one is "whole" and the all is "whole"—or, in our process philosophical account of wholeness, "not-yet whole". It would not be amiss to see the helix as a drawn-out projection into four-dimensional time-space of the taijitu, the yin-yang symbol, which visualizes the dialectical dependency of the two poles and the birth of one in the other. In this way, the model relates to the idea of Dao, or the all-pervasive way of the being, another articulation of perfective drift, and one that the *Dao De Jing* already recognizes to be of an intuitive nature that has to be grasped directly and cannot be discursively and conceptually pinned down: "Way-making (*dao*) that can be put into words is not really way-making, And naming (*ming*) that can assign fixed reference to things is not really naming".[31] The addition that the theory of perfective drift makes is not at all the claim that the eternal Dao will once be spoken but rather the realization that this opening statement of the *Dao De Jing*, when taken as an indication of how it is with perfection in this world, implies the communicative, gap-like and drift-like nature of the real. As we said, perfection becomes visible and real only in the communicatively maintained lack of it: but no communicative event is without a reference to perfection, to totality, to the whole. In Daoist terms: no "eternal name" without "the ten thousand names", no ten thousand names without the eternal name.

The theory of perfective drift has to be understood in exactly the same way as the status of the helical model, namely as a speculative theory that assigns the status of analogue to what it terms "perfective drift", a fundamental feature of the process of becoming, a dialectical movement between a singular and an infinite pole which exists in the spiral-like transgressive process by which the new comes into being. Dance's model can be used as a model of perfective drift when we make it explicit that the helical movement is driven by the two becoming poles of the helix; the singular and the infinite. This is implicit in the model, because also for Dance there would be no reason for the helix to unfold or contract if there were no bi-directional lure behind. But that lure is the persuasion Burke spoke about and the—also ontologically generalized—erotic pull, the seductive structure of the ideal, of Plato's *Phaedrus* and *Symposium*. When seen in this way, the model acquires another connection, namely to the structure of the process of self-realisation of the individual event, the "actual entity" or "occasion" of Whitehead's process philosophy. This is the process by which a new self-creative event realizes itself as its own connection to the totality of being and in doing so creates unbounded, infinite novelty. The process is driven by a lure for realization, an aim of something that represents a value, and perfection. We can now expand Dance's model in a simple way to articulate this process-like relation of singularity and infinity, to finally yield a *model of perfective drift*:

Figure 19.4 Model of Perfective Drift

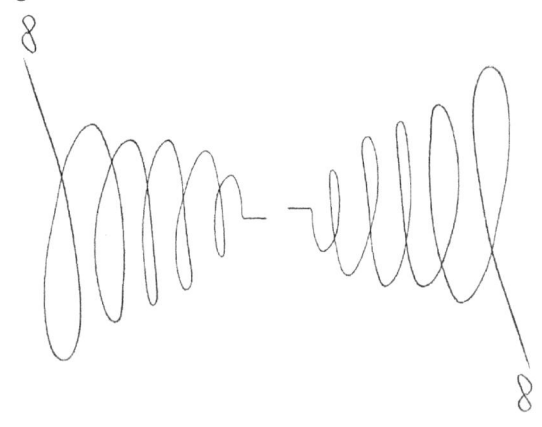

Source : Author

The great advantage of this model is that it visualizes two further dimension of perfective drift that have remained implicit until now, namely the pulsating nature of the perfective dialectic and the encounter structure of communication. Perfective drift is not a gradual evolution of the universe towards an Omega point, as was noted before. The structure of negativity implies that all communication, and hence all processual realization, has the structure of a rupture of the fabric of the given, it is a transgression. The rupture is included in the fabric, and a new rupture arises. The spring-like pulsation that is given with the model we have now produced captures this moment; it captures the specific nature of the temporalisation of communication. Secondly, the communicative relation is an encounter; it is as it were bi-directional. The spiraling towards singularity and infinity, and vice versa, happens in a dimension of "over-againstness", itself a gap, at the meeting point of which communication occurs, paradigmatically in an I-Thou dialogue but also, analogically, elsewhere. Without this moment (which can still be a moment of recognition, relation, or of its opposite: as noted perfective drift does not mean harmony if harmony be taken merely in a classical way), communication would become appropriation. (Here we see the value of Buber's conceptualization of the difference between the I-It relation and the I-Thou relation.) The theory of perfective drift is a theory of the universe in dialogue. At its most abstract level this dialogue is that between past and future, no longer and not yet, which is the present moment. In its religious manifestations, the bi-directionality is that between god and world, grace and nature, freedom and necessity, as in Rosenzweig's reading of Star of David, which we can connect to the event cone and the model of perfective drift in a movement like this[32]:

Figure 19.5 Star of David with the Event Cone

Source : Author

The communicative event arises in freedom and is liberation from the given, unto the new; it is contingent, although not unconditioned, like the hope of which it testifies and to which it gives rise. The theory of perfective drift translates into the realm of praxis by giving us a handle with which to critique images of perfection that so easily become oppressive or ideological—a critique that does not remain merely diagnostic, but because of the subjunctive nature of the theory itself is intrinsically practical, action to transform the world. The theory of perfective drift encompasses a praxis of dialogue and educated hope, using the speculative understanding of communication to examine our visions of liberation and redemption: this is where its main use as a critical communication theory lies, and where it can contribute to existing ways of critically understanding communicative practices. Its knowledge is thus that of the subjunctive, hope as knowledge, a kind of knowledge without which we cannot understand communication, without which we cannot understand critique or indeed human existence. Adorno was aware of this type of knowledge when he wrote:

> The only philosophy which can be responsibly practised in the face of despair is the attempt to contemplate all things as they would present themselves from the standpoint of redemption. Knowledge has no light but that shed on the world by redemption: all else is reconstruction, mere technique. (…) But beside the demand thus placed on thought, the question of the reality or unreality of redemption itself hardly matters.[33]

The theory of perfective drift gives this statement hands and feet in an age in which the standpoint of redemption is not so easily articulated anymore. It shows the light of knowledge to reside in the subjunctive activation of the perspective of hope that dwells in all communication. It stands up for the invocation, the exhortative, the desiderative—without which no knowledge can be gained—and it widens these to encompass reality as a whole. It does not paint a programmatic picture of the goal of our actions, it does not stipulate an endpoint of history or simply condone our desires; it seeks to sensitize us to the flowing, creative movement in which we become ourselves and are together, and in which the new may occur in its peculiar, itself inexhaustible relation to wholeness, and to use this awareness as a source of critique of domination, exploitation, idolatry and dogmatism, but also as a wellspring of creativity itself. In this way, like all philosophy, it seeks to sensitize us to the hidden depths of reality, in this particular case to what happens when we communicate. The fact that the widest speculation possible comes to be the prerequisite for a practical critical theory that aims to liberate is the specific advance made by the theory of perfective drift as a philosophical theory of communication.

NOTES

1. Alfred North Whitehead, *Modes of Thought* (New York: The Free Press, 1968), 69.
2. Richard Lanigan, *Phenomenology of Communication; Merleau-Ponty's Thematics in Communicology and Semiology* (Pittsburgh, PA: Duquesne University Press, 1988).
3. Richard Lanigan, "Merleau-Ponty's Phenomenology of Communication," *Philosophy Today* 14, no. 2 (1970): 79–88.
4. Maurice Merleau-Ponty, "In Praise of Philosophy," in *In Praise of Philosophy and Other Essays*, trans. John Wild, James M. Edie, John O'Neil (Evanston: Northwestern University Press, 1988), 3–64. (Citations from the text are my own translations.)
5. Merleau-Ponty, "In Praise of Philosophy," sections 5 and 6.
6. Merleau-Ponty, "In Praise of Philosophy," section 7.
7. Merleau-Ponty, In Praise of Philosophy," section 3.
8. Wayne Booth, *The Rhetoric of Rhetoric: The Quest for Effective Communication* (Oxford: Blackwell, 2004), 76.
9. Booth, *Rhetoric of Rhetoric*, 153–169.
10. See for example Stephen Mulhall, *The Great Riddle: Wittgenstein and Nonsense, Theology and Philosophy* (Oxford: Oxford University Press, 2015) for a reflection on the perfections in metaphysics and ethics that seeks to articulate the relation between classical (Thomist) metaphysics and Wittgenstein.
11. Jan Aertsen, *Medieval Philosophy as Transcendental Thought* (Leiden: Brill Publishers, 2013).
12. The theory of perfective drift includes the claim that the psychoanalytic idea that the desire of the whole, as a constant factor in human mentality, can be reduced to a desire for a symbiosis with the mother, from which all separation is an undialectical negation, is a form of psychologism that needs to be repudiated in philosophy, while recognizing its proper sphere of application. Wholeness and the kind of separation by which we become autonomous individuals do not exclude, but rather presuppose each other, in many (analogously related) ways. We can envisage an "ethics of solidarity and separation" as part of a fully developed theory of communication as perfective drift.
13. Merleau-Ponty, "In Praise of Philosophy," section 7.
14. David Bohm, *Wholeness and the Implicate Order* (London: Routledge, 1980).
15. Alfred North Whitehead, *Process and Reality, Corrected Edition*, ed. David Ray Griffin and Donald W. Sherburne (New York: The Free Press, 1978), 4.
16. Robert Craig, "Communication Theory as Field," *Communication Theory* 9, no. 2 (1999): 119–160.
17. Ernst Bloch, *The Principle of Hope*, trans. Neville Plaice, Stephen Plaice, and Paul Knight (Cambridge: MIT Press, 1986), 12.

18. Kenneth Burke, *A Grammar of Motives* (Berkeley, University of California Press, 1969); *A Rhetoric of Motives* (Berkeley, University of California Press, 1969).
19. Burke, *Rhetoric of Motives*, 172.
20. The theory of perfective drift includes the claim that is better to say that the negative and symbolic are equiprimordial and imply each other.
21. For an insightful exploration of the application of process philosophy to communication theory which stresses the subjunctive, see Cathy B. Glenn, "A Middle Way: Process Philosophy and Critical Communication Inquiry," *Empedocles: European Journal for the Philosophy of Communication* 4, no. 2 (2012): 113–132.
22. Ernst Bloch, *The Spirit of Utopia*, trans. A. Nassar (Stanford: Stanford University Press, 2000), 82.
23. Indeed, the attitude of *perfectionism*, which causes so much imperfection, is unrelated to what we mean here by perfective drift.
24. Bloch, *Principle of Hope*, 239.
25. Craig, "Communication Theory as Field.".
26. Frank Dance, ed., *Human Communication Theory: Original Essays* (New York: Holt, Reinhart and Winston, 1967).
27. Ludwig Wittgenstein, *Tractatus Logico-Philosophicus*, trans. C. K. Ogden (London: Kegan Paul, 1922).
28. A personal communication by David Pears, the late Wittgenstein scholar.
29. Ludwig Wittgenstein, *Philosohical Investigations*, trans. G. E. M. Anscombe (Oxford: Blackwell Publishers, 1958), 194.
30. Craig, "Communication Theory as Field," 124.
31. Roger Ames and David Hall, *Daodejing, "Making this Life Significant", A Philosophical Translation* (New York: Ballantine Books, 2003), 77. Is it here necessary to refer as well to David Hall's superb essay on Taoism, process philosophy and creativity: "Process and Anarchy: A Taoist View of Creativity," *Philosophy East and West* 28, no. 3 (1978): 271–285, in which Hall presents an interpretation of the central place of chaos in the concept of Dao as self-creative event and uses it to articulate a conception of the relation between radical novelty and togetherness that echoes central claims of the theory of perfective drift.
32. Franz Rosenzweig, *The Star of Redemption*, trans. Barbara E. Galli (Madison: University of Wisconsin Press, 2005).
33. Theodor W. Adorno, *Minima Moralia: Reflections from Damaged Life*, trans. E. F. N. Jephcott (London: Verso Books, 2005), 247.

BIBLIOGRAPHY

Adorno, Theodor W. *Minima Moralia: Reflections from Damaged Life*, 247. Translated by Jephcott. London: Verso Books, 2005.

Aertsen, Jan. *Medieval Philosophy as Transcendental Thought*. Leiden: Brill Publishers, 2013.

Ames, Roger, and David Hall. *Daodejing, "Making this Life Significant", A Philosophical Translation*. New York: Ballantine Books, 2003.

Bloch, Ernst. *The Principle of Hope*. Translated by Neville Plaice, Stephen Plaice, and Paul Knight. Cambridge: MIT Press, 1986.

Bloch, Ernst. *The Spirit of Utopia*. Translated by A. Nassar. Stanford: Stanford University Press, 2000.

Bohm, David. *Wholeness and the Implicate Order.* London: Routledge, 1980.
Booth, William. *The Rhetoric of Rhetoric: The Quest for Effective Communication.* Oxford: Blackwell, 2004.
Burke, Kenneth. *A Grammar of Motives.* Berkeley: University of California Press, 1969.
Burke, Kenneth. *A Rhetoric of Motives.* Berkeley: University of California Press, 1969.
Craig, Robert. "Communication Theory as Field." *Communication Theory* 9, no. 2 (1999): 119–160.
Dance, Frank, ed. *Human Communication Theory: Original Essays.* New York: Holt, Reinhart and Winston, 1967.
Glenn, Cathy B. "A Middle Way: Process Philosophy and Critical Communication Inquiry." *Empedocles: European Journal for the Philosophy of Communication* 4, no. 2 (2012): 113–132.
Hall, David. "Process and Anarchy: A Taoist View of Creativity." *Philosophy East and West* 28, no. 3 (1978): 271–285.
Lanigan, Richard. "Merleau-Ponty's Phenomenology of Communication." *Philosophy Today* 14, no. 2 (1970): 79–88.
Lanigan, Richard. *Phenomenology of Communication; Merleau-Ponty's Thematics in Communicology and Semiology.* Pittsburgh: Duquesne University Press, 1988.
Merleau-Ponty, Maurice, "In Praise of Philosophy", In *In Praise of Philosophy and Other Essays.* Translated by John Wild, James M. Edie, John O'Neil. Evanston: Northwestern University Press, 1988.
Mulhall, Stephen. *The Great Riddle: Wittgenstein and Nonsense, Theology and Philosophy.* Oxford: Oxford University Press, 2015.
Rosenzweig, Franz. *The Star of Redemption.* Translated by Barbara E. Galli. Madison: University of Wisconsin Press, 2005.
Whitehead, Alfred North. *Modes of Thought.* New York: The Free Press, 1968.
Whitehead, Alfred North. *Process and Reality, Corrected Edition.* Edited by David Ray Griffin and Donald W. Sherburne. New York: The Free Press, 1978.
Wittgenstein, Ludwig. *Philosohical Investigations.* Translated by G. E. M. Anscombe. Oxford: Blackwell Publishers, 1958.
Wittgenstein, Ludwig. *Tractatus Logico-Philosophicus.* Translated by C. K. Ogden. London: Kegan Paul, 1922.

Afterword

Richard L. Lanigan: A Fifty Year Legacy

THOMAS J. PACE, JR.[1]

When Richard Leo Lanigan first sat down in my SIU office in the Fall Quarter of 1967, little did I realize the influence he would have on our graduate program, our students, and the field of human communication. The "Richard Influence" is clearly evident in the contributors to this volume. Many were privileged to be in Richard's classes and others were impacted by his extensive involvement within philosophical and semiotic circles.

During that initial visit, Richard indicated he was from the University of New Mexico. I figured his application was likely accelerated because Professor Eubanks, from that Speech Department, was a close friend of Earl Bradley, SIU's graduate director. Both were officers in Tau Kappa Alpha Honorary Speech Society, an organization to which Richard himself was initiated. I was so pleased to meet this young man from New Mexico, hoping he might enhance my love of the enchanted State. A more pleasant surprise came when he proposed doing his dissertation on Maurice Merleau-Ponty, the continental philosopher who contributed significantly to my exploration of existential communication.

My own interest in Merleau-Ponty began when I was a Visiting Scholar at Northwestern University studying Existentialism in the Philosophy Department and it continued during my study of Communication in the Northwestern Speech Department. During my earlier PhD years at the University of Denver as a student of Elwood Murray, I was exposed to communication methodologies, something very different than the rhetorical tradition. Murray introduced me to *Communication: The Social Matrix of Psychiatry* by Jürgen Ruesch and Gregory Bateson. The discussion of the various levels of communication—intrapersonal, interpersonal, group and cultural—emphasized the study of interpersonal communication as a separate entity. Murray's interpretation of General Semantics theory, however, indicated that all four levels were involved in the communication experience.

After teaching Murray's communication methodologies for several years, I contemplated expanding that modality to "authenticity" within individual choice and communication practice. This quest motivated my trek to Northwestern, where I took my first course in Existentialism from Visiting Professor Calvin Schrag, a contributor to this volume. Murray later retired from Denver, then served as a Visiting Professor at Southern Illinois University, and he retired from that position in 1965. To my good fortune, I was asked to fill his position at SIU and to continue his work in communication methodologies along with my newly formed philosophical perspectives.

During my first few quarters at SIU I introduced in my graduate courses selections from Merleau Ponty's *Phenomenology of Perception*, *Signs*, and especially George Gusdorf's *La Parole*. Richard Lanigan's matriculation into our graduate program provided me with a wonderful opportunity to exchange ideas with a knowledgeable person in continental philosophy. Richard understood and appreciated the value of studying the "[hu]man speaking," not just the transmission of messages. He also had the more traditional background in argumentation, classical rhetoric, and dialectics, a combination of academic areas rarely found in beginning PhD students.

In the latter part of the 1960s decade, there was significant turmoil in race relations in Chicago. The SIU Department of Speech began conducting field studies that focused on situational analysis, which utilized theoretical constructs from symbolic interaction scholarship out of the University of Chicago. Members of our faculty contributed to the Speech Association of America Field Study Conference on Relevance in Minneapolis. Also, in 1968 our department brought to campus several community action leaders from Chicago to expound on their action agencies' situational perspectives on racial problems. These types of academic endeavors underscored the department's research on relevant contemporary topics. Such nontraditional efforts in our field, at SIU and elsewhere, brought about the controversial address by Marie Hochmuth Nichols, entitled "The Tyranny of Relevance." Richard Lanigan was a part of SIU's historic seminar and his final paper provided an analysis of the polarization and communication within the Chicago community. It was an outstanding paper, later revised and published in the Central States Speech Journal in 1970.

It should be noted Richard was the first graduate student to finish course work, comprehensive examinations, and his dissertation in *two academic years*. His first academic appointment, after completing his PhD in 1969, was with the University of Texas at El Paso. Richard was again in a culture he understood so well. He was geographically close to Santa Fe where he was born and Albuquerque, a city where he was schooled and played sports. El Paso bridged the Hispanic and American Indian cultures. These two sociocentric cultures were part of Richard's early life and provided him lived-world experiences that enabled him to explicate brilliantly the comparisons between the United States' ego-centric cultures and the Chinese socio-centric cultures. And, of course, this location in El Paso was close to his immediate family with whom Richard devoted much special time and assistance, even bringing his mother to live in Carbondale during the later portion of her life.

From there, Richard's sights focused academically in another direction. He was selected to teach and study Philosophy at the University of Dundee and at St. Andrews University, both in Scotland. It was there he began research for *Speech Act Phenomenology* published in 1977, which followed the publication in 1972 of his dissertation on Merleau-Ponty as *Speaking and Semiology*. After two years of teaching, studying, and writing in Scotland, Richard returned in 1972 to teach at Chicago State University.

During Richard's years in Scotland, the Vietnam War was creating havoc in the U.S. and especially at Southern Illinois University, Carbondale. Destructive violence toward the University's Center for Vietnamese Study caused the university to close for five weeks in the Spring Quarter of 1970. It was difficult to get students to study philosophy or theory when the "world was burning." Academic departments focused on modes of participatory democracy in institutional decision making.

In 1974, as the war waned in Vietnam, a faculty member who was previously involved in our field studies research, chose to pursue opportunities in a nonacademic arena. It was my belief we needed a time of reflection and to take another look at theories and practices. With this in mind and with a faculty position vacancy, I made the case to our administration that Richard Lanigan would be a highly desirable candidate. My persuasion was successful and Richard agreed to join us. Thus, a new world of communication theory and practice commenced.

When Richard joined the faculty in 1974, departmental graduate programs were in disarray, which drew critical attention from the central administration. Edward McGlone was brought in as chairman in 1975. New graduate degree requirements were formulated as well as discussions about various concentrations. No one could construct charts and diagrams to explain and differentiate theories as could Richard Lanigan. His structural vision gave shape to the department's new concentration called Philosophy of Communication. Marvin Kleinau, later our department chair and dean, claimed that Richard's gift to organize and reorganize was a credit to his knowledge of our field and his ability to see new vistas. As the new graduate director, I concurred with chairman McGlone that the two most important graduate concentrations in the department were Performance Studies and Philosophy of Communication. My dream of seeing the Philosophy of Communication emphasis become a reality was fulfilled. Much of that can be attributed to Richard's knowledge and persuasive skills.

Richard's ability to construct organizational proposals was demonstrated once again at the International Communication Association conference in (West) Berlin, May 1977. His convincing proposal to form the Division of Philosophy of Communication was accepted by ICA. Richard was the chairperson of the PhilComm Division for several subsequent years. I was privileged to be at that conference to assist Richard. Elwood Murray also attended the conference and gave his support to the proposal.

Richard always paid tribute to the line of teachers and their teachers who influenced his life. In Philosophy, for example, he paid homage to his great teacher Hubert Griggs Alexander from the University of New Mexico, whose teacher was Wilbur Marshall Urban from Yale. In the ICA room that day were three generations of the lineage leading to the teaching of Communicology. I was Richard's teacher at Southern Illinois University and Elwood Huey Allen Murray from the University of Denver was my teacher. And now, a number of the contributors to this work are Lanigan's legacy.

I should mention that Richard gives credit to Elwood Murray as being one of the first in the field of Speech to create a program in the communicology framework. Murray's reaction to the traditional Speech Association of America was to organize in 1950, with Paul Bagwell of Michigan State University, the National Society for the Study of Communication. That organization later became the International Communication Association. Bagwell was its first president and Murray was the second. Notably, Murray was never elected president of the traditional Speech Association of America due to his active restructuring of speech pedagogy.

At the West Berlin Conference, I assisted my colleague, the late Keith Sanders, in establishing the Division of Political Communication. This marked two ICA divisions our department was responsible for creating—Philosophy of Communication and Political Communication, both of which still stand. At that meeting Keith and Richard stayed at the same hotel and visited together the sights of Berlin. I believe their interpersonal encounters helped solidify their mutual interests in theory. In later years Richard accompanied Keith and other scholars to a conference in Paris at the Sorbonne to compare the French and U.S. elections held during the same year, 1988. I should mention that at that conference, Richard was the only one of our delegates who was fluent in French, a tribute to the early days when a foreign language was a graduate tool requirement for the PhD.

Through Keith's contact, Richard attracted the attention of the late Dan Nimmo, a noted scholar in Political Communication, then at the University of Tennessee. My conversations with Dan often centered on his understanding and admiration of Richard's work. Keith, after serving on our faculty and as our dean, left to become an academic administrator in Wisconsin. At each subsequent visit I had with him, Keith always inquired about Richard, his family, and his academic pursuits. Richard authored an article in 1981 in Nimmo and Sanders' *The Handbook of Political Communication* and his presentation at the Sorbonne Conference was published in *Semiotica*.

Richard was my departmental colleague for 20 years. We were able to enjoy seeing the growth of the Philosophy of Communication program, one of the first to be so named in the field of Speech Communication. Chairman Kleinau often remarked that our program was of enormous importance to the university and its reputation extended beyond the borders of the United States. Richard and I served on many dissertations together, either as director or co-director. With few exceptions, other members of the committee would concur with our assessment of the acceptability of a dissertation, and they often commented on the research's creative contribution. This gave credence to the program and it allowed our students to take risks in exploring new vistas in the interpretation and significance of relationships found through communicology as a human science.

Two of my sabbaticals were spent at Duquesne University in Philosophy and in Psychology. Richard and other of our graduates continue to have close relationships with Duquesne's Department of Communication and Rhetorical Studies. It was at Duquesne I learned much from the professors that employed description, reduction, and interpretation as modalities in phenomenological research. As I now look back, two major theoretical constructs evolved which I was able to develop and teach and these reflect Richard's influence. The first was Richard's illustrative diagram of "The Dialectics of Thought and Life." With Phenomenology and Existentialism as dialectical extremes and with essence and concreteness as inner dialectical positions, his diagram provided understanding of the philosophical foundations of our research philosophy. The second contribution was Richard's development and elaboration in discovering "revelatory phrases" as existential signifiers. Often that phase of this method is taught as an objective thematization, as in social science qualitative research. For me, the revelatory free variation modality permits interpretation whereas existential universals are explicated from the lived world embodied in the discourse. Richard's presentation and article on Attica and Tom Wicker's book, *A Time To Die*, offered an example of imaginative free variation at various levels that grounded my thinking in discovering revelatory phrases.

One might think my relationship with Richard is based only on academic and departmental discussions. Far from it. Topics for our conversations included real estate, sports, family, medical items and yes, home plumbing, believe it or not. His two sons went to the same elementary school as my children did earlier, and I am aware he helped structure their education there as we did. Richard's academic accomplishments are noteworthy, but he is the "everyman" and is conversant with individuals in all walks of life.

Departmental graduate programs are created by groups of likeminded individuals and as they retire, the programs, like the Philosophy concentration, may fade in interest if not direction. With my retirement in 1994 and the retirements of other faculty interested in the Philosophy concentration, Richard was able still to maintain student interest and to encourage those in and outside the department who conducted research in communicology as a human science. During these last few years, Richard has been freed to develop what I believe to be his most productive years. His publishing, professional travel, including extensive intercultural consultations, and other work within semiotic organizations are monumental. To establish the International Communicology Institute at SIUC, then to move it to Washington DC upon his retirement in 2009, has kept Richard and his colleagues actively involved in current world affairs.

Since I started teaching communication in 1953, I probably have attended more conferences and conventions than most. I have heard more academics respond to presentations and argue points of view than I wish to remember. Some responders love the attention and often their egos get the best of them and we cringe in the audience. I have been to many sessions in the last few years where Richard and colleagues are present. I marvel that Richard, as an oral responder, can clarify, give criticism about, and enlighten a difficult topic. Yet, he does it in such manner as not to offend but to be supportive in his criticism. The members of the session seem to be so pleased and encourage him to continue. This is a communication ability with ethos few academics are capable of doing. Richard does it so well!

How appropriate that these essays are FOR Richard! Appropriate because for 40 years Richard was and is there FOR his students, his graduates, and his Communicology colleagues. The advice, the editing, the recommendations, the Fulbright applications, this goes on and on FOR me and countless others. As Richard's friend and colleague, and with me knowing for years most of the contributors to this volume, I wish to join with them in affirming our love and gratitude for Richard Lanigan being such an important part of our academic and personal lives.

NOTES

1. I wish to thank William "Bill" Smith, longtime friend and colleague, for his editorial suggestions.

APPENDIX A

Richard L. Lanigan's Biography and Curriculum Vitae

Professional Biography

Updated: July 8, 2017

RICHARD LEO LANIGAN 蓝 瑞 德 博 士
E-MAIL: RLANIGAN@MAC.COM

B.A. (Majors: Communicology and Philosophy, University of New Mexico, USA **1967**),
M.A. (Major: Communicology; Minor: Philosophy, University of New Mexico, USA **1968**),
PhD (Major: Communicology; Minor: Philosophy, School of Communication, Southern Illinois University, USA **1969**).
Postdoctoral Fellow: Philosophy (U. Dundee; St. Andrews U., Scotland, UK **1970-1972**); Philosophy (UC—Berkeley **1982**).
Languages: English, French, Spanish, Latin; limited German, Chinese, and Navajo (Diné).
Born: 31 December 1943, Santa Fe, New Mexico, USA.

He was granted the PhD at age 25 (the first person to complete courses, dissertation, and two foreign languages in two years), and, appointed Full Professor at age 35. Currently he is University Distinguished Scholar and Professor of Communicology (Emeritus), Dept. of Communication Studies, School of Communication, Southern Illinois University, USA where he completed forty-one years of university teaching and research in 2009. As a member of the Graduate School at SIU, he directed *35* PhD dissertations and served as an external examiner (abroad and in the USA) for an additional *64* doctoral dissertations. In 2000 he became founding Executive Director, of the International Communicology Institute [国际交流学学会] at SIU, an internet research and conference coordination group (http://www.communicology.org), now located at Capitol Hill Tower, Washington, DC, USA.

He is past Vice President of the International Association for Semiotic Studies, and now serves on the IASS Executive Committee representing the USA. On request by the U.S. Department of State, Bureau of Cultural and Educational Affairs, he served as a Senior Fulbright Fellow (P.R. China 1996, Cross-Cultural Communication) at Sichuan Union University in Chengdu City, and again as a Senior Fulbright Program Specialist (Canada 2007, Intercultural Communication) at Brock University to assist the Vice President for Research and International Affairs with Chinese student instruction. He was the first communication scholar invited to lecture at CASS, the Chinese Academy of Social Sciences, Beijing, PR China (2 March 2004). He is an elected Fellow of the International Academy for Intercultural Research (1998).

In 2012, he was elected a Fellow of the Polish Academy of Science (Philology). He is a past President (1994) of the Semiotic Society of America and past Editor (10 years) of *The American Journal of Semiotics*. He was Guest Editor and contributed to *Semiotica* (Vol. 41: "Semiotics and Phenomenology" 1982); and *Schutzian Research* (Vol. 3: "Phenomenology of the Human Sciences", 2011). He is an elected member of the American Philosophical Association. He was the founding Chair of the Philosophy of Communication Division (#9) of the International Communication Association (First World Congress on Communication Science, Berlin, Germany, 1977; re-elected Chair in 1978, 1979, 1980).He was a founding member of the Philosophy of Communication Division of the National Communication Association (USA). His academic awards include: Winchell Research Award (2013) of the General Semantics Institute (USA), International Scholar Award in Philosophy of Communication (2011), Duquesne University, Phi Kappa Phi Outstanding Scholar Award (1999), National Communication Association (USA) Spotlight on Scholarship Award (1995), Delta Award for Scholarship (1988), S.I.U. He was twice an Andrew Mellon Fellow at Vanderbilt University (Linguistics 1981; Philosophy 1984).

PUBLICATIONS:

The Human Science of Communicology (Duquesne University Press 1992). *Phenomenology of Communication* (Duquesne University Press 1988); *Semiotic Phenomenology of Rhetoric* (University Press of America 1984); *Speech Act Phenomenology* (Martinus Nijhoff 1977); *Speaking and Semiology* (Mouton 1972; 2nd ed. 1991); He has authored 45 Book Chapters, 91 Journal Articles (print and electronic), 22 Encyclopedia Entries, 170 academic Conference Papers, and 167 Invited Public Lectures in some 30 countries. He serves on the Editorial, Scientific, or Advisory Board of 18 international journals and 3 book series.

PROFESSIONAL BIOGRAPHY | 401

PDF Vita and Publications: https://siucarbondale.academia.edu/RichardLanigan

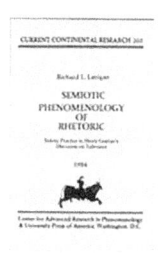

Richard L. Lanigan

Curriculum Vitae

[UPDATED: JULY 8, 2017]

REFERENCE INFORMATION:

Name:	Richard Leo Lanigan, Jr.
Birth Date:	31 December 1943; Age = 73
Birth Place:	Santa Fe, New Mexico (U.S.A.)
Postal Address:	1000 New Jersey Avenue, SE; Capitol Hill Tower, Suite PH06; Washington, DC 20003-3377, USA
Voice/Message	[001] **(202) 506-4048** (land line)
Mobile/Text/Message	[001] **(571) 439-6290**
E-mail: Professional:	rlanigan@mac.com [or] rlanigan@siu.edu
Years of Teaching:	Forty-One (University Level) [34 at S.I.U.; 3 years abroad]

CURRENT POSITIONS:

(1) Executive Director and Laureate Fellow,
   International Communicology Institute (Washington, DC, USA)
   ⌘ http://www.communicology.org

(2) Distinguished University Scholar and Professor of Communicology (Emeritus), *Southern Illinois University* (Carbondale, Illinois, USA)

⌘ https://itmfs1.it.siu.edu/php/details.php?sf=employee&cn=Richard%20L%20Lanigan&campus=Carbondale
⌘ http://www.siuc.edu/ExcellenceAwards/Scholar/index.html [1995]

Online Vita:

⌘ siu.academia.edu/RichardLLanigan [includes Vita and PDF publications]
⌘ http://myprofile.cos.com/rlanigan (COS = Community Of Science Profile)

PROFESSIONAL EDUCATION:

Degrees: PhD {1969} *Southern Illinois University* (USA)
School of Communication
Major: Communicology
Minor: Philosophy
Languages: French and Spanish [Chinese, German, Navajo (Diné)]
[at age 25, first person to complete the PhD in two years]

M.A. {1968} *University of New Mexico* (USA)
Major: Communicology
Minor: Philosophy
(Language Study: Navajo [Diné] and German)

B.A. {1967} *University of New Mexico* (USA)
Majors: Philosophy, and, Communicology
Language: French [High School Language: Latin]

Post-Doctoral Study: {1970–72} *University of Dundee* and *St. Andrew's University* (Scotland, UK)
Joint-Post Graduate Program in Philosophy
{1982} *University of California at Berkeley* (USA)
Department of Philosophy, Graduate Division

Certification: {1996} *English Language Examiner* (bilingual announcers) **Sichuan State Television (Channels 1 and 2)**, Division of China Central Television
Chengdu City, People's Republic of China

{2004,5,6,7,8} *State of Illinois Ethics Training Program* for University Employees, **State of Illinois**, Office of Executive Inspector General, 28 October.

{July 2007} *Instructional Skills Certification*, [Required for teaching at Canadian Universities], Center for Teaching, Learning, and Educational Technologies, *Brock University*, St. Catharines, Canada

{2008} *Experts Directory Listing*, Foundation for Educational Exchange between Canada and the United States, *Network on North American Studies* in Canada http://nnasc-renac.ca/

ACADEMIC APPOINTMENTS:

EMERITUS	2009 *SOUTHERN ILLINOIS UNIVERSITY*
UNIVERSITY DISTINGUISHED SCHOLAR and PROFESSOR OF COMMUNICOLOGY	2004 *SOUTHERN ILLINOIS UNIVERSITY*
OUTSTANDING SCHOLAR	1995 Graduate School *SOUTHERN ILLINOIS UNIVERSITY*
PROFESSOR	1980 [at age 35] *SOUTHERN ILLINOIS UNIVERSITY*
ASSOCIATE PROFESSOR	1976 *SOUTHERN ILLINOIS UNIVERSITY* [Tenure Granted]
ASSISTANT PROFESSOR	1974 Department of Speech Communication; *SOUTHERN ILLINOIS UNIVERSITY*
ASSISTANT PROFESSOR	1972 Department of English *CHICAGO STATE UNIVERSITY*
RESEARCH ASSOCIATE	1970 Joint PhD Program, Department of Philosophy *UNIVERSITY OF DUNDEE;* and Department of Moral Philosophy, *UNIVERSITY OF ST. ANDREWS* [Scotland, United Kingdom]

ASSISTANT PROFESSOR	**1969** Department of Speech and Theatre *UNIVERSITY OF TEXAS at El Paso*
TEACHING ASSISTANT	**1967** School of Communication *SOUTHERN ILLINOIS UNIVERSITY*

COTERMINOUS ACADEMIC APPOINTMENTS:

SENIOR FULBRIGHT FELLOW (Cross-Cultural Communication)	**2007** [May–July] Fulbright Program Specialist (Cross-Cultural Communication) *BROCK UNIVERSITY* St. Catharine's, **Canada**
SENIOR FULBRIGHT FELLOW (Cross-Cultural Communication)	**1996** [January–July] College of Foreign Languages and Cultures;
(DISTINGUISHED PROFESSOR and RESEARCH FELLOW)	Center for American Studies *SICHUAN UNION UNIVERSITY* Chengdu City, **People's Republic of China**
Expert Consultant	*Sichuan State Television* (Channels 1 and 2) {Examiner English Language Anchors, 25 April 1996]
VISITING PROFESSOR	**1994** [October] Department of Communication and Theatre *MILLERSVILLE UNIVERSITY*, Pennsylvania
UNIVERSITY DISTINGUISHED VISITING PROFESSOR	**1988** [March] Dept. of Human Communication Studies, College of Communication, *CALIFORNIA STATE UNIVERSITY at Chico*
INSTITUTE PROFESSOR	**1986** [June] Institute for Human Sciences [School of Interpersonal Communication and Department of Philosophy] *OHIO UNIVERSITY*

VISITING PROFESSOR	1985 [21–23 March] Short Course: "Semiotic Phenomenology of Communication" Department of Psychology *DUQUESNE UNIVERSITY*, Pittsburgh, PA Online: http://www.duq.edu/academics/schools/liberal-arts/academic-departments-of-liberal-arts/psychology/faculty-and-staff/visiting-faculty
VISITING SCHOLAR	1983 [May] 4th International Summer Institute for Semiotic and Structural Studies *INDIANA UNIVERSITY*
RESEARCH ASSOCIATE	1982 [January–August] Department of Philosophy, Graduate Division, *UNIVERSITY OF CALIFORNIA at Berkeley*
RESEARCH ASSOCIATE	1981–1998 Center for the Study of Cultural Transmission; (Departments of Anthropology, Communication, and Linguistics), *STATE UNIVERSITY OF NEW YORK at Buffalo*
VISITING SCHOLAR	1981 [June] 2nd International Summer Institute for Semiotic and Structural Studies *VANDERBILT UNIVERSITY*
PROFESSIONAL ASSOCIATE	1980 [December] Institute of Culture and Communication *EAST-WEST CENTER at Honolulu* [Federal Agency]
VISITING SCHOLAR	1980 [June] 1st International Summer Institute for Semiotic and Structural Studies *UNIVERSITY OF TORONTO, Canada*

ACADEMIC HONORS AND RESEARCH AWARDS:

2017 *Laureate Fellow,* International Communicology Institute, Washington, DC.

2013 *J. Talbot Winchell Award,* "Recognizing his many years of indispensable Contributions, Accomplishments, and Time-binding Efforts in Service to The Institute of General Semantics", presented October 25, 2013, The Princeton Club, New York City.
Online: http://www.generalsemantics.org/our-offerings/prizes-awards/j-talbot-winchell-award/

2012 *Fellow* (member by election), *Polish Academy of Science,* Philology Division, Wrocław Branch, Poland, June 2012.
Online: http://www.english.pan.pl/index.php?option=com_content&view=article&id=79:the-wroclaw-branch-of-the-polish-academy-of-sciences&catid=40:territorial-branches&Itemid=49

2011 First annual *International Scholar Award in Philosophy of Communication, "for Communication Excellence in Education for the Mind, Heart, Spirit",* Department of Comunication and Rhetorical Studies, Duquesne University, Pittsburgh, Pennsylvania, 4 November 2011. **2014:** Award renamed *"Richard L. Lanigan International Scholar Award in Philosophy of Communication".*

2008 *Who's Who in America* (61st ed., New Providence, NJ: Marquis Who's Who)

2007 *Senior Fulbright Fellow,* Brock University, St. Catharine's, Ontario, Canada.
Online: http://brocku.ca/brock-international/archives/past-events/other-events/-the-home-world-model-of-cultu

2006 *Senior Fulbright Program Specialist,* U.S. Dept. of State, Bureau of Educational and Cultural Affairs; Council for International Exchange of Scholars (CIES)
Online: http://eca.state.gov/fulbright

2006 *Who's Who in America* (60th Diamond ed., New Providence, NJ: Marquis Who's Who)

2005 *Who's Who in America* (59th ed., New Providence, NJ: Marquis Who's Who)

2004 *Vice President,* Executive Bureau; Scientific Committee for Congresses, International Association for Semiotic Studies [2004–2009]
Online: http://iass-ais.org

2004 *Who's Who in America* (58th ed., New Providence, NJ: Marquis Who's Who).
2000 *Fellow and Executive Director,* International Communicology Institute
Online: [www.Communicology.org]
1999 *Phi Kappa Phi Outstanding Scholar,* Southern Illinois University
Online: http://pkp.siuc.edu/pkpsub/scholarartistawards.html
1998 *Fellow,* International Academy for Intercultural Research
Online: http://www.intercultural-academy.net
1996 *Senior Fulbright Fellow,* Dept. of Foreign Languages, School of Foreign Languages and Cultures, Center for American Studies, Sichuan Union University, Chengdu City, Sichuan Province, People's Republic of China. [First Speech Communication scholar to be selected by the Fulbright Program to go to China; the only social science scholar approved by the Chinese government for 1996. Research and Lecturing Grant: (1) Philosophy of Communication; (2) Sociology of Language.] [SIU sabbatical leave] Online: http://eca.state.gov/fulbright
1995 National Communication Association *Spotlight on Scholarship*; "The Semiotic Phenomenology of Richard L. Lanigan," a peer reviewed and presented program on published research screened by the National Communication Association for sustained contribution [publications from 1967 through 1995] to the discipline, NCA Annual Conference, San Antonio, Texas.
Online: https://www.natcom.org
1995 *Outstanding Scholar of the University Award* (an occasional award that may be given only once to an individual, sponsored by the Graduate School, Southern Illinois University); $5000.
Online: http://excellenceawards.siu.edu/pastwinners/scholar/
Print: Marylin Davis, "Portrait: Richard Lanigan, The Culture of Communication" *Perspectives* [magazine of the SIU Graduate School] Fall 1995, pp. 22–24.
PDF: https://siu.academia.edu/RichardLLanigan
1995 Biographical references, *The Encyclopedia of Phenomenology,* editor-in-chief, Lester Embree. Kluwer Academic Publishers (1996), pp. 109, 319, 683, 721.
1994 *President,* Semiotic Society of America
Online: http://semioticsocietyofamerica.org
1988 *Delta Award,* 26 April 1988, Southern Illinois University, Friends of MorrisLibrary, "in recognition of your expertise in the field of communicology and philosophy, and your publications on the semiotics and phenomenology of communication».
Online: http://www.lib.siu.edu/departments/development/delta87

1988   Biographical and Intellectual History Listing, *AMERICAN PHENOMENOLOGY*, volume 26 in the series *Analecta Husserliana; The Yearbook of Phenomenological Research* , ed. Eugene F. Kaelin and Calvin O. Schrag. Hingham, MA and Dordrecht, The Netherlands: D. Reidel Publishing Co., pp. 424–429.

1984   *SIU Mini-Sabbatical:* Center for the Study of Cultural Transmission, Dept. of Anthropology, State University of New York at Buffalo. [March]

1984   *Andrew Mellon Fellowship* in Philosophy: Vanderbilt University. [May-June]

1983   Invitational Participant, *National Science Foundation*, Short Course "Science, the Media, and the Public", University of Georgia. [March]

1982   Biographical and Publication Listing, *Directory of American Scholars*, 8th ed.,Vol. II (Tempe, AZ: Jacques Cattell Press, A Xerox Publishing Co.).

1982   Appointment as visiting *Research Associate*, Dept. of Philosophy, Graduate Division, University of California-Berkeley; sponsored by Hubert L. Dreyfus. [SIU sabbatical leave]

1981   *Andrew Mellon Fellowship* in Linguistics: Vanderbilt University. [May-June]

1981   Biographical Listing, *Men of Achievement*, 8th ed.(Cambridge, England: International Biographical Centre).

1980   *SIU Mini-Sabbatical:* Toronto Semiotic Circle, University of Toronto, Canada.

1979   Biographical Listing, *Who's Who in International Education*, (Cambridge, England: International Biographical Centre).

1977   Invitational Participant, Cross-Cultural Seminar, *International Communication Agency [U.S. Information Agency]*, Washington, D.C. [November]

1977   *SIU Mini-Sabbatical:* Dept. of Film, San Francisco State University; and, Dept. of Rhetoric and Dept. of Philosophy, University of California-Berkeley.

1977   Founding Chair, Philosophy of Communication Division, International Communication Association, Berlin, Germany, *First World Congress on Communication Science*; re-elected 1978, 1979, 1980.

1976   Biographical Listing, *World Directory of Linguistics*.

1970   Elected to Membership: *American Philosophical Association* [Nomination by: Prof. Hubert Griggs Alexander] Online: http://www.apaonline.org

1966   Elected to Membership: Phi Sigma Tau, *National Scholastic Honor Society in Philosophy*. Online: http://phi-sigma-tau.org/membership.html

1963 Elected to Membership: Tau Kappa Alpha, *National Scholastic Honor Society in Communication. Online:* http://www.kappataualpha.org/membership.html

GRANTS FUNDED:

38. Third ROASS International Conference (Romanian Association of Semiotic Studies) "Alexandru I. Cuza" University, Iasi, **Romania**, 4–7 November, Lecture-Travel Grant, $1000, **2010**.
37. International Research Arts Project METAMIND: "Metamorphoses of the Absolute", Latvian Academy of Culture, Riga, **Latvia**, 5–10 Oct., Lecture-Travel Grant, $500, **2010**.
36. Faculty of Management, Czestochowa University of Technology, Czestochowa, Poland, 21 May; Philological School of Higher Education, Wroclaw, Poland, 19 May; Karkonosze College, and, State Museum "Gerhard Hauptmann House", Jelenia Góra, **Poland**, 15–18 May, Lecture-Travel Grant, $1,000, **2010**.
35. Universidad de la Coruña, **Spain**; Research-Travel Grant, International Association for Semiotic Studies, 10th World Congress, "Culture of Communication, Communication of Culture", $1,200, **2009**.
34. Nanjing Normal University; Research-Travel Grant, International Institute for Semiotic Studies, International Symposium on Cultural Semiotics, Nanjing, **P. R. China**, 15–17 November, $1000, **2008**.
33. Council for International Exchange of Scholars/U.S. Dept. of State, Bureau of Educational and Cultural Affairs: *Fulbright Senior Specialist Program* (**Canada**, Brock University, St. Catharines), $8,776, **2007**.
32. University of Helsinki and the International Semiotics Institute (Imatra), **Finland**, 11–17 June: Research-Travel Grant, International Association for Semiotic Studies, 9th World Congress, "Communication: Understanding/Misunderstanding", $3000, **2007**.
31. Universidad Autónoma de Nuevo Leon, **Mexico**, 19–22 October: Research-Travel Grant, 2nd World Congress on Semiotics and Communication, $3,000, **2005**.
30. Finnish Network University of Semiotics; University of Helsinki, **Finland**, 11–19 June: Research-Travel Grant, International Semiotics Institute at Imatra, $3,000, **2005**.
29. International Association for Semiotic Studies, 7–12 July: Research-Travel Grant, Université Lumière Lyon 2, **France**, 8th World Congress, $2,000, **2004**.

28. Downs School of Human Communication, Arizona State University, 26–28 February: Distinguished Professor Lecture and Seminar, $4,000, **2003**.
27. International Association for Semiotic Studies, 13–18 July: Research-Travel Grant, Guadalajara, Jalisco, **Mexico**, 6th World Congress, $3,000, **1997**.
26. Mercer University, Georgia, 24 April: National Endowment for the Humanities (NEH) Distinguished Lecture, $3,000, **1997**.
25. Council for International Exchange of Scholars/U.S. Dept. of State, Bureau of Educational and Cultural Affairs: *Senior Fulbright Fellow* (**P. R. China**, Sichuan Union University, Chengdu), $33,000, **1996**.
24. Federal University of Rio Grande del Sol, **Brazil**, 4–6 September: Research-Travel Grant, Instituto de Psicologia, $1,000, **1996**.
23. Pontifica Universidade Católica de Sao Paulo, **Brazil**, 31 August-3 September: Research-Travel Grant, 3rd Congresso International Latino-Americano de Semiótica, $2,000, **1996**.
22. Catholic University of Portugal, Oporto, **Portugal**, 25–28 September: Research-Travel Grant, International Conference: Perception and Consciousness in the Arts and Sciences, $3,000, **1995**.
21. University of Kassel, **Germany**, 20–23 March: Research-Travel Grant, International Conference: Semiotics of the Media, $1,000, **1995**.
20. International Association for Semiotic Studies, 12–18 June: Research-Travel Grant, University of California, Berkeley, 5th World Congress, $1,000, **1994**.
19. University of Toronto, **Canada**, 12–16 October: Research-Travel Grant, International Congress: Michel Foucault and Literature, $1,000, **1994**.
18. Universidad Autónoma de Nuevo Leon, **Mexico**, 19–22 October: Research-Travel Grant, 1st World Congress on Semiotics and Communication, $2,000, **1993**.
17. Office of Research and Development, Southern Illinois University: Research Grant, $6,000, **1992**.
16. *Inter-University Centre of Dubrovnik*, **Yugoslavia**, March: Research-Travel Grant, International Conference: Maurice Merleau-Ponty, $2,000, **1991**.
15. California State University, Chico, California, 15–19 March: Distinguished Visiting University Professor, $5,000, **1988**.
14. *Indian Council for Philosophical Research*, New Delhi, **India**, 5–8 January: Research-Travel Grant, International Conference: Phenomenology and Indian Philosophy, $3,000, **1988**.
13. Institute for Human Sciences, Ohio University, 15–28 June: Distinguished Institute Professor, $6,000, **1986**.

12. Office of Research and Development, Southern Illinois University: Mini-Sabbatical Research Grant, $1,000, **1986**.
11. Duquesne University, Pittsburgh, Pennsylvania, 14–18 March: Distinguished Visiting Professor of Psychology, $3,000, **1985**.
10. Mellon Foundation/ Vanderbilt University, Nashville, Tennessee, June: MF Summer Institute Fellow (Philosophy), $3,000, **1984**.
9. Center for the Study of Cultural Transmission, State University of New York, Buffalo, New York, 1–10 March: Distinguished Visiting Professor of Anthropology, $1,000, **1982**.
8. Office of Research and Development, Southern Illinois University: Mini-Sabbatical Research Grant, $790, **1982**.
7. *Mellon Foundation/* Vanderbilt University, Nashville, Tennessee, June: MF Summer Institute Fellow (Linguistics), $3,000, **1981**.
6. *Danforth Foundation:* Communication in the Classroom Research Grant, $1,000, **1981**.
5. Institute for Culture and Communication, *East – West Center,* Honolulu, Hawaii, 15–23 December: Research Associate, $3,000, **1980**.
4. *National Endowment for the Humanities* (NEH): Primary Consultant, Access and Ability: Whose Judgment [PI = J. Thomas Lijewski], $33,460, **1977**.
3. *Rockefeller Foundation:* Instructional Materials Grant, $500, **1976**.
2. Office of Research and Development, Southern Illinois University: Research Grant, $400, **1974 to 1975**.
1. *Rockefeller Foundation:* Instructional Materials Grant, $500, **1974 to 1975**.

MEMBERSHIP IN LEARNED SOCIETIES AND PROFESSIONAL ASSOCIATIONS:

COMMUNICOLOGY:

Fellow, Polish Academy of Science, Wrocław Division (Philology)
Fellow, International Academy for Intercultural Research
International Association for Intercultural Communication Studies
Human Science Research Conference
Society for Phenomenology and the Human Sciences
Semiotic Society of America; Founding Member (1976), Past President, Journal Editor, Institute of General Semantics
International Association for Semiotic Studies/Association Internationale de Sémiotique

Toronto Semiotic Circle (Canada)
International Society for General Semantics
International Communication Association: Divisions: (9) Philosophy of Communication, Founding Chair; (8) Intercultural & Development Communication
National Communication Association: Divisions: (1) Philosophy of Communication; (2) International & Intercultural Speech Communication
Rhetoric Society of America

Past Memberships:

Central States Communication Association: Interest Groups:
(1) Communication Theory;
(2) Mass Communication
Canadian Semiotic Society
International Society for Intercultural Education, Training, and Research

PHILOSOPHY:

American Philosophical Association
(Elected Member; nominator: Hubert Griggs Alexander)
Society for Phenomenology and Existential Philosophy
The Charles S. Peirce Society
The International Merleau-Ponty Circle (Past Chair)
The International Alfred Schütz Circle for Phenomenology and Interpretive Social Science

Past Memberships:

Central States Philosophical Association
British Society for Phenomenology
The Husserl Circle
The International Husserl and Phenomenological Research Society

PROFESSIONAL:

Fulbright Association (Life Member)
United States—China Friendship Association
Network on North American Studies in Canada (NNASC)
Experts Directory (www.nnasc-renac.ca)

Past Memberships:

American Association of University Professors
SIU Chapter President (1984–1987)
Illinois Conference of the A.A.U.P.
Illinois Education Association/National Education Association

TOPICAL RESEARCH AND TEACHING INTERESTS:

COMMUNICOLOGY: Theories and Models of Human Communicology
Cross-Cultural, Intercultural, International Communication
Group Process and Interpersonal Communication
Philosophy of Communication; Semiotics
Visual Arts and Media in Critical-Cultural Studies
Qualitative Research Methodology; Normative Logics
Semiotic Phenomenology
Rhetoric and Discourse Studies

PHILOSOPHY: Contemporary Continental Philosophy
– French: Maurice Merleau-Ponty; Michel Foucault; Julia Kristeva; Pierre Bourdieu; Georges Gusdorf; Claude Lévi-Strauss, Ferdinand de Saussure
– German: Ernst Cassirer; Karl-Otto Apel; Jürgen Habermas; Alfred Schütz; Aldoph Lowe
American Phenomenology and Semiology
Charles Sanders Peirce; Wilbur Marshall Urban; Hubert Griggs Alexander; Edward Sapir; Benjamin Lee Whorf
Language and Logic of Communication; Speech Acts
Human Sciences; Philosophy of Science

PUBLICATIONS: LIST IS PROVIDED AS A SEPARATE DOCUMENT

TEACHING: Graduate Dissertation / Thesis Direction

SIU Graduate Faculty Status: Category I – Direct PhD Dissertation
Total of Committee Memberships: PhD = 99
[Author/Title List available on request] M.A. M.S. = 38

Director:
PhD Dissertation: 35 [since 1979; 3 Published]

M.A. and M.S. Thesis: 9 [since 1977]
M.A. and M.S. Research Report: 8 [since 1976]
External Examiner on Committee:
PhD Dissertation: 29 [since 1975] [3 at other universities]
M.A. and M.S. Thesis: 4 [since 1979] [1 at another university]
M.A. M.S. Research Report: 3 [since 1988]
Committee Member:
PhD Dissertation: 35 [since 1975]
M.A. and M.S. Thesis: 4 [since 1979]
M.A. M.S. Research Report: 10 [since 1978]

TEACHING: Pedagogy and Postgraduate Seminars

Courses Taught:
[Courses taught since 1974 at **Southern Illinois University;**
* = created the course; ** = taught abroad at foreign universities]

Undergraduate Courses:

152 – Interpersonal Communication
153 – Public Speaking
221 – Advanced Public Speaking
230 – Introduction to Communication Theory
261 – Small Group Communication
262 – Interpersonal Communication II
280 – Business and Professional Communication
341 – Introduction to Intercultural Communication* [*cross list,* **Linguistics Dept.**]
361 – Nonverbal Communication [cross-cultural]
362 – Communication and Social Process*/**
383 – Interviews and Interviewing
390 – Applied Communication

Undergraduate / Graduate Courses:

401 – Communication Theories and Models*
411 – Rhetorical Criticism
421 – Studies in Public Address
440 – Language Behavior
441 – Intercultural Communication*/**
442 – Psychology of Human Communication*
446 – Sociology of Language, Discourse, and Signs*/** [*cross list,* **Sociology Dept.**]
460 – Small Group Communication: Theory and Research
465 – Philosophy of Communication* [*cross list,* **Philosophy Dept.**]

490 – Communication Practicum
494 – Internship

Graduate Courses:

501 – Introduction to Speech Communication Research
503 – Communicology as a Human Science*
504 – Seminar: Empirical Phenomenological Research Methods*
505 – Seminar: Semiotic Phenomenology and Critical-Cultural Research*/**
510 – Seminar: Rhetoric and Communication*
526 – Seminar: Studies in Persuasion
540 – Seminar: Language, Culture, and Semiology*
545 – Seminar: Semiology and Semiotic Communication*
551 – Phenomenology Seminar I: French Communicology*
552 – Phenomenology Seminar II: German Communicology*
561 – Studies in Small Group Communication
562 – Philosophy of Human Communication* [*cross list*, **Philosophy Dept.**]
593 – Research Problems in Communication
595 – Research Report [MA. MS]
599 – Thesis [MA, MS]
598 – Proseminar in Human Communication*
600 – Dissertation [PhD]

Graduate Seminars:

[unless noted, taught at **Southern Illinois University**; masters students, doctoral students, faculty auditors]

2007 — In **Canada** at *Brock University*,(as Senior Fulbright Specialist), Center for Teaching, Learning, and Educational Technologies, St. Catharines, Ontario.
Faculty/Administrative Development Workshops: [graduate and in-service credit]
— Nonverbal Communication: An Overview of Applications
— The Body in the Classroom: Considerations for Teaching and Learning
— Intercultural Communication and Instructional Strategies
— Small Communication Communication: Teaching and Learning Considerations
— Nonverbal Communication: Visual/Image Analysis
— Intercultural Communication and Research Contexts
— Small Group Communication and Multidisciplinary Research Teams
— Public Speaking and Presentation Skills and Research Contexts

— Academic Writing for Publication
— Validity and Reliability in Qualitative Methodology
— Pedagogy, Teaching, and Learning Strategies with Chinese Students

2000 — "Communicology as a Human Science"
1998 — "Umberto Eco's *A Theory of Semiotics* and Related Books"
1997 — "Michel Foucault's Theory of Discourse"
1996 — In **Brazil** at *Federal University of Rio Grande del Sol* (**Psychology Dept.**):
"The Discourse of Subjectivity in the Human Sciences"
1996 — In **P. R. China** at *Sichuan University* (**Chengdu City**):
— "Communication and Social Process in the USA"
— "Intercultural Communication and Comparative Social Values"
1995 — "Charles Sanders Peirce's Argument Cycle: Abduction, Induction, Deduction"
1994 — "Vincent Descombes' *Le Même et L'Autre*"
1993 — "Chaim Perelman's *The New Rhetoric*"
1992 — "A. J. Greimas' Semiotic Square"
1990 — "Jürgen Habermas and Communication Ethics"
1989 — "Contemporary Perspectives on Rhetoric
(Richards, Weaver, Toulmin, Perelman, Grassi, Burke, Foucault, Habermas)"
1988 — "Merleau-Ponty and Foucault on Discourse"
1988 — At *California State University at Chico*:
"Communicology as a Human Science"
1987 — "Julia Kristeva's Theory of Intertextuality/Transposition"
1986 — At the **Institute for the Human Sciences,** *Ohio University*:
"Michel Foucault's Communicology"
1985 — "Phenomenology of Rhetoric: Chaim Perelman"
1985 — In Pittsburgh at *Duquesne University* (**Psychology Dept.**):
"Semiotic Phenomenology of Communication"
1984 — "Ways of Seeing: The Phenomenology of Art"
1982 — "The Attica Prison Rebellion and Metajournalism"
1980 — "Maurice Merleau-Ponty's *Phenomenology of Perception*"
1979 — "Validity and Reliability in Qualitative Research"

SERVICE: ADMINISTRATIVE

(3) Southern Illinois University

DEPARTMENT:

Director of Undergraduate Studies {1974; 1981; 1985; 1986; 1987; 1988}
Director of Graduate Studies {1980}

Assistant Chairperson {1975}
Standing Committees {one or more of these each year):
Personnel; Grievance; Graduate Program; Undergraduate Program; General Education Textbook Selection; Planning and Development; Space Utilization; Computer.

COLLEGE:

College of Communications and Fine Arts:
Promotion and Tenure Committee {1983; 1985}
International Committee {1980; 1981; 1985}
College of Liberal Arts:
Faculty Mentoring Program {1998; 1999}
Outstanding Scholar Award Selection Committee {2001–2009}

UNIVERSITY:

Search Committee, Dean of the College of Mass Communication and Media Arts [Faculty Senate Representative], Office of the Provost and Vice Chancellor, {2007–8}
Phi Kappa Phi Outstanding Scholar and Artist Awards, Selection Committee, SIU, Chapter 72 {2000–9}
University Outstanding Scholar Award Selection, *Committee, Graduate School* {1996–9}
Chair (1993), Promotion Grievance Committee (Richard Lawson), Office of the President [Appointment by President].
Chair (1990–1995), Committee on Honorary Degrees and Distinguished Service Awards {Graduate Council Representative, 1989–1995}
Search Committee, Associate Dean of the Graduate School [Graduate Council Representative] {1989}
Faculty Senate {1988–1991}
Governance Committee {1988–91}
Chair, President's Committee on Enhancement of the Scholarly Environment at SIU-C [Graduate Council Representative] {1986–87}
Search Committee, Associate Vice President for Academic Affairs and Research, and, Dean of the Graduate School [Graduate Council Representative] {1986}
Chair, Ad Hoc Promotion Review Committee [for the Department of Community Development], Office of the Associate Vice President for Academic Affairs and Research {1987–88}
Graduate School, Office of Research Development and Administration, Review Committee for Business, Education, and Social Science [internal grants; Summer and Sabbatical Research] {1981–87}

Graduate Council {1980–81; 1984–87}
- Educational Policies Committee {1980–81; 1984–87}
- Research Committee {1980–81}
- Degree Program Review Committee:
    - Dept. of Community Development {1980–81}
    - Dept. of Mathematics {1986–87}
    - Dept. of Educational Psychology {1990–91}
    - Dept. of Linguistics {1991–92}

Undergraduate Honors Program:
- Program Review Committee {1977}
- Editorial Board, student journal *Papyrus* {1985–1995}

Ad Hoc Committee on Support for Organized Research, Office of the Associate Vice President for Academic Affairs and Research [Faculty Senate Representative] {1983–84}

Committee on University Research Policy, Office of the Vice President for Academic Affairs and Research [Graduate Council Representative] {1980–81}

(2) Chicago State University

DEPARTMENT:

Assistant Director, Speech Communication Program, Dept. of English {1973–74}
Curriculum Committee {1972–74}
Advisor {1972–74}

COLLEGE:

Chair, Committee to Draft College Working Paper {1972}
Faculty Council, College of Liberal Arts {1973–74}

UNIVERSITY:

Chair, Oversight Committee on Student Union Operations {1973–74}

(1) University of Texas – El Paso [Cuidad Juarez, Mexico; twin city on the Rio Grande]

DEPARTMENT:

Curriculum Committee {1969–70}
Advisor {1969–70}

COLLEGE:

College of Liberal Arts, Teaching Member, Interdisciplinary
Program Committee; Teacher (joint English-Communication courses) {1969–70}

UNIVERSITY:

Faculty-Student Film Society {1969–70}
Chair, Dean of Students Committee on Stress and Suicide {1969–70}

SERVICE: ACADEMIC AND PROFESSIONAL

CAMPUS (Southern Illinois University):

Executive Board, United States -China Friendship Association, SIU Carbondale
    Chapter {1992–95}
President, SIU Chapter, American Association of University Professors {1985–92}
Chair, Committee on Collective Bargaining {1984–86}
Legislative Liaison, State of Illinois {1983–88}

NATIONAL:

Executive Council, *Society for Phenomenology and Human Science* {1981–84; 1990–94}
President, *Semiotic Society of America* {1993–1994}
    Executive Board {1989–1992; 2014–2016}
    Chair, Finance Committee {1991–1993}
    Member, Awards and Recognition Committee {1991–1992}
    Founding Member {1976}
National Communication Association (formerly *Speech Communication Association*).
    Commission on Semiotics and Communication {1991–1993}
        Member, Conference Program Committee {1991–1994]
        Founding Member {1991]
    Philosophy of Communication Division [2012-present];
        Publication Awards Committee [2012–2015; Chair 2014]
        Founding Member [2010]
Center for Advanced Research in Phenomenology [CARP], Department of Philosophy,
    Florida Atlantic University, Boca Raton, Florida
        Member, International Board of Advisors (1981-present)
        Member, Committee on Cultural Studies, Department of Philosophy,
        Ohio University, Athens, Ohio (1980–1998)

Faculty, *Institute for Human Science* [CARP], School of Interpersonal Communication, School of Telecommunications; and, Dept. of Philosophy, Ohio University (1986).

INTERNATIONAL:

Member, International Advisory Council, Dept. of Semiotics and Communication Theory, *St. Petersburg State University*, **Russia** [2008-present]

Fellow and Executive Director, International Communicology Institute, http:www.Communicology.org [2000-present]

Member, Advisory Council, World Association for Massmediatic Semiotic and Global Communication, Institute for Semiotics and Mass Culture, *University of Monterey, Nuevo Leon,* **Mexico** [2003-present]

Scientific Committee, Second World Congress on Semiotics and Communication 2005, Institute for Semiotics and Mass Culture, *University of Monterey, Nuevo Leon,* **Mexico** [2003–2005]

Vice President, *International Association for Semiotic Studies,* {2004–2009}
  Executive Bureau {1994-present}
  Assistant Treasurer (North & South America) {1994–2004}
  Member of Scientific Committee [program planning and review for International Congresses every 3 to 5 years]

Executive Board of Advisors, International Merleau-Ponty Circle {1986-present}
  Coordinator, 10th International Conference {1985}

Founding Chair, Division 9: Philosophy of Communication, *International Communication Association*
  {Interest Group Chair 1976–1980; Division 9 Chair 1981–1983}

Liaison, Council of Philosophical Societies, World Congress of Philosophy {1984–86}

Invited Scholar, 50th Anniversary Conference, Edmund Husserl Archive, *University of Leuven,* **Belgium** {1989}

SERVICE: ACADEMIC EVALUATION

GRANT AGENCIES:

Proposal Reviewer, *National Science Center,* Polish Ministry of Science and Higher Education, **Poland** [2014-present]

National Screening Committee, *Fulbright Grants for Graduate Study Abroad: P.R. China,* Institute of International Education (New York), Fulbright Program, Bureau of Educational and Cultural Affairs, U.S. Dept. of State [2009–2010].

Proposal Reviewer, ESF Research Conference Scheme and Research Conference Series, *European Science Foundation*, Brussels, **Belgium** [2010-present]
Nominator, The Kyoto Prize Committee, *The Inamori Foundation*, Shimogyo-ku, Kyoto 600, **Japan**. {The Kyoto Prize is an international award of $100,000 given to one person each year in one subject area of art or science.} {1996–2006} [popularly known as "Asia's Nobel Prize"]
Proposal Reviewer, *National Endowment for the Humanities*, Interpretive Research Program, Division of Research Programs {1986}
Nominee Consultant, Vanderbilt University -*Mellon Foundation Summer Humanities Institutes* {1984; 1986; 1987; 1988]
Project Consultant, *NEH-Minnesota Humanities Commission* {1977; 1978]
Project Consultant, *NEH-Illinois Humanities Council* {1977; 1978]

DEGREE PROGRAMS:

External Consultant, Proposal for a Phenomenology of Communication Course Series, Center for Advanced Research in Philosophy and Department of Philosophy, *Jadavpur University,* Calcutta, **India** {1989}
External Consultant, Proposal for a Department of Communication, *University of California at Santa Cruz* {May 1985}
External Consultant, Proposal for a Philosophy of Communication Major, *Goldsmith's College*, London, **United Kingdom** {1980}
Consultant, Proposal for the Model Graduate Major in Semiotics, *Semiotic Society of America* {1977}

FACULTY: [historical selection of interdisciplinary and rank examples]

External Evaluator, Promotion of candidate to **Professor,** School of **Communications,** Grand Valley State University, Allendale, Michigan {August 2010}
External Evaluator, Promotion of candidate to **Professor,** Department of **Communication,** University of Oklahoma, Norman, Oklahoma {October 2002}
External Evaluator Promotion of candidate to **Associate Professor (tenure),** Department of **Communication,** University of Toledo, Toledo, Ohio {November 2002}
External Evaluator, Promotion of candidate to **Professor,** School of **Interpersonal Communication,** Ohio University, Athens, Ohio {January 1997}

External Evaluator, Promotion of candidate to **Associate Professor (tenure)**, Department of **Rhetoric,** University of California, Berkeley, California {August 1995}
External Evaluator, Promotion of candidate to **Endowed Chair,** School of **Politics** and **Communication Studies,** University of Liverpool, United Kingdom {July 1994}
External Evaluator,Promotion of candidate to **Professor (Phenomenology Specialization),** Department of **Behavioral Medicine** and **Psychiatry,** School of Medicine, University of Virginia, Charlottesville, Virginia {November 1991}
External Evaluator, **Chairperson** nominee for the Department of **Speech Communication,** Office of the Dean, College of Liberal Arts, Pennsylvania State University, College Park, Pennsylvania {March 1991}
External Evaluator, **Chairperson** nominee for the Department of **Communication,** Office of the Dean, Faculty of Social Science, State University of New York at Buffalo {March 1989}
External Evaluator, Promotion of candidate to **Associate Professor (tenure),** School of **Interpersonal Communication,** Ohio University, Athens, Ohio {January 1989]
External Evaluator Promotion of candidate to **Associate Professor (tenure),** Department of **Communication,** University of Massachusetts, Amherst {January 1989}
External Evaluator, Promotion of candidate to **Associate Professor (tenure),** Department of **Communication,** University of New Hampshire, Orono {January 1988}
External Evaluator, Promotion of candidate to **Professor,** Department of **Sociology,** Florida State University, Tallahassee {May 1988}
External Evaluator Promotion of candidate to **Associate Professor (tenure),** Department of **Communication** Studies, Northwestern University, Evanston, Illinois {January 1988}

FOREIGN TRAVEL EXPERIENCE:

Americas:
Brazil	1996
Canada	1980; 1984; 1987; 1988; 1994; 2001; 2002; 2003, 2007, 2010; 2015

Mexico	1960–68 [multiple visits]; **1969–70** [in residence El Paso, Texas; Cuidad Juarez, Mexico]; 1974; 1978; 1989; 1993; 1997; 2005

Africa:

Cameroon	(pending)
South Africa	(pending)

Asia:

Bangladesh	1987
P. R. China	**1995–96** [in residence Chengdu City, Sichuan Province], 2004, 2008 [2 trips], 2012
India	1987 [New Delhi]; 1988 [Mysore]
Japan	1989

Europe:

Austria	1991
Belgium	1970; 1972; 1988; 1989
Czech Republic	2011; 2012
Denmark	1988; 2006
Estonia	2007; 2012
Finland	1988; 2005; 2007
France	1970; 1971; 1972; 1977; 1987; 1988; 2004
Germany	1971; 1977; 1988; 1995; 2006; 2007; 2010; 2011; 2012
Korea	2012
Latvia	2010
The Netherlands	1970; 1972; 1988
Spain	2009
Portugal	1995
Poland	1988; 2010; 2011 [3 trips]; 2012
Romania	2010
Sweden	1988; 2007
Switzerland	1970; 1972;
United Kingdom	**1970–72** [in residence Dundee, Scotland]; 1977; 1987; 1988; 1991; 2011 (Oxford, Saint Catherine's College)

U.S.S.R. (CCCP)   1988
Russian Federation   2005; 2006
Yugoslavia   1991 (Dubrovnik Interuniversity Center)

APPENDIX B

Richard L. Lanigan's Publications, Presentations, Thesis and Dissertation Direction

Publication List—
Richard L. Lanigan

University Distinguished Scholar and Professor of Communicology (Emeritus)
Southern Illinois University
School of Communication, Department of Speech Communication
Carbondale, Illinois, 62901–6605, USA
E-mail: rlanigan@siu.edu

Director and Fellow,
⌘ *INTERNATIONAL COMMUNICOLOGY INSTITUTE*
Communicology.org
Capitol Hill Tower, Suite PH06
1000 New Jersey Avenue, S.E.
Washington, DC 20003–3377, USA
Tel: (202) 506–4048 Mobile: (571) 439–6290

E-Mail: rlanigan@mac.com

[Updated: Saturday, July 8, 2017]

Curriculum Vitae, Many Articles, Book Chapters and Book's *Table of Contents* are available as PDF files @
https://siucarbondale.academia.edu/RichardLanigan
ALL ENTRIES ARE CHRONOLOGICAL PRESENT TO PAST

BOOKS [5]

5. *THE HUMAN SCIENCE OF COMMUNICOLOGY:* **The Phenomenology of Discourse in Foucault and Merleau-Ponty** (Pittsburgh, PA: Duquesne University Press, **1992**; ISBN: 0–8207-0242-0).
   ☐ *Review Essays:*
   1. Craig R. Smith, *Quarterly Journal of Speech*, Vol. 79., No. 4 (November 1993), pp. 509–511.
   2. Thomas F. N. Puckett, "Reclaiming the Person in Communication: Lanigan's Semiotic Phenomenology of Communicology", *Semiotica*, Vol. 107, Nos. 1/2 (1995), pp. 171–178.
   3. Gary Genosko, "Gaps" in *The Semiotic Review of Books*, Vol. 6, No. 1 (January 1995).
   4. David James Miller, *Philosophy and Rhetoric*, Vol. 28, No. 4 (1995), pp. 423–425.

4. *PHENOMENOLOGY OF COMMUNICATION:* **Merleau-Ponty's Thematics in Semiology and Communicology** (Pittsburgh, PA: Duquesne University Press, **1988**; SBN: 0–8207-0199-8). [*Korean Translation* by DuWon Lee and Kee-soon Park; Seoul, Korea: Naman Publishing House, 1997; ISBN: 89–300-3554-X].
   ☐ *Review Essays:*
   1. David Descutner and Richard Letteri, *Phenomenology and the Human Sciences: Journal of Reviews and Commentary*, Vol. 15, No. 1 (January 1990), pp. 7–17.
   2. Graeme Nicholson, "Communication Theory", *The Semiotic Review of Books*, Vol. 2. No. 3 (Sept. 1991), pp. 8–9.
   ☐ *Review:*
   3. *The Chronicle of Higher Education*, (27 April 1988), p. A16.

3. *SEMIOTIC PHENOMENOLOGY OF RHETORIC:* **Eidetic Practice in Henry Grattan's Discourse on Tolerance** (Current Continental Research, No. 203: Washington, DC: Center for Advanced Research in Phenomenology; University Press of America, **1984**; ISBN: 0–8191-4295-6).
   ☐ *Review Essay:*
   1. Stephen Tyman, *Phenomenology + Pedagogy*, Vol. 3, No. 1 (1985), pp. 57–59.
   ☐ *Reviews:*
   2. *LLBA: Language and Language Behavior Abstracts*, Vol. 20, No. 2 (1986), p. 555; 8603607.
   3. *Poetics Today*, Vol. 8, no. 2 (1987), p. 458.

2. *SPEECH ACT PHENOMENOLOGY* (The Hague: Martinus Nijhoff Publishers, **1977**; ISBN: 90-247-1920-8). E-BOOK available at Springer Book Archives: Springer.com

☐ *Review Essays:*
1. Jerry H. Gill, *International Studies in Philosophy*, Vol. 11 (1997).
2. Bryan K, Crow, *The Southern Speech Communication Journal*, 45.3 (Spring 1980), 316–318.
3. A Colloquy Review, Robert N. Gaines review, *Quarterly Journal of Speech*, Vol. 64, No. 4 (December 1978), pp. 465–466; Lanigan response, pp. 466–467.

☐ *Reviews:*
4. *Choice*, Vol. 15 (March 1978), p. 62.
5. C. Struyker Boudier, *Tijdschrift Voor Filosofie*, Vol. 1978, No. 3 (1978), pp. 529–530.
6. I. Ribeiro, *Brotéria*, Vol. 109 (October 1979). p. 334.
7. A.v.d.M., *Bibliographie de la Philosophie*, (January 1980).
8. Johan Van der Auwera, *Journal of Pragmatics*, Vol. 4, No. 6 (December 1980), pp. 560–562.

1. *SPEAKING AND SEMIOLOGY:* Maurice Merleau-Ponty's Phenomenological Theory of Existential Communication (No. 22: Approaches to Semiotics; The Hague, Paris, and Hawthorne, NY: Mouton, **1972**; 2nd Reprint Edition, 1991; ISBN: 3-11-012864-0).

☐ *Review Essays:*
1. Gerald J. Carruba, *Kinesis* Vol. 6, No. 1 (Fall 1973), pp. 56–61.
2. John O'Neill, "Philosophical Speech and the Poetry of Review", *Semiotica*, Vol. 10, No. 3 (1974), pp. 283–291.
3. Sebastian Mariner Bigorra, *Revista Española de Linguistica* Vol. 4, No. 2 (1974), pp. 510–512.

☐ *Reviews:*
4. Robert Lechner, "M. Merleau-Ponty", *Philosophy Today*, Vol. 17, No. 4 (Winter 1973), p. 271.
5. *Choice*, (June 1973), p. 635.
6. Charles E. Regan, *Philosophical Studies (Ireland)* Vol. 23 (1975), pp. 299–302.

BOOK AND JOURNAL EDITING [24]

BOOKS

1. Honorary Editor; Current ms. Reviewer [All Vols.]
   Series: *Languages in Contact (Poland)*
   Edited by Piotr P. Chruszczewski;
   Committee for Philology, Polish Academy of Science; Philological School of Higher Education, Wrocław;
   International Communicology Institute, Washington)
   Vol. 1, Languages in Contact 2012 (2014) {Lanigan contributed Chapter]
   Vol. 2, Ways to Protolanguage 3 (2014)
   Vol. 3, Konrad Klimkowski,
   Toward a Shared Curriculum in Translator and Interpreter Education (2015)
   Vol. 4, Paulina Kłos-Czerwińska,
   Discourse: An Introduction to Teun Van Dijk, Michel Foucault, and Pierre Bourdieu (2015)
   Vol. 5, Piotr P. Chruszczewski, Richard L. Lanigan, John R. Rickford, Katarzyna Buczek,
   Aleksandra R. Knapik, and Jacek Mianowski (eds.),
   Languages in Contact 2014 (2015)

2. Advisory Board, Current ms. Reviewer {All Vols.]
   Series: *Philologica Wratislaviensia: From Grammar to Discourse (Germany)*
   (Edited by Zdzisław Wąsik ; Peter Lang GmbH Internationaler Verlag der Wissenschaften)
   Vol. 1, Zdisław Wasik and Tomasz Komendzinski (eds.)
   Metaphor and Cognition (2008)
   Vol. 2, Elzbieta Magdalena Wasik,
   Coping with an Idea of Ecological Grammar (2010)
   Vol. 3, Zdisław Wasik, with Daina Teters (eds.)
   Unfolding the Semiotic Web in Urban Discourse (2011) {Lanigan contributed Chapter]
   Vol. 4, Ryszard W. Wolny and Zdisław Wasik (eds.)
   Faces and Masks of Ugliness in Literary Narratives
   Vol. 5, Magdalena Zabieiska
   Searching for the Patient's Presence in Medical Case Reports (2014)

3. Scientific Board, Current ms. Reviewer [All Vols.]
   Series: *METAMIND: International Research Arts Project (Latvian Academy of Culture)*

(Edited by Daina Teters, LAC Associate Director (Riga: Latvian Academy of Culture; Metamind Project Press)
Vol. 1, Metamorphoses of the World: Traces, Shadows, Reflections, Echoes, and Metaphors (2010)
Vol. 2, Metamorphoses of the Absolute (2011) {Lanigan contributed Chapter]
Vol. 3, The Order in Destruction and the Chaos of Order: Freedom (forthcoming 2016)

4. Current ms. Reviewer: University and Commercial Presses {Discipline Subject Matter}
    Duquesne UniversityPress {Communication; Philosophy; Linguistics}
    Elsevier {Language, Linguistics, Semiotics}
    Indiana University Press {Semiotics}
    Longman, Inc. {Communication Theory}
    Martinus Nijhoff {Philosophy; Merleau-Ponty; Communication}
    Mouton; Walter de Gruyter {Philosophy; Communication}
    Ohio University Press; Center for Advanced Research in Phenomenology {Phenomenology; Communication; Semiology}
    Southern Illinois University Press {Philosophy; Linguistics; Semiotics}
    State University of New York Press {Philosophy; Merleau-Ponty}
    University of Alabama Press {Communication}
    University of California Press {Communication; Philosophy}
    University of Notre Dame Press {Philosophy; Communication}
    University Press of America; Center for Advanced Research in Phenomenology {Phenomenology; Communication; Semiology}
    University of Toronto Press {Communication, Merleau-Ponty, Foucault}
    Yale University Press {Communication}

JOURNALS: Editorial Boards

1. Past Journal Editor; Current ms. Reviewer
    The American Journal of Semiotics (Semiotic Society of America; USA)
    Vol. 11, Nos. 3/4 (Spring **1994**) [1998], (316 pp.)
    Theme: *Semiosis and Cultural Construction*
    Vol. 12, Nos. 1/4 (Summer **1995**) [1998], (452 pp.)
    Theme: *History and Semiotics*
    Vol. 13, Nos. 1/4 (Fall **1996**) [1998], (320 pp.)
    Theme: *Signs in Musical Hermeneutics*
    Vol. 14, Nos. 1/4 (Spring **1997**) [1998], (234 pp.)
    Theme: *Trickster: Cultural Boundaries and Semiosis*
    Vols. 15 and 16, Nos. 1/4 (**2000**), (362 pp.)

Theme: *French Semiotics*
Vol. 17, No. 1 (Spring 2001), (293 pp.).
Theme: *Rhetorical Semiotics*
Vol. 17, No. 2 (Summer 2001) (428pp.) [Printed May 2002]
Theme: *Communication and Culture*
Vol. 17, No. 3 (Fall 2001) (294pp.) [Printed August 2002]
Theme: *Semiotics of the Image*
Vol. 17, No. 4 (Winter 2001) (384pp.) [Printed December 2003]
Theme: *The Body as Sign and Embodiment*

2. Journal Guest Editor; Current ms. Reviewer
   Semiotica—Journal of the International Association for Semiotic Studies (Germany)
   Special Issue: Semiotics and Phenomenology, 1982, Vol. 41, nos. 1–4, pages 1–335.

3. Journal Guest Editor
   Schutzian Research—A Yearbook of Lifeworldly Phenomenology and Qualitative Social Science [Alfred Schutz] (USA and Romania)
   Special Issue: Phenomenology of the Human Sciences Vol. 3 (2011), pp. 1–259.
   The American Journal of Semiotics (Semiotic Society of America; USA)
   Special issue: Cassirer on Communicology: The Symbolic Forms of Language, Art, Myth, and Religion in Culture (2017, forthcoming)

4. Editorial Board; Current ms. Reviewer
   Text and Talk (United Kingdom)

5. Editorial Board; Current ms. Reviewer
   The Russian Journal of Communication (Russia and USA)

6. Advisory Board; Current ms. Reviewer
   Chinese Semiotic Studies
   (Institute for Semiotic Studies, Nanjing Normal University, People's Republic of China)

7. Advisory Board; Current ms. Reviewer
   Language and Semiotic Studies
   (The Chinese Association for Language and Semiotic Studies [CALSS], Soochow University, People's Republic of China)

8. Board of Reviewers
   Academic Journal of Modern Philology (Poland)

9. International Advisory Board
   Chinese Semiotic Forum (People's Republic of China)

10. Advisory Board
    Empedocles—European Journal for the Philosophy of Language (European Communication Association [ECU], United Kingdom)

11. Scientific Board
    Athanor: Semiotica, Filosofia, Arte, Letteratura (University of Bari, Italy)

12. Scientific Board
    Styles of Communication (Poland and Romania)

13. Advisory Board
    Cultura: International Journal of Philosophy of Culture and Axiology (Romania)

14. Past Editorial Board; Current ms. Reviewer
    Communication Theory (USA)

15. Past Editorial Board
    Critical Studies in Mass Communication (USA)

16. Past Editorial Board
    Human Studies (USA)

17. Past Editorial Board
    Signifying Behavior (Canada)

18. Past Editorial Board
    Scripta Semiotica (Germany)

JOURNALS: Ad Hoc ms. Reviewer

Atlantic Journal of Communication (National)
American Journal of Semiotics (International)
Critical Studies in Mass Communication (National)
Communication Studies (Regional)
Communication Theory (National)
Human Studies (International)
International Journal of Qualitative Studies in Education [Pedagogy]
Journal of Communication (National)

Journal of Family Communication (National)
Journal of Phenomenological Psychology (International)
Journal of Pragmatics (International)
Philosophy and Rhetoric (International)
Philosophy and Social Science (National)
Pennsylvania Speech Communication Annual (State)
Qualitative Research in Psychology (National)
Qualitative Sociology (National)
Quarterly Journal of Speech (National)
Social Theory and Practice (International)
Western Journal of Communication (National)

BOOK CHAPTERS [45]

45. "The Rhetoric of Discourse: Chiasm and Dialogue in Communicology" in Dialogic Ethics (Dialogue Series), ed. by Ronald C. Arnett and François Cooren. Philadelphia, PA: John Benjamins Publishing Co., **1918**) (2017 submitted)

44. "La teoría de la comunicología: el método de la fenomenología semiótica" in *Communicación, campo(s), teorias y problemas*, ed. by Carlos E. Vidales Gonzáles and Eduardo Vizer (Salamanca, Spain: Comminicacíon Social, **2016**), pp. 293–306 [trans. by Carlos Vidales with R. Lanigan]

43. "Contact Confusion in Perception: West Meets East, One Actuality Becomes Two Realities" in *Languages in Contact 2012* (Languages in Contact, Vol. 1), ed. Piotr P. Chruszczewski and John R. Rickford .Wrocław, Poland: Philological School of Higher Education in Wrocław Publishing, **2014**), pp. 103–125.
ISBN: 978-83-60097-26-7

42. "Familiar Frustration: The Japanese Encounter with Navajo (Diné) "Code Talkers" in World War II" in *Languages in Contact 2011* (Philologica Wratislaviensia: Acta et Studia. Vol. 9), ed. Zdzisław Wąsik and Piotr P. Chruszczewski (Wrocław: Philological of Higher Education Publishing **2012**), pp. 47–69.
ISBN 978-83-60097-15-1

41. "Information Theories" in Paul Cobley and Peter Schulz (eds.), *Theories and Models of Communication, Vol. 1* (Handbooks of Communication Science, 22 vols., 2012–2019), (Berlin, Germany; Boston, USA: De Gruyter Mouton, **2013**), pp. 58–83. [Chapter 4]
ISBN: 978-3-11-024044-3

40. "Communicology and the Mother of Civilization: The Semiotic Phenomenology of Human Embodiment as Cultural Media" in *Humans, Media and Communication Paradigms: Respecification of Printing Media in the Age of Smart Media* [International Conference Proceedings, 17—18 September 2012] (Chengju, Korea: Chengju Early Printing Museum and Korean Communication Association, 2012), English and Korean bilingual keynote address, pp. 7–32. ISBN: 73–4360039-000019-01.

English reprint: Korean Journal of Communication Studies 20. No. 5 (December 7, **2012**), pp. 5–16.

39. "Communicology and Culturology: Roland Posner's Semiosphere" in *Sign Culture / Zeichen Kultur*, ed. Ernst W. B. Hess-Lüttich (Würzburg: Verlag Königshausen and Neuman GmbH, **2012**), pp. 265–282.

ISBN: 978-3-8260-5076-1

38 "Husserl's Phenomenology in America (USA): The Human Science Legacy of Wilbur Marshall Urban and the Yale School of Communicology"in *Schutzian Research—A Yearbook of Lifeworldly Phenomenology and Qualitative Social Science*, 3 (**2011**), pp. 203–217.

37. "Defining the Human Sciences," in *Schutzian Research—A Yearbook of Lifeworldly Phenomenology and Qualitative Social Science*, 3 (**2011**), pp. 9–11.

36. "Absolute Human: The Communicology and Intentionality of Embodiment" in *Metamorphoses of the Absolute*, ed. Daina Teters (Riga: Latvian Academy of Culture; Metamind Project Press), [submitted **2011**; in press for 2017].

35. "Solomon Marcus: A Profound Voice for Understanding Communicology"in *Întâiniri cu Solomon Marcus = Meetings with Solomon Marcus*, 2 vols., ed. Lavinia Spandonide and Gheorghe Păum (Bucureşti: Spandugio, **2011**), vol. 1, pp. 902–906. [plus: backcover quotation]

ISBN: 978-606-92895-6-3

34. "Small Group Communicology: Nominal Group Technique for Conflict Management in Work Groups" in *People and the Value of an Organization*, ed. Felicjan Bylok and Leszek Cichobłaziński (Częstochowa, Poland: Faculty of Management, Częstochowa University of Technology, **2011**), pp. 124–139.

ISBN: 978-83-61118-39-8

33. "On Homeworld and Community Models of the City: The Communicology of Egocentric and Sociocentric Cultures in Urban Semiotics" in *Unfolding the Semiotic Web in Urban Discourse*, {Philologia Wratislaviensia: From Grammar to Discourse, No. 3], ed. Zdzisław Wąsik [in scientific cooperation with Diana Teters], (Frankfurt am Main: Peter Lang Internationalaler Verlag der Wissenschaften, **2011**), pp. 11–46.

ISBN: 978-3-631-61626-0

Reprint: "Communicology as a Human Paradigm for Urban Semiotics", (Section 2.1. Signs in the City. *In honor of Jeff Bernard*) *TRANS: Internet-Zeitschrift für Kulturwissenschaften* no. 18 (June 2011). Available online: http://www.inst.at/trans/18Nr/II_1/lanigan18.htm

32. "*Slugging:* The *Nonce Sign* in an Urban Communicology of Transportation" in *Unfolding the Semiotic Web in Urban Discourse,* ed. Zdzisław Wąsik [in scientific cooperation with Diana Teters], (Frankfurt am Main: Peter Lang Internationalaler Verlag der Wissenschaften, **2011**), pp. 143–161.

ISBN: 978-3-631-61626-0

31. "Theoretical and Applied Aspects of Communicology" in *Consultant Assembly III: In Search of Innovatory subjects for Language and Culture Courses,* ed. Zdzisław Wąsik (Wrocław, Poland: Philological School of Higher Education in Wrocław Publishing, **2010**), pp. 7–32.

ISBN: 978-83-60097-03-8

30. "The Verbal and Nonverbal Codes of Communicology: The Foundation of Interpersonal Agency and Efficacy" in *Communicology: The New Science of Embodied Discourse,* ed. Isaac E. Catt and Deborah Eicher-Catt (Madison, NJ: Fairleigh Dickinson University Press, **2010**), pp. 102–128. ISBN 978–08386-4147.7

29. "The Cultural Semiotics of the City as a Homeworld" in *Global Signs; Acta Semiotica Fennica XXIX* (Proceedings from the ISI Summer Congresses at Imatra in 2003–2006), ed. Eero Tarasti (The Finish Network University of Semiotics, Imatra; International Semiotics Institute at Imatra, Imatra; Semiotic Society of Finland, Helsinki, **2008**), pp. 64–72.

28. "The Phenomenology of Embodiment in Communicology" in *Phenomenology 2005: Vol. V, Selected Essays from North America, Parts I and II,* 5 vols., ed. Lester Embree and Thomas Nenon (Bucharest, Romania: Zeta Books, **2007**), Vol. 5, Part 2, Chapter 15, pp. 371–398.

ISBN: 978–9738863262

[e-book edition available from www.zetabooks.com]

27. "Communicology: The French Tradition in Human Science" in *Perspectives on the Philosophy of Communication,* ed. Pat Arneson (West Lafayette, IN: Purdue University Press, **2007**), pp. 168–184.

ISBN: 1557534314

26. "The Human Science of Communicology (Semiotic Phenomenology)" in *Semiotics Beyond Limits* (Proceedings of the 1st Romanian Association of Semiotic Studies), (Bacau: Slanic-Moldova, **2006**), pp. 779–783.

25. "The Semiotic Phenomenology of Maurice Merleau-Ponty and Michel Foucault" in *Signs of the World: Interculturality and Globalization,* ed. Louis Panier and Bernard Lamizet (Lyon: Université Lumière—Lyon 2, 2005). [Abstracted version; CD imprint **2006**, Proceedings of the 8th World Congress on Semiotics and Structural Studies, July 2004, Lyon, France.]

24. "Transcultural Communication in an Internet World: Semiotic Perspectives in the PRC and the USA" in *Intercultural Semiotics and the Human Sciences,* ed. Roland Posner (Munster-Hamburg-Berlin: LIT-Verlag; (simultaneous Chinese translation edition) Beijing: Chinese Academy of Social Sciences, 2005-submitted. [Book was never published due to lack of funding; ms. was published as an article in *Chinese Semiotic Studies,* see no. 33 below in the "Print Articles" section.]

23. "Fabulous Political Semiotic: The Case of George Orwell's *Animal Farm*" in *Semiotics 2003: "Semiotics and National Identity",* ed. Rodney Williamson, Leonard G. Sbrocchi, and John Deely (Ottawa, Canada: Legas Publishing, **2005** [appeared 2006]), pp. 421–435.
ISBN: 1894508645

22. "Applied Creativity in PR and R&D: Pierce on *Synechism,* Fuller on *Synergetics,* Gordon on *Synectics,* and Alinsky on *Socialism*" in *Semiotics 1999,* ed. Scott Simpkins, *et al.* (New York: Peter Lang Publishers, **2000**), pp. 94–106.
ISBN: 0820452262

21. "Television: The Semiotic Phenomenology of Communication and the Image" in *Semiotics of the Media: State of the Art, Projects, and Perspectives,* ed. Winfried Nöth, No. 127: Approaches to Semiotics (New York & Berlin: Mouton de Gruyter, 1997), pp. 381–391.
ISBN: 3110155370

20. "A Semiotic Perspective in China from a 'Big-Nose'" in *Semiotics 1996,* ed. C. W. Spinks and John Deely (New York: Peter Lang Publishers, **1997**), pp. 249–255.
ISBN: 0820440450

19. "Embodiment: Signs of Life in the Self" in *Semiotics 1995,* ed. John Deely (New York: Peter Lang Publishers, **1996**), pp. 354–364. [A paper originally presented at the University of Chicago]
ISBN: 0614178541 Online: http://www.focusing.org/apm_papers/lanigan.html

18. "*STAR TREK:* The Child and the Semiotic Phenomenology of Choosing a Family," in *Semiotics 1993,* ed. John Deely and Robert Corrington (Lanham,

MD: Semiotic Society of America; University Press of America, **1995**), pp. 223–230.

ISBN: 9995686589

17. "From Enthymeme to Abduction: The Classical Law of Logic and the Postmodern Rule of Rhetoric" in *Recovering Pragmaticism's Voice: The Classical Tradition, Rorty, and the Philosophy of Communication*, ed. Lenore Langsdorf & Andrew R. Smith (Albany: State University of New York Press, **1995**), pp. 49–70; (notes) 278–283.

ISBN: 0791422143

16. "A Good Rhetoric Is Possible: Ricoeur's Philosophy of Language as a Phenomenology of Discourse in the Human Sciences" in Lewis Hahn, Editor, *The Philosophy of Paul Ricoeur* (a volume in series The Library of Living Philosophers), (Chicago: The Open Court Publishing Co., **1995**), pp. 309–326. {A reply by Ricoeur occurs on pp. 327–329} [Chapter invited by Prof. Hahn who was the external examiner for my doctoral dissertation on Maurice Merleau-Ponty]

ISBN: 08126692594

15. "Thomas D'Aquin and the Semiotic Phenomenology of Discourse at the *Université de Paris*," in *Semiotics 1991*, ed. John Deely and Terry Prewitt (Lanham, MD: Semiotic Society of America; University Press of America, **1993**), pp. 61–70.

ISBN: 0819188700

14. "The Algebra of History: Merleau-Ponty and Foucault on the Rhetoric of the Person" in *The Critical Turn: Rhetoric and Philosophy in Contemporary Discourse*, ed. Ian Angus and Lenore Langsdorf (Carbondale, IL: Southern Illinois University Press, **1993**), pp. 140–174. Review by John L. Sloop, *Quarterly Journal of Speech* (February 1994), p. 120.

ISBN: 080931844X [*Reprint* from Lanigan 1992, Chapter 6, pp. 114–141.]

13. "Is Irving Goffman a Phenomenologist?" in *Beyond Goffman: Studies on Communication, Institution, and Social Interaction*, ed. Stephen Riggins (Berlin and New York: Mouton de Gruyter, **1990**), pp. 99–112. {*Reprint* from *Critical Studies in Mass Communication*, 5, no. 4 (December 1988), pp. 335–345.}

ISBN: 978-3110122084

12. «Le Même et L'Autre: Michel Foucault's Semiotic Quadrilateral of the Phenomenology of Discourse" in *Semiotics 1989*, ed. John Deely (Washington, D.C.: Semiotic Society of America; University Press of America, **1990**), pp. 117–123.

ISBN: 0819178403

11. "Popular Political Signs: Jesse Jackson's Presidential Candidacy as Depicted in Editorial Cartoons" in *Semiotics 1988*, ed. Terry Prewitt (Washington, D.C.: Semiotic Society of America; University Press of America, **1989**), pp. 501–506. An extended version with all images and cartoons is available at siu.academia.edu/RichardLLanigan
    ISBN: 0819174785
    Historical Note:
    Lynda Lee Kaid, Jacques Gerstlé, and Keith r. Sanders (eds.), *Mediated Politics in Two Cultures: Presidential Campaigning in the United States and France* [1988] (New York, NY: Praeger Publishers, 1991); ISBN 0-275-93595-7
    The papers published in *Mediated Politics in Two Cultures* are the result of a Franco-American project initiated at a coordinating conference in the Fall of 1987 at the *Université de Paris I (Sorbonne)*. I was the only American there who spoke French and I led the American participation (a professional translator was hired for the other Americans). My paper was on *"Popular Political Signs"*, an analysis of *visual semiotics* (which was paired in the project with the paper by my friend and colleague Henri Quéré *(Sorbonne)*, an original member of the *A. J. Greimas Group* in Paris). My paper was rejected by the project editors because the white versus black racism I demonstrated in a semiotic analysis of American political Cartoons [including the Rev. Jesse Jackson] was felt to be too controversial at the time (politically incorrect). The newsmagazine covers and cartoons were used as examples of overt racism compared to the covert racism apparent in, e.g., the cover images and text in *Time* and *Newsweek* magazines at the time. In response to this overt censorship by the book editors, my paper was immediately published by the Semiotic Society of America in 1988 because of its timely *in situ* analysis. Unfortunately at that time, there was no possibility of printing the all the images referred to in the analysis (they are included in the PDF version of *"Popular Political Signs"* online at Academic.edu/Lanigan). Ironically, no publisher could be found initially for *Mediated Politics in Two Cultures*. Eventually, Praeger Publishers agreed to print it in 1991, some four years after the project started. My analysis was later confirmed by Susan J. Dougles, *"Time* does Jackson in with subliminal message", *In These Times* [Washington, DC newspaper], April 20—26, 1988, page 16.

10. "Self-Presentation" in *American Phenomenology (Analecta Husserliana: The Yearbook of Phenomenological Research)*, Vol. 26, ed. Eugene F. Kaelin and Calvin O. Schrag (Hingham, MA and Dordrecht, The Netherlands: D. Reidel Publishing Co., **1989**), pp. 424–429. [Intellectual history entry discussing my role in the development of phenomenology and communicology written by invitation of the Editors. An entry by my friend and colleague at SIU, Dr. Prof. Hans Rudnick, follows mine.]
    ISBN: 9027726906

9. "From Saussure to Communicology: The Paris School of Semiology" in *Hermeneutics and the Tradition* (Proceedings of the ACPA, Vol. 62), Daniel O. Dahlstrom (ed.)., (Washington, D.C.: American Catholic Philosophical Association, **1988**), pp. 124–135.

8. "Précis of Alfred Schütz on Semiotic Phenomenology" in *Semiotics 1984*, ed. John Deely (Washington, D.C.: Semiotic Society of America; University Press of America, **1987**), pp. 393–399.

   ISBN: 0819148792

7. "Communication Science and Merleau-Ponty's Critique of the Objectivist Illusion" in *Horizons of Continental Philosophy: Essays on Husserl, Heidegger, and Merleau-Ponty,* Hugh Silverman, Algis Mickunas, Theodore Kisiel and Alphonso Lingis (Eds.). (= Martinus Nijhoff Philosophy Library Vol. 30). (Boston: Martinus Nijhoff, **1988**), pp. 205–226.

   ISBN: 902473651X; Reprint **2011** by Springer, ISBN: 9048183081.

6. "Précis of Merleau-Ponty on Metajournalism" in *Semiotics 1981*, ed. John N. Deely and Margot D. Lenhart (New York: Plenum Press, **1983**), pp. 39–48.

   ISBN 0306412705

5. "A Critical Theory Approach" (with Rudolf L. Strobl) in *The Handbook of Political Communication*, ed. Dan Nimmo and Keith Sanders (Beverly Hills, CA: Sage Publications, **1981**), pp. 141–167.

   ISBN: 0803917147

   [*Review:* Bruce E. Gronbeck, *Quarterly Journal of Speech* 69.4, 452–454. "Lanigan and Strobl's clarity makes their essay the definitive reference on Critical Theory available for theorist and critic alike."]

4. "*Discussion:* Subdued Thought as Discourse" in *Phenomenology in Rhetoric and Communication,* [ed.] Stanley Deetz (No. 3: Current Continental Research; Washington, DC: Center for Advanced Research in Phenomenology; University Press of America, **1981**), pp. 47–50.

   ISBN: 081912088X

3. "Communication Models in Philosophy: Review and Commentary" in *ICA Communication Yearbook 3*, ed. Dan Nimmo (New Brunswick, NJ: International Communication Association; Transaction Books, **1979**), pp. 29–49.

   ISBN: 087855341X

   [*Review:* John E. Bowes, *Journal of Communication* 32.1, 219–224.

   "Lanigan constructs 'communication models in philosophy' as a way of showing the parallel quality of communication to philosophical research. The effort is helpful in adding depth to that which, as communication research, is often a disembodied exercise in empirical description."]

2. "The Phenomenological Foundations of Semiology" in *A Semiotic Landscape/ Panorama Sémiotique: Proceedings of the First International Congress of IASS-AIS,* Milan, 1974, (No. 29: Approaches to Semiotics), ed. Seymour Chatman,

Umberto Eco, and Jean-Marie Klinkenberg (The Hague and New York: Mouton, **1979**), pp. 304–308.

ISBN: 9027979286

1. "Merleau-Ponty on Signs in Existential Phenomenological Communication" in *Studies in Language and Linguistics 1972–1973*, ed. Ralph W. Ewton and Jacob Ornstein (El Paso, TX: Texas Western Press, **1972**), pp. 53–88.

ISBN: 874040183

ENCYCLOPEDIA ARTICLES [22]

22. "Netizen" in *The SAGE Encyclopedia of the Internet*, ed.Barney Warf (Beverly Hills, CA: Sage Reference, April **2019**). (2016 submitted).

21. "Maurice Merleau-Ponty", *An Encyclopedia of Communication Ethics*, eds. RonaldC. Arnett, Annette M. Holba,and Susan Mancino (New York, NY: Peter Lang Publishing) (2017 submitted)

20. "Stephen C. Pepper", *An Encyclopedia of Communication Ethics*, eds. RonaldC. Arnett, Annette M. Holba,and Susan Mancino (New York, NY: Peter Lang Publishing) (2017 submitted)

19. "Communication Theory"in *The SAGE Encyclopedia of Theory: Vol. 1: Humanistic and Vol. 2: Scientific Perspectives*, ed.James Mattingly (Beverly Hills, CA: Sage Reference, March **2019**). (2015 submitted), Vol. 1, pp. 00.

18. "Structuralism"in *The SAGE Encyclopedia of Theory: Vol. 1: Humanistic and Vol. 2: Scientific Perspectives*, ed.James Mattingly (Beverly Hills, CA: Sage Reference, March **2019**). (2015 submitted), Vol. 1, pp. 00.

17. "Alfred Schütz (1899—1959)" in *International Encyclopedia of Communication Theory and Philosophy*, ed. Klaus B. Jensen (Malden, MA: Wiley-Blackwell, **2016**), Vol. 4, pp. 1808–1816.

ISBN: 978-1118290736

16. "Charles Sanders Peirce (1839—1914)" in *International Encyclopedia of Communication Theory and Philosophy*, ed. Klaus B. Jensen (Malden, MA: Wiley-Blackwell, **2016**), Vol. 3, pp. 1413–1418.

ISBN: 978-1118290736

15. "Jean Jacques Maurice Merleau-Ponty (1908—1961)" in *International Encyclopedia of Communication Theory and Philosophy*, ed. Klaus B. Jensen (Malden, MA: Wiley-Blackwell, **2016**), Vol. 3, pp. 1213–1219.

ISBN: 978-1118290736

14. "Immanuel Kant (1724—1804)" in *International Encyclopedia of Communication Theory and Philosophy*, ed. Klaus B. Jensen (Malden, MA: Wiley-Blackwell, **2016**), Vol. 2, pp. 1035–1043.
    ISBN: 978-1118290736

13. "Phenomenology" in *The Concise Encyclopedia of Communication*, ed. Wolfgang Donsbach (Oxford, UK and Malden, MA: Wiley-Blackwell Publishing Co.; International Communication Association, **2015**), pp. 448–449.
    ISBN: 978-1118789308

12. "Communicology" in *The Concise Encyclopedia of Communication*, ed. Wolfgang Donsbach (Oxford, UK and Malden, MA: Wiley-Blackwell Publishing Co.; International Communication Association, **2015**), pp. 102–103.
    ISBN: 978-1118789308

11. "Mind-Body Problem" in *Encyclopedia of Identity*, (2 Vols.), ed. Ronald L. Jackson II (Thousand Oaks, CA: Sage Publications, Inc. **2010**), vol. 1, pp. 450–454.
    ISBN: 978-1412951531

10. "Erving Goffman (1922–1982)" in *The Routledge Companion to Semiotics*, ed. Paul Cobley (Abingdon, UK: Routledge/Taylor & Francis Group, **2009**), pp. 225–226.
    ISBN: 978-0415440721

9. "Phenomenology" in *International Encyclopedia of Communication* (12 Vols.), ed. Wolfgang Donsbach (Oxford, UK and Malden, MA: Wiley-Blackwell Publishing Co.; International Communication Association, **2008**), vol. 8, pp. 3595–3597.
    ISBN: 978-1405131995

8. "Communicology" in *International Encyclopedia of Communication* (12 Vols.), ed. Wolfgang Donsbach (Oxford, UK and Malden, MA: Wiley-Blackwell Publishing Co.; International Communication Association, **2008**), vol. 3, pp. 855–857.
    ISBN: 978-1405131995

7. "Charles Sanders Peirce (1839–1914)" in *Encyclopedia of Communication and Information*, ed. Jorge Reina Schement (New York: Macmillan Library Reference USA, **2001**), vol. 3, pp. 705–707.
    ISBN 0028653866

6. "Structuralism" in *Encyclopedia of Phenomenology*, ed. Lester Embree (Boston; Norwell, MA: Kluwer Academic Publishers, **1997**), pp. 683–689.
    ISBN 0792329562

5. "Communicology" in *Encyclopedia of Phenomenology*, ed. Lester Embree (Boston, Norwell, MA: Kluwer Academic Publishers, **1997**), pp. 104–110.
ISBN: 0792329562

4. "Phenomenology,"in *Encyclopedia of Rhetoric and Composition: Communication from Ancient Times to the Information Age*, ed. Theresa Enos (New York: Garland Publishing Co., **1996**), pp. 512–513.
ISBN: 0824072006

3. "Thomas Albert Sebeok [1920—2001]" in *The International Encyclopedia of Language and Linguistics*, ed. R. E. Asher (Oxford: Pergamon Press, **1994**), vol. 7, pp. 3710–3711.
ISBN 0080359434

2. "Phenomenology" in *Encyclopedic Dictionary of Semiotics*, (3 Vols.), ed. Thomas A. Sebeok (Berlin; Hawthorne, NY: Mouton de Gruyter, **1986**), T. 2, pp. 695–701.
ISBN: 0899251374

1. "Maurice Merleau-Ponty" in *Encyclopedic Dictionary of Semiotics,(*3 Vols.), ed. Thomas A. Sebeok (Berlin; Hawthorne, NY: Mouton de Gruyter, **1986**), T.1, pp. 527–528.
ISBN0 899251374

ARTICLES IN PRINT JOURNALS [46]

46. "Ernst Cassirer's Theory and Application of Communicology: From Husserl via Bühler to Jakobson", (Special Issue: Cassirer on Communicology, ed. Richard l. Lanigan) *The American Journal of Semiotics* (forthcoming **2017**)

45. "Crossing Out Normative Boundaries in Psychosis: The Logic of a Social Semiotic Passage in Dickens' *Bleak House*", *The American Journal of Semiotics* (forthcoming **2017**)

44. "John N. Deely: A Thomistic Voice for Semiotics", [Festschrift for Deely] *Chinese Semiotic Studies* 12, no.3 (**2016**), pp. 279–291.

43 "Philosophy of Communicology: 'Discourse which Expresses Itself is Communication' [Heidegger]", *Review of Communication*, vol. 15, no. 4 (October **2015**) pp. 332–358.

42. "Semiotic Paradigms of Self and Person: The Perspectives Model of Communicology as the Logic Foundation of Human Science", *Language and Semiotic Studies* [China], 1, no. 1 (Spring **2015**), pp. 106–129.

41. "Human Embodiment: An Eidetic and Empirical Communicology of Phantom Limb", *Metodo: International Studies in Phenomenology and Philosophy*, 3, no. 1 (**2015**), pp. 257–287.
40. "Netizen Communicology: *China Daily* and the Internet Construction of Group Culture", *Semiotica*, Vol. 2015, Issue 207, pp. 489–528.
39. "Convergence Constitutes the Horizon of Divergence: In Dialogue with Calvin O. Schrag", *Russian Journal of Communication* , 7, no. 1(**2015**), pp. 94–101.
38. "Semiotic Confusion in the Phenomenology of Perception West Meets East, One Actuality Becomes Two Realities", *Chinese Semiotic Studies*, 11, no. 2 (**2015**), pp. 227–262.
37. "Charles S. Peirce on Phenomenology: Communicology, Codes, and Messages, or, Phenomenology, Synechism, and Fallibilism", *The American Journal of Semiotics*, 30, nos. 1–2, (**2014**), pp. 139–158.
36. "The Two Senses of a Phenomenology of the *Weltanschauung:* An Essay in Honor of Émile Benveniste", *The American Journal of Semiotics*, 28, nos. 1–2, (**2012**), pp. 63–72.
35. "Communicology and the Mother of Civilization: The Semiotic Phenomenology of Human Embodiment as Cultural Media", *Korean Journal of Communication Studies*, 20, no. 5 (December 7, **2012**), pp. 5–16.
34. "The Logic of Phenomena: Semiotic Structures of West and East in Communicology and Culture", *Chinese Semiotic Studies* [Journal of the Nanjing University International Institute of Semiotic Studies] 6, no. 1 (June **2012**), pp. 39–77.
33. "Noam Chomsky's Complaint About Media Communicology", *Glimpse: Journal of the Society for Phenomenology and Media*, 11 (**2009–2010**), pp.
32. "Cosmology and Communicology in an Internet World: Semiotic Perspectives of the East (PRC) and the West (USA)", *Chinese Semiotic Studies* [Journal of the Nanjing University International Institute of Semiotic Studies], 1 (June **2009**), pp. 228–254.
31. "Communicology: Towards a New Science of Semiotic Phenomenology", *Cultura: International Journal of Philosophy of Culture and Axiology* [Romania], No. 8 (**2008**), pp. 212–216, 218.
30. "The Semiotic Phenomenology of Maurice Merleau-Ponty and Michel Foucault", *Sign Systems Studies*, 33, no. 1 (**2005**), pp. 7–25. [Distributed: April 2006; Dept. of Semiotics, University of Tartu, Estonia].
29. "Paradigm Shifts: Recalling the Early ICA and the Later PHILCOM", *The Communication Review*, 8, no. 4 (**2005**), pp. 377–382.

28. "Media Freedom and Terror, Mediated Order and Chaos: A Comparison of P. R. China and the U.S.A.," *International Journal of Communication*, guest ed. Igor E. Klyukanov, 11, nos. 1–2 (January-December **2001**), pp. 7–25. [Distributed: 2002; New Delhi, **India**; Bahri Publications].
27. "The Postmodern Author: Foucault on Fiction and the Fiction of Foucault," *The American Journal of Semiotics*, 17, no. 1 (Spring **2001**), pp. 253–271.
26. "The Self in Semiotic Phenomenology: Consciousness as the Conjunction of Perception and Expression in the Science of Communicology," *The American Journal of Semiotics*, 15–16, nos. 1–4 (**2000**), pp. 91–111
25. "Media Order and Chaos: A Comparison of the People's Republic of China and the United States of America," [Ordem e Caos na Midia: Uma comparação das Pessoas da Repúblic da China e dos Estados Unidos] *Face: Revista de Semiotica e Comunicaçao* (Ediçao Especial **1999**,"Chaos and Order in Media, Culture and Society"), ed. Lucia Santaella, (Sao Paulo, **Brazil**: Pontifica Universidad Católica).
24. "Michel Foucault's Science of Rhetoric: The Contest between Practical Discourse and Discursive Practice," *Symploké: a Journal for the Intermingling of Literary, Cultural, and Theoretical Scholarship*, 4, nos. 1–2 (1996), pp. 189–202. [Distributed: 1997] Available Online: http://www.jstor.org/stable/40550393
23. "Time Binding: The Conjunction of Semiotics and Communicology," *Cruzeiro Semiótico* [**Portugal**], (Special Issue: Essays in Honor of Thomas A. Sebeok), No. 22–25 (**1995**), pp. 325–336. ISBN: 0870–6832
22. "The Postmodern Ground of Communicology: Subverting the Forgetfulness of Rationality in Language," (*Presidential Address to the Semiotic Society of America*) *The American Journal of Semiotics*, 11, nos. 3–4 (**1994**), pp. 5–21.
21. "Capta Versus Data: Method and Evidence in Communicology," *Human Studies: A Journal for Philosophy and the Social Sciences*, 17, no. 1 (January **1994**), pp. 109–130; **Printers Erratum** for p. 119 published in *Human Studies*, 17, no. 2 (April **1994**), p. 285.

Reprint Portuguese Translation:

"Capta versus Data: Método e Evidência em Comunicologia" *Revista "Psicologia: Reflexão & Critica"* [**Brazil**], 10, no.1(**1997**), pp. 17–46.
20. "Is Irving Goffman a Phenomenologist?", *Critical Studies in Mass Communication*, 5, no. 4 (December **1988**), pp. 335–345. {*Reprint* in *Beyond Goffman: Studies on Communication, Institution, and Social Interaction*, Stephen Riggins [ed.]. Berlin and New York: Mouton de Gruyter, **1990**, pp. 99–112}

19. "Foundations of Communicology as a Human Science," (Special Series on Foundations of the Human Sciences), *The Humanistic Psychologist*, 15, no. 1 (Spring **1987**), pp. 27–37.

18. "Structuralism and the Human Science Context of Semiology and Phenomenology," *Review Journal of Philosophy and Social Science*, (Special Issue on Modern Social Theory), 11, no. 1 (**1986**), pp. 55–70.

17. "Merleau-Ponty on Metajournalism: Signs, Emblems, and Appeals in the Poetry of Truth," *Communication*, 7, no. 2 (**1983**), pp. 241–261.

16. "Talking: The Semiotic Phenomenology of Human Interaction," *International Journal of the Sociology of Language*, 43 (**1983**), pp. 105–117.

15. "Semiotic Phenomenology in Plato's *Sophist*," *Semiotica*, 41, nos. 1–4 (**1982**), pp. 221–246. {*Reprint* as "Semiotics, Communicology, and Plato's *Sophist*" in John Deely (ed.), *Frontiers in Semiotics*. Bloomington: Indiana University Press, **1986**, pp. 199–216.}

14. "Semiotic Phenomenology: A Theory of Human Communication Praxis," *Journal of Applied Communication Research*, 10, no. 1 (Spring **1982**), pp. 62–73.

13. "A Semiotic Metatheory of Human Communication," *Semiotica*, 27, no. 4 (**1979**), pp. 293–306. [Lead article featured in this ten year Index issue of *Semiotica*.]

12. "The Phenomenology of Human Communication," *Philosophy Today*, 23, no. 1 (Spring **1979**), pp. 3–15.

11. "Contemporary Philosophy of Communication," *Quarterly Journal of Speech*, 64, no. 3 (October **1978**), pp. 335–347.

10. "The Speech Act Theory of Interpersonal Communication: Stimulus for Research," *Journal of Applied Communication Research*, 3, no. 2 (November **1975**), pp. 98–101.

9. "Merleau-Ponty, Semiology, and the New Rhetoric," *Southern Speech Communication Journal*, 40, no. 2 (Winter **1975**), pp. 127–141.

8. "Enthymeme: The Rhetorical Species of Aristotle's Syllogism," *Southern Speech Communication Journal*, 39, no. 3 (Spring **1974**), pp. 207–222.

7. "The Phenomenology of Speech and Linguistic Discontinuity," *Dégrees: Revue de synthese a orientation sémiologique*, 1, no. 2 (Avril **1973**), pp. 1–7. [Brussels, **Belgium**]

6. "Maurice Merleau-Ponty Bibliography," *Man and World*, 3, no. 3 (Fall 1970), pp. 289–319.

[Bibliography covers eight languages; There have been many unauthorized reprints]

5. "Semiotic Expression and Perception: Merleau-Ponty's Phenomenology of Communication," *Philosophy Today*, 14, no. 2 (Summer **1970**), pp. 79–88.
4. "Urban Crisis: Polarization and Communication," *Central States Speech Communication Journal*, 21, no. 2 (Summer **1970**), pp. 108–116.
3. "Aristotle's Rhetoric: Addendum to the Organon," *Dialogue: Journal of Phi Sigma Tau*, 11, no. 2 (November **1969**), pp. 1–6. [Authored as a PhD Student]
2. "Rhetorical Criticism: An Interpretation of Maurice Merleau-Ponty," *Philosophy and Rhetoric*, 2, no. 2 (Spring **1969**), pp. 61–71. [Authored as a PhD Student]
1. "Two Species of Style in Aristotle," *Dialogue: Journal of Phi Sigma Tau*, 10, no. 1 (May **1968**), pp. 1–5. [Authored as a Masters Student]

ARTICLES IN ELECTRONIC FORM (INTERNET) [24]

Abbreviations:
ERIC   Educational Resources Information System, Department of Education, United States Federal Government. Online: http://www.eric.edu.gov/
FAR   Foreign Affairs Research Documentation Center, Bureau of Intelligence and Research, Department of State, United States Federal Government. This data base is no longer available online; it was originally a contract project of the Corporation for National Research Initiatives: http://www.cnri.reston.va.us/

24. "Communicology and Culturology: Semiotic Phenomenological Method in Applied Small Group Research", *The Public Journal of Semiotics*, IV, no. 2 (February **2013**), pages 71–103. http://pjos.org/issues/pjos-4-2.pdf
23. "Communicology as a Human Paradigm for Urban Semiotics", *TRANS: Internet-Zeitschrift für Kulturwissenschaften*, Nr. 18 (Juni, **2011**). http://www.inst.at/trans/18Nr/II-1/lanigan18.htm
22. "Communicology: Approaching the Discipline's Centennial", Special Issue: "Semiotica y Comunicologia", *Razón y Palabra*, No. 72 (Mayo-Julio **2010**), Coordinacíon: Carlos Vidales, on-line journal: www.razonypalabra.org.mx/
21. "Communicology: Lexicon Definition" (**2007**), [International Communicology Institute]
    http://www.communicology.org/content/definition-communicology
20. "Communicology: Précis (**2005**)", [International Communicology Institute]
    http://www.communicology.org/content/précis-communicology
19. "Embodiment: Signs of Life in the Self" (**1995**) [University of Chicago]

http://www.focusing.org/apm_papers/lanigan.html

18. "Capta Versus Data: Method and Evidence in Communicology,"
    ERIC ED355567 (3 February **1993**).
17. "The Library and the Museum Become Tele-Vision,"
    ERIC ED356500 (October **1992**).
16. "Roman Jakobson's Semiotic Theory of Communication (Revised),"
    ERIC ED355570 (19 November **1991**).
15. Is Erving Goffman a Phenomenologist?",
    ERIC EJ386836 (**1988**).
14. "The Convention of 'Conventions': A Phenomenological Reflection on the Ideology of Professional Mass Communication,"
    ERIC ED266493 (**1985**).
13. "Can An American Do Semiotic Phenomenology?",
    ERIC ED265594 (**1985**).
12. "Unreflected Ideology and the Subversion of Conventional Critique,"
    ERIC ED172268 (**1979**).
11. "A Semiotic Metatheory of Human Communication,"
    ERIC ED146637 (**1977**).
10. "Communication Theories and Models: A Bibliography of Contemporary Monographs,"
    ERIC ED145494 (**1977**) and
    FAR (**1978**).
    Print publication in Spanish translation in the journal *Communication e Informatica* (**1982**). [**Mexico**]
9. "Discovering Phenomenology as a Research Methodology: An Introductory Bibliography,"
    FAR (**1977**).
8. "Critical Theory as a Philosophy of Communication,"
    ERIC (**1977**) and
    FAR (**1977**).
7. "The Future of Communication Theory: Phenomenology and Semiology,"
    ERIC (**1977**) and
    FAR (**1977**).
6. "Phenomenology of Human Communication as a Rhetorical Ethic,"

ERIC ED136314 (**1977**) and
FAR (**1977**).
5. "Communication and Austin's Notion of 'Uptake',"
ERIC ED136313 (**1975**).
4. "The Speech Discipline in Crisis--A Cause for Hope,"
ERIC ED120866 (**1975**).
3. "Existential Speech and the Phenomenology of Communication,"
ERIC ED103921(**1975**).
2. "The 'Speech Act' Paradigm in Current Analytic Philosophy,"
ERIC ED093004 (**1974**).
1. "A Suggestion on Method: The Ethics of Persuasion in the Beginning Speech Course,"
ERIC ED079801 (**1973**).
Review published in *Speech Teacher*, Vol. 24, No. 4 (November **1975**), p. 304.

BOOK REVIEW ARTICLES, NOTES, NEWSLETTER ARTICLES [23]
(All items were written by invitation of the respective journal Editor)

23. Article, "*Semiotics Education Experience* by Inna Semetsky (ed.)" in *Russian Journal of Communication*, 4, nos.1/2 (Winter/Spring 2011), pp. 129–135. [Igor Klyukanov, Editor]
22. Review of "*A Body* by John Coplans" in *American Journal of Semiotics*, 17, no. 4 (**2001**), pp. 371–1373. [Distributed December 2003]
21. Article, "The Communicology of the Image", a review of *Instantanes* [Snapshots] by Alain Robbe-Grillet in *American Journal of Semiotics*, 17, no. 3 (**2001**), pp. 255–265. [Printed August 2002]
20. *Note*, "In Memoriam — Thomas F. N. Puckett", *American Journal of Semiotics*, 15–16, nos. 1–4 (**2000**), pp. 249–250.
19. Article, "Postmodern Memories of Discourse in the Flesh: Merleau-Ponty on the Esoteric Body and Foucault on the Exoteric Body", a review of *Merleau-Ponty Vivant* by M. C. Dillon (ed.) and Merleau-Ponty, *Hermeneutics, and Postmodernism* by Thomas W. Bush and Shaun Gallagher in *Semiotica*, 107, no. 1/2 (**1995**), pp. 147–169. [Thomas Sebeok, Editor-in-Chief]
18. Article, "The Two Mysteries, or, This is Not Narcissistic Nominalism", a review of *Inscriptions: Between Phenomenology and Structuralism* by Hugh J. Silverman

in *Semiotica,* 103, no. 1/2 **(1995)**, pp. 193–200. [Thomas Sebeok, Editor-in-Chief]

17. **Article,** "Somebody is Nowhere: Foucault on the Human Sciences and the Discourse of Subjectivity", a review of *Communicative Praxis and the Space of Subjectivity* by Calvin O. Schrag in *Semiotica,* 101, no. 1/2 **(1994)**, pp. 139–162. [Thomas Sebeok, Editor-in-Chief]

16. **Article,** "On Discourse: A Phenomenology of Rhetoric and Semiotic", a review of *Communicative Praxis and the Space of Subjectivity* by Calvin O. Schrag (1986) in *American Journal of Semiotics,* 9, nos. 2–3 **(1992)**, pp. 241–251.

15. **Article,** "Culture and Communication: The Phenomenological Approach to the Human" in *Gebser Society Newsletter,* 6, no. 2 **(1989)**, pp. 4–8. [Michael Purdy, Editor] (Published version of a paper presented at the conference "Phenomenology and Indian Philosophy", Indian Council of Philosophical Research, New Delhi, India, 5–8 January 1988.)

14. *Note,* "On the Goals of Semiotics" in *Semiotica,* 61, no. 3 **(1986)**, p. 381. [Thomas A. Sebeok, Editor-in-Chief] Text Online @ communicology.org See "Definition: Communicology", scroll down to "1980s" then entry "1986".

13. Review of *"How Natives Think* by Lucien Lévy-Bruhl" in *International Journal of Intercultural Relations,* 10, no. 4 **(1986)**, pp. 512–516. [Young Y. Kim, Editor]

12. **Article,** "A Short History of Division 9: Philosophy of Communication in the International Communication Association" in *Communiqué* [Division 9 Newsletter] no. 1 **(1985)**, pp. 5–12. [Thomas Cooper, Editor]

11. Review of *"Possibilities and Limitations of Pragmatics"* [Proceedings of the Conference on Pragmatics, Urbino, July 8–14, 1979] by Herman Parret, Marina Sbisa, and Jef Verschueren (eds.)" in *American Journal of Semiotics,* 2, no. 4 **(1984)**, pp. 171–176. [Henryk Baran, Editor]

10. Review of *"Interpersonal Communication: Essays in Phenomenology and Hermeneutics* by Joseph J. Pilotta (ed.)" in *Philosophy and Rhetoric,* 16, no. 4 **(1983)**, pp. 262–265. [Herman Cohen, Editor]

9. Review of *"Structuralism and Semiotics* by Terence Hawkes" in *International Journal of Intercultural Relations,* 6, no. 1 **(1982)**, pp. 107–109. [Young Kim, Editor]

8. Review of *"Radical Reflection and the Origin of the Human Sciences* by Calvin O. Schrag" in *Quarterly Journal of Speech,* 67, no. 3 (August **1981**), pp. 342–343. [Michael C. Leff, Editor]

7. Review of *"Beyond the Letter: A Philosophical Inquiry into Ambiguity, Vagueness and Metaphor in Language* by Israel Scheffler" in *Journal of Pragmatics,* 4, no. 6 (December **1980**), pp. 555–560. [Jef Verschueren, Editor]

6. *Note,* "The Development of Speech 445: Semiology and Semiotic Communication" in *Semiotic Scene,* 1, no. 3 (September **1977**), pp. 43–44. [Daniel Laferriere, Editor]

5. «*Dialogue Note*» [author reply to a review of *Speech Act Phenomenology*] in *Quarterly Journal of Speech,* 64, no. 4 (December **1978**), pp. 466–467. [John Stewart, Editor]

4. Review of "*Beyond Culture* by Edward T. Hall" in *American Anthropologist,* 80, no. 2 (June **1978**), p. 403. [Edwin Cook, Editor]

3. Review of "*The Prose of the World* by Maurice Merleau-Ponty" in *Journal of the Illinois Speech and Theatre Association,* 28, no. 2 (Fall **1974**), pp. 44–45. [Janet McHughes, Editor]

2. Review of "*Speech and Reality* by Eugen Rosenstock-Huessy" in *Philosophy and Rhetoric,* 6, no. 2 (Spring **1973**), pp. 124–125. [Henry W. Johnstone, Editor]

1. *Note,* "Merleau-Ponty Bibliographies," *JBSP: Journal of the British Society for Phenomenology,* 3, no. 1 (January **1972**), p. 108. [Wolfe Mays, Editor]

Public Lecture and Paper Presentation List

RICHARD L. LANIGAN

University Distinguished Scholar and Professor of Communicology (Emeritus)
School of Communication
Southern Illinois University
Carbondale, Illinois, 62901–6605, USA

Director and Fellow,
⌘ **INTERNATIONAL COMMUNICOLOGY INSTITUTE**
Capitol Hill Tower, Suite PH06
1000 New Jersey Avenue, S.E.
Washington, DC 20003–3377, USA
Tel: (571) 439–6290

E-Mail: rlanigan@mac.com

VITA and Publications (PDF): siucarbondale.Academia.edu/RichardLanigan

{"Response" papers given at conferences are not listed; * = an invited paper;
*P = invited Plenary Session Paper; *PK = invited Plenary Keynote Paper}
[Updated: July 8, 2017]

Scheduled _____

2017

173. "History and Discourse: The Memory and Memorial of John N. Deely", 42nd Conference of the Semiotic Society of America, Universidad

Popular Autónoma del Estado de Puebla (UPAEP), Puebla, Mexico, 25—29 October 2017

172. "Communicology Chiasm: The Play of Tropic Logic in Bateson and Jakobson", 42nd Conference of the Semiotic Society of America, Universidad Popular Autónoma del Estado de Puebla (UPAEP), Puebla, Mexico, 25—29 October 2017

Presented _____

2017

171. "John N. Deely: A Voice for Semiotics in the Catholic Tradition", Third Biennial Philosophy of Communication Conference: The Catholic Intellectual Tradition, Duquesne University, Dept. of Communication & Rhetorical Studies, Pittsburgh, Pennsylvania, 5—7 June 2017.*PK

2016

170. "Immanuel Kant on the Philosophy of Communicology", Outstanding Papers in the Philosophy of Communication, Philosophy of Communication Division, 102nd Annual Convention, National Communication Association (USA), Philadelphia, Pennsylvania, 10–13 November 2016.

169. "John N. Deely: A Thomistic Voice of Semiotics", 41st Conference of the Semiotic Society of America, Delray Beach, Florida, 28 September – 2 October 2016.

168. "The Rhetoric of Discourse in Dialogue: A Semiotic View of the Phenomenology of Axiology", 14th National Communication Ethics & International Association for dialogue Analysis Conference, Duquesne University, 1–4 June 2016.

167. [with Jacqueline M. Martinez] "Applying Phenomenology to 'Cultural Experience': Semiotic Phenomenology and Communicology in the Study of Embodiment", [Workshop], Interdisciplinary Coalition for North American Phenomenology, Arizona State University (Downtown Phoenix Campus), 28 May 2016.

166. "New School Comportment Collaborators: The Confluence of Phenomenology and Semiotics in Communicology", Interdisciplinary Coalition for North American Phenomenology, Arizona State University (Downtown Phoenix Campus), 26–30 May 2016.

2015

165. "The Three Great Absurdities", National Communication Association (USA), 101st Annual Convention, LasVegas, Nevada, 19–22 November 2015.*

164. "Bateson on Difference: Past, Present, Future", Eastern Communication Association Pre-Conference: "Patterns of Connection: Contextualism, Bateson, and Husserl/Foucault", Pennsylvania State University (York), 8–9 October 2015. *PK

163. "How Americans and Chinese See Each Other: What You Always Wanted to Know, But Were Afraid To Ask!", Campus Lecture, International Teaching Event: China Series, International Office, Pennsylvania State University, York, Pennsylvania, 7 October 2015.*P

162. "Visualizing Semiotic Models for Applied Research" [Workshop], The Semiotic Society of America, 40th Annual Meeting, Theme: "Evolutionary Love Relations and Identities in a Virtual World", Pittsburgh, Pennsylvania, October 1–4, 2015.*PK. Included workshop booklet, 44 pp.

161. "Semiotic Paradigms of Self and Person: The Perspectives Model of Interpersonal Communicology as the Logic Foundation of Human Science", The Semiotic Society of America, 40th Annual Meeting, Theme: "Evolutionary Love Relations and Identities in a Virtual World", Pittsburgh, Pennsylvania, October 1–4, 2015.*

160. "The Phenomenology of Rhetoric: Noam Chomsky's Complaint About Media Communicology" 2nd Biennial Philosophy of Communication Conference, Department of Communication & Rhetorical Studies, Duquesne University, Pittsburgh, Pennsylvania, 3–5 June 2015.

159. "Ernst Cassirer's Communicology and Culturology: The Theory and Method of Semiotic Phenomenology", ICNAP VII Conference, Theme: "Facticity and Transcendence", The Interdisciplinary Coalition of North American Phenomenologists, Brock University, St. Catharines, Ontario, **Canada**, 22–24 May 2015.

2014

158. "Philosophy of Communicology: "Discourse which Expresses Itself is Communication", National Communication Association *Centennial Celebration Series Panel:* "Being (T)here", Philosophy of Communication Division, Chicago, Illinois, 21 November 2014.*P

157. "Netizen Communicology: *China Daily* and the Internet Construction of Group Culture", 40th Annual Conference, Semiotic Society of America, Seattle, Washington, 1–5 October 2014.

156. "Communicology Paradigms of Self: The Perspectives Model of Interpersonal Communication as the Foundation of Human Science", 1st International Communicology Institute Colloquium, Department of Communication

Studies, Eastern Washington University, Cheney, Washington, 13–15 October 2014.*PK

2013

155. "Meaning Models for Coping with Nonsense Signification: Postmodern Logics of Culture, Perception, and Expression", *Pre-Conference: "Applied Semantics and Practical Communication Across the Disciplines"*, 99th Annual Convention, National Communication Association, Washington DC, 20 November 2013.*

154. "Family Finitude on the Frontier: Immigrant Communicology and Culturology", 38th Annual Conference, Semiotic Society of America, Dayton, Ohio, 25 October 2013.*

153. "C. S. Peirce on Communication, Codes, and Messages, or, Phenomenology, Synechism, and Fallibilism", 38th Annual Conference, Semiotic Society of America, Dayton, Ohio, 24—27 October 2013.*PK

152. "Hermeneutic Rhetoric: Michel Foucault's Model of the Human Sciences", International Conference: "Rhetoric in Europe", Europäisches Institut für Rhetorik, Universität des Saarlandes; Institut Européen de Rhétorique, Université du Luxemborug, Gebäude, **Luxemborug**, 9–13 October 2013.*

151. "Human Embodiment: An Eidetic and Empirical Communicology of Phantom Limb", "Philosophy of Communication", 6th I.C.I. International Summer Conference—1st Duquesne Philosophy of Communication Conference, Dept. of Communication & Rhetorical Studies, Duquesne University, Pittsburgh, PA, 9–13 July 2013

2012

150. "An Eidetic and Empirical Communicology of Phantom Limb", 5th Annual Conference, Interdisciplinary Coalition of North American Phenomenologists (ICNAP), Ramapo College, Mahwah, NJ, 24–26 May 2012.*

149. "Phenomenological Methods: Descriptive Phenomenology versus Semiotic Phenomenology in Applied Human Science", Panel: "Confluences of Philosophy of Communication, Communicology and Contemporary Human Science: Reflections on Research Methods, Group Cultures and Selfhood, and Mental Health Communication", Eastern Communication Association, Pittsburgh, PA, 24—28 April 2012.*

148. "The Human Group as a Medium of Communicology", 37th Annual Conference, Semiotic Society of America, Toronto, **Canada**, 1–4 November.*

147. Special Round Table: "Communicology and Semiotics: The Phenomenological Heritage in Cultural Discursive Patterns and Practices" [Zdzisław Wąsik,

co-chair]. The Nanjing 11th World Congress of Semiotics, Theme: "Global Semiotics: Bridging Different Civilizations", International Association for Semiotic Studies, Nanjing Normal University, Nanjing, **P. R. China**, 5–9 October 2012.*

146. Special Round Table: "Semiotics in the USA" [John Deely, co-chair], Special Round Table: "Communicology and Semiotics: The Phenomenological Heritage in Cultural Discursive Patterns and Practices" [Zdzisław Wąsik, co-chair]. The Nanjing 11th World Congress of Semiotics, "Global Semiotics: Bridging Different Civilizations", International Association for Semiotic Studies, Nanjing Normal University, Nanjing, **P. R. China**, 5–9 October 2012.*

145. "Communicology and the Mother of Civilization [Printing]: The Semiotic Phenomenology of Human Embodiment as Cultural Media", International Conference: "Humans, Media, and Communication Paradigms: Respecification of Printing Media in the Age of Smart Media", Cheongju Early Printing Museum (CEPM) and Korea Communication Association (KCA) 20th Anniversary of Jikji Museum, Cheongju City. **South Korea**, 17–18 September 2012. *PK

144. "Contact Confusion in Perception: West Meets East, One Actuality Becomes Two Realities", 3rd International Conference: "Languages in Contact", Philological School of Higher Education at Wrocław, in cooperation with the Polish Academy of Sciences (Wrocław Division), Wrocław, **Poland**, 26–27 May 2012. *P

143. "Intercultural Communicology: Juri Lotman's Logic of Apperception and Apposition", International Conference "Cultural Polyglotism" dedicated to Juri Lotman's 90th Anniversary, Department of Semiotics, Tartu University, Tartu, **Estonia**, 28 February to 2 March 2012.*

2011

142. "Philosophy of Communicology: The Rhetorical Branch of Linguistics", Program of the Philosophy of Communication Division: "Defining Philosophy of Communication: Process Contexts of Culture, Language, and Practice", 17–20 November 2011, New Orleans, Louisiana.*PK

141. "Communicology: The Semiotic Phenomenology of Human Communication", lecture on the occasion of receiving the first annual "International Scholar Award in Philosophy of Communication, for Communication Excellence in Education for the Mind, Heart, Spirit", Department of Comunication and Rhetorical Studies, Duquesne University, Pittsburgh, Pennsylvania, 4 November 2011.

140. "Communicology and Semiotic Hypercodes: The Example of Schizophrenic Discourse", 36th Annual Conference, Semiotic Society of America, 27–30 October 2011, Duquesne University, Pittsburgh, Pennsylvania.*

139. "The Two Senses of a Phenomenology of the *Weltanschauung*", Roundtable: "Can or Should We Have a Worldview?", 36th Annual Conference, Semiotic Society of America, 27–30 October 2011, Duquesne University, Pittsburgh, Pennsylvania.*P

138. "Communicology and Phenomenological Method in Small Group Cultures", 30th International Human Science Research Conference: "Intertwining Body-Self-World", organized by the Open University, London, venue at St. Catherine's College, Oxford University, Oxford, **United Kingdom**, 29 July 2011.*

137. "Communicology and the Theory of Culture: Applied Phenomenological Method in Small Group Semiotic Research", 5th International Communicology Institute Summer Conference, organized by the Dept. of Linguistic Semiotics and Communicology, Philological School of Higher Education at Wrocław, in cooperation with the Town Museum "Gerhart Hauptmann House" and the Karkonosze State Higher School, Jelenia Góra, Silesia, **Poland**, 15–22 July 2011.*P

136. "Small Group Communicology: Nominal Group Technique for Conflict Management in Work Groups", International Conference: "People and the Value of anOrganization: Social, Human, and Intellectual Capital", Dept. of Sociology and Psychology, Faculty of Management, Częstochowa University of Technology, Częstochowa, **Poland**, 16 June 2011.*P {Included visit to *The Pro Memoria Edith Stein Museum,* Lubińcu, Poland]

135. "Familiar Frustration: The Japanese Encounter with Navajo (Diné) "Code Talkers" in World War II", 2nd International Conference: "Languages in Contact", Philological School of Higher Education at Wrocław, in cooperation with the Polish Academy of Sciences (Wrocław Division), Wrocław, **Poland**, 12 June 20111. *P

134. "Communicology Paradigms of Self: The Perspectives Model of Interpersonal Communication", at the "Workshop: The Semiotic Self in Communicative Interactions", 42nd Poznań Linguistics Meeting, Theme: "Language, Discourse, and Society: Collective and Individual Aspects of Social Dynamics", Adam Mickiewicz University, Poznań, **Poland**, 3 May 2011.*P

133. "Phenomenology of Art: Communicology, Pedagogy, and Research", 3rd Annual Conference: The Interdisciplinary Coalition of North American Phenomenologists, Washington, DC, 6 May 2011.

132. "Sexuality: Consciousness of Individuality Confronts the Silence of Culture", New Book Symposium: Jacqueline M. Martinez' *Communicative Sexualities: A Communicology of Sexual Experience*, 3rd Annual Conference: The Interdisciplinary Coalition of North American Phenomenologists, Washington, DC, 7 May 2011.*P

2010

131. "The Basics of Communicology", Departments of Communication and Philosophy, Al. I. Cuza University, Iasi, **Romania**, 8 November 2010.*P

130. "Communicology: The Apperception and Apposition of Communication Theory and Information Theory", 3rd International Conference: Romanian Association of Semiotic Studies, Al. I. Cuza University, Iasi, **Romania**, 4 November 2010.*PK [A Public Lecture in Honor of Solomon Marcus, Chair in Mathematics, Romanian Academy of Science.]

129. "Absolute Human: The Communicology and Intentionality of Embodiment", International Conference: "Metamorphoses of the Absolute", *Latvian Academy of Culture*, Riga, **Latvia**, 8 October 2010.*

128. "Netizen Communicology: *China Daily* and the Internet Construction of Group culture", 9th Chinese Internet Research Conference: "Global Public Goods, National Policies, and Private Interests", Institute for the Study of Diplomacy, E. A. Walsh School of Foreign Service, Georgetown University, Washington, DC, 23 May 2011.*P

127. "Theoretical and Applied Aspects of Communicology", Consultant Assembly III: In Search of Innovatory Subjects for Language and Culture Courses, Karkonosze State Higher School, Jelenia Góra, Silesia, **Poland**, 15 May 2010.*P

126. "Proto-Phenomenology, Rationality, and Schizophrenia", 2nd Annual Conference: The Interdisciplinary Coalition of North American Phenomenologists (ICNAP), Brock University, St. Catharines, **Canada**, 28 May 2010.

2009

125. "Slugging: The Nonce Sign in an Urban Communicology of Transportation", 10TH World Congress of the International Association for Semiotic Studies, "Culture of Communication, Communication of Culture", Plenary Round Table on Urban Discourse, La Coruña, **Spain**. 22–26 September 2009.*P

124. "Semiotic Phenomenology as the Methodological Foundation of the International Communicology Institute", 10th World Congress of the International Association for Semiotic Studies, "Culture of Communication,

Communication of Culture", Plenary Round Table on Communicology as Science, La Coruña, **Spain**. 22–26 September 2009.*P

123. "The Logic of Phenomena: Comparing West (USA) to East (PRC)", Inaugural conference of the Interdisciplinary Coalition of North American Phenomenologists, Ramapo College, New Jersey, 8–9 May 2009.*

122. "Noam Chomsky's Complaint About Media Communicology", The Society for Phenomenology and Media, 11th Annual Conference: "Philosophy, Politics, and the Media", Washington, DC, 26–28 February 2009.*

2008

121. "Husserl's Phenomenology in America (USA): The Legacy of Wilbur Marshall Urban and the Yale School of Communicology", OPO III World Conference on Phenomenology (in Celebration of the 60th Anniversary of the Department of Philosophy, The Chinese University of Hong Kong (under the auspices of the Hong Kong Society for Phenomenology and the Organization of Phenomenological Organizations), Hong Kong, **People's Republic of China**, 15–20 December 2008.*

120. "Cosmology and Communicology in Cultural Semiotics: A Comparison of West (USA) and East (PRC)", Nanjing International Symposium on Cultural Semiotics, and, Eighth Annual Conference of the China Association for Linguistic and Semiotic Studies, Nanjing Normal University, Nanjing City, **People's Republic of China**, 15–17 November 2008.*

119. "The Verbal and Nonverbal Codes of Communicology: The Foundation of Interpersonal Agency and Efficacy", 33rd Annual Conference of the Semiotic Society of America, St. Thomas University, Houston, Texas, 16–19 October 2008.*

118. "An Intellectual History of Communicology and Phenomenology", Invitational conference to found a Society for North American Phenomenology, Center for Advanced Research in Phenomenology, Florida Atlantic University, Boca Raton, Florida, 19–21 June 2008.*P

2007

117. "Graduate Student Research Writing for International Journals", 13th Biennial Conference, International Study Association on Teachers and Teaching: "Totems and Taboos: Risk and Relevance in Research", Brock University, St. Catharine's, **Canada**, 4–9 July 2007.*P

116. "The Homeworld Model of Intercultural Communication", public lecture funded by the Foundation for Educational Exchange between Canada and the United States of America (Ottawa), The Canada-U.S. Fulbright Program, at Brock University, St. Catharine's, **Canada**, 25 June 2007.*P

Press release and Photographs online:
http://www.brocku.ca/brockinternational/richard_reception.php

115. "H. G. Alexander's Communicology: A Semiotic Theory of Human Communication", 9th World Congress of the International Association for Semiotic Studies, University of Helsinki, **Finland,** 11–17 June 2007.*

2006

114. "Ernst Cassirer's Theory and Application of Communicology", "Language Beyond Power", Fourth Biennial Summer Symposium and Professional Development Seminar, International Communicology Institute in collaboration with the Centre for Philosophy and Science Studies, Aalborg University, Aalborg and Skagen, **Denmark,** 25 June – 2 July, 2006.*p

113. "Foucault Dialogues with Aristotle: Both Have an Identity Crisis", Symposium on Gesture, Conversation, and Dialogue", Toronto Semiotic Circle, Victoria College of the University of Toronto, Toronto, **Canada,** 28–29 April 2006.*PK

2005

112. "The Matrix of Semiotic Systems in Communicology", Semiotic Society of America, University of West Florida, Pensacola, Florida, 22 October 2005.

111. "Television After Umberto Eco: The Communicology of Roman Jakobson", Second World Congress on Semiotics and Communication, Universidad Autónoma de Nuevo León, Associación Mundial de Semiótica de los Mass-Media & Communicación Global, Monterrey, **Mexico,** 20 October 2005.*

110. "The Communicology Homeworld Model of Globalization for Media Semiotics", Second World Congress on Semiotics and Communication, Universidad Autónoma de Nuevo León, Associación Mundial de Semiótica de los Mass-Media & Communicación Global, Monterrey, **Mexico,** 19 October 2005.*

109. "The City: A Human Group Paradigm for Cultural Semiotics" International Summer School for Semiotic and Structural Studies of the International Semiotics Institute, University of Helsinki, Imatra Congress Center, **Finland,** and, European University of St. Petersburg, **Russian Federation,** 15 June 2005.*P

2004

108. "Methodological Applications of the Nonce Sign", Signs, Signing, and Signage, 3rd International Summer Symposium of the International

Communicology Institute, Bemidji State University, David Park House, Bemidji, Minnesota, 21 July 2004.*

107. "Aberrant Signs in Hypercode Transformations", Signs, Signing, and Signage, 3rd International Summer Symposium of the International Communicology Institute, Bemidji State University, David Park House, Bemidji, Minnesota, 19 July 2004. *PK

106. "The Semiotic Phenomenology of Maurice Merleau-Ponty and Michel Foucault", Signs of the World: Interculturality and Globalization, 8th Congress of the International Association for Semiotic Studies, Université Luminère Lyon 2, Lyon, **France**, 10 July 2004.*

105. "Paradigm Shifts: Recalling the Early ICA and the Later PHILCOM", Philosophy of Communication Division 9, International Communication Association, New Orleans, Louisiana 27 May 2004. *PK

104. "Transcultural Communication in an Internet World: Semiotic Perspectives in the PRC and the USA", International Congress on Semiotics and the Humanities, *The Chinese Academy of Social Sciences* [CASS], 28 March 2004, Beijing, **People's Republic of China**. [Congress limited to 36 invited speakers; 2 from USA. Co-sponsored by the International Association for Semiotic Studies.] *PK

2003

103. "Fabulous Political Semiotic: The Case of George Orwell's *Animal Farm*", Semiotic Society of America Annual Conference, University of Ottawa, **Canada**, 11 October 2003.

102. "Fabulous Habits in the Contest between Culture and Communication", Keynote for the *Jeanne Herberger Lecture Series:* "Communication, Culture, and Conflict", Hugh Downs School of Human Communication, College of Public Programs, Arizona State University, 27 February 2003, *PK

2002

101. "Crossing Out Boundaries in Psychosis: A Semiotic Passage in Dickens' *Bleak House*", Semiotic Society of America, San Antonio, Texas, 18 October 2002.

100. "Communicology: Past, Present, and Future", Communicology Summer Symposium: Cultural Constructions of Technology and Human Relations: Healthy and Unhealthy, Strange and Familiar Bodies, International Communicology Institute, Brock University, St. Catharines, Ontario, **Canada**, 8 July 2002, *PK

99. "Reflections on Communicology", Communicology Summer Symposium: Cultural Constructions of Technology and Human Relations: Healthy and

Unhealthy, Strange and Familiar Bodies, International Communicology Institute, Brock University, St. Catharines, Ontario, **Canada**, 15 July 2002, *PK

98. "The Logic of Communicology", Communicology Summer Symposium: Cultural Constructions of Technology and Human Relations: Healthy and Unhealthy, Strange and Familiar Bodies, International Communicology Institute, Brock University, St. Catharines, Ontario, **Canada**, 19 July 2002, *P

2001

97. "A Bag of Marbles and a Pile of Salt: Cities as a Human Group Paradigm for Cultural Semiotics", Semiotic Society of America, University of Toronto, **Canada**, 19 October 2001.

2000

96. "The Postmodern Author: Foucault on Fiction and the Fiction of Foucault", Semiotic Society of America, Purdue University, Lafayette, Indiana, 29 September 2000.

1999

95. "Cultural Codes and Messages, or Where's the Toilet?", Outstanding Scholar Award Lecture, Honor Society of Phi Kappa Phi, Southern Illinois University, Carbondale, Illinois, 1 November 1999.

94. "Applied Creativity in PR and R&D: Peirce on Synechism, Fuller on Synergetics, Gordon on Synectics, and Alinsky on Socialism" Semiotic Society of America, Duquesne University, Pittsburgh, Pennsylvania, 30 October 1999.

1998

93. "Carnival and Festival: The Reading Group and the Academic Conference", 6th Annual Philosophical Collaborations Conference, Theme: "Selves and Others", Southern Illinois University, Carbondale, Illinois, 20 March 1998.*

1997

92. "Embodied Phantasm: The Signs of Intentionality," Semiotic Society of America, Annual Conference, Louisville, Kentucky, 23–26 October 1997.

91. "Body Signs of Culture: The Home World Model of Intercultural Communication," Sixth International Congress: Semiotics Bridging Nature and Culture, International Association for Semiotic Studies, Guadalajara, **Mexico**, 13–18 July 1997.*P

90. "Foucault's Law of Communication," *National Endowment for the Humanities Distinguished University Lecture*, College of Liberal Arts, Mercer University, Atlanta, Georgia, 24 April 1997.*

1996

89. "A Semiotic Perspective in China from a "Bignose", Semiotic Society of America, Annual Conference, University of California, Santa Barbara, 17–19 October 1996.

88. "The Conjunction of Communicology and Psychology," Institute of Psychology, Pontifical Catholic University, Rio Grande do Sul, **Brazil**, 6 September 1996.*

87. "The Subject of Discourse in the Human Sciences," Research Seminar, Institute of Psychology, Federal University, Rio Grande do Sul, **Brazil**, 5–6 September 1996.*

86. "Media Order and Chaos: A Comparison of China and the United States," Third International Latin-American Congress of Semiotics & Fourth Brazilian Congress of Semiotics, Pontifica Universidade Católica de Sao Paulo, **Brazil**, 31 August to 3 September 1996. *P

85. "Cross-Cultural Communication: The American Experience of Chinese Culture," Distinguished University Lecture (sponsored by Dept. of Foreign Languages and Cultures), Yunnan University, Kunming City, Yunnan Province, **People's Republic of China**, 13 June 1996.*

84. "American (USA) Culture and Communication," Distinguished University Lecture (sponsored by the College of Foreign Languages and Cultures, and, The Center for American Studies), Sichuan Union University, Chengdu City, Sichuan Province, **People's Republic of China**, 12 June 1996.*

83. "American Verbal and Nonverbal Communication," Distinguished University Lecture (sponsored by the Dept. of Philosophy, Dept. of Chinese, Dept. of Foreign Languages, and the Center for Comparative Literature), Suzhou University, Suzhou City, Jiangsu Province, **People's Republic of China**, 24 May 1996.*

82. "American Semiotics: The Signs and Symbols of Culture," Distinguished University Lecture (sponsored by the Dept. of Philosophy, Dept. of Chinese, Dept. of Foreign Languages, and the Center for Comparative Literature), Suzhou University, Suzhou City, Jiangsu Province, **People's Republic of China**, 23 May 1996.*

81. "Cross-Cultural Communication and Intercultural Communication," Distinguished University Lecture (sponsored by Dept. of Foreign Languages

and Cultures), Chongqing University, Chongqing City, Sichuan Province, **People's Republic of China**, 17 May 1996.*

80. "Cross-Cultural Communication: America (USA) and China (PRC)," Distinguished University Lecture, sponsored by Sichuan International Studies University (formerly Chongqing Research Institute for Foreign Languages and Cultures), Chongqing City, Sichuan Province, **People's Republic of China**, 16 May 1996.*

79. "American Culture and Communication," 1896–1996 Centennial Distinguished Lecture Series, Southwest (Tangshan) Jiaotong University, Chengdu City, Sichuan Province, **People's Republic of China**, 19 April 1996.*

78. "Intercultural Communication and Contemporary Technology," 1896–1996 Centennial Distinguished Lecture Series, Southwest (Tangshan) Jiaotong University, Chengdu City, Sichuan Province, **People's Republic of China**, 5 April 1996.*

1995

77. "Embodiment: Signs of Life in the Self," Semiotic Society of America, Annual Conference, San Antonio, Texas, October 1995.

76. "Consciousness and Communication," International Association for Semiotic Studies, Catholic University of Portugal, Oporto, **Portugal**, September, 1995.*PK

75. "Television: The Semiotic Phenomenology of Communication and the Image," International Conference on the Semiotics of the Media: State of the Art, Projects, and Perspectives, University of Kassel, Kassel, **Germany**, 20–23 March, 1995. Sponsored by the *Deutsche Forschungsgemeinschaft*.*P

1994

74. "Is Communicology a Human Science or a Social Science?", Dept. of Communication, Millersville University, Pennsylvania, 24 October 1994.*

73. "Michel Foucault's Science of Rhetoric: Critical Discourse and Discursive Practice," International Congress on Michel Foucault and Literature, University of Toronto, **Canada**, 12 October 1994.*P

72. "Merleau-Ponty and Semiotics," Semiotic Society of America, Philadelphia, Pennsylvania, October 1994.

71. "Communicology and the Forgetfulness of Rationality," Presidential Address, Semiotic Society of America, Philadelphia, Pennsylvania, October 1994.*PK

1993

70. "STAR TREK: The Child and the Semiotic Phenomenology of Choosing a Family," Semiotic Society of America, St. Louis, Missouri, October 1993.

69. "The Cartoon and Caricature Campaign: Notes on Jesse Jackson's Candidacy in the American Presidential Election of 1988," First World Congress on Semiotics and Communication: The Educational Dimension, sponsored by the Institute for Semiotics and Mass Culture and the Governor's Office of the State of Nuevo Leon, in Monterrey, **Mexico**, 16–19 June 1993.*P

1992

68. "The Abortion Aphorism: A Preliminary Semiotic Analysis of PRO-Choice and NO Choice," Semiotic Society of America, Chicago, Illinois, October 1992.

67. "The Library and the Museum Become Tele-Vision," Mass Communication Division, Speech Communication Association, Chicago, Illinois, October 1992.*

1991

66. "Roman Jakobson's Semiotic Theory of Communication", Language and Social Interaction Division, Speech Communication Association, Atlanta, Georgia, November 1991.*

65. "Thomas D'Aquin and the Phenomenology of Discourse at *L'Université de Paris*", Semiotic Society of America, University of Maryland, October 1991.*

64. "Roman Jakobson's Communication Theory: The Motivated Logic of Semiotics and Phenomenology", Philosophy of Communication Division, International Communication Association, Chicago, Illinois, 23–27 May 1991.*

63. "The Contingency of the Flesh: Merleau-Ponty's Discourse on the Esoteric and Foucault's Discourse on the Exoteric", Colloquium on "Sozialphilosophie und Lebenswelt; Maurice Merleau-Ponty", Directors: Joseph Bein (University of Missouri), Gvozden Flego (University of Zagreb), Gerard Raulet (Université de Rennes II), & Hauke Brunkhorst (Freie Universität Berlin), *Inter-University Centre of Dubrovnik*, **Yugoslavia**, 25 March – 5 April 1991.*P

1990

62. "Somebody Is Nowhere! Recentering the Decentered Subject in Research: The Case of Michel Foucault", Hollins College Communication

Studies Colloquium: "Communication Studies and the Liberal Arts", 26–28 October 1990.*PK

61. "The Voiceless Name (Asyndeton) and the Nameless Voice (Prosopopoeia): Michel Foucault's Semiotic Phenomenology of Discourse", Semiotic Society of America, and, Centennial Conference ["Crossing the Disciplines: Cultural Studies in the 1990s"] of the University of Oklahoma, Norman, Oklahoma, 19–21 October 1990.

1989

60. "Semiotic Phenomenology", International Symposium on "Japanese and Western Phenomenology", Niigata — *Kansai Interuniversity Conference Center*, Sanda City, Japan, 24–27 October 1989. [Invitational conference sponsored by the Japan Phenomenology Association and the Center For Advanced Research in Phenomenology (USA)].*P

59. "Foucault's Quadrilateral Model of the Phenomenology of Discourse" [Session: The Convergence of Rhetoric and Philosophy in the Twentieth Century], Society for Phenomenology and Existential Philosophy, Duquesne University, Pittsburgh, Pennsylvania, 14 October 1989.*

58. "The Two Mysteries, Or, This Is Not Narcissistic Nominalism" [Current Research Session: Hugh Silverman's *Inscriptions: Between Phenomenology and Structuralism*], Society for Phenomenology and Existential Philosophy, Duquesne University, Pittsburgh, Pennsylvania, 12 October 1989.*

57. "Le Même et L'Autre: Foucault's Quadrilateral Model of Discourse", Semiotic Society of America, Indiana University—Purdue University at Indianapolis, Indiana, 14 July 1989.

1988

56. "Popular Political Signs: Jesse Jackson's Presidential Candidacy as Depicted in Editorial Cartoons", Semiotic Society of America, University of Cincinnati, Ohio, 27–30 October 1988.

55. "The Interpretation of Political Reality: Fantasy in Presidential Elections: Two Perspectives (France—USA)", International Communication Association, New Orleans, Louisiana, 31 May 1988.*

54. "History and Prospect: The Emergence of Phenomenology in the Communication Discipline" [one of four papers; others were by Fred Dallmayr, John O'Neill, Eugene T. Gendlin], Keynote Program "The Experience of Phenomenology in the Human Sciences", annual conference of the Society for Phenomenology and the Human Sciences, Ontario Institute

for Studies in Education, University of Toronto, Toronto, Ontario, **Canada**, 19 May 1988.*PK

53. "From Saussure to Communicology: the Paris School of Semiology", American Catholic Philosophical Association; Conference on "Hermeneutics and the Tradition", Louisville, Kentucky, 8 April 1988.*

52. "Communicology as a Human Science: The Semiotic Turn in French Phenomenology", 1988 University Distinguished Visiting Professor Lecture, California State University at Chico, Chico, California, 17 March 1988.*

51. "French Phenomenology and Literary Criticism", *American Institute for Indian Studies*, Calcutta, **India**, 14 January 1988.*

50. "Contemporary Phenomenology of Communication", National Center for Advanced Studies in Philosophy, and, Department of Philosophy, Jadavpur University, Calcutta, **India**, 14 January 1988.*

49. "Culture and Communication: The Phenomenological Approach to the Human", First Binational Conference of the Indian Council for Philosophical Research (India) and the Center for Advanced Research in Phenomenology (USA) on "Phenomenology and Indian Philosophy" at the Jawaharlal Nehru National Museum and Library, *Teen Murti House*, New Delhi, **India**, 6 January 1988.*P

1987

48. "Is Erving Goffman a Phenomenologist?", International Symposium on Institution, Communication, and Social Interaction: The Legacy of Erving Goffman", *Central Institute of Indian Languages* (Ministry of Human Resource Development, Department of Education, Government of India), Mysore, **India**, 27 December 1987.*P

47. "The Algebra of History: Merleau-Ponty and Foucault on the Rhetoric of the Person", Twelfth Annual International Conference of the Merleau-Ponty Circle, University of Rhode Island, Kingston, Rhode Island, 17–19 September 1987.

46. "Silent Science: On the Semiotic Phenomenology of Cultural Media", Sixth International Human Science Conference, University of Ottawa, Ottawa, **Canada**, 26 May 1987.P

45. "Praxis for What? A commentary on Calvin O. Schrag's *Communicative Praxis and the Space of Subjectivity* ", 37th Annual Conference of the International Communication Association, Montréal, **Canada**, 22 May 1987.*

1986

44. "A Treasure House of Preconstituted Types: Alfred Schutz on Communicology", International Invitational Symposium, "Worldly Phenomenology--The Continuing Influence of Alfred Schutz on North American Human Science", Ohio University, 28–30 June 1986.*

43. "Michel Foucault's Communicology: The Semiotic Turn in French Phenomenology", Institute for Human Sciences; Center for Advanced Research in Phenomenology, Ohio University, Athens, Ohio, 15–28 June 1986. *Short Course:* Faculty development seminar and graduate credit course in the Department of Philosophy and the School of Interpersonal Communication.*

42. "Commentary: Discourse as Creative Axiology", 36th Annual Conference of the International Communication Association, Chicago, Illinois, 24 May 1986.

41. "Somebody is Nowhere: Michel Foucault's Rhetoric of the Human Sciences," Case Studies in the Rhetoric of the Human Sciences; Seventh Annual Invitational Conference on Discourse Analysis, Temple University, Philadelphia, Pennsylvania, 10–12 April 1986.

1985

40. "Michel Foucault's Rhetoric as a Human Science," Planning Conference of the Institute for Human Science (a division of The Center for Advanced Research in Phenomenology), Ohio University, 12 July 1985.*P

39. "A Short History of Division 9: Philosophy of Communication in the International Communication Association," International Communication Association Conference, East-West Center and University of Hawaii, 26 May 1985, Honolulu, Hawaii.* {Published: Division 9 newsletter *Communiqué* no. 1 (1985), pp. 5–12}

38. "Can an American Do Semiotic Phenomenology?," International Communication Association Conference, East-West Center and University of Hawaii, 26 May 1985, Honolulu, Hawaii.

37. "The Convention of 'Conventions': A Phenomenological Reflection on the Ideology of Professional Mass Communication," International Communication Association Conference, East-West Center and University of Hawaii, 26 May 1985, Honolulu, Hawaii.

36. "Freedom and Field: Merleau-Ponty's *Sinngebung* as the Essence of a Semiotic Phenomenology of Human Communication," International Communication Association Conference, East-West Center and University of Hawaii, 26 May 1985, Honolulu, Hawaii.*P

35. "Semiotic Phenomenology of Communication," a graduate credit and faculty development *Short-Course*, Department of Psychology, Duquesne University, 21–24 March 1985, Pittsburgh, Pennsylvania.*
34. "Phenomenology and Semiology in the Discipline of Communication," University Lecture, Department of Psychology, Duquesne University, 20 March 1985, Pittsburgh, Pennsylvania.*

1984

33. "Freedom and Field: Merleau-Ponty's Sinngebung as Semiotic Phenomenology," The Merleau-Ponty Circle Annual International Conference, Concordia University, 29 September 1984, Montréal, Canada.
32. "Guess at the Words, or, How to Phenomenologically Research the Hermeneutic Experience," Midwest Sociological Association, 19 April 1984, Chicago, Illinois. *Revised* draft presented as the Conference Keynote paper, Conference on "Research Practice in the Human Sciences," Pennsylvania State University, 13 July 1984.*
31. "Communication Science and Merleau-Ponty's Critique of the Objectivist Illusion," International Communication Association Conference, 26 May 1984, San Francisco, California.
30. "Alfred Schütz on the Semiotic Phenomenology of Communication," International Human Science Research Conference, West Georgia College, 16 May 1984, Carrollton, Georgia. *Revised* draft presented at Semiotic Society of America Conference, 12 October 1984, Atlanta, Georgia.
29. "The Phenomenological Interview: An Oral Protocol for Life Experience Research in the Social Sciences," Conference on "Oral History: Theory and Practice," Center for the Study of Cultural Transmission, State University of New York, 2 March 1984, Buffalo /Amherst, New York.*P

1983

28. "Life-Histories: A Teaching and Research Model for Semiotic Phenomenology", Semiotic Society of America, 8th Annual Conference, 9 October 1983, Snowbird, Utah. *Revised* draft presented at Society for Phenomenology and the Human Sciences Conference, 23 October 1983, St. Louis, Missouri.
27. "Merleau-Ponty on Semiotic Methodology: Implications for Communication Studies," Colloquium on the Theory and Practice of Semiotics, Fourth International Summer Institute for Semiotic and Structural Studies, Indiana University, 5 June 1983, Bloomington, Indiana.*P

1982

26. "Philosophy of Communication: From Phenomenology—to Ethnomethodology—to Semiotics," Research Series Workshop, Speech Communication Association Conference, 4 November 1982, Louisville, Kentucky. [with Profs. Michael Hyde and Wayne Beach]*

1981

25. "Report on the 'Task Force on the Phenomenology of Communication and Instruction': A Danforth Foundation College Fund Project," Speech Communication Association Conference, 13 November 1981, Anaheim, California. [with Prof. Randall Bytwerk]

24. "Hearing the Invisible: Semiotic Matrices of the Verbal and Visual in Videotape Data," Society for Phenomenology and the Human Sciences Conference, Northwestern University, 1 November 1981, Evanston, Illinois.

23. "Précis of Merleau-Ponty on Metajournalism,"'Semiotic Society of America Conference, Vanderbilt University, 3 October 1981, Nashville, Tennessee.

22. "Philosophers Who Cannot Tell a Lie and Rhetoricians Who Can: A Commentary on Plato's *Sophist*," Dept. of Linguistics Colloquium, Southern Illinois University, 25 September 1981, Carbondale, Illinois.*

21. "Logic in Plato's *Sophist*," Second International Summer Institute for Semiotic and Structural Studies, Vanderbilt University, 9 June 1981, Nashville, Tennessee.*

1980

20. "Semiotic Phenomenology and the Theory of Human Communication," First International Summer Institute for Semiotics and Structural Studies, Victoria College, Toronto University, 5 June 1980, Toronto, **Canada.***P

1979

19. "Phenomenological Method in Communication Science," Society for Phenomenology and Existential Philosophy Conference, Purdue University, 2 November 1979, West Lafayette, Indiana.

18. "The Objectivist Illusion in Therapeutic Philosophy," The Merleau-Ponty Circle Annual International Conference, State University of New York, 12 October 1979, Stony Brook, New York.*

17. "Semiotic Phenomenology in Plato's *Sophist*," Semiotic Society of America Conference, Indiana University, 6 October 1979, Bloomington, Indiana. *Revised* drafts presented at [1] The Merleau-Ponty Circle Annual International Conference, Pennsylvania State University, 5 September 1980, University

Park, Pennsylvania, and [2], Conference on "Communication Theory from Eastern and Western Perspectives," Center for Culture and Communication, East-West Center, 16 December 1980, Honolulu, Hawaii.*P

16. "Unreflected Ideology and the Subversion of Conventional Critique," Southern Speech Communication Association Conference, 13 April 1979, Biloxi, Mississippi.

1978

15. "Phenomenology and Semiotic Communication," Society for Phenomenology and Existential Philosophy Conference, Duquesne University, 2–4 November 1978, Pittsburgh, Pennsylvania.

1977

14. "Critical Theory as a Philosophy of Communication," First World Congress on Communication Science (27th Annual Conference of the International Communication Association), 29 May-4 June 1977, Berlin, **Germany**.*P

13. "The Future of Communication Theory: Phenomenology and Semiology," The Future of Communication Theory Conference (held in conjunction with the Southern States Speech Communication Conference), 6–8 April 1977, Knoxville, Tennessee.*P

12. }Phenomenology of Human Communication as a Rhetorical Ethic," Central States Speech Communication Conference, 15 April 1977, Southfield (Detroit), Michigan.

1975

11. "The Speech Discipline in Crisis—A Cause for Hope," Conference Keynote Address, Illinois Speech and Theatre Association Conference, 7 November 1975, St. Louis, Missouri.*PK

10. "Speech Acts," Dept. of Linguistics Colloquium, Southern Illinois University, 14 March 1975, Carbondale, Illinois.*

9. "Communication and Austin's Notion of 'Uptake' ", Dept. of Philosophy Colloquium, Southern Illinois University, 13 February 1975, Carbondale, Illinois.*

1974

8. "The Phenomenological Foundations of Semiology," First World Congress of the International Association for Semiotic Studies/Association Internationale de Sémiotique, 21–23 February 1974, Milan, **Italy**. [invitation of Umberto Eco]

7. "The 'Speech Act' Paradigm in Current Analytic Philosophy," International Communication Association Conference, 18 April 1974, New Orleans, Louisiana.

6. "Merleau-Ponty, Semiology, and the New Rhetoric," Dept. of Speech and Theatre Arts, University of Pittsburgh, 15 March 1974, Pittsburgh, Pennsylvania.*

1972

5. "Nonverbal Communication: A Comparison of America and Britain," Psychological Society, Dept. of Psychology, University of Dundee, 3 February 1972, Dundee, **Scotland**, UK.*

1971

4. "Phenomenological Existence and Communication," Faculty Research Seminar, Dept. of Philosophy, University of Dundee, and, Dept. of Logic and Metaphysics, St. Andrews University, 12 May 1971, Dundee, **Scotland**, UK*

1970

3. "The Meaning of Existential Phenomenology for Speech Communication," University Lecture Series, Humboldt State University, 29 May 1970, Arcata, California.*P

2 "Semiotic Expression and Perception: Merleau-Ponty's Phenomenology of Communication," New Mexico and West Texas Philosophical Society Conference, University of Texas, 2 May 1970, El Paso, Texas.

1969

1. "Merleau-Ponty on Interpersonal Communication," Texas Speech Association Conference, University of Texas, 2 October 1969, El Paso, Texas.

Richard L. Lanigan

University Distinguished Scholar and Professor of Communicology
(Emeritus)
Department of Speech Communication
Southern Illinois University, Carbondale, IL 62901-6605

Director, International Communicology Institute
http://www.communicology.org
E-mail: rlanigan@mac.com
Vita: http://myprofile.cos.com/rlanigan

Graduate Student Research
Service on Dissertation, Thesis, and Research Report Committees

S.I.U. Graduate Faculty Status: Doctoral Director (Category I)

Summary Count:

Total Doctoral Committees: 99

PhD Director = 35
PhD External Examiner = 29
PhD Committee Member = 35

M.A./M.S. Thesis Director = 9
M.A./M.S. Thesis External Examiner = 4
M.A./M.S. Thesis Committee Member = 4
M.A./M.S. Research Report Director = 8
M.A./M.S. Research Report External Examiner = 3
M.A./M.S. Research Report Second Reader = 10

[Updated: Wednesday, 26 July, 17]

DOCTORAL DISSERTATIONS

PhD Dissertation Director:

1. **GAVIN C. WHITSETT** [†], "A Phenomenology of Human Sexuality," PhD Dissertation, Dept. of Speech Communication, SIU, **1979**. Initial professional placement: Dept. of Speech Communication, University of Evansville, Evansville, Indiana.
2. **ERIC E. PETERSON**, "A Semiotic Phenomenology of Performing," PhD Dissertation, Dept. of Speech Communication, SIU, **1980**. [SIU Graduate School Doctoral Fellow, 1979]. Initial professional placement: Dept. of Speech Communication, University of Maine, Orono, Maine.
3. **KRISTIN M. LANGELLIER**, "The Audience of Literature: A Phenomenological Poetic and Rhetoric," PhD Dissertation, Dept. of Speech Communication, SIU, **1980**. [SIU Graduate School Doctoral Fellow, 1979]. Initial professional placement: Dept. of Speech Communication, University of Maine, Orono, Maine.
4. **MICHAEL L. PRESNELL**, "Sign, Image, and Desire: Semiotic Phenomenology and the Film Image," PhD Dissertation, Dept. of Speech Communication, SIU, **1983**. [SIU Graduate School Dissertation Research Award, 1982]. Initial professional placement: Dept. of Communication, Tulane University, New Orleans, Louisiana.
5. **CORRINE M. CAHILL**, "A Phenomenology of Feminism," PhD Dissertation, Dept. of Speech Communication, SIU, **1983**. [SIU Graduate School Dissertation Research Award, 1982]. Initial professional placement: College of Speech, Marquette University, Milwaukee, Wisconsin.
6. **WILLIAM B. GOMES**, "Experiential Psychotherapy and Semiotic Phenomenology: A Methodological Consideration of Eugene Gendlin's Theory and Application of Focusing," PhD Dissertation, Dept. of Higher Education, SIU, **1984**. [Emil Spees, Co-Director]. Initial professional placement: Departmento de Filosofia e Psicologia, Universidade Federal de Santa Maria, Santa Maria, [Brazil]
7. **VIVIAN C. SOBCHACK**, "The Address of the Eye: A Semiotic Phenomenology of Cinematic Embodiment," PhD Dissertation, Dept. of Speech Communication, SIU,**1984**. [SIU Graduate School Doctoral Fellow, 1982; Dissertation Research Award, 1983] {**Published** as *The Address of the Eye: A Phenomenology of Film Experience*, Princeton University Press, 1992; ISBN 0–691–00874–4}. Initial professional placement: Theatre Arts Board (Cinema),

Porter College, University of California, Santa Cruz, California. As of 1987, full Professor; as of 1988, Dean of Porter College.

8. **HALINA ABLAMOWICZ,** "An Empirical Phenomenological Study of Shame," PhD Dissertation, Dept. of Speech Communication, SIU, **1984.** [SIU Graduate School Dissertation Research Award, 1983]. Initial professional placement: Dept. of Communication and Media, State University of New York, Fredonia, New York. **[Poland]**

9. **YUKIO TSUDA,** "Language Inequality and Distortion in Intercultural Communication: A Critical Theory Approach," PhD Dissertation, Dept. of Speech Communication,SIU, **1985.** [SIU Graduate School Doctoral Fellow, 1984] {Nominated by the departmental Faculty for the 1985 Dissertation Award of the Speech Communication Association}. {**Published** under the same title by Benjamins, The Netherlands, 1986; ISBN: 1–55619-008-5}. Initial professional placement, as **Associate Professor**: College of Economics (Intercultural Communication),University of Nagasaki. **[Japan]**

10. **JENNY LEE NELSON,** "The Other Side of Signification: A Semiotic Phenomenology of Televisual Experience," PhD Dissertation, Dept. of Speech Communication, SIU, **1986.** [SIU Graduate School Doctoral Fellow, 1984; SIU Graduate School Dissertation Research Award, 1985]. Initial professional placement, Department of Communication, University of New Hampshire, Durham, New Hampshire. As of 1990, Director of Graduate Studies, School of Telecommunications, Ohio University, Athens, Ohio.

11. **JOLANTA DZIEGIELEWSKA,** "The Intercultural Dimension of Friendship: A Study in the Phenomenology of Communication", PhD Dissertation, Dept. of Speech Communication, SIU, **1988.** [SIU Graduate School Dissertation Research Award, 1986]. {Second place selection; 1989 Outstanding Dissertation Award of the SIU Graduate School.} **[Poland]**

12. **PETER M. KELLETT,** "Conversion and Organizational Communication: The Process of Becoming a Member in a Religious Organization", PhD Dissertation, Dept. of Speech Communication, SIU, **1990.** [SIU Graduate School Dissertation Research Award, 1988] Initial professional placement, Department of Communication, Clemson University, Clemson, South Carolina. **[United Kingdom]**

13. **ANDREW R. SMITH,** "A Theory of Transcultural Rhetoric: *Poiesis* and Mishima Yukio's Textuality", PhD Dissertation, Dept. of Speech Communication, SIU, **1990.** [SIU Graduate School Doctoral Fellow, 1988; SIU Graduate School Dissertation Research Award, 1989; *Finalist*, Outstanding Dissertation Award, SIU Graduate School,1991] Initial professional place-

ment, Department of Communication Arts, Villanova University, Villanova, Pennsylvania.

14. **ABDULLAH M. AL-TIWERQI**, "Phenomenology of Self-Disclosure: An Existential Explication of the Structure of Self-Disclosure as Lived in the East and West by Saudis", Dept. of Speech Communication, SIU, **1990**. [Thomas J. Pace, Co-Director]. [Saudi Arabia government Dissertation Completion Award, $10,000]. Initial professional placement, Department of Mass Communication, Riyadh University, Riyadh. **[Saudi Arabia]**

15. **MACHIKO TAKAYAMA**, "Poetic Language in Nineteenth Century Mormonism: A Study of Semiotic Phenomenology in Communication and Culture," PhD Dissertation, Dept. of Speech Communication, SIU, **1990**. {Dissertation published in Japanese by Edogawa University, Tokyo, Japan, 1991}. Initial professional placement, as joint full Professor, Department of Applied Sociology and Department of Mass Communications, College of Sociology, Edogawa University, Tokyo. **[Japan]**

16. **ROBERT E. WEST**, "Electronic Signs and Meaning: A Semiotic Phenomenology of Communicative Praxis in an Electronic Church," PhD Dissertation, Dept. of Speech Communication, SIU, **1991**. Initial professional placement, Department of Communication, University of Evansville, Evansville, Indiana.

17. **CHRIS B. GEYERMAN**, "The Discourse of Intercollegiate Athletics: Jan Kemp and the Genealogy of Corruption, PhD Dissertation, Dept. of Speech Communication, SIU, **1991** [Thomas Pace, Co-Director] Initial professional placement, Department of Communication Arts, Georgia Southern University, Statesboro, Georgia.

18. **JOSEPH GEMIN**, "Science and Con-Science: A Semiotic Phenomenology of Cultural Organization", PhD Dissertation, Dept. of Speech Communication, SIU, **1991**. Initial professional placement, Department of Communication, University of Wisconsin-Parkside, Kenosha, Wisconsin. **[United Kingdom]**

19. **THOMAS FREDERICK N. PUCKETT** [†], "Phenomenology of Communication and Culture: Michel Foucault's Thematics in the Televised Popular Discourse of *Star Trek* ", PhD Dissertation, Dept. of Speech Communication, SIU, **1991**. [Research Assistant to Lanigan 1990–1991] Initial professional placement, Department of Communication Studies, Eastern Washington University, Cheney, Washington. [Research Assitant to Lanigan]

20. **IAN CLARKE HENDERSON**, "Rock Goes Pop: Rock Music, Post-Modernism and Popular Culture", PhD Dissertation, Dept. of Speech Communication, SIU, **1991**. [SIU Graduate School Doctoral Fellow, 1988; Research Assistant to Lanigan, 1990–1991] Initial professional placement,

Department of Communication, University College, Mercer University, Forsyth, Georgia. [Research Assiatant to Lanigan] **[United Kingdom]**

21. **CHANDRASHEKHAR ASHOK DESHPANDE,** "Historical Representations in the Cinematic Apparatus and the Narratives of Popular Memory," PhD Dissertation, Dept. of Speech Communication, SIU, **1991.** SIU Graduate School Dissertation Research Award, 1985; Initial professional placement, Department of Communication Studies, Chatham College, Pittsburgh, Pennsylvania. **[India]**

22. **JACQUELINE M. MARTINEZ,** "Feminist Communication Theory: A Semiotic Phenomenological Explication of Feminist Academic Theorizing," PhD Dissertation, Dept. of Speech Communication, SIU, **1992.** [Awarded 1990 Chicana Dissertation Research Fellowship (one of two awards in national competition; $16,000), University of California, San Diego; Awarded 1990 Elizabeth Eames Dissertation Fellowship, Women's Studies Program, SIU]. Initial professional placement, Division of Liberal Arts, Babson College, Wellesley, Massachusetts.

23. **FRANK J. MACKE,** "Speech, Communication, and Pedagogy: A Genealogy of Speech Communication as an Academic Discipline," PhD Dissertation, Dept. of Speech Communication, SIU, **1993.** Initial professional placement, Mercer University, Macon, Georgia.

24. **DU-WON LEE,** "A Semiotic Explication of Communicative Competence: Respecifying Human Communication in Communicology," PhD Dissertation, Dept. of Speech Communication, SIU, **1993.** SIU Graduate School Tuition Scholarship Award, 1992, 1993]. [Research Assistant to Lanigan]. Initial professional placement (tenured assistant professor), Kyongju University, Kyong-Ju City, **South Korea.**

25. **CAROL A. RICHARDS,** "The World Is the Basic Unit of Communication: A Semiotic Phenomenology of Commonplace Echolalia," PhD Dissertation, Dept. of Speech Communication, SIU, **1993.** Initial professional placement, Bemidji State University, Bemidji, Minnesota.

26. **JANET K. MORRISON,** "Teachers' Lived Experience of Communication Rupture in the University Classroom: A Semiotic Phenomenological Explication," PhD Dissertation, Dept. of Speech Communication, SIU, **1995.** Initial professional placement, University of Maine, Orno, Maine.

27. **HAMMOUD AL-KHAMENIS,** "University Instruction: The Relationship Between International Teachers' Communication Competence and Teaching Performance as Perceived by Students," PhD Dissertation, Dept. of Speech Communication, SIU, **1995.** [Saudi Arabia government Dissertation

Completion Award, $10,000]. Initial professional placement, Muhammed Iben Saud University, Riyadh. [**Saudi Arabia**]

28. **HASSAN OMAR BASFAR**, "A Phenomenological Study of Intercultural and Cross-Cultural Interpersonal Communication Experience: Uncertainty Reduction as Perceived by Saudi Arabian Students in the U.S.A.", PhD Dissertation, Dept. of Speech Communication, SIU, **1995**. [Saudi Arabia government Dissertation Completion Award, $10,000]. Initial professional placement, King Abdulaziz University. [**Saudi Arabia**]

29. **DEBORAH L. EICHER-CATT**, "Searching for the Sacrality of Motherhood: A Semiotic Phenomenology of Non-Custodial Mothers," PhD Dissertation, Dept. of Speech Communication, SIU, **1995**. Awardee 1992–1995, Forgivable Loan/Doctoral Incentive Loan Program [to attend SIU], Office of the Chancellor, University of California System (Berkeley); $30,000. Initial professional placement, Rowan College of New Jersey, Glassboro, New Jersey.

30. **MICHAEL R. DICKMAN**, "The Structure of Argument Used in Intercollegiate Debate Rounds," PhD Dissertation, Dept. of Speech Communication, SIU, **1997**. Initial professional placement, Cumberland College, Williamsburg, Kentucky.

31. **DR. THOMAS DARRAND CRAIG**, "When the Absent Body Presents: A Critical Phenomenology of Communication and Chronic Disabling Conditions," PhD Dissertation, Dept. of Speech Communication, SIU, **1997**. Initial professional placement, Dept. of Physical Education, Brock University, Canada. [Research Assistant to Lanigan] [PhD, Religion, Vanderbilt University, 1991].

32. **ERIC DAVID FOX**, "Signs of Memory: A Semiotic Phenomenology of the United States Holocaust Memorial Museum," PhD Dissertation, Dept. of Speech Communication, SIU, **1998**. Initial professional placement: University of Richmond, Virginia.

33. **HONG WANG**, "Constructing a Sign of *Dignity:* A Semiotic Approach to Understanding and Intercultural Communication", PhD Dissertation, Dept. of Speech Communication, SIU, **2001**. Initial professional placement: Shippenburg University, Shippenburg, Pennsylvania. [Research Assistant to Lanigan] [**P.R. China**]

34. **YUN XIA**, "Participation and Learning Effectiveness: Computer-Mediated Communication in Group Learning", SIU Graduate School Dissertation Research Award, 2001. PhD Dissertation, Dept. of Speech Communication, SIU, **2002**. Initial professional placement: Rider University, Lawrenceville, New Jersey. [**P.R. China**]

35. HEATHER A. HOWLEY, "A Communicology of Childhood Attention Deficit Hyperactivity Disorder (ADHD)", PhD Dissertation, Dept. of Speech Communication, SIU, 2004. Initial professional placement: Cazenovia College, Cazenovia, New York.

PhD Dissertation External Examiner:

1. ELIZABETH BOEWN GURLEY, "The Size of Freedom [in Merleau-Ponty's Philosophy]," PhD Dissertation, Dept. of **Philosophy,** SIU, 1975.
2. DAVID L .EASON, "Metajournalism: The Problem of Reporting in the Nonfiction Novel," PhD Dissertation, School of **Journalism,** SIU, 1977.
3. SAN JIN HAN, "Discursive Method and Social Theory: Selectivity, Discourse, and Crisis: A Contribution to a Reflexive Sociology which Is Critical of Domination," PhD Dissertation, Interdisciplinary-Dept. of **Sociology [Philosophy; Political Science],** SIU, 1979. [South Korea]
4. REBECCA STODDART, "Communicative Responsiveness in Preschool Children: Individual Differences in Nonverbal and Verbal Conversational Behaviors," PhD Dissertation, Dept. of **Psychology,** SIU, 1980.
5. ELEANOR DOUGHERTY, "Cognitive Models of Face-to-Face Interaction: A Semiotic Approach," PhD Dissertation, Dept. of **Anthropology, State University of New York at Buffalo,** 1984.
6. MARIO SAENZ, "The Problem of the Conditioned and Unconditioned: Philosophical Justification of Freedom in Marx and Habermas," PhD Dissertation, Dept. of **Philosophy,** SIU, 1985.
7. EFTHIMIOS D. ZAHAROPOULOS, "Foreign Mass Communication in Greece: Its Impact on Greek Culture and Influence on Greek Society," PhD Dissertation, School of **Journalism,** SIU, 1985. [Greece]
8. PYUNG-JOONG YOONG, "Rationality and Social Criticism: Habermas, Foucault, and Beyond," PhD Dissertation, Dept. of **Philosophy,** SIU, 1988. [South Korea]
9. AHRAR AHMAD, "India's Underdevelopment: An Application of the World System and Dependency Perspectives," PhD Dissertation, Dept. of **Political Science,** SIU, 1988. [Bangladesh]
10. CHONG-HWAN OH, "Some Problems of Reference and Truth in Putnam's Internal Realism", PhD Dissertation, Dept. of **Philosophy,** SIU, 1990. [South Korea]

11. **KATSUHITO AOKI**, "Topological Twist in the Heart: Reading Heidegger," PhD Dissertation, Dept. of **Philosophy**, SIU, 1992. [Morris Eames Graduate Award in Philosophy, SIU, 1991. [**Japan**]
12. **HONG-PIL LEE**, "Self, World, and Language: Robert Lowell's *Life Studies*," PhD Dissertation, Dept. of **English**, SIU, 1993. [**South Korea**]
13. **YANGJIN NOH**, "Relativism Without Confrontation: Putnam, Rorty, and Beyond," PhD Dissertation, Dept. of **Philosophy**, SIU, 1993. [**South Korea**]
14. **NAN-NAN LEE**, "The Adventure of Thinking: An Introduction to the Critical Theory of T. W. Adorno," PhD Dissertation, Dept. of **Philosophy**, SIU, 1993. [**South Korea**]
15. **ROBERT A. RUSSELL**, "The Promise of Philosophy: Adorno and the Possibility of Normative Critical Social Theory ," PhD Dissertation, Dept. of **Philosophy**, SIU, 1995.
16. **GREGORY MICHAEL HOLDEN**, "System, Science, and Truth: Fichte's Reflections on the Distinction between Form and Content in Kant's Critical Philosophy," PhD Dissertation, Dept. of **Philosophy**, SIU, 1995.
17. **PING LEUNG TSO**, "Habermas's Theory of Communicative Action and the Problems of Modernity," PhD Dissertation, Dept. of Philosophy, SIU, 1995. [**P.R. China**]
18. **TIMOTHY CROWE**, "An Examination of Three Strategies for Dealing with [Quine's] Normativity within Naturalized Epistemology," PhD Dissertation, Dept. of **Philosophy**, SIU, 1995.
19. **DONNA MAURER**, "The Vegetarian Movement in North America: An Examination of Collective Strategy and Movement Culture," PhD Dissertation, Dept. of **Sociology**, SIU, 1997. Dissertation Research Award Fellowship, SIU Graduate School, 1995.
20. **KATHERINE L. TIETGE**, "Ontology and Genuine Moral Action: *Jñāna* (Intuitive Perception), Ethics and *Karma-Yoga* in Sankara's *Advaita Vedanta* and Schopenhauer's *On the Basis of Morality*," Dept. of Philosophy, SIU, 1996.
21. **VICTOR PAUL HITCHOCK**, "'Now the shadow' passes over the 'age of transition' into the 'Chair at the well': The Politics of Experimentalism in Alain Robbe-Grillet, Christine Brooke-Rose, and Wilson Harris," PhD Dissertation, Dept. of **English**, SIU, 1997.
22. **STEPHEN A. CARELLI**, "The Last Moderns: Bergson, Freud, Nietzsche, Weber and the Emergence of the Postmodern Paradigm," PhD Dissertation, Dept. of **History**, SIU, 1997.
23. **PRIYA BANERJEE**, "Assessing the Effects of Learning Styles and Attitudes toward Computers on Users' Evaluation of Three Computer Assisted

Instruction Modules in Health Education," Dept. of **Health Education,** SIU, 1999. [**India**]

24. GARY A. MULLEN, "The Eschatological Dimension of Adorno's Thought," PhD Dissertation, Dept. of **Philosophy,** SIU, 2000.

25. JANET R. HURLEY, "Health Education and Computer Technology: The Qualitative Methodology of Phenomenology and Identified Experts," PhD Dissertation, Dept. of **Health Education,** SIU, 2000.

26. L. KURT ENGLEHART, "Wholeness and the Rational Structure of Inquiring Systems," PhD Dissertation, **Psychology Dept., Graduate School and Research Center, Saybrook Institute,** San Francisco, California, 2001.

27. STEPHEN LONG, "Harmartia Poetics in Three Victorian Novels", PhD Dissertation, Dept. of **English,** SIU, 2002.

28. CHRISTOPHER A. P. NELSON, "Our Author's Voice: The Quest of the Actual Veronym in the Writing of Søren Kierkegaard", PhD Dissertation, Dept. of **Philosophy,** SIU, 2003. Morris Doctoral Fellow, SIU Graduate School; SIU Alumni Association Outstanding Masters Thesis, 1998.

29. MARC CALDWELL, "Journalism as a Practice of Strong Evaluation: An Analysis of Journalists Conversation", PhD Dissertation, Dept. of Culture, Communication, and Media Studies Graduate Programme, University of KwaZulu-Natal, Durban, **South Africa,** 2009.

PhD Dissertation Committee Member:

1. FRANK J. CHORBA, "Student Dissent as Viewed through Marx's Theory of Alienation," PhD Dissertation, Dept. of Speech Communication, SIU, 1975.

2. JAMES M. DORRIS, "A Phenomenological Explication of Masculinity," PhD Dissertation, Dept. of Speech Communication, SIU, 1975.

3. JAMES L. SPENGLER, "A Phenomenological Explication of Loneliness," PhD Dissertation, Dept. of Speech Communication, 1975.

4. PHIL D. BOROFF, "Joshua Logan's Directional Approach to the Theatre and Motion Pictures," PhD Dissertation, Dept. of Speech Communication, SIU, 1975.

5. RUSSEL PAUL WESTBROOK, "A Thematic Analysis of the Advocacy of Thomas Emmet Hayden as a Radical Intellectual Activist in the New Left Social Movement," PhD Dissertation, Dept. of Speech Communication, SIU, 1976.

6. RONALD W. DeFORD, "Contemporary Poetic Drama: Three Original Verse Plays," PhD Dissertation, Dept. of Speech Communication, SIU, 1977.

7. **DIANNE BRITWIESSER,** "Silent Reading as Dramatic Experience," PhD Dissertation, Dept. of Speech Communication, SIU, 1977.
8. **NANCY A. SOCHAT,** "Teaching Medical Diagnostic Interviewing Skills: An Application of Semiotic Theory and Practice," PhD Dissertation, Dept. of Speech Communication, SIU, 1978.
9. **ISAAC E. CATT,** "An Existential Phenomenological Interpretation of Narcissism," PhD Dissertation, Dept. of Speech Communication, SIU, 1982.
10. **KAREN C. EVANS,** "Woman's Experience of Woman: A Phenomenological Explication," PhD Dissertation, Dept. of Speech Communication, SIU, 1984.
11. **CAROLE J. SPITZACK,** "The Subjects of Weight Consciousness: A Discursive Analysis of Experiential Unity," PhD Dissertation, Dept. of Speech Communication, SIU, 1985.
12. **WILLIAM NEVIOUS,** "A Phenomenological Explication of the Meaning of the Decisive Moment in Photography," PhD Dissertation, Dept. of Speech Communication, SIU, 1986.
13. **GORDON NAKAGAWA,** "The Politics of Narratives: Stories of Japanese American Internment," PhD Dissertation, Dept. of Speech Communication, SIU, 1986. {Second place selection; 1987 Outstanding Dissertation Award of the SIU Graduate School.}
14. **BRENDA K. DeVORE MARSHALL,** "A Semiotic Phenomenology of Directing", PhD Dissertation, Dept. of Speech Communication, SIU, 1988.
15. **CAROL L. BENTON,** "Raised Eyebrows: The Comic Impulse in the Poetry of Margaret Atwood", PhD Dissertation, Dept. of Speech Communication, SIU, 1988.
16. **DONALD R. HINTON,** "An Empirical Phenomenological Investigation into the Phenomenon of Hurt in Close Interpersonal Relationships," PhD Dissertation, Dept. of Speech Communication, SIU, 1989.
17. **ELIZABETH HILL,** "A Semiotic-Phenomenological Analysis of the Self-Reflexive Messages of Adult Children of Alcoholics", PhD Dissertation, Dept. of Speech Communication, SIU, 1990.
18. **EMILY HUEI-LING HER,** "A Phenomenological Explication of Shame in a Shame Culture: A Cross-Cultural Perspective", PhD Dissertation, Dept. of Speech Communication, SIU, 1991. **[P.R. China]**
19. **GARY T. MARSHALL,** "William Stafford: A Writer Writing", PhD Dissertation, Dept. of Speech Communication, SIU, 1991.
20. **GEORGE ERICH KORN,** "Everett C. Parker and the Citizen Media Reform Movement: A Phenomenological Life-History", PhD Dissertation, Dept. of Speech Communication, SIU, 1991.

21. **BEATE ELIZABETH THARANDT,** "Walter Gropius' Totaltheater Revisited: A Phenomenological Study of the Theater of the Future", PhD Dissertation, Dept. of Speech Communication, SIU, 1991. [Germany]
22. **JAY R. MOORMAN,** "Doorway to the Promised Land: A Phenomenological Explication of the Epiphanic Experience in Cross-Cultural (China–USA) Adaptation", PhD Dissertation, Dept. of Speech Communication, SIU, 1992.
23. **THADDEUS D. MARTIN,** "A Semiotic Phenomenology of the Will-to-Communicate in the Philosophy of Karl Jaspers," PhD Dissertation, Dept. of Speech Communication, SIU, 1992.
24. **JAMES C. LUNDY,** "What is the Pedagogical Experience of 'Answering'?: A Phenomenological Explication of Intentionality as an Experience of the Flesh," PhD Dissertation, Dept. of Speech Communication, SIU, 1992.
25. **JACQUELINE DOBYNS DeHON,** "A Phenomenological Explication of Women's Choosing to Attend College as a Nontraditional Age," PhD Dissertation, Dept. of Speech Communication, SIU, 1993.
26. **PAMELA R. McWHERTER,** "A Phenomenology of the Communication Process in Age-Gap Marital Relationships," PhD Dissertation, Dept. of Speech Communication, SIU, 1993.
27. **JULIA V. PACHOUD,** "A Radical Romance: An Existential Phenomenological Investigation of Feminist Playwrights Whose Works Appeal to Children," PhD Dissertation, Dept. of Speech Communication, SIU, 1994.
28. **CYNTHIA M. BISHOP,** "Argumentativeness and Verbal Aggressiveness: Aspects of Speech Communication's Raison d'Etre," PhD Dissertation, Dept. of Speech Communication, SIU, 1999.
29. **EDWIN D. PHILLIPS,** "Defining Leadership Communication: A Qualitative Investigation of Leadership in a Non-Profit Service Organization", PhD Dissertation, Dept. of Speech Communication, SIU, 2000.
30. **TONY L. ARDUINI,** "Interpersonal Communication Motives and Channel Selection: An Investigation of Student-to-Teacher Out-of-Class Communication," PhD Dissertation, Dept. of Speech Communication, SIU, 2000.
31. **LU XIN-AN,** "'Public Secrets' as a Phenomenon in Organizational Communication", PhD Dissertation, Dept. of Speech Communication, SIU, 2000. [P.R. China]
32. **STEPHANIE CHANEY HARTFORD,** "Employee Perceptions of Leader Credibility and Its Relationship to Employee Communication Satisfaction in a Health Care Organization", Dept. of Speech Communication, SIU, 2000.

33. **TEDDI A. JOYCE**, "Perceptions of Departmental Chairs and College and University Administrators toward Issues and Activities of Shared Governance," PhD Dissertation, Dept. of Speech Communication, SIU, 2000.
34. **MICHELLE WILKES-CARILLI**, "Student Motivation: An Assessment of What Motivates Today's College Students in the Classroom," PhD Dissertation, Dept. of Speech Communication, SIU, 2000.
35. **HANSON PAUL LeBLANC**, "Family Boundary Negotiation in Parent-Adolescent Interaction", PhD Dissertation, Dept. of Speech Communication, SIU, 2000.

MASTERS THESES

M.A. and M.S. Thesis Director:

1. **ANDREW R. SMITH**, "A Phenomenology of Confinement," M.S. Thesis, Dept. of Speech Communication, SIU, 1977. Placement: PhD program [Communication], SIU.
2. **RICARDO de la PIEDRA**, "Phenomenology of Xenophobia," M.S. Thesis, Dept. of Speech Communication, SIU, 1977. Placement: Private industry, Lima. Peru.
3. **CHARLES M. CARROLL**, "A Phenomenology of Suicide," M.S. Thesis, Dept of Speech Communication, SIU, 1979. Placement: Officer Candidate School [Intelligence], U.S. Air Force.
4. **CORINNE M. CAHILL**, "A Phenomenology of Alienation," M.S. Thesis, Dept. of Speech Communication, SIU, 1979. Placement: PhD program [Communication], S.I.U.
5. **SHARON F. KIRK**, "A Phenomenology of a Child of Holocaust Survivors," M.S. Thesis, Dept. of Speech Communication, SIU, 1981. Placement: PhD program [Communication], Pennsylvania State University, State College, Pennsylvania.
6. **JAMES T. EDWARDS**, "Rock'n'Roll, the Gig, and Time: An Investigation of Live Communication as Guerrilla Rhetoric," M.A. Thesis, Dept. of Speech Communication, SIU, 1984. Placement: PhD program [Communication], University of Texas, Austin, Texas.
7. **PATRICK F. SULLIVAN**, "Peirce's Theory of Signs as Framework for a Theory of Human Communication," M.A. Thesis, **Dept. of Philosophy,** SIU, 1984. Placement: PhD program [Philosophy], University of Kentucky, Louisville, Kentucky.

8. **MICHIKO HAMADA,** "Speaking as Embodiment: Japanese Terms for Self-Reference and Address", M.A., Thesis, Dept. of Speech Communication, SIU, 1988. Placement: PhD program [Linguistics], University of California at Berkeley [Awarded Graduate Assistant ship; and, Non-Resident Scholarship]. [Japan]
9. **ERIC DAVID FOX,** "The Reflexivity of Time and Technology: Intensional and Extensional Descriptions in Human Communication Theory," MS., Thesis, Dept. of Speech Communication, SIU, 1992. Placement: PhD program [Speech Communication], Southern Illinois University, Carbondale, Illinois.

M.A. and M.S. Thesis External Examiner:

1. **CAROL M. JORDAN,** "The Person as Open System: A Neglected Factor in Economic Theory," M.S. Thesis, Dept. of **Economics,** SIU, 1979.
2. **NAN-NAN LEE,** "Heidegger on Thinking," M.A. Thesis, Dept. of **Philosophy,** SIU, 1980. [South Korea]
3. **DU-WON LEE,** "The Zero Sign in Semiotics," M.A. Thesis, Dept. of **Communication, Sangamon State University,** Springfield, Illinois, 1991. [South Korea]
4. **ROY EGGENSPERGER,** "Glossolalia: The Footprints of God," M.S. Thesis, Dept. of **Anthropology,** SIU, 1995.

M.A. and M.S. Thesis Committee Member:

1. **ELIZABETH DUNCAN (MOSER),** "A Phenomenological Explication of the Experience of True Friendship," M.S. Thesis, Dept. of Speech Communication, SIU, 1979.
2. **LYNN PHILLIPS,** "A Phenomenological Inquiry: Identification and the Mother-Daughter Relationship," M.S. Thesis, Dept. of Speech Communication, SIU, 1980.
3. **JOHN KOLE KLEEMAN,** "An Existential Phenomenology of Interpersonal Therapy and Love," M.S. Thesis, Dept. of Speech Communication, SIU, 1983.
4. **ANNA HIRATA SMITH,** "Voice To My Silence" [The Communicative Meaning of Silence in Interpersonal Communication], M.S. Research Report, Dept. of Speech Communication, SIU, 1990. [Japan]

MASTERS RESEARCH REPORT

M.A. and M.S. Research Report Director:

1. **SUSAN McHUGH,** "The West Coast Women's Studies Conference: A Demonstration of Feminist Rhetoric," M.S. Research Report, Dept. of Speech Communication, SIU, 1976. Placement: Private industry, Boston, Massachusetts.
2. **MICHAEL PRESNELL,** "Reason, Insanity, and Psychiatry's Self-Understanding," M.S. Research Report, Dept. of Speech Communication, SIU, 1976. Placement: PhD program [Communication], S.I.U.
3. **KRISTIN M. LANGELLIER,** "The Chamber Theatre Model as Viewed from a Social Systems Perspective," M.S. Research Report, Dept. of Speech Communication, SIU, 1977. Placement: PhD program [Communication], S.I.U.
4. **ERIC E. PETERSON,** "A Communication Model Perspective on Oral Interpretation," M.S. Research Report, Dept. of Speech Communication, SIU, 1977. Placement: PhD program [Communication], S.I.U.
5. **JEANMARIE COOK,** "Conflict in Long-Distance Romantic Relationships: A Multi-Theory Approach," M.A. Research Report, Dept. of Speech Communication, SIU, 1984. Placement: Instructor, Dept. of Speech Communication, St. Cloud State University, St. Cloud, Minnesota.
6. **LARRY PENROD,** "Moscow-Tartu Cultural Semiotics: Its Relation and Significance to the Intercultural Communication Discipline," M.S. Research Report, Dept. of Speech Communication, SIU, 1986. Placement: Private industry, Mississauga, Ontario, **Canada.**
7. **DANIEL H. LEYES,** "Vygotsky and Merleau-Ponty: Toward Semiotic Phenomenology as a Communicological Research Methodology," M.S. Research Report, Dept. of Speech Communication, SIU, 1988. Placement: PhD program [Communication], S.I.U.
8. **HEATHER A. HOWLEY,** "Spinning the Threads of Prophecy: An Exploration of Native American Fiction and the Prophetic Tradition," M.S. Research Report, Dept. of Speech Communication, SIU, 1998. Placement: PhD program [Communication], S.I.U.

M.A. and M.S. Research Report External Examiner:

1. **YOUNG HEE KIM**, "A Study of the Impact of Communication on the New Community Movement in the Republic of Korea," M.S. Research Report, Dept. of **Community Development**, SIU, 1988. [**South Korea**]
2. **HIROMI NAGASHIMA**, "The Kanji (Chinese Characters) as an Image-Based (Pictographic and Ideographic) System of Communication," M.S., Thesis and CD-ROM, **Interactive Multimedia Program, College of Mass Communication and Media Arts**, SIU, 2000. [**Japan**]
3. **LEAH STONE**, "Poetry Audience and New Media Textualities," M.S., Thesis and CD-ROM, **Interactive Multimedia Program, College of Mass Communication and Media Arts**, SIU, 2002

M.A. and M.S. Research Report Committee Member:

1. **BRENDA L. BERTELSEN TRUEBLOOD**, "An Analysis of Humor in Walt Disney Films," M.S. Research Report, Dept. of Speech Communication, SIU, 1978.
2. **JANICE L. SETHNE**, "Being-and-Choice: A Communicative Model," M.S. Research Report, Dept. of Speech Communication, SIU, 1979.
3. **MARK R. CYR**, "The Unconscious Level of Communication Based on the Hypotherapeutic Work of Milton Erickson," M.S. Research Report, Dept. of Speech Communication, SIU, 1979.
4. **DENNIS K. MUMBY**, "Bernstein's Deficit Hypothesis: Towards a Critique of Linguistic Deprivation," M.S. Research Report, Dept. of Speech Communication, SIU, 1981. [**United Kingdom**]
5. **CAROLE SPITZACK**, "The Masking of Interpersonal Magic: Or Rationalizing Irrationality," M.S. Research Report, Dept. of Speech Communication, SIU, 1981.
6. **IAN HENDERSON**, "The Body: Merleau-Ponty and Foucault," M.S. Research Report, Dept. of Speech Communication, SIU, 1986. [**United Kingdom**]
7. **RUI-HONG GUO**, "An Existential-Phenomenological Study of the Experience of Comforting between Friends," M.S. Research Report, Dept. of Speech Communication, SIU, 1987. [**P.R. China**]
8. **ERIC W. MARLOW**, "A Phenomenological Approach to Academic Value Debate Case Construction: A Case Study," M.S. Research Report, Dept. of Speech Communication, SIU, 1993.

9. **PRIYA R. BANERJEE,** "An Empirical Phenomenological Explication of the Experience of Watching An Other Culture Interpretation of One's Culture: A Study in Intercultural Communication," M.S. Research Report, Dept. of Speech Communication, SIU, 1995. **[Bangladesh]**

10. **TODD J. SZELUGA,** "Conversation—Free: An Ethnographic Analysis of Joking Behavior in an Afircan-American Barbershop", M.S. Research Report, Dept. of Speech Communication, SIU, 1999.

Index

Note: Page numbers in italics indicate figures; page numbers followed by "t" indicate tables.

A

abduction, 24, 28–31, 111, 112, 126, 135, 138–41, *139*
abjection, 299
aboutness, 71, 76–77, 86, 333
absolute beginnings, search for, 8
abstraction, 253, 345–46n15
Achilles and the tortoise, paradox of, 135
Ackerman, Nathan, 95, 103
acta, 207, 291
action
    bodily, 243–63
    discourse and, 277
    information and, 244–45
    reflection in, 307–8
    reflection on, 306–7
    of sign, 330
    of signs, 346n17
    signs and, 243–44
actuality, 221, 236n1
actualization model, 126

Addressee, 256
Addresser, 256
adduction, 13, 24, 28–31, 111, 112, 126, *139*
    as critical, 126
    monstrosity of, 133–46
    non-normal, 139
adolescent adjustment, 93
Adorno, Theodor, 95, 386
Aertsen, Jan, 373
aesthetics, 10
Africana scholars, 223–24
agency, 272, 329, 330–31, 332, 340, 345n12, 346n17
Alexander, Hubert Griggs, 12, 223, 394
allegory, 380–81
Allport, Gordon, 112
alphabetic literacy, 59–62
alterity, 193
American dream, 101, 105
American pragmatism, 4, 5, 6–7, 26, 352
American Psychiatric Association, 95
Amerindians. *See* Native Americans

analogical relations, 52–53
analogy, 380–81
analytical method, 126
Analytic philosophy, 354
Ancient Greeks, 150–51, 184, 188. *See also specific philosophers*
animism, 365
anthropology, 4, 8, 9–10
antidepressant medicine, 204–6, 209–10, 214. *See also* Prozac
Anton, Corey, 13
Anzaldúa, Gloria, 238n32
apperception, 256–57
appositions, 4, 14, 52, 57, 59–60, 268, 269
appresentation, 50, 51–54
Argentina, 223
Aristotle, 137, 138, 269, 313, 372, 376
Arneson, Pat, 14
Arnett, Ronald, 13–14
articulation, 372–73
asynchronization of perception and expression, 215
asyndeton, 314
attending, 283–90, 294
    attending-away, 286–87
    central, 286
    identifying in, 286–87
attention, 294. *See also* attending
    inner, 288
    objects of, 288–89
    visual, 283, 286–87
Augenblick, 98
"author," vs. "writer", 272–77
author discourse, 315
author function, 275, 276, 277–78, 313–14, 315
authoring
    as technology of self, 273–77
    vs. writing, 273–74
authority, 274, 355, 357
authorization, 272
authorship, 273–74, 321
    postmodern, 315
    by signature, 321
autobiographical subject, 270–71, 272
autonomous discourse, 59–62
axiology, coding and, 173

B

Baden (Southwestern) School, 111
bad infinity, 382
Bagwell, Paul, 394
Bakhtin, Mikhail, 334, 335, 347n32, 383
    critique of scientism, 347n31
    "Discourse on the Novel," 333
Baldwin, James, 361
Bales, Robert, 93–94
ballet, 300
Barthes, Roland, 273, 274, 315, 318, 321
Bateson, Gregory, 5, 9–11, 15n2, 51, 56, 95, 202
    Communication: The Social Matrix of Psychiatry, 9, 50, 65n13, 67n4, 391–92
Baudrillard, Jean, 253
becoming, 373
behavior, 4, 125
behaviorism, 8, 10
Being/being, 284, 293
    being-for- itself (*l'être-pour-soi*), 285
    being-for-the-Other, 193
    being-in- itself (*l'être-en-soi*), 285
    Being-towards-death, 315, 319
    conscious, 284
    feelings of being, 206, 207, 216n17
    modes of, 84–85
    in speech, 351–67
    transcendental predicates of, 372–73
    unconscious, 284
Benveniste, Émile, 7
Bergo, Bettina, 188
Bernstein, Richard, 352
Bhaskar, 124
biologism, 207, 208
Blaug, Mark, 137
Blick, 287
Bloch, Ernst, 374, 375, 378–79
Boas, Franz, 8, 9
bodily expressive movement, 300, 308
the body. *See also* embodiment
    bodily limits, 254–55
    experiential body (body-for-itself), 301
    meaning-making body, 299
    as sign, 302

sign and, 10
  as subject/object, 301
body-lived, 206–7
Böhme, Jakob, 379
Bogost, Ian, 363
Booth, William, 372
borders, 14
border thinking, 12, 23–48
boundaries, 14, 35
Bourdieu, Pierre, 4, 8, 10, 11, 34–35, 202, 213
Bowen, Murray, 96, 98, 103
Bowles, Paul, *The Sheltering Sky*, 13, 148, 152–55, 156
Bradley, Earl, 391
braidedness, 288, 294
Brandom, Robert, 15, 352–53, 355–62, 364
  historicism and, 362
  making explicit, 353–54
  Making it Explicit, 353–54
  rationality and, 362
  Tales of the Mighty Dead: Historical Essays in the Metaphysics of Intentionality, 354–55
Bryant, Levi, 363
Buber, Martin, 385
Buchler, Justus, 341
Bühler, Karl, 7
Burke, Kenneth, 372, 375–77, 384
Burling, Robbins, 73
Butler, Judith, 167, 169

C

Cabot, Meg, 216n15
Calderoni, Mario, 137
California missions, 227
Campbell, W. Keith, 244
capability. *See* capacity
capacity, 221, 236n1
  perceptual, 232–35
capta, 207, 291
Carey, James W. 382
Carushe, Paul, 137
Casey, Edward S., 283, 285–90, 294
Cassirer, Ernst, 10, 11, 223

categories, 160
categorization, 160
  common sense, 164–65
Catt, Isaac E., 14, 133, 170, 180, 181, 182
change
  information and, 249–50, *250*
  as performative phenomenon, 14
  problem of, 13–14
Charmaz, Kathy, 159, 168
chemical imbalance hypothesis, 204, 206, 209–10
chiasm of flesh, 202
childhood, 93
children
  antidepressant medicine and, 209–10
  child as icon, 103–6
  lived communicative experience of, 93–108
China, 136
"choice of context," 302
Chomsky, Noam, 73
choreology, semiotics and, 300
Choreutics, 310n13
Christianity, 227
Cixous, Hélène, 267, 279n23
climate change, technical risk communication about, 14
clinical practice, phenomenology of signs in, 9
codes/coding, 53–56, 60–61, 68, 249, 256–57, 291, 300, 302
  axiology and, 173
  context and, 66–67n29
  dialectical construction of, 7
  epistemology and, 171
  logic and, 171–72
  ontology and, 170–71
  practice of, 13, 159–76
  as a system of pragmatic elements, 167–70
  as a system of semantic elements, 163–67
  as system of syntactic elements, 161–63
  in theory of communicative acts, 170–73
codification, 7
cognition, experimental phenomenological studies in, 13, 111–32
Colapietro, Vincent, 15
colonialism, 222, 223, 225–27, 228
  21st-century, 225–28

violence of, 225–28
commodities, 253–54
Common Sense Categorization, 164
communicability, 72
    conditions of, 72
    experience and, 85
    as ground of communicology, 71–92
    horizons of, 15
    impediments to, 72–75
    principles of, 76–81
    three seminal impulses for communicability as ground of communicology, 81–85
    universal, 85
communication, 329, 334
    as concept and phenomenon, 369
    connecting classical view of being and its "perfections," 372–73
    culture and, 10
    democracy and, 358–61
    depression and, 213
    desire and, 375–77
    discipline of, 3–4
    experience of, 133, 141
    as ground of communicology, 13
    helical model of, 380–84, *380*
    heterosemiotic analysis of, 72
    hypoiconic analysis of, 72
    information and, 118
    instead of information transmission, 245
    limits of, 133
    lived experience of, 11
    media of, 11
    as process, 258
    psychology of, 13
    reality of, 342
    repression of, 215
    semiotic phenomenology and, 255–58
    as social vs. human science, 3
    theories of, 369
    universality and, 374
communication levels, distinction between, 15n2
communication matrix, 14
    mental health in, 14, 201–19
    possibility in, 213–15
    risk in, 213–15

communication research, qualitative, 13, 159–76
communication studies, 93, 201
communication theory, 6, 170–73, 373–75
    dialogical-dialectical coherence of field of, 379–82
    field of, 379–82
    logic of, 67–68n38
communicative acts
    as ontological and transcendental moment of self-expression and communication, 373–74
    theory of, 170–73, 373–74
communicative context, meaning and, 63
communicative networks, 290
communicative praxis, critical theory of, 15
communicative relationships, 202
communicative universality, 85
communicology, 33, 41, 133, 222, 224, 233, 327, 341
    coding and, 13, 159–76
    communicability as base line of, 72
    communicability as ground of, 71–92
    communication as ground of, 13
    in context of life itself, 93–108
    cultural, 232–35, 237n13
    cultural matrix of, 379
    decolonial project and, 221–41
    definition of, 1
    direction of, 93
    discipline of, 1–3, 5–15
    German tradition of, 13
    history of, 4–5
    human science of, 41–42
    interpretation of, 5
    intrapersonal, 283
    Lanigan's pioneering conception of, 179–80
    new territory of, 15
    normative logic in communicology praxis and theory, 256
    perceptual component of, 290–91, 293
    semiotic phenomenology and, 255–58
    terminology, 1, 3–4
Communicology (journal), 5
communicology.org, 2–3

community, 341, 342
community consensus, 85
complementarity of pairs, 374
complex entities, ontic heterogeneity of, 72
computer-assisted qualitative data analysis software (CAQDAS), 159
concepts, 355–57
    dimensions of, 354–58
    historical dimension of, 357–58
    inferential dimension of, 356
    meaning of, 359
    normative character of, 354–55
    vs. norms, 356
conceptual follow up, 126
conceptual normativity, 355–56
Confucius, 329
Connolly, Maureen, 14, 299–300, 301, 304–5, 306–7
consciousness, 10, 11, 67n35, 133, 203, 328, 333, 375
    core attributes of, 125
    culture inherent in, 211
    embodied, 301
    embodiment and, 125
    environmental education and, 258
    levels of, 363
    lived, 202
    ontic heterogeneity of acts of, 71
    phenomenology and, 362–63
    philosophy of, 213
    universal, 210–11
"conservation education," 244
consumerism, 253–54
context, 7, 9, 202
    code and, 66–67n29
    "contexts of choice," 302
Continental philosophy, 4, 5, 33, 354
contingent rights, 362
"continuism," 8
conversation, 330, 333, 338, 340, 345n13
Cosmic Anomaly, 136
Cox, J. Robert, 244, 258
Craig, Robert, 374, 379–80, 381–82
Craig, Tom D., 14, 301
Critical Disability Studies, 302
critical experimentation, 126

cultural (intergroup) domain, 290
cultural communicology, decolonial project of, 232–35, 237n13
cultural difference, understanding at level of perceptual capacity, 232–35
cultural hierarchies, reproduction of, 14
cultural other, 11
cultural semiotics, 93
Cultural Studies, 4, 7
culture, 85, 258, 300, 302, 333
    communication and, 10
    cultural predispositions, 11
    inherent in consciousness, 211
    language and, 8–9
    as matrix, 379
    person and, 9
    psychology and, 9–10
culturology, 8
dance, 300, 305–9

D

Dance, Frank, 380–81, *380*, 382–84
Dao, 384, 388n31
Dao De Jing, 384
Darstellung, 28
Darwin, Charles, 352
Dasein, 315, 319, 362
data, 207, 291
Davidson, Donald, 352
decolonial phenomenological practice, 221–41
decolonial production of knowledge, 24–25
decolonizing research praxis, 23–42, 221–41
deduction, 111, 112, 126, 137, 138–41, *139*
    non-normal, 139
deductive entailment, Aristotelian/Scholastic theory of, 138
deixis, implicit, 77–78, 86
Deleuze, Gilles, 38
democracy
    communication and, 358–61
    theory of, 359–60
    as tradition, 358–61
    tradition and, 358–61
denotation, 54–59, 58–62

Department of Communicology at University of Hawaii, Manoa, 5
depression, 14
  communication and, 213
  depressive mood disorder, 201–19
  disease model of, 210–11
  from phenomenological point of view, 207
  relapse of, 209
depression medicine, 201–19
"derivative I," 179, 183, 195
derivative response, 194
Derrida, Jacques, 56, 136, 140, 147, 188, 315
Descartes, René, 335
description/Description, 39, 179, 180–81, 292, 293
descriptive reduction, 187
desire, 208
  communication and, 375–77
  of the whole, 387n12
De Smet, Pierre Jean, 317
"desynchronization," 215
Dewey, John, 2, 4–5, 7–11, 201, 202, 343, 345n12, 348n57, 352
Diagnostic and Statistical Manual of Mental Disorders (*DSM*), 207, 214
dialogical-dialectical coherence, 379–82
dialogism, 335
différence, 56, 315
Dilthey, Wilhelm, 79–81
direct intuition, 15
disciplinary language, 13
disconnection, 208, 209, 214–15
discourse, 10, 11, 63, 268, 271, 275, 333
  action and, 277
  autonomous, 59–62
  constraints of, 206
  dialectical practice of, 14
  history of, 357–58
  human model of, 256
  language and, 268, 269–70t, 271–72
  postmodernism and, 275
  theory of, 93
  voice as discursive praxis, 268–69
discursive, vs. non-discursive, 351–53
discursive beings, 362
discursive capacity, 353

discursive formation (message as code), 314
discursive model of being human, 256
discursive practices, 271, 272, 275, 277
discursive transformation (code as message), 314
disease model hypothesis, 210–11
disembodiment, 203, 209
dispositif(s), 34, 39
Doctorow, E.L., 163
documents, 320
Dostoyevsky, Fyodor, 188
Dreyfus, Hubert, 8, 11, 171
dualism, 8, 335
Duquesne University, 395
Dussel, Enrique, 222–25, 236
  Ethics of Liberation in the Age of Globalization and Exclusion, 222
  Lanigan and, 222–25
  philosophy and ethics of liberation, 228–32
Dyer, Alan W., 254
Dynamic Object, 141

E

Eco, Umberto, 4, 141, 160, 168–71, 249
ecology, 203–4
écriture, 273–76, 315
edgelessness, 288–89, 294
education, on "zero nature," 245–50
egocentricity, 234
Eicher-Catt, Deborah, 14, 181, 182
eidetic approach, 24–25, 32–33, 39, 42, 52–53, 55, 58–59, 62, 65n14, 111, 300, 301
Eisenstadt, Oona, 188, 189
Ellison, Ralph, 361
elusiveness, 288, 294
embodied coercion, in educational contexts, 299
embodied conceptual insight, particularity of, 180–81
embodied human discourse, 1
embodied transgression, 307–8
embodiment, 11, 12, 23–48, 271, 301
  bodily limits and, 254–55
  consciousness and, 125

dialectics of, 10
expression and, 300
perception and, 290–91
predispositions of, 202
shared by humans and non-humans, 364
stressed, 302
theories of, 363–64
voice and, 14
embodiment studies, 125
embodying voices, 14
Emerson, R.W., 361
"Literary Ethics," 328
"Spiritual Laws," 328–29
emic approach, 24–25
emotions, 207
Empedocles, 150
empirical, meaning of, 3
empirical approach, 23, 24, 25, 111
"Encyclopedic Dictionary," 13, 49–70
the Enlightenment, 237n13
énoncé, 269, 271, 275, 315
énonciation, 269, 271, 315
entelechy, 347–48n46
environmental education, 14, 243–63
Environmental Protection Agency (EPA), 244, 245–65, 256
epistemic disobedience, 24
"epistemic pathology," 206, 214–15
epistemology, 206
coding and, 171
epoché, 235, 292
equality, evolutionary history of, 357–58
equity, 234
Erfahrung (experience), 286
Eskin, Michael, 198n91
ethics, 10, 236. *See also* semioethics
"derivative I" and, 195
ethical signification, 183–91
ethical theory, 358
as first philosophy, 179, 180
Levinas, Emmanuel and, 198n91
of liberation, 228–32
performative, 180
as preceding being, 190

Eurocentrism, 223–25, 228–29, 235, 237n13, 365
Euro-Modernity, 222–23, 224, 225, 229, 233, 235
evanescence, 288, 294
event cone, 385–86, *386*
events, 332
Evernden, Neil, 253
exchange value, 253–54
existence, 11, 203, 206–7, 235–36
existential moments, 84–85
existential philosophy, 15
Existenzen, 315
experience, 4, 8, 11, 133, 203, 286, 291
actuality of, 221
attending to, 283–90, 294
communicability and, 85
of communication, 133, 141
as discursive, 271
as embedded, 9
embodied phenomenological, 133
existence and, 11
of non-human beings, 364
perception and, 301
phenomenology and, 93, 362–63
as reflexive condition of consciousness, 8
reversibility of, 206–7
as semiotic, 9
semiotics and, 93
social reality and, 63–64
experiential body (body-for-itself), 301
experimental design, 126
experimental phenomenological laboratory, 125
experimental phenomenological methodology, 111–12, 125
experimental psychology, 125
experimentation, 117–18
explicit deixis, 71
expression, 10, 201, 215, 268, 299, 300, 346n19
cultural, 10
embodiment and, 300
perception and, 203–4, 207–8, 213, 268, 272, 277, 291–93, 369–70
exteriority, 195

F

face
    representation of, 187–88
    as sign, 180
families, 13
    cultural theory of, 93
    familial relations, 14
    iconography of family life, 99–101
    lived communicative experience of, 93–108
    normality of, 101–3
"family system," 95
family therapy, 95
Fanon, Franz, 35
"fearless speech," 272, 276
feminism, 267–81
feminist life writing, 14
feminist voice, 267–81
Feyerabend, Paul, 359
first-person perspective, 111–12, 123–25, 126
Fitch, Tecumseh, 75
flesh, as tissue of the world, 202
Fodor, Jerry, 79–81
Food and Drug Administration (FDA), 204–5
fore-conception (*Vorgriff*), 33
fore-meanings, 33
Foucault, Michel, 4, 13, 33–34, 94, 100, 195, 267–72, 283, 294, 321, 342
    apposition between library and museum, 313, 318
    author function and, 275, 276, 277–78
    The Birth of the Clinic, 284–85
    distinction between "writer" and "author," 272–77
    on "fearless speech," 272, 276
    on the gaze, 284
    Lanigan and, 362
    oppositions/appositions of language and discourse, 268, 269, 269–70*t*
    The Order of Things, 270
    technologies of self and, 272
    theory of agency and, 272
    theory of discourse, 93
    What is an Author? 273–74, 318
fourfold, 13, 147–58

Francis, Pope, 226–28
Frankfurt School, 5
Frazer, James George, 55
free imaginative variations, 301
Freeman, Elise C., 244
Frege, Gottlob, 73, 75, 76, 78, 354
French communicology, 13, 317
French feminism, 279n23
French philosophy, 5
Freud, Sigmund, 95, 100, 375
Fromm, Erich, 378
Fuchs, Thomas, 215

G

Gadamer, Hans-Georg, 33–34, 81–82, 360
Gallagher, Shaun, 125
Gass, William, 58
the gaze, 283, 284–86, 290, 294
Geisteswissenschaften, 72, 80–81, 333
Gemeinsamkeit, 79
Gendlin, Eugene, 113
General Semantics theory, 392
General Systems Theory, 93–94
generational time, 103–6
German communicology, 13
German philosophy, 5
Gesellschaft (aspects of society), 314, 321
Gestalt (form), 50, 51–54, 55, 65n13, 151, 299
Gibbs, Robert, 189
Gibson, James J., 125
Giorgi, Amedeo, 114
the glance, 284–86
    around, 287
    as communicative event, 291–93
    communicative possibilities of, 14, 283–98
    concerted, 287–88
    vs. gaze, 285–86, 290
    glancing-after, 288, 289
    glancing-along, 289–90
    glancing-at, 288, 289
    glancing-in-depth, 289
    glancing-into, 289
    glancing-through, 289

Globalization, 222, 229
God, 184–85, 189–90
Gomes, William, 13
Gordon, Lewis, 223
Greek, 188
Greimas, A.-J., 147, 148–49, 155
Grillo, Eric, 252
Grounded Theory, 159
Group for the Advancement of Psychiatry (GAP), 95
Gusdorf, George, *La Parole*, 392
Gutenberg, Johannes, 62

H

Habermas, Jürgen, 5, 71, 79–80, 347n37, 359
  Knowledge and Human Interest, 333
habits, 5, 213
  of culture, 8
  dispositions of, 202
  habit formation, 7
  as predispositions of custom, 8
habitual logics, 8
habituated practices, transcendence of, 13
habitus, 5, 10, 11, 35, 202, 203, 208, 213
Haley, Jay, 95
Hall, David, 388n31
Hall, Edward T., 50–51, 66–67n29, 95
Hamilton depression scale, 209
Hammersley, Martyn, 162
Hammoudi, Abdellah, 32–33
Hannan, Jason, 15
Harman, Gilbert, 359
Harman, Graham, 363
Hatley, James, 189
Hauerwas, Stanley, 360
health communication, 202
hearing, vs. listening, 208
Hebrew, 188
Hegel, G.W.F., 6, 8–9, 352, 353, 354, 358
  bad infinity and, 382
  conceptual idealism of, 354
  conceptual normativity and, 355–56
  description of expressive rationality, 353–54

Science of Logic, 353
Heidegger, Martin, 33, 51, 81, 96, 186, 206, 287, 290, 315, 319, 321
  Building, Dwelling, Thinking, 147
  communicability and, 354
  communicology and, 13
  dynamism and, 150
  fourfold model of, 147–58
  Lanigan and, 362
  The Thing, 147
Heilbrun, Carolyn, *Writing a Woman's Life*, 267
helical model of communication, 380–81, *380*, 382–84
hermeneutic imperialism, 185
hexis, 11, 35, 36, 202, 203, 208, 213
Hilgard, Ernest, 114
historicism, 15, 351–67
Hjelmslev, L., 51, 148
Holenstein, Elmar, 51, 55, 65n19, 66n24
  Roman Jakobson's Approach to Language, 51
Holmes, Oliver Wendell, 6
homoiomata, 71. *See also* resemblance relations
hope, 378–79, 386–87
Horkheimer, Max, 95
Hornborg, Alf, 258
the human, decentering, 364
human beings
  vs. non-human beings, 351–53, 363–64
  as sign-using organisms, 328
humanism
  nature and, 361–62
  phenomenology and, 362–63
humanities, 333–34
  vs. human sciences, 126
human model of discourse, 256
human science, philosophy of, 213
human sciences, 4
  vs. humanities, 126
  as "living philosophy," 201
  models of human science studies, 256
  vs. natural sciences, 347n32
  social sciences and, 25–28
  theory construction in, 23–48
Hume, David, 335
Husserl, Edmund, 30, 51–52, 74, 77–79, 84, 89n78, 95–96, 114, 243, 254, 287

communicology and, 4–6, 8, 10–11
conception of eidetic science, 32–33
dictum that "subjectivity is intersubjectivity," 362–63
epoché and, 235
intentionality and, 33
Lanigan and, 362–63
Logical Investigations, 147
London lectures of 1922, 11
philosophy of transcendental subjectivity, 32–33
on protention and retention, 38
on subjectivity as intersubjectivity, 317
hypoiconicity, 72, 82–84, 86
hypotheses, proposal of, 126

I

icons, 10, 66n26, 86, 93, 95–98
  child as, 103–6
  frozen, 101–3
ideality, 71
identification, 375–77
identity, 14, 379
ideologemes, 37
idiographic methods, 111
idiographic science, 112–17
Ihde, Don, 125
images, 95–98, 380–81
imaginability, 72, 78–79, 86
the "imaginary," 67–68n38
immanent criticism, 360
imperialism, hermeneutic, 185
implicated agency, 329
implicit deixis, 71, 77–78, 86
incommensurability, of thought, 8
Independence Rock, 14, 313–14, 317–19, 320, 321
index, 10, 66n26, 86
indexical marking, 161
indicative, vs. subjunctive, 378
indices, 334
induction, 111, 112, 126, 137, 138–41, *139*
infantile attachment, 93
inferentialism, 351–67

information, 52–54, 59–61, 258, 314
  action and, 244–45
  change and, 249–50, *250*
  communication and, 118
  evolution within communication, 54–59
information theory, 6, 67–68n38
informed choices, 202, 213–14
infusion- and inclusion-based and cultural/social minority perspective approaches, 302
Ingarden, Roman, 72, 84–85, 89n78
injustice, interventions against, 14
insistence, 346n19
intentional arcs, 14, 252, 257–58. *See also* intentionality
intentionality, 11, 33, 71, 85, 208, 252–53, 257–58, 344n5, 362, 363. *See also* intentional arcs
  of act, 243, 254
  intention-reading, 71, 72
  metaphysics of, 351–67
  operative, 243
  of others, 71
  social conventions and, 252
  synergic function of, 369–70
interdisciplinarity, 4
internal/manifest conversation, 118
International Communication Association
  Division of Philosophy of Communication, 394
  Division of Political Communication, 394
International Communicology Institute, 2–3
interpersonal (self-other) domain, 290
interpersonal communication, 9
interpersonal other, 11
interpersonal reasoning, 362
interpersonal relations, 14
interpretants, 7, 202, 230, *250*
interpretation, 179, 181, 258, 292, 293
intersubjective mentalism, 72, 86
intersubjective recognition, 362
intersubjective relations, 41
intersubjectivity, 126, 290, 317
interviews, as collaborative practice, 168–70
intrapersonal (self) domain, 290
introjection, 71, 86
intuition, 15, 372–73, 374

invention, coding and, 170–73
I/Other relations, 193
Irigaray, Luce, 279n23
Italian experimental psychologists, 125

J

Jackson, Don, 95
Jahoda, Gustav, 95
Jakobson, Roman, 7, 13, 51, 62, 181–82, 256–57
    context and, 55–56, 60
    Holenstein on, 51
    Lanigan and, 362
    six functions of communication, 60
    Wilden on, 51
James, William, 2, 3, 6–7, 27, 51, 231, 286, 341, 352
Jaspers, Karl, 315
Jewish hermeneutics, 185
Jews, 188
Johns Hopkins University, 7–8
jouissance, 308
Judaism, 184–85, 188–89
judgments, 354–55
    analytic a priori, 139
    complex, 72, 81–82, 86
    four kinds of, 139–41, *139*
    mediate vs. immediate, 356–57
    synthetic a priori, 140
the just, 24

K

kabbalism, 379
Kant, Immanuel, 6, 75, 81–83, 85, 137, 139, 141, 335, 373
    conceptual normativity and, 355–56
    Critique of Judgment, 72, 81–82
    Critique of Pure Reason, 137
    on judgments, 354–55
    non-formal pure reason, 85
    tools for dealing with complex judgments, 72

Karolak, Hannah, 13–14
Karp, David, 204, 210, 213, 214
Katz, Claire Elise, 188–89, 195
Katz, David, 125
Kierkegaard, Søren, 98
Killingsworth, M. Jimmie, 258
Kleinau, Marvin, 393, 395
Kleinberg-Levin, David, 285–86
Klyukanov, Igor E., 13
knowledge, 111, 381–82. *See also* epistemology
Körper, 301
Korzybski, Alfred, 9, 11, 208
Kozin, Alexander, 13
Kramer, Peter, 205, 207, 209–10, 212, 213
    Listening to Prozac, 204
    Ordinarily Well: The Case for Antidepressants, 205
Krippendorf, Klaus, 29
Kristeva, Julia, 279n23, 307
Kuhn, Thomas, 359
Kull, Kalevi, 248–49, 258n10

L

Laban, Rudolf, 14, 299–311, 310n13
Laban Movement Analysis (LMA), 302–3
Laban movement theory, 300, 301, 304–5
labeling, 163–64
Lacan, Jacques, 51, 67–68n38, 95, 283, 285, 294
    Four Fundamental Concepts of Psycho-analysis, 285
    on the gaze, 284
    Lacanian psychoanalytic theory, 95
Lakoff School, 75
langage, 7
Langellier, Kristin, 13
Langer, Susanne K., 56, 65n14, 66n21
Langley Porter Institute, 10
language, 7, 268, 271, 275, 332–33, 334. *See also* linguistics
    as "actuality of culture," 8–9
    agon of, 272
    children's acquisition of, 60
    culture and, 8–9

discourse and, 268, 269–70, 269–70t, 271–72
inferential dimension of language use, 356
Lanigan on, 206
memorialization and, 315–16
natural language, 86, 89n78
positivity of, 126
The Postmodern Author: Foucault on Fiction and the Fiction of Foucault, 318
as primary but nonexclusive semiotic system, 8
social, 256–57
langue, 7, 256–57
Lanigan, Richard L., 23, 25, 41, 42n5, 86, 163–64, 169, 172, 203–4, 215, 277, 294
on abductive and adductive inferences, 28
adduction and, 28, 138, 140–42
apposition between library and museum and, 314
cognition and, 111–15
commitment to radical scientific inquiry, 235
communicability and, 341
communicology and, 4, 11, 13, 15, 97, 99, 101–6, 180, 183, 222, 224, 233
"Communicology: An Encyclopedic Dictionary of the Human Sciences," 49–70
on concept of "icon," 93
contributions of, 72, 237–38n16, 343–44, 369
cultural matrix of communicology and, 379
de-centering of Eurocentrism and, 237n13
decolonial project and, 235–36
on distinction between writing and speaking, 269–70, 271
Dussel and, 222–25
early life of, 392–93
on egocentricity and sociocentricity, 234
"Encyclopedic Dictionary," 13
epistemological view, 111–12
establishes International Communicology Institute at SIUC, 396
"Figure 15. Phenomenology: The Form and Structure of Appearances," 64, 66–67n29

Foucault and, 269–71, 273–74
on four phases of scientific work, 126
graduate work, 391–93
Greek Voices of Discourse and Epistemology Explicated in French Discourse, 317
humanism and, 362
The Human Science of Communicology, 1, 365
on human sciences, 201
interest in interpretation of human experience, 364
interpretation of Foucault's writings on rhetoric, 268
intersection of ontological levels and, 117–18
joins faculty at SIU, 393–94
Laban and, 14, 299–311
on language, 206
legacy of, 391–96
Levinas and, 180–81, 183, 191, 195
Lévy-Bruhl and, 365
logos and, 327
on meta-theory construction, 40
mind-body dualism and, 363
"phenomenalism" and, 26
phenomenology and, 362–63
Phenomenology of Communication, 309–10n12
pioneering conception of communicology, 179–80
on postmodern authorship, 315
research praxis and, 37
retirement of, 396
on reversibility, 203
in Scotland, 393
semiotic phenomenology methodology and, 255–56, 290, 302, 309–10n12
at SIU, 391–93
The Social Matrix of Psychiatry, 5
Speaking and Semiology, 393
Speech Act Phenomenology, 72, 393
theories of communication and, 369
three acts of description and, 180–81
tripartite methodology of description, reduction, and interpretation, 300
at University of New Mexico, 12, 391, 394

upbringing in New Mexico, 236
West-East interrelations and, 222
"The Yale School of Communicology," 4
Last Tango in Paris, 308
Law of Contradiction, 26, 38
Law of Identity, 42n5
Law of Non-Contradiction, 31, 42n5
Law of Participation, 31, 42n5, 365
learning, 299–300. *See also* education
Lebenswelt, 72. *See also* lived experience; lived world (*Lebenswelt*)
Leibniz, Gottfried Wilhelm, 354
Leopold, Aldo, 244
Levinas, Emmanuel, 13–14, 36, 179–99
  conception of face as sign, 180
  critique of rhetoric, 179–80, 195
  ethics and, 179–99, 198n91
  interpretation of his project, 195
  Jewish context of, 189
  Jewish texts of, 188–89
  reduction of his project, 191–94
  scriptural references in, 188–89, 195
  semioethical conception of, 186
  semiotics and, 180, 198n91
  signification and, 190
  Totality and Infinity, 147, 179, 187
Lévi-Strauss, Claude, 51, 148
Lévy-Bruhl, Lucien, 42n5, 55, 365
Lewis, David, 352
lexis agonistike, 269, 270, 313–23
lexis graphike, 269, 313–23
Liaozhai zhiyi, 136
liberal democracies, 358–59
liberation, 228–32, 236
library, 313–23
Lieb, 301
life worlds, 208, 292
  occupation and exploitation of, 24
  phenomenology of the, 201
life writing, 14, 267–68, 272, 277
  as discursive, 269–70
  as discursive praxis, 271
  practical discourse of, 272
  as technology of itself, 267–81
limen, 142
limit, 142

Lin, Maya, 314–17
Lindlof, Thomas R., 159–65, 167–68
linearity, transgression of, 382
linguistics, 4, 334
  linguistic determinism, 8
  "linguistic illusion," 179
  linguistic pragmatism, 7
listening, 203
  vs. hearing, 208
literacy, 57, 60–61
  history of, 64–65n6
literality, 380–81
lived-body, 206–7, 301
lived communicative experience, 93–108, 183
lived experience, 23, 24–25, 289, 292, 301. *See also* lived world (*Lebenswelt*)
  within codes and signs of given culture, 302
  consumerist, 253
  of learning, 299–300
  of meaning, 299–300
  understanding of, 222
lived meaning, 13
lived world (*Lebenswelt*), 72, 78, 290
living-in-the-world, 255
Locke, John, 72, 359
logic, 10, 13, 171–72, 381
logos, 317, 327, 337, 341, 342–43
longing, 375
Lotman, Yuri, 149, 248
Luhmann, Niklas, 363–64
Lynch, David, 105

M

MacIntyre, Alasdair, 359, 360
Macke, Frank, 13, 291
magikos, 317
making explicit, 353–54
Mancino, Susan, 13–14
Martin, Thaddeus, 14
Martinez, Jacqueline, 14, 181–82
Marx, Karl, 254
Maslow, Abraham, 112
materiality, 71
The Matrix, 94–95

"matrix," 10
  definition of, 10
"maximum gripping," 255
McGlone, Edward, 393
McLuhan, Marshall, 64, 65n11
Mead, George Herbert, 2, 8, 118, 352
Mead, Margaret, 93, 95, 103–4
meaning, 85, 292, 293, 301, 375
  communicative context and, 63
  contextualized, 23
  lived, 13
  perceptions and, 10
  surplus of, 184
meaning ideality, 89n78
meaning identity, 89n78
meaning making, 180, 256, 299–300
  phenomenal world conditioning, 251–55
mediations, 11, 14, 253–54, 257, 272
medical model, 210–11, 213
medicine, 201–19
melancholy, 213, 215
memorialization, language and, 315–16
mental (internal) glancing, 294
mental health, 14, 201–19
mental scenarios, projection of, 72
Merleau-Ponty, Maurice, 43n16, 74, 202–4, 215, 235, 252, 255, 257, 269, 271, 291, 293, 300
  on abduction and adduction, 28–30
  "the body is our general medium for having a world," 362–63
  communicability and, 328, 343
  communication and, 369–70
  communicative dimension of philosophy and, 370–72
  communicology and, 4–5, 8, 10, 13, 15
  conception of embodiment, 301
  distinction between "speech spoken" and "speech speaking," 61
  expression and, 369–70
  Lanigan and, 362–63, 369–70, 391–92
  Levinas and, 181–82, 195
  perception and, 369–70
  phenomenological analysis and, 291
  Phenomenology of Perception, 201, 392
  In Praise of Philosophy, 370–72
  on research praxis, 35, 37
  retrospection and, 38
  Signs, 147, 392
  The Structure of Behavior, 299–300
  synergic function of intentionality, 369–70
  on theory construction, 37–38
  theory of perfective drift and, 373, 383
Merrell, Floyd, 137
"The Message Mystique," 133
message reification, 133
meta-cognitive strategy, 302
metaphor, 380–81
Metaphysical Club, 4, 6
metaphysics, 374
metaphysics of intentionality, 351–67
meta-theory, 25, 42, 112
methodology, 111
Mexia Movement, 227
Middelthon, Anne-Lise, 333, 345n13
midrash, 188–89
Mignolo, Walter, 23
Milbank, John, 360
mime, 300
mind-body dualism, 301, 363
Minuchin, Salvador, 95, 96, 98, 103
"mixed methods," 159
modernity, 223, 225–28, 237n13. *See also* Euro-Modernity
modes of being, 84–85
money, as sign, 253–54
monstration, 135–37
monuments, 14, 313–23, 320
Moraga, Cherríe, 238n32
Morris, Charles, 8, 11
motivation, 375–76
movement, 14
  movement analysis, 300
  qualities of, 304–5
Movement Education, 301, 302–3
Murray, Elwood, 391–92, 394
Murray, Elwood Huey Allen, 394
museums, 313–23
muteness, 333–34, 335, 347n31
mystos, 317
myth (parole), 11
mythos, 317

N

Nagel, Thomas, 364
"nameless voice," 272, 314
Nancy, Jean-Luc, 134, 142
National Society for the Study of Communication, 394
Native Americans, 227–28, 321–22
natural language, 86, 89n78
natural sciences, vs. human sciences, 347n32
nature, 258
    Burke and, 376
    commercialization and, 253
    humanism and, 361–62
    mediated by products, 253
    responsibility toward, 362, 364
    "zero nature," 258n10
the negative, 388n20
negativity, 376–77, 378, 385
Neo-Kantians, 111
networks, 15n2, 290
neuropsychology, 111, 125
New Mexico, 223
new pragmatists, 6
"new traditionalists," 360, 361
Nichols, Marie Hochmuth, 392
Nietzsche, Friedrich, 269, 270
Nimmo, Dan, 394–95
no-longer conscious, 375
nomothetic methods, 111
nomothetic science, 112–17
non-discursive, vs. discursive, 351–53
non-formal sign exchange, 85
non-human beings, 351–53, 362, 363–64
normality, ambiguity of, 99–101
normative commitments, 362
norms, 355–56
    vs. concepts, 356
North-South interrelations, 222
the not-yet, 375–76, 378
not-yet conscious, 375
noumenon (*data*), 111

O

objectification, dialectics of, 10
objective exterior institutionalized body (the body-in-itself), 301
object-oriented ontology, 363–64
objects, 7, 10, 331–32
    of attention, 288–89
    as function of mind, 95
    as mute, 333–34, 335
    mute, 347n31
    of perceptions, 95
    phenomenology of, 364
Oehler, Klaus, 347n37
oeuvre, 192–93
Old Oregon Trail, 318
Ong, Walter J., 68n47
ontic heteronomy, 72, 84–85
ontology, 206
    coding and, 170–71
    object-oriented, 15, 363–64
    of possibility and process, 374
open-ended, transformative exchanges, 330–41
open-mindedness, 3
openness, 287
oppositions, 268
oppression, 308
"originative I," 179
the Other, 93, 179, 183, 189–90, 194, 317
    face of, 182–83, 187–88, 191, 192, 194, 195
    responsibility for, 190–91
other(s), 11
    intentionality of, 71
    problem of, 13–14
    problem of researching, 32–37

P

Pace, Thomas J., 12, 114, 391–96
Palestinians, 184
Palo Alto School, 95
paradigmatic axis, 67n35
paradox, 134–35

Parmenides, 151
parole, 7, 256–57
parole parlante, 35, 38, 269, 271, 272, 275, 277
parole parlée, 35, 269, 270, 271, 272, 277
parrhesia, 272, 276
Parsons, Talcott, 93–94
Peirce, Charles Sanders, 24, 72, 85, 93, 97, 106, 202, 208, 225, 229, 231–33
    on abduction and adduction, 28–30, 37, 135
    adduction and, 28–30, 37, 133, 135, 137–41
    communicability and, 328, 330, 333, 335, 342, 343, 346n27, 348n54
    communicology and, 2, 4–5, 6–7, 10, 11, 13, 15, 243–44, 251
    concept of semiosis, 11
    critique of nominalism and positivism, 347n31
    definition of abduction, 138
    definition of truth in non-formal sign relations, 85
    developmental teleology and, 347–48n46
    on doubt, 338
    on four phases of scientific work, 126
    Habermas and, 347n37
    heterosemiotic analysis of, 73
    hypoiconicity and, 72, 75, 82–84
    on induction and deduction, 137
    on the Interpretant, *250*, 230
    Lanigan and, 362
    model of semiosis, 329, 330–41
    on perfect signs, 339–40
    power and, 348n67
    on pragmatistic sensibility, 24
    on *precission*, 345–46n15
    sign types and, 83
    on theory construction, 40
    theory of signs, 327, 335–41, 346n24
    triadic model of reflexive dialogue, 118
    tuism of, 347n37
    use of *entelechy*, 347–48n46
Peircean realists, 338
perception, 10, 201, 215, 268
    embodied, 8
    embodiment and, 290–91
    experience and, 301
    expression and, 203–4, 207–8, 213, 268, 272, 277, 291, 292–93, 369–70
    meaning and, 10
    objects of, 95
    perceptual capacity, 232–35
    perceptual component of communicology, 290–91, 293
    perceptual frame, 95
    primacy of, 271
perfection, 376–77, 378
perfectionism, 388n23
perfective drift
    model of, 384–85, *385*
    theory of, 15, 369–89
perfect signs, 339–40
performative style (*lexis agonistike*), 313–23. *See also lexis agonistike*
Perpich, Diane, 187–88
persistence, 346n19
person
    culture and, 9
    as living body, 202
    world and, 8
personhood, individuals as signs of, 7
perspective, 221–22, 258
    presumptions and, 235–36
persuasion, 375
Peterson, Eric, 13
Petit, Jean-Luc, 125
Petrilli, Susan, 186–87, 191–93
phaneroscopy, 6–7
pharmaceutical industry, 204–6
pharmacology, 215
    philosophy of, 203
pharmakon, 203, 213, 215
Phenomenological Description, 292
Phenomenological Interpretation, 293
phenomenological methodology, 3, 10–11
phenomenological practice, decolonial, 221–41
phenomenological realism, 126
phenomenological studies
    communicational aspects in, 13, 111–32
    experimental, 111–32
phenomenology, 23, 26, 30, 32, 72, 95, 126, 252, 258, 271, 291, 300–301

communicability and, 327
communicology and, 3, 6–7, 9–11
consciousness and, 362–63
experience and, 93, 362–63
historicism and, 361
human conscious experience and, 362–63
humanism and, 362–63
of the lifeworld, 201
of objects, 364
posthumanism and, 361, 363–64
as "radical empiricism," 3
semiotic approach to, 15
semiotics and, 147
of the sign, 8
phenomenon (*capta*), 111. *See also capta*
philosophy, 333. *See also* Analytic philosophy; Continental philosophy; *specific philosophers and schools*
    communicative dimension of, 370–72
    of consciousness, 4, 8, 213
    existentialist view of, 371
    of experience, 4
    of human science, 213
    as indicative, 371–72
    intuition and, 372
    of liberation, 228–32
    of logic, 4
Philosophy and Rhetoric, 187–88
placebo effect, 208–9
Plato, 151, 152, 337
    Gorgias, 187
    Phaedrus, 187, 375, 384
    The Republic, 187
    Symposium, 373, 384
plurality, unity and, 374
poesis, 268
Polanyi, Michael, 360
political theory, 358
politics, 307–8
Ponzio, Augusto, 186–87, 191–93
positivism, 376
positivity, 378
possibility, in communication matrix, 213–15
postcolonial approaches, 302
posthumanism
    historicism and, 361

phenomenology and, 361, 363–64
posthumanist ethics and politics, 15, 361, 363–64
postmodernism
    discourse and, 275
    postmodern authorship, 315
poststructuralism, 7, 273–74
post-WWII America, 96, 101
power, 308, 338, 348n67
    apparatuses of, 41
    reality and, 337
practical discourse, 270, 271, 272, 275, 277
pragmaticism, 7, 341
pragmatics (*acta*), 291
pragmatism, 6–7, 8, 9, 10, 85, 201, 232. *See also* American pragmatism
praxis, 268
precission, 345–46n15
pre-consciousness, 192
"pressing," 300, 304–5
presumptions, perspective and, 235–36
"primitive" minds, 365
The Princess Diaries, 209–13, 214, 216n15
printing press, 62
process philosophy, 384, 388n31
projection, 71
    of mental scenarios, 72
Promethean humanism, 332
Propp, Vladimir, 148
prosopopeia, 314
protention, 38
Prozac, 204–6, 207, 208–9, 214
psychiatry, 4, 9–10, 201–19
    politicization of, 205
    theory in, 207
psychoanalytic theory, 95
psychologism, 207, 208, 387n12
psychology, 4
    of communication, 13
    culture and, 9–10
    reflex arc in, 8
psychotherapy, 10, 112–17, 211–12
public discourse, history of, 357–58
punctuation, 161–63
Pu Songling, 136

Q

Quadrilateral Discourse Model of Même et L'Autre, 124
qualitative analysis, 126
quality, 111
quantitative analysis, 126
quantity, 111
questions
    answering, 167–68
    asking, 168
quiddity, 35
Quine, Willard Van Orman, 74, 84–85

R

racism, 224
radical perspectivism, 363–64
Ransdell, Joseph, 332
Ratcliffe, Michael, 206, 207, 213–15, 216n17
rationality, 360, 362
Raven test, 118, 120–23
Rawls, John, 359, 360
reaching out, 370
Reagan, Ronald, 104
the "real," 67–68n38
realism, 338
reality, 328, 333, 338, 343
    of communication, 342
    power and, 337
    symbols and, 379
realization, 377–78
realization model, 126
"real symbol" (*Realsymbol*), 379
reason(ing)
    abduction, 126, 138–41, *139*
    adduction, 126, 138–41, *139*
    deduction, 126, 138–41, *139*
    dialectic between reflective and teleological reasoning, 85
    four kinds of, 138–41, *139*
    induction, 126, 138–41, *139*
    interpersonal, 362
    non-formal pure reason, 85

reciprocal recognition, 355
reciprocity, 71, 79–80, 86
recognition, 248
    impersonal, 194
    intersubjective, 362
    reciprocal, 355
redemption, 386–87
reduction, 39, 179, 181, 186–87, 292, 293
reflectivity, 125, 221
reflex arc, 8, 11
reflexive relations, 15
reflexivity, 125, 221
le regard, 284–85
relativism, 358–59
religious language, 372
religious studies, 358
representation, 249
researching others, 32–37
research praxis, 12, 23–48, 221–41, 237n13
resemblance, 85
resemblance relations, 71, 85, 86
resources, 253–54
retention, 38
retrospection, 37–38
"revelatory phrases" as existential signifiers, 395
reversibility, 125, 203, 206–7, 221, 271
rhetoric, 179, 187, 193–94, 375
    conventional, 187
    Foucault on, 268
    Levinas's dismissal of, 179, 195
    Orthodox, 187
    reduction to, 186–87
rhetorical demand, 180, 191–94
rhetorical theory, 375
Rich, Adrienne, 279n23
"Richard Influence," 391
rights
    contingent, 362
    pluralism of, 362
risk, in communication matrix, 213–15
Rogers, Carl, 112, 113–14
Rorty, Richard, 334–35, 342, 347n31, 347n32, 352
Rosen, Jonathan, 205, 206–7, 208, 209, 212, 213
Rosenzweig, Franz, 385–86, *386*

RRQ, 120
Ruesch, Jürgen, 5, 9–10, 11, 15n2, 202
    Communication: The Social Matrix of Psychiatry, 9, 50, 65n13, 391–92
Russia, 5
Russian formalists, 148
Russian philosophy, 26
Ruthrof, Horst, 13

S

said, vs. saying, 188, 189–91, 193–94
Saldaña, Johnny, 159, 172
Sanders, Keith, 394–95
sapience, 353, 354, 362
Sapir, Edward, 4–5, 8–9, 10, 11, 95, 223
Sartre, Jean-Paul, 184, 186, 283, 284, 285, 294
Satir, Virginia, 95
Saussure, Ferdinand de, 7, 8, 73, 148, 181, 225, 243, 251
saying
    vs. said, 188, 189–91, 193–94
    showing and, 381
Scandinavia, 5
Schiller, Friedrich, 6
Schleiermacher, Friedrich, 81
Schmicking, Daniel, 125
Schrag, Calvin, 12, 392
Schutz, Alfred, 319
scientific work, four phases of, 126
s-codes, 160
Sebeok, Thomas A., 186, 257–58
second-person perspective, 112
the Self, 11, 13–14, 93, 100, 141, 317
    technology of, 267–81
    technology of self, 14
self-expression, 374–76
Selfhood, 100, 104–5
self-illumination, 288, 289, 294
self-other relations, 13–14. *See also* I/Other relations
self writing, 267–68, 272
Sellars, Malcolm, 359
semantics (*capta*), 291. *See also capta*
"semethics," 198n91

semioethics, 13–14, 179–99, 180, 186–87, 191–94
semiology, 8
semiosis, 7, 10, 11, 72, 141, 243–44, 329, 345–46n15, 347–48n46
Semiotica, 395
semiotic choreology, 300
semiotic code, 212
semiotic phenomenology, 23, 51, 54, 93–108, 181, 202, 206, 290, 300–303, 309–10n12
    as communication paradigm, 255–56
    communicology and, 7, 15
    of depression medicine, 201–19
    global context of, 42
    guide to doing, 23–42
    vécu of, 93–108
semiotics, 4, 8–9, 10, 11, 23, 93, 300
    choreology and, 300
    experience and, 93
    Levinas and, 180
    phenomenology and, 147
    reduction to, 186–87
semiotic square, 13, 138–41, 147–58, *149*, 155–56
Semiotics Society of America, 186
semiotic systems, 8
semiotic theory, Levinas and, 198n91
sensus communis, 85
sentience, 353, 354
Serra, Junipero, 225–26, 227–28
Shapiro, Susan, 187
Sheridan, Alan, 284–85
Shklovsky, Viktor, 148
showing, saying and, 381
Shweder, Richard, 37
Siebers, Johan, 15
sign action, 7
sign-activity, 329
signatura rerum, 379
signatures, 320
    vs. souvenirs, 320–22
sign embodiment, 7
signification, 94–95, 187, 189, 193, 194
    preoriginary, 189–90
    reduction to sign game devoid of meaning, 179

Signified, 181, 243, 254–55
Signifier, 243, 254–55, 292
signifying, 7, 330–31
sign of action, 244
sign of thoughts, 244
sign(s), 7, 243, 253, 302, 328, 338, 346n24. *See also* linguistics; semiosis; semiotics
   action of, 330, 346n17
   agency of, 346n17
   the body and, 10
   kinds of, 66n26
   linguistic, 332–33
   phenomenology of, 8
   reliance on, 331–32
sign systems, 302
Silverman, Hugh, 169
situatedness, 364
sixth extinction, 361
Smith, Andrew R., 12
Smith, David Woodruff, 251
Smith, John E., 346n19
Smith, Sidone, 270–71, 273
Snow, C.P., 80
the social, as "interpretant," 7
social (group-organizational) domain, 290
social language, 256–57
social life (*Mitwelt*), 23
social practices, habitual patterns of, 8
social reality, experience and, 63–64
social reciprocity, 71, 79–80, 86
social sciences, 25–28, 126
society, 9, 341
sociocentricity, 234
sociology, 4
Socrates, 151, 370, 371, 375
Socratic position, 373, 382
Sokolowski, Robert, 248–49
Sørensen, Jesper Brøsted, 125
Southern Illinois University at Carbondale, Illinois, 12, 391–96
souvenirs, vs. signatures, 320–22
Spanish colonialism, 225–27
Spanish missions, 225–27
speaking, 27, 203, 269, 271
speaking speech, 35, 271, 272, 275, 277
speech, power of, 351–52, 362

Speech Association of America, 394
speech pedagogy, 394
Spees, Emil, 113
Spinoza, Baruch, 354
spirit (sign), 11
spoken speech, 35, 68n47, 270, 271, 272, 277
SSRIs (serotonin reuptake inhibitors), 205
Stanford University Medical School, 95
Star of David, 385–86, *386*
Stellen, 151
Stiegler, Bernard, 103–4, 203, 213, 215
stigma, 299
storytelling, 165–66
Stout, Jeffrey, 358
   Democracy and Tradition, 359–61
   Ethics After Babel: The Languages of Morals and their Discontents, 358–59
structural-functionalist approach, 94–98
structuralism, 7
structures, fluid, 101–3
Stumpf, Carl, 125
subject, 337
subject at hand, 15, 327–50
subject function, 314, 315
subjectivity, 15, 317
   transcendental, 32–33
subject-predicate relations, instability of, 85
subjects, sorting, 165–67
subjunctive, vs. indicative, 378
substitution, 67n35
suffering, 202, 364, 378
Sullivan, Harry Stack, 5, 9–10
surveillance, 299
sustainability, 243–63
the symbolic, 67–68n38, 388n20
symbolism, 11, 66n26, 376–77
symbolization, 348n57, 379
symbols, 10, 11, 86, 332–33, 346n24, 348n57, 376–77, 379
SYMLOG (SYstematic MultiLevel Observation of Groups) method of group observation, 94
synergic function of intentionality, 369–70
syntactics (*data*), 291
synthetic method, 126
systems approach, 93–94, 95–98

T

taijitu, 383, *383*
Tango, 305–9
task-ordering, 167
Taylor, Bryan C., 159–65, 167–68
technical risk communication, 14, 243–63, *248*
technology of self, 14, 267–81, 271, 273–77
Tezcatlipoca, Olin, 227
theoretical models, 14
theory, 111
    as consensual criteria of judgment, 112
    theory construction, 12, 23–48
Theory of Codes, 170
theory of perfective drift, 369–89
    claims of, 377–78
    model of, 384–85, *385*
theory of signs, 327, 335–41, 346n24
third-person perspective, 111–12, 121–23, *122–23*, 126
thought, 8, 10
Tolstoy, Leo, 188
Tomasello, Michael, 77, 79
Tönnies, Ferdinand, 313, 321
Torah, 184
trace, 193–94
tradition, democracy and, 358–61
transcendental esthetic, Kantian notion of, 43n16
transcendental subjectivity, 32–33
transformational theory, logic of, 67–68n38
transgression, 35, 307–8, 378, 385
translation, 313–23
triadic model of reflexive dialogue, 118
tropologics, 13, 24
Twenge, Jean M., 244
Tynjanov, Yu., 148

U

Umwelten, 332
United States, 5, 6, 10
unity, plurality and, 374
universality, 85, 374, 379
universal truth, 85
University of Chicago, 9
University of Denver, 394
University of Freiburg, 4
University of Göttingen, 4
University of New Mexico, 12, 391, 394
Urban, Wilbur Marshall, 10, 12, 223, 394
    Language and Reality, 10–11

V

Van Kaam, Adrian, 114, 115
the Vatican, 320
vécu, 93–108
Verstand, 28
Verständigung, 80
Verstehen, 28, 79
Vietnam War, 393
Vietnam War Memorial, 14, 313–19, 321
violence, 299
visual (external) glancing, 287, 294
visual attention, 283, 286–87, 294
voice, 71, 76–77, 86
    as communicative phenomenon, 278
    concept of, 267–81
    as discursive praxis, 268–69
    embodiment and, 14
    as emergent discursive phenomenon, 269–73
"voiceless name," 271–72, 314
voicing bodies, 14
Von Uexküll, Jakob, 211, 363–64
Vorhabe (fore-having), 33
Vorsicht (fore-sight), 33
Vorstellung, 73, 75, 78, 82

W

Wang, Hong, 14
Watson, Julia, 270–71, 273
Weinstein, Deborah F., 95, 106
West-East interrelations, 222
wetlands, 254

Whitehead, Alfred North, 369, 374, 379, 384
Whitman, Walt, 361
wholeness, 373–74, 376, 377, 383–84, 386–87, 387n12
Whorf, Benjamin Lee, 5, 8–9, 11, 223
Wicker, Tom, 395
Wilden, Anthony, 51, 162
Wiley, Norbert, 114, 118, 119
Windelband, Wilhelm, 115
Wirth, Uwe, 126
Wittgenstein, Ludwig, 74, 75, 354, 359, 381
women's writing, 267–81
Wong, David, 359
words
    choice of, 67n35
    empirically employed, 67n37
    images and, 380–81
works, 273–74
world, person and, 8
"world of signification," 147
World War II, 95
Wright, Chauncey, 6
"writer," vs. "author", 272–77
writing
    vs. authoring, 273–74
    as discursive practice, 272–77
    speaking and, 269
writing life, 272
writing process, 273–76
written style (*lexis graphike*), 313–23. *See also lexis graphike*

Y

Yale University, 10, 12
yin-yang symbol, 383, *383*

Z

Zachary, Adam, 189
"zero nature," 258n10
    education on, 245–50
zhinguai (Jer-Gwai), 136